9/12

MW00356625

Warriors Without War

Warriors Without War

*Seminole Leadership in
the Late Twentieth Century*

PATRICIA RILES WICKMAN

THE UNIVERSITY OF ALABAMA PRESS
Tuscaloosa

Typeface: Caslon

∞
The paper on which this book is printed meets the minimum requirements of Ameri-
can National Standard for Information Sciences-Permanence of Paper for Printed Library
Materials, ANSI Z39.48-1984.

Front cover photograph: James Billie, the tribe's future, drives his airboat across the Florida
Everglades. Photograph courtesy of the author.
Back cover photograph: Henry John Billie poles his cypress dugout canoe across the
Everglades. Photograph courtesy of the author.

Wickman, Patricia R. (Patricia Riles)
Warriors without war : Seminole leadership in the late twentieth century / Patricia Riles
Wickman.
p. cm.
Includes bibliographical references and index.
ISBN 978-0-8173-1731-7 (cloth : alk. paper) — ISBN 978-0-8173-8539-2 (electronic)
1. Billie, James, Seminole chief. 2. Billie, James, Seminole chief—Influence. 3. Seminole
Indians—Kings and rulers—Biography. 4. Seminole Indians—Florida—Social
conditions—20th century. 5. Seminole Indians—Oklahoma—Social conditions—20th
century. 6. Seminole Nation of Oklahoma—History—20th century. 7. Indian leadership—
Florida—History—20th century. 8. Indian leadership—Oklahoma—History—20th
century. 9. Gambling on Indian reservations—Florida—History—20th century. 10.
Gambling on Indian reservations—Oklahoma—History—20th century. I. Title.
E99.S28B459 2011
976.6004'973859—dc22
[B]
2010053743

Contents

Illustrations

Acknowledgments

Almost a complete generation of adventure-filled and intensive years have passed since that day when James Billie told me that I ought to move out to "BC Res" (the Big Cypress Seminole Indian Reservation, that is) and teach the Indians their own history. The memory alone still startles me. When I make a public presentation and people ask me, as they inevitably do, how I came to live and work with the Indians, I can only respond that James Billie opened a Cosmic Door for me, and I walked through, and I can never go back. Nor would I want to, even if such were possible.

Now-former chairman James E. Billie (à la Harry "S." Truman, the "E." stands for nothing—except perhaps "energy," which you'll recognize if you ever get caught up in the vortex) is a visionary. He's not long on planning, and he rolls through life like a human juggernaut, bent on forcing his visions into reality—by the power of his single will, if necessary. It's a risky business, based sometimes on a canny sense of using his Indianness to buffalo white politicians and lawyers, and at other times, on a pure love of the adrenalin rush. Either way, his visions and his accomplishments—and his failures—dominate the entire landscape of the last quarter of the twentieth century in the history of the Florida Seminoles, and for half of that time he provided me personal access.

And the impact of his visions has been felt not by the Florida Seminoles alone. His charisma and force have been felt all the way across Indian Country, and as high up as the U.S. Supreme Court, and across several oceans.[1] Unfortunately, as much of an impact as he had, he still realized no more than about a quarter of the power that he could have had. Part of this fact stems from the intensely combative and disempowering nature of his upbringing, and another part from the intensely combative nature of Seminole culture and society, in the twentieth or any other century. And the two are inextricably bound, as we shall see.

All of which is to say, circuitously, that my first and last acknowledgments must be to James Billie for his entrée to his world. All the rest of my acknowledgments go to the Seminole people, first, of Florida, and second, of Oklahoma, who may or may not always have been well served by their political leaders—a not unusual statement in any culture, but when Congressman Tip O'Neill said, "All politics is local," he still was laughably unaware of the labyrinthine nature of politics in Indian Country.

A Note on Language

The subject of American Indian languages, particularly as regards the Seminole people of Florida, is a complex and oftentimes confusing one and, so, bears a few words of explanation. First and foremost, there is no such thing as a "Seminole" language. Further, there is no single language spoken by the Seminole Indian people of Florida, regardless of what it might be called. There are, in point of fact, two languages still in active use among the Indian people who comprise the closely related citizens of the Seminole Tribe of Florida and the Miccosukee Tribe of Indians of Florida. These are the only federally recognized (FR) Indian tribes headquartered within the state of Florida, and neither language is exclusive to either tribe. One language is known as Creek and the other as Miccosukee, but these two terms obscure much of their history.

The two languages, mutually unintelligible today, were once the same language. The "mother" tongue, Maskókî (inaccurately known among English speakers as Creek), was the language spoken by culturally related tribes all across the lower Southeast long before the coming of the Europeans half a millennium ago. At various times both before and after that event, separate communities and villages and towns and cities began to shape dialects of Maskókî, and over time these dialects evolved into completely separate languages. The language popularly called Miccosukee today was spoken historically by the Hitchiti people—members of the Maskókî cultural family. It was one of the dialects that, over time, became a separate language and is today referred to as Miccosukee.

In the 1840s, in Indian Territory (soon, Oklahoma), the Rev. R. M. Loughridge, a non-Indian Protestant missionary, began to assemble a lexicon of the core Maskókî language. For this work he created a syllabary using the English letters v and r, two sounds not used in Maskókî, to represent Maskókî sounds not used in English. Many writers will use this system of transcription today, with varying degrees of resulting intelligibility. I view this system of transcription as entirely too precious. Hitchiti/Miccosukee has never been completely codified in writing, although the Hitchiti-speaking Seminoles do themselves write words in a mostly ad hoc manner, for various social, educational, and artistic reasons. Consequently, for purposes of the present work, in which relatively few Maskóki or Miccosukee words are necessary, the following protocols are considered sufficient.

> *s* is equivalent to the English sound of *sh,* spoken as an aspirant, from the back of the mouth
> *k* equals the soft *g* sound of the English *gull*
> *c* equals the hard English *c* of *cat*

Warriors Without War

I   An Alternate Universe

Imagine the beauty of a placid lake, amid dense woods, in the early morning. Imagine the dark water, as smooth as glass and so still that the first curved rays of the sun reflect brilliantly from a hundred shimmering points on its surface. The serenity seems all-pervasive. It also is deceptive. The peace is only as deep as that crystalline surface, and the serenity is belied by the teeming cycle of life and death that occurs and recurs everywhere beneath it. That submarine kingdom exists in purposeful contrast to its exterior and, moreover, is a world apart from all that happens on its shores and beyond. This is the functional reality of the Seminole world—a world apart from the gargantuan non-Native world that surrounds and unceasingly presses upon it.

The contrast between the facade created by the surface and the reality of the depths is a chosen one—a social construct that has served the Seminole people and their ancestors, the Maskókî peoples of the lower Southeast, for many centuries, at least, as an ongoing process of maintaining cultural distinction and social equilibrium. The water metaphor is apt, given their long imaging of their world as water based and water bound. The depths absorb the cycles and shocks of quotidian human existence and, as long as those cycles and shocks are not permitted to break the surface, the Seminole world continues in balance—and in apparent serenity. This philosophy is no mere whim or passing fancy. It is the keystone of the Seminole world and, perforce, of the world the ancestors created.

To carry the metaphor of the lake one final step further, it is important to realize that the placid exterior of the Seminole world was not created to impress or deceive those who looked at it from the outside. It was created as an internal mechanism, designed to contain and control all of the inherent centrifugal forces of Maskókî culture. Over the centuries these have been codified, element by element, as systems for perpetuating intra- and interclan relations, settling grievances, expiating and closing the grieving process, regulating even the most intimate of personal relations, recovering from the imbalances of illnesses and deaths and natural disasters, and regulating myriad other facets of life among the ancestors of today's Seminole society.[1]

~

In the larger view, however, the single most essential force in the Maskókî world was, arguably, warfare. By the late pre-Contact period, in the 1400s CE, warfare among the Maskókî ancestors was, in fact, "endemic, widespread, and an integral component of many aspects of daily life."[2] During the sixteenth through the nineteenth centuries, the period of European colonialization and U.S. nation building, the most powerful of the centrifugal forces of the southeastern Maskókî character was, and remained, warfare.

This quintessential characteristic of Maskókî life in the Southeast ended abruptly, and unnaturally, in 1858, with the unilateral decision of the U.S. government to withdraw its forces from Florida and end the final or Third Seminole War. Even though the withdrawal of U.S. troops ushered in a period of military peace (absence of physical warfare) that has endured into the present day (in Florida, at least), the social void created by the loss of warfare as a principal element of the Maskókî world has been detrimental to the continuity of the overall Seminole culture. Despite the fact that we (as non-Native observers) may reason from the vantage point of our twenty-first-century attitudes that peace is preferable to war (despite our obvious determination to perpetuate it), no such fine distinction can be applied retroactively to the lives of the Seminoles' ancestors, either across time or space. "From time to time, the earth needs to drink blood," the Seminoles say.[3]

This centrality and social utility of warfare has never been sufficiently appreciated by non-Native observers, however. A reductionist fallacy, based upon an overemphasis on the value of sedentary agriculture as the principal determinant in shaping southeastern Indian society, has institutionalized an external historical imaging of the Maskókî peoples in which warfare, although significant, has been assigned a secondary role. That is to say that Euro-Americans have, once again, transferred their own beliefs onto another culture instead of examining that culture closely to discover its own beliefs. The documentation, moreover, provides no basis for such an assumption other than an interpretive choice. While the value of sedentary agriculture (the ability to harness Nature for increased production and, therefore, increased human survival) should not be underplayed, the centrality of warfare in Maskókî life could hardly be overplayed. This latter understanding reverberates throughout the history of the Seminoles and provides the touchstone for the present work.

Warfare calibrated and recalibrated intertribal relations. It provided the single most valuable, and viable, path to preferment for males (and, in certain instances, for females), and mixed and remixed marriageability options for females, among other critical processes. The core and plurality of items wrapped into the Medicine bundle, the "ark of the covenant" in Maskókî spirituality, always were war-related items. The attrition of these war items, following the end of tribal warfare in the lower Southeast in 1858, has weakened the Seminole people in their own eyes even as the social memory of the void continues to occupy them, reverberating daily across the generations, in their discourse.

The numerous and militarily superior tribes of the lower Southeast had been the first North American Natives to meet and interact with the Europeans on a sustained basis. It was they who resisted colonialization the longest, and whom Euro-American social scientists today characterize as the *Maskókî* (var., *Muscogee*) peoples. The external relations of these tribes with the earliest European colonizers, the Spaniards, and with the later French, English, and European Americans, has been documented extensively by each of these powers, albeit within the framework of their own sociopolitical objectives. Historians and other writers, over time, have used and reused these early cross-cultural misunderstandings. As but one case in point, the Europeans' rhetorical attempts to image women in Maskókî society as second-class citizens have not yet managed to completely erode the power of Seminole women. Failure to understand on the part of the Europeans, obviously, has not necessarily implied a failure to sustain on the part of the Indians.

This ultimate series of the United States' Wars of Indian Removal east of the Mississippi River would be fought against descendants of many of these same Maskókî tribes, as the Creek War of 1813–14 (in Alabama); the Creek War of 1836 (in Georgia); and the First (1817–18), Second (1835–42), and Third (1856–58) Seminole Wars (in Florida).

These conflicts constituted a watershed era in the modern history of the Indian people of today's Florida. The effects of these Wars of Removal, perpetrated upon the Indian people in blatant determination to remove them from the paths of white settlement, were geographically definitive. At least three thousand of their Creek relatives were deprived of their ancient lands in Alabama and Georgia. During the second quarter of the century, several thousand were forced westward, completely leaving their ancestral homes for Indian Territory in the West. Following 1814, about three thousand or so moved southward into Florida, however, to join several thousand Florida Indians still surviving in their own ancient, peninsular, homelands. Euro-American politicians and historians would quickly begin to speak of them all generically as "Seminoles" despite the fact that the Indians themselves knew quite well that they were Coça, Abalache, Hitchiti, Yamassee, Yuchi, Calusa, and other members of the larger Maskókî cultural family of tribes.[4]

These Wars of Removal were, inarguably, socially disruptive. Clans and nuclear families were ripped apart. Animosities between those who outfought the United States to remain in Florida and those who were removed to Indian Territory reverberate to the present day. Indeed, the former still view the latter as "traitors" for having left Florida, despite the fact that those who did so were either physically captured or so psychologically debilitated that they could no longer resist U.S. military power. We shall view the ongoing impact of this fierce and continuing antagonism, set in motion over 160 years ago, from events as relatively small as the ongoing interactions of the Florida and Oklahoma Seminoles at annual "Tribal Fairs" and "Nation Days," to those as large as the final disposition of the Indian Land Claims Case and U.S. government awards of millions of reparation dollars (in chapter 5).

The wars were not, however, either culturally, socially, or politically destructive in any definitive sense. The descendants of those who remained in Florida would take refuge in the southern peninsula and, ultimately, in the impenetrable Everglades and reemerge, in the middle of the twentieth century, in U.S. political terms, as three separate entities: the Seminole Tribe of Florida, a federally recognized (FR) tribe comprising mainly Miccosukee speakers, together with a minority of Maskókî or Creek speakers; the Miccosukee Tribe of Indians of Florida, a politically separate FR tribe; and a tiny group of "independent Seminoles," who meet the requirements for enrollment in either FR tribe, but never have joined either, and are not federally recognized as anything other than individual Indians. Despite political differences, they are nevertheless all the same people, culturally. Since the 1950s, however, they have charted separate political and economic courses. All, nevertheless, have maintained the same overarching objective: the cultural survival of the people as Indians and as sovereign nations, politically separate from the United States.

Students of southeastern history will be familiar with numerous tribal "names" that have disappeared over the centuries, such as the Escampabas or Calusas, the Tequestas, Jeagas, Ais, Abalaches, Abalachicolas, and many others. Today, however, the surviving descendants of the southeastern Maskókî peoples are known to Euro-Americans, and recognized by the U.S. government, as the following separate FR tribes.

Seminole Tribe of Florida (governmental offices in Hollywood, Florida)
Miccosukee Tribe of Indians of Florida (Tamiami Trail, Florida)
Poarch Band of Creek Indians (Atmore, Alabama)
Mississippi Band of Choctaw Indians (Philadelphia, Mississippi)
Seminole Nation of Oklahoma (Wewoka, Oklahoma, a removed tribe)
Muscogee (Creek) Nation (Ocmulgee, Oklahoma, a removed tribe)
Chickasaw Nation (Ada, Oklahoma, a removed tribe)
Chitimacha Tribe of Louisiana (Charenton, Louisiana)
Choctaw Nation of Oklahoma (Durant, Oklahoma, a removed tribe)

Thlopthlocco Tribal Town (Okemah, Oklahoma, a removed tribal town)
Alabama Coushatta Tribe of Texas (Livingston, Texas, a removed tribe)
Kialegee Tribal Town (Wetumka, Oklahoma, a removed tribal town)
Jena Band of Choctaw Indians (Jena, Louisiana)
Coushatta Indian Tribe (Elton, Louisiana)
Tunica-Biloxi Tribe (Marksville, Louisiana)

Some of these are tribal designators that have been used by the Indians for hundreds of years, at least. Others have been wholly applied by Europeans and Euro-Americans over time. Related by culture and speaking dialects of a core language (*Maskókî*, erroneously called Creek by English speakers since the eighteenth century), their villages, towns, and cities ranged across what are today five complete states (Florida, Alabama, Georgia, South Carolina, Mississippi) and parts of four others (North Carolina, Tennessee, Kentucky, and Louisiana). The Spaniards recognized immediately that these tribes were different from all of the other peoples whom they had met in the Americas, and that the systems of confrontation and control that had been successful for them (the Spaniards) in Central and South America would not be successful here because of these Natives' especially high degree of sociopolitical organization and their abilities and willingness to confront the Spaniards in battle.

Consequently, the title of this book, *Warriors Without War*, is meant to reflect a deeper and more fundamental imaging of the Seminole people and, particularly, their leadership, than could be conveyed by any other term. Without the critical outlet that war provided historically, male paths to preferment and power became attenuated during the century between 1858 and 1957, after which a new path opened up. From 1957 and the creation of the political entity, based upon the institution of a white-man's-style constitution and bylaws, the concomitant growth of a Euro-American-style bureaucratic infrastructure created brand new avenues to power and preferment for "politicians" in the new "Seminole Tribe of Florida." And although neither the form nor the function were their own, culturally, they accepted the form and began to adopt and adapt the function in order to fulfill the requirements of the U.S. government, as they imperfectly understood them.

The "fit" never was a good one. This new and imposed system of governance, accepted specifically to satisfy yet another pressure placed upon them by the U.S. government, was meant neither to augment nor to replace traditional forms of governance. In point of fact, not all FR tribes have agreed to accept written, U.S.-style constitutions. These tribes are known across Indian Country simply as "traditional government" tribes. And, even among those with written organizational documents, in recent years a number of tribes have reasserted their autonomy by removing from their constitutions former U.S. requirements that they obtain the formal approval of the U.S. secretary of the interior for various tribal actions.[5]

Seen through Seminole eyes, their new constitution and bylaws preserved many elements of governance that appeared to be analogous or adaptable to traditional forms and ignored or buffered the people from those elements that were not understandable or were antithetical. In other words, the documents sheathed the Seminole world in a layer of bureaucracy that could protect it, for as one prominent Medicine man expressed it, "the Indian world and the white man's world are like two rivers, running parallel, never flowing together."[6] As one result, there arose a new breed of warrior—not *in place of* a traditional style of leader but *in addition to it*. And, in limited ways, purely political warfare began to fill the void created by the end of military warfare. The major concern for the Seminole people, in the twentieth century as in the twenty-first, was whether these new warriors would, indeed, use the white man's political systems to protect the people, or be co-opted by the outside system to the detriment of the people and the demise of the Seminoles' culture.

∼

With the advice of officials of the U.S. Department of the Interior's Bureau of Indian Affairs (BIA), the Florida Indians formed a two-headed government in 1957. Today, after some procedural modifications enacted over the years, the first of these, the Seminole Tribal Council, is led by a chairman elected at large by the tribal citizens, and by reservation representatives, elected by each of the three "big Res's," Big Cypress (BC), Brighton, and Hollywood. The council directs the internal affairs of the tribe as well as many of the external business affairs. The second, a Board of Directors, with a president and representatives elected in the same manner as the members of the council, was envisioned originally as the entity that would direct the external or business affairs of the tribe. This seemed especially viable in the mid-twentieth century when cattle raising was a central element of the tribe's burgeoning economy. Since the FR Indian tribes are acknowledged as sovereign nations by the U.S. government, the Board of Directors would (it was first thought) oversee the Seminole Tribe of Florida, Inc.—a corporate entity that would be able to enter into contracts without the complete legal shield of sovereign immunity that clothed the sovereignty of the tribe itself.[7] To provide continuity of action between the two bodies (Tribe and Tribe, Inc., or, more simply, Council and Board, as they are known within the tribe), the council chairman sits also as the board's (voting) vice president, while the board's president also functions as the (voting) vice chairman of the council.

But neither the U.S. government, generally, nor the BIA, specifically, reckoned with the warrior tradition of the Florida Indians. In the nearly half-century since the imposition of this bureaucratic system, the power of the two entities, council and board, never has been determined completely by the function of each as initially conceived by white men and codified on white man's paper. Rather, the power of each has waxed and waned depending directly upon the imaging of its leaders as more or less powerful, personally, as defined by the Indian people themselves. Among the leaders, two men and one woman, who exercised varying degrees of power as council chairmen or board presidents between 1957 and the end of the millennium, the skills of the warrior have been less or more visible in each. Certainly struggle has been the basic requirement of their survival in every instance, but strong leaders have made decisions and taken actions regardless of whether such decisions and actions were officially allocated to council or board. In the process they have aggrandized themselves and protected the people to varying degrees.

Inadvertently, in the process of creating their founding documents the Seminoles also damaged non-Indians' imaging of their tribal sovereignty by accepting and using the English word *member* rather than *citizen*—a choice that hinders their exercise of sovereignty even as the political will and financial wherewithal to rely upon that exercise increases today. According to the corporate memory of current BIA officials, the BIA representative who was sent out from Washington, DC, in the 1950s to assist the Seminoles and other tribes in formulating their constitutions and bylaws was given as a "boiler plate" document the constitution and bylaws of the American Legion.[8] This was and remains a voluntary association, based upon membership by choice rather than citizenship by birth. Many Indians, not understanding the social and legal implications of English words, and valuing English little, accepted the word and, in so doing, codified an imaging by non-Indians of tribes as social clubs, with permeable borders that could be crossed at will. This continuing use of the concept of a *member* as opposed to a *citizen* has engendered ongoing problems for the FR tribes, especially as regards the cavalier attitude of the U.S. Bureau of the Census and the importunities of thousands of outside individuals determined to assert their Indianness based on nothing more than family anecdotes and, all too often, greed.

In 1957, the Seminole people could not yet envision a moment when individuals totally unknown to them, from all over the world, would unilaterally choose to image themselves as Seminoles and seek enrollment in the tribe. The Seminoles of the mid-twentieth century set their requirements for "membership" in terms of the Seminole people and the tribe as they knew it then. And fortunately, in so doing, they created a solid, protective barrier against the outside world that served them well then, and better to the present day, even as perceived economic rewards have spurred enrollment attempts from what one federal official refers to facetiously as "the two largest tribes in the U.S.: the Wannabes and the Outalucks!"[9] We will return to this theme of Seminole and pan-Indian awareness of sovereignty repeatedly throughout this work. We will also discuss further the dangerous aspects of current and growing attempts by non-Indians to breach sovereignty and share in the putative benefits of Indian-ness by clamoring to be let in to FR tribes.

~

After only a few months of working with the Seminoles, in the 1960s, one researcher wrote: "Those who do accept the leadership role, such as the tribal officers, find themselves in a difficult position. They are under constant pressure from the Bureau of Indian Affairs and other white officials to be active, efficient, and decisive. The Seminoles, however, expect them to conform to their idea of a leader, which is quite a different concept."[10] Each individual who asked for the settlement of a dispute genuinely expected a judgment in his own favor and bitterly resented any other result. New projects and new ideas could not simply be introduced and implemented by tribal officials. They had to be introduced first to the people, slowly and directly, sometimes one person at a time. Definitely, each Res expected officials to travel there and meet with the people, personally, and satisfy all the local concerns. By the end of the twentieth century, these expectations would continue to exist, but they would be in open conflict with the changing elements of Seminole life.

Under no circumstances did the Seminole people of the mid-twentieth century expect leaders to act rapidly and without the direct consent of the governed. Individuals who did so were "foolish people"—the most heartfelt insult that the Seminole elders use. This requirement to consult is a basic facet of the horizontal power structure that has long functioned among the people. Theirs is, at basis, still a consensus form of decision making. Over the decade of the 1970s, however, tribal leaders very slowly increased council decision making, in parallel with the demands of the numbers of programs becoming available through various departments of the U.S. government.

As one researcher has commented, it was through the numerous War on Poverty programs of the Kennedy-Johnson era that many later tribal officials got their training in tribalwide administration.[11] Programs such as the Comprehensive Education and Training Act (CETA), the Neighborhood Youth Corps (NYC), and the Community Action Program (CAP) permitted tribal citizens to find income-producing employment without leaving the reservations. The federal reporting requirements that came with each program introduced the tribal administrators to the expectations of the outside world. These non-Indian, bureaucratic expectations would clash, directly and forcefully, with traditional Seminole leadership requirements. Early tribal leaders quickly would tire of being buffeted from both sides—from inside the tribe as well as outside.

When it came to acting on behalf of all the people, *against* the outside "white" world, however, rapid and unilateral action by tribal officials was, and continues to be, not only permitted but also expected. This is the classic "double bind" in which the Seminoles place not only their elected officials but also the Christian preachers whom they permit to work among them and any other non-Indians in whom they choose to repose any degree of confidence. Loyalty to the people is paramount. Individuals who cannot manage to walk this thin line risk running afoul of public sentiment and losing the trust of the people. One BIA staff member stated this situation most clearly. He wrote: "Seminole political life is, frankly speaking, the most vicious type of thing yet observed by the Community Services officer. Political dissent or defeat is expected to result in the most deep-seated resentments, interestingly enough, usually in the surface atmosphere of extreme quiet. Retaliation may take forms from deliberate slander and the spreading of baseless accusations to the utilization of witchcraft [that is, "bad" medicine]. The latter technique has been practiced and condoned [even] by Seminole Baptist leaders."[12] This observer has recognized the same model that I recognized as still functioning more than a quarter of a century later: the subsurface turmoil of the water in conjunction with the social requirement that the surface of the lake should remain placid. Further, he has realized another fact that became clear to me very early on in my years with the Seminoles. Even among those Seminoles who have converted to Christianity, the conversion is only skin deep.

An excellent example from as far back as the eighteenth century comes to mind. It is an incident that occurred during the destruction of San Marcos de Apalachee Mission by British Carolina General James Moore in 1704. The mission was in flames as one of the Franciscan friars saw an ostensibly converted Indian running away from the debacle. The friar called to the Indian and reminded him that he was a Christian and should stay to help combat the flames. With no need to stop or think about it at all, the Indian paused only long enough to strike his forehead with his fist three times and proclaim: "Water be gone! Water be gone! Water be gone! I am no Christian." Neither the power of Christian baptism, the Spanish god, nor the might of the Spanish king's army had produced any basic, cultural change in his worldview.[13]

In almost a decade and a half of my own intimate association with the Seminole and Maskókî people, I have yet to find an Indian who has accepted white man's Christianity in an orthodox manner, despite the constant pressures of the Christian missionaries to coerce them to do so. Their beliefs remain heterodox—a syncretism of the Indian worldview with which and into which they were born, and those parts of Christianity that do not conflict absolutely with their continuing imaging of themselves as Indians. In Oklahoma, for example, I have waited patiently in the side yard among the weeds for many hours to talk to "Baptist preachers" who had just conducted Sunday services and were now busy collecting Medicine plants to make Indian Medicine for their constituents. In Florida, the quickest way to determine the degree of traditionalism of any individual is to ask if they still participate in the annual Green Corn Ceremony. If they have embraced Christianity, they usually will respond with, "No man can serve two masters."[14] In the interest of "serving only one master," they may not attend Green Corn but they will, as the BIA staffer noted, watch, condone, and participate in the use of good—and sometimes *bad*—Medicine. This entails, as its name implies, drawing upon the power of Indian Medicine for positive purposes, or for the "bad" purposes of personal gain or revenge. (We will revisit the topic of Indian Medicine below.)

There is, undoubtedly, a positive aspect to this system of accepting only parts of the white man's world. As I have said before, the Seminoles continue to view themselves as independent actors in the process of intercultural relations. This is an amazing statement given the lengths to which the Spaniards, the French, the English, and the Americans have gone, over almost half a millennium, to force them to assimilate—to "turn white and be right," as the Indians indignantly say. Through the 1970s, at least, they determinedly continued to choose those parts of the non-Indian world that they did not view as disruptive or destructive and ignored the rest. This process has constituted a critical element of their cultural survival.

Other variables have begun to have an impact upon this process since that time, however, and they do not necessarily bode well for the cultural future of the Seminoles. These variables, which range from the indiscriminate acceptance of everything from white man's sneakers to white man's cocaine, have become more and more available as a result of increased demographic pressures—that is, white development that crowds in upon the reservations or beams directly into Seminole homes via television and radio and increased resources as a result of rapidly increasing revenues from gaming and other Seminole business ventures but, predominantly, from gaming. We will examine these variables and their impact upon the Seminoles as a cultural group as we begin to examine the inner workings of the tribal government in the late twentieth century.

⁓

It is useful to image the political leadership of the Seminole Tribe, since its creation in 1957, as comprising three phases or generations in the second half of the twentieth century. Council chairman Billy Osceola (1957–66) was indicative of this first generation of political tribal leaders. His was a philosophy of leadership based on an acceptance of Euro-American Christianity, coupled with a certain sense of cultural pride, but with only the most limited sense of "sovereignty." The Seminoles, isolated geographically for most of the previous century and with only the barest awareness of pan-Indian nationalism and political activism that had been growing since the mid-twentieth century outside of Florida, were neither socially nor economically ready to confront the power of the U.S. government in this era. As one historian has realized, however, among the individuals who stepped forward to become the first political leaders of the Seminole Tribe of Florida: "The Seminoles' willingness to accept their leadership may also indicate that Christianity provided a vehicle for legitimizing a behavior pattern—telling others what to do—that was objectionable in traditional Seminole culture."[15] Christianity, never more than a heterodox practice—a syncretism, at best, among the Florida Seminoles, as I have said before—tried to influence the Indians away from their culture and heritage, but with only minor successes, principally among the middle generations of tribal citizens. As long as the reservations persisted and the people maintained their collective affinity and, above all, as long as the clans persisted and the elders remembered, the Old Ways would survive.

The political leaders of the 1950s and 1960s engaged, rather than confronted, the white men's laws and sought conformity with them insofar as they could provide an economic stability understood as critical to the ability of the Seminoles to protect themselves against increasing white settlement pressures. But Seminole social traditions, based as they were on the legitimizing power of consensus, were antithetical to individual initiative and decision making. Billy Osceola and the first generation of overtly Christian leaders would give way over the coming decade to a new generation of predominately politicized business leadership. The cattle business, for which the Seminoles and their ancestors had had an affinity since cattle first were introduced to them by the Spaniards in the sixteenth century, served as a conduit and transitional arena for this second generation of leaders.

Board president Fred Smith (1939–1996), who entered tribal government in 1968 and served in various capacities until his death, in office, almost three decades later, was a harbinger of this next generation and a powerful leader who came out of the cattle owners, or "the hat men" as many Seminoles jokingly call them because of their attachment to the wearing of expensive Stetsons. Smith was from the same generation as Howard Tommie (b. 1938), who would serve as council chairman from 1971 until 1979. The two, both Bird Clan, had many of the same aims and managed their political power bases, the board and the council, amiably and successfully. Both men were actively engaged in taking advantage of U.S.-government-funded programs that would bring white men's money to the tribe principally as an outgrowth of U.S. President Lyndon B. Johnson's Great Society programs and his promulgation of a self-determination policy for FR tribes.[16] Both Seminole leaders were interested in advancing their personal images nationally, meanwhile taking the Florida Seminoles into the national arena of Indian Country and the larger, non-Indian United States. In this process, this second generation of leaders began to move away from the intensely personal style of leadership that remained within the expectations of the Seminole people. Both men fought for the Seminole people, but without directly "telling [the people] what to do." Consequently, both men managed to walk the fine line between the internal expectations of the people and the external requirements of the U.S. government. This style of leadership occurred, and succeeded, however, before gaming revenues upped the ante—for both sides—exponentially.

Without a doubt, however, the leader who would complete the second generation of leadership styles and introduce the third was James E. Billie, tribal chairman from 1979 to 2003, who dominated the tribe's political landscape throughout all of the late twentieth century, leading the tribe through its greatest battles to its greatest successes, and its greatest failures, and projecting the quintessential image of a warrior. Part of that imaging was born of his unique life story and his innate charismatic nature. A significant portion was the result of his inborn intellect and political savvy and his excellent understanding of the requirements of leadership among his people, which is to say, of the expectations of the people and the imaging to which their leaders should conform. It was a facade that he went to great lengths to maintain, often at the risk of his personal health and safety. It was a success he knew that only he, himself, could ever destroy. It was, consequently, his own choices and changes in leadership style that set the stage for his ultimate downfall and the end of the third phase of modern Seminole leadership, in 2003.

∽

Much of the story of the Seminoles' political emergence into visibility in the non-Native world in the late nineteenth and early twentieth centuries has been well recounted elsewhere, and the story closes with the end of the tenure of council chairman Howard Tommie, the immediate predecessor of James Billie, in 1979.[17] This moment puts a finis to the second generation of tribal leadership, although we can understand this now only with the clear vision of hindsight. The rise to power of James Billie would usher in a brilliant new era in tribal politics and, far beyond that, a new era of tribal visibility and influence—the way the tribe saw and was seen—across Indian Country and among non-Indians.

My association with the Seminole people and the tribe's administration occurred during the last half of this third generation, because I was hired and directed by Chairman James Billie (some called him the "Chief," but he and I had a long-running discussion about that, about which more later). As a result I had a direct relationship with him and with the Seminole people during roughly the whole second half of his political career, from 1992 to 2003. These were the years of the zenith of his personal and corporate power, and of his fall. During these years, his power and the image that he projected were so pervasive, both inside and outside the tribe, that, as a result, the story I have to tell focuses, to a great extent, on James and the internal structure of his administration and administrators.

My role was never one of the wielding of direct power. It was more the part of the éminence grise, with only the power of access, and the very limited power of influence. It was, nevertheless, an excellent vantage point from which to observe and learn. James has a mind that is omnivorous and will seek out information on *any* topic. Let me repeat: *any topic that enters his consciousness.* (Among others, for example, the words prurient, salacious, scatological, rude, crude, and personal do not occur in his vocabulary.) His is the joy of the completely unfettered mind. Further, it is a mind couched in the circular Indian world where all things are connected and no subject is wholly separate from any other.

Some of our most exciting conversations took place outside of the mainstream of his public life: in his kitchen at 8:00 a.m., when he would awaken and come down to make coffee, and before the favor seekers began to line up on his porch; in his pickup, bouncing across his cattle pasture, avoiding armadillo holes. We had numerous discussions about sovereignty, too, that mysterious and powerful force that surrounds nations and protects their actions from the invading tentacles of other nations. We discussed fear and greed and the strange actions of all human beings, especially at exalted political levels. He told me stories of his life and the world of the Seminoles that have enriched my life immeasurably. He remonstrated with me on myriad occasions, to "stop thinking inside the box!" The Seminole world is distinctly not box-shaped; it is circular.

He only half jokingly announced at a tribal Christmas party that the Seminoles had a new clan that would henceforth be known as the Armadillo Clan, and I would be its only member. It made sense, he said, because, like the armadillo, I was always "going around poking my nose into everything!" Afterward, tribal citizens, whose traditions do not permit the making of totem images (despite the patchwork stylizations of panthers and birds that have begun appearing on skirts and vests recently) generously began bringing me gifts of stone, plush, and wooden armadillos, or joking that they has passed one of my cousins—flattened—on Snake Road, on the way in to Hollywood!

My personal relationship with James (the single name by which he is always recognized) and the Seminole people continues to the present day and, I hope, will do so for many days to come. I lived and worked with the Seminole people for a total of fifteen years. In all those years, I never considered them to be subjects of a study—that is, as distanced from myself. Nor would the Seminole people have permitted me to stay with them if I had; the final choice for me to be with them was always theirs—not mine. My relationship with them transcended that of a social scientist, as I have tried to make clear throughout the text, and was conditioned on their acceptance of my personal, far more important even than my professional, respect for, and understanding of, the invaluable social and cultural information that they were sharing with me as they came to know me. I have outlined my relationship in this area in my introduction to a previous publication, *The Tree That Bends: Discourse, Power, and the Survival of the Maskóki People* (The University of Alabama Press, 1999).

The Florida Seminoles are people whose memories of the wars against them waged by non-Indians are very strong and, as I stated in the text, even an entrée provided by the tribal chairman would not have been enough to persuade them to accept me, at any level, if they had believed that I was simply there to study them. As a consequence, they made their trust in me exceedingly clear (over the years, as I slowly earned it) and I, in turn, have not divulged numerous pieces of cultural information that they expressly desired not to have divulged. These, I have recorded and reserved, at their request, on their express behalf only. At the same time, I have never attempted to hide my profession and, indeed, wrote *The Tree That Bends* while living with them and discussing my theses with them in numerous instances and settings.

Finally, in a significant number of instances the people have gone so far as to send me out over the years to represent them in non-Indian settings. In this regard I served for several years as Tribal Historical Preservation Officer (THPO) for the tribe, and as an alternate delegate to the Culture and Heritage Committee of USET, the United South and Eastern Tribes. I have always felt honored to represent the Seminole people in any setting, and have understood quite clearly the "balance of trust" that existed in this process: I understood the fiduciary responsibility that resided in me to represent their information and their interests fairly, and they realized that their trust was conditioned on my sense of maintaining, in the most public settings, that responsibility. All of which is to say that the things, persons, events, and attitudes presented in this book are not items that I have taken away surreptitiously; they are the results of years of close discussions with many, many Seminole people, and I do not feel in any way that I am breaking trust with them now. In the writing, it was never my intention to make the book a personal memoir; it was not my story, even though it is my story to tell. Nor did I want to make the work so heavily academic as to distance the overall story from the intense humanity of my experiences. I trust that I have succeeded in walking that fine line.

Far beyond my own considerations, however, there is the uniqueness of the story itself that absolutely compels telling. In many aspects, it fairly defies credulity. It parallels the stories of sultans and potentates of fabulously wealthy, small, third world nations. And, indeed, it is the story of a small nation, awakening from the shock of prolonged physical warfare and the torpor of geographical and cultural isolation—an overwhelming reaction to the white man's fierce commitment to dominate—and seeking not the *assumption* of sovereignty but its *reassertion* in the face of continuing and mounting attempts from the white man's government to suppress its exercise and force the assimilation of its citizens.

Two major factors, and many minor ones, account for a death-defying rise to prominence of the Seminole Tribe of Florida, across Indian Country and in the larger Floridian and U.S. national consciousness in the last quarter of the twentieth century. One of these was the personal magnetism of James Billie, and his determination (albeit ultimately imperfect) to understand and use the prerogatives of sovereignty in order to secure the cultural survival of the people. The other—and, again, in great measure due to the determinism of James Billie—was the growth of bingo into Indian gaming, a source of annual gross revenues that provided what can only be termed a phenomenal power base for himself and the tribe. The annual budget of the tribe in 1979, when James first became chairman, was just passing $1 million for the first time. When he was forced out of office in 2003, the budget had risen to at least three hundred times that amount, with all the attendant notoriety and power that such an income inevitably brings.

Despite his centrality in the story, however, James Billie was not the only figure on the political landscape of the Seminole Tribe of Florida in the late twentieth century. The complex relationship between the chairman of the Tribal Council and the president of the Board of Directors of the Seminole Tribe of Florida, Inc., in itself provides an excellent example of internal tribal politics and the continuing value of a warrior posture among the people. Further, the smaller, internal, political machinations of the council and board representatives, each with a (family) clan at its base, constituted largely independent power spheres that had to be taken into account and manipulated—or co-opted—with great care by the chairman and the president. White men had, to a great extent, influenced the shape of the tribal government that was established in 1957. They could not, however, control its functioning because they could never control the internal cultural mechanisms by which the Seminole people chose their leaders. In half a millennium neither Europeans nor Euro-Americans had been able to do that.

Long before the external functions of the warriors began to change with the Seminoles' adoption of a white-man's-style governmental structure in 1957, however, the nature and requirements of the wars themselves had already begun to change radically as well. Shortly after 1858 and the end of its Indian Wars of Removal in the East, the United States plunged itself into the horrors of the American Civil War. A significant part of its aftermath was the second phase of the Indian Wars of Removal, culminating in yet another clash between expansionist white Americans and Native Americans, this time in the Indian Territory west of the Mississippi River.[18] By the 1870s, however, this phase of national growth was winding down, and the U.S. government had officially eschewed treaty making with the Indian nations, principally as a way of denigrating sovereignty, and was embarking upon a new phase of relations with Native Americans that I characterize as the period of Conquest by Legislation.[19] This is the phase that continues to the present day. In the case of the Seminole people, I frequently have characterized the resulting political aggressions of the twentieth century to them as the Fourth Seminole War.

It is to the process of cultural survival in the face of these new and profound pressures that Seminole leadership since 1957 has had to respond. Forms of traditional governance had overt warfare and the prowess of warriors as their touchstone. Consequently, the leadership styles required by the people have continued to focus on the characteristics of traditional warriors. As U.S. governmental pressures have increased, over the second half of the twentieth century, the Seminole people have looked more and more to their leaders to fulfill the traditional roles of warriors, but within a white man's legal and political system that they (the people) simply do not understand and still, for the most part, do not wish to understand. Therefore, the abilities of the elected leaders to respond to inside expectations and outside requirements all at the same time have determined the degrees to which they have had success as leaders. As the current chairman of the Tribal Council, Mitchell Cypress, once told me, "A man has to have two heads!"[20] That is to say, one head for the Indian world and the other for the white man's world. He has to learn how to navigate the two rivers that never meet—not an easy task.

If you want to understand the indigenous people of Florida, you can't escape the need to understand the land that sustains them, and the conditions of their lives. It is the unrelenting heat that sets the tone for all of life in South Florida. Below Orlando and Yeehaw Junction, the Hawthorne Formation or the Great Sandy Ridge, the topographic backbone of Florida, begins to slope off. Higher "piney woods" give way to sandy deposits overlaying deep calciferous layers formed from the marriage of warm and cold bodies of water. Swamplands, drained over the last century with no clear understanding of their ecological value to sustainable settlement, have survived mostly as agricultural fields. Thousands of acres of this rich black muck are farmed intensively as sugarcane and are burned several times annually as a thick, acrid, yellow smoke stings the eyes and sends the sinuses into brain-splitting spasms. More and more, the acres are covered or are being covered with the stubble of "development." It was, to a great extent, air conditioning that made this possible. The heat is a cloying presence that gums up the mind and drags at the arms and legs, establishing a top end for motion that promises heat stroke to anyone who tries to exceed it. People who have never experienced the heat's omnipresence imagine life in

South Florida as consisting entirely of beautiful sandy beaches and a laid-back lifestyle that one cannot find in the industrialized centers of the North. And this is a valid image, as far as it goes, but it reckons without the terrain and the climate.

Especially for the Indians the heat is a palpable actor in the drama of survival in South Florida. Their home for the last one and a half centuries has been almost exclusively the Everglades and the Big Cypress, the home also of a large percentage of the state's alligator, snake, and mosquito populations. The Seminoles managed to make a home out of it and, against the omnipresent backdrop of danger, have evolved a symbiosis. Sawgrass prairies shimmer in the heat, finally giving way, after miles and miles, to cypress domes that have become the northern frontier of the Everglades since nineteenth-century "reclamation" destroyed so much of the natural South Florida swampland that had lain to the north of it. The Seminoles define the spaces they occupy relative to the water that covers it, rather than the land. To them, the Everglades signify not land covered with water but, rather, *water*, with land *under* it. This distinction is critical to a people, some of whom (admittedly fewer each year) still orient their lives to the water, watercourses, and daily travel by dugout canoes.

In the 1930s some interested whites began to realize the pressures being placed upon the Indians by increasing white settlement, and they lobbied state and federal governments to formally set aside lands that would buffer the Indians from the pressures of future development.[21] The Indians who would choose, slowly, to move onto the Res lands preserved for them did so for a variety of reasons, principally in chain migrations that followed clan lines.

By 1979, when James Billie first took office as Tribal Council chairman, there were four reservations spread across the peninsula. Today there are six, still separated by wide distances of South Florida wilderness and a patchwork quilt of spreading white development. Tribal elders frequently refer to white people as "ants"—busily moving, building, crowding the landscape. In the 1970s the Seminoles still had the option to maintain their isolation on most of the "Res's" but that became well nigh impossible as the century drew to a close.

There remains today only a minimum of order underlying the who-lives-where of the reservations. There is, however, a great deal of order in the Seminoles' *process* of living. In two cases, the Indians' settlement patterns followed separate social lines. The Brighton Res, on the northwest shore of Lake Okeechobee, became the center of Maskókî or Creek amalgamation. These were, for the most part, descendants of those people who had migrated southward as a result of the Creek War of 1813–14 in Alabama and the Creek War of 1836 in Georgia. They were, as I have pointed out, cultural kin to the Hitchitis (today's Miccosukees). Their languages, however, once mother and child of the same tongue, had grown apart over time into mutually unintelligible languages. Further, there was a deep rift and a great lack of trust between the two groups, which had solidified over centuries, at least, of intertribal warfare and contentious experiences. As a reminder of this rift we may recall the anger of the Seminoles, who were mostly removed Miccosukees, at the determination of the U.S. government to place them on Creek lands in Indian Territory in the 1830s.[22]

This whole discussion of Maskókî/Creeks, Hitchitis/Miccosukees, and Seminoles is very confusing to nonhistorians (and still contentious even among historians). Such complex information is nevertheless valuable to our understanding of late twentieth-century Florida Indian politics for several reasons. For one reason, it helps us to understand why there are two separate Indian languages still spoken by the Indians of Florida today, and why neither of them can properly be called "Seminole."

Further, language does not define tribal affiliation. The Indians enrolled in the Miccosukee Tribe are almost exclusively core Mikísuukî speakers. But the great majority of the Indians enrolled in the Seminole Tribe are core Mikísuukî speakers also. The base language of the rest (the minority) of the Seminole tribal citizens is Creek, and most of these Seminole tribal citizens live on Brighton Res. Through culture and heredity, the citizens of both tribes are closely related. Through intermarriage, especially over the last century, many citizens of both tribes speak both languages today, and about one-third of these speak no English. Through political choice, clan kin and blood kin are split between the two political tribes. In many instances, fathers are enrolled in the Seminole Tribe while children are enrolled Miccosukee. Grandparents are in one, while grandchildren are in the other. It is a situation rather strange in Indian politics today, but no stranger (to us non-Indians) than many other relations shaped by the unique processes of Seminole politics today, as we shall see.

~

Comments on several social issues will be useful at this point. Throughout the book I refer to all the Florida Natives as "Indians," rather than as Native Americans or Indigenous Peoples, because they image themselves that way (just as they image their cultural "others" as white men and black men). Indian is a historical and geographical misapplication that they have taken to their hearts and reframed as a point of honor. In addition it is a constant reminder to non-Indians that "political correctness" is just another of our own imagings, and not theirs. There is no universal consensus across Indian Country concerning the cultural term by which they should be known. There is consensus, however, that no matter what the epithet, it should be used with respect. No amount of political correctness will ever equate with respect, and the Indians are exceedingly aware of this fact. They have had almost half a millennium to learn to recognize one from the other.

It also will be useful to understand the uses of "names" among the Seminoles and their ancestors, because the referents I have chosen to use in this work are those that are used by the Seminoles themselves. Although I have covered the larger traditional forms and uses in my earlier work, *The Tree That Bends*, the Indians' transition to persistent (not universal, just persistent) use of English or "white men's" names requires a little discussion as well. Obviously, the transition to English usages began as soon as there were more-or-less permanent settlements of English speakers encroaching upon the Maskókî territories, that is, from 1670 onward in the lower Southeast, and from 1763 onward in the area today comprising Florida. Spanish baptismal names and nicknames had been the first to compete with traditional naming forms as early as the Spaniards arrived, in the sixteenth century. But even these were transliterated at the whim or convenience of later English speakers.

Despite more than two centuries of English usage, however, Seminoles still really care little for white men's names, even today. Patterns of use shift in recognizable, if not traditional, manners but names shift at the whim of the wearer. Only private "Indian names" are constant, more or less in accordance with tradition, and even these still respond to a traditional system of change over the life of the bearer. White men's names oftentimes "flip" over generations. Thus, a Jim surname remains today, quite possibly descended from the "Jim Boy" or "High Head Jim" of Creek War notoriety. But succeeding generations have produced a Boy Jim, Johnny Jim, John Jimmie, and families with the surnames John and Johns, which are used by some, but not all, of the family today. Since we will be dealing principally with the later twentieth century in the present work, most of the individuals will be referred to by English names. If it becomes appropriate or useful to use an Indian name I will provide it, along with an explanation.

In the case of English names, however, single names are sometimes favored rather than forenames and surnames by Indian speakers. In other instances, two names, not necessarily including a surname, may be used in conversations to singularize an individual within a system with many repeated names. (Thus, "Henry" and "Henry John," and "Joe" and "Joe Junior.") Included in this system is the facet of social recognition. This is the primary reason why it is entirely appropriate to refer to Council Chairman the Honorable James E. Billie simply as "James." This fact creates a great deal of difficulty if the hearers are not all fully aware of the individuals under discussion. It also provides a simple method of excluding English-speaking hearers from understanding a conversation fully and keeping Indian business private. Consequently, my use of single names at various places in the text should not confuse readers and I will do my best to clarify subjects in their contexts.

∾

Next, it is important to understand the meaning and functioning of clans. Beyond the bounds of white-man's-style blood kinship and the system of patrilineal descent, which is only secondary today and traditionally was nonexistent in the Seminole world, clan kinship is the bond that ties together the citizens of both the Seminole and Miccosukee tribes, irrevocably.[23]

A clan is an extended family, but clan affiliation is passed exclusively through the mother.[24] If your mother is of Deer Clan, then you are a member of Deer Clan, and you will be all your life. If you are a male Deer, you must marry a woman of another clan, and certain clans are preferential to each clan. People who have sexual relationships, of any duration, with members of their own clans are branded *if'athi*, or "Dog People" (but such relationships have occurred nonetheless, human sexuality being what it is). Each clan is a matrilineal (but *not* matriarchal) social grouping, which constitutes the core element for social and political interactions in all larger settings. Individual rights exist, but must always be balanced against the good of the clan. Clan interactions are regulated by cultural value structures that place high positive value on communal concepts of order and balance. That is to say that equilibrium and reciprocity are core values in the Seminole worldview and their consequent imaging of (social) law and (political) order are modeled in the workings of the clan.

In Oklahoma the clan system has largely been lost and its function replaced by the non-Indian term "Bands" and Band affiliation, due to the pressures of the U.S. government over the last century and a half since Removal. In Florida, however, the traditional clan system and clan affiliations continue in use to the present day, and they continue to have a direct and powerful—and often precarious—impact upon Seminole politics. As one researcher noted, "For a Seminole, the position of leader is a position of jeopardy. He must be careful to offend no one, for he can easily become a hated object in a community where an entire extended family [clan] will take the side of an offended relative."[25]

Among the Seminole people, sociopolitical groups, historically, have ranged from the most basic unit, a camp comprising members of a single clan, to complex communities and cities embracing multiple clans, to even more complex regional groupings of cities, towns, and villages, all maintaining intra- and interclan relationships.[26] Regardless of the size of the grouping, however, each clan carries within itself the template for sociopolitical interaction and, consequently, can be replicated as required at successive levels of complexity in the larger society, and can be transmitted over space and time—that is, from place to place and generation to generation.

Clans cut across political lines and supersede all other considerations, as I have said before. Bear Clan, for example, did not and does not exist wholly within a single tribe. Bear and Panther and other clans could be found in various tribes among the ancestors of the Seminoles. Traditionally, members of a clan made seasonal "rounds," visiting with other members of their clan in other camps, communities, and cities, an ordered process that Europeans have arrogantly mistaken for nomadism.[27] If two culturally related tribes were not in a state of belligerence, then Bear Clan members had host and guest responsibilities during trading or ball games or other types of visits. This system continues to the present day in Florida and functions well even within the political system mandated by the U.S. government. It particularly creates difficulties, however, each month when dividends need to be distributed, and at election times when peripatetic voters must be located and relocated on whichever Res they are living on at the moment.

Tradition demanded that men should move to the clan camp of their wives at marriage. Men never gave up their own clans, but husbands and wives lived in the camps of her clan and the children she bore were *her* children, not *theirs*. Moreover, they were raised by her clan and not by the biological mother or by the biological mother and father. Each day, in the formal and informal processes of living in the clan camp, children received information transmitted from generation to generation by the elders of their clan.

This process of cultural and social transmission has been materially harmed—but *not* destroyed—as one result of the introduction of the U.S. government's Department of Housing and Urban Development's (HUD) housing program in the mid-twentieth century. HUD administrators mandated construction without regard for traditional clan residential systems. Living patterns were fragmented and generations were separated. Many Seminoles continued to live in a traditional *chiki(t)* (palm-thatched, open-sided hut) rather than in their cheap, hot, cramped HUD houses, which they used mostly as storage units. The clan camps are used less frequently but still are used as gathering places on formal occasions, although the clan system remained, and remains, strong.

Neither the core Maskókî language, now known as Creek, nor its Hitchiti dialect, today known as Miccosukee, and still spoken by the citizens of the Seminole Tribe of Florida, contains any specific word for "politics" or for the function of "democracy," or even for the core concept of "sovereignty." The people never have viewed such compartmentalizations as necessary. Nevertheless, these concepts and their practices have long been integral to the social functioning of the Seminoles and their ancestors. Thus the core concepts of "political" decision making and governance remain as viable today as they have been throughout the previous centuries. Numerous intricately layered interclan responsibilities order the governmental workings of the larger community. As but one example, certain elements of civic, spiritual, governmental, and military responsibilities have rested with specific clans and are assigned to specific positions within various clans. These positions, in turn, were filled by successive individuals. That is, it is not the individuals who are central to the process. Rather, it is the process and its continuation that are central to the cultural perpetuation of the people.

Within this system power was transmitted in a prescribed fashion from generation to generation. Power was never absolute, however, in that every hereditary responsibility or privilege had to be confirmed by the people and reconfirmed annually at four major liturgical events, the most important of which took place in early or late summer (depending on geography and climate), at the time when the corn was green. This *búsketau,* "fasting time," or busk, known to English speakers as the Green Corn Ceremony, and witnessed or alluded to over the centuries by Europeans and Euro-Americans, continues to take place to this day.[28] In fact, at the time of this writing, there are four separate Green Corn Ceremonies in four separate geographic locations, serving four separate communities served by four separate Medicine men and their acolytes, holding four separate Medicine bundles. Thus the reciprocity and equilibrium of the circular Seminole world were embodied in the functioning of the clans and were echoed in public rituals performed by the clans at the communal and regional levels.

~

Within the clans, individuals obtained status by their prolonged commitment to the welfare of the people. Among these individuals, *hilíswa haya* (shamen, or "Medicine people") were, and remain, the most powerful. "Medicine" was the realm of life that connected the seen and the unseen worlds. Much more than Christian "priests" or "preachers," Medicine practitioners might be generalists or specialists, and each clan might have one or more of such individuals. Medicine people might be either male or female. Medicine practitioners frequently had and have specialties, some focusing their powers on war Medicine, a position of especial status whose practitioners were said to be able to stop bullets, raise a fog to hide the Indians from their enemies, and make guards fall asleep so Indian prisoners could escape, among other critical abilities. Others specialized in female health, some in the curing of specific or general illnesses, some functioning as "seers" of the future, and so on. Certain clans, however, held primary responsibility for practicing, renewing, and safeguarding the ceremonies and rituals that kept, and continue to keep, the people strong. As but one historical example of this specialization process, the Guale people of the Sea Islands (off today's Georgia) were so called by the Maskókî people because *oówali(t)* (transliterated as Guale) meant (and means) "seer."[29]

A principal actor among these was and is Panther Clan, a "red" clan because red is the color of blood—living blood as well as blood shed in warfare. Panthers live close to the ground and, therefore, are especially knowledgeable about plants and their uses. Panthers fight for the people in two ways: as warriors who protect the people from the aggressions of other people, and as Medicine people, that is, as warriors who protect the people from personal illnesses, which can come from many sources. When Panthers make Medicine for the people during the rituals of the Green Corn Ceremony, omnipowerful Wind Clan stands alongside. Bird Clan, the lawgivers and a "white" or peace clan, organize and arrange the rituals, maintain order, and arbitrate disputes according to a clan-specific system. Their realm is the air, with Wind and, so, they have a grand vantage point for seeing overall processes. Wind, however, goes everywhere, to places where no other clan can go and so has predominant powers, powers allotted to no other clan.

No clan makes arbitrary decisions in matters of ritual and ceremony, however. Each is following age-old requirements. Even when Bird sends out the man designated as the *tastenaki* (var., *tustenakee*) to inform the people of the next event during the Green Corn Ceremony, each of these messengers carries a wand or shaft of power (a cane in Oklahoma), holding it up before him to remind the people that he speaks not for himself but only by the power of the Medicine man who, in turn, speaks not from his own authority but with the authority of tradition—tradition established by the superordinate power *hisáki(t) imisit* (Maskókî) or *fosáki(t) oómichet* (Mikísuukî), the Maker or Giver of Breath.

Bears are powerful, but only within their own earthly realms. Otters are playful, but dangerous because of their mercurial natures: they bite. Deer are gentle unless and until provoked. Tradition demands great respect for Snakes. In the old days, warriors carved the heads and tails of their long bows in the shapes of *chinti chobi* (Mikísuukî) or *chitto thlocco* (Maskókî), the Big Snake, the southeastern diamondback rattler. Seminoles do not generally kill snakes today, although they seem to have done so in past centuries—perhaps except the *chinti chobi*. Currently, there are very few Snakes left, but among them was Betty Mae Tiger Jumper, who proved herself a warrior of the first magnitude for her people.

Each Medicine man who directs a Green Corn ceremonial ground is, as a principal responsibility inherent to his position, also a "bundle carrier." This Medicine bundle is the focus of all the power of the people, as a people, and contains items of power that preserve and increase the strength of the people necessary to maintain themselves as a people. The majority of its contents traditionally have been war-power items. Each year, at the Green Corn Ceremony, the central ritual is the unwrapping and examination and replenishment of the Medicine bundle, following which it is secreted again for another year. The Seminoles today quietly mourn the diminishing number of war-related items in the bundle. Their slow attrition over the last century and a half during which the warriors have been without military warfare has created a *basso continuo* of anxiety among the Seminole people. Without the continuing presence of military warfare to sustain the Medicine's power, and without its power to sustain the people, the Seminoles believe that their survival as a culture is materially weakened.

To the present day the continuing strength of the clan system also constitutes political power bases to a great extent. Much of Fred Smith's power base came from within his Bird Clan, in Brighton. Howard Tommie, also Bird Clan, told a reporter upon his first election, in 1971, "I do belong to a large clan and that was very helpful."[30] James Billie, Howard's successor and yet another member of Bird Clan, also depended on his clan in maintaining his power. Mitchell and David Cypress's Otter Clan, of moderately large numbers, has provided support, but Mitchell and David's power bases have also crosscut clan lines. David, council representative from BC Res, has the support of the elders there, to whom David caters liberally (although hardly exclusively) with his annual discretionary Reservation Allotment. Mitchell's clan was helpful, but his success also had a great deal to do with Fred Smith's tutelage. As we shall see, however, during the final quarter of the twentieth century almost every tribal politician began to make personal use of growing tribal revenues—counting on the support of his or her clan to support his actions actively and buying much of the rest. (David Cypress would blatantly attest to this process in federal court testimony, discussed later in chapters 10–13.)

Today the Seminole Tribe of Florida is composed of nine major clans and three minor clans, although one hundred or more clans may have existed over time. Segments of these same clans exist also within the Miccosukee Tribe of Indians of Florida. The major clans are: Wind, (Big) Bird, Panther, Bear, Deer, Otter, Snake, Big Town (earlier known as Toad Clan), and Mole. The minor clans are (Little) Bird, Bobcat, and Wolf. They are minor clans because over the past century or so their numbers have diminished to the point where it was necessary to fold them in to their affinity clans in order to keep from losing them entirely. Consequently, Little Bird Clan was subsumed by Big Bird Clan. Wolf became a part of Bear, and Bobcat was folded into Panther. When their numbers once again become large enough to sustain them independently, they will reemerge as separate clans. Biologically speaking, the size of a clan is dependent upon the number of females produced in any generation and the number of female offspring they produce. Women sustain the clan and, therefore, the tribe. But, ultimately, the moment when a subsumed clan is strong enough to reemerge will come when the people decide that it has come.

Tahkósai(t), or Mole Clan, presents a special illustration of this process, as well as an excellent example of the political power of the clans. Social tradition has it that the *tahkosî(t)*, or Mole (the totem), did not come out of the ground at the same time as the other clan totems. Indeed, Mole came out so much later that the people of the other clans were not sure that he was a man, like them. So they threw him some meat, to see if he would eat it and, therefore, prove that he was one of them. He did take the meat and, so, his people were accepted among the clans, but they are still referred to, to this day, as "found people."

Over the years Mole Clan people proved themselves to be staunch keepers of tradition but, unfortunately, their righteous ways were accompanied by an ever-increasing amount of overbearing righteousness. The other clans tired of being upbraided by them for every perceived transgression and began to kill them off. Finally, when only a few of them were left, it was decided that their hubris had been sufficiently quelled, and they were left alone. Almost extinct, they were subsumed by their uncles, the Otter Clan. In traditional Seminole fashion, no timeframe is attached to these events. They may well have been recent, however, as *tahkósai(t)*, or Mole Clan, was well known during the Seminole Wars and represented in Oklahoma when John Swanton of the Bureau of American Ethnology worked there in the first half of the twentieth century. They were not identified as an autonomous clan in the late nineteenth and early twentieth centuries in Florida, however. It was not until the 1980s, after almost a century of genetic renaissance, that they had regained sufficient numbers as to constitute a separate clan once again, and so became able to function as a viable political force. Billy Cypress, chairman of the Miccosukee Tribe until 2010, is *tahkósai(t)*, and his chairmanship was very much the result of the size, ergo, the political strength, of his clan.[31]

One further group must be discussed here as well. It is what I refer to as "Clan X," or the "No Clan Clan." This is not, properly, a clan at all, and the group of people represented by it is in a very precarious position socially within the tribe. Nevertheless, it exists, and its numbers are growing rapidly and radically. Clan X did not exist until the early 1970s, when social standards shifted sufficiently as to permit a growing number of Seminole males and females to partner sexually with non-Seminoles and to produce offspring. During the years of the Wars of Removal, such fraternization would have been punished by ostracization of the Seminole parent or execution of both parent and child. In fact, the latest case I have heard of, of a mixed-blood child's being left on the banks of a canal, its mouth filled with mud, to be eaten by alligators—a process the Seminoles refer to as being "let go"—was in the 1950s. The occasion and increase of mixed-blood offspring appears to have coincided with the rise of migrant labor camps in Immokalee and Palm Beach County, and the extension of railroad lines (requiring white, male workers) southward on both the east and west coasts of the Florida peninsula.

If a Seminole woman had a child whose biological father was non-Seminole (regardless of whether he was black, white, Asian, or of any other ethnicity), the problem was not so great because clan kinship passes through the mother, and the child would, therefore, have a Clan affiliation. If, however, the Seminole biological parent was a man and his female partner was a non-Seminole, the child would be destined to suffer from significant social displacement because it would have no clan. In the mid-1970s, the numbers of such children were few. By the mid-1980s the numbers had grown sufficiently as to overtake Otter Clan as the (distant) third-largest clan in the tribe, after Panther Clan and Bird Clan. As this book is being written, unfortunately, Clan X rivals Panther Clan for plurality in the tribe.

Clan consensus was, and continues to be, carried forward to the community level, where it is the continuing expectation of the Seminole people that the good of the whole always will be the primary consideration of the people and the touchstone by which leadership is judged. The process of consensus decision making, a horizontal power structure that contrasts starkly with the vertical power system of Euro-Americans, was modeled first within the clan and, then, mirrored in the early Tribal councils. This conciliar format for consensus decision making has existed for at least half a millennium among the Seminoles and their ancestors. In earlier days, individuals were admitted to the council because of their experiences as warriors and/or civic leaders and clan representatives, but always with the approbation of the community. With the inception of the fictitious political agency, the Seminole Tribe of Florida, in the mid-twentieth century, the people transferred some (but not all) of their leadership and decision-making expectations to their elected Tribal Council, on the premise that the white-man's-style entity would not transfer white men's laws into the tribe but, rather, would serve to buffer the Seminoles *from* white men's laws. Therefore, a new form of council emerged, but the expectations of the people did not change.

Specific public ceremonies and rituals attended law making, law giving, and the process of dispensing justice, which, rather than a mere rule of law, or law enforcement, always has been the basis of Seminole order. These rituals and public processes of order and community renewal and reaffirmation continue to be enacted each year, as central elements of the Green Corn Ceremony, from which many citizens continue to draw strength and renew their commitments to the larger community.

Medicine men and women continue to occupy positions as statused social figures, preserving and practicing rituals and ceremonies that have given form and coherence to Seminole society for thousands of years. Their province is to keep individuals and, thereby, the larger community, in balance. Their work is neither in place of nor in opposition to the responsibilities of the chairman and the Tribal Council, just as the Medicine practitioners, clan elders, and the *mikkó* did not function in opposition to one another. In the Seminole world, the efforts of each are required to maintain the balance of all. As we shall see, however, by the late twentieth century, the lure of the non-Indian world had begun to exert a potent force on this new breed of political warriors, and the resulting social tension would erupt, for the first time ever, in the suspension and impeachment of a chairman, James Billie.

~

The ancestors of the Seminoles never considered it necessary to develop systems for writing down their languages and history or documenting their social systems. Oral transmission of information has been sufficient and eminently successful for them and their ancestors for thousands of years. No society is static, however, whether Indian or non-Indian. Neither is any body of sociocultural information transmitted in pristine form over generations. Certainly, no Euro-Americans today maintain information across generations in exactly the same form in which their own ancestors knew it, centuries earlier, even with the assistance of written records.

Such a requirement is implicit, nevertheless, in the U.S. government's forcing the Seminoles (and other FR Indian tribes) to create and function upon a written, constitutional form of government, on the Euro-American model. In yet another response to this assimilative pressure, the Seminoles have accepted this external requirement but melded it, in every way possible, with traditional internal systems of self-governance, as I have outlined here. Whenever the functional requirements of the U.S. constitutional template have come into direct conflict with overarching traditional requirements for the greater welfare of the people, the Tribal Council has expressed the sovereign right of the Seminole people to alter or abolish it as *they* see fit.

In practice, what matters ultimately is not whether a social system is perfectly or imperfectly transmitted from generation to generation. What matters is that *a system is transmitted.* In the case of the Seminole people, a system for replication of information existed and continues to exist because its principal elements—the clans, Medicine men and women, a generation of elders, and the warrior mentality—continue to exist.

2   Coming of Age in the '70s

In 1565, Don Pedro Menéndez de Avilés's Spanish soldiers tried to make a deal with the Indian whom they called "Felipe," one of Carlos's people, later to be known as the Calosa or Calusa, whose territory centered near present-day Fort Myers on Florida's lower west coast. The Spaniards had killed Carlos, believing that he plotted against them, and installed Felipe, thinking that they could direct him as their puppet. Felipe balked. He could not do as the Spaniards directed him, he said, because the things they wanted would not meet the expectations of his people. The people, he said, would kill him. The Spaniards pressed and threatened violence. The people threatened violence. Felipe demurred but would not acquiesce. The Spaniards killed him.[1]

The story, even though greatly simplified here, has changed little in its principal elements since then. In 1954, while the U.S. Congress was attempting to force its Termination Acts upon the FR tribes, the annual report of the Seminole Agency director to the Muscogee (Oklahoma) Area Office had stated baldly, "The basic Federal policy for all Indians recognizes that they will eventually have to participate more or less in the non-Indian's way of life."[2] In 1977, however, when the tribe celebrated the twentieth anniversary of its political incarnation, the Seminoles told the world, "Essentially the reservation Indians have accepted the policy of self-determination, attempting to be as self-sufficient as possible and to foster non-interference with their historic culture and traditional way of life while [at the same time] embracing 20th century living."[3] In 1987 the great historian of American Indian history, Francis Paul Prucha, summed up not only the BIA's attitude, but also that of the larger U.S. government when he wrote: "The best term for this persistent attitude is paternalism, a determination to do what was best for the Indians according to white norms, which translated into protection, subsistence of the destitute, punishment of the unruly, and eventually taking the Indians by the hand and leading them along the path to white civilization and Christianity."[4]

Two elements are important in the Seminoles' response, above. First is the traditional value of equilibrium: twentieth-century non-Indian living absolutely balanced against traditional Indian culture. Second is the aggressive commitment to "non-interference." Even as the Seminoles accepted what the white man viewed as beneficence, they asserted their determination to accept only on their own terms, reverberating the same attitude espoused by their ancestors four centuries earlier.

Each non-Native power seeking dominion over the land and the Native peoples has, nevertheless, sought to control the processes of interaction inside the group. Each of these interlopers has failed to understand, however, the vitality and durability of the group's systems, and the depth of their warrior commitment to the preservation of their culture. As a consequence of this "simple" fact, the Indians of Florida remain, to this day.

Demographic Impact

What might euphemistically be called "The Hundred Years' Solitude" of the Florida Indians, from the end of the U.S. Wars of Removal in 1858 through the Indians' reentry into the full-body contact sport of white men's politics in 1957, was a double-edged sword. For most of its years, the isolation of the Indians on the southern peninsula, in areas of little or no white settlement, protected the Indians from extracultural pressures and gave them precious time to recoup and reassert their fractured social systems. Above all else, it gave the Indians time to recover demographically. Adult males relied upon the traditional system, so frustrating to European Christians, of taking multiple wives, and the birth rate, as a result, generally exceeded the death rate. As a result, a population that Euro-Americans smugly asserted would decline rapidly, instead grew slowly but surely.

By the end of 1977, the population of the Seminole Tribe had reached 1,283: Hollywood Res, 364; BC Res, 319; Brighton Res, 284; and off-Res, 316. (Totals adjusted for death and relinquishments to Miccosukee.) Including also the number, nearly five hundred, who had enrolled in the Miccosukee Tribe, this meant that the number of South Florida Indians had increased more than fivefold since the end of the United States' Wars of Removal, in 1858.

The population had grown slowly over the second half of the nineteenth century, but the fact that it had grown at all was, in itself, nothing short of a miracle. After 1858, all actions of U.S. governmental and military officials had been grounded in the assumption that mortality rates would sufficiently exceed birth rates so that the remaining Florida Indians would suffer a steady and inevitable decline into oblivion.

Several factors combined to thwart this ethnocentric expectation. One was the fact that the harshness of the Florida Everglades was neither a new nor an unmanageable reality for the Indians. The so-called Seminoles—the core group of the survivors who had coalesced in the Everglades—had long known "the Pointed Land," and even those whose more northerly Maskókî (Creek) families had moved southward in the century between 1715 and 1815 had hunted deep into the peninsular lands across the generations and the centuries before.

Another survival factor was contained in the age-old marriage traditions of the Maskókî peoples whose lifeways were shaped by the centrality of warfare. The loss of men in battles resulted in a superfluity of marriageable women. The practice of taking kidnap brides added to the situation. The practice of polygamy, therefore, including sororate polygyny, relieved the sexual imbalance. It was a prerogative of statused warriors to take multiple wives and, particularly, wives who were sisters. Women captured as spoils of battle were distributed as battle honors. Further, marriage was traditionally matrilocal. That is, upon marriage, men went to live in the clan camps of their wives, where clan sisters were readily available for widowers, under certain circumstances. A choice of wives was not the unilateral prerogative of the male, however. The clan camp was a well-ordered social grouping, not a singles bar. If a wife died, and her clan elders so chose, they could keep the husband (rather than return him to his own clan), and provide him with another, or other, clan wives. Then, if an unusually large number of prime-aged males was lost at any time—due to disease or the vicissitudes of war—young males took older women as partners, or older men took much younger female mates, as the tribal elders felt necessary.

Most important for the survival of the Florida Indians after the end of the Wars of Removal is the fact that these long-established social practices did not end with the end of the wars. Of the thirty-seven separate families (certainly an undercount) enumerated on the U.S. Census of 1880 for Florida, six included a male head and two or more sisters or wives at the same time.[5] By 1914, the practice had diminished as the number of males available was once again increasing, but the practice persisted into the middle of the twentieth century.

By the moment of the formation of the political entity, the Seminole Tribe of Florida, in 1957, although infant mortality rates were undoubtedly significant, demographic growth was a product of a slow but steady incline in the number of births over deaths.[6] At this time, this demographic growth was based almost entirely upon marriages between and among Indians. Even up to this moment—the mid-twentieth century—sexual relations between Indians and non-Indians was a serious and punishable social offense. Infants born as a result of an Indian–non-Indian sexual liaison still were being "let go" by strongly traditionalist families. That is, the babies were suffocated by filling their mouths with mud and their tiny bodies were left on river or canal banks to be eaten by alligators. This was a desperate response of a group under profound cultural pressure to survive.

The decade of the 1970s, however, became a cultural, social, and demographic watershed for the Seminoles. During this decade the population of the state grew by 43.3 percent, from 6.8 to 9.8 million residents. A concurrently sharp rise was occurring in the populations of the non-Indian towns surrounding and encroaching upon the reservations. Increasingly efficient forms of transportation were ending even the old illusions of isolation that had buffered Indians from the non-Indians in South Florida. The populations of Hollywood and Dania and greater Fort Lauderdale, together with the rest of Broward County, rose 62 percent in the short decade of the 1970s. The populations of Hendry, Glades, and Okeechobee counties, pressure points for the Big Cypress, Immokalee, and Brighton reservations, rose 46.1, 24.4, and 74.9 percent, respectively.[7]

As Christian values and other nontraditional white legal and social pressures mitigated against infanticide and in favor of fraternization and assimilation, traditional tribal sanctions against intercourse with non-Indians were less determinedly enforced by traditionalist elders. As late as the 1930s and 1940s, as the South Florida Indians had been forced into the agricultural workplace, their relations with non-Indians still had been suppressed by force of traditions and by the social ascendancy of the Medicine people and the clan elders. By the 1970s, however, citizens were looking to the new political elites for exercise of some of the authority previously held by traditional power elements, and certain of the Old Ways were less stridently enforced.

Changes in crops and in Florida state laws governing the introduction and movements of migrant workers over the period of the 1960s and into the 1980s resulted in dramatic increases in the numbers of Mayans and other Mexican Indians, Cubans, Haitians, and American blacks in the nearby Collier, Hendry, and Palm Beach counties, creating the occasion for an increasing amount of social and physical intercourse with the Seminoles.[8] The Seminole Tribe experienced a direct impact from these demographic changes as a dramatic and rapid upsurge in the instances of out-marriages and casual liaisons with non-Indians rapidly increased the birth of half-blood-quantum (Q) children, including a growing percentage of children without clans.

This last fact has occasioned a constantly exacerbating social situation within the tribe. First and foremost, because until the early 1970s there was almost no Seminole citizen who did not have and know his or her clan affiliation. The Florida Seminoles have been justly proud of this fact, particularly since the Oklahoma Seminoles have almost completely lost their clan connections and replaced them with fictive "band" affiliations. As Seminole females began, in the 1970s, to take non-Indian male sexual partners, the situation was annoying but not critical. Mixed-blood children have always constituted a diminished social caste and have been subject to derision both from inside and outside the tribe, but, at least, mixed-blood children of Seminole mothers still had a clan.

As the number of Seminole males taking non-Seminole women as sexual partners began to rise, however, the situation worsened appreciably. Clan membership is the sine qua non of Maskókî social placement. Without it individuals are untethered, free floating in the social cosmos, and their existence harms both themselves and the tribe. A child with no Seminole mother has no clan. In 2005, Clan X, as I have dubbed it, had risen in numbers sufficiently as to become the second largest "Clan" in the Seminole Tribe. This threatens the equilibrium of the tribe. At the same time, however, it would contravene all of Seminole tradition for the Tribal Council to attempt to legislate interpersonal relationships between Seminoles and non-Seminoles, even though they certainly had been expected to do so, and had done so, in the past, in times of war. At one point in the later 1990s I presented James with statistics on the growing Clan X problem. His response was to openly but unofficially promulgate the idea of a Seminole Full-Blood Sperm Bank that could guarantee the permanent availability of a full-blood gene pool. James has understood the value of DNA science since he first heard of it (although there are other aspects of the DNA subject that he knows to have severely negative value for the Seminoles and Indians generally). The idea was before its time, however: Seminole men didn't understand it, and Seminole women had a wonderful laugh.

Readers should be aware that, throughout this discussion, I have used the term "marriage" only in a generic sense, rather than in the formalist terms of the non-Indian world. Traditionally, and even up to the mid-twentieth century, Seminoles have had only a limited interest in white man's "marriage." They have kept to their own arranged marriages and traditional commitment rituals that the Europeans had been able to do very little to change. Modern Christian missionaries, however, have sought to impose Christian marriage requirements, especially including premarital celibacy, upon converts, but with only limited success. Regardless of their most stringent admonitions, sexual repression has not been a traditional feature of Seminole life. Among the Old Ways were certain socially acceptable sexual activity patterns, but these were neither based upon, nor necessarily consistent with, non-Indian beliefs, despite more than four centuries of Christian contacts and proselytization. In the Florida Boom Period of the 1920s, South Florida tourist attraction owners began the practice of hiring Seminole families to "live" on site in exhibition camps during the winter visitor season and also staged Seminole "weddings" for the tourists, in which an uncomfortable looking man and woman donned white man's wedding finery and permitted themselves to be photographed for embarrassingly unusual postcards.

In the second half of the twentieth century, specifically during the watershed decade of the 1970s, two major changes began to occur, as the Old Ways, some new Christian requirements, and increasingly easy and frequent access to non-Indians collided. The idea of a formalized marriage ceremony including the gown, flowers, and celebratory trappings of white man's weddings began to appeal to some of the Seminoles, first and foremost those on the Hollywood Res where non-Indian newspaper accounts and photographs touted such events. The syncretistic result made a minor ripple on the greater Seminole lake.

A major and, unfortunately, still growing wave was created in this same decade by the growing importance of South Florida agriculture and its increasing need for migrant labor. There are no figures available from any source on the ethnic origins of the males whose genes paired with those of Seminole women to produce offspring of diminishing Q beginning in this decade. Neither are there figures available on the ethnic origins of the women who were taken as sexual partners by Seminole men, except in several broad categories. Seminole enrollment records sometimes indicate whether a non-Indian biological father or mother was Indian (other than Seminole), black, or white.

The single overarching requirement that remains within today's Seminole society is that the facade of propriety should be maintained. This stricture extends as well to the gay and lesbian population of the tribe, which, I believe to be (on the basis of my own observations and information) slightly less than that of the non-Indian population but significant nonetheless: Don't ask, Don't tell. Everybody knows, but nobody knows. The surface of the lake *must* remain placid.

Recognition and Enrollment

The history of U.S.-Indian relations notwithstanding, by the 1970s the Seminole people of Florida had moved into and through the first half of the twentieth century in a relatively positive manner. In response to evolving U.S. social attitudes, the Florida Indians had received help from non-Native support groups of concerned white citizens, from the State of Florida, and from the U.S. government, and both their demographics and their economic base were slowly (very slowly) climbing upward. According to the BIA/Seminole Agency's 1957 Census of Florida Indians, there were at least 977 Seminole Indians in Florida by midcentury—an increase of more than 300 percent over their post–Removal Wars low of two hundred to three hundred individuals.

This number ostensibly represented all of the South Florida Indians, at this time generically referred to by non-Indians as Seminoles. It almost certainly was not a precise number, owing to the fact that the Indians lived in widely separated camps and on geographically distant Res's, which made finding all of them extremely difficult. Further, many of the Indians were not interested in being found by the white government, and never had been.[9] The white men's wars, still too recent in their memories, had taught them the value of not being found.

It is important to realize also that the BIA's 1957 census was only that, a census, a *head count*—not a Tribal Roll, another cultural misunderstanding that has bedeviled the Seminole Tribe for almost sixty years thus far. In 2006 I was asked by the office of the tribal secretary to review the tribal constitution, by-laws, and council ordinances and resolutions pertaining to tribal enrollment, and to prepare a Tribal Enrollment Officer's Protocol Manual. My review and assessment could only clarify the process and its problems as they currently stand, however; constitutional revisions will be necessary to align the conflicting elements, several of which have been occasioned by the failure to differentiate between a *census* and a *roll*.

As I have indicated earlier, when the original constitution was created, in 1957, the Seminoles were not envisioning any future moment when they would not know, personally, individuals who would seek tribal enrollment. They were envisioning neither the children who would be born to tribal citizens and partners outside of the tribe, nor the outside individuals who would be driven by the possibility of free money from a share of gaming dividends to seek enrollment. Nor were they envisioning, even in 1957, the moment a short five years later when their population would be split because of the U.S. government's recognition of a second tribe in Florida, one that would be composed of grandmothers and sisters and brothers of the Seminole people themselves. Over the last quarter of the twentieth century all of these elements would become factors of serious concern for the Seminole Tribe in regard to its enrollment policy.

As the process of U.S.-style political affiliation began in 1957, each one of those 977-plus people had to make a choice whether to request enrollment (parents made the request for children under eighteen) in the new political organization, the Seminole Tribe of Florida, and the Tribal Council had to agree to their enrollment by individual council resolutions. Thus began the creation of a separate Tribal Roll, the tribe's base citizenship roll, which is the core of its sovereign nationhood to this day. The constitution required that applicants for citizenship should have a minimum quantum (Q) of one-quarter *tribal* blood—not a total of one-quarter *Indian* blood. (Tribal Q refers only to the total of Florida Seminole blood a person carries. Indian Q is the total of Indian blood quanta that an individual might derive from several FR tribes. For example, if a person's mother was one-half Florida Seminole and one-half Seneca, and their father was one-half Mescalero Apache and one-half Shawnee, then that person's Indian Q would be 4/4 or 100 percent, but their Florida Seminole Q would be only 1/4 or 25 percent.)

This process would go on for years as, one by one, the Florida Indians decided upon whether or not they saw a value in tribal affiliation. The benefits of such an affiliation might seem obvious to non-Indians, but to the Indians the principal negative factor lay in being branded "government Indians," a tag that remained a blasphemy to those whose anger at the memory of the Removal Wars remained high.

Nevertheless, over the first five years of the tribe's political existence, several hundred Florida "Seminoles" applied for citizenship and were enrolled in the Seminole Tribe of Florida. By 1962, several hundred others had enrolled in the new and separately recognized Miccosukee Tribe of Indians of Florida instead. Over the ensuing years, a few dozen others eventually changed their minds and relinquished their citizenship in the Seminole Tribe to enroll Miccosukee. In a unique element of tribal government, the Florida Seminoles, in recognition of the single cultural identity from which both tribes derived, codified the right of each person to change tribal citizenship, but only once. That is, an enrolled citizen of the Seminole Tribe had the right to withdraw—to relinquish Seminole citizenship—and seek enrollment with the Miccosukee Tribe. Miccosukees, if they had never been enrolled earlier with the Seminoles, could pursue the same course, if they could meet the other requirements as specified in the tribal constitution, bylaws, ordinances, and resolutions. A degree of contentiousness was associated with this decision originally, born of tribal pride and the ages-old belligerent warrior mentality, and that contention, and contentiousness, has blossomed into open animosity over the years.

Two factors in particular have exacerbated this condition. One has been the revenues generated by gaming since 1979 and, especially since the introduction of high-stakes gaming in 1989, the parallel increases in dividends offered to tribal citizens by each tribe (the Miccosukee Tribe would not begin its own bingo operation until 1990). The other factor has been the increasing intransigence of the Miccosukees as they have attempted to position themselves as the true and only keepers of the Old Ways. This has resulted in their raising the minimum Q for enrollment eligibility from one-quarter to one-half, in what they announced as a determination to purge their nation of mixed bloods and, as a consequence, disenrolling some citizens who immediately sought citizenship with the Seminoles. The Seminoles were not amused. They passed a resolution banning enrollment by erstwhile Miccosukees, on the premise that they did not want the other tribe "dumping their trash" on the Seminoles.[10] That resolution technically remains active today but is enforced selectively by the Seminole Tribal Council, despite warnings from some tribal officials that selective enforcement leaves the Seminole Tribe open to charges of discrimination. Such a charge would be hard to make "stick," however, because of the sovereignty, ergo, sovereign immunity, of each tribe.

One family, however, never enrolled in either tribe, and some of their children and grandchildren remain "independent" to this day. Mike Osceola, a member of the original 1957 Constitutional Committee, clashed with the other members over restrictions that he viewed as preferential to Res residents. In anger, he refused to participate further in the formation of the tribe.[11] Some Seminole elders today recall that the choice for his leaving was theirs rather than his. Today, his descendants still live almost entirely in a single camp along the western end of the Tamiami Trail. This tiny group of approximately one hundred today, unfortunately, is not only determined to maintain its independence but also to position itself as the only "true" Indians in Florida, notwithstanding the same claims by the Miccosukees, and the fact that both the Seminoles and the Miccosukees—but not the "independents"—are FR tribes, and despite the close clan and blood kinship of all these groups. This boast on the part of the independents has caused very little inconvenience to the citizens of the Seminole Tribe or to the citizens of the Miccosukee Tribe, which provides limited benefits and resources to the independents regardless of their nonenrollment, but it has inconvenienced the U.S. government considerably, in one regard at least, which we will discuss shortly.

The Indian (Land) Claims Act

When the U.S. Congress passed the Indian Claims Act in 1946, its aim was to settle, once and for all, suits being brought by tribes in the U.S. Court of Claims.[12] These suits had arisen on such grounds as treaty fraud and duress, the taking of lands without payment, and any other claim for which a tribe might have cause to bring suit against the U.S. government in a federal court, if the United States had not been protected from such suits by its own sovereign immunity. A handful of Florida lawyers, supporters of the Florida Indians, helped them to bring a claim in 1949, asking recompense for the historic taking of the Indians' Florida lands. The fact that the U.S. Congress was willing to entertain such suits, however, did not mean that the U.S. government was prepared to admit culpability and pay awards for such suits.

By the time the Seminole case was favorably adjudicated twenty-one years later, the Seminole Nation of Oklahoma (SNO), the Miccosukee Tribe, and the independent (by then also referred to as Trail) Indians had all joined the suit to claim that they were the only Indians who had suffered from the taking of Florida lands, as evidenced by their removal (in the case of the SNO), or to forward a claim to recover the lands themselves (as in the case of the independent Indians of the Trail). The award, in 1970, was $12,262,780.[13] Unfortunately, the tribes and the independents—albeit unhappy with the final award amount—fought among themselves over the way in which the judgment funds should be distributed. This wrangling among the tribes and the independents resulted in the U.S. government's withholding distribution of the settlement funds until Congress, finally, forced a distribution on the tribes, another twenty years later, in 1990, forty years after the claim originally had been placed with the Indian Land Claims Commission (ILCC).

Ultimately, Public Law 101-277, 104 Stat. 143, split the settlement (plus interest) 75 percent/25 percent between the SNO and the Florida Indians. Of the 25 percent of the award earmarked for the Florida Indians, 77.2 percent went to the Seminole Tribe, 18.6 percent to the Miccosukee Tribe, and 4.64 percent was earmarked for the independent (Trail) Indians. The total funds to be distributed to the Miccosukee Tribe and to the independents were to be held in trust pending the submission of a distribution plan from each of the recipient groups. But the independent or Trail Indians refused to accept their portion and continue to refuse it to this day, claiming that their acceptance of the award would negate their claim to recovery of the land itself.[14] The untenability of their position seems to have escaped them: the government's premise of their having been permitted to bring suit to begin with was that an award would negate their land claim. Periodically, the BIA sends a representative to attempt to negotiate their acceptance of the money, which amount, plus interest, is growing annoyingly large (and embarrassingly large, no doubt, in the light of the Cobell case that hinged on mismanagement of funds by the BIA), but with no success thus far.[15]

In mid-1994, the BIA gave public notice that the Seminole Agency in Hollywood, Florida, was preparing a descendancy roll of the "independent individuals of Seminole Indian descent" from which the U.S. secretary of the interior would prepare a list of persons eligible for per capita payments from the ILC case. The independent Indians did not comply, preferring to reiterate their desire for the return of lands rather than monies. Another BIA attempt—again unsuccessful—was made in 2006. Since much of the struggle for settlement of this case was led by Chairman James Billie, however, we will revisit this case and the actions of the independents, among others, in chapter 4.

Res Indians

Over the second quarter of the twentieth century more and more of the Florida Indians gravitated toward the Brighton, BC, and "old Dania" (later Hollywood) Res's as non-Indian settlement pressed them from all points of the compass. In some cases, internal pressures dictated the migration process as well. The family of Betty Mae Tiger Jumper, which became an anchor of the old Dania Res, only agreed to move from their Indiantown (Martin County) camp because traditionalists threatened to kill Betty Mae (1922–2011) and her younger brother,

Howard (1925–1967), whose biological fathers were white men. About two years after Betty Mae was born, her mother, Ada Tiger, began to work with a white woman who took in washing from men who worked on Henry Flagler's Florida East Coast Railway. Ada had a short relationship with one of the men; he was killed in a railway accident before she might have told him of his impending fatherhood. The offspring were twins: Howard and a sibling, who was "let go."[16] Howard and Betty Mae were staunch defenders of their people and very active politically for all of their lives. Howard was much beloved of all who knew him, and his death, in a heavy equipment accident, still is remembered sadly today.

Distances between the reservations remained significant, however. The completion and opening of the Tamiami (Tampa–Miami) Trail, in 1928, still left the majority of the Indians too far north to make reasonable use of the state's first road across the Everglades, although a small number of them worked as hired laborers on the construction. The construction of I-75, running northward from Miami and turning westward for 140 miles across the peninsula as "Alligator Alley" before resuming its long northward run, made a huge difference to the Indians of the Big Cypress after its opening in the 1960s. Frank J. Billie (Wind Clan, b. 1925), who operated heavy machinery in the construction of the Tamiami Trail, and other Seminole elders recall that, prior to its completion, they had to spend a complete day poling their dugout canoes across seventy miles of sawgrass to get from BC to Hollywood. If they were fortunate enough to have a car, the trip still required them to leave Hollywood on old Highway 27 and drive at least sixty-five miles to the northwest, to Clewiston, and another fifty-five or so miles southward, splashing through puddles and bumping across potholes (nowadays, still forty-two miles of proverbial bad road), to get into the BC community.

Either way, the sawgrass—not actually a grass but definitely sawlike—tricks the eye immediately. From a standing position in a dugout canoe, it rises as high as a grown man's shoulders. It grows thick enough to look like an interminable field of buff-colored grain and is light enough to be swayed by the winds that sweep across it, usually from the Gulf coast on the west toward the Atlantic coast on the east. More than a hundred years earlier, soldiers in the Third Seminole War had complained constantly of the excruciating difficulty of marching through a land that was not all water, and a water that was barely land. Most often too shallow for boats, soldiers had to slog along in single file. Every five minutes or so the point men had to rotate to the back of the file because the sawgrass tore at their clothes and their skin unmercifully. The brackish water, in many areas up to their knees at least, supported the growth of algae that seeped into their boots and made their feet itch so powerfully that their sergeants had to restrain them at gunpoint from throwing off their boots and scratching their feet until they bled.[17] The conditions were no less arduous for the Seminoles in the twentieth century, but they still had the advantage of their skill with dugout canoes that swept with such streaming grace through the *pahe oki*, the grass water.

Both highways—U.S. 41/Tamiami Trail and I-75's Alligator Alley—were "mixed blessings," of course. Even as they greatly simplified travel across Florida's southern peninsula for human beings, they impeded the sheet flow of water so necessary to maintain the strength of the mighty Everglades and created dangerous obstructions in the natural migratory paths of animals and disrupted the roosting patterns of fowls. In terms of the Seminoles, the roads opened doors into their personal lives and permitted a stream of non-Indian tourists to pass through—a stream that has only grown to a torrent today.

Despite the positive and negative aspects of the roads' constructions, distances between and among Seminole tribal reservations remain tiresomely long, and to the present day many tribal resources are used in maintaining communications and providing support across the entire Florida peninsula. When James Billie first became chairman in 1979, acquisition of autos for his new law enforcement agency was an important issue for the economically struggling tribe. By the decade of the 1990s, automobile purchasing and leasing had become significant line items in tribal program area (departmental) budgets. In this decade as well, travel and communication difficulties would be ameliorated for many by a special agreement with a south Florida cable company to provide closed-circuit broadcasting to tribal citizens on several of the reservations, especially broadcasting of council and board meetings, thus eliminating some of the travel requirements.[18] For this reason, among others, political emphasis also continues to be placed upon the election of officials who speak one or both of the tribe's remaining languages.

By the 1970s, Hollywood (old Dania) Res, where the Seminole Tribe had maintained its bureaucratic headquarters since its establishment, comprised almost five hundred acres where approximately one-third of the tribe's population lived in what was rapidly becoming and is today an intensely pressured urban setting of west central incorporated Hollywood (an adjunct of greater Fort Lauderdale). A significant portion of its land had been leased to non-Indian business interests as part of providing a stable basis of annual income for the tribe. In its early days, the Tribal Council had considered granting ninety-nine-year leases to these businesses, but the BIA advocated much shorter leases on the premise that times and land values would change and the tribe should not lock itself in to such limited returns. This turned out to be a positive consideration. In the late 1990s and early 2000s, James Billie and the council would begin to buy out old leases, for far less than they might have had to pay for the extended leases, in order to accommodate the rapidly growing population and business interests of the tribe. More of that later, also.

BC Res, the most isolated of the three big reservations, supported about the same population as the Hollywood Res, but on 42,700 (ultimately, today, 70,700) acres, almost one-quarter of which was cypress swampland. Via Alligator Alley and Snake Road, BC was seventy miles (one way) just slightly north of due west from Hollywood Res, literally in the middle of the peninsula and the Big Cypress, the northern frontier of the Everglades, mostly within Hendry County and partly within Palm Beach County.

One of the first pieces of information I was given when I went to live with the tribe was that the people who lived in BC were "strange." Naturally, this pronouncement was made by people living on the other reservations. I quickly found that the conclusion was right—if you understood the point of view of the pronouncers. The people who lived in BC were there seeking isolation from white settlements, and they clung even more determinedly to their traditions than did people on other reservations. This certainly made them different from the residents of the Hollywood Res, for example, who were pressed in on all sides by non-Indians. It made them different from the Brighton residents, who were almost entirely Creeks, and the Creeks had traditionally been more open to non-Indian interactions than had the Miccosukees. The people of Immokalee, however, were also relatively isolated and were satisfied to remain so. The immense growth of the migrant labor camps in the tiny town in the second half of the twentieth century, however, made inroads into their isolationism. From BC Res to the tiny Immokalee Res (population 200) was another thirty-six miles west and north, mostly over two-lane roads bisecting pasture lands, into Lee County.

From BC, groceries were and are forty-two miles of some paved road and too many potholes away to the north, in Clewiston. The Brighton Res, 35,805 acres and population another third of the total, is yet another thirty-five miles north-by-northwest beyond Clewiston, on the northwest shore of Lake Okeechobee (the largest body of water on the Florida map, although drought conditions and pollution levels current at the time of this writing make the future of the lake uncertain), and twenty-five miles below the town of Okeechobee. Although there is no reservation for them yet, a small number (fewer than one hundred) Seminole tribal citizens continue to live "out the Trail"—Tamiami Trail, that is, which parallels Alligator Alley about twenty-five miles south of it, into the Everglades, and forty to fifty miles west to Ochopee (the town with the United States' smallest post office) and Fort Myers. These are enrolled citizens of the Seminole Tribe, and not to be confused with the independent or

Trail Indians discussed earlier who have the genetic and cultural credentials to enroll in either the Seminole or the Miccosukee tribes but, for their own political reasons, choose not to affiliate with either.

The Miccosukees, those who chose to leave the larger number of their cultural kin in 1962 and create their own FR tribe, by the mid-1970s were a group of the same size as the residents of the Seminole Tribe's Hollywood Res: 430. They occupied 333.3 acres of land inside Everglades National Park, set aside for them by "Special Use Permits" in perpetuity. Three other small tracts of land along the trail were also set aside for their commercial use, by the State of Florida. Another state parcel, much larger and connecting the trail land and the BC Res was taken into trust status by the federal government in this period.[19]

The distances among the reservations have only been made greater over recent years by the fact that there are now two more reservations, at Tampa and Fort Pierce. Tampa, established in 1984, is a steady four-hour drive from Hollywood, almost two hours beyond Brighton, or across Alligator Alley and on up the seemingly interminable I-75, on the west coast of the peninsula. Its residents are essentially a single extended family whose members only agreed to move there when James promised the clan elder that she could take along her pigs if they would leave their old camp in the woods. The Tampa Res was the outcome of a deal with the City of Tampa. In 1980, the city was preparing a downtown lot for a city parking garage, when Indian skeletal remains were encountered. (The lot had been a part of the Seminole Wars Fort Brooke reservation.) The tribe agreed to quietly take back the remains and protect them and, to this end, purchased a small parcel of land adjacent to Tampa's Florida State Fairgrounds, on the far east side of the city, on which it constructed a small building to house the remains.[20] This was the core to which more land, a casino, and a hotel would be added (more of this later).

Fort Pierce, the newest Res, established in 1995, is two hours up the east coast from the Hollywood tribal offices and, again, was added to accommodate an extended family. Earlier in the twentieth century, four sisters, of the Tommie family, married four American black men, and the Fort Pierce community is entirely their progeny. Only their children and grandchildren and some great-grandchildren are eligible for tribal citizenship, however, since the minimum Q required for citizenship is one-quarter Seminole. (Each of the children was only one-half Q because their biological fathers were non-Seminole, and the grandchildren are therefore one-quarter Q, if the Seminole child also took as partner an individual, male or female, who was not Seminole. Great-grandchildren might or might not be eligible for enrollment, depending upon whether their Seminole parent chose a partner who was also a Seminole and of equal or greater Q.) Further, in this situation, the incidence of Clan X offspring is higher than usual, and disconcerting to many Seminoles. Nevertheless, the Seminole Tribe does not prevent family members who are not eligible for tribal citizenship from living with parents who are.

The Fort Pierce community is an anomalous group within the tribe because the Tommie sisters moved from Brighton to Fort Pierce to accommodate their non-Indian husbands who, by tradition, should have gone to live with their Indian wives and, therefore, did not provide their children with sufficient access to their Indian culture. The cultural and social differences are visible in any tribalwide setting, and the subject of much controversy. This controversy delayed council acceptance of citizenship for a number of the community members for almost a decade, from the mid-1980s through the mid-1990s, and continues to disconcert older tribal citizens who look down upon Fort Pierce residents for their lack of traditionalism. The fact that Sally Tommie (Bird Clan, daughter of one of the four sisters) has been the principal assistant to Mitchell Cypress since he took office as president of the board and has continued with him in his chairmanship of the council, has given the Fort Pierce community a direct and powerful conduit to council support, but neither her advocacy nor council support has diminished negative feelings toward the Fort Pierce community.

Nowadays, ribbons of white men's highways have put an end to all-day trips by dugout canoes to get from camp to camp, and cars and trucks and helicopters have managed to shorten the trip tremendously for the modern Seminoles. The only thing that still manages to travel faster in the Seminole world is news—positive or negative. I used to kid my Seminole friends that if someone sneezed in Tampa, someone would respond from Hollywood. On the second day after I had gone to live on the BC Res, I walked in to Ahfachkee School and the secretary, whose name I did not even know yet, said, "Oh, good. You're here. They're looking for you." I said, "How can anyone be looking for me? They don't even know who I am!" As I soon discovered, however, Betty King was the nexus of all BC information (and much tribal information) and she was right: she *did* know who I was, and "they" *were* looking for me. And, one further concomitant of this information process is: don't ever park your car anywhere on a Res where you don't want it to be seen. That just speeds up the communication process.

~

By the 1940s the hunting-based economy of the Indians, another and most basic facet of past survival, was being destroyed by outside forces. The continuing problems of livestock rustling in Florida generally, coupled with sporadic outbreaks of tick fever among the cattle, spelled the end of open range and, along with it, the end of one of the critical remaining elements of Indian male society. By tradition, men lived in their wives' camps and had no authority in the raising of their children or the running of the camp. Their principal, and overlapping, spheres of interest were hunting—to support the camp; warfare—to keep the world of the clan and camp in balance; and civic administration—to balance the needs and interests of the clans, specifically, and the people, generally.

Warfare had ended, unnaturally, as I have said, almost a century earlier. War Medicine was disappearing from the Medicine bundles. Now, even the ability to hunt, as men should, was being taken away from them. Today's elders recall this period as "the Sad Time." Men sat around the fires in their camps with their rifles across their knees, and stared sadly at the ground, and waited for death. Hunting, to provide food for the clan's cook fires, had been one of the warrior's proud roles for centuries. It was shameful that women now had to take up the slack. Diminution of some, and loss of access to other, wild food resources increased the necessity to buy more of white men's food in grocery stores, and buying more food required more of white men's money. Trading hunted skins and feathers for staple foods was no longer sufficient. Truck farms in Immokalee and Palm Beach County provided hard work for an increasing number of Indian women who picked tomatoes and other vegetables.[21] The fires of old anger at white men only burned higher.

By the 1950s and 1960s, with the advent of U.S. government programs and the concomitant increased U.S. government oversight, the level of anger at white society and white men's government reached a boiling point. Younger men, especially those in the under-fifty generation, were facing amputated lives. Their traditional social outlets were almost entirely gone. They lashed out, directly, at federal authorities, whom they saw as attempting, yet again, to suppress, assimilate, and destroy them. No matter how benign or potentially enjoyable the program might be, outsiders—non-Indians—faced almost insurmountable hostility. In the 1960s, on the Hollywood Res, which was very close to white, urban development, recreational program equipment was repeatedly hacked up and shredded, until the program director quit trying to implement outside ideas. One community services officer was physically attacked and had his arm broken. His attacker, a young Seminole who wanted to go to college, became furious because federal program regulations restricted his freedom by requiring him to attend a precollege workshop.[22] Bobby Henry (Otter Clan, b. 1937), a Medicine man who, for many years, would not accept citizenship in either the Seminole or Miccosukee tribes, responded to the Seminole tribal secretary each time she asked him to consider enrollment with, "Don't you understand? I am your anger!"[23] (His anger would finally be mitigated and he would accept enrollment, in 2007, with the purchase by the tribe of the entire Hard Rock corporation, but by then, Seminole tribal leadership would have passed into a fourth generation and, of this, much more later.)

The final value of U.S. government programs depends, once again, on whether the evaluator supports tribal autonomy and cultural preservation or views as-similation as the ultimate good for the Seminoles. As one historian has summed it, "The history of [U.S.] government relations with the Indians over two centuries points with considerable clarity to the long-standing pressures for assimilation of the Indians into the mainstream of white American society."[24] Do the Indians have the right to maintain their own cultural uniqueness and, therefore, sovereignty, within the larger sovereignty of the United States, or should they finally commit what, to them, clearly constitutes cultural suicide and "turn white and be right," as they sardonically phrase it? U.S. government programs have provided much-needed funds to support the people as the surrounding non-Indian world has left them fewer and fewer opportunities to survive in their own traditional manners. At the same time, however, it has created internal pressures to build bureaucratic infrastructure (among other assimilative requirements), and this requirement has had its own positive and negative aspects.

Federal programs of the 1960s and 1970s introduced many Seminoles to the processes and requirements of work, in white man's terms, in the white man's world. Government administrators thought that they were preparing the Indians to leave the reservations and function as other U.S. citizens. The Indians had no such idea. By the mid-1970s, of 1,232 tribal citizens, less than one-third lived on the urban Hollywood Res. The rest still lived in the relative isolation of the BC, Brighton, and Immokalee reservations and preferred their isolation as a vehicle for cultural preservation. "Work" was no stranger to them; they were surviving in what is arguably the most inhospitable environment on earth. Their daily work of basic survival was never ending. But what white men called work involved wearing tight clothes, going inside a building, and thinking in an abstract, detailed, and repetitive manner for a set number of hours every day. White man's work required schedules and rules and deadlines.

Totally antithetical to tradition, whites expected Indians to put job loyalty before family loyalty. If even the smallest family emergency occurred, however, Seminole workers would always choose family over job. Most difficult, white men expected "their workers" to view themselves as subordinates within a vertical, hierarchical power structure, when Seminole life was strongly horizontal, and the Indians refused to see themselves or act as anything other than peers. As I have explained earlier, neither of the languages still in use among the Seminoles had or has needed words for politics, democracy, or sovereignty. But neither have they needed words for "hour," "minute," "second," or "deadline." These concepts directly oppose the freedoms of life outside of offices.

My friend, Henry John Billie, in his seventies when I first met him and born so far down the southwest coast of Florida, in the Thousand Islands, that it took his family an entire day to pole their traveling canoe to the nearest trading post at Everglades City, where they traded furs and skins for sugar and coffee and flour, spent his last years sharing a trailer on the old Wind Clan camp on BC Res with friends. Henry's bed was a single cot—hard as a rock, or, more accurately, hard as the raised floor of the chikî(t) on which he had slept growing up—next to a window at the west end of the trailer. The window was never closed; winter, spring, or hurricane season, it stayed open. "So, what do you do when it rains?" I asked him in all my naïveté. His eyes crinkled; he had a mischievous sense of humor. He responded, simply, "Turn over!"

Henry John was the last of the great dugout canoe carvers among the Florida Indians. His clan uncles had taught him how to choose and cut the tree and wait for the summer rains to raise the water level until it could be floated back to the camp on the hammock (a hillock rising above the swamp water, with specific vegetation and just enough dry land for a family camp) for shaping. On a heart-stoppingly hot day in 1994, Henry drove his battered old black pickup truck five miles out into the Big Cypress to choose a tall cypress tree for a new canoe. The truck mired down in the muck (the rainy hurricane season begins on 1 June and frequently earlier). Henry had absolutely refused to be bothered with carrying a cell phone, and it wouldn't have worked in the middle of the swamp anyway, so he simply left the truck where it was and walked the five wet, steamy miles back to his camp. By the standards of most white people, working in offices, such travail would have been unthinkable. By traditional Seminole standards, working in the confined spaces of a white man's office also was unthinkable.

Even before the 1930s, private groups together with state and local funding agencies began to assist the Seminoles to build white-men's-style houses.[25] By the mid-1970s, numerous of President Lyndon B. Johnson's Great Society programs were reaching inside the FR tribes. Couched in a sincere desire to make Indians partners in the benefits of U.S. citizenry (all U.S. Indians had had dual citizenship since 1924), all such programs were nonetheless double-edged swords as they blurred cultural lines to offer more and more nontraditional elements to Indians.

The U.S. government's HUD system, as but one example, put tiny, poorly built houses in tracts on the reservations, without regard to the cultural order of clans or clan camps. Construction programs began as early as the first federal reservations, in the early twentieth century, and were still the basic housing program in the late 1980s, when the tribe took over housing under a "638" or self-determination contract that they continue to administer today. For many years, the Indians disdained the structures in favor of the traditional palm-thatched, open-sided chikî(t) (or *chokó* in Maskókî), called a "chickee" by English speakers. HUD houses were tiny and enclosed and very, very hot. Aesthetically they had nothing to recommend them. They were uncomfortable to remain inside and had opaque walls that separated people from their extended families. A chikî(t) (at least by comparison) is visually pleasing as a part of nature, and open and cool. It is a rare Seminole family that does not have at least one chikî(t) in its yard now, and does not spend a significant amount of time under its cool shade.

Frank Shore (Panther Clan, 1900–1986), one of the most powerful Medicine men of the twentieth century, simply refused to move into a house. His family did, but Frank continued to live and sleep in his chokó (he was a Brighton Creek) until his final days, when he was too weak to care for himself and the family moved him inside to make caring for him easier on themselves.

When I first moved out to the BC Res to live, in 1992, I saw many of these ugly little boxes, but it was some time before I was invited inside of any of them. The Miccosukee-speaking Seminoles frequently protect their houses with Indian Medicine and do not permit non-Indians inside of them for this reason. When I finally began to be invited in, I was surprised, at first, to see boxes and boxes of unopened merchandise sitting on counters and cluttering the floors to the point of restricting any daily living. The merchandise was, I realized quickly, the result of indiscriminate purchasing power resulting from increasing gaming dividends. The fact that the majority of the boxes were unopened was typical of people who had had nothing for a very long time and were now excited by their own access to consumerism, an access that far outdistanced their social ability to internalize the uses of the goods.

But the fact that the goods cluttered the living space almost entirely took a bit more thought to understand. There was virtually no room left for living! The simple answer that I finally reached, of course, was and is, that the "default setting" for Seminole life is out of doors. Euro-Americans have long focused their lives on the indoors, especially as technology spawned by the Industrial Revolution of the latter nineteenth century made cooking and other previously dangerous tasks safer and cooler indoors, and as air-conditioning technology advanced. The Seminoles, however, are only now (literally, as this book is being written) transitioning to an indoor focus, and this transition still is not universal and may never be. Their lives are gregarious and centered in the air and sun and water rather than in the isolated spaces delineated by solid walls.

Even those Seminoles who began, over the twentieth century, to consider the luxuries that a house could afford encountered difficulties in taking their ideas to fruition, for two main reasons. First, the reservations are lands held in commonalty. That is, Seminoles' houses are not on individually owned parcels of land; therefore, an individual citizen might, in some instances, own the house but not the land it is built on. That land is leased from the tribe. Second, since all FR tribes are sovereign entities, they have sovereign immunity in this regard and therefore can shield their citizens from foreclosure or prosecution for de-faulted mortgages. Consequently, until the 1990s, U.S. banks and other lending institutions were loath to finance construction for tribal citizens on tribal reservations. This obstacle finally would be negotiated, nationally, with the critical support of the U.S. Veterans' Administration, in the passage of the Native American Housing Assistance and Self-Determination Act, in 1996.[26]

To say that the 1970s were an era of profound change in U.S. policies toward Indian tribes would be a vast understatement. Following its most recent era of congressional attempts to relocate Indians to areas away from their tribes and terminate federal relations with the FR tribes, and the strident actions of angry tribes and American Indian Movement (AIM) members who physically occupied BIA headquarters in Washington, DC, in 1972 and, in the following year, fought the FBI at Wounded Knee, the U.S. government now began to espouse a policy of what it chose to view as inclusion.[27]

President Lyndon B. Johnson ushered in this next era by publicly including American Indians in his "Great Society" programs. On 6 March 1968, he presented his "Special Message to Congress on the Problems of the American Indian: 'The Forgotten American,'" in which he proposed "new goals" for the Indians that ostensibly erased paternalism and stressed "self-determination" and "partnership self-help."[28]

The Indians were not to be taken in, however, by even the most benign sounding rhetoric. They met the government's vaunted profession of caring with "outright suspicion."[29] Indian self-determination was yet another dubious offering to the tribes. Wrapped in the language of enlarged autonomy (read: sovereignty), a concept dear to the hearts of all Indians, it appeared to encourage economic growth on the reservations. From the viewpoint of white culture, this was undoubtedly a worthwhile prospect. And, from the point of view of thousands of impoverished Indians whose traditional economic bases had been severely eroded or destroyed by the pressures of the white U.S. government and white settlement for almost three centuries up to this point, anything that could bring monies to Indians who now had to purchase their groceries and pay for utilities could only help. The thinly veiled reality of self-determination was, however, that it was conceived as a Trojan horse, meant to addict Indians to a white lifestyle that would, in time, completely replace tribal identities with the "civilized" lifestyles of non-Indians.

When President Johnson spoke of Indians as "Forgotten American[s]," the Seminole Tribe of Florida was one of the FR tribes that had already fought the U.S. government over proposed termination—a congressional proposal to terminate economic support to as many tribes as possible—and negotiated the continuance of its relationship with the federal government and the BIA. Arguably, the turning point of that negotiation occurred when Laura Mae Jumper Osceola (Panther Clan, 1932–2003), mother of current council representative from Hollywood, Max Osceola Jr. (a.k.a. Max Jr., Panther Clan, b. 1950), told the congressional committee debating termination of the Florida Seminoles that the U.S. government should continue their support of her people for another twenty-five years but, that, "in twenty-five years they won't need your help. We will be giving you help!"[30] Laura Mae was boastful but prescient: exactly twenty-five years later, the Florida Seminoles would begin their lucrative gaming operations.

That termination negotiation ended with the Seminoles' consent to create a white man's constitutional form of government, in 1957, that they named the Seminole Tribe of Florida. It is a fine, but important, legal distinction to understand that by this agreement the Seminoles were not being federally recognized as a tribe. Before the BIA created its Branch of Acknowledgment and Research (BAR), in 1978, Indian groups were de facto recognized as sovereign tribes if the United States had ever fought a war against them, signed a treaty or treaties with them, or sent an Indian agent and monies to them. The Florida Seminoles met all of these requirements and, therefore, did not, in the strictest sense, need federal recognition. By their 1957 agreement with the United States, however, the Seminoles did agree to accept the requirements of the earlier Indian Reorganization Act (IRA), or the Wheeler-Howard Act of 1934, that had reversed earlier Indian policy and had begun to encourage the organization of tribal governments, albeit in the image and likeness of white men's government.[31] This act did not find universal favor among Indian tribes, and in fact only twenty-one Florida Seminoles had voted for it, but the BIA chose to view the entire group as having supported it. Regardless, the Seminoles accepted its major tenets and moved into yet another phase of their cultural existence.[32]

By the 1970s the greater national social changes that resulted in President Johnson's self-determination policy in turn prompted numerous self-identifying groups across the United States to assert a tribal identity that might or might not exist in historical reality. In response to this fact, and in a desire to limit the number of tribes for which the United States accepted trust and government-to-government responsibilities, the BIA promulgated an official threshold for groups seeking federal recognition as Indian tribes.[33] The BIA's new Branch of Acknowledgment and Research was created and charged with employing the BIA's requirements for federal recognition and, ultimately, making recommendations to the Department of the Interior/secretary of the interior and the assistant secretary for Indian Affairs (the head of the BIA) regarding applications for federal recognition. Even though the BAR's new policy required nothing of the Seminoles, whose status as an FR tribe was unquestioned, the new process for recognition would reverberate unfavorably across Indian Country, and the more politically engaged the Seminoles would become over the last two decades of the twentieth century, the more political interest they would absorb.

By 1977, however, the tribe already was a full generation into its own bureaucratic era and, therefore, was one of many FR tribes ready to look toward Washington for increased possibilities of exercising its autonomy without fear of retribution. That facet of self-determination was quite appealing. Howard Tommie (son of Mildred Bowers Tommie, and Tribal Council chairman 1971–79) purposely took advantage of many of the U.S. government's offerings. In fact, Howard became known across Indian Country as "Mr. Self-Determination" for his public advocacy of federal funding and programs newly available to tribes. These included federal programs such as the Comprehensive Education and Training Act (CETA), the Neighborhood Youth Corps (NYC), and the Community Action Program (CAP), which funneled national dollars directly to tribes. Incidentally, one of the Seminoles who benefited from the NYC in the 1970s was a young man named James Billie, not long back from two tours with the U.S. Army in Vietnam, and a course in hairdressing. He was a young energetic man who was searching for a place where he could exercise his talents within the tribe. We'll take a close look at his background and life in the next chapter.

As tribal chairman throughout the 1970s, Howard Tommie personified the second generation of tribal leadership. In his personal philosophy he turned the tide of the tribe's political trajectory against the earlier Christian control. He told the Christian faction that "I am an Indian too. . . . Just because you go to church and have your values does not mean that I would not like to have these benefits at my disposal."[34]

His political philosophy was that the Seminoles should take advantage of every dollar the Indians could get *from* the U.S. government as their right after so many years of being warred upon *by* the U.S. government. "We have expert contracting programs," he wrote in 1977, "to service the people and create employment, while reserving as much of the resources, human and natural, as possible for the exclusive benefit of the people."[35] This included a determined effort to place tribal citizens in as many positions as possible inside the bureaucracy, except where that created a political dilemma. As his own secretary Howard hired a white woman on the premise, it appeared, that having an Indian as his personal secretary would endanger the confidentiality that the chairman needed to maintain in business relations. His successor would espouse that philosophy also, and even more adamantly.

Nevertheless, Howard was frustrated with what he saw as yet another determined, and competing, attempt by the U.S. government, through the BIA, to manipulate the Indians to its own ends. The BIA, he felt, was directing its funding principally to those programs that were most aggressively consistent with BIA objectives, especially cattle and heavy construction equipment operation. "But a lot of times it [the funding] would benefit the present [tribal] administration's personal pocketbook," he asserted.[36]

This was neither a new nor an unfounded charge. Reginald ("Rex") Quinn, superintendent of the Seminole Agency, told listeners in a 1981 speech how he had been sent to Florida by the BIA in 1957 to discover firsthand the Seminoles' attitude toward the formation of a constitutional form of government. He found that tribal citizens were angry, above all, because BIA "Area Director Paul Frickinger had been withdrawing Tribal funds from the United States Treasury without the knowledge or consent of the Tribe. Paul Frickinger was strongly opposed to self-government for the Seminoles. Several of the BIA employees of the Seminole Agency were also opposed."[37] Quinn was not alleging that Frickinger was receiving the Seminole monies for his personal use, but to the Seminoles such an action was tantamount to malfeasance. The Seminoles had (and have) too many memories of being betrayed by white men.

Allegations of personal profits aside (and such allegations would only increase as annual revenues increased over the coming years, but aimed at their own Indian politicians as well as white men), this was not only thinly veiled assimilation pressure from the BIA, it was also a manifestation of what was already recognized as the theory of diminished expectations. By 1992, when I arrived in BC, the Ahfachkee School was still laboring to educate Indian children under the same low expectations that had hampered Seminole children for generations. Annual events such as "Career Day" touted the benefits of no professions other than those involving manual labor and mechanical occupations. Howard Tommie's greatest failure, he later recalled, was his inability to convince the Tribal Council and the tribe to take over administration of Ahfachkee Day School in BC. Built and maintained by the BIA since the 1940s, many citizens were afraid that the tribe did not have adequate resources with which to take over its running themselves. Howard asserted, however, that the U.S. government employees were afraid of losing their jobs and, so, frightened the tribal citizens into opposing the tribe's takeover. Only in the 1980s, with the advent of high-stakes gaming revenues, would the tribe be able to take over its own educational program, under a 638 contract, and break away from these diminished expectations and begin to offer its young citizens educational opportunities more consistent with their intellectual abilities and aspirations.[38]

These educational opportunities, including tribal support for any of its citizens who wished to attend "white men's schools" and white men's institutions of higher education, were and continue to be materially hampered, however, by many of the tribal citizens' traditional attitudes that mitigate against opening one's self to white men's ideas. Betty Mae Tiger (later Jumper) and two of her

Snake Clan cousins, Mary Parker (later Bowers) and Agnes Parker (later Denver) were the first in the modern era to leave Florida in order to study white man's information. They went to Cherokee, North Carolina, in the 1940s to the BIA's Indian school there, of their own volition. They were among the very few at the time who cared to learn more about the white men or their knowledge.

I asked Henry John one time if he had ever considered going to a white man's school and how his Wind Clan family felt about the subject. He said that a clan uncle had told him that "if I went [away] to a white man's school, a man on a horse would ride up, with a big stick [spear] and stick me under the arm and I would die." As fascinating as this image is in its reverberations of a sixteenth-century Spaniard in armor, it is also quintessentially indicative of the traditional, embedded attitude of the Seminoles against opening one's self to the culture of white men. Albeit an attitude expressed in the mid-twentieth century, many Seminole children encounter this attitude, at best, in their families today or, at worst, they find a corporate lassitude and ambivalence that does not require them to make a decision one way or another. We shall revisit the tribe's educational policies in the 1980s, as gaming revenues became increasingly available to support on- and off-Res educational programs.

Even so, the dropout rate for Indians enrolled in institutions of higher learning in the United States was, and remains, high (well over 50 percent), and the rates for Seminole students parallel this statistic. Indian students are not linear learners, and few non-Indian institutions offer Indians a culturally and intellectually supportive atmosphere, although that situation is changing slightly now. Consequently, obtaining a white man's education has negative as well as positive aspects, as the Seminoles know all too well. In its positive aspects, it would fall under Mitchell's "two head" theory. In its negative aspects, it would come under Sonny Billie's "two river" theory. There is no clear good in the process.

Chairman Tommie's tenure ended in 1979 when he chose not to seek a third four-year term, even though the Tribal Constitution and Election Ordinance contained no term limits for any elected officials. His programs of bureaucratic expansion had laid the foundation for the next generation of leadership and infrastructure growth. His creation of the tribe's sales-tax-free tobacco sales would engender opposition from non-Indians that would be left to his successor to overcome. James Billie would be the one to take advantage of this significant source of tribal income, and the tribe would finally enter a period of economic stability that would only increase over the coming years of the century. Two programs as well awaited James's aggressive personal and professional style. Those were Howard's first step to the creation of a tribal law enforcement program and an offer, made in the closing months of Howard's last term by an associate of Myer Lansky, to open a bingo parlor on tribal lands. Each would send ripples across the still waters of the great Seminole pond for many years to come and take the tribe's promulgation of its sovereignty all the way to the U.S. Supreme Court.

~

The 1975 elections had changed the composition of the Tribal Council almost completely, but, at the same time, the changes were indicative of the new access to preferment that had been created by the tribe's foray into white-man's-style government. This second generation of leaders was no longer dominated by the tribe's Christian converts, nor was it drawn completely from the revolving group that had managed the tribe's affairs in close association with the BIA since 1957.

Howard Tommie received another term as chairman, his second and last four years, and Bill Osceola returned to tribal government as board president and, therefore, council vice president, replacing Fred Smith, who focused on managing the tribe's federal Food Stamp Program and put much effort into improving the Brighton cattle program. Rounding out the council, however, three political first-timers stepped into tribal politics: Paul Buster, Stanlo Johns, and James Billie.

Bill "the Rev. Bill" Osceola (Bird Clan, 1919–1995) replaced Fred Smith as board president, although Fred remained involved in tribal government. Rev. Bill had never really left the political arena and had been on and off the Tribal Council for a dozen years. Rev. Bill's family was from the western side of Broward County. Bill had married by 1938 and lived "down the Trail" with his wife, Annie. By 1940, Bill had a new wife, Charlotte (Mary Tommie; Snake Clan, 1921–1999), and they had moved to the old Dania Res. He and Charlotte accepted white man's Christianity and eventually had five children, three boys and two girls, and stayed together for the rest of their lives. Charlotte also served on the corporation's board of directors from 1957 to 1960, when she resigned.

Bill had been involved in the political organization of the tribe since the beginning of the movement, but his work was controversial. As an Indian who had accepted white man's Christianity, he was among the small coterie of tribal citizens who were viewed as "progressives" by BIA staff and were favored by the BIA for their willingness to accept BIA direction, and their growing power angered the traditionalists. Many Seminoles did not appreciate an Indian who appeared to be siding with non-Indians. The Christianized Indians' sense of their own rightness authored a degree of decision making in them that ran counter to traditional laissez-faire attitudes that left clans to make their own separate decisions. This core attitude had been echoed down through the ages, in varying ways since the first recordings of white men, in the sixteenth century: the Indians don't want anyone telling them what to do!

Paul Buster (Otter Clan, b. 1950), representing the Hollywood Res, was a young man with three great loves: his family, the Christianity he had accepted, and his music. Even though his family composition has changed over the years, Paul's commitments have not. He has been in and out of the political arena, mostly out, but he continues to preach in the various Baptist churches in BC and Brighton and Hollywood, especially at funerals, where he also plays his guitar and sings hymns in Miccosukee and in English. He is hired by the tribe to provide entertainment at various tribal functions as well, and he is a gentle man with a unique facility for singing the blues in Miccosukee. Strangely, even when he performs songs in English, his renditions are also unique—opening on tempo, mysteriously wandering off tempo, and even key, in midsong and, then, just as mysteriously homing back in on the tempo and key for a strong finish. Paul also rents out his audio equipment and sets it up and runs it for various events, from clan gatherings to Veterans Day celebrations. When he performs, his son, "Chunky," often accompanies him. This is a great victory since Chunky, born in 1968 to Paul and the passionate Daisy Mae Jumper (Panther Clan, b. 1948), suffered a serious traffic accident in the late 1980s and there was much doubt whether he would be able to survive without serious impairment. The young man defied all odds, however, and has become a regular in his dad's current band, Cow Bones.

Stanlo Johns (Panther Clan, b. 1935) represented Brighton Res, where the extended Johns family was and is large, active, and powerful. Stanlo, although fifteen years older than Paul and even three years older than Howard, was just of an age to be considered an adult, in traditional terms. Stanlo has worked hard and played hard all his life, and although he has never been an ardent politician, he has remained vocal and active in his allegiance to the Brighton Creeks and their needs.

It was the Rev. Bill, father of current tribal secretary Priscilla Osceola Sayen, and politician and cattleman Fred Smith, who first encouraged the young veteran, James Billie, to become involved in Seminole politics. Voters knew that James had the Rev.'s approbation, even though James never accepted the Rev.'s Christianity—not then or since. But it was the Rev. Bill who first took James with the tribal delegation to Washington, DC, and encouraged him to become a tribal leader. He told the young man: "There's only one thing you need to know about running this Tribe and that is, make money!"[39]

Fred Smith, as president of the board, had helped James to take charge of the board's Okalee Village enterprise, a tourist attraction on the Hollywood Res that was not doing well. Both the Rev. Bill and Fred had clan duties toward James: they were his Bird Clan uncles. Fred's connection went even further, however; his Bird Clan "grandfather" was Morgan Smith (1900–1979), one of the people who had befriended and protected James in his youth.

James replaced Jimmy Cypress (father of later council chairman Mitchell Cypress and BC council representative David Cypress) on the council for a single term, and Jimmy was reelected in 1977, while James became director of the tribe's Okalee Village tourist attraction in Hollywood, which was a board project, under the direction of board president Rev. Bill Osceola.

By the end of the 1970s, the tribe had well established the basic social services programs that would continue to grow throughout the rest of the twentieth century, slowly being assumed by the tribe itself as funds became available and as it expanded exercise of its innate sovereignty. Indian Health Service (IHS) clinics had been set up on the three larger reservations. Federal Head Start programs cared for many children. BIA recreation programs and HUD housing offices had been set up, and the elementary education program on BC Res expanded. Tribal infrastructure expanded to take over the personnel and accounting functions formerly controlled by the BIA. Tribal revenues were such that the tribe could provide twice-annual dividends to elders of a maximum of $300 each (payments were indexed by age). The stage was set for the next generation of growth and expansion inside the tribe, all of which would require the leaders to remember centuries of warfare in order to continue to protect the people.

~

On a classically hot, muggy Monday, the 4th of June 1979, as the inauguration of the newly elected council and board was taking place under the old Council Oak on Hollywood Res, Howard Tommie became uncharacteristically emotional. His political tenure was at an end; he had chosen to leave politics and turn his attention to his business interests, which were growing and lucrative, and which included income from leasing a Smoke Shop, for which he was criticized. He also had tried, two years earlier, to establish another personal business, a retail package liquor store, on the Hollywood Res. Public Law 277, known as the Federal Indian Liquor Law, had established ground rules for the sale of alcoholic beverages on Indian reservations, and the tribe had amended those rules to conform to its own requirements.[40] Ultimately, however, tribal feeling was against it, even though the subject would be introduced again periodically until it was ended by tribal referendum in 1985.[41] Despite these first stumbles, Howard's business acumen and the tacit permission of the tribe in other areas would make him a very wealthy man over the coming years, with business interests in both Florida and Oklahoma.

"It took a lot of hard work and blood, sweat and tears to get where we are," he said. The next day's edition of the *Miami Herald* reported: "The 41-year-old former chairman sees threats to the Seminoles' rights and, in turn, their revenues. . . . Tribal leaders are upset over proposals that would eliminate some of what they consider their rights. Without taking action, Florida lawmakers this legislative session discussed requiring Indian cigaret [*sic*] sellers to impose state taxes."[42] That would be one of the major issues facing the new chairman. In the same period, the U.S. Congress had introduced bills that, if they had passed, would have abolished reservations completely. Further, Howard and the council were concerned that courts might reconsider decisions of recent years that had upheld Indians' special status.

"When you're an Indian, a situation is never resolved finally. You're tested every day," said Mike Tiger (Clan X, b. 1950), director of the tribe's Human Resources Division. Mike, a son of Howard Tiger and his Cherokee wife, Winifred, would leave the tribe and Florida within a few years, in an ongoing feud with James over conflicting political styles. He would spend most of his career in a management position with the federal Indian Health Service in Washington DC, and Nashville, Tennessee, and return to the tribe only during the early years of the twenty-first century, when James was being removed from office. At this moment, however, they both were young men eager to prove themselves and to protect the tribe.

In a U.S. political philosophy that I have characterized as Conquest by Legislation, the FR tribes were being besieged by yet another wave of political and economic attempts to force assimilation. Their discourse clearly was filled with their recognition of themselves as warriors for the people. "There is a backlash going on," Howard told the citizens assembled. "White people are tired of having Indians exercise their rights. We're being constantly attacked."[43] Howard had led the tribe to fight back, legally, and he was passing the torch to the next generation of leaders. Tax-free cigarette sales provided the bulk of the tribe's rapidly growing annual revenues. Trailer park leases provided another, but much smaller, source of income. The federal government's offered portion of the ILCC judgment was $16 million (although the actual award was still years away); the tribe had taken on the state over Everglades lands illegally flooded; a full-time lawyer was now on staff. The financial stability of the tribe was growing, but so was its national visibility, and that was a dangerous thing in the jealous, non-Indian world.

"I tell you this job can get to you," Howard admitted. "It's not an easy job anymore." James told him, "You've brought this Tribe from almost nothing to what it is today. We're going to fight for the highest potential of our tribe, Howard, I want you to know that."[44]

Certainly, James E. Billie has not been alone on the Seminoles' political landscape fighting that fight. But all of the other figures—among them board president Fred Smith, BC council representative David Cypress and his brother and now council chairman Mitchell Cypress, and James's "brother" (in the Cinderella sense, as James so often comments) Max Osceola Jr.—were clearly supporting actors rather than principal characters. James and Fred Smith quickly arrived at a modus vivendi for council and board, which was beneficial for the tribe. In the case of David Cypress, however, his deep dislike of James—a man who also disliked him—finally boiled over into political intrigue and (with a significant outside push) the incitement of a "palace coup" that would succeed, with the help of the other two, in ending James E. Billie's long political tenure, in 2003. We shall review these events in the final chapters of this book.

3   James "E." Billie:

The Man Who Would Be King

Between 1979, when he rose to power, and the date of his final fall, in 2003, so little was known of the reality of James Billie that he had already begun to pass into legend. His story was the story of the Seminole people in the entire last quarter of the twentieth century. His deeds and misdeeds (perceived or otherwise) set the tone for the twenty-first century for the Seminole people and their leaders.

When the council took its final vote on the impeachment of James Billie, in 2003, gross gaming revenues were estimated (by the press; tribal officials would not give a specific figure, even to tribal citizens) at somewhere between $370 and $480 million annually. This figure then constituted slightly over 96 percent of the tribe's annual gross revenues and, moreover, made the tribe one of the top five businesses in the entire state. Regardless of this latter reality, this single-source income put the Seminoles in a highly risky economic position given the variables surrounding gaming in the state of Florida. Three past referenda on legalizing gaming in Florida had failed, but the point is almost moot today, given pari-mutuel betting at horse tracks, and jai alai fronton betting, and Broward County's recently passed "gambling for scholars" referendum. Sooner or later high-stakes gaming will be legal statewide, and the tribe will lose its edge. James knew this, and he tried to broaden the economic base so all of the tribe's eggs would not be in one basket. Ultimately, however, his business choices were dictated too often by personal considerations or associations, and as his assistant of many years, Pat Diamond, used to say, rather than successful income producers, they became monuments that littered the landscape as reminders of his failures. His successes, however, were even larger and much easier to see, and they compensated for a multitude of failures.

When Howard Tommie was first elected, in 1971, the salaries of the council chairman and the board president were $10,660 each, and the annual gross revenues of the tribe were only slightly over their 1968 level of $600,000, mostly from land leases and loans from a governmental revolving fund. By 1977, half-way through Howard's second and last term, annual gross revenues had reached $4.5 million, from federal loans and contracts, grants, and land lease incomes, and the chairman's and president's salaries had been raised to $13,000 per annum. In James Billie's first year the tribe's annual budget reached $9 million, and the salary of the chairman, on the premise that he was not only a tribal administrator but also principal administrator of government contracts, was raised to $35,000. Periodic revenue shortfalls had made the rises in incomes and salaries tenuous up to that point, but the tribe was slowly beginning to feel the sweet rewards of white man's money. Who was the unique and popular leader who had taken the tribe so rapidly to this point?

~

James Billie is not handsome in any conventional sort of way. He's about five feet ten inches tall and uncomfortable if he carries more than 175 pounds, which he does from time to time because he really likes to eat. He especially likes overcooked beef—a critical requirement for all Seminoles and the one that, in the Seminole worldview, distinguishes humans from other forms of life. He has a face that most frequently is described as "rugged." But he exudes a kind of sexuality that is so potent that both women and men recognize it. He knows this. He capitalizes on it.

He plays guitar and writes and sings his own songs. His voice is deep and resonant and so powerful that it lingers in the mind. There was a time in his early political years when he bought tuxedos and ruffled shirts and saw himself as an Indian Tom Jones. In 1993, he went onstage with country music star John Anderson at the Country Music Awards in Nashville, to accept a platinum record for the album *Seminole Wind,* much of which Anderson, a Florida native, wrote in James's front yard in BC. There's a scene in the music video of the title cut where John and James are each driving airboats, flat out, across the sawgrass behind James's house. It is the quintessential James Billie moment: he has power; he has glory; he has music.

He flies his own airplanes, both rotor and fixed-wing aircraft. These are interests that he was able to exercise fully only after he became chairman and later as tribal gaming began to bring in sufficient income. I was standing beside him in 1994, just after the little BC landing strip, built in 1987 with U.S. Economic Development funding, had been lengthened to accommodate jet aircraft. The tribe's first jet, an eight-passenger British Hawker, was being brought in for a landing. The tribe already had a small Bell helicopter, mostly for the use of its Forestry Department in fire control, and a Cessna that James used frequently. Earlier fixed-wing aircraft—a Cessna T210M and a Beechcraft Queen Air—had been forfeited to the tribe by alleged drug runners (but more of this in chapter 5).[1] But the jet was a real step up for the tribe, even if no one else actually understood that at the moment except James. I just couldn't help smiling as the sleek, trim Hawker glided down onto Seminole national territory. "James," I said, "why do I get the feeling that you're starting your own air force?" He didn't miss a beat. He turned and stepped right up in my face, with an expression of the utmost hardened determination, and growled: "Hell, honey, I'm not going to fight 'em for it. I'm just going to buy the damn state back!"

～

James's infancy and youth were not auspicious. But neither were they particularly unusual in the world of the Florida Seminoles in the 1940s and '50s. They were, however, unbelievably hard to imagine for those of us not born to Indian life and survival in the Everglades. His story includes incest, abandonment, and years of hardscrabble survival in Florida and Oklahoma, being "pitched from pillar to post" as the old saying goes. For years he suffered the taunts and beatings of other Indians because of his white blood, even as whites frequently assaulted him for being an Indian. James has managed to outlive much of the taint, but not the memory, which lingers on.

Tommie Doctor (Bird Clan, 1906–1958), mother of James Billie's mother, was herself the child of incest between her maternal grandfather, Tommy Lusti (Panther Clan, d. 1918) and his own biological daughter, Mamie Lusti (Bird Clan, 1896–1979). Mamie subsequently became a wife of Little Doctor (Otter Clan, 1876/88–1967).

Traditionally, "children of incestuous matings used to be killed, the father killed and the mother given as wife to the executioner, a man of low status."[2] This does not seem to have been quite the case for Mamie, however. Her daughter, Tommie, was, indeed, given to a man much older than herself, John Billie (Wind Clan, 1845–1936). Nevertheless, Tommie's only two children, Effie, known later as Annie (Bird Clan, 1925–1948), and Agnes (Bird Clan, 1927–1953) may have been the children of a much younger man. Tribal memory indicates that Agnes, at least, was the child of Jimmie Billie (? Clan, d. 1934), who killed his brother-in-law and then killed himself in the white man's prison.[3] Tommie's clan may have given her to old John Billie because it satisfied the circumstances of her birth, but Tommie was not Mamie's only child; there were four siblings in all, three sisters and one brother.

Tommie was formally with John Billie until about 1934, two years before his death at about eighty-nine years, when she had a short-lived relationship with Willie Billie (Panther Clan), who died in that same year. For the next two or three years, Tommie was the partner of John Philip Billie (Otter Clan, 1906–1938), who attacked another woman and was sentenced to death by the aggrieved clan and the Green Corn Council for his action. On several tribal records, including the 1937 Florida Seminole Census, Tommie is shown as wife of Johnny Buster (Wind Clan, 1897/1909–1961). Tommie and Johnny Buster were still together at the time of her death, in 1958. He was working for the MacMillan family on their ranch in Delray Beach.

Both of Tommie's daughters had suffered from rheumatic fever as children, and it left them with weakened hearts that foreshortened their lives considerably. As a young woman, Annie worked in Miami at Musa Isle, one of the winter tourist camps, with clan members. These camps were actually public tourist attractions, owned and operated by white men, where the Indians were lured out of obscurity to the fascination of the winter tourists. The Florida Indians, in particular, had an international image as exotic, and in addition, their beautiful patchwork garments were unique draws as souvenirs. Tommie and little James would visit Annie there sometimes. Annie soon married an Eastern Cherokee, Richard Wolfe, whom she met in school in North Carolina, and lived out her short life there with him. Annie died in North Carolina in 1948, at only twenty-three years of age, and her only son, Larry, died shortly thereafter. Both are buried there.

Agnes, a strikingly lovely young woman, was much attracted to white men for their novelty value, as were a number of her peers. She was in her late teens when the U.S. military began a buildup of bases and service personnel in the areas of north Dade and south Broward counties. Opa Locka Air Base sent aircraft pilots and navigators a few miles northward to train at Perry Airfield, and at Foreman Field, a tiny "touch-and-go" training field not half a mile from the old Dania Res (now the property of Nova Southeastern University), and all within twenty miles of one another. A military bus took servicemen from these two sites into Fort Lauderdale regularly, to the movies. No civilians were supposed to ride the bus, but the young and exotic Seminole women could usually catch a ride into town anyway.

Each winter Agnes and Tommie, together with the families of Betty Mae Tiger and a few others, spent the tourist months working at the Thunderbird Indian Trading Post on the Davie Cutoff Canal at Federal Highway in Dania, established and run by the Barnhill family. Ada Tiger, Betty Mae's mother (Snake Clan, 1889–1970), was the organizer of the group and known to the camp as "the Sheriff." The Thunderbird Indian Trading Post included a large property with a house, several cabins for tourists, caged animals, a central fire pit, and the Indians' exhibition "camp."

"My father was a monkey," James says publicly, in front of me, as soon as he figures out that it annoys me and he can get a rise out of me with such a silly story. His father most certainly was not a monkey, although he doesn't know who his father was. That's why he has had people looking for his dad for some

Figure 1. Agnes Billie (1927–1953), mother of James Billie. (Photograph courtesy of James Billie.)

years now. I'm the latest. The closest thing he has had to a clue is the information given to him by Betty Mae Jumper, and it is ephemeral at best.

By 1943 the teenaged girls, Betty Mae Tiger, Agnes Billie, and Mary Parker, were leaving each September for school in North Carolina. They attended Cherokee school, because there they had the company and support of other Indians; and, besides, the local schools would not admit Indians. It seems that Betty Mae Tiger (as she was before she married Moses Jumper Sr.) was on a bus traveling back to South Florida with a pregnant Agnes Billie in January of 1944. The girls had left for school in the previous September and Agnes either had not realized that she was pregnant or had not been concerned. When her condition became apparent in the fall, her school counselor advised her to stay as long as she wished. She stayed until January and then asked Betty Mae to accompany her on the long bus ride back to South Florida and her mother.

At one point during the dull ride back, Agnes said to Betty Mae: "I'm sorry I took your friend away from you."[4] She did not add any further details about what she meant. Betty Mae interpreted that statement to mean than Agnes had had a physical relationship, at least at one moment, with a certain sailor with whom Betty Mae also had had a relationship—one of the servicemen they had met when he came to buy cold drinks from a little roadside stand on the Old Davie (Hollywood) Res operated by Betty Mae's clan uncle, Jimmy Gopher. It appears that Agnes never said anything else to anyone else about James's paternity; Seminole tradition did not require women to focus on paternity because their children were their own alone. Nevertheless, in later years every time they would see white servicemen, Grandmother Tommie would say to little James, "Those men are your uncles!" Throughout his youth the story of his parentage was even enlarged to include his sailor-father's having been killed in World War II, in an enemy attack on his ship. The people around James felt that he would be better off not worrying about a non-Indian father. In James's case, however, that didn't work.

Seminoles, not much interested in white men's names, had supplied an approximate surname, but over the years no one, including U.S. Navy contacts in Washington, DC, had been able to find the man whom Betty Mae envisioned as the one to whom Agnes had been referring. I found him. He was married, with a large and loving family, and for many years had been living only five miles away from the house in which I had grown up.[5] I was almost as shocked as he was, and James was cautiously excited. The gentleman remembered Agnes. He remembered Betty Mae. He admitted his relationships with each of them. But the DNA test was negative: he was not, after all, James's father. Whatever Agnes had meant about Betty Mae's "friend," she had not been referring to this man. James's disappointment was deep, and obvious, but he asked me to give the man a profound message that provided a view into the depths of the real James Billie. "You tell him," he said thoughtfully, as we sat in the gentle heat and late afternoon quiet on an old oak log under the trees in his front yard in BC, "that I honor him for letting me use his image and his name in Vietnam. When things got bad there, I would think of him in the war, and he would give me the courage I needed to keep going." When I delivered James's message, the gentleman cried.

The Thunderbird Indian Trading Post, where James was born, was a product of the continuing 1930s tourist boom in South Florida. Begun by an entrepreneur named Barnhill, who had established other tourist "trading posts" across the peninsula, several Seminole families were hired to "live" there, à la Musa Isle and Coppinger's Tropical Garden and other tourist attractions a few miles farther south, in Dade County.[6] The idea was to provide an exotic experience for visitors. It was a poor experience for the Seminoles; all needed the money; many drank away their days as tourist attractions.[7] Some others enjoyed the experience and the information that it provided them about white men and their ways. The money was very useful also, given the degree to which the money-based world was daily encroaching upon their traditional lifestyle.

The Thunderbird was right on Federal Highway in old Dania, at what was known as "the big bend," just on the north side of the canal and almost under the branches of Dania's "million dollar Banyan tree." The property backed on the plant nursery of the Shaw family of now former U.S. Senator Clay Shaw (R, FL). In 1944, in the disruption of World War II, the animal farm attached to the trading post was sold to Armand and Leila Roosevelt Denis. Leila's mother, the famous sculptor Adelheid Lange (Mrs. André Roosevelt, 1878–1962), lived and worked in one of the cabins. Mr. Denis raised rhesus monkeys for scientific research, under the not-for-profit name of the Anthropoid Ape Research Foundation, and was known nationally for his knowledge of animals. He served as a technical adviser on the hit Hollywood film *King Solomon's Mines.* Around 1951 Denis sold the foundation and the property to an employee who by 1949 had already leased the trading post. The attraction closed permanently in 1956 when the Florida Power and Light Company (FP&L) condemned the land as right of way for a power corridor. FP&L still owns and uses the land today.

It was on the far back side of the old Thunderbird property, next to the canal, where the Seminoles made their annual camp, on a bed of palm fronds or "fans" laid over a lime-rock outcropping, that Agnes gave birth to her baby boy on 20 March 1944. Her mother, Tommie, was her midwife and only attendant.

From the first moment of his coming into this world, the baby's life would be a fight. Seminole traditionalists visited Tommie and wanted the half-blood infant to be "let go"—that is, they wanted to put mud in his mouth and leave him on the canal bank to die and be eaten by alligators. Betty Mae and her mother, Ada, fought this possibility. Some of Ada's family had accepted Christianity. Ada's two children, Betty Mae and Howard, were half white, their fathers white men who had worked near the family's old camp at Indiantown (in Palm Beach County). Indian men who adhered to the Old Ways had visited their camp with shotguns to take the half-white babies away. For other traditional reasons, Howard's half-blood twin had, indeed, been let go (as has been mentioned earlier). The threats had been a major impetus for the family to relocate to the new Res in Old Dania. Her family had fought for Betty Mae and Howard, and Betty Mae would fight for James. Betty Mae told this story over and over throughout the early years of James's life and, in so doing, bound him to her in a sincere loyalty that would last for half a century.

Almost from the time when he was born, Agnes left the baby often with Tommie, or took him traveling and left him for long periods with others. By Seminole tradition, biological parents are not supposed to be responsible for raising their children; the entire clan camp, especially the elders, assumes that responsibility. In 1948, when Agnes's sister, Annie, died, James had been living in Cherokee with his aunt for several months at least. James recalls her death, although he was no more than four years old.

Shortly after their return to Florida, Agnes joined the Oklahoma Seminole preacher Webster Wise and his wife, Nancy, and a few other Florida Seminoles on a church-sponsored trip to Oklahoma. There, Agnes and James stayed with the family of Jimpsey Carbitcher. One of Jimpsey's sons, Jimmy, married a cousin of Nancy Wise. James lived with the Carbitcher family for over a year and never forgot their generosity.

His return to the Old Dania Res was short-lived. In September of 1950, six-year-old James was enrolled in the Delray Beach Elementary School by his grandmother, Tommie, with whom he was living. The following year, Agnes married Sonny Billie (Panther Clan, 1935–2003). Sonny was from the family of infamous Medicine man Josie Billie (Panther Clan, 1887–1980), who had served as principal informant for Dr. William Sturtevant in the 1950s, and Josie's brother Ingram Billie (Panther Clan, 1890–1996).

Josie had been very controversial in the tribe, for several reasons. First and foremost, he was respected for his tremendous knowledge and for his powerful Medicine, but, at the same time, he was feared because it was known that he practiced bad Medicine as well as good. The controversy surrounding him only increased in 1945, when he "put down his [Medicine] bundle" and accepted white man's Christianity. In subsequent years, in a drunken rage, he had killed a woman who would not have sex with him, and other deaths were attributed to him as well, and many in the tribe said that it was all too convenient that his disavowal of Indian Medicine and acceptance of Christianity had placed him beyond the jurisdiction of the Green Corn Council and a potential sentence of death.[8]

As a clan nephew of this family, Sonny was in line to be taught Medicine, but as a teenager, at the time when his training should have begun, he was not interested, he said. He wanted to go into some business. It was, ultimately, Agnes who convinced him that he should begin to study Medicine. When he approached Josie to teach him, however, Josie told him that he should go to Ingram to learn because, Josie said, "He [Josie] had done too many bad things in his life, and Ingram would teach [me] right."[9]

Sonny, never one to be impeded by humility, said that he "chose" Agnes to be his wife (although, by tradition, it was not his decision alone) because he wanted to marry an older woman, one who could teach him about life and be "a better guide" to him than could a younger woman. Also, Agnes had learned some English at school, and Sonny had ambitions and felt that she could be a help to him. Some people spoke poorly of Agnes, principally because of her past involvement with white men, but Sonny prevailed. His mother, he said, supported his choice.

Shortly after they were married, in 1951, Sonny got paid work as an extra in the filming of the movie *Distant Drums,* starring Gary Cooper, which was filmed in the Everglades and in St. Augustine. I often smile at this memory because the St. Augustine scenes in the movie focused on the old Fort Marion (El Castillo de San Marcos National Monument) and were to simulate an engagement between the Indians and the U.S. troops, with cannon balls exploding on the Fort Green. I was six years old at the time, but I can still remember the parents and children of the city leaving home early in the morning, while the city was still peaceful, to gather excitedly along San Marco Avenue beside the fort to watch the filming. My mother wore her housecoat and slippers; most of the parents and children were still in morning house-wear. We hurried the five blocks or so across the Plaza and up the Bayfront. She held my hand tightly as the simulators, strategically placed under the grass of the glacis (the "Fort Green") burst around us. Now, I imagine that a young, tall, good-looking Seminole man named Sonny Billie was there also, and it took us forty-five years to meet.

Sonny used his "extra" pay to take himself and his new wife, Agnes, to Oklahoma. He believed that the job possibilities would be greater there, but, he said, he also wanted to place Agnes and himself beyond the antagonisms against their union of some in Florida. They stayed in a tiny wooden house in Seminole, Oklahoma, owned by the Carbitchers, that James would buy, in 1996, for sentimental reasons. When their money began to run out, Sonny found enough work to pay for their return to Florida. Meanwhile, James was living with his clan grandmother, Tommie, in Delray Beach. Her partner, Johnny Buster, was a foreman on the MacMillan family's ranch.

Neil MacMillan, a lawyer in Delray, and his wife, Nell, owned a working ranch that they called "Cabbage Palm Ranch" out in what was the scrub that characterized so much of old South Florida, where he ran cattle and had a few horses, only about fifteen minutes west of the city. Now, of course, like so much else of native Florida, the area has been taken over by development and is nearer to downtown than to the remaining areas of scrub palmettos and hardwood hammocks. Johnny Buster managed the ranch for them. Johnny and Tommie Buster built two chickees out in the short grass and cabbage palms and lived there. Frequently, Agnes and young James would stay out there with them; it was James's joy to ride the horses around the patches of cabbage palm, across the hammocks, and through the ponds, and James recalls "Mr. and Mrs. Mac" very kindly. Agnes would sit on the chickee platform and work her little hand-crank sewing machine, making patchwork. She sent James to Delray Elementary School for a couple of years.

It was just before Christmas one year when "Jimmy" stole into the barn and found a stash of brand new toys there, under the floorboards. He was frightened that he might be doing something wrong by taking them out, but the attraction of the toys was just too strong, so he had to play with them. Inevitably, Mr. Mac caught him with the toys, and James was sure he was in trouble. So he still remembers the moment when Mr. Mac smiled at him and said, "Son, it's all right. They're your toys. They're your Christmas presents."

His time in Delray, at white man's school and on the ranch, would be very important to James for at least two reasons. First, because of his opportunity to learn and practice English. Second, or perhaps first, because of the valuable lessons concerning business and running a ranch that he would learn firsthand from Mr. Mac. "Jimmy" Billie was nine and a half years old and Charles, his new little brother, was only a few months old when they last stayed with Tommie at the Cabbage Palm Ranch. By then their mother, Agnes, had passed away. The MacMillans sold the Cabbage Palm Ranch in 1961.[10]

By 1951 Agnes and Sonny Billie were married and Agnes became pregnant again. Her second son, Charles, was born on 6 August 1952 but, within a couple of months, Agnes began to sicken. With hindsight, it is possible to understand that her heart, weakened in childhood by fever, simply could not sustain the stress of another birth. In fact, it is surprising that she was able to survive the birth of her first child. Her sister had been less strong.

When Agnes died, at 3:05 p.m. on 7 April 1953, Sonny was devastated. So was her young son, James. He recalls the moment when someone put her into a car to take her to the hospital. She looked out of the window at James, and waved. He waved back. It was the last time he saw her alive. Since that time, some older Seminoles, mostly women, have recalled his mother, Agnes, as a "whore," and this has stung him badly. I have heard him repeat this publicly on a number of occasions, throwing out a tiny bit of the anger that he has clung to ever since her death. As soon as he realized that it offended me, it became a game between us. His mother's sexuality was of no concern to me; such a pejorative was a white man's social judgment and not really valid in Indian terms anyway, nor could any epithets change the past. I was annoyed, nevertheless, to see him prod the pain that I knew was all too real in him and hovered all too close to the surface of his reality. Agnes died when James was only nine years old, and he has never really gotten past his anger at her for deserting him, although he has intellectualized it over the years.

We had a conversation once about "cosmic will" and the power of concentrating one's cosmic will, and it brought up an important anecdote in this regard. James recalled an event that occurred when he could have been no more than six years old, and Agnes had taken James with her to BC to stay for a short while. (The myth that Seminoles' lives are static is just that—a myth. They are a dynamic society, frequently on the move from one clan camp to another and consequently, in Florida, from one Res to another.) James and his mother had gone out to BC and were sleeping under a chikî(t), on a typical sleeping platform about three feet off the ground. "I remember one night," James said, "waking up and a man was beating my mom. He was beating her with his fists." James does not recall why no one else had yet awakened and come to her aid. Unless the two were surrounded by other Bird Clan members, however, others probably would have considered the event none of their business. Regardless, feisty little James was ready to defend his mother. "I grabbed a flashlight—you know, one of them big ol' heavy kinds with the long handle—and jumped up and started beating him over the head with it! So he let go of her and backed off. So, my mom grabbed my hand and we ran away and hid.

"But, you know, after that I watched that man [for years and years], and I stayed real close to him. You know why? So I could remind him all the time of that night. And I really wished he would die. He had diabetes, so I used to take him little pieces of candy and things like that, whatever I could do. And I would smile and say 'How are you doing today?' So, before long, they cut off one of his legs, and then they cut off the other one, and then he died. So, I have to be careful what I ask for, because I might get it. One time I wished that my mom would die—and she did." "Why were you so angry with her?" I asked. "Well, you know, you get pretty upset when you're little and your mom is supposed to be around for you and she's not. I understand that now, but I didn't then. So I have to be careful."

When nine-year-old James next saw his mother after she was taken to the hospital, she was in her casket. He remembers her body stretched out in front of the church altar and the light pouring in through the stained glass windows. This was Rev. Lucius Crenshaw's little white-painted Baptist church on the Old Dania (Hollywood) Res. The minister lifted the "mosquito netting" away from her face so everyone could see her, and just at that moment a bolt of lightning struck, very close by. Tommie told him: "God has just taken your mom away with him." That made the little boy feel good—and feel good about lightning and thunder. Years later, when he was serving with the U.S. Army in Vietnam, he was always able not only to sleep through lightning but actually to like it because he could smile and think that it was his mother looking out for him.

This memory provides a critical element in our understanding of James Billie. He has maintained a strong and vital love-hate relationship with women for all of his life. Numerous moments in his life, past and present, may be responsible for this as we can see, but James's sexuality is so visible and vital a part of his personality and his actions that no imaging of him without an imaging of this aspect of his character would be possible. He uses sexuality, both his and others', as a social and a political tool.

To understand this, first and foremost, it is important to realize that, among the Indians generally and the Seminoles specifically, human sexuality is just one more valid part of the circle of life, and not the cause for fearful repression and prurient interest that it too often is in the Euro-American world. This is the philosophical basis of the world in which the Seminoles were and, for the most part, still are, raised. Nevertheless, that reality does not make the Seminoles any less human, that is, any less subject to everything along the spectrum from innocent human foibles to abject weaknesses.

Sonny seems to have lost a true love in Agnes. He told me how he would visit her grave from time to time, to talk things over with her. He had never told James this, and visiting a grave is not at all in keeping with Seminole tradition, especially for a Medicine practitioner, but he wanted James to know that now and asked me to tell him. I said that perhaps he had unfinished business with her because she had died too soon, and he agreed.

Technically left with two sons, Sonny told me that he gave James to his grandmother, Tommie, to replace the child she had lost. Such an act could have sounded magnanimous if it were not for the fact that Agnes already had left James with Tommie some years earlier, and fathers were not traditionally responsible for the care and raising of children anyway. Charles, the new baby and clan brother to James, also was given to Tommie, but Tommie's life would end within a few years, and eventually Charles was given over to a white family "down the Trail" to raise, a couple whom the Indians knew and trusted. This created a permanent estrangement between Charles Billie Hiers (he has respectfully kept the white family's surname) and his biological father, Sonny Billie.

Sonny became a prominent but controversial Medicine man. He accepted Christianity and continued, nevertheless, to practice a syncretistic form of Indian Medicine. He remonstrated with me, frequently, saying that I had no "focus" in my life because I did not accept Christianity, as he had. I, in return, chided him each time for purporting to practice Indian Medicine and white man's Christianity at the same time. He asserted, each time, that the two did not conflict, and in his combination of the two I am sure that the parts of Christianity that he accepted did not, in practice, conflict with his Indian Medicine. It was a friendly give-and-take that we had.

The Seminole people respected the tremendous knowledge that Sonny had obtained from Ingram and Josie who were, themselves, keepers of knowledge obtained from the old practitioners of early nineteenth-century war Medicine. But Sonny ran a business, hauling fill dirt, in addition to his attention to the people's needs, and was completely open about his desire for white man's money. This desire, unfortunately, extended to his Medicine practice. By tradition, Medicine practitioners are supposed to make Medicine (which includes far more than the basic use of herbs and other plants) in exchange for certain items, such as bolts of cloth of prescribed colors, or chickens or horses, rather than for any direct payment. Sonny eschewed barter for cash. Over the years James acquiesced to Sonny's desire for payment, taking his fees for treating tribal citizens out of tribal coffers. Naturally, rumors grew, as James's political successes grew, that Sonny was using Medicine to help James stay in power. I never found any evidence to support this allegation, but Sonny did support James politically, and James did look after Sonny. After all, regardless of its tenuousness, and the fact that they were not of the same clan, they had a history together.

Sonny's power and prominence remained high within the tribe for the rest of his life. In the late 1980s and 1990s, when the Green Corn Ceremony had reached the nadir of its attendance, and many of those who did attend did so primarily to spend four days drinking, it was James and Sonny who worked to clean it up. James posted Seminole Police Department (SPD) sentries to search cars for alcohol, and Sonny called for and led community talks to teach and remind people of their traditions and duties. Between them, they revitalized some of the Old Ways that were not being sufficiently regarded. When the sixty-eight-year-old Sonny collapsed and died instantly in his backyard in BC, on a hot August day in 2003, the BC Green Corn Ceremony was strong again, and he had instituted tribalwide programs that brought together multigenerational groups to revitalize others of the Old Ways as well.

∽

By the late 1950s, young James was passing through what he refers to wryly as his "Cinderella years." He was on the Old Dania Res, living with the family of Laura Mae Jumper Osceola (Panther Clan, 1932–2003), sister of Moses Jumper Sr. and, therefore, sister-in-law of Betty Mae Tiger Jumper, although they were of different clans, and Laura Mae's husband, Max B. Osceola Sr. (Bird Clan, 1930–1994). These were the parents of current Hollywood council representative Max Jr. The reference to Cinderella should not be interpreted to mean that James was experiencing good fortune. To the contrary, James uses the allusion to make clear that his was as Cinderella's position was in the household, cleaning and doing menial tasks that left Max Jr. free to enjoy the position of favored son. In classic political style, nevertheless, Max Jr. has made much of his early connection to James, as did Laura Mae, over the years. They were perfectly satisfied to bask in the limelight of "their" James's successes. Unfortunately, Max Jr. also was perfectly satisfied to be one of the council members who would vote with Mitchell and David Cypress to suspend and, then, impeach his vaunted "brother" in 2003.

The social value of riding on the coattails of James's successes over the years was especially dear to the two tribal doyens, Betty Mae Tiger Jumper and Laura Mae Jumper Osceola, and their oft-times not-so-friendly rivalry became a standing tribal joke. They vied, privately and publicly, time and again, to identify themselves with James and, in their loyalty to his (and, obviously, their own) causes, received numerous dividends as a result of James's loyalty. In addition to asking for and receiving whatever favors they wanted at any given moment, from gifts of money to VIP inclusion in tribal events, each quickly took every opportunity to support James publicly in return. It was all too obvious, however, that their loyalty owed at least as much to the vaunting of their own images as to that of their longtime benefactor.

One hilarious moment stands out. The tribe staged a fiftieth birthday celebration for James, on 19 March 1994, in the arena of the old Hollywood rodeo grounds. Neil and Nell MacMillan were special guests. Betty Mae was courteously asked up to the podium to offer her comments, and Laura Mae could not let the opportunity pass to add her comments as well. Each began to vie with the other to convince the crowd that she had known James longer, and more intimately, than the other. One spoke of recalling him as a child, and caring for him; the other spoke of a closeness to Agnes, his mother; each had been there at the major events of his life—and on and on. The Seminoles took it all in with inured patience. We all laughed together, however, when I commented, "Any minute now, I think that one of them is going to say that she was there at his conception!"

Laura Mae passed away just a few years later, in the same year in which her son voted to suspend her "adopted son" from office. Betty Mae lived on, until 2011, but her life was radically constricted as a result of recurring bouts of cancer. Her relationship with James became severely constricted as well, after the 1995 elections, when her son, Moses Jumper Jr., known to the tribe as "Big Shot" (Snake Clan, b. 1950) made a serious political blunder. In an unsuccessful attempt to have himself appointed head of the tribe's Recreation Department (he was serving already as head of recreation for BC), he spoke out loudly and petulantly against James's candidacy, and to add insult to injury, he spoke in support of one of James's opponents. James was furious. He made comments repeatedly about the meanness of being bitten by a Snake that he had fed! Betty Mae was sick over her son's actions and expressed her regret to me repeatedly, asking me to pass her feelings on to James in the hope of preserving the protection and deference she had received over the years. I had no intention of getting caught in a feud between James and Betty Mae. As soon as James was reelected, as everyone knew he would be, one of his first actions was to remove Big Shot from the Recreation Department altogether and ignore him henceforth in every way possible. Betty Mae's relationship with James was never the same after that time.

～

Even off the Res, life in Hollywood in the 1950s had its ups and downs for a proud Indian boy. The growing towns of Hollywood and Davie were unfriendly neighbors to the Seminoles in these days. When he was about thirteen or fourteen, Mrs. Ivy Stranahan, owner, with her husband, of an early twentieth-century Indian trading post on the New River in old Fort Lauderdale and driving force behind a small local support group that called themselves the Friends of the Seminoles, collected $10 so that James could have a pair of shoes to wear to school. Thinking that a young man should develop his own authority, she gave the cash to James rather than possibly embarrass him by accompanying him to the shoe store.

So James went alone and told the fat, white man in the store what he wanted. The man asked him how much he had to spend; a classic ploy, but James was young and he fell for it, and told him. The man went into the stock room and came out with what James recalls as an ugly pair of shoes that were at least two sizes too large for the teenager's feet. The man tore up newspaper and stuffed the toes full of it and told James that this pair was just right for him and cost exactly the amount he had to spend, and James walked out with the shoes, feeling angry and foolish and embarrassed to have permitted the white man to take advantage of him.

Not knowing how else to express his frustration, he walked straight to the nearest borrow pit and threw the big ugly shoes as far out as he could into the dark water. When Mrs. Stranahan asked, he said that he had lost the shoes, and she knew that there was more to the story than that, but she didn't press. He admired her for that more than for anything else. Years later, when the City of Fort Lauderdale needed money to restore the historic Stranahan House, James saw to it that the council voted a sizeable contribution to the project. James is loyal to an amazing degree, and he prizes loyalty above all other virtues. Unfortunately, the city's project occurred at a moment when James and the council were parting ways, and the council ultimately rescinded the contribution.

Tommie Billie Buster passed away in 1958, at the age of only fifty-two, when James was still a teenager. By then, James had had enough of being the virtual chimney sweep in the Osceola household and had left Old Dania Res for BC and high school in Clewiston. He wasn't all that interested in high school; his quick mind made him impatient with any formal educational setting. He did, however, want to play football, and the forty-two miles separating BC and Clewiston made it imperative that he live closer to the school.

Lloyd Pershing "Pete" Turner and his wife, Nina, were among the first to offer James another stable home, albeit short-lived. They ran a bar/restaurant and gas station at the spot known as "Earl Henry's Corners," also known just as "the Big Bend" on Highway 27, about halfway between Clewiston and Moorehaven, Florida, where there also was a dance hall and a junkyard full of old cars. Pete and Nina already had seven children, of whom their son, Ard, was about thirteen or fourteen, just James's age, when they learned from him that James was living out in one of the derelict, rusted out, junked cars. One night, there was a terrific lightning storm, and Pete went out to the car and said to James, "Son, come on inside with me. You're not going to stay out here anymore."

This caused some consternation on the BC Res because the Seminoles there did not want an Indian living with white people they did not even know, but the Turners and James prevailed. The Turners were impressed with the young man's ambition, and they loved him. He felt close to them also: they called him "son" and he called them "mom" and "dad." They did acquiesce to the Indians' decision that James should be sent to school in Oklahoma, lest he become too close to whites. All throughout his political career James has had to deal with this fine line between being loyal to the tribe and being seen by his constituents as too close to non-Indians. The Indians have been betrayed so many times that they are constantly suspicious of any perceived deviation. Even I felt this requirement. Once, after a public tribal event attended by many non-Indians, Mitchell Cypress let me know that I was being watched, and repeatedly tested. He told me: "Yeah, I saw you over there talking to those white people, and I thought, 'What's she doing over there with them; she one of us!'" It was a double-edged compliment. I got the message. That same subject, of loyalty to the Indians versus involvement with non-Indians, would also build resentment against James that would become a significant element of his ultimate loss of power.

Pete drilled it into James that he could do anything—if he wanted it enough. He had to study and prove himself though, more to himself and the Seminoles than to anyone outside of the tribe. One summer when he returned to the Turners, he told them that he was determined to be "chief" one day, "to be something that nobody ever thought I could be," and they knew he meant it.[11] He had a lot of people to prove himself to. David Jumper recalls how much abuse James took from the Indians for being half white, and he believes that this, rather than the factor of James's impoverished circumstances, is responsible for the anger that James sometimes expresses.

These were the years when James bounced back and forth, from BC and swiping cold drinks from Morgan Smith's little store, where he got the nickname *hokípi(t)*, meaning "thief," a play on his Indian baby name; to high school in Clewiston; to college in Haskell Indian School in Kansas; to a couple of semesters at Rollins College in Winter Park, Florida, and, in 1965, to a hitch in the U.S. Army—just in time to be sent straight to Vietnam.

∽

Even as the United States has systematically destroyed the roles of Indians as warriors in their own right over the last century and a half, the same United States has been perfectly pleased to welcome Indian warriors into its own ranks, to fight and die for the putative conquerors. In the case of the Florida Seminoles, Howard Tiger, Betty Mae's brother, was the first in the twentieth century to choose to fight, enlisting in the U.S. Marine Corps. I found the process ludicrous—the idea of Indians fighting *for* the United States seemed too strange to reckon with—until the tradition of warriorhood was factored in to the subject. Then James explained it even more clearly.

"The U.S. Army did two things for me that I never could have done by myself. First, it sent me to places that I never would have gotten to see otherwise. Then, it let me kill people." Pure James: boastful, shocking, on the edge, in your face, true. I remembered his oft-repeated maxim that he had heard from his Seminole elders that "from time to time, the earth needs to drink blood," the mantra of the warrior spirit. He spent almost his entire hitch (1965 to May 1968) in Vietnam, rising from private to sergeant, most of the time heading a long-range reconnaissance patrol. "I wasn't the only Indian in the Army, but I had a big advantage over all of them. They were used to living on the open plains, and I was from the Everglades. They saw all that dense jungle terrain, and they thought they were walking into another world. But I got under that heavy tree cover, and it felt like home!"

He never lost a man when he was leading his patrols, he says. He chose his men carefully: by taking them out and getting them drunk. "That's the quickest and best way to find out what a man is really like," said the man who drinks rarely and, even then, little. "Some men get drunk, and they're just no good. Some men get drunk too easily and lose their senses. Other men just won't let themselves get drunk at all. Those were the men I liked best, and I chose them first." He also judged men by the way they moved and walked and held themselves. Years later, as he and I were walking out of his Hollywood office and up toward the helipad on the roof, he pointed to a tribal supervisor, a non-Indian whom he liked. We were talking about this ability to identify others through their experiences. "See that?" James said, looking at the man and nodding (Seminoles never use their fingers to point; it isn't polite). "You can just look at a man and see if he has killed another man by the way he stands and holds himself. There's a whole different look about him."[12]

He lost men only once, and that was when he went on R&R and a temporary leader was assigned to take them out. The temp took the men up the same path that they had just reconnoitered previously, and the enemy spotted them and killed them, in a particularly vicious manner. "I never used the same path twice," James said. You didn't want the enemy to think you were predictable.

In the war, he used all of the swamp lore that he had been taught in his twenty years of life in South Florida. "I liked to get out on patrol very early in the morning. That way, the dew was still fresh, and I could see it hanging on the trip wires put out by the VC." He also used the Medicine that he had been studying for many years. James is very closed about the exact nature or extent of his studies, but he has learned a great deal and that is obvious, therefore, undeniable. A basic requirement of Medicine at the outset of any enterprise involves the use of tobacco. The smoke carries the words of the participants directly up to the Giver of Breath and binds the people involved in purity of intent and honesty to one another. His men quickly realized the value of the small ceremony and asked him to include them in it as a ritual. His very existence today seems to provide evidence of his ability to use his knowledge to survive.

Bears, traditionally, for example, have special importance to the Seminoles. Bears have the power to foresee events. "There's a little chant that you can use in Medicine, in which you ask the bear for help. It's just little and repeats 'Oh Bear, let me see tomorrow,' because bears can 'see.' If you shoot at a bear but can't hit him, you should quit, because it's not his day to die. If he lets you kill him, it's because he already knows that it's his day to die." James often thought of the bears and asked them to help him see ahead before he went out on those dangerous recon patrols. One night he dreamed that he saw an enemy soldier with a machine gun, crouched under the ledge of a rock face. Next day, his patrol needed to climb up a ravine and James decided, in an unusual move, to divide them into two groups of three each. As they began to climb they reached an area of rock overhangs, just as he had seen in his dream. Suddenly, he realized that an enemy soldier with a machine gun had spotted one of the patrol groups and was climbing up behind them. James was able to fire a grenade from his launcher and kill the enemy soldier, ending the danger to his own men.

One of the Seminole power figures, Ingram Billie, brother of Josie, taught the young man another valuable hunting lesson that stood him in good stead in war. Ingram commanded patience in hunting, requiring James to hold his fire until he was very sure of his shot. "He would send me out hunting with three shotgun shells, and expect me to bring two back. Anything else meant that I had wasted shots." James recounted a moment later, in Vietnam, when he had fallen asleep on sentry duty and awakened to see a figure moving toward him in the dark. Four times, he recalled, he put his rifle to his shoulder and four times had the shot but remembered Ingram's admonition. When the man finally got close enough for James to see clearly, he realized that it was a comrade, coming to relieve him. If he had taken the shot, he laughed anxiously, he would probably still be in Fort Leavenworth today.

He had a reason to survive, as least as he saw it. "Some of the men who came back from Vietnam died over here. They didn't have any more battles to fight or a tribe to care for them like I did with the Seminoles."[13] Nevertheless, the years between mid-1968, when he returned from his military service, and the major political victory of his election as chairman in 1979, were years of trial and error for the restless young man. He had proven himself as a warrior in physical warfare, and his experiences with the non-Indian world gave him a certain cachet with tribal citizens—coming under the heading of "know your enemy," as they saw it—but he still had to find a place for himself within the tribe. In the tradition of Seminole warfare, there is no such thing as a permanent rank. No one gets to rest on his laurels. Every day and every deal is a new battle.

He tried a wide range of activities. First he became a coordinator of the federally funded Youth Camp. "'But that job wasn't paying the bills and I knew that wherever women are concerned, there's money to be made,' he grins, 'so I decided to go into the beauty salon business.'"[14] "'I figured since I was a veteran, I'd have a head start in getting a $25,000 loan to get started. But they wanted collateral.'"

"So he took the 1,200 hours of beauty school, graduated and worked for about six months. 'I wasn't all that terrific with a head of hair, but I did get an overall sense of the business aspect.' He then decided on the landscaping business ('because the two jobs are really very similar') but was unable to get a loan to expand the business."[15] The tribe hired him to serve as employment assistance director, another of Chairman Howard Tommie's federally funded positions, but, after a year, James moved again, this time to the directorship of Okalee Village, a visitor attraction on Highway 441 operated by the board. There he did everything from supervising the gift shop to "wrestling" alligators for the tourists. It was a fight of a very different, but also dangerous, kind. "'There's a trick to wrestling 'gators, you know. You have to study them and learn their moves. There's really not much that a 'gator can do—except bite hell out of you. When you learn to avoid that, you've got it made.'"[16] (There really is no such thing as "wrestling" a 'gator. The epithet was dreamed up by those tourist attraction owners in the 1920s to create the image of man fighting beast. Flipping a 'gator over causes his small reptilian brain to rest against the cranium and restrict the blood and oxygen flow, thereby inducing unconsciousness. It's not good for the 'gator to be placed in this state repeatedly, and the Indian "wrestlers" know it, and change 'gators frequently.)

James took a $4,000 cut in pay to wrestle the 'gators and stock the gift shop, but he learned a lot more about business and became a great deal more proficient in alligator and snake handling. At one point, he almost lost a thumb to an alligator, but that wouldn't happen again for about thirty years, by which time he felt that his debt to the 'gators had mounted up sufficiently that he "owed" them.

The story of James and the 'gator is, however, quintessentially James, and deserves telling, even if we must skip ahead a few years to tell it. It happened on a bright afternoon in early 2000. A film crew had asked permission to visit the BC Res to film a segment of *Extreme Contact;* in this case, contact between man and alligator. James, always excited by the possibility of being on camera, decided to star in the role himself and chose to ignore several basic admonitions that he had received long ago. First, the 'gator was about seven feet long—a teenager in human terms—and just as full of aggressiveness as any teenaged boy and, so, a dangerous choice for handling. Then, the 'gator was in water deep enough to obscure his head and body and make the enterprise even more dangerous. Finally, James's knees had been operated on by this time, and he was not as flexible as he had been in past years. All in all, a poor situation from the outset.

James stood over the 'gator's back and thought that he had one hand on the 'gator's jaws as he looked up at the video crew and reached down into the water with the other. Unfortunately, his one hand was not where he thought he had it. A 'gator's jaws are very sensitive and very powerful. One of his fingers went right into the 'gator's mouth, and the 'gator took a bite. James quickly spun away from the cameras and, clutching his hand, got out of the arena. The SPD and James's brother, Charles, were standing by; they recovered the finger segment and rushed James to the hospital. Doctors advised against reattaching the segment of the finger (only about an inch) because of the high risk of infection from the particular bacteria that live in a 'gator's mouth. Afterward, James carried the dried finger segment in his pocket for a year or so, showing it gleefully to anyone who happened to ask. Images of the event meanwhile went round the world; even a Japanese TV station requested the video.

∽

In the 1970s, however, James still held tight to his old determination to run the tribe, however long his apprenticeship in tribal administration might be. "I was on the outside in a sense [since he was not yet an elected official] but I still knew what was going on here. Maybe not the fine details, but enough to keep tabs. I knew I was going to run for chief one day—I prefer to call it 'chief' rather than 'chairman'—but I never knew when."[17]

That was the topic of yet another of our ongoing discussions, James and mine. The word "chief" is the symbol for a concept that really only works in the white man's world: it implies a vertical hierarchy and a degree of unilateral power that simply does not translate accurately into the Seminole world. I wouldn't use it, and sometimes that annoyed James. Finally, however, he found a rationalization that satisfied both of us. "Well," he said one day, "I am the *Chief* Executive!"

When his opportunity to become "chief" finally arrived, in 1979, James learned a lesson about the value of loyalty, especially to one's clan. He told me about his relationships to other people in the tribe whom he does not like or whose limitations he definitely recognizes, but to whom he owes debts. And he pays off his debts. He recalled the first time he ran for chairman. He went out to speak and there were other candidates: Fred Smith, Jack Smith Jr., Alice Snow, and three others. James, naive as a politician, began spouting off about his negative opinions of others. Shortly, Fred and Jack Smith took him aside and told him, quietly, "We're not going to dump you out of this race and forget you, but we're going to teach you something and help you to remember to be respectful toward your clan." Jack and Fred and Alice were all related because they were all Bird Clan. "And you are Bird Clan. And we're going to take care of you because you're Bird Clan. But we want you to remember never to make this mistake again." And James stood there, his face falling, turning paler, feeling more and more like a jerk, he said, as they reminded him of the importance of being loyal to one's clan.

∽

It was in the period when James's political life was just taking shape, shortly after his return from army duty, that his personal life also entered a new era. His sexuality, which had been expressing itself at every opportunity since he had been about fourteen years old, entered a formal stage with the establishment of his relationship with Bobbie Lou Bowers (Panther Clan, b. 1949). Their first child (not his, but theirs) was stillborn, although they would go on to have others, all girls. Their relationship seems to have been a truly loving one although, according to James, it began to diminish in intensity over the coming decade because James did not want to stop having children until they had a boy. Their last daughter was still very young when they hired a beautiful young woman, Lesley Garcia (Panther Clan, b. 1972), to babysit. The arrangement was too convenient for James, and Lesley became an acknowledged lover, finally, about 1990, causing Bobbie Lou to depart the house and the relationship.

The Seminoles were very displeased with these events and quietly expressed their disapproval by ignoring the new partner. Lesley, in a show of good political sense (and some say, aided by Medicine provided by her mother, Agnes Jumper), did not flaunt herself or her new access to power and preferment. She quietly attended events, always pitched in to work wherever she was permitted, and over the 1990s, was also quietly accepted by the tribe. Sentiment remained with Bobbie Lou, however, and James supported her and his daughters, although his relationship with his girl children always has been a rough one.

Lesley and James eventually had children of their own; James finally got his sons, two of them. For the first time James seemed to see the tribe as made up of individual persons and to focus on their needs, at least for a while. But James and Lesley's relationship inevitably would become more and more turbulent as James's commitment to his own sexual expression became more and more flagrant, outside of the tribe as well as in. As one close observer noted, once Lesley transitioned from mistress to mother, the position of mistress was once again open, and James was quick to fill it, and not merely once. The tribe's revenues were becoming larger and larger; James's visibility in the non-Indian world was growing rapidly; and his reputation within the tribe as a generous lover all combined to make the number of his already easy conquests increase, almost exponentially. Lesley was not amused. As their relationship deteriorated, she became more and more voluble in her unhappiness, even to the point of physically threatening one tribal lover who openly expressed her determination to supplant Lesley.

Amazingly enough, in the midst of their domestic disharmony, James agreed to officially divorce Bobbie Lou and marry Lesley. This arrangement would last for another few years only, as James's personal and political lives began to crumble apace. Not until 2007, four years after his impeachment, did James and Lesley finally divorce. By that time, she had left the BC Res and moved closer in to Fort Lauderdale, in a spacious house financed by a tribal loan. Shortly, she would remove even farther away, to Orlando. Well before then, however, in the last couple of years of his chairmanship, James would have found another partner with whom he would appear to find contentment. This relationship is with a young Hispanic woman with whom he also has had children, including sons. They still live together at the time of this writing, off-Res, on a small "ranch" that he bought. Even when, just before his ouster, James engineered the tribal acquisition of properties in Honduras and one of the perks of traveling there for some of James's business associates was easy access to sex, James sometimes preferred the faithfulness of his new relationship at home. Perhaps he's slowing down. Perhaps he's jaded. Perhaps he's finally past his old anger at his mother and able to form an authentic relationship with a woman. Perhaps not.

Nevertheless, James requires DNA testing for each of his putative children, regardless of the conditions of his relationships with their mothers. As for his own "relationships," I can't help recalling a tired old joke that he liked to tell repeatedly. Two bulls—one young and virile and the other older and experienced—are standing on a hilltop looking down on the herd of cows. The young one says to the older: "How about if we run on down there and get us one of them!" The older-and-wiser bull smiles knowingly at the younger, brash bull and says, "How about if we just walk on down there and get us *all* of them!"

∼

When the "palace coup" that ousted James took place, in 2003, the tribe's annual gross revenues had grown to at least $400 million. Whatever charges have been leveled against him, accurately or inaccurately, this fact was irrefutable.

Figure 2. For his 1993 chairman's Christmas card, James sent warm wishes from "James, Micco, and Hul-pah-te-cho-bee" (Big Alligator). The baby alligator Micco is holding bit him during the photo shoot, but did little damage. The Big Alligator, fortunately, was cooperative. (Photograph by Peter B. Gallagher, courtesy of James Billie.)

Many times James said, echoing the Rev. Bill Osceola, "I'm a Cash Cow! That's what they want me to be, and that's what I am."

Considering the precariousness of leadership among the Seminoles, James had maintained a continuous position of leadership longer than any other Seminole. For twenty-four years up to that point, he had led the Seminole people to greater and greater economic success, even when that required him to challenge the State of Florida and the U.S. government in legal combat. Even he had no real idea of how great was the visibility and how large the image—not only across Indian Country but across the non-Indian world also—that he had given to the Florida Seminoles in those years. He never turned away from a fight. James Billie was the quintessential Warrior Without War. He projected his own special combination of leadership skills but quietly manipulated them to fit the expectations of the people.

What neither he nor the people realized, however, is that they wanted conflicting results—the outgrowth of changing (that is, conflicting) values. James would give them what they said they wanted for as long as he could. But, when he finally began to realize, even dimly, the need for substantive change—a sea change—in the system of governance, to support the infrastructure of the tribe over the next level of its growth and meet the challenges of the outside world, it was too late; the people balked. He had been the Prophet rather than the Pastor for far too long.

Now, he began to ask things of the tribe (especially the tribal employees who also were enrolled citizens and, therefore, could vote and could be fired but could not be disenrolled and, therefore, felt little or no impetus to change) that they did not want to give. Essentially, in white man's parlance, they wanted to have their cake and eat it too, and that was not going to work as well as it had in the past, when there had been very little cake to share. By the end of the twentieth century the Seminoles, with no real experience whatsoever in the uses—and misuses—of white man's money, were spending at an alarming rate. Only the fact that the revenues were coming in at such a flood rate mitigated the fact that the outgo was profligate (in white man's terms). As the Seminole Tribe's revenues climbed steadily through the 1980s and '90s, the U.S. Congress would determinedly step up its efforts to have access to those revenues and to legislate the sovereign Seminole Tribe into the same legal requirements as those of non-Indian U.S. citizens. The more money the Indians earned, the more the United Stated validated its own view that they should be treated just like other U.S. citizens—which is to say that they should be just like other U.S. citizens rather than "special" Indians.

In order to deal with constant and increasing pressures from the U.S. government, the tribe repeatedly was pressured to tighten up its business practices, clamp down on wasteful infrastructure, and put its government on a solid white-man's-style business footing. This was not going to be a popular process. Especially when, far more than other U.S. citizens, Indians were aware of the examples of duplicitous dealings of white men, both past and present, in their own businesses and in their own governments.

Interestingly, James chose several white men to become the harbingers of the sea change that he envisioned, if only imperfectly, and in the process of implementing the new policies, James and they would become the targets for almost all of the tribe's dissatisfactions with the process. In a series of rapid political moves that bore the mark of significant behind-the-scenes maneuvering—and not all by the Indians—the white men were pushed out of tribal business in 2003. James, however, would bear the brunt, and his twenty-four-year career would topple in the process. The fact that the palace coup that finally unseated him would be led by old enemies was, we are supposed to believe, simply coincidental.

4   Hitting the Big Time

The theme of Chairman James Billie's first and, indeed, subsequent administrations would be the increasing exercise of tribal sovereignty by the Seminole people in order to provide the economic security that would protect their future, and specifically, their cultural survival. Although he could not depend on any other members of the council, whose visions tended more toward the parochial, to grasp the intricacies of that exercise and its potential ramifications, for the most part they accepted his leadership because they recognized the growing power accruing to the tribe as a result and could see its real value in economic returns to the tribe. As James told a reporter in 1986, "So all any of us can do is fight as hard as we can to hold on to what little the white man has left of our culture and our blood."[1]

In these early days of this next generation of leadership, any personal antagonisms that would later explode among council and board members still took a backseat to the newness of the tribe's rapidly expanding economy. Outsiders were quick to grasp the tribe's burgeoning potential as well. White men with grandiose business ideas that might or might not be viable were increasingly accosting James, and he was not always able to distinguish among them. As a reporter would sum it up later, "Billie has always been a man who does it now and thinks about it later."[2] Even though his experiences with the non-Indian world were greater than those of the rest of his current political colleagues, James still stumbled through his early years of leadership. He developed a style of leadership based upon his own bravado, his innate and intense and growing commitment to tribal sovereignty, and a style of decision making based on personal choices that did not always serve him or the tribe well, but the positive aspects of a large and growing income can mitigate a number of negative aspects.

∼

Some FR tribes in the U.S. Northwest have taken to referring to white men's money as "green frog skins." This epithet is valuable of itself because it highlights the underlying mindset: most Indians do not see money as inherently valuable, as white men so often do. They see it as leverage: white men value it and, therefore, the more Indians can get, the greater is the possibility that white men will respect the Indians. This respect, in turn, translates into two critical, long-range, Indian goals: second, to permit each tribe to be left alone to determine its own future; and, first, to use all of that future to secure the preservation of its own culture and traditions. From these interlocking objectives we may not infer, however, that all tribes knew, or know, how to protect their cultural characteristics from the onslaught of those harmful as well as those valuable non-Indian elements. For the Seminoles of Florida, whose geographic isolation had buffered them from the non-Indian world for much longer than other, especially western, tribes, there was a great deal of "catching up" to do.

Even James did not completely understand the full details of the exercise of sovereignty, but he certainly did grasp the "bottom line" of the fight. He knew that its value to the Seminole people was profound and absolute. He knew that the social matrix of the larger non-Indian world was finally expanding to include Indians' long-awaited access to the exercise of inherent powers that white men had long sought to deny them. He knew that he would have to fight the white men, yet again, for their exercise. He just wasn't completely sure of how and how far he could push.

One day, almost two decades after James had begun his fight for autonomy, he and I were sitting in his sumptuous new office in Hollywood. It was late in the afternoon of a very busy day, but one of those luxurious moments when the meetings with white men—the "suits"—were over and even the Indians were tired of trying to get to him. Yet again his mind went to the subject of sovereignty, and he asked me to go over the list of inherent national powers once again. I launched into a recitation, and he became very impatient and agitated. He lunged forward across the desk toward me and said, forcefully, "Hell, honey—so, what I hear you sayin' is that sovereignty ain't nothing but who's got the biggest gun!" There was no arguing with that.

In the process of navigating not only his first term but also his second and third, several major themes and a number of minor ones would consume James and the council. These were, for the most part, themes that had begun during Howard Tommie's administration, but they quickly became fugues as the tribe made its rise from relative obscurity to an object of national interest. The intertwining themes were the fight to recover reparations from the U.S. government for their taking of Indian lands, known as the Indian Land Claims Case (which quickly became a fight among the Indians, as well); tobacco sales, or Smoke Shops, which brought the tribe its first substantive revenues; "bingo," or gaming in the larger sense; a fight over water rights and control among the tribe, the State of Florida, and the U.S. government, known legally as the East Big Cypress Case (EBCC); and law enforcement on the reservations, especially in response to a growing drug problem both inside and outside the tribe, and a subject tremendously complicated by federal and state interventions.

From these very earliest moments of tribal involvement, both state and national law enforcement agencies began to turn the intense light of their interest upon the tribe, as rumors of organized crime involvement in tribal enterprises spread. The FBI, in particular, focused on the tribe generally, and James specifically, sending undercover agents onto the reservations, a practice they would continue up to and including the moment of his impeachment. "God knows how many times we've been investigated," James told a reporter in 1986, "but they've never been able to prove a thing." That would continue to be the case from 1986 to the present day. By this time, the tribe, directed by James, had taken the state and the U.S. government each to court several times, and James had been under indictment for killing an endangered Florida panther. But the tribe was just beginning to flex its sovereign muscle. "It's funny how the white men never bothered with us as long as we were just a bunch of Indians selling trin[k]ets along the side of the road," James said smilingly.[3]

The Indian Land Claims Case

The first issue to bring the Florida Seminoles out of their cultural isolation of the late nineteenth and early twentieth centuries and back into the national arena had been the possibility of obtaining reparations from the U.S. government for the lands taken from them, by earlier treaties and wars. The case began for the Florida Seminoles almost as early as the passage of the Indian Claims Commission Act, on 13 August 1946, more than two generations before James Billie had even come on the political scene, but it would devolve upon his determination to fight the issue to its conclusion—almost half a century later.[4]

It was an outgrowth of a much larger issue, in the eyes of the U.S. Congress; it was part of the latest movement on the part of the U.S. government to divest itself of any economic and political responsibilities toward Indian tribes. The premise was that the government would create a special tribunal to adjudicate tribal suits for disputed claims as a result of broken treaties, or alleged takings of lands on the part of the U.S. government over past years, whether arising from "fraud, duress, unconscionable consideration," or other claims "with respect to which the claimant would have been entitled to sue in a court of the United States if the United States was subject to suit."[5] The sovereign immunity of the U.S. government had prevented settlement of these claims, and Congress believed that final adjudication by a freestanding commission and a Court of Claims, ergo, relinquishment of the claims, would relieve the United States of a significant portion of its responsibilities toward Indian tribes.

In the 1950s the United States would next introduce a series of so-called Termination Acts, in which Congress would target tribes that it claimed were economically viable—sufficiently self-supporting, it claimed—that federal jurisdiction could be withdrawn, that is, the U.S. government could cease any economic responsibility for the tribes and any responsibility for government-to-government relations. This would relieve the United States of yet another, and significant, portion of tribal responsibilities.[6] The Seminole Indians of Florida, targeted in the second of these groups, entered into a negotiation with the U.S. government that ended with their continuing a direct relationship with the United States and their agreement to create a governmental entity based on a white-man's-style governmental structure with a constitution and bylaws. This governmental entity the tribe called the Seminole Tribe of Florida.

Meanwhile, in the same decade, the BIA obtained funding to initiate a relocation program, intended to provide relocation support and help in job placement for any Indians who were willing to leave their tribes and resettle in urban areas, thereby (the BIA believed) assimilating into the larger non-Indian world. In the fiscal year 1954, some 2,163 Indians accepted BIA-promulgated resettlement. Almost 100 percent of those relocated came from the Northwest and the West. Their principal centers of relocation were California and Illinois.[7] The Florida Seminoles, still determinedly insular in their outlook, did not participate.

Over the ensuing two decades, as it became obvious that all of these attempts by the U.S. government were falling far short of their objectives, and as U.S. society once again shifted in its attitudes toward Indians, President Lyndon Johnson's Great Society programs espoused a new national policy of tribal "self-determination." If the United States couldn't get rid of the Indians by simply cutting them adrift, or by forcing them into assimilation, then it would "return" governmental responsibilities to the tribes and, subsequently, enact legislation upon legislation to subsume them into submission on an equal legal footing with all other U.S. citizens rather than permit them to retain their current status as "special" Indians. It was the beginning of the modern process that I have dubbed Conquest by Legislation.

In the earliest of these themes, the Florida Indians, at the urging of BIA Seminole agent Kenneth Marmon, entered into a contract with white attorneys to place a claim before the Indian Land Claims Commission (ILCC). In 1950 the claim was filed, asking for compensations totaling $47,782,975 and arising from four separate causes of action.[8] Three of the four arose out of broken treaties and wars, especially the Second Seminole War (1835–42), and the fourth action arose from the alleged taking of Indian lands during the creation of Everglades National Park in 1944.

Accepted by the ILCC, what we might term the first phase of the struggle for a favorable judgment from the ILCC went on for a quarter of a century with several battles impeding the larger conflict. The first was an outgrowth of the anger that still existed between the Oklahoma Seminoles who had been removed from Florida during the Seminole Wars and the Florida Seminoles who had successfully resisted removal. In 1951 the politically separate Seminole Nation of Oklahoma (SNO) entered its own petition. Not only did the Oklahoma tribe assert their right to reparations, their petition asserted that it had the only right and asked for dismissal of the Florida Seminoles' claim on the grounds that they (the Oklahoma tribe) were the only Indians with the right to place the claim. The motion to dismiss the original Florida Seminoles' claim was denied in 1953, but the SNO would remain a party to the petition, although the internecine war over the ultimate settlement split between the Florida and Oklahoma tribes would go on and on, until the U.S. Congress finally put an end to it almost half a century later—in 1990.

As if the intertribal wrangling were not enough, between 1950 and 1953 the U.S. government itself attempted to have the Seminoles' claim dismissed in summary judgment. The ILCC supported the tribe's right to claim, however, and denied the government's motion. In addition to the attempts of the U.S. government to sabotage the Seminoles' case, over the years 1950 to 1968, several significant events occurred, each of which had an impact upon the case.

Between 1957 and 1962, a social rift among dissident Florida groups became a permanent political split. In 1957 the U.S. government agreed to recognize the Seminole Tribe of Florida, and the tribe offered citizenship to any of their South Florida kin who chose to request enrollment. Meanwhile, most of the disaffected Indian families "down the Trail" chose not to seek enrollment but, rather, to ask the federal government for separate recognition, which finally was granted in 1962, as we have discussed earlier. This splinter group adopted the political title the Miccosukee Tribe of Indians of Florida. A third group, however, consisting of a single extended family, chose to hold itself aloof from either of the other two and continues to exist to this day as so-called independent Indians.

The Miccosukees, the group of Indians living "down the Trail"—the Tamiami Trail, or Highway 41—who would obtain separate federal recognition in 1962, attempted to quash the claim placed by their cultural kin. Then, the small group of "independent" Indians attempted to intervene in the claim on the premise that receiving any monetary settlement from the U.S. government would preclude their getting back the land itself, which was their overarching interest. Despite the factionalizing that this clearly indicated among the Florida Indians, the ILCC and the U.S. Court of Claims rejected the attempts of the separate groups to intervene in the case on the premise that they were adequately represented by the original petitioner.[9]

In 1970, the ILCC ruled in favor of a $12.5 million settlement, but the Florida Seminoles appealed the amount as far too small, and the ruling was overturned by the federal Court of Claims. Five years later, the ILCC made the Indians another offer of a $16 million settlement. In November of 1975 the SNO voted to accept the amount and in January of 1976, the Florida Seminoles voted to accept the offer also, on the premise that the longer they held out the smaller the offer might become. Howard Tommie and the council, including James Billie and Mike Tiger as Hollywood Res representatives, explained the offer to a crowd of about 250. The general sentiment was that the fight had gone on long enough and it should be ended, even though the figure still was far too small.[10]

Belief that the case had come to an end was precipitous, however. The crux of the problem was the division of the funds between the Florida Indians and the Seminole Nation of Oklahoma's citizens—a detail that was not addressed in the ILCC's final judgment. The larger of the contentions was between the SNO and the Seminole Tribe of Florida specifically, but, before this problem could be addressed, yet another schism invaded the process, one that had existed for over a century in Oklahoma between the Indian citizens of the SNO and two bands of Freedmen descendants whose citizenship had been forced on the tribe, SNO asserted, in the 1866 treaty between the United States and the Seminoles at the end of the American Civil War.[11]

On several separate occasions in the twentieth century (at least, during this case and since, in a tribal vote to disenroll them by instituting a blood quantum requirement), the SNO attempted to divest itself of any tribal responsibilities to the descendants of those slaves who had been transported to Indian Territory with them during the Seminole Wars of Removal in Florida.[12] With the treaties of 1866, forced upon each of the Five Tribes at the close of the Civil War, the United States, for complex but transparently self-serving reasons, at once managed to punish not only the Indians who had fought with the Confederacy but those who had supported the Union as well and to limit its future responsibilities to blacks in the Indian Territory by transferring those responsibilities to the Indians. Now, as the Freedmen saw a significant settlement in the offing, they sought to intervene in the case in their desire to protect a share of the final award.

The SNO rebutted the Freedmen's petition and the ILCC eventually rejected their claim to intervene as a separate party.[13] This did nothing, however, to ameliorate the historical estrangement that had existed and continued to exist between the two groups in Oklahoma. Even I would become a minor party to the fights—social, political, and legal—among the Florida Seminoles, the Oklahoma Seminoles, and the two Freedmen's Bands of the Seminole Nation of Oklahoma. Waged as economic fights, as they surely were at basis, they were nevertheless wrapped in the cultural warfare that was a continuing aspect of the United States' nineteenth-century Seminole Wars of Removal. These blacks—some descendants of the slaves and free blacks who had been transported to Indian Territory along with the forcibly removed Seminoles, and others, freedmen from the American Civil War era—were caught between the proverbial rock and a hard place. The rock being the Indians—who knew the Freedmen were not Indians—and the hard place being the U.S. government, which conveniently chose to see them as equal to the Indians for economic and political purposes.

We shall revisit this struggle between the Indians of Florida and Oklahoma shortly, as they attempt to negotiate some fair split of the award monies that were drawing massive amounts of interest in federal holding accounts. By 1987, the original $16 million award, drawing interest in an escrow account, had reached about $40 million. During the entire decade of the 1980s, however, the settlement problem dragged on as a result of infighting among the Indians themselves. Congress was forced to intervene—eventually to impose its own distribution plans—as the SNO fought the Seminole Tribe of Florida over appropriate shares; the Florida independents repeatedly claimed the land itself and eschewed any share in the settlement; and the tiny Miccosukee Tribe, whose council is the entire adult tribe rather than a few elected representatives, voted against taking any part of the settlement funds.

James Billie had a relatively good relationship with Buffalo Tiger, who served as chairman of the Miccosukees from 1961 to 1985. Buffalo, an intelligent and gently spoken man who espouses traditionalism even as he enjoys a lifestyle outside the Res, married to a white wife, had to accept the vote of his tribe as final. James was hardly bothered by the Miccosukee or independents' stands. His concern was the citizens of the Seminole Tribe and getting the best deal he could for them. Despite quiet discussions with Buffalo and with Sonny Billie (James's erstwhile stepfather), who replaced Buffalo as chairman for a short period in 1986–1987, and, ultimately, with Billy Cypress (not the same as the Billy Cypress who directed the Seminoles' tribal museum) who led the Miccosukees until 2010, James was not able to reconcile all the Florida Indians' views. James's most pressing concern, however, was with the SNO and with the various Oklahoma congressmen, Florida congressmen, and Florida legislators whose attempts to devise settlement plans were sometimes more and often less supportive of the Florida Seminoles.

Within two quick years of the final award, it became obvious to all concerned that the Oklahoma and Florida Indians were not going to find an easy accommodation on the subject of the division of monies. The U.S. Senate Subcommittee on Indian Affairs tried, and failed, to reach settlement. After another two years of quiet discussions, by which time the $16 million award had collected another $4 million in interest, James made the SNO an offer, over which it vacillated under pressure from the Freedmen's Bands.

By the time James took over the chairmanship, the subject of water management—the East Big Cypress Case—had entered the discussions among the Florida Indians, the State of Florida, and the U.S. government, and this topic threatened to derail the ILCC settlement process. From this point through the final settlement, in 1990, the process would take on added dimensions because of the Seminoles' determination to counter what they viewed as the arrogant and high-handed attempts of the state to use and control thousands of acres of their Big Cypress Reservation lands. Any final arrangement that would end the ILCC case would have to include some settlement of the East Big Cypress Case.

Beyond all of the minor skirmishes of the larger war, however, this case nevertheless constituted a landmark for the Florida Indians and especially for the citizens of the Seminole Tribe. It was one of their largest battles since 1858 and the end of their warfare, in traditional form, against the white men. This, however, was a new form of war and one that the Indians would understand only imperfectly, at first. Eventually, before it was settled, the original suit would subsume the East Big Cypress Case as well and make the Seminoles the first tribe east of the Mississippi to forge a precious water compact with its state and the federal governments. In the process of both of these fights, some aspects of which would linger on for another decade, the tribe would wage war on other but allied fronts, fighting to protect revenues from economically important tobacco sales, and taking the state all the way to the U.S. Supreme Court in a landmark case, to protect its quickly increasing gaming revenues, the proceeds from which were critical to paying white lawyers to protect the Indians against the increasing pressures of the white governments. In every instance, however, the overarching theme of every battle was protection and exercise of national sovereignty. In the second decade of his tenure, and on through the turn of the twenty-first century, James's exercise of those powers would reach their zenith.

～

Over the years James frequently referred to himself publicly and privately as the "Cash Cow." He understood what his people expected of him, in economic terms, and he knew how to exude the aura of power and manipulate the social expectations of the people to keep himself in power. He was quite a showman. The other council members enjoyed the fruits of the tribe's growing income but were very low-key in their political pursuits. Personal animosities always existed among the council members—and more and more particularly between James and David Cypress—especially as revenues increased and the possibilities for the individual council members' control of monies and largesse and access to personal wealth increased. Nevertheless, in the 1980s, the potential for revenues and the value of a common enemy (the white man's government) united them. By the end of the next decade, with the tribe's quantum leap in gaming income, the very same considerations would begin to divide them, and James would pay a high price for his warrior's determination and the aggrandizement it had provided him personally.

Under James's leadership, in the 1980s the council's actions began to outdistance those of the board. As I have outlined earlier, the actual power of the board to be the business arm of Seminole governance was never the same as the rhetorical powers assigned to it in the constitutions and bylaws of the two entities. In reality, the power of each—council and board—depended upon the personal power and clan support of its constituent members and, especially, the personal characteristics of its chairman and president. While Fred Smith was still alive, which was for much of the same time when James was in office, the board was content to manage the cattle program and a few business interests in Hollywood, the most lucrative of which were the Smoke Shops, and especially the Okalee Village tourist attraction, which required an intermittent infusion of board cash to supplement its chronically poor income, and various marginal business interests to which it leased Res lands to non-Indians for short terms.

A small but growing concern for the council was directly related to Fred Smith, and to the growing demand for money in the form of internal tribal loans. Ellen Click, a non-Indian employee at the Brighton Field Office, soon would become Fred Smith's second wife. She quietly had instituted a personal system of loans to tribal citizens that would run parallel to the council's system of loans and sometimes eclipse it. In the late 1990s, following Fred's death, the council would finally be forced to come to grips with Ellen's determination to collect on monies owed her by negotiating directly with her and committing council funds to a citizen bailout. In the meantime, the board's income from Smoke Shops, fortunately, became a significant element of tribal income, but in short order it would be eclipsed by an even more anomalous income source—gaming—the control of which James would keep for the council.

A Bumper Crop

The possibility that the tribe's fortune might be built on tobacco and gambling seemed inconceivable to almost all tribal citizens, even as late as the mid-1970s. Most tribal citizens were not interested in white men's pursuits, nor were they even interested in white men, generally (and generically) speaking. But the tribe acquired a new and heightened visibility with the U.S. government's final award of $16 million in the Indian Land Claims Case in 1976—even though it would ultimately take another fourteen years before the Seminoles would actually receive monies—due to the battle among the litigants over distribution of the award monies, as I have described earlier.

Further, by the 1970s the social attitudes of the larger non-Indian nation were becoming slightly more inclusive as regarded Native tribes, and recognition of some tribal rights were beginning to be viewed as rewarding economic shelters for outside investors. Suddenly, non-Indians saw fresh and potentially lucrative business prospects where an FR tribe could become involved.[14] One reporter characterized the Seminole's Hollywood Res as "an investment haven for non-Indian businessmen seeking quick profits."[15]

Howard Tommie, as the chairman and a figure of growing status across Indian Country, became the focal point for these overtures. Ultimately, he had sufficient difficulty in separating his personal and official interests that he engendered much criticism, and he chose to step out of tribal politics and cultivate several of the more lucrative possibilities for himself. He has used his business acumen to expand them over the years, providing solid benefits for himself both in Florida and in Oklahoma, and for his (now estranged) wife and his son and daughter. Mrs. Dorothy Tommie (née Osceola, Panther Clan, b. 1935), an excellent business person in her own right, has actively pursued interests as well, independently of her ex-husband, spinning off Smoke Shops and off-Res real estate holdings.

James would, for years afterward, denigrate Howard's business skills. The two men were powerful and very self-directed, and they walked warily around each other. It also was James's recollection that the reason why the council had not already accepted Howard's negotiated deal with the outside backers to begin tribal bingo was because the deal was highly unfavorable to the tribe. James would renegotiate it, over physical threats from the outsiders, to favor the tribe.

Further, after James was elected, he said that he (James) waited for Howard to make some overture, offering help to make a smooth transition from one chairmanship to the other. But it was not forthcoming. That was, James recalled, when he realized that Howard was still "very sure of himself and only waiting for a chance to make another bid for power."[16] Howard would, indeed, make two further bids to return to tribal politics, one in the 1980s and another in the 1990s, each unsuccessful. James, to whom loyalty is a paramount issue, recalled a supporter of Howard standing up in a crowd during the 1987 reelection campaign and attempting to discredit James with a charge that Howard, not James, was the successful businessman and, therefore, knew what he was doing. The attempt was unsuccessful. In both instances, James was far too firmly entrenched by then and the tribe's economic base was growing too well for the people to "change horses in midstream."

Popular attitudes notwithstanding, the tribe's first tax-free tobacco shop was on tribal land leased in 1976 to Marcellus ("Marcy") Osceola, a close friend of Howard, and his deal with the council gave him an "exclusive" right to sell cigarettes to any other tribal citizens who might want to go into the tobacco business themselves. By 1979, when Howard opted out of tribal politics and James

Billie replaced him as chairman, a small number of Smoke Shops had blossomed on the Hollywood Res.

In short order, however, the council would have to face two challenges to its new and lucrative business, one from within the tribe and the other from without. Other Seminoles did, indeed, want to get in on the potentially lucrative venture. They quickly began to complain to the council that Marcy refused to sell them cigarettes at his wholesale rate but, rather, offered them such a small discount as to make it impossible for them to realize any profits. Marcy quickly challenged the council, however, on the grounds of what he had understood as an exclusive right to tobacco sales. The council mitigated his charges by explaining that their understanding of "exclusive" was that Marcy would "exclusively" provide cigarettes, *wholesale,* to other tribal citizens who might be permitted by the council to operate Smoke Shops. The council voted, three to two, to revoke the word "exclusive" in Marcy's empowering resolution, and eventually the council would make the tribe itself, rather then any individual, the wholesale purveyor to tribal citizen owners of Smoke Shops.[17]

Almost as quickly as he got into the business, Marcy opted out. The impetus was a generous offer from the powerful Howard—the same person who had gotten him into the business. Howard is rumored to have paid Marcy $500,000 for his business and stock. A few short months later, and just prior to Howard's leaving office, the council—ever influenced by a strong leader—voted obligingly to transfer Marcy's land lease to Howard as well.[18]

The financial backing for Howard's buyout of Marcy's interests came not only from his own pockets but also from outside of the tribe, however, from three individuals whose involvement with tribal income would grow tremendously over the coming decade. George Simon, a Miami CPA; Jack B. Cooper; and Eugene Weisman of Pittsburgh and Florida, incorporated Seminole Management Associates, Ltd., in May of 1979. Simon had been questioned by a congressional committee investigating the Bobby Baker influence-peddling scandals of the 1960s. Weisman was a bingo operator from Pittsburgh with alleged ties to mob figures. Cooper, who died in 1983 but whose financial interest in tribal income lingered on, was a well-known associate of Meyer Lansky.[19] Jack Skelding, the tribe's first Tallahassee lobbyist, had introduced the backers to tribal legal counsel, Steve Whilden, who had introduced them to Howard. We shall revisit Seminole Management Associates, Ltd., as we discuss the operations of the tribe's gaming industry in the next chapter.

Howard's business acumen, his powerful Bird Clan affiliation, his forceful nature, and his size (he's a tall man with a deep and resonating voice) have earned him a high degree of deference in the tribe, even among council members who have for the most part left Howard alone over the years. Even when his land lease payments began to fall behind, in the mid-1990s, the council was loath to exert any pressure on him to bring his payments up to date. Even James was quiet about Howard, perhaps because of their clan bond, but it was in the mid-1990s, when demographic increases pushed land values to a premium on the Hollywood Res, that the council finally required Howard, by resolution, to pay his outstanding debts or return his Smoke Shop property leases to council control. And possibly for reasons of health—his had deteriorated profoundly in the 1990s—he chose to return the properties to tribal control.

～

The challenge from outside the tribe came quickly also, in 1977, from Broward County sheriff Edward Stack, who, backed by a local cigarette vendor, would bring suit as a private citizen against the Florida State Beverage Division director Charles Nuzum, in order to require that agency to force the tribe to collect taxes on tobacco sold to non-Indians.[20] As an all-too-oft-repeated charge, the basis for Stack's challenge was his allegation that the state was losing "staggering" amounts of money. When the suit was subjected to a change of venue, from Fort Lauderdale to a Tallahassee court, he told reporters, "What [the transfer of the case] will mean is we will have to do more traveling, but we plan to win the suit in Leon County just as we would in Broward County."[21]

His confidence was entirely misplaced. In March of 1978, the Leon County Circuit Court ruled for the tribe in the case of *Vending Unlimited vs. State of Florida,* confirming that the state could not tax tribal cigarette sales. Later that year the Florida 1st District Court of Appeals affirmed the county court's decision.

In another, and separate, issue, 1978 also was the year in which Robert A. ("Bob") Butterworth was appointed sheriff of Broward County (county seat, Fort Lauderdale). Butterworth and the Seminoles would not remain separate issues for long, however. Butterworth had served for the previous four years as a judge in the county and circuit courts of Broward County. As sheriff, he opposed tax-free tobacco sales by the Seminoles, and he would soon become a vocal opponent of Seminole gaming, and the new chairman, James, and the council would become embroiled in lawsuits on two fronts. Although the tribe would prevail, and by 1981 the courts would confirm the inability of the State of Florida to control gaming on the Seminoles' sovereign reservations, Butterworth would remain a foe of these tribal enterprises, especially after his election as state attorney general, in 1986. (See chapter 5.)

In addition to receiving the favorable court decisions, the cases occasioned the Tribal Council's next active steps into white man's politics. Paid lobbyists worked on behalf of the tribe to secure a binding agreement with the state legislature on the subject of tobacco sales, and a permanent agreement was reached in 1979.[22] The council then began to turn part of its growing revenues outward, to support local non-Indian political candidates who would, in turn, support the tribe's objectives. The Seminoles were becoming more engaged in white men's political processes. By 1979, there were five Smoke Shops, all on the Hollywood Res, and the tribe had weathered the legal battle with the state to keep the businesses and avoid state taxes. The court had, once again, strengthened the image of Indian tribal sovereignty by confirming the inability of the state to control tribal business on a Res.

While the agreement between the State of Florida and the Seminole Tribe of Florida has remained in place since that time, the victory for Indian sovereignty was a Pyrrhic one. Over the remainder of the twentieth century, numerous state and federal courts, aided by the U.S. Congress, continuously would seek to make inroads into this much-battered Indian bastion in a determination to bring tribes completely under non-Indian jurisdiction. It was a new kind of battle in a very old war, and the Seminoles would become yet again, as they had historically, among the most passionate of warriors in Indian Country.

In the short term, however, tobacco sales provided the tribe's first quantum leap into solvency. By 1978, annual revenues had reached $600,000, slightly over 50 percent of the tribe's total revenues, and by the next year tribal revenues, with the significant assistance of tobacco sales, topped the $1 million mark for the first time. Within another year, revenues from tobacco profits provided $1.6 million to the tribe. The tiny little ragtag group of "tourist attraction" Indians headquartered on land *in* Hollywood but not *of* Hollywood was suddenly becoming serious economic competition for the surrounding community and the county.

~

Along with a significant and growing economic base and legal battles, tobacco also brought the tribe another spate of problems that James and the council would have to fight to overcome in the first decade of his chairmanship. The perceived taint of organized crime involvement in the inception and early management of Seminole Smoke Shops and, soon, Seminole Bingo, had a basis in fact, however, but one that James was willing to accept as a necessary evil, although not one that he was willing to accept as a permanent part of tribal business.

In the 1980s commercial banks and public lenders still were not ready to provide entrepreneurial capital to FR tribes because along with sovereignty came sovereign immunity: investors were loath to extend financing for ventures in which they had no legal recourse in the case of any defaults. Tribal lands were sovereign lands—held in commonalty rather than individually and, in addition, protected by federal trust status. Further, the federal government had and has fiduciary responsibilities to protect tribal lands. Indian businesses were potentially high yield but, also, very high risk. "That leaves only one possibility," said the tribe's legal counsel, Steve Whilden, "private investors." In the case of the

Smoke Shop deals, as we have learned, the tribe's Tallahassee lobbyist had introduced investors, albeit dubious, to Whilden, who had given them entrée to Howard.

As he assumed the chairmanship in 1979, James told reporters that he had attempted to check into the backgrounds of the individuals who put up funds and held 49 percent of the Smoke Shop businesses. Tribal citizens always held the remaining 51 percent, and the tribe took a varying percentage of the gross profits from each business lease.

The ultimate deal with the state decreed that revenues from tobacco sales had to directly benefit the tribe as a whole. Strictly speaking, this was not the case if individual operators were permitted to make and keep individual profits, but the tribe as a whole benefited by the percentages of profits that the individuals paid to the tribe. James never had any intention of allowing the non-Indians to become permanent parts of the Seminole economy. He envisioned their participation as lasting about three years, or over the time it would take the tribe to build enough equity in the process to become its own backer and make the tobacco business wholly its own. But profits were good and non-Indian interests were not to be as easily unseated as he or the council hoped.

"There's an old saying [in Indian Country]," James told reporters, speaking of the white men who backed the new tribal enterprises: "They'll shake your hand, then take your land. We watch them with both eyes."[23] He added, "It would have been great if Billy Graham had come over and invested in a smoke shop—but he didn't."[24] James admits today that he realized how questionable were the backgrounds and connections of many of the individual backers who provided funding for the tribe's first steps into big business, but he saw their involvement as a necessary evil; especially after a statewide referendum voted down casino gaming in 1978 (with heavy combined opposition from the pari-mutuel interests already involved in horse and dog racing, and jai alai wagering). Floridians have voted down legalized statewide gambling a total of three times over the late twentieth century, even as pari-mutuel wagering and a state lottery flourish, and South Floridians most recently have accepted slot machines, with profits ostensibly dedicated to supporting statewide education.[25] James was very aware of the tenuousness of the tribe's corner on the market in tobacco and gaming and, over his tenure, was constantly on the lookout for enterprises that would diversify the tribe's economic base.

James is still quiet about his long and dangerous process of getting the organized crime connections out of the Smoke Shops. His longtime administrative assistant, Patricia Diamond, is not so reticent. "Several times, they threatened to break his legs," she recalls.[26] But he was determined. For gaming, the story would evolve differently. Eventually, he would also succumb to the economic lure, and open his own Smoke Shop, but he did this quietly, in a shop "down the Trail," based on a quiet agreement with the Miccosukees. The agreement would hold until shortly after James's impeachment by the council in 2003, when financial needs caused James unwisely to dip so far into the business as to leave it without sufficient operating funds, and Billy Cypress would reclaim the contract (see chapter 10). Nevertheless, Seminole Smoke Shops continue to do business to the present day, although the income they produce constitutes less than 2 percent of the tribe's annual gross revenues. Gaming, producing more than 98 percent of the tribe's revenues, has become the tribe's "Cash Cow" now.

The "East Big Cypress Case," Water Compact, and ILCC Settlement

Another major opportunity for the exercise of tribal sovereignty was realized near the end of Howard's tenure, after the council had hired its first full-time legal counsel, Stephen Whilden, who went to work for the tribe in August of 1977. Whilden was energetic in defense of the tribe, even though his personal style was abrasive, and that, eventually, became the centerpiece of his undoing. Whilden advised the council that the state and its Water Management District were making arbitrary use of tribal lands. This attitude on the part of white men's administrations was part of an old pattern of cultural high-handedness that was rapidly losing some of its old hold as social attitudes broadened across the larger, non-Indian, nation in the 1970s. The council decided to fight back. In 1974, the tribe brought suit against the state and its Water Management District in Broward County Circuit Court. Known as the "East Big Cypress Case," this name identified the Seminoles' Big Cypress (BC) Reservation, as opposed to the West Big Cypress, an area of land set aside for the Florida Indians and allocated to the Miccosukee Tribe. The suit, *Seminole Tribe of Florida v. State of Florida et al.*, was shortly moved to federal jurisdiction, in the U.S. District Court for the Southern District of Florida.

Ultimately, the tribe asserted its rights in 16,000 acres of Res lands currently being controlled by the state and the South Florida Water Management District (SFWMD) which, the tribe asserted, constituted an illegal taking of tribal lands.[27] In particular, flooding of various parts of these lands at the unilateral determination of the SFWMD ruined large portions of the tribe's cattle pasturage. Further, the state was receiving monies from mineral leases on these lands that should rightfully have gone to the Seminoles. Not the least of the tribe's positions, in addition, was that the Seminole Tribe's primary relationship was with the federal government—not the state—and the tribe had certain protections in this and allied regards that had been codified in the U.S. Constitution.

Thus would begin thirteen years of litigation and negotiation, giving James and the council, over three terms, one of many opportunities to come for exercising their autonomy in very clear and unmistakable ways. Further, pressing their claim to control over the water rights on their own reservations would, ultimately, coalesce with several other major disputes among the tribe and the State of Florida and the U.S. government that would consume the entire decade of the 1980s.

In 1980 the new council acted on its own behalf to assert control in the area used by the state when it began to grow sugarcane in the portion of the acreage designated by the SFWMD as Conservation Area 3-A. The state claimed that this was an "incompatible use" of the land and attempted to assert its own control, based upon its interpretation of U.S. Public Law 280. This was a weak argument, particularly considering the fact that state control on Florida Indian reservations currently was being adjudicated in the tribe's tobacco and the gaming suits, as we have discussed earlier. The core of Public Law 280 concerned criminal jurisdiction rather than civil-regulatory jurisdiction, and even the state's criminal jurisdiction was not subject to state interpretation unilaterally. We shall explore the ramifications of this federal law and its applications to the Florida Indians more fully as we examine the beginnings and growth of the tribe's law enforcement agency and its fight to preserve gaming (in chapter 5).

From a U.S. legal standpoint, two factors were paramount here. Under a doctrine set forth by the U.S. Supreme Court in 1908, in *Winters v. the United States*, "American Indians have the unique rights to use the waters that arise on, border, traverse, or are encompassed within their reservations."[28] Specifically, "The *Winters* case and its progeny recognized that lands set aside as reservations for Indian tribes to have as homelands would be worthless to the Indians unless they were assured adequate water to sustain their lives and livelihoods."[29]

In the eastern United States, however, since the numbers of tribes were fewer and water supplies greater, the subject of tribal water rights had not yet been the subject of major litigation. The State of Florida had passed its own major legislation governing the use of state waters in 1972, but the law did not include any specific application of the subject to the reservations of the Florida Indians.[30] Either the state legislature was reticent to broach the subject because of the lack of applicable federal law, or legislators simply assumed that their power extended to all lands within the state. Given the subsequent actions of the SFWMD, it would seem that the latter mindset prevailed.

The tribe boldly asserted its control in the disputed area by initiating sugarcane planting there. In response, a series of legal challenges by the state and its SFWMD embroiled the tribe, the State of Florida, and, as the patience of the U.S. Congress began to flag over the inability of the Florida and Oklahoma tribes to reach agreement on division of the ILCC award, the federal government. To further complicate the issue, the State of Florida and Governor (later,

U.S. Senator) Bob Graham's "Save Our Everglades" Program—a popular but underfunded initiative—seemed threatened if the state could not control such a large and integral area. The tribe was rapidly being buffeted on all sides by the assertion of white men's legal control.

Actions by the SFWMD had flooded portions of tribal lands over which the state claimed that its duty to "protect the Tribe's use and benefit of the Big Cypress lands forever" provided what the state asserted as an inherent water flowage easement.[31] Howard and the council had countered that the state had violated its fiduciary responsibilities by claiming that any such easement existed or that it gave them (the state) any unilateral decision-making control, and the tribe filed suit, in 1978, to eject the state, and obtain other relief.

Meanwhile, after 1979 the ILCC was still in a precarious state and the new chairman, James, was quietly attempting to talk the Oklahoma Seminoles into a settlement, even as lawmakers at the state and federal levels weighed in to impose an agreement that the Indians could not achieve.

A subset of the disagreement involved demographics. The ILCC award split would be based on ratios of SNO citizens to Seminole Tribe of Florida citizens, to Miccosukee citizens, to Florida independents. The BIA established 1914 as the most recent year in which population statistics might be established and correlated for purposes of finding such ratiocination. In this year, the number of Seminoles in Oklahoma was approximately three times as great as the number of Florida Indians (2,146:700), so the BIA recommended that there should be a 75:25 percent split between Oklahoma and Florida, with the Florida portion distributed among the Seminole Tribe, the Miccosukees, and the independents. The Florida Seminoles balked.

Following this initial contretemps, various distribution plans were introduced by U.S. congressional members from Florida and Oklahoma, none of them ultimately acceptable to the tribes. Oklahoma congressmen essentially accepted the BIA proposal. Florida senators Lawton Chiles and Richard Stone introduced legislation that included a differential settlement, based on the fact that Oklahoma Seminoles had already received various benefits (reparations) from the U.S. government over the intervening years following the Removal to Indian Territory, while the Florida Seminoles had been virtually ignored for most of those years. Therefore the Florida Indians should be indemnified differentially for their losses.[32]

The independent Indians continued to press their own particularist point of view that accepted the possibility of a congressional distribution plan even as it asserted the right to maintain a claim to the land itself rather than a financial settlement. U.S. government representatives told the independents, clearly, that they could not have it both ways, but the independent Indians determinedly refused to see the untenability of their position then, even as they continue to do so to this day.

By 1980 the original award had accrued interest to the total of $20 million, and James offered a 60:40 split to the Oklahoma Seminoles.[33] His overtures were not acted upon, however. Indecision has ever been the strong suit of the Oklahoma people. By 1987, the award monies had grown to $40 million. Neither a revised plan submitted to Congress by Oklahoma delegates nor a Florida delegates' submission was acceptable to the tribes. The Oklahoma people balked over language that would have included the Freedmen in the distribution of the award. They accepted, however, the requirement that they must submit a plan for use of the monies to the secretary of the interior for approval. The Florida Seminoles balked absolutely at the possibility of having to seek permission from the Department of the Interior for their use of their own monies.

On 14 September 1989, the U.S. House of Representatives Committee on Interior and Insular Affairs held hearings on final bills submitted to the House and Senate from the Oklahoma and the Florida delegations. Chairman Billie placed a formal statement before the committee asking that the record of the hearing should be kept open for thirty days while Florida and Oklahoma made one final attempt to settle their differences. James told the committee members that even though the Florida Seminoles had "sharp disagreement" with "our Oklahoma brethren . . . we have not lost sight of the fact that we are all one people."[34]

Nevertheless, James cited his opposition to any "straight population division" of the award because of the disparate blood quantum standards used by the two tribes. He doubted the validity of the Reconstructed 1914 Florida Seminole Roll that led the BIA to recommend a 75:25 percent split, calling it "arbitrary and inequitable" and questioned any logical connection it might have to the award, whether it was accurate or not. He asked for an impartial judge to assess the difference in treatment between the two tribes over the years since the Oklahoma Seminoles had been removed. He sharply opposed language that would distribute the claim award on the basis of individual descendancy, rather than making the award directly to the tribe. Finally, he offered alternative language that would close a loophole by tightening a test for entitlement through the "independent" category of Florida award recipients.[35]

The thirty days passed without any agreement between the Seminoles of Florida and Oklahoma. On 30 April 1990, the U.S. Congress imposed a final settlement (codified as Public Law 101-277, 104 U.S. Statute 143) that was a compromise that everyone had to live with, rather than one that anyone wanted to live with. First, it maintained the 75:25 split, with Oklahoma receiving the larger share. Then, it stipulated the way the Florida award would be divided, with 77.2 percent going to the Seminole Tribe, 18.6 percent to the Miccosukees, and 4.64 percent reserved for the independents. For the Seminoles, this ultimately meant an award of almost $10 million.[36]

The final bill did, indeed, tighten the language of entitlement to preclude potential outside attempts to claim Seminole heritage and, therefore, a right to a share of the award. Finally, the Florida Seminoles retained the right to accept the award with no strings attached. That is, as a sovereign nation, they would not be required to submit any plans for the use of the monies but, rather, to have the funds "allocated or invested as the tribal governing body determines to be in the economic or social interests of the tribe." This alone was a signal victory for tribal sovereignty.

Pursuant to Section 7 of the Act, the BIA created a Public Notice announcing its intention to "compile a roll of independent individuals of Seminole Indian descent," from which the secretary of the interior would prepare a list of those independents eligible to receive award funds. The requirements for inclusion in the roll were three. First, individuals had to have been born on or before, and living on, 30 April 1990, the date when Congress passed the settlement bill. Second, applicants had to have been "listed on or lineal descendants of persons listed on the annotated Florida Seminole Agency Census of 1957 as independent Seminoles." This was an unrealistic requirement, given that (a) the Seminole Agency's 1957 Census was not a Tribal Roll, (b) the Seminole Tribe accepted "membership" (that is, citizenship) applications from persons on the census for another six years, and (c) "independent" Indians were undifferentiated in 1957. Third, applicants could not be "members" of any other FR tribe. Applicants were required to obtain forms for application and provide supporting documentation. The burden of proof lay completely with the applicant.

To anyone who actually knew the Florida Indians, not to mention the group that called itself "independents," this process was clearly beyond their interest or ability. Speaking in English was beyond the knowledge of many. The possibility that they had maintained paper documents, or knew how to interact with non-Indian officials to obtain paper documents, was highly improbable. (Life in a chikî[t] exposes one to the elements, and the South Florida climate is not kind to paper.) Beyond all other considerations, however, is the fact that the tiny independent group was not interested in the money—not in 1946, not in 1957, not in 1990. Not now. From time to time the BIA sends a representative down from Washington to make another attempt at establishing a definitive list of eligible recipients. The tiny group refuses to cooperate. Their share of the award monies sits in U.S. government bank accounts, earning interest, to the continuing annoyance of BIA and U.S. government officials.

∿

All of the problems in this internecine Indian struggle stemmed principally from the unresolved feelings engendered by the actions of the U.S. government during the Seminole Wars of Removal—a century and a half before. The

Florida Indians continued to image the Oklahoma Seminoles as traitors who had given up the fight to protect their homelands in the Southeast and, therefore, had relinquished any right to be compensated for their losses. The Oklahoma people, hurt and angry over being forced out of their homelands, felt that their rights were the greater as they were the more transgressed upon. Former principal chief of the Seminole Nation of Oklahoma, Richmond Tiger, was only one of a number of the people who expressed these feelings to me even after the settlement had been finalized in 1990. The pain of the U.S. government's actions, on every front, would never diminish in the hearts of the Indians of Florida or Oklahoma.

In 1997 I had this view impressed upon me yet again—in the most formal and traditional of terms—during a visit to Oklahoma with James and other tribal representatives, and the situation is illustrative of the depth and durability of the Indians' feelings and the extent to which it continues to color all of their dealings. James, in a gracious move to introduce me formally to the people of Oklahoma and make public his approbation of my presence and researches, had introduced me at a public event during the SNO's annual Nation Days celebration in September. The Oklahoma Seminoles had a great deal of respect for James because of his strong leadership and also because of the tribal revenues earned by the Florida people. Oklahoma was, and is, a poor state, compared to Florida, but the Florida people also saw the relative penury of the Oklahoma people as further evidence of the degree to which they had been cowed by the U.S. government: they had caved in to the demands of the white men that they leave their homelands in the Southeast, and they had never recovered.

I wanted to interview Chitto Hajo, or Tom Palmer, himself a former principal chief of the Seminole Nation. James asked Lottie Coody, a Nation citizen who lived sometimes in Florida and had married a Florida Seminole, to guide me and introduce me to the chief, as it was not considered courteous to approach him (or anyone) directly, without an intermediary, to vouchsafe my intentions. After some days of negotiation by my intermediary over the time and place of our meeting, the arrangements were finally fixed. We would meet in my motel room (one of only two motels in the tiny town of Seminole, Oklahoma). I had been advised by James and by other Seminole friends in Florida about how to deport myself in Indian terms, that is, in a womanly and respectful manner.

At the appointed day and hour, my liaison arrived with a formal party that included Chief Palmer, his wife, and his wife's sister. Lottie arranged chairs for them, with their backs to the outside wall, Lottie nearest the door and Chief Palmer quietly in the corner, not looking at me. The curtains and door would remain open. I had long known by this time that the social norm was to lower my head and not to look anybody straight in the eye. That would be an insult, and moreover, I might learn, to my detriment, how much "power" a person had. I sat quietly, hands folded in my lap, awaiting their pleasure. Slowly, Chief Palmer began to speak, in Creek (Maskókî) to his wife and she to her sister and they to Lottie, who translated their questions to me, and translated my answers. What was I doing there? Why did I want information from them? How did I intend to use the information? Within each direct and truthful answer, I sought to introduce small bits of traditional information that would help them understand that I already understood, and respected, much of their culture and traditions. By this time, many people had "spoken" to me in Florida and some in Oklahoma, and I wanted the chief to realize the extent to which I knew and respected them and the Old Ways.

The questioning went on for about half an hour, with the chief speaking only his own language, and only to them and not to me, and never realizing that I knew that he could speak English very well. Finally, he satisfied himself that I might be worth speaking with, but his first words to me in English were forceful and memorable, not to mention indicative of all the other complications that had, and still, embroiled the two tribes: "All right," he said in clear English. "I'll speak to you, but I want you to promise me something first." He paused. I lifted my eyes momentarily and nodded my head slowly, to give assent. "I want you to go back to Florida and tell those people that we are not cowardly dogs! We did not put our tails between our legs and run to this place!" There was only one possible response to that: "I promise that I will tell them," I said. "I will do everything in my power to make that clear." Thereafter, we spoke amiably for another hour or so. I offered food and drink, they accepted water.

From then on I enjoyed a most friendly relationship with Chitto Hajo, as he preferred to be called. Each time I visited in Oklahoma, which was at least once a year for a month or so each time, we sat together and laughed, and he and James let me see the cordiality of their association as well. They were friendly enemies who respected each other's intellectual acumen, who had fought the good fight for their people to secure as large a share as possible of the ILCC award, and, now that their fight was over, for the moment at least, they could laugh together, although James said to me privately at one point, "Remember, his name is *chitto:* he's a Snake!"

Chitto Hajo had one other request of me that I alone, unfortunately, was not able to fulfill. He was a long-standing opponent of the inclusion of the two Freedmen's Bands in tribal life and politics. He believed that the 1866 treaty forced upon the Five Tribes by the United States, an article of which required the Seminoles to give the Freedmen full rights of citizenship in the Nation, was an illegality. (We have discussed this before.) He wanted me to prove that the people never had legally ratified it. If he had remained in power, I do not doubt that he would have had the strength to carry the fight to the U.S. government. As it was, a successor, Jerry Haney, attempted to lead a tribalwide charge that resulted in a vote by referendum in the 1990s that, among other important changes, set a blood quantum requirement for the Nation that would disenroll not only the Freedmen but also other enrolled citizens who did not have sufficient Q. The U.S. government fought back, viciously, withholding tribal funding for Head Start and Hot Meals programs and threatening other clearly punitive actions until Chief Haney succumbed and dropped the suit. This is, of course, a much simplified recounting of the legal war, but the outcome was that the SNO backed down, and the Freedmen retained their tribal status and seats on the Tribal Council.

~

In the midst of all these events, which had become so intertwined, James suffered a personal—but fortunately temporary—setback when he was charged by both the state and federal governments with killing an endangered Florida panther (*Felis concolor coryi*) in December 1983.[37] State environmental officials claimed that as few as thirty individual panthers were extant. The Seminoles did not accept this estimation and cited the fact that Florida panthers, especially the males, had such a broad range that counting them was almost impossible. This, however, was not the crux of the cases against James.

Both state and federal officials brought charges. The case hinged on another heretofore untested legal point, regarding the rights of Indians "to take any game found within the boundaries of the reservations, because of the status of their reservations as Indian homelands and the settled principle that states lack regulatory jurisdiction over Indian hunting and fishing on Indian lands within reservation boundaries."[38] James pled not guilty to the two separate misdemeanor counts of killing an endangered animal and of possessing it, which could have brought him five years in prison or a $5,000 fine, or both, and was released on a $10,000 surety bond.

The charge actually stemmed from an act of revenge on the part of a tribal citizen and was tied intimately to the critical subject of drug running on the BC Res and the tribe's rapidly growing need for its own law enforcement agency— yet another pressing concern for the council in the early 1980s. Despite the internal politics of the charges, however, the incident fit nicely with the determination of federal officials to find some evidence of wrongdoing by James, specifically, and the Seminoles, generally, that would shine a legal spotlight inside the tribe.

The *New York Times,* in its report on the arrest of the Seminole chairman, which event had national prominence, said: "Acting on an informer's tip in December [1983], officers of the Florida Game and Fresh Water Fish Commission discovered the panther's hide and skull in Mr. Billie's camp in the Big Cypress Indian reservation about 55 miles [actually 70] northwest of Fort Lauderdale."[39] The tribe's own newspaper, the *Seminole Tribune,* added the critical piece of information that permitted tribal citizens to identify the informer—if they didn't already know: "It is reported that a certain ex-deputy for Hendry County who for reasons of vengence [*sic*], is responsible for the 'anonymous tip' and led to the eventual arrest of Chairman Billie."[40]

The ex–Hendry County deputy was none other than Jimmy Cypress (Panther Clan, 1924–1998), a tribal citizen and father of the current chairman, Mitchell Cypress, and his brother, David Cypress, then council representative from BC. After twelve years as a deputized Hendry County sheriff on the BC Res, Jimmy had succumbed to the lure of drug money and had been arrested in a drug bust in 1978.[41] He spent a year and a half in jail in Hendry County and another year in a federal prison. As Mitchell would tell me some years later, "I don't think he ever really got over that time in jail." Jimmy blamed James for organizing and permitting his arrest, although according to one former Hendry County sheriff's deputy, there were many others who knew about Jimmy's involvement, and his consequent act of vengeance is important to understand as it would have an impact upon later events.[42]

James would describe Jimmy some years later: "Jimmy Cypress was, to use a hunting metaphor, like the man who never goes hunting. However, he waits for the hunter to return with meat, then looks for some way to take the meat away from him."[43] When he returned to the tribe following his incarceration, Jimmy led a petition drive, ultimately unsuccessful, to impeach James. For the rest of Jimmy's life, his smoldering anger at James over his arrest was only one of numerous elements in the antagonism that divided James and the Cypress brothers. Their dislike of one another would remain a well-known part of tribal politics up to and after their engineered final ouster of James from his chairmanship in 2003.

Though they later tried the case, at the outset the state decided not to prosecute, perhaps because of having the larger issues of water rights and land claims on the table at the same time. Nevertheless, the Florida District Court of Appeals reversed the state's decision and remanded the case for trial.[44] In the federal case, the federal District Court denied a motion to dismiss, entered by Bruce Rogow, James's legal counsel. Even though Jim Shore had become the tribe's chief in-house legal counsel by this time, Shore was not, and never has been, a litigator. Rogow, a law professor at Nova Southeastern University in Davie, Florida (greater Fort Lauderdale), had come to the attention of James and the council as a result of Rogow's connections to the tribe's lobbyist, Jack Skelding; the former Cherokee leader, Osley Bird Saunooke (who also had been the first president of United Southeastern Tribes); and some of the principals of the gaming arrangement. Mr. Rogow has continued to work with the tribe on its larger legal suits since this time, and we will review his legal involvements later.

The charges, taken in their entirety, had national impact, and the cases dragged on for a total of four years—tumultuous years for James and the council even without this tumult. Both the state and the federal courts went so far as to intimate that James and by extension the tribe were out to exterminate an already threatened species. In this they were harking to another recent Indian case involving fishing rights of the Puyallup Tribe.[45] But as one legal reviewer has seen it, their rhetoric certainly was "more phrase making then legal analysis."[46]

The larger issue in the case, that of Indian rights to birds and animals considered endangered by non-Indians, would overshadow the issue of the rights of Indians on their own reservations. Despite the fact that a state law clearly assigns to the Seminoles the right "to hunt in [their] usual and customary way" on the BC Res, and even specifically includes the right to "traditional tribal ceremonials," both the state and federal judges saw the need to preserve panthers as the overarching issue.[47] In James's defense, Rogow asserted that the state really had no rights to regulate hunting or fishing on the Indians' land.[48]

In a pertinent case with ramifications all across Indian Country, *United States v. Dion*, the Eighth Circuit Court of Appeals, in 1985 initially had ruled in favor of the Indians: "In *Dion*, the Eighth Circuit held that neither the Eagle Protection Act nor the Endangered Species Act extinguished Yankton Sioux Indian treaty hunting rights on their reservations, provided that such hunting was for non-commercial purposes only."[49] A year later, however, the U.S. Supreme Court reversed the Court of Appeals ruling on a unanimous decision written by Associate Justice Thurgood Marshall.[50]

At one point James asserted in his own defense (through his legal counsel; he never took the stand in either case), that the slaying of the panther was based in the traditions of Indian Medicine, which he had been studying for some years, under the tutelage of Ingram Billie Jr., son of the powerful Ingram Billie Sr. and nephew of the equally powerful Medicine practitioner, Josie Billie. Sonny Billie, James's stepfather (erroneously identified as a cousin for the *New York Times*), told reporters that James was, indeed, studying Indian Medicine and that the procurement of a panther was strong Medicine in the Seminole world.

The tribe's newspaper, the *Seminole Tribune*, told its citizens that Medicine men Pete Osceola (a powerful and outspoken bundle carrier, a principal position), Guy Osceola, Jimmy Bert, and Joe Cypress, all concurred. "The Indians didn't make the panther endangered," Guy told the *New York Times*. "The white man did by hunting the panther to near extinction."[51]

A vice president of the Florida Audubon Society, Charles Lee, saw James's actions only through the lens of non-Indian society. He said of James's traditionalist Medicine defense, that James was a Vietnam veteran who flew his own plane and directed a lucrative bingo industry and, therefore, "The image of a noble savage pursuing his religious beliefs stretches things a bit from my point of view."[52] In this, Mr. Lee certainly did not grasp the centrality, or the durability, of what the Seminoles still refer to as the Old Ways.

In a further refinement of his defense, Rogow told jurors that James did not even realize that he was killing an endangered Florida panther. Rather, he fired at an animal that could just as well have been another member of the cougar family, one that had been introduced into Florida in recent years to bolster the declining population of *Felis concolor coryi*. Federal jurors accepted this and James's other arguments and, on 27 August 1987, deadlocked over a verdict. According to one juror, the vote was seven to five for acquittal. Twice the jurors returned to the courtroom to report that they could not reach a verdict, and twice the judge sent them back to deliberate further. After two days, they sent a final note to Judge James C. Paine advising that they were "absolutely deadlocked," and the word "absolutely" was underlined twice. The judge declared a mistrial.[53]

The federal authorities were equivocal about whether they would retry, waiting instead to see what would happen in the state case. James was sure they would retry. Less than two weeks later, however, the State Circuit Court jury voted for acquittal, after deliberating for only one hour and forty minutes. The next day, U.S. Justice Department officials announced that they would drop their charges also. There would be no retrial. The state jury's acceptance of the defense's assertion that James did not realize that he was killing an endangered animal "appeared to have decided" the Justice Department. According to James Kilbourne of the Justice Department, "Beating it [the prosecution] to a final conclusion wasn't going to serve any useful purpose." Rogow saw it another way. "The case was like a railroad train, once it started to move down the line the government bureaucracy couldn't stop it," he told reporters. "They just wanted to prove a point, that they could convict an Indian for killing a Florida panther."[54]

James has an anecdote about the trial that he still tells to anyone who asks. It certainly illustrates his penchant for shock and the lengths to which he easily went in his unwillingness to share traditional information with outsiders. In the courthouse hallway, after the federal mistrial had been declared but while the state still was deliberating its case, a reporter asked if it was true that he had eaten the panther and wanted to know what it tasted like. James didn't miss a beat; he probably had been hoping for the question all along. "Well," he drawled, "it tasted a lot like manatee."

The state and federal charges in this issue provided a convenient weapon—valid or invalid—for non-Indian officials to use against James and the tribe at a moment when the same officials already were seeking avenues that would permit them to delve into tribal affairs regarding possible ties to organized crime. It was just one more of the many opportunities that federal agents would seize over the coming years to invade tribal business. In reality, however, James Billie was never shy about creating opportunities that would challenge outsiders to rise in opposition—"pushing the edge of the envelope" we would call it today. In 2002 his enemies inside the tribe, most particularly Jim Shore, the tribe's chief legal counsel and a man whom James had helped greatly, would ignore tribal sovereignty and personal loyalty and provide total access to tribal affairs to the FBI, though even that would not be enough to convict James of any wrongdoings under white man's law (more of this subject in chapters 10 to 14).

James's traditional love of hunting and his ego would result in a legal confrontation for him once again, almost ten years later. For most of the 1980s and early 1990s, James led annual hunting parties to Idaho and a few other areas of the Northwest. Each year he chose a young man to accompany the party, guiding him in the hunting in a fatherly manner. James, who had never had a father to teach him, felt a responsibility to other young men. In most years, this was a positive element of his leadership, but there was never a single agenda for these trips. For example, James laughed and retold the story many times of the year he assigned Chris O'Donnell and Robb Tiller to a single tent, just to see what would happen—how they would handle each other. Chris, a longtime assistant and intermittent paramour of James, loathed Tiller, and she was furious about being required to share a tent with him. Tiller, whose personal proclivities were omnivorous and legendary, was completely nonplussed. It was a tense time for everyone on the trip, except James, who was delighted with what he thought of as a great show.

By 1993 the adventure of the trip had pretty well run its course for James. He had a definite interest limit to everything he did. In that year, Lesley, his new partner, went along to hunt in Idaho's Clearwater National Forest. The outfitter who guided the tribal party, Gordon Frost, was one whom the tribe had paid more than $800,000 over the most recent three years for such trips. The U.S. Fish and Wildlife Service, however, viewed Frost as an outfitter who allowed clients to kill animals illegally, and they arrested James and Lesley on charges that he and she and another Seminole member of the party had killed a black bear, more elk than they were permitted for, and had transported an elk across state lines. Lesley also killed a female elk without a permit.

James blamed the outfitter for the violations. Paul Weyland, a U.S. Fish and Wildlife officer, disagreed. "They didn't come up here to play by the rules," he said. "I know James Billie didn't. I know from his arrogant attitude, like he could do whatever he wanted, when we interviewed him."[55] Ultimately, James, Lesley, and other members of the party pled guilty to hunting infractions, and James was fined $3,000 and placed on two years' probation, which included the injunction not to hunt outside of the Seminole reservations. Needless to say, the event ended his annual hunting trips to the Northwest.

In the meantime, by 1984 the EBCC had become even more complicated as the tribe challenged state officials over plans for a flood control project that required a dredge and fill permit from the U.S. Corps of Engineers. The tribe threatened to require a full administrative hearing. The state saw negotiations with the tribe potentially dragging on indefinitely and involving issues that never had been litigated in the East before—and issues regarding which the outcome was not certain. Citrus growers pressured the state too, as some of the state's largest landowners, because they believed that the delay of an administrative hearing would seriously delay their plans to increase their landholdings for citrus production.[56] The state and the Water Management District (WMD) moved to have the tribe's suit dismissed. The tribe's lawyers, however, aware of several pending cases in the U.S. Supreme Court that could have an impact on the outcome of the Seminoles' case, sought and obtained a stay order in May 1984.[57]

The cases on point before the U.S. Supreme Court were *County of Oneida, New York, et al. v. Oneida Indian Nation* (known as *Oneida II*), and its predecessor, *Oneida Indian Nation of New York v. State of New York* (*Oneida I*).[58] In these related cases, the Oneidas obtained a ruling that the State of New York had illegally taken possession of a large portion of lands secured to them by a 1795 treaty with the United States. In the earlier case, the court had accepted a tribal argument that the state had obtained possession of a large part of their land in direct violation of the United States' 1790 Non-Intercourse Act.[59] Citing similarities between the Oneida and Seminole positions and their bases in law in regard to state control of Indian reservation lands, Seminole tribal attorneys asked the federal court for a partial summary judgment. The state countered that this was a state, not a federal, matter. The judge withheld a decision. Questions of ownership of reservation lands and the rights to jurisdiction plagued the proceedings, and the state and tribe returned to what had heretofore been fruitless talks.

At this point the state and the WMD authorities "blinked." The state turned on its own agency, charging that the WMD from the outset had exceeded its own authority for the use of Indian lands by requiring the tribe to apply for permits to graze their cattle, among other excesses. In addition, the argument over water flowage easement and sheet flow of water also involved questions of purification of waters as they entered the aquifer. The WMD officials countered that the state had no right to assume to speak for the Seminoles, who had their own attorneys.

By 1985 the state and its WMD reached a compromise between themselves, but one that still did not recognize the rights of the Indians to have a seat at the bargaining table. The WMD held public hearings on their intention to move forward with a modified water management plan—"public" hearings to which the Seminoles had not been invited, nor of which they had even been notified. When the tribe announced that it would seek a further public hearing and that it would push for an Environmental Impact Survey (EIS), which would stall the WMD's plans for a significant amount of time, the state and the WMD went back to the negotiating table to sit down—finally—with the tribe.

This was not only a moment when Seminole warriors were finally being taken seriously by the non-Indian authorities. This was also an important time, nationally, for bringing Indians to the table to assert their authority over their own lands and over sites of historical/cultural importance to them and, in the much larger sense, for being taken seriously as arbiters of their own cultural and political destinies. As early as 1968, Council Chairman Betty Mae (Tiger) Jumper had met with leaders of three other tribes—Mississippi Choctaw, Eastern Band of Cherokee (North Carolina), and Miccosukee—to discuss and consolidate political agendas. The outcome of this meeting soon would be the formation of the United Southeastern Tribes (in 1979, the United South and Eastern Tribes [USET]). By the 1980s, USET was fast on its way to becoming the powerful political action group representing almost all of the FR tribes east of the Mississippi that it is today. Through its early actions, for example, headquarters for the group was established at Nashville, Tennessee, and the BIA was induced to settle its Indian Health Service (IHS) there also. Seminoles would be represented at IHS for over a decade by Mike Tiger, son of Howard Tiger and nephew of Betty Mae Jumper, who would finally return to his tribe in 2001.

At the national level, the U.S. government was enacting broadening legislation—from the American Indian Religious Freedom Act (AIRFA, of 1978), to the Native American Graves Protection and Repatriation Act (NAGPRA, which would be enacted in 1990), to a spate of other pieces of confirming legislation and executive orders; the Indian tribes finally were being recognized as active partners in charting at least some elements of their cultural destinies. The non-Indian citizens of the United States and the U.S. government were finally beginning to take Indians seriously, and the Indians were learning how to engage the white men on their own terms.[60] Needless to say, as FR tribes followed the Seminoles' lead in the 1980s and expanded their own economic horizons to include lucrative gaming, their ability to afford white lawyers to press their legal interpretations, rather than simply accepting the white men's interpretations of white men's law, began to increase as well.

This shifting national attitude was undoubtedly of benefit to the tribe as it stood against the state to defend its sovereign rights. The stage was now set for the WMD to reach some kind of agreement with the tribe, and the tribe was ready to end the standoff, as long as it did not simply have to give in to the state.

A new negotiator with "a more flexible approach" was assigned to the talks and was able to win the trust of the tribe—an element always critical to working with the Seminoles, specifically, and Indians, generally. By 1986 it became obvious that it would be beneficial to link the several critical elements of the multiple state-federal-tribal negotiations in order to achieve a workable conclusion, and on 5 September an agreement with the state was reached.[61] Early in the next month a Tribal Council resolution ended the tribe's lawsuit against the SFWMD.[62]

The outcome of the resulting successful linkage of the EBCC and the ILCC cases was the Seminole Indian Land Claims Settlement Act. On 31 December 1987, U.S. President Ronald Reagan signed the agreement into law, which agreement included a historic Water Rights Compact, binding the tribe, the state, and the U.S. government to the first such agreement created by any tribe east of the Mississippi.[63] Within the coming year, as a part of the agreement, the tribe created its own water management infrastructure—a Water Code, a Water Commission, and a Water Office.[64]

Water Resources director for the tribe, Craig Tepper (a non-Indian), who is profoundly loyal to his boss, Jim Shore, also has been assiduous in his work on behalf of the tribe since that time, establishing a beneficial laissez-faire working relationship with the Florida unit of the U.S. Army Corps of Engineers that has been useful in facilitating tribal projects. Surrounded, as the reservations are, by several large and powerful neighbors whose interests do not coincide with those of the tribe, Tepper has been successful in containing or defeating their antienvironmental actions.

The water compact was a true compromise. "In the settlement achieved under the Compact, the tribe relinquished the possibility of establishing broader rights in exchange for early resolution of tribal claims without the uncertainty and delay of litigation. Similarly, the State forfeited the possibility of defeating tribal claims to superior federal water rights in return for tribal compromise and an immediate agreement to conduct tribal activities affecting state waters in harmony with the state system."[65]

"Conflict between the Tribe and the State can never be fully eliminated. Some conflict may be inevitable due to the Tribe's special status as a semi-autonomous sovereign and the fact that its reservations in Florida are not under state civil regulatory authority."[66]

5   Dollars and Drugs

Seminole Gaming

In a political move not at all unlike those of his non-Indian counterparts, candidate Billie made it a plank in his premier election campaign for the chairmanship: he pledged to oppose gambling and the sale of tax-free liquor. By the congressional act of 15 August 1953, known as the Federal Indian Liquor Law, the U.S. government had codified requirements for the sale of liquor on FR tribal reservations, tying sales to state laws.[1] The Florida Seminoles, however, enacted their own ordinance, C-02-65, taking responsibility for controlling sales into their own hands.[2] By Resolution C-43-78, on 16 December 1977, the council amended the ordinance to remove requirements for state concurrence and implement tribal approval and licensing.

Just four months earlier Howard Tommie and (ostensibly non-Indian) partners had received approval from the council and board to lease three acres of land on State Road 7/Highway 441, on the Hollywood Res. The purpose of the lease was the operation of a package liquor store business, at a fee of $6,000 or 10 percent of the net profit, per year, whichever was greater, plus a 4 percent tribal tax. The approval, however, required the agreement of the non-Indian businessman whose leased mobile-home-park land abutted the parcel, and the package store never materialized.[3] During the next summer, and Howard's last in office, he once again proposed liquor sales on the Res's, at a joint meeting of council and board, and the two bodies voted to take the issue to the people at community meetings.[4] The highly vocal Baptist segment shouted it down and Howard backed off the issue (for the moment).

Within James's first term, however, the subject of liquor sales continued to be an issue for the council; the prospects of the revenues to be had from such business were entirely too enticing. A "group of Seminole businessmen" approached the council in November of 1980, asking for the right to market alcohol on the reservations. The council demurred, considering a tribalwide referendum. The actual reason for their demurral was not public opinion, however. Four months earlier, the council already had entered into a venture agreement and a management agreement with Jim Clare and Pan American & Associates ("Pan Am"), doing business as "Seminole Energy Company" for the construction and management of an alcohol production plant on properties owned or being purchased by the tribe northward up the coast from Hollywood.[5]

The management agreement gave Pan Am 45 percent of the net profits and assigned the other 55 percent to the tribe. By an amendment to the agreement, however, passed by the council in the following November, the tribe required Pan Am to kick back a full one-half of its profits to the tribe as a fee for tribal "consulting services."[6] The alcohol production business never materialized, but within a calendar year Pan Am did obtain the management contract for gaming on the new Tampa Res and begin an extremely lucrative relationship with the tribe that would endure for twenty years.

The subject of potential liquor sales would not be quelled permanently, however, even though tribal citizens were all too well aware of the damage caused by alcohol. They watched their peers and children and grandchildren die of its effects far too often. The BC cemetery, in particular, has a disproportionate number of graves of people far too young to be there naturally, their lives, rather, curtailed by alcohol-related deaths. Nevertheless, in 1981 the council would amend, and in 1983 and '85 the council would promulgate yet another tribalwide referendum on alcohol sales, which would yet again be voted down. Only in the gaming venues would alcohol be permitted by the tribe; catering to the gambling/smoking/drinking triad being quintessential to successful gaming operations.

Over the years, even though James has served wine at various of his political functions for nontribal guests, tribal citizens have continued to resist offering alcohol at any internal tribal functions or selling alcohol as a tribal business. James, himself only a minimal wine drinker, has publicly and privately railed against tribal drunks and done everything in his power to embarrass them. This was yet another bone of contention between James and David Cypress.

Yet the gaming industry, also an ostensibly unpalatable acorn, has nevertheless since grown into a mighty oak. In the fall of 1978 Howard presented an economic development proposal to the council in which he appeared as the majority owner (51 percent) of "Seminole Management Association." The plan was based on an initial investment of $2.5 million from Tommie and white backers, and called for allocating nineteen acres of prime frontage along State Road 7/Highway 441 (the major north–south axis through the Hollywood Res) for a Hollywood Bingo Hall and a strip shopping center, Seminole Indian Plaza, that would include a Smoke Shop as well. The white backers were linked to crime, but they had provided quiet funding for one or two of the Smoke Shops since 1977.[7] The council agreed to it. Only Joe Dan Osceola (Panther Clan, b. 1936) was critical. Joe Dan, an intelligent and always hustling entrepreneur, and a former chairman, was outspokenly critical of many things, which diminished his popularity. He had been sidelined by the council during the setup of the Smoke Shops and eventually established his own business on 441, the Anhinga Gift Shop, among other enterprises.

On 3 January 1979, the Tribal Council had passed Resolution C-79-79 by which it enacted its first Bingo Licensing Ordinance, at a joint meeting of the council and the board, by a unanimous council vote of 5 for and 0 against.[8] According to the resolution the tribe recognized that it needed "additional revenue to carry out our needed social programs" and declared that the proceeds, after operating costs, would go to support "Tribal, Health, Education and Welfare programs." Further, the resolution asserted that "this activity is not prohibited by the State of Florida, and the Tribe needs to regulate the conduct of this activity in keeping with the customs, traditions and mores of its own Seminole people." This latter was certainly a specious argument, given that gaming of this nature did not exist within the traditions of the Seminole people, although wagering on sports and games of chance certainly did. On another level, however, the desire for its own governmental regulation was inarguable, as well as the need to funnel revenues back to the welfare of the greater tribe.

This was a full four months before the coming tribal election, which would bring a change of administration to the tribe, although, to Howard, it was an important prelude to his ability to secure for himself a share of gaming revenues after he left office. Campaigning was, at this time, still a matter of a short sequence of events among tribal citizens. The election was held early in May, and qualifying occurred only one month prior with, subsequently, just a few weeks of campaign events. These latter were predominantly dinners sponsored by the candidates and their supporters on each of the Res's. Food is a central and critical element of all tribal events, and the candidates were already so well known to all the tribe that public speeches were neither traditional nor necessary among the modern Seminoles. Campaigns were low-key, one-on-one, contact processes, although they have become more protracted and formalized over time.

By the early May elections of 1979, no gaming contracts had been signed. By the end of the month, however, once elections were out of the way and the new officials were formally inaugurated, plans clearly were moving forward, rapidly, and the non-Indian backers of the first (Hollywood) bingo hall were setting up for business. Seminole Management Associates, Ltd., was incorporated and was composed of five general partners who would receive 60 percent of the profits. Four of these five were enterprises controlled by either George Simon or

Eugene Weisman, both non-Indians. Howard Tommie was a quiet fifth partner. Over 1979 to 1994, other minor partners have come from Atlanta, Chicago, Aspen, and Hong Kong, but Howard has derived significant continuing benefit from his partnership.

Simon was a Miami Beach CPA who had been questioned in 1964 in congressional hearings regarding his "financial involvement in a corporation tied to influence-peddling charges against Bobby Baker."[9] Weisman was a commercial bingo operator from Pittsburgh, with alleged ties to Pittsburgh mobsters.[10] Weisman vehemently denied such allegations. Some years—and many investigations—later, he blamed the Las Vegas gaming kingpins for the negative publicity. He told one reporter, "Vegas didn't want the Indians to succeed. Vegas hired—and you can check on this—great PR people to put out that all Indian bingos are rampant with organized crime, prostitution, drugs, every other damn social evil that you can think of. They did a great job, all over the country."[11]

Despite his protestations a 1983 *Arizona Daily Star* article examining the background of an unrelated management company would later mention that Simon and Weisman's Seminole Management Associates had been investigated by the FBI, the federal Organized Crime Strike Force in Miami, and the Broward County sheriff's office.[12] No charges were ever filed.

As late as July of 1979, James still denied to reporters that any gaming operation was planned. This was, of course, wholly inaccurate. He said that he had pledged to oppose gambling and liquor sales when he ran for tribal chairman. Even as he issued his denial, nonetheless, James and the council contracted with the newly incorporated Seminole Management Associates to run tribal bingo for a more favorable 45 percent of the profits.[13]

The first Seminole gaming facility opened on the Hollywood Res on 14 December 1979, only five months after James's statement. The seeds of contention between the tribe and Broward County, which would lead to the spectacular and groundbreaking court decisions, with national ramifications, had already been planted before the doors ever opened. According to James, then–Broward County sheriff Robert Butterworth had approached him on behalf of a business associate who wanted to obtain the tribe's contract for construction of the "bingo hall." When James quietly decided against him, Butterworth became angered and turned against the project, despite the fact that it was on a sovereign Indian Tribal Res in federal trust, rather than in the larger Broward County.[14]

Federal authority for states to enforce laws on Indian reservations was—in the view of the state—couched in a state statute, and in what is known as U.S. Public Law 280.[15] By this latter act, passed in 1953, Congress had unilaterally extended states' jurisdiction over offenses committed by or against Indians into

Indian Country. (We shall examine the ramifications of this act for the Seminoles further, as we discuss the evolution of tribal law enforcement, below.) Public Law 280, however, was silent on issues surrounding gaming on Indian reservations. At the time when the Seminoles were creating their first gaming operation, the legal boundary between the state's exercise of authority on sovereign tribal lands in federal trust regarding gaming had not yet been tested in the courts. The Seminoles, therefore, would battle the State of Florida to the promulgation of a landmark decision, one of which other FR tribes would be quick to take advantage, and on the one subject that has, arguably, become the single most contentious issue between Indians and the U.S. government today, and the one that has the most transparently economic basis: the issue of Indian gaming.[16]

As his medium of control, Butterworth contended that tribal gaming was in violation of Florida Statute § 849.093 and that he intended to arrest violators. This statute provided, in pertinent part, that bingo could be conducted on only two days per week; that only one jackpot per night could be won, and that it was not to exceed $100 in value; and that no members of any sponsoring organization could be compensated for their operation of the games. In the case of the Seminoles, their operation exceeded all of these limits.

The Florida attorney general was granted permission to enter an amicus curiae brief in support of Butterworth's contention. The basis of the state's case was their contention that the state had the legal right to control gaming, on Res as well as off. The tribe asked the U.S. District Court for the Southern District of Florida to issue a preliminary injunction against Sheriff Butterworth, and in December of 1979, the court complied.[17] Judge Norman C. Roettger Jr. noted that the tribe had already invested $900,000 in construction of the bingo hall. He also noted that the tribe's operation was clearly in violation of Florida Statute § 849.093 in several respects. Reviewing these respects, however, the court found them accurate but not overarching. He reminded the defendant that Indian nations had always been dealt with exclusively by the federal government, not by states. (Even this latter position would begin to shift within a few years, however, as gaming revenues would begin to skyrocket across Indian Country.)

Ultimately, therefore, the question arose of whether the state could apply U.S. Public Law 280 in order to obtain control of gaming on Indians lands, and for that it was necessary to determine if the state's statutory authority under Florida Statute § 849.093 was criminal/prohibitory (as was Public Law 280) or civil/regulatory. The judge concluded: "Having made the determination that [State Statute] § 849.093 should be classified as a civil/regulatory scheme, it is a simpler task to determine if Congress has authorized Florida to impose its civil regulatory schemes on Indian land. The answer is clearly no."[18]

At the outset the tribe estimated that gaming would generate annual revenues of $1.5 million. Reluctant to let go of this lucrative new venture, even as the tribe's case against Butterworth wound its way through the appellate system, the bingo hall remained open. The Seminoles were publicly denying gaming plans, constructing a gaming casino, and fighting legal battles against the Broward County sheriff and the State of Florida—all at the same time. From the relative lethargy of the past century and their lack of experience in political acumen, in white men's terms, the Seminoles now were rapidly approaching warp speed.

Sheriff's Appeal against Seminole Bingo Heard in Atlanta
from the tribe's newspaper, the *Alligator Times*
ATLANTA, GA—March 19 [1981]—the case of Seminole Tribe of Florida vs. Robert Butterworth (Sheriff of Broward Co.), appealant [*sic*], came before the United States Court of Appeals for the 5th circuit. Presiding on the court were their honors: Judge Lewis R. Morgan from Newnan, Ga., Judge Paul H. Roney from St. Petersburg, FL., and Judge Phyllis Kravitch from Georgia.

Phillip Shailer attorney for Sheriff Butterworth was assisted by Florida Assistant Attorney General Kent Zaiser. Both argued against the decisions made earlier by U.S. District Judge Norman C. Roettger, Jr., and Judge Alcee Hastings who both have ruled in favor of the Seminole Tribe. Mr. Shailer began the case by trying to make the Seminole Bingo case seem similar to a decision hand [*sic*] down in the 9th circuit court. Where in the state of Washington the sale of fire works was halted by a court order—the reason being the danger involved with fireworks.[19] The question of whether this was a Criminal Prohibitory Statue [*sic*]—which the sheriff would like—or a Civil Regulatory—which the courts maintain, was asked by the sheriffs' attorneys.

The difference between the two being—Criminal Prohibitory Statues (Laws) can be enforced on the reservation, these are laws for criminals [growing out of the enforcement of Public Law 280], on the other hand, Civil Regulatory Laws aren't applicable to the Tribe due to the Federally Recognized Sovereignty of Seminole [n]ation. While giving the oral presentation for the Tribe, attorney Marion Sibley brought out a few interesting points that the sheriff's lawyers failed to mention. Such as, "Constitution of State of Florida permits gambling under certain circumstances," before the state wanted gambling they depended upon a law dated in 1885.

Mr. Sibley also mentioned that the Supreme Court of the State of Florida has said that, "Bingo is of the same nature and character of Pari-Mutual Betting." Pari-Mutual Betting grosses anywhere from [$] 40 million on Jai-Alai, to [$] 50 million on Horse Racing, per year. Of all the statements made, the one that sticks to mind was when he answered the argument that the Washington State Fireworks case, was similar to this case, Mr. Sibley, "The sheriff and the state have tried to draw an analogy . . . absurd, I think that the people of Florida have been polluted or damaged by a Seminole game in which the prize is more than $100 and people can play more than two or three times a week." At this time there is no firm indication when the judges would rule.

Attending the hearings were Chairman James Billie, President Fred Smith, Councilman Jacob Osceola, Tribal Counsel Stephen H. Whilden and Jim Shore.[20]

On 5 October 1981, the Fifth Circuit Court issued its opinion, affirming the lower court's decision in favor of the tribe, by a vote of two judges to one (Roney dissenting).[21] Not only could the Seminoles continue to operate their bingo game but also non-Indians, as well as Indians, could play at the casino. Indian Country took notice.

The tribe's lead counsel for this issue, Steve Whilden (1940–1995), was an assiduous force on behalf of the tribe. James liked him because "he was good at getting information on people and I also had access to all that information." James has used this particular yardstick by which to test associates all too frequently. Unfortunately, Whilden also was good at rubbing people the wrong way, and in the case of tribal citizens that was not a hard thing for a non-Indian to do. The tribe had hired Whilden in August of 1977 after he had answered an ad in the *Florida Bar Journal* for a tribal attorney. Whilden, a California native, had been a foreign service officer for the U.S. State Department, and had worked in the Office of Management and Budget, serving as White House liaison in the later days of the Nixon administration. He had twice been a diplomatic officer in Vietnam (undoubtedly the basis for another bond between himself and James). In a 1983 interview with the *Miami Herald*, Whilden laid out his philosophy as he had explained it to the Seminoles. "The Indians can sit up there on the moral high ground and stay poor. But if they want their fair share, they have to learn to use the modern tactical methods. They have to get into politics."[22]

Whilden encouraged the tribe to hire lobbyists in Tallahassee, the state's capital, and to contribute to political campaigns. He fought very successfully for the tribe in municipal, state, and federal arenas during his five-year tenure. It was Whilden who negotiated the acquisition of the human remains that led to the creation of the Tampa Res for the tribe, after the City of Tampa encountered a significant number of Indian skeletal remains downtown, during construction of a city parking garage in 1980. The remains were vestiges of an Indian burial ground that had been attached to the nineteenth-century military reservation of Fort Brooke, the nucleus of the modern city of Tampa. Fifteen years later I would field calls from representatives of the Tampa Bay Lightning hockey team, whose stadium was not far from this burial site. The owner's wife was absolutely convinced that any team loss was the result of the stadium's proximity to an Indian burial ground, and I never was able to convince them otherwise. But, then, Indian burial grounds have dotted Florida over thousands of years, and people still contact the tribe regularly in the belief that the unhappy spirits of the old warriors are responsible for their family illnesses, divorces, and crumbling houses. Tribal Medicine practitioners will not, however, agree to exorcise the spirits, in any instance. As Sonny Billie told me, "People must seek answers to their questions inside their own cultures."

Rather than risk adverse publicity, the city agreed to turn the remains over to the tribe for a promised memorial burial.[23] The tribe purchased 8.5 acres on the far east side of the city, next to the fairgrounds, for the purpose. The money for the land purchase—$185,000—came from three investors, incorporated as Pan American & Associates: the now familiar Jim Clare, together with Donald Valverde, and Alfred Estrada, who were already involved with the council on a project to produce gasohol.[24] In another guise, as Seminole Energy Co., they had already partnered with the council for the abortive alcohol production project. Their willingness to support the tribe was their entrée into much bigger things.

The new Tampa Res was taken into federal trust on 5 May 1984, but not before James contacted an elder who lived in the Florida woods near the site and the tribe constructed apartments for her and her clan family on the new Res. (He used to laugh about that memory, as the woman, Ruby Tiger Osceola [Panther Clan, b. 1914] refused to move to the new site unless she was permitted to take along her pigs. So the pigs went too.) The tribe did, indeed, reinter the remains, and, in addition, constructed a small "museum" and gift shop, followed quickly by a bingo casino in 1982 and a high-rise 150-room Sheraton Hotel and Convention Center, completed in 1987.

State leaders felt that they had been tricked by the tribe, they said, into using the property as they had neither intended nor envisioned it. A tribal lawyer and citizen, Jim Shore, told the press, "If the shoe were on the other foot, I'm sure they would have done the same thing. They say we pulled a fast one on them, which we didn't. But if we did, that's part of the game."[25]

The management contract for the casino was given to Pan Am, whose principals had no experience in casino management before beginning their involvement with the Seminoles. But the Seminoles like to establish a personal relationship with individuals before doing business with them. And, once established, they prefer not to go outside of those relationships for any needs, whether the individuals involved have experience in those other areas or not. In many ways, it's reminiscent of Lyndon Johnson's oft-repeated working philosophy: "I want *can do* people," he would pronounce, stridently, "only *can do* people!"[26] James Billie, not one to require experience as a prerequisite for action, liked "can do" people. (As we shall find later this was not the only point of comparison between James Billie and Lyndon Johnson.)

The relationship between the tribe and Pan Am grew only closer and more profitable over the years, despite some tense moments. The tribe would acquire thirty-one additional acres of land in Tampa, adjacent to the tiny parcel already in trust and bearing the bingo hall managed by Pan Am. The plan for ten of the thirty-one acres was the construction of a hotel and restaurant. The project was estimated at a total cost of $10,430,000 that would be funded partially from a grant from the U.S. Department of Housing and Urban Development, partly from a bank loan to the tribe, and partly by equity financing directly from the tribe.

Pan Am offered to arrange a $2 million loan for the tribe, and in return the tribe would extend Pan Am's first management contract for another three years.[27] The tribe set aside the ten acres and guaranteed the $2 million contribution. The project stumbled, however, five months later, when Pan Am failed to provide the loan, and James and the council canceled Pan Am's management contract extension.[28] The next month, the council turned the hotel/restaurant project over to its own Seminole Economic Development, Inc. (SED, Inc.), a wholly owned tribal corporation, with a twenty-five-year lease renewable for twenty-five years. Over the coming year, SED, Inc., moved rapidly to secure the necessary funding and proceeded with construction on the hotel complex that it would lease to the Sheraton hotel chain. The Sheraton East complex would remain a part of the tribe's economic family until the entire Res was cleared for the new Hard Rock Tampa project, in 2003.

The management contract with Pan Am was, however, renewed after all, and by the end of the decade the Tampa Seminole Bingo Palace had become so much more lucrative than had been expected that the operation was running twenty-four hours per day. The tribe planned a six-thousand-square-foot expansion for "improvements and additional gaming machines."[29] A short four months later, the tribe would make its first overture to the State of Florida for a Class III gaming compact.[30]

∽

Despite his utility to James, personally, and the tribe, attorney Steve Whilden's brusque manner eventually antagonized tribal citizens once too often. James later told a writer the story of what he characterized as "Whilden's last blunder."

In 1980 the council had hired a second attorney, Jim Shore, who was a blind tribal citizen and recent graduate of Stetson University College of Law (in Winter Park, Florida). This was in keeping with the Seminoles' tradition of putting non-Indians in positions only until they could find (but too rarely train)

Figure 3. The first tribal headquarters building also housed the BIA's Seminole Agency until it was replaced by the new building in 1995. (Photograph courtesy of the BIA Seminole Agency.)

Seminoles for the positions. At the time, Jim was married to a white woman, also a lawyer. One day she visited Jim in his tribal office in the old, dark tribal headquarters building on the northwest corner of Stirling Road and Highway 441 in Hollywood. "Jim Shore's wife came into the office. Both he and Steve were working for the tribe at that time. Jim's office was smaller than Steve's. Jim's wife didn't like that. She complained about it being too dark. Steve replied by asking what difference it made since Jim couldn't see anyway. Word of that story got around the tribe. Marcellus Osceola fired him."[31] Marcy, then a council representative from Hollywood did, indeed, lead the council charge to fire Whilden, in May of 1982.

Jim Shore's story is a fascinating chapter in the history of the tribe (several chapters, actually). Jim (Bird Clan, b. 1945) comes from a prestigious Creek Medicine family at Brighton. He was one of eight children born to Lottie Bowers Shore (Bird Clan, 1912–2000) and Frank Shore (Panther Clan, 1900–1986), arguably one of the three most powerful Medicine men of the twentieth century. Frank Shore had the added advantage of being highly respected, which another preeminently powerful Medicine practitioner, Josie Billie, did not. A brother of Frank Shore, Sam Jones (Panther Clan, 1894–1959) was the third of the powerful Medicine triumvirate. When Jim Shore, son of Frank, was in his mid-teens, he was drunk and driving a motorcycle and suffered a severe accident as a result of which both of his retinas became detached. He opted for a risky operation that was not able to restore his sight, and he has been blind ever since.[32]

Jim Shore and James Billie have another of the many love/hate relationships that characterize James's interactions, both personal and professional. Since Jim is a Creek (Maskókî) rather than a Miccosukee, his people are regarded with suspicion by the majority of the tribe's citizens, who are Miccosukee, even though intermarriage over the last century has mitigated that feeling somewhat. The historical relationship between the Seminoles and their cultural kin the Creeks (so-called by English speakers) has been one of mutual distrust, at least, and open animosity, at most. In the case of Jim Shore, however, the aura of respect that continues to surround his father and his paternal uncle, Sam Jones, is so great as to mitigate much of the distrust. After the dismissal of Whilden, Jim became the lead general counsel for the tribe and continued in that position through the years of his pivotal role in the permanent ouster of James, in 2003. Since that time, his influence had been eclipsed. Initially, his relation with James was a positive one, James frequently telling listeners how he (James) had helped to secure funding for Jim to attend Stetson University College of Law and had gotten him his position with the tribe upon his graduation in 1980. Jim is a slow-talking, lugubrious person, whose intellect is obvious. He is quick with a chuckle and notorious for his anger that once turned against a person (for reasons usually known only to Jim) is not likely to change.

Jim's anger, which began to turn against James in the 1990s, became a central element of the process of James's eventual fall from power. Jim became a greater and more and more vocal—and vitriolic—critic of anything James did. He repeatedly told certain confidants that James lied so much that his lies were like "land mines, laid across the countryside. After a while," he drawled, "he's going to have so many that he'll forget where he buried them and, sooner or later, he's bound to step on one of them!"[33]

From my standpoint, as an observer with a close vantage point in this personal struggle between the two powerful individuals, it seemed that their positions became more and more obstreperously entrenched. Jim had something negative to say about everything James did; he seemed never to suggest remedies, he just always found fault. James tried to consult with Jim, as counsel to the chairman and to the Tribal Council, but found Jim timorous and too slow moving for the swift, decisive actions that James wanted more and more to take. Eventually James would anger Jim even further by hiring another attorney, Robert Osley Saunooke, son of Osley Bird, specifically for the chairman's office, in an attempt to circumvent Jim altogether. Jim saw James's actions as precipitous and freewheeling and, therefore, dangerous. By the turn of the millennium, Jim had begun actively to work against James in ways that smacked more of personal animosity than of a regard for the greater welfare of the tribe. One repercussion of his outspoken animosity would be an attempt—fortunately unsuccessful—on his life by person or persons still unknown. We shall watch these unfortunate events unfold in the coming chapters.

On 9 May 1983, James was reelected to a second term as tribal chairman. "Let's do it again, together for progress, stability, and a stronger economic future," he proclaimed on flyers that he passed out across the reservations during the weeks prior to the election. With a final 233-vote margin over his closest opponent, a broadside *News Brief* reported, "With the results of the elections, one could venture to say that the tribal members were confident that the Chairman can lead the Seminole Tribe into the future."[34]

Almost as soon as the decision handed down in 1981 by the Court of Appeals Fifth Circuit clarified and confirmed the relationship (or, rather, the nonrelationship) of the FR tribes with their states on the issue of reservation gaming, James began to export gaming to other tribes, with the backing of Pan Am, in ventures that were only somewhat lucrative to himself personally. The council agreed to a number of consultation agreements—with the Sandia Pueblo, Hopi, Soboba, Muscogee (Creek), Muckleshoot, Colusa, Sisseton-Wahpeton, and Otoe-Missouria tribes, and Thlopthlocco Tribal Town—by which the Florida Seminoles sought to export their gaming experience outward across Indian Country, with an ultimate lack of success.[35]

Roy Diamond, ex-husband of James's administrative assistant Patricia ("Pat") Diamond, was hired by a group called Bingo Entertainment, in which James had a significant interest, in March 1985. (In 1981, the council had agreed to the establishment of an executive office for the chairman, with its own line item appropriation and giving the chairman the right to hire and fire his own staff. Throughout his entire tenure, this would provide James with a high degree of independent action. His successor has assumed its autonomy unquestioningly.) For years Roy had worked for Eastern Airlines, headquartered in Miami, until company layoffs in the 1980s caused him to seek other employment. Pat didn't want James to hire Roy; she thought it would be bad business to have herself and her ex-husband both working for the tribe, but James persisted. James never saw obstacles when he had decided on something, and nepotism is not a word in the Seminoles' lexicon.

Roy was first sent to be the general manager of a tribal bingo hall in Auburn, Washington, for the Muckleshoot Indian Tribe, which proved not to be a lucrative venue. He was there for only a short time before he was sent on to Red Rock, Oklahoma, where James had formed a joint venture with the Otoe-

Missouria Tribe. Bingo there closed in September 1986. Roy then was sent to Watertown, South Dakota, for a very short time, and then in January 1987 he was sent back to Florida to run the new BC Res's "Million Dollar Bingo" hall. Conflicts with the management caused him to quit very soon, however, and BC bingo, partly because of its location—seventy miles from either coast of Florida's peninsula—or because management was greedy (Pat Diamond's viewpoint), soon closed. In April of 1989, a new management company, Investment Resources, owned by Stan Trilby, reopened the BC bingo hall and once again hired Roy to manage it, but this attempt also failed. In each instance, BC community residents cited unsavory management practices as the basis for the short-lived ventures. By 1992, these practices would become very public.

In September 1989, Roy went to North Carolina for the tribe to work on a joint venture with Bob Tate, to be called Bonus Bingo. A million dollar jackpot would be offered once a month. This time, the project was defeated by Hurricane Hugo, and by December 1990, Roy became tribal representative for the Miccosukee Tribe at their bingo hall on the Tamiami Trail. It was a turbulent time for the Miccosukees who finally, in 1993, ousted their management partners, Tamiami Partners, Ltd., for their failure to cut ties with the Genovese organized crime family of Pittsburgh.[36] Roy wanted to get out of the situation, and James brought him back to the Seminoles to oversee final construction on a controversial new enterprise on the BC Res called the Kissimmee Billie Swamp Safari. (More on this venture in chapter 6.)

In the meantime, the Seminole Tribe had become a role model for generating revenues, even if James's personal involvement had not provided the expected returns. In the mid-1980s, both the FBI and the IRS opened investigations of the Seminoles' Hollywood gaming operation, "triggered in part by findings from the Tribe's own police force."[37] Ultimately, a report on the investigation, dated 7 February 1990, cited an unnamed Seminole informant as saying that profits were being skimmed from the Hollywood and Tampa casino operations. The investigation was not carried further, however, due to "lack of manpower and resources."[38] Certainly, the recent panther case and the court decisions in support of James and the tribe would have had some impact upon the allocation of federal funding for these continuing investigations.

For much of the 1980s, as interest in the lucrative business of gaming grew across Indian Country, the BIA had maintained a laissez-faire stance asserting that its permission was not even a prerequisite for any tribe to open a bingo hall. And the BIA would review management contracts only "in cases where tribes request approval."[39] Although consistent with the larger reality of U.S.-Indian relations, this attitude could not survive for long. In 1988, after the national rumors of criminal involvement reached the ears of Congress, the Indian Gaming Regulatory Act (IGRA) was passed, and the first of a continuing series of strictures on Indian gaming was applied.[40]

The IGRA stated clearly that the goal of federal Indian policy (at that moment, at least) was to promote tribal economic development, self-sufficiency, and strong tribal government. To that end, it was necessary to clarify the U.S. government's role relative to gaming. The secretary of the interior, as the United States' liaison with tribes, it said, was charged with reviewing and permitting gaming management contracts but had no explicit standards for review and approval. The purpose of the act, therefore, was to provide a statutory basis for the regulation of Indian gaming that would ensure that gaming was conducted "honestly and fairly," that the tribe was the primary beneficiary of revenues, and that the tribes were adequately protected from "organized crime and other corrupting influences." In other words, the act was passed to provide the U.S. government with an ever-enlarging control over tribes on the unspoken premise of protecting Indians from themselves.

With an obvious nod to the recently decided Seminole case from Florida, the United States pronounced itself the arbiter of these subjects even as it declared the exclusive right of the tribes to regulate gaming on Indian lands—as long as it was conducted within a state that did not "as a matter of criminal law and public policy, prohibit such gaming activity." To further these ends, the act established a National Indian Gaming Commission (NIGC), of three members. For its first three years, the tribal representative on this NIGC would be Joel Frank (Panther Clan, b. 1950), formerly tribal administrator for the Florida Seminoles.

The act defined three "classes" of gaming—I, II, and III. Class I included "social games" in connection with tribal ceremonies or celebrations, and would remain basically unregulated. Class II gaming was bingo, with or without electronic aids, which, while remaining within the jurisdiction of the tribes, would also be subject to the provisions of the act. Class III gaming was defined broadly as anything that was "not Class I gaming or Class II gaming." The differentiation between Classes II and III, in practice, has come to mean games of chance that one plays against one's self or other players (Class II) as opposed to games that are played against the "House," such as Blackjack (Class III).

Finally, the act stipulated one requirement that opened the door to an entirely new vista of obstacles for all of the tribes as they sought the "economic development . . . self-sufficiency . . . and strong tribal government" that the United States purported to encourage. According to Sect. 11(a)(3)(A): "Any Indian tribe having jurisdiction over the Indian lands upon which a Class III gaming activity is being conducted, or is to be conducted, shall request the *State* in which such lands are located to enter into negotiations for the purpose of entering into a *Tribal-State compact* governing the conduct of gaming activities. Upon receiving such a request, the State shall negotiate with the Indian tribe *in good faith* to enter into such a compact" (emphasis added).

The requirement that tribes should negotiate with their states placed a tremendous burden on the tribes' practice of sovereignty. As Judge Roettger had noted in his earlier decision permitting Seminole gaming, Indian nations had always been dealt with exclusively by the federal government, not by states. It was a long-established tradition in law that unless authorized by Congress, the jurisdiction of state governments and the application of state laws did not extend to Indian lands.[41] In a germane case, *California v. Cabazon Band of Mission Indians,* in 1987, the U.S. Supreme Court had upheld tribal sovereignty, declaring that "the State's interest in preventing the infiltration of tribal bingo enterprises by organized crime does not justify state regulations of the tribal bingo enterprises in light of the compelling federal and tribal interests supporting them. State regulation would impermissibly infringe on tribal government."[42]

The IGRA requirement, enacted in the following year, that tribes negotiate a state compact, therefore seriously debased tribal sovereignty by requiring that a sovereign tribe seek permission from a state government for the conduct of its affairs rather than dealing directly and only with the federal government. Further, in its ostensible determination to protect tribes, the IGRA opened the financial dealings of sovereign tribes to attempts at oversight by other federal agencies such as the IRS, the Justice Department, the U.S. Treasury Department, and the FBI. Further, as we shall see, the requirement that states should negotiate with tribes "in good faith" was constitutionally unenforceable and, therefore, had ramifications of national significance well beyond the bounds of Indian Country.

In 1988, the same year in which Congress passed IGRA, these onerous requirements had limited impact upon the Seminole Tribe, but that would change rapidly. By 1986 erstwhile sheriff Bob Butterworth had become Florida's elected attorney general. He would remain in office until 2002. In 1989, one short decade after their opening, the Seminoles would push their gaming operations to the next level, with "high stakes" bingo. As soon as those games were functional, James would begin to plan for further increases that would bring the tribe, once again, into open political warfare with the state and the federal government. As James confided to me in the early 1990s concerning his plans, "I have the room, I have the machines. All I have to do is unlock the door and flip on the light switch. So, I'm just gonna try it, and see what they [the NIGC] do!" This time, the case would go all the way to the U.S. Supreme Court for a decision that some legal minds have dubbed one of the most important decisions of the twentieth century.

Law Enforcement and SPD

The entire confused and confusing extension of non-Indian law enforcement onto Indian reservations across Indian Country is based upon two major legislative attempts (and numerous subsequent legislative refinements) by the U.S. Congress, the purpose of which has been—ostensibly—to bring Indians completely under the laws of the larger non-Indian nation. That is, to end any special treatment of Indians even though that treatment was based upon a historical acceptance of tribes' sovereignty that dated to the moment of creation of the United States and its founding document, the Constitution.

The "carrot" that always accompanies this "stick" is the assertion that the Indians, as citizens of the United States (albeit also dual citizens of their own separate and sovereign tribes) would only gain full benefits of U.S. citizenship if they accepted full responsibilities, which they apparently could not do while also maintaining their tribal citizenship. This subliminal message seems to echo the overused old Christian proselytizers' mantra that "no man can serve two masters" (as I mentioned in chapter 1). Such binary applications are not a traditional part of the Indian worldview, however.

The first major legislation was the limited Major Crimes Act of 1885, by which the U.S. government gave itself permission to assert jurisdiction on Indian reservations in cases where any of seven stipulated crimes were committed by one Indian against another Indian "or other person." The seven major crimes were murder, manslaughter, rape, assault with intent to kill, arson, burglary, and larceny. "This was a major encroachment upon traditional tribal autonomy."[43] The Indian Crimes Act of 1976 eventually extended the number of included major crimes to fourteen.[44] Further, it stipulated that any of the crimes not punishable under the exclusive jurisdiction of federal law would be punished according to state law.

The second major, and broader, act is known simply as Public Law 280 and was passed in 1953.[45] Initially it gave five states the right to assert the same civil and criminal jurisdiction on reservations (with a few exceptions) as the states exercised in their larger, non-Indian spheres of control. In addition, the bill permitted other states to pass their own legislation assuming the same control. The most egregious part of this legislation (if any part could be said to have been more egregious than any other) was the fact that it gave states the right to decide unilaterally to assert their authority. There was no requirement to even consult with the tribes, much less to seek their consent. U.S. President Eisenhower expressed "grave doubts" about this part of the legislation. The Department of the Interior, however, supported this move. An attempt during the Eighty-fourth Congress to require the consent of Indian tribes failed, and it would not be until the passage of the Indian Civil Rights Act of 1968 that states would be required to obtain the consent of tribal governments.[46]

This latter requirement harkens back to the understanding born of a policy established by the U.S. Supreme Court and known as "the canons of treaty construction."[47] This policy required that, in questions of treaty interpretation, Indians should receive the benefit of the doubt. The spillover from this policy has colored U.S.-tribal relations in other areas. This policy was, unfortunately, itself based upon the supercilious premise that the United States, with (ostensibly) superior knowledge and language skills, should not take advantage of poor and uncivilized Indians. Nevertheless, the policy has been beneficial to tribes, especially in the U.S. Northwest, as regards treaty interpretations. As the policy has impact upon law enforcement, it reminded President Eisenhower and legislators that they had a responsibility to pay attention to the values and views of tribes that could be culturally quite different from their own. Despite paying lip service, however, this awareness did not necessarily cause the U.S. government to color its actions accordingly.

Within a few months of taking office for the first time, Chairman James Billie turned his attention to the need for law enforcement on the reservations. As early as 1974, his predecessor, Howard Tommie, had applied for and received funds from the United States' Law Enforcement Assistance Administration to begin a tribal law enforcement program. In the 1970s, the state was furnishing law enforcement to the reservations. Local law enforcement agencies from the various involved counties cooperated with the Seminoles and appointed and trained deputies for work on each Res or deputized tribal citizens to patrol the vastnesses. The federal government was willing to train Indian deputies at a school in New Mexico, but the states would have to pay them for their work afterward.[48]

The U.S. Indian Civil Rights Act of 1968 also authorized the creation of model codes for courts of Indian offenses and, finally, required that tribal consent, not just consultation, should be given in order for states to assume jurisdiction over Indian Country.[49] In the case of the Seminole people, they had always had their own internal systems for establishing and maintaining rules regarding social boundaries among the tribal citizens and for punishing transgressors. Clans kept order within themselves. Each clan had at least one powerful and respected Medicine practitioner; grandmothers and grandfathers; and uncles who were charged with "scratching" a young person whose actions were, as English speakers might say, getting out of hand. Beyond the quotidian, once each year larger issues having impact upon the entire tribe were adjudicated by the principal Medicine man and clan elders during the Green Corn Ceremony. This system was damaged during the United States' Wars of Removal, but not destroyed. Its most potent forms of punishment, meted out only after serious considerations, were ostracism or, ultimately, execution. These and, more frequently, minor forms of penance continued to be imposed upon miscreants well past the midpoint of the twentieth century.

"This issue would be satisfactorily addressed only when the Seminoles could provide their own police force. That became possible in 1974, when the Florida Legislature made statutory provisions, as a result of which the tribes could obtain federal funding to handle law enforcement on their reservations."[50] Howard decried the fact that the incidence of drug and other crime problems was rising on the reservations, and he had only seven tribal deputies to patrol 100,000 acres of tribal lands. He requested funding from the national Law Enforcement Assistance Administration to establish a tribal law enforcement program, but it would be left to James and the council to take serious action on the development of the Seminole Police Department (SPD) during the next decade.

When James took office in 1979, the Res patrols were essentially the same as they had been throughout part of the 1960s and all of the 1970s. Tribal designates patrolled each of the reservations and called in law enforcement agents from the pertinent county for arrests. In most instances, tribal citizens were designated "special deputies" by the appropriate county for each Res. For example, BC patrols called in Hendry County sheriff's deputies; from Brighton, Glades County was called in; from Hollywood Res, Broward deputies were relied upon; calls from Immokalee might involve Collier County; certain lands might also involve Palm Beach County. James took the next step when he spoke to a white man, husband of a tribal citizen, who had just returned from U.S. Marine Corps duty in 1979. Once again, he looked to warriors who had proven themselves in war.

The man was Gustavus Adolphus "Pete" Baker III, who was married to Judy Ann Billie (Panther Clan, b. 1943).[51] Pete was a native of Beaufort, South Carolina, who had moved to South Florida with his father and stepmother when he was about eight years old. As a young man of seventeen, he worked very close to the Old Dania (Hollywood) Res and began to meet the Seminole people casually. They went to the drive-in movies together and ate hamburgers at the Blue Parrot Café, across Highway 441 from the Res. He and Judy quickly began to care about each other deeply, and their relationship lasted for the rest of his life. Shortly, he enlisted in the U.S. Marine Corps and would spend a total of thirty years there and in the Fleet Marine Force; his service included security training, brig guard duty at sea, three tours of duty in Vietnam, and a stint in the Military Police.

In 1978, Pete and Judy returned to Hollywood, and Pete went to work building chickees with a tribal builder until Hollywood council representative Cecil Johns (Bird Clan, 1935–2001) asked him to serve as a security guard on the Hollywood Res. The tribe was having increasing problems with break-ins there, especially in the clinic. Drugs were becoming a serious problem on Brighton Res also. Tom Bowers (Bird Clan, 1920–2000) was patrolling there. On the BC Res, Jimmy Cypress was the Hendry County special sheriff's deputy and had been since 1966.

Pete used his own car to patrol in Hollywood each night until the council eventually acquired an auto for him, just before the 1979 elections. A short three months following his election, James asked Pete to begin an official police department for the tribe. In cooperation with another tribal employee who was willing to handle the paperwork, the tribal police began its operations with a $99,000 budget (small enough but still more than double the appropriation for fiscal year 1974), from which came uniforms, autos, guns, and radios (that functioned only because of the large system of repeater towers in place for the use of the U.S. Forest Service).[52] Pete completed a course at the Indian Police Academy in Utah. Training for the new officers was provided by Broward County sheriff Bob Butterworth, who set up a forty-hour course for new tribal officers. This was the same sheriff who so vehemently opposed the Smoke Shops and gaming but was a strong supporter of law enforcement. After a year and a half of applications and forms, the Seminole Police Department was certified, and the council acted rapidly to dismiss law enforcement personnel who were not certified.[53]

The first major problem for tribal law enforcement came from drug gangs—at least nine separate gangs, it was determined—who were using the remote sections of the BC Res as landings strips or dropping grounds for drug shipments. Since most of BC was remote and heavily forested, it was a major chore to police the entire area. The problem only surfaced because tribal officers began stopping and inspecting cars entering the BC Res and finding weapons and aircraft radios. In addition to support from Sheriff Butterworth, Broward Organized Crime Agency director (later Broward County sheriff) Nick Navarro and the Broward County SWAT team cooperated also. Only limited help was available from the Hendry County Sheriff's Department, unfortunately, where Sheriff Earl Dyess, an incumbent of almost twenty years, was strongly suspected of participating personally in the drug trafficking. Sheriff Dyess was stabbed to death in a drug-related incident, in 1980, before anything could be proven, however, and was succeeded in office by a son, Earl Sermon Dyess Jr., who was indicted and finally pled guilty in 1993 to four counts of cocaine trafficking stemming from events dating back to 1979 and 1988.[54]

The problem was so large and so lucrative that Pete was unable to control it. He recalled an incident one steamy summer night when police officer Jerry Seeley of Hendry County came upon three Cuban males, sitting down among the heat and the mosquitoes at the end of a small landing strip on the BC Res, ostensibly fishing in a canal. The officer told the men to lift their fishing poles out of the water, only to discover that they had no hooks or other fishing paraphernalia. He immediately handcuffed them and began to search their vehicle, only to discover weapons and aircraft radios. He could hear a pilot coming down, reporting that he was running out of fuel and was going to dump his load across the Everglades. Bales of marijuana began to rain into the water, and the plane soon set down on the west coast, at Punta Gorda. The plane's crew escaped but drug residue in the aircraft proved it to be the same one that had dropped its load over BC.

The arrest of tribal citizen and Hendry County special sheriff's deputy Jimmy Cypress in 1978 (discussed in chapter 4) would follow the same pattern. Jimmy's arrest followed an eight-month investigation led by Clewiston officers and included the capture of two Miami men and a plane loaded with five hundred pounds of marijuana. Jimmy was turned over to the state attorney general's office and temporarily released on $50,000 bond.[55] Ultimately, he would serve time in Hendry County and in federal prison.

Drug control on the Res's did not always end in arrests, but SPD kept up its surveillance. The state had passed a law making it legal for law enforcement to confiscate items, such as guns, autos, and airplanes, captured in the commission of crimes, and the tribe was able to take some advantage of this. On 11 February 1980, the council enacted Ordinance C-134-80, empowering the tribe to retain aircraft and other vehicles used in the commission of crimes on tribal lands. In the event of seizure, the appropriate local, state, or federal authorities were notified, and the owners of record of the vehicles were notified and given the opportunity to claim their property by applying to the council and paying an appraised value. If unclaimed, the tribe retained the right to use or destroy the vehicle.[56] Pete recalled how, on some moonlit nights, he and James would fly together over BC Res. The quality of the moonlight on cloudless nights is brilliant over the Big Cypress, where it is unimpeded by ambient light levels from the coastal cities.

The key to keeping order on the reservations, as Pete saw it, was, first, understanding that the social nature of each Res is different and, second, working directly with the people and getting to know them personally. This certainly is in keeping with the tradition of working one-on-one with the people regardless of the subject. Seminoles want personal service. The earliest officers were both Indians and non-Indians, but the non-Indians were offered materials that would help them to learn of the history of the Seminole people. This process of intercultural awareness would be ignored by some of the succeeding SPD police chiefs, but in the late 1990s I would have the opportunity to work with SPD officers as they sought to learn more about the ways of the people. It was a critical element of policing on the reservations.

In addition to police work, Pete also ran background checks on prospective employees of the bingo halls on the Hollywood, Tampa, and Brighton reservations. When the BC bingo hall first opened, in the 1980s, SPD turned out thirty-nine armed security guards and five helicopters to cover the arrival of more than two hundred Greyhound buses—full of gamblers. It was an auspicious beginning but a short run: the BC bingo hall would reopen several times over the coming few years, each time unsuccessfully—partly because of the obscure location in the middle of the Big Cypress and partly because of poor (or greedy) management.

It was the political aspects of the work that finally led to Pete's being moved out of SPD. In his three-and-a-half-year tenure, the department had grown to thirteen officers, but the drug problems had grown even faster. James was content for SPD to arrest nontribal lawbreakers, but tribal citizens began to cash in on the deals also, and their arrests created political problems. Pete said, "I was really strict about the drug thing and I confiscated peoples' cars. . . . And, then, all of a sudden, Tribal members got involved, and Councilmen that was in charge of different reservations, their kids got involved. And one day I went in and my office was locked up. Changed the lock."

Pete and Judy sat down with James and had a "heart-to-heart talk." James informed them that the stringent arrest policies were "bothering his politics. And he was the one who had ordered it [the changing of the locks]. So politics is strong." Pete and Judy continued to live on the Hollywood Res, raising their children and running a security company in South Florida, with additional accounts across several states in Indian Country. Pete, a licensed private investigator, operated his security firm for a total of twenty years.

On 10 November 1983, six months into James's second term, the tribe, by referendum, passed Amendment No. 18, to Article 5, Sections 11 and 12 of the Tribal Constitution, codifying the power of the Tribal Council to create a tribalwide law enforcement agency and empowering the creation of a Tribal Court. Control of the tribal police force had been placed in the hands of the former deputy, Jerry Seeley, after Pete Baker's tenure, but was shortly turned over to a succession of new men.[57] By the end of James's second term, SPD had grown to a force of twenty-five state-certified police officers, and the department had a budget of $650,000, from gaming proceeds. "A lot of white men criticized me for those bingo halls,' Billie says. 'But our tribe needed money, and bingo was the easiest way for us to get it without having to go begging from the government again.'"[58]

The concept of a Tribal Court was one that has not come to fruition during James's tenure or since, however. Many Seminoles repeatedly asked for a court system—a body apart from the council that wielded more and more power and left tribal citizens with no right of redress inside the tribe. Thus, we see a part of the reason why some felt the impetus to take their cases outside of the tribe to the next available authority, white men's court. The reason regularly advanced for the council's failure to create a Tribal Court was the difficulty of finding Seminoles of sufficient impartiality not beholden to their clans.

Nevertheless, the council's moves to create the tribe's own internal law enforcement system in the early and mid-1980s precluded complete control of law and order on the reservations by the State of Florida. By the end of the decade, however, the council had encountered a period of financial overextension, and SPD was cut back to accommodate economic retrenchment. At least this was the rationale provided. The need for economic retrenchment was real; an over-exuberant rush into construction and other development deals and moves into gaming management agreements with other tribes across Indian Country had extended the tribe's resources to the point where it became necessary to seek extensions of bank loans. (More on this later.) Whether such a financial position warranted cutbacks in such critical services as law enforcement is another discussion.

Regardless of this latter consideration, law enforcement on the five reservations at this time was consuming a budget of $849,000 (tribal) and $223,100 (BIA). This was "scaled down" by entirely deleting SPD enforcement on all but the BC and Tampa reservations and leaving control on the Hollywood, Brighton, and Immokalee reservations to the local sheriffs' offices. The resolution pointed out that tribal citizens had failed to enlist in the police force as it had been expected they might, but this seems a specious argument for such a drastic cutback, especially given the fact that the establishment of a court had been impeded all along by more or less the same reason.[59]

The economic problems that ostensibly caused the cutbacks would be alleviated within a very few years, however, as tribal gaming shifted into the "high stakes" arena (see chapter 9), even though this move would, once again, pit the tribe against state and federal authorities.

6   Home, Home on the Res

In most ways, the major topics that absorbed the Tribal Council in the decade of the 1980s were completely alien to almost all tribal citizens. Their lives were consumed with the quotidian—and the quality of their lives depended principally on their relationships to one another and to the land that continued to sustain them. It was the job of the council and the board to buffer them from the outside world—to keep the white man's world from intruding upon the placid waters of the Seminole lake. The buffer that ostensibly insulated them was a growing layer of administrative infrastructure at the political frontier of the tribe. This was only "ostensible" because that same layer of infrastructure connected them to the non-Indian world regardless of their desire to remain aloof. Elements of their lives were changing, further, as the society and technology of the outside world changed, and as dividend dollars from gaming revenues offered them greater access to the goods and services to be found in the outside world.

≈

The tribe's infrastructure had expanded significantly by the time of its thirtieth anniversary, in 1987. Tribal elections returned Fred Smith to the presidency of the board, for his third term, along with Henry Gopher (Panther Clan, b. 1939) as the Hollywood representative, Mitchell Cypress as the BC representative, and Joe Lester Johns (Panther Clan, b. 1918) from Brighton. Mitchell would tell me later of the ways in which Fred had encouraged his interest in tribal politics. Ethel Santiago (Panther Clan, 1938–1993) served as elected but nonvoting representative from the burgeoning Immokalee community. The board's principal domain, the cattle program, had been turned over to the individual cowmen (tribal joke: "It might take a cow*boy* in Texas but to work cattle in Florida, it takes a *man!*").

In 1983, Agnes Billie Motlow (Bear Clan, b. 1950) had been chosen by the board to administer their remaining programs, consisting mainly of some Smoke Shops and business land leases. The frequently failing Okalee Village visitor attraction in Hollywood would be turned over to the board in 1993.[1] Agnes was from Hollywood and is an intelligent and beautiful woman who had been among the first Tribal Princess winners. She had attended local public schools to the eighth grade and graduated from Sequoyah High School in Tahlequah, Oklahoma. She continued her education a bit further at Stetson University in Deland, Florida, and entered an Emergency Medical Technician training program in South Florida before several years of work with the BC EMT program. Always a caring and dedicated person, Agnes switched shortly to work as personal secretary and assistant to Jim Shore, where she has remained ever since. She is dignified and organized, and has formed a very close working relationship with Jim over the years. Her husband, Bob Motlow, lives in BC and they have one son, David Jr. A few years ago, Agnes made local news when she donated a kidney to her ailing husband—an act thoroughly consistent with her sense of responsibility. In a parallel way, she protects Jim Shore professionally as closely as she protects her personal family.

The tribe's next administrator would be Joel Frank Sr. (Panther Clan, b. 1950), an old friend of James and staunch supporter of his programs. It was his responsibility to see to it that council programs were carried out on each Res, thus creating a "functional rapport" across the many miles geographically separating the various reservations. Joel would leave the administrator's position in 1991, with the passage of the Indian Gaming Regulatory Act (IGRA) and the concomitant establishment of the three-person IGRA Committee, of which he would become an original member.[2] His immediate successor, Larry Frank (Otter Clan, b. 1953) would be far less forceful, and, subsequently, successive tribal administrators would be increasingly challenged by the power and autonomy associated with each council representative's office, as discretionary funds allocated to each representative increased over the last decade of the twentieth century. In fact, the increasing appetite of the representatives for discretionary funds and their increasingly unrestrained spending of those funds would become a flashpoint in the growing tensions between Chairman James and the representatives, especially Mitchell and David Cypress.

~

The persistent failure of the Okalee Village visitor attraction was only partly due to insufficient visitation. ("Okalee" is just a variant spelling of the same Hitchiti word as the name of the small town in central Florida, Ocala, or *Ocali* as it was spelled in some sixteenth-century Spanish documents. It means "my camp" and is related to the slightly more expressive version, and other town name, Immokalee or *Immokali(t)*, "my camp, the place where I lie down.")

Mostly, the failure of Okalee Village was due to the same inherent problems that non-Indians have identified as they have tried to deal with the Seminoles in other business venues over the years. One problem is that it is impossible to keep Seminole-specific stock on the shelves, for one or both of two reasons. The first reason is that numerous social and cultural injunctions restrict the times when tribal citizens may gather grasses (for baskets, dolls, and such) or purchase textiles (for patchwork, for example), or begin new items or finish new items, or even make such seemingly innocuous items as lids for grass baskets, or undertake new projects of various sorts, small or large. The second reason is the fact that neither the word nor the concept of "deadline" occurs within the Seminole lexicons. Consequently, it is all but impossible to keep sufficient stock on the shelves to entice buyers. (Joe Dan Osceola's shop, Anhinga Gifts, always has stock but the belief around the reservations is that Joe Dan and Virginia buy from both the Seminoles and the Miccosukees—that is, from "down the Trail"—and that they also provide raw patchwork strips and patterns to non-Indian seamstresses who supply finished clothing items on schedules that would be impossible to require of Seminoles, thus leaving buyers to believe that their items are all made by Seminoles.)

The second problem pertaining to why Okalee Village periodically failed was because of the near impossibility of getting and keeping staff on a regular basis. Again, the concept of adhering to specific hours of work, in white man's terms, always takes a backseat to family interests or requirements or any other more promising tribal interests that appear. In the case of alligator "wrestling," which is always a draw among visitors, a special case occurs and the attrition rate among wrestlers is high because of the inherent danger and concomitant stress of the work. The general rule of thumb in employment inside the tribe, however, has been (and frequently still is) if one person won't do the job, hire two. If two still can't cover the job requirements, hire three. From the point of view of a manager, this creates serious persistent problems. From a cultural point of view, however, such "problems" illustrate the persistence and durability of Seminole cultural values and the continuing determination of the Seminoles to view white men's requirements in Indian terms, first and foremost.

At the time of this writing, the old Okalee Village has disappeared from the corner of Highway 441 and Stirling Road. This is now the site of the Hollywood Hard Rock complex of casino, restaurants, and shopping arcade, which has incorporated (at tribal insistence) a small "museum" (actually, a preview center for the tribe's BC Ah-Tah-Thi-Ki Museum), a tiny multiseat "stadium" for alligator shows, and a gift shop, all the old Okalee Village elements. This small complex has been created at the far back of the Hard Rock's foot-traffic pattern, that is, far off the beaten path, and transparently as an afterthought of the powerful developer, David Cordish, of whom more later.

Council program areas inside the tribe expanded quickly under James Billie, who was eager to provide opportunities for tribal citizens to prove themselves in any areas that interested them. Unfortunately there was rarely any training for them except whatever they might learn as assistants to nontribal department heads whom James often expected to be eclipsed as soon as possible by the tribal citizens. This irrational but hopeful process would be repeated over and over, giving preference to tribal citizens who jumped into a position, untrained, and failed quickly, only to be succeeded by another untrained tribal citizen. It was part and parcel of James's personal process: he relied constantly on natural intellect and strength of enthusiasm to supersede the need for training. Overall, he maintained a determination that the Indians would prove to outsiders that they could take care of themselves. Unfortunately, without any near-term reliance on training to shorten the prospect of this entirely realistic hope, the process has taken more than a generation to come to any semblance of fruition.

One area in which a successful program was established, at least nominally under the leadership of a tribal citizen, was the tribe's newspaper. Originally established in 1973 as the *Alligator Times,* former council chairman and tribal activist Betty Mae Jumper controlled the newspaper as head of the Seminole Communications Department. With her leadership and council support, the paper grew over the years from a simple black-and-white newsletter, typed and photocopied, to a full-sized, full-color newspaper. On 14 October 1983, volume 1, number 1 of the new edition appeared, with the name on the masthead changed to the *Seminole Tribune.* Myriad reporters, photographers, and layout artists have passed through the paper's staff offices, most consistent of all being a non-Indian reporter and close confidant of James, Peter B. Gallagher. James never made any secret of the fact that he looked upon the tribal newspaper as an extension of his personal and political politics, and this fact frequently was contentious among tribal citizens over the years, especially among those who did not always agree with James's politics (more later on this topic).

Nevertheless, the newspaper earned a visible place for itself in Indian Country, receiving the prestigious Robert F. Kennedy journalism award in 1990. Betty Mae retained the editorship until she was physically unable to continue, leaving the paper in the hands of Virginia Mitchell (Panther Clan, b. 1955), a controversial individual in her own right.

The newspaper never has had a readership of more than a few thousand, at the most, but this limited number includes individuals from around the world, as well as officials and politicians from the local to the national level who are more and more interested in the views and priorities of an FR tribe with a relatively small population and impressively high revenues. Except for a few years immediately before James was suspended in 2001 and Pete Gallagher was fired for his strident loyalty to James, the *Trib* only occasionally evinced any interest in the goings-on of the outside world. Its outlook and editorial policies have been distinctly parochial. Nor has the *Trib* considered the potentially negative ramifications of publishing socially and culturally proprietary information that tribal traditions require not be made public to the non-Indian world.

But one critical example of this latter concerns names and dates of birth and clan affiliations of tribal citizens—information both private and proprietary. These began to appear as more Seminoles began to celebrate birthdays toward the end of the century. Requests to withhold such private information from the office of the council secretary brought no cooperation but, instead, a stinging rebuke from Jim Shore disclaiming the right to privacy on behalf of the tribe's citizens. Jim's strange rebuke will, perhaps, become more clear as we review his involvement with the FBI and his cooperation in its attempts to gain access to tribal business. Picture this situation in counterpoint to the situation of the Miccosukees, who even refused to respond to the requests of the U.S. Bureau of the Census in the 2000 census for data concerning tribal citizens. One charge the Miccosukees make regularly against the Seminoles is that the Seminoles are far too quick to interact with non-Indians. In this instance, however, the Seminole problem seems to have stemmed originally from acute political naïveté rather than from any direct interest in non-Indians. Jim Shore's failure to protect Seminoles' privacy seems to have been connected, rather, to an apologia for his own actions.

In the late 1980s, the Seminole Communications Department, formerly the umbrella for the *Seminole Tribune,* was spun off to create Seminole Broadcasting, a separate program area for television and video.[3] It became the purview of Seminole Broadcasting to videotape council meetings, to interview elders on cultural preservation issues, to videotape tribal events, and to establish a process for making such meetings and events available tribalwide. This last requirement never came completely to fruition, although various working contracts with cable companies provided closed-circuit programming for Hollywood and BC reservations for the better part of a decade. No one cable company covers the entire peninsula of Florida, and the head of the broadcasting department, Danny Jumper (Panther Clan, b. 1951), never managed to establish a system that would serve all the reservations.

Tribal citizens were particularly interested in hearing meetings and commentary in their own languages, and elections have generally favored politicians who were fluent in one or both tribal languages. Max Osceola Jr., Hollywood council representative since 1985, is one of the few who have been elected, and reelected, without speaking either language, although this is one factor that has come close to excluding him in a couple of past elections. Despite this fact, Max Jr. has never made any serious attempt to learn his language (his mother,

Laura Mae, and his father, Max Sr., certainly were fluent), preferring rather to be especially generous with his representative's discretionary funds, to ride motorcycles, play golf, and sponsor golf tournaments. Meanwhile, his wife, Marge, a non-Indian, manages his Smoke Shops very successfully.

James, by contrast, was and is proficient in both tribal languages, although he has been very reticent to publicize his knowledge of Muscogee/Creek. On many occasions, he has preferred to remain quiet when conversations were struck up around him in Creek, acting for all the world as if he did not know what was being said, especially when it was being said about him. This brings up an interesting situation about which he and I and others have commented with some regularity. In addition to a traditional mistrust of the Creeks, such as all Miccosukees have, James somehow came to believe that the Creeks did not like him, personally. In my experience, this does not seem to have been the case at all and so may arise from memories of incident or incidents in his past. Moreover, the Brighton Creeks were aware of his feelings and sought to ameliorate them time and again. They did feel that he tended to disregard their Brighton Res, and they attempted with some regularity to tempt him there to hear their concerns, with only irregular success. Despite our discussions about this point, James never revealed any basis for his negative feelings.

⌒

Despite a chronic lack of training in infrastructure positions, James did make it his policy to support any citizens who unilaterally sought outside education. In line with tradition, he felt that he could not require anyone to seek education, but he would support individual efforts. Howard Tommie had obtained federal funding for numerous tribal programs, and in 1979 the tribe had negotiated a 638 contract (see below) with the BIA to manage several educational programs serving various age groups, from Head Start programs through adult education. At mid-decade Seminole students were obtaining higher education through Pell Grants, Florida Student Assistance Grants, U.S. Department of Education fellowships, and even funding from the Daughters of the American Revolution.[4] In addition, grants from the State of Florida supported both adult and vocational education programs.

From 1945 to 1977, 146 persons had graduated from high school, principally in Indian schools in Cherokee, North Carolina; in Tahlequah, Oklahoma; and in Haskell, Kansas. From 1977 through 1985 another 102 Seminoles were graduated from all high schools, both Indian and non-Indian. Under the policies of James and the new council, almost 150 percent of that number was graduated in the following two years alone, by which time 58 Seminoles had earned college degrees, and the number would only increase gradually over the last decade of the millennium.

On the flip side, in the mid-1970s, the high school dropout rate for Seminole students was approximately 70 percent, but more and more were trying out white men's education, even if they quickly judged it unsatisfactory. Several variables certainly accounted for this situation. One is the disparity between the linear and circular worldviews held by non-Indian and Indian cultures, respectively. Indians are not raised to see the world in a linear (unfolding, developing) fashion. They have difficulty viewing the world as a disarticulated series of subjects. For example, the words "politics," "economics," and even "history" do not occur in either tribal language. Further, their clan-centered lives provide a pervasive family support system that is not available to them in nontribal settings, such as those that exist as non-Indian educational systems. Then, in the case of the Seminoles in particular, the Indians are not raised to question, or to be especially introspective about, their world. The world *exists*, it doesn't *unfold*, and questioning is discourteous and disrespectful. This view is too often antithetical to the requirements of a white man's classroom setting, and this disparity is one with which students would have to come to grips over the coming generations.

Within another decade, as the number of Seminole children who were attending white men's schools rose and students became more conversant with outside educational requirements, the dropout rate fell to 30 percent, but it would rise again by the end of the millennium, both in Florida and across Indian Country. The council periodically had passed resolutions in support of white men's education, but by tradition it would not mandate attendance.[5] The Seminoles still did not want to tell one another what to do any more than they wanted outsiders telling them what to do.

By 1983 the tribe had begun the contracting process to take over control of the only remaining school on the reservations, Ahfachkee Day School on the BC Res. The BIA had opened the school in the 1940s, and by the end of Howard Tommie's tenure as chairman, the tribe still had not considered itself to be in a sufficiently stable economic position to take over its running. Ahfachkee means, loosely, "a happy place." This does not indicate a place of laughter but, rather, commemorates a tract of land once owned by a white rancher who permitted the Indians to camp on his land in peace and safety—it was "happy" for the Indians because they were safe there. By the end of the decade tribal attendance at Ahfachkee had risen sufficiently that the tribe expanded classes from K–6 to pre-K–12.[6] The council further requested support from the BIA to expand Ahfachkee to include a boarding facility for the high school.[7] Neither came to fruition, however.

In the late 1970s tribal income had topped $1 million, from Smoke Shops and from eighty-eight U.S. government contracts. By the end of the 1980s annual gross revenues had soared to $10 million, mostly from gaming, and James and the council were ready to take yet another leap into solvency with "high stakes" bingo. Within five years the revenues from this next form of gaming would reach $31 million, 60 percent of the annual budget, with almost $1 million dedicated by the council to its educational system.

As the end of the 1980s neared, the tribe's Education Department offered Early Childhood and Head Start programs, an Individualized Manpower Training program, and employment assistance, including a partially federally funded Head Start program, in addition to an adult literacy program, and the pre-K–12 program at Ahfachkee. More than 400 Seminoles worked directly for the tribe, out of a total population that would shortly top 1,800. James was almost always willing to provide support for any Seminoles who wished to attend institutions of higher learning, anywhere, as long as they could meet the qualifications of the institution and be accepted. He frequently dipped into his chairman's discretionary budget to provide apartments, food, clothes, books and supplies, and computers, and sometimes even autos. Frequently, his support for students was politically partisan, that is, tied to parental support for James's politics, but he was the only council member providing such support. By the end of his tenure the Education Department would take over much of this process and establish regulations that were frequently less generous but more evenhanded than his own policies, but the educational support system continues nonetheless.

As noted in a booklet produced by the tribe in 1987, "Chairman Billie is anxious to see his people learn to survive in a contemporary world, but also would like to see the traditional customs and values retained. To support that objective, Chairman Billie initiated a cultural heritage and enrichment program. The program is designed to educate the younger members of the Tribe in the importance of retaining the language, practices and the traditional organization of the Seminole people."[8]

This commitment to a program of cultural education has taken on a life of its own over the years. The original "cultural heritage" program languished for a short period, until it was revived in the early 1990s and run by the council-appointed cultural director, Louise Jones Gopher (Panther Clan, b. 1945), of Brighton, who had been involved in cultural and educational development for the tribe since 1982. Louise, who has a strong commitment to the power of education, in both Indian and white man's terms, received an associate of arts degree from Indian River Community College in 1965 and a bachelor of arts degree from Florida Atlantic University in 1970.

Culture programs were set up on each Res, run by local residents who were required to have their language (either one or both). In Brighton the project began as an after-school program set in an isolated demonstration camp at an edge of the Res. The Brighton Creeks are traditionally a more socially active group than the socially conservative Miccosukee Seminoles. By the early 1990s,

the enterprising Brighton Creeks had removed their children from the culturally unfavorable atmosphere of Moorehaven's school system (to the south of
the Res) and had established a positive working relationship with the City of
Okeechobee (a shorter trip to the north). The city's high school system provided one class-hour of release per week for tribal students that the tribe could
use to bring its own cultural programs into the classroom. These programs were
funded on each of the reservations partially by a system of discretionary funds
allocated to the council representative on each Res and partially by the council's
line item educational budget. Louise Gopher's excellent work was succeeded
in 2001 by that of Lorene Gopher, who had long been an active partner in the
tribe's "Princess Contest" program, an event that is almost universal across Indian Country.

~

The origins of the Florida Seminole Princess Contest can be seen as early as
the 1950s, when Seminole women were competing in local, non-Indian-style,
swimsuit "beauty pageants," but these rapidly shifted focus from non-Indian
to Indian standards. By the early 1970s contests were staged for tribal citizens
rather than for non-Indian viewers and included "talent" portions wherein the
contestants explained traditional processes such as tanning deer hides and making patchwork clothing.

Princess Contests from that point forward were an excellent example of the
ability of the Indians to capture a non-Indian cultural non sequitur and adapt
it to their own cultural ends. The program offers them a cross-cultural point of
pride in ways that, perhaps, no other current tribal program can—certainly not
one centering on women. It takes a specifically non-Indian form and restates
it in Indian cultural terms, buttressed with tribal social values. The pageant-
centered program places little or no emphasis on beauty in the non-Indian social lexicon; beauty in the Indian world is couched in a comeliness born of humility and a broad facility with traditional female roles. Dress size is practically
irrelevant and white man's beauty standards have only recently infiltrated the
judging process, as tribes increasingly have become aware of the public relations
value of having winners who have what can be termed "crossover value" in the
non-Indian world.

Much more pertinent to the Indian process are traditional female values,
such as knowledge of tribal traditions. Among the Florida Seminoles these often include demonstrations of *sofkee* making (a ground and boiled corn drink,
a Seminole staple), patchwork sewing, speaking or singing in a tribal language
(although sometimes, ironically, this is singing of a Christian hymn in an Indian language), dancing (which is principally ritualistic rather then social), or
providing an audience with a short history talk about the tribe and some aspect
or aspects of its culture. Interestingly, the 2008 contest saw the inclusion of a

talent *video* rather than a live demonstration—of the contestant demonstrating alligator handling. Although some women have handled alligators out of necessity in the past (Betty Mae Jumper used to take over her husband's tourist shows when he was too drunk to go on), the field has been left predominantly to the males.

In the 1980s the Princess Contest still was a single evening affair, with contestants sometimes being required to present themselves in (non-Indian) "business" attire, sometimes in formal wear (also non-Indian, of course), and always in tribal traditional clothing. In addition, some talent of the sort mentioned earlier was required. Emphasis in this segment of the contest was on traditional knowledge, with preference given to entrants who exhibited skill in such areas. These events were unsophisticated in terms of technology and presentation but were greeted with great enthusiasm by tribal citizens. It was a point of pride to see young people exhibiting their interest in learning about and becoming proficient in the Old Ways. This process partially fulfilled the requirement of transmitting the Old Ways, of actively passing cultural information from generation to generation, in a historical moment when the process of transmission of such information was being buffeted, especially by changing living patterns.

Contests were moveable feasts, being held each succeeding year near another Seminole Res, in rotating fashion. Following the construction of field offices on each Res and construction of a new building (with "cafetorium") for Ahfachkee School in BC in the late 1980s, sufficient viable spaces became available on-Res, and the contests no longer needed to use spaces in any surrounding non-Indian communities. After the tribal headquarters were moved into the beautiful new building in Hollywood in 1995, the contest was held in the council chambers, a large auditorium attached to the rear of the headquarters office building, with every state-of-the-art technical amenity. This pattern would shift again at the end of the century, as tribal funds became available to spread the contest over several days and treat contestants to luxury stays in upscale non-Res hotels, but the construction of the Hard Rock complexes in the early years of the twenty-first century (in Hollywood and Tampa) would, once again, return the contests to tribal venues.

The winner of the Florida contest was invited to attend the Oklahoma Seminoles' Nation Days celebration, and since the Florida Seminoles could afford to sponsor the trip, she did attend, with clan accompanists. The Oklahoma Seminole Princess, representative of a less solvent tribe, was not able to visit Florida in the early years of the Oklahoma contest, although she was invited. It would remain for the SNO to finally agree to provide support for the trip when their gaming revenues eventually reached a moderate level of income, in the mid-1990s. It should be remembered that even when the ILCC case was finally settled in 1990, the SNO, unlike the Seminole Tribe of Florida, bound itself by an agreement with the Department of the Interior to establish a use plan for the award monies and to seek the approval of the secretary of the interior for spending. The SNO has always been timid about its expenditures, obviously still locked in the anxieties of post-Removal poverty, intimidated by the power of the U.S. government, and hampered by the ethnic hostility and economic malaise of the state generally.

In addition to tribal contests across Indian Country, a pan-Indian contest has been introduced over the last quarter of the century, at the huge Gathering of Nations Powwow, in Albuquerque, New Mexico. (Powwow, or Pow Wow, is a western Indian term, and not much used in the East or Southeast by FR tribes. It is, however, a catchphrase and a term of fictitious association among wannabes.) Among the dozens of so-called powwows and Indian festivals staged across the United States each year, Gathering of Nations, held at the University of New Mexico Arena (the "Pit") since 1983, and the Red Earth Cultural Festival, staged at the Cox Cultural Center in downtown Oklahoma City, Oklahoma, established in 1986, are the more prestigious of the events. Red Earth focuses on fine arts and dance, among other facets of Indian culture.[9] Gathering of Nations also includes the Miss Indian World contest, and the winner has achieved higher and higher visibility in the non-Indian world as the annual revenues and political awareness of FR tribes has risen over the last quarter of the twentieth century. In 2005, Miss Florida Seminole, Christine McCall (Clan X, b. 1986), daughter of Wanda Bowers (Clan X, b. 1951), was among the twenty-eight contestants and represented the tribe at the Miss Indian World pageant.

Over the years as increasing annual revenues have provided funds for increased panoply, the Florida Seminoles have expanded their contests to include Junior and Little Mr. and Miss Seminole contests, with particular emphasis on the creation and wearing of traditional clothing, which typically means patchwork and styles from the 1920s and '30s when capes were in fashion for women. Boys' styles tend to reach back further, to the turbans and silverwork conchos of the turn of the twentieth century. Clan grandmothers and aunts have regained a dimension of demand once again, using their memories and talents to provide the clothing and unique hairstyles. The increasing visibility, economic power, and political awareness of the Florida Seminoles have induced them to reinsert non-Indian dimensions to the current contests (the 2007 judges included Miss Florida USA), but their focus remains on tribal culture.

∽

In 1976, pursuant to the U.S. government's Indian Self-Determination and Education Assistance Act (Public Law 93-638), the tribe had negotiated a contract with the BIA to administer its own health program.[10] It would be the first of a number of moves toward increasing the exercise of its autonomy taken by the tribe as its economic base increased. Known simply as "638 contracts," these returned infrastructure initiatives to the control of the tribes, while maintaining a liaison with the BIA and the Indian Health Service and other pertinent federal agencies. The tribe's Health Department provided services to Seminoles on each of the tribe's reservations as well as to Seminoles living off-Res. The system was, and remains, minimal in too many ways, nevertheless.

A chief medical officer, at first a family practitioner, visited the clinics one day per week to see patients. The chief value of this process was and is to provide basic health care services on-Res and to funnel Seminoles who require more treatment into the larger non-Indian local systems of health care. This referral system can be useful—or obstructive, depending on its personnel. Its value depends also on the traditionalist attitudes of the people themselves.

Many Seminoles simply do not wish to become entangled with white man's medicine: recall Sonny Billie's admonition that the worlds of the Indians and white men are like two rivers running parallel, never meeting. Betty Mae Jumper, the tribe's first female chairman of the modern era, spent many of her early years traveling the back roads of South Florida to Seminole camps, encouraging the Seminoles to avail themselves of white man's medicine. Sometimes she succeeded and transported her patients over miles of dirt roads to hospitals in Miami or Dania; sometimes she was repelled by traditionalists with shotguns and was forced to beat a hasty retreat.[11] The traditionalists—even today—will defer to Indian Medicine practitioners in most situations and accede to non-Indian medicine only as a last recourse and, sometimes, not even then.

The negative interface between Indian Medicine and white man's medicine stems also from the traditional Seminole view of illness. Illness is rarely physiologically based in the Seminole worldview. It is more likely the result of some personal imbalance on the part of the ill person, something that he or she has done to impel themselves out of the natural equilibrium of the seen and unseen worlds. Even war Medicine had its basis in the failure of an individual to be properly balanced before placing himself in harm's way. Frequently, illnesses also may be the result of bad Medicine, itself the result of an individual's having excited the animosity of another, and the possible rationales for this condition are numerous.

For all these reasons traditionalists consult with a Medicine practitioner, male or female, first to reestablish the universal equilibrium that they have wittingly or unwittingly disrupted or, if necessary, to remove the effects of the bad Medicine. Clan relatives often feel that the disequilibrium or the bad Medicine may be contagious, and so they often decline to visit ill persons, whether in camp or in a white man's hospital, for fear of upsetting the natural universal order further and thereby bringing illness upon themselves. For those who choose to submit to white man's medicine and enter a hospital, this makes for a lonely and isolating experience, especially for those who have little or no English skills. Only at this moment in time are these traditional feelings mitigating somewhat, as some clan relatives and friends begin to visit hospitals in support of loved ones.

The other edge of the problem concerns non-Indian medical personnel who have no frame of reference for Indians, the Indian languages, or Indian cultural values. It has been my honor to interact with, and provide information for, numerous non-Indian medical practitioners who honestly strive to understand the ill persons who come to them from cultures other than their own with language and value barriers to understanding. Unfortunately, I also have dealt with too many who are blinded by scientific arrogance, or who are visibly angered by the prospect of dealing with people born "in the United States" who neither speak English nor share their Euro-American values. This is not only a barrier to understanding; it is also a barrier to survival for the patients.

The broadest and most inclusive part of the tribe's non-Indian-medicine health care system (as opposed to the tribe's traditional Medicine system) involves the network of health aides on each Res. These are tribal citizens who speak one or both languages, have their own automobiles, and perform a variety of personal and professional tasks for ill tribal citizens. They make home visits to see that patients are taking medicine (white man's, that is), which frequently involves negotiating with clan relatives who sometimes support and sometimes oppose involvement with white men. They pick up and deliver patients, especially elders (or "elderlies" as they are often referred to), to outside health care facilities. They translate the patients' problems to the doctors and the doctors' medical terminology into terms the patients might understand. At the same time, they may also serve as the initial liaison between a sick person and a tribal Medicine practitioner. Many Seminoles who do think of availing themselves of the dual systems do so as a form of what we would call "hedging their bets." Regardless, the health aides are the unsung heroes of the tribal heath care system.

Dental services are provided to tribal citizens on approximately the same basis as other health services. A nutritionist also travels from Res to Res, attempting to convince citizens to change harmful diets. Interactions with non-Indians over the twentieth century shifted cooking patterns away from boiling foods to an unhealthy reliance on frying and, since their creation during World War II, to an unhealthy reliance on "junk foods" as well, with disastrous results for the Seminoles. In the last quarter of the twentieth century, the main health problems, in addition to alcoholism and substance abuse, were obesity and resultant diabetes, and its by-products such as renal failure and hypertension, and the incidence of HTLV II (human T-lymphotropic virus), a retrovirus (identified in research in which I participated in 1995).[12] Adult onset diabetes, especially, has exploded like a bomb among the Seminoles in the twentieth century, but the tribe has, once again, chosen not to make any direct, corporate attempts to steer citizens away from their harmful eating patterns, other than paying the salary of the nutritionist, who is a non-Indian and, therefore, in a position to try to influence people directly. Interestingly, non-Indian health practitioners recognize the etiology of certain of these diseases as being distinct from the etiology of the diseases as they occur among the non-Indian population.

Human services and social services programs, staffed principally by non-Indian professionals and funded by a combination of tribal and federal monies, had greater or lesser success over the last quarter of the twentieth century depending principally, yet again, upon the individuals involved. Seminole tradition relies heavily upon pairing individuals in need of certain services (especially certain types of counseling) with those who have had personal experiences in those specific areas. Consequently, staff members of the social services program regularly have been rejected by tribal citizens, even though their training and credentials might have been sufficient in the non-Indian world, if they were too young or inexperienced in the eyes of the Seminoles.

One counselor, employed by the social services program, who had greater longevity than any other staff member, was a Vietnam veteran whose personal background gave him obvious credibility in the eyes of those who counseled with him. Further, he truly liked the Seminole people and spent significant time outside of formal work hours attending tribal activities and getting to know, and be known by, the people. Less successful counselors insisted on maintaining a non-Indian-style "professional distance" between themselves and their "clients" that marked them, in the eyes of the Seminoles, as uncaring. These are the keys to any success in working with the Seminoles, even after half a millennium of non-Indian interactions: personal, one-on-one relationships fostering trust.

A federally funded food distribution program, initiated in January of 1981, provided food packages (frequently commodity cheese and peanut butter) to families who qualified as economically needy. At the outset of the program, ninety-six households qualified for assistance. In six years, 275 households had qualified, for a total of 650 recipients. The commodity foods program was consolidated with the federal Nutrition Program for Women, Infants, and Children (WIC), and a warehouse was set up in Brighton as a distribution center.

Senior programs, an outgrowth of the health system, provide activities for the "elderlies," everything from outings, picnics, dinners, and trips, to the currently popular bowling. As tribal resources increased over the last two decades of the twentieth century, an unspoken commitment to support and care of the elders has increased as well. David Cypress, BC council representative, has his largest power base, outside of his Otter Clan, in the BC elders to whom he actively—financially—pays court. BC elders remain faithful to him, and he remains faithful to them. Buses transport them to Swap Shops and flea markets across the state. They visit the Indian casinos of Foxwoods and Mohegan Sun. Walmarts have been especial favorites of the Florida Seminoles because of the variety of colorful fabrics they offer, and the Seminoles buy, for the production of patchwork. It used to be a regular joke on trips that Seminoles had "special Indian power" to tell when a Walmart was nearby.

I created a series of "Time Travel Tours" that was quite generously supported by David and the council over seven years. I took busloads of citizens annually for special "behind the scenes" tours to places in and out of the state that have significance to their history, from Tallahassee to New Orleans to Cahokia Mounds, Illinois. On our second trip, over one hundred Seminole citizens and officials visited Charleston, South Carolina, to commemorate the imprisonment of the Seminoles at Fort Moultrie in Charleston Harbor during the 2nd Seminole War and the 160th anniversary of the death of the warrior, Osceola, who is buried there.

Groups still travel to Oklahoma each year just after Labor Day for the Oklahoma Seminoles' Nation Days celebration. Florida Seminoles continuously deride the patchwork produced by the Oklahoma Seminoles, which they view as being a poor imitation of Florida Seminole patchwork and produced in a clear attempt to reconnect themselves with their southeastern homelands. (The trained eye can distinguish immediately among Florida Seminole patchwork, patchwork made "down the Trail" in Florida, and Oklahoma patchwork. Even patchwork made in Immokalee has begun to take on its own aesthetic characteristics.) So, Florida Seminoles always carry raw Florida patchwork and finished patchwork garments with them to Oklahoma to sell, and it sells immediately. But, despite the negative feelings each group has for the other, the one group wants to go to Oklahoma each year, and the other group expects to see them.

In terms of caring for their elders, however, one important goal had yet to be reached by the end of James's tenure. This is the construction and operation of extended care facilities on-Res. The subject has been discussed numerous times over the years, but never brought to fruition. Across the 1980s and most of the 1990s as tribal revenues made such possible, tribal elders who required extended care still were placed in non-Indian facilities across South Florida, making travel and visitation difficult for clan members and leaving elders lonely for their outdoor lives and their relatives and friends in the woods. By the late 1990s, the council had found a limited compromise that alleviated the least welcome parts of life in nursing homes. The council began to pay for in-home skilled nursing care or home helpers (almost always non-Indians) who could provide food and personal care for individuals without requiring them to leave the Res. In addition, tribal Hot Meals programs, partially federally funded, gave both ambulatory and nonambulatory citizens local social venues with close ties to tribally funded senior programs.

~

In addition to its major program areas, tribal infrastructure in the late 1980s was expanded to include a number of other federally funded and tribally funded programs. Employment assistance provided training for students in or recently out of high school whose interests were in the vocational and technical areas. In the 1980s this training clearly was predicated upon the lower expectations of non-Indians, whose imagings of Indians' intellectual abilities were pitched principally toward manual labors. Clerical, mechanical, and industrial courses were offered, and the program touted a 90 percent employment rate. This employment was almost completely within the tribe, however, where the majority of Seminoles continue to work. The old cycle of lowered expectations began to change in the early 1990s, as a concomitant of radically increasing revenues from gaming and as tribal enterprises became available to expand training programs, and with the expansion of Ahfachkee School to a K–12 structure, with a series of principals whose expectations of Indian students were significantly heightened.

The tribe began its own Construction and Development Program in May of 1979 as the new council began its activities, and this had a direct impact on the tribe's ability to provide jobs for, and services to, its citizens. Their initial construction projects created community buildings that are only now being superseded by the next generation of buildings supporting community-wide program areas and activities. The first community health clinics were completed on the BC and Brighton reservations. In addition, multipurpose centers were constructed for Hollywood, Brighton, and BC.

All of these projects were funded in part by Community Development Block Grants from the U.S. Department of Housing and Urban Development. In Hollywood, the council subsidized the construction of a planned "shopping center," a short strip mall on Sixty-Fourth Avenue that wound up as office space for tribal program areas that could not be housed in the tiny, old, tribal headquarters building on the corner of Stirling Road and Highway 441. These included, among others over time, the Seminole Police Department, the Tribal Utilities Department, and a temporary working office for the planned Ah-Tah-Thi-Ki Museum (which we will revisit later). Today a more modern building has been constructed on the site as headquarters for the Seminole Police Department and Emergency Services.

Early in 1979 the Department of the Interior had taken into trust five acres of land in the tiny migrant town of Immokalee, fifty miles west by northwest from the BC Res, accepting the utilitarian view that it was "contiguous" to the BC Res, as, indeed, it continued to be, at least in political terms, for some years.

By 1989 the tribe had expanded its Immokalee Res land base to more than six hundred acres and the elected council representative from BC was charged with serving the community of about 123 residents until, by 1987, a nonvoting Immokalee representative was added to the Tribal Council. Today, this representative is elected but continues to be nonvoting until such time as the population of that Res reaches parity with the three "big reservations," BC, Brighton, and Hollywood.[13] By the last decade of the century, Immokalee Res comprised not only detached housing but also a field office, a Smoke Shop, an arts and crafts center, and a small clinic.

Tampa Res, the result of the deal with the City of Tampa to re-inter Indian remains found downtown, remained an extended-single-family Res throughout the 1980s and 1990s. Medicine practitioner Bobby Henry, an adept at rainmaking—and rain preventing—who was hired from time to time by the Miami Grand Prix to ensure good weather, was an early entrepreneur. He managed an "Indian Village" behind the Sheraton Hotel complex and beside the casino, with a gift shop including arts and crafts, outdoor live animal exhibits, and a rudimental "museum" whose central element was the re-interred Indian remains recovered from the City of Tampa. There was, of course, the ubiquitous Smoke Shop as well.

Also too small demographically for an elected council representative of its own, Tampa is represented in council meetings by an appointed liaison who, for all its years, has been Richard Henry (Panther Clan, b. 1964), a young and active member of the Tampa Res family. With the deposing and impeachment of James Billie and the planned construction of the Tampa Hard Rock, however, the council moved to disperse the residents of the tiny Tampa Res. The council subsidized alternative housing for Res residents, but not in any manner consistent with an objective of maintaining tribal coherence.

Well into his third term in office, James saw to it that BC, an old Res, obtained its share of tribal largesse. In addition to Ahfachkee School, BC had its own field office, clinic, fire station, SPD office, and EMT service. The Forestry Service, a function of the U.S. Forest Service and a cooperative tribal program, had and has its headquarters there as well. Joe Frank (Panther Clan, b. 1954) remains the "Monarch of the Glen." In addition, individual businesses blossomed (and frequently died) over time, with unfortunate regularity, from gas stations to small grocery stores. As BC is the most isolated of the reservations—its nearest town, Clewiston, being forty-two miles of bad road away, any local amenities are a boon to residents.

James would have been pleased to see BC, his personal headquarters, also become the administrative center for all tribal operations, rather than Hollywood, but his visions were hampered continuously by the facts that water, electrical, and telephone services were always problematic on BC Res (being controlled by white men in Hendry County), and by two other realities. One was the simple fact of distance: employees who did not live on BC Res would be obliged to drive as many as 140 miles round trip to work there. The other was local tribal resistance to the alternative possibility of having large numbers of non-Indians living in BC. Some non-Indians who were the partners or spouses of tribal citizens lived there, as did a few non-Indian or non-Seminole teachers who were working at Ahfachkee School (one of whom was engaged in a long-term relationship with Mitchell Cypress), but these were obliged to do so very quietly in order not to flaunt their presence, which could easily turn locals against them.

BC also became the center of the tribe's agricultural industries, citrus in particular, begun in 1980 and surviving to become a stable, revenue-generating industry. As BC has grown over the 1990s, its economic base augmented by the Kissimmee Billie Swamp Safari visitor attraction and the Ah-Tah-Thi-Ki Museum (more of these in chapter 7), the need for nontribal employees has continued. This has been supplied, principally, by Mexicans from the nearby Montura trailer park that has grown up along Highway 833 between BC and Highway 27 to Clewiston/Moorehaven, and by transient labor forces from Immokalee. The Seminoles feel a slight kinship to the Mexicans, generally, and to the Nahuatl-speaking Mayans, because of their Indian heritage. This does not necessarily make it any easier to maintain a stable workforce, however.

⁓

Over the first three decades of their political existence, the tribe's corporation, the Seminole Tribe of Florida, Inc., reached the zenith of its enterprises and control functions. Overseeing much of this growth was Bill Osceola, who was succeeded in 1987 by Fred Smith, who was succeeded following Fred's passing in 1996 by Mitchell Cypress, whom Fred had groomed. Originally funded and run principally by the BIA, by the 1970s the corporation was organized as separate offices of Planning and Development, and Management Services, both funded by the Economic Development Administration of the U.S. Department of Commerce. However, reduced federal funding caused the tribe to consolidate the offices, and tribal growth allowed the tribe to shift control of the offices to the tribe itself. It was the purview of the board to oversee tribal enterprises, the earliest being the cattle program, Smoke Shops, and land leases (principally trailer parks and businesses). The board also oversaw the tribe's insurance program, Worker's Compensation office, and a sheltered annuity retirement program that was available to senior employees. These latter were managed for the tribe as self-insurance programs by various outside insurance agencies over the years.

The tribe's modern tribal cattle programs began in the 1960s when, following the creation of the political tribe, herds were divided among individual owners. The ancestors of the Seminoles had tended cattle since their introduction to Florida by the Spaniards in the sixteenth century. The Indians' association with their herds was completely interrupted by the U.S. military, however, during its Wars of Seminole Removal in the first half of the nineteenth century, and not recovered by the Florida Seminoles until the reintroduction of herds by the U.S. government in the third decade of the twentieth century.

The modern tribal program of the late 1980s and 1990s focused on herd improvement, which was managed in cooperation with the University of Florida. Herdsmen on each Res oversaw the program, and individual Seminole owners of cattle herds asked the tribe for support in the introduction of such other strains as Angus, Hereford, Brahma, and Beefmaster in order to strengthen the tribe's bull herd, and, therefore, the entire herd in South Florida where "scrub cattle" traditionally have had to battle flea and tick infestations for survival. The two principal cattle herds in the late 1980s were at Brighton Res, where there were 120 cows, and at the BC Res, where another herd of about 160 cows was enrolled in a master Beefmaster Breeder's Universal Association upgrading program.

In addition to the breeding association, a 4-H program opened the door to the education of future Seminole cattlemen and the entrée of Seminole youngsters to the larger non-Indian world of breeding and showing cattle. Sponsored by the Florida Cooperative Extension Service (FCES) at the University of Florida (UF), the program offered learning opportunities that placed the tribe's 4-H program on an equal footing with the programs of Florida's counties and offered tribal programs led by UF/FCES personnel that also included technical training in agriculture and agribusiness-related areas.

In order to increase marketing exposure for tribal herds, the tribe incrementally purchased 51 percent of the stock of First American Video, an Oklahoma-based video marketing venue for livestock. Next, the tribe entered into an enhanced marketing arrangement with the Amarillo (Texas) Livestock Market to conduct sales, with First American Video taping and shipping the cattle to buyers. By 1985 tribal cattle were being sold via satellite, anyone in the western hemisphere could participate in the sale, and the tribe had sold 80,000 cattle.

In another of its moves to reconsolidate its own tribal control, and in conjunction with its cattle program, the tribe had established the Brighton and Big Cypress Land Use Program in the 1970s, a land management program formerly run by the BIA. Funding came from grazing fees charged to individual cattle owners and supported water and weed control, development of farm leases and new acreage, and maintaining pasturage. Grazing fees were sufficient for most of these processes until the East Big Cypress Case drew to a close in the period 1986–87, when the tribe's new water compact with the state and federal governments was finalized, and the tribe began to take greater control of land development programs.

During the first three decades of its infrastructure life, the tribe developed approximately 27,000 acres of improved pasturage on Brighton and BC, leased to seventy-four cattle owners. A few major herd owners ceased paying grazing fees and began to pay lease fees for the land only, assuming responsibility for total management of their pastures and herds. Herd owners in Brighton, in particular, began to contract with the tribe to provide some services, thereby increasing income to the tribe, and the tribe created five water management districts in Brighton, assessing the owners for fees in each of these districts. Tribal revenues from these services were returned to the Res citizens in the form of renovated pastures and increased pasturage. The tribe's exercise of this increasing degree of control over its lands was also, indirectly and directly, an important facet of its ability to forge a water compact with Florida and the federal government.

Despite the fact that, for almost all of its twentieth-century existence, the tribe's cattle program was a money-losing proposition, the council supported it in any necessary way. Cattle raising was an integral part of the post-Contact history of the Seminoles, and no one questioned it. By the end of the century, the tribe would finally have the eleventh largest cattle operation in the United States and the third largest herd in Florida.[14] More than 10,500 head lived on 35,000 acres of grazing land on the Brighton and BC reservations. The tribe's herds are termed a "cow-calf operation." Despite regular dipping for ticks, a major protection for cattle and cattle raisers mandated by the state since 1940, Florida cattle still have many natural obstacles to overcome in the process of survival in the Florida "scrub," and calves are regularly sent away to western feedlots to be fattened for sale.

The tribe has never hesitated to invest in the cattle-raising and sales process. In 2004 it decided to participate in an electronic tagging program that permits individual cattle to be "source verified," that is, tracked throughout their lives as a method of controlling potential cases of mad cow and other diseases.[15] By 2006, the tribe's cattle operation ranked twelfth in the nation and fourth in Florida in cow-calf production.

⁓

From the inception of the political "Tribe" and especially throughout the lean economic years of the 1960s and 1970s, significant support for tribal infrastructure and enterprises was provided by the U.S. government and the BIA through a revolving credit fund available to FR tribes.[16] In the case of the Florida Seminoles, the BIA instituted this funding in the year following the establishment of the political tribe in 1958. As the first two decades of tribal

Figure 4. Tribal headquarters building, Hollywood Res, opened in 1995. (Photograph by P. R. Wickman.)

enterprise were lean ones, the interest on the federal loan rose even as the principle decreased very little. By the mid-1960s, the tribe had received slightly more than $1 million, which it used at the rate of approximately 60:40 percent for tribal:individual business loans. At this point the tribe chose to invest the funding in infrastructure and report the interest on the loan as delinquent.

By 1970 the BIA agreed to renegotiate the principle and interest downward, and the tribe confidently expected to be able to meet the new debt threshold with incomes from real estate leases and oil exploration leases.[17] These expectations were not met, however, and delinquency on the loan continued to grow each year. In 1977 (fiscal year 1978), the council and board, at a special joint meeting, passed resolution No. C-3-78/BD-1-78, asking the U.S. government to modify the tribe's loan agreement in order to permit the tribe to pay off the mounting interest ($236,343.64) in equal installments over the coming five years and, then, to continue with repayment of the principal. Neither this nor the previous plan worked out.

In 1979, as James and the new council began their work, the U.S. government required the Seminoles to develop another plan for retiring the debt, which had reached $1.5 million, including $330,000 in interest. These monies had underwritten construction of a new tribal headquarters complex on the northwest corner of Highway 441/State Road 7 and Stirling Road, support for the

Okalee Village and arts and crafts enterprises, and various cattle programs among other enterprises.

The resultant plan to repay the debt required fixed amounts from each of the supported program areas, with the resultant expectation that the tribe would be able to become current on both principal and interest by 1982. Once again, the plan was dependent upon the tribe's business programs being successful, but this time, the expectations were met. The tribe's image was expanding positively with its successes in its lawsuits against the federal and state governments over gaming rights and water control. Gaming, of course, was the goose that had begun to lay not only eggs but also golden eggs, and James and the council and board were finally beginning to see the production of sufficient revenues as to be able to meet their revolving fund expectations. The result was that on 20 September 1993, the tribe issued check number 331553, made payable to the BIA, in the amount of $60,177.19, in complete retirement of the revolving credit fund that had encumbered the tribe since 1958. It was a moment of great pride for the council. The fund had underwritten many major elements of tribal infrastructure development from sewerage systems to field offices, but above all, its retirement represented the cutting of one more thread that had bound the tribe to the white man's government.

7 One Too Many Alligators

Sovereignty and Citizenship

The subject of sovereignty was always much in James's mind, as I have mentioned before, although it did not appear to be an issue germane to the thoughts of the other council representatives, or its weight did not seem to them to be as pressing. They turned their thoughts inward; he turned his outward. James and I had many conversations about the meaning and exercise of sovereignty by the tribe. He wanted only "bottom lines" and grasped complex subjects in their entirety if they were presented in a very basic and straightforward manner. It was not that he did not understand complexity but, rather, that he had no patience for it. He has, however, a subtlety of thought that is clearly Machiavellian in many ways. For example, the axiom "Keep your friends close, but your enemies closer" was one of his guiding philosophies, but as he did not always know how to recognize the former and had too many of the latter, his practice of this philosophy was constant. But the concept of tribal independence of action, that is, sovereignty, was not one that he had had the opportunity to explore intellectually in breadth, even though he had fought the U.S. government—and won—over several critical elements of the sovereignty issue and would soon fight for more.

I made lists of points and faxed them to him, wherever he was, for later discussions by telephone or in person. The kitchen of his house in BC early in the morning over a fresh cup of hot coffee was always the best time and place for exploration of this or any subject or, secondarily, in his black pickup truck, bouncing across his cattle pasture. We discussed the power to impose individual taxation. The tribe had codified its authority to tax in Article V, Section 6 of its constitution and already had used the concept of business taxation by requiring Smoke Shop lessees to pay a percentage of profits to the tribe. Further, by Ordinance C-01-78, the tribe had imposed a 4 percent sales tax on retail sales of tangible property by persons doing business on the Hollywood, Brighton, and BC reservations. This ordinance excluded taxations on food, livestock, gasoline, or beverages. Interestingly, the term *beverages* was left ambiguous.[1] Three years into James's chairmanship, tribal taxation was expanded to include mobile homes, trailers, RVs, and gasoline.[2] Further ordinances in these regards would earmark funds for restored support of the SPD and other municipal services.[3] Over the coming development of the tribe as a business entity, taxation would be one of many ways that the council would use to increase income.

The power to determine its own form of government and to be free from the U.S. government's attempts to interfere with tribal government were the fronts on which the tribe's protection of its sovereignty were pressed hardest every single day. As early as 1956 the U.S. Supreme Court had enunciated the policy that individual Indians must pay federal taxes unless a treaty or statute gave them an exemption.[4] Today, the U.S. government taxes the incomes of individual Indians under most circumstances, although state governments do not have this same authority except in certain states and certain instances. The tribe itself, however, as a sovereign nation, is not taxed. The situation is extremely complex—not unlike all other aspects of Indian/tribal–U.S. relations.

The inherent sovereign power to regulate domestic relations among its citizens was another right the Seminoles were not ready to exercise at the time either and, perhaps, might never be, at least in its broadest sense. With the critical exception of regulating citizenship/enrollment issues, the council was still, in the early 1990s, not ready to tell its citizens what to do, and it would be left to the pressures of the outside U.S. government to make requirements upon the citizenry that tribal officials were loath to make (such as, for example, attempts by the U.S. Bureau of the Census to obtain proprietary information concerning individual tribal citizens).

One internal ramification of the Tribal Council's unwillingness to "regulate domestic relations" among its citizens is the astounding rise in the number of Clan X individuals since the 1970s, as we have discussed earlier (see chapter 2). This fact, in turn, has reduced the Q of numerous tribal citizens, placing more and more of them on the threshold of citizenship eligibility (see figure 5). Seminoles love children and nowadays, for the most part, still do not consider it appropriate to specify to their own children where the next generation should come from, ethnically. This is in direct opposition to the stringent requirements imposed a short century ago, during the Wars of Removal, when fraternization of any degree might bring ostracization, at least, or the death penalty, at worst, but conditions seem less bellicose now. Emphasis is on the word "seem."

It is the province of the tribal secretary/treasurer to record the relations of tribal citizens, and so this office became the earliest arena in which registration and regulation most nearly intersected. Priscilla Osceola Sayen (Snake

Clan, b. 1941, daughter of Charlotte Tommie and the Rev. Bill Osceola), tribal secretary/treasurer from 1982 until the two offices were split in 2003 and Mike Tiger became tribal treasurer, was caught constantly between the assertion of tribal sovereignty and the ever-increasing demands of the U.S. government for information, regulation, and, ultimately, control, of tribal citizenry.[5] (You may recall that Mike Tiger, son of Winifred and Howard Tiger, was politically averse to James and was brought back into tribal administration by the council that removed James.)

Fortunately for tribal sovereignty the increasing revenues of the tribe have made it possible for the tribe to protect vital statistics somewhat by taking over clerical and statistical functions heretofore assumed by the BIA/Seminole Agency. For example, copies of birth and death certificates, forwarded to the agency from the Florida Bureau of Vital Statistics in Jacksonville, were slowly redirected to the office of the secretary of the tribe itself in the 1990s. Then, as tribal enrollment issues became more complex, in the 1990s, with an increase in enrollment requests from children born to, and raised by, a nontribal parent; with the question of increasing reliance upon DNA testing as proof of paternity; and even the need to untangle issues created by such scientific techniques as in vitro fertilization, the degree of control vested in the tribe, through the functions of its tribal secretary, rose exponentially.

Regulations regarding tribal citizenship are codified in the constitution, which is a founding document of the political tribe, and in subsequent ordinances and resolutions. Requisites for enrollment are four, and they are clear. First, the individual seeking enrollment must be able to prove a direct descendancy from an individual listed on the 1957 Seminole Agency census. Second, the generational and Q (blood quantum) attributes of the individual seeking enrollment must leave that individual with no less than one-quarter Florida Seminole Q. (For a discussion of this computation, revisit chapter 2, and for comparative statistics, see figure 5.) Third, the individual seeking enrollment must have a current Seminole parent, grandparent, or other close relative, of the appropriate clan, who is willing to act as sponsor in the enrollment process. Fourth, and finally, it must be recalled that, despite the fact that the tribe has a solid constitutional basis in which it codifies these enrollment regulations, the final authority to accept or decline citizenship rests always with the Tribal Council. That is, whether an individual applicant meets all of the other qualifications or not, the sine qua non of tribal enrollment is a sociocultural one: acceptance by the Tribal Council. This point is entirely misunderstood by non-Indians, whose economically driven determination to breach the walls of Seminole tribal sovereignty leads many to purposely ignore the dictates and rights of sovereignty in the area of citizenship and enrollment.

This is an especially important point today when the subject of DNA test-

Clan	R1914 #	% of Tot.	R1968 #	% of Tot.	R1979 #	% of Tot.	R1997 #	% of Tot.	R2001 #	% of Tot.
Bird	137	19.6	229	22.9	275	19.8	407	17.0	420	15.4
Panther	204	29.2	504	50.5	620	44.6	904	37.8	985	36.2
Snake	24	3.4	58	5.8	50	3.6	48	2.0	49	1.8
Wind	32	4.6	55	5.5	78	5.6	97	4.1	125	4.6
Otter	65	9.3	130	13.0	201	14.5	231	9.7	250	9.2
Bear	24	3.4	21	2.1	30	2.2	38	1.6	45	1.7
Deer	15	2.1	1	0.1	29	2.1	65	2.7	72	2.6
Big Town	40	5.7	?	—	1	0.1	98	4.1	107	3.9
Tahkoshat	0	0	?	—	0	0	13	0.5	13	0.5
Clan X	0	0	?	—	107	7.7	489	20.5	658	24.2
Total Pop.	698	—	998	—	1390	—	2390	—	2724	—
Q = 1.00	541	77.5	—	—	858	31.7	865	36.2	848	31.1
Q = 0.250	0	0	—	—	78	5.6	553	23.1	735	27.0
Clan/Q Unknown	157	22.5	?	?	0	0	0	0	0	0

Figure 5. Populations. Comparisons, and Q Statistics. Slight changes in Clan numbers may be accounted for by decease or withdrawal from the Seminole to the Miccosukee Tribe. Larger changes rely on births. The C1957 (BIA Census; there is no "R1957") is not included here because it counted all the Indians, including those who soon formed the Miccosukee Tribe. The 1970s were also a watershed era: the number of Q0.50 (half-bloods) had increased radically, setting the stage for the coming drop to the minimum Q0.250 (quarter bloods) in the next generations, precipitated by the growing number of offspring born with/to a non-Seminole parent.

R = Roll/Year; Q = Blood Quantum

(Prepared by the author.)

ing is being touted more and more often as if it were a definitive basis for obtaining citizenship in any FR tribe. It most especially is not. Genetic information aside, and beyond even social recognition, the last hurdle remains: will an applicant be accepted by the tribe as it is represented by its Tribal Council? The decision of the council is final; there is no appeal. Nothing can make a person an "Indian" if the tribe will not accept him or her.

In the case of DNA testing, and the ostensibly resultant use of any DNA test as sufficient basis for citizenship in any FR Indian tribe, the process has value only if the individual seeking enrollment is so generationally close to tribal relatives that a test can be conducted using two individuals: one already inside the tribe and the other out. Otherwise, the process has no merit on its face. First and foremost, the validity of DNA testing, in any instance, lies in the ability to test one sample *against another.* A single test proves nothing in and of itself. Certain DNA results *may* indicate *some* genetic connections to *some* known group but, first, the group *must be known.*

Even then DNA results cannot indicate the *degree* of connectedness—that is, even if your DNA looks somewhat like the DNA to be found in another group, how long ago did your DNA and that of the others intersect? Upon this answer rests the Q of each applicant, and each FR tribe sets its own threshold in this matter. This is an arena in which the state of current technology has outstripped the social basis for its application. Only greed and an unrealistic belief in the power of science lead non-Indians to clamor at the gates of tribal sovereignty today. Unless and until such time as *every* enrolled citizen of *every* FR tribe in the United States has contributed DNA that may be used as baseline data, no definitive use may be made of *any* DNA test for the specific purpose of enrollment in any FR tribe.

Some FR tribes have begun to seek avenues of limited acceptance for individuals with severely restricted Q on the premise that sheer numbers equate with political power. In no instances, however, are these diminished-Q individuals given access to positions of power within the tribe. (When the Western Band of Cherokee dropped their Q requirement to 1/64 a few years ago, in order to increase their political numbers, they became the butt of even more jokes from their old enemies, the Seminoles. Q: What do you get if you put 64 "Cherokees" in a room? A: One Full-Blood!) A few politically intimidated FR tribes have permitted the BIA to express, at least, or enforce, at most, their opinions regarding tribal citizenship, in other words, appropriating yet another sovereign function of the tribe. The Florida Seminoles are not among them. They maintain their own sovereign control in this core national matter.

❧

As the last decade of the twentieth century opened, a number of shifts and changes had taken place in the world outside of the tribe, most of which would have an impact on the conduct of life and business inside the tribe. In 1984, for example, the BIA and the secretary of the interior had agreed to recognize yet another tribe, this one literally on the doorstep of the Seminoles. This "new" FR tribe was the Poarch Band of Creek Indians, headquartered in Atmore, Alabama. Genetically and politically, it is possible to think of these people as sisters (English speakers would say "cousins") of the Seminoles and Miccosukees. Since Atmore and the tribal lands are in Escambia County, Alabama, very close to the West Florida border, a growing number of Poarch Creeks began to take up residence across the Florida line, mainly in Escambia County, Florida. At the time of this writing, the Poarch Band Tribal Council is seriously considering creating housing near Pensacola, Florida, for the more than five thousand Poarch Creek citizens who today reside there. They may or may not have spoken to the Florida Seminoles about this.

Eddie Tullis, who ultimately led his tribe for twenty-six years, and James had much in common, and they have had much in common with another powerful southeastern tribal leader, Philip Martin of the Mississippi Band of Choctaw Indians. Betty Mae Jumper, Philip Martin, Buffalo Tiger, and a representative of the Eastern Band of Cherokee Indians had been the founders of the United Southeastern Tribes, expanded in 1978 as the United South and Eastern Tribes, or USET, which was rapidly growing into one of the two most powerful consortia of FR tribes in the nation and the only one exclusively representing FR tribes east of the Mississippi. By 1990, James and the Seminoles already had gaming. They had, in fact, one casino each on three of the tribe's reservations (Hollywood, Tampa, Brighton, and a fourth, in Immokalee, was in negotiation). The Poarch Creeks had their first "bingo hall" as well. Philip Martin had a solid and expanding manufacturing base on the reservations. In 1990, Billy Cypress, successor to Buffalo Tiger, opened the first (and, thus far, only) Miccosukee gaming casino on the far western edge of Miami and Dade County, about thirty miles southwest of Hollywood.

Eddie Tullis wanted gaming for the Poarch Creeks and set about negotiating with the United States/Department of the Interior and his state for their agreement. Already several thousand of his tribal citizens were living across the Florida border, but he had no intention of attempting to move into "Seminole territory." (Such a view, of course, partially accepted a white man's imposition—a state boundary line, as a tribal boundary, even though such boundaries are not consistent with tribal territories, historically. Political necessity, however, is often the mother of invention.) The obstacle to his plans centered on the land that he proposed to use and its potential historical value to all Creeks. It was a portion of the land historically known as the Hickory Ground—an area of high cultural value to the Muscogee people of both Alabama and Georgia—and the Muscogee (Creek) Tribe of Oklahoma entered a brief with the Department of the Interior in opposition to the Alabama band's plans. The Poarch Creek Band's position was that archaeological research had gleaned from the area of contention all existing information, leaving it available for development.

After a battle that included a legal suit analogous to that of the Seminoles (see below), the Alabama band prevailed, and today the tribe has three gaming facilities, all in Alabama: the Creek Entertainment Center at Atmore, the Riverside Entertainment Center at Wetumpka, and the Tallapoosa Entertainment Center at Montgomery. This evolution of events has done nothing to lessen the long-standing animosity that exists between the largest FR Creek tribe in Oklahoma, the Muscogee (Creek) Nation of Oklahoma, and the only remaining FR Creek tribe in Alabama, the Poarch Band of Creek Indians. A simmering discontent, based upon the same feelings of dispossession felt by the SNO, usually leads the Oklahoma Nation to dispute or disavow any actions taken by the Alabama Creeks.

(Please recall that the terms "Nation," "nation," and "Tribe," or "tribe," are the same legal denominators of a sovereign entity, as has been mentioned before. In the case of the uppercase "N" or "T" the term also may be an element of the name of a political entity. An example would be the name, the "Seminole Tribe of Florida," that is the name of the political governmental entity, as separate from the Seminole people who form a sovereign tribe or nation and, as has been stated earlier, would continue to exist even if the political entity ceased to exist or changed its name.)

One leader who was not above attempting to enter Florida Seminole territory, however, was Jerry Haney of the Seminole Nation of Oklahoma. Many of the Oklahoma (removed) Seminoles still cling to their memories of their birth lands in the Southeast. Jerry, by nature a cautious leader, economically shy and very concerned about the possibility of antagonizing the U.S. government in any way, and not given to the boldness of a James Billie or the political sagacity of an Eddie Tullis or a Philip Martin, nevertheless was one of those who felt the strong draw of Florida as the ancestral home of the Oklahoma Seminoles and constantly was on the lookout for business opportunities that would permit his tribe to regain any foothold in the state. One such foothold offered itself in the form of outside backers for a proposed gaming casino complex in the West Florida Panhandle, relatively close to the tribal lands of the Poarch Creek Band.

James publicly encouraged Jerry. I knew that James did not want the Oklahoma Seminoles anywhere near Florida, as I realized that he privately saw them as traitors and interlopers—the proverbial "poor relations"—just as did so many of the rest of the Florida Seminoles. Further, in the guise of looking like a decisive leader, Jerry had announced his plans to James rather than first seeking permission of the Florida tribe. James nevertheless used each opportunity to encourage Jerry, and I finally—naively—asked why he would do something so duplicitous. It was a simple political ploy, he said laughingly. James felt quite confident that the Oklahoma Seminole Council, large and unwieldy and extremely conservative fiscally, would never vote to permit Jerry to dip into the tribe's ILCC award to support any part of such a plan, no matter how lucrative it might seem and how much outside help they could get—particularly since they had committed themselves to obtain approval of the U.S. secretary of the interior for use of the funds. Therefore, James knew that he could afford to look like Jerry's friend because it wasn't going to cost him and the Florida tribe anything in the final analysis. And, in fact, such was the case as the SNO council dithered and the backers backed away, and the project died a quiet death.

Indian Images and Sports Mascots

The subject of tribal territories brings up another subject that had begun to arise a decade earlier at least, but continued to play itself out on the stage of Indian Country and the non-Indian nation in this period, finally involving the tribe directly: that of the use of Indian mascots by non-Indian sports teams, generally, and the Florida Seminoles' controversial stance on the issue, specifically. It is a stance that has made the Florida Seminoles the target of much derision, both across Indian Country and the non-Indian nation ever since.

The subject had begun to arise to the level of national awareness in the 1960s as an element of the civil rights movement. It was the moment when, among other issues, African Americans arose to challenge the Little Black Sambo logo figure at Sambo's Restaurants nationally. The American Indian Movement (AIM) and the National Congress on American Indians (NCAI), the elder and only national consortium of Indians in the United States, began separate campaigns to eliminate negative stereotyping of Indians that focused on the media, especially movies, cartoons, and sports. Over the ensuing decade the issue of stereotyping in sports, among fans and with sports mascots, gained the most attention.

Supporters of the images argue that such elements as drumming tom-toms, war paint on the faces of fans, tomahawk chops, and team mascots in varying degrees of Indian caricature, are meant to highlight the bravery, courage, and fighting skills of Indians rather than any derogatory aspects of Indian life. And, indeed, it is sometimes difficult to judge the intentions of individuals and groups from the outside. Sometimes. Opponents of the images aver that such uses demean Indians and their traditions and rituals. In 2005, after more than a quarter of a century of the ongoing fight, Clyde Bellecourt, AIM director, explained: "It's the behavior that accompanies all of this that's offensive. The rubber tomahawks, the chicken feather headdresses, people wearing war paint and making these ridiculous war whoops with a tomahawk in one hand and a beer in the other—all of these have significant meaning for us. And the psychological impact it has, especially on our youth, is devastating."[6]

The University of Oklahoma—in a state where more than three-dozen FR tribes still reside—dropped its mascot, "Little Red," in 1972, but it would be another generation before the issue would become really heated. In Florida, the single focus of growing national Indian activism was the "Seminoles"—the successful and highly visible football team of Florida State University (FSU) in Tallahassee. The Florida Seminoles (the real Indians) were not opposed to FSU's use of the tribal name, at least not officially; nor was the Florida Seminole Tribe politically involved in the pan-Indian antimascot movement.

In 1958 school leaders had bowed to mounting pressures from state citizens and the legislators and first sanctioned an annual football contest between the two state universities: Florida State University at Tallahassee and The University of Florida at Gainesville ("The 'Gators"). Representatives of the teams approached the Seminoles to obtain an authentic dugout canoe that would serve as the trophy for the winners. This would be the extent of Seminole Indian involvement in a white man's sports process for a few years to come.

The history of FSU and their Indian image dates to that same year, a moment when the political Seminole Tribe of Florida was only just coming into existence and tribal leaders were not interested in becoming politically engaged at any level beyond the territories inhabited by the Seminoles themselves. FSU adopted two images for their sports programs, those of "Sammy Seminole" and "Chief Fullabull." Neither, as might be inferred from the names, evidenced any regard for the actual Indians living in the southern end of the state. Neither was adopted pursuant to any discussion with the actual Indians either. Not until fourteen years later, in 1972, did tribal representatives, during the early years of Howard Tommie's tenure and at a time of growing Seminole awareness of Indian Country attitudes, attend a basketball game in Tallahassee and see for themselves the offensive nature of the images. At the urging of the tribe, both images were retired that year.[7]

In 1978, FSU hired a new football coach, Bobby Bowden, who accepted an idea put forward by an FSU alumnus and booster club member, Bill Durham. Henceforth, the opening of each home game would be heralded by the galloping arrival on field of an individual dressed (very loosely) as the Seminole war leader Osceola (ca. 1804–1838), who would be riding an Appaloosa horse called Renegade and who would plant a flaming spear in midfield. The image, much more indicative of respect than had been the earlier ignominious images, caught the hearts and egos of FSU fans, and the image has remained, through at least two evolutions in appearance.

The first evolution took place in the mid-1980s, while I was the senior historian at the state's Museum of Florida History in Tallahassee, and before I had any direct connection to the tribe. Lane Green, then director of the Tallahassee Junior Museum and an ardent FSU booster, approached me about providing research that could assist FSU in making the clothing and overall image of "Osceola" and "Renegade" more consistent with historical reality. I provided historical images and citations and also stated my problems with the characterization, based on the facts that Osceola had neither horse nor lance during the Second Seminole War and the fact that the rider was a white student and not actually an Indian, but FSU was already wedded emotionally to those elements of the image and was not going to be dissuaded from using them.

Not long after that time, I found out much later, James directed Jim Shore to consult with outside counsel concerning the legal possibility of trademarking or obtaining other proprietary control of the name "Seminole." Jim was told that it could not be done.[8] And there, he let the matter rest, permanently. Publicly, however, Jim has been complimentary of FSU. Nevertheless, he transparently mitigated his support of the school with the comments: "And then there's the university's impact in Tallahassee. Hundreds of Florida government officials are [FSU] graduates and supporters. We [the Tribe] deal with these people every day."[9]

During this same period, the FSU marching band also began the tradition of playing the repetitive musical phrase that has become FSU's "war chant" and is always accompanied by the arm-waving motion known as the "tomahawk chop." FSU officials assert today, as both chant and chop continue, that the chop is "a term we did not choose and officially do not use."[10] Unfortunately, it is a term that the school does not attempt to stop either.[11] The chant, moreover, is recognized as sounding "more like American Indians in western movies." Which is to say, more accurately, that it sounds like white men trying to sound like Indians on the warpath in western movies, where Indians were always the villains.

The argument rumbled on across the non-Indian nation. In the mid-1990s, pro-Indian activists sued the Washington Redskins for trademark infringement, but the suit was finally unproductive. In Tennessee, early in the new century, the state's Human Rights Commission received a petition on the issue from the state's unfunded Commission on Indian Affairs, but neither action carried any political or legal weight. Some national and collegiate teams did, however, recognize the negativity of their images and names were changed.

In Florida the controversy reached a head in 1993 when Oklahoma part-Seminole Mike Haney, one of the more strident Indian activists, gave a public talk at FSU. It took place on the evening of 8 February 1993, in the cramped quarters of the B. K. Roberts Hall of the FSU Law School. I had flown up with James and tribal citizen Steven Bowers. James had a point that he wanted to get across, but not to FSU officials or the non-Indian public; rather, he wanted Mike Haney to hear his words, and as usual, James had choreographed the process.

Above and far beyond the heat in the body-filled room and the smell that adrenaline creates, there was virtual electricity in the air of the small auditorium. Mike Haney billed himself as "Second Chief of the Newcomer Band of the Seminole Nation in Oklahoma, and Chairperson of the National Coalition Against Racism in Sports and Media." The event was sponsored by the National Lawyers' Guild. Despite the fact that the national controversy was at its zenith at this moment, and despite Mike's credentials, however, he was the wrong person to bring the fight to Florida. His touted Seminole attachment had cachet for his non-Indian audience, but not for the Florida Seminoles.

First and foremost, he was not regarded by Florida Indians as one of their own despite a modicum of Florida Seminole ancestry. In other words, he was not on his own territory. Further, and insultingly, he had not asked permission of chairmen James Billie or Billy Cypress to come onto their tribes' territories. According to time-honored tradition, if an Indian of one tribe wanted to do so much as fish in a stream running through the territory of another tribe, courtesy demanded that he ask permission of the other tribe before doing so. Many of the Florida Seminoles were very annoyed with Mike Haney for failing to follow the prescribed protocol. In their eyes, his actions were transparently self-serving. He was courting the press in a blatant gambit to position himself among the leaders of the national Indian antimascot movement.

That's the way James Billie saw it. But James also knew that his own attitude and the attitudes of a majority (albeit not all) of Seminole Tribe of Florida citizens were supportive of FSU. This was the moment when I would finally understand just how supportive, and why.

James's way, when controversy reigned and negative publicity might ensue, was to choose a champion—a speaker for the nation—and send that person out to the fray while he (James) remained behind the scenes, anonymously if possible, manipulating the process, and commanding the action. In this he was following time-honored tradition. This was exactly the way in which his ancestors had functioned for hundreds, perhaps thousands, of years. In this instance, the speaker sent out publicly to engage Mike Haney was Steven Bowers (Clan X, b. 1949). Steven, who had served in a succession of diplomatic roles for the tribe—as a legislative lobbyist in Tallahassee, and as a tribal liaison with Broward County and Fort Lauderdale municipal governments—spoke English with a greater degree of fluency than many tribal citizens and had the ability to be a cogent advocate, when he chose to be.

In a public setting marked by high emotions and publicity, Steven made the critical argument that Mike had no right to be agitating in Florida, on territory other than his own. But non-Indian emotions ran too high at the moment, and Mike—either unaware of or uninterested in tradition—was able to deflect tribal considerations as students and locals rose to shout out their support for FSU, waving everything from notebooks to boxer shorts splashed with their pseudo-Indian logo. Steven also made the point that the tribe had already, a generation ago, given FSU permission to use their name, and they had no intention of withdrawing that permission now. Few people in the room knew James Billie by sight, so he and I were able to stand in the back of the crowded hall with our backs against the wall, literally and figuratively, and survey the action. After thirty minutes or so of shouted invective—indicative far more of emotion than of reason—the meeting broke up with intransigents on each side still intransigent.

James and I moved out with the crowd and made our way to the speakers' exit at the back of the stage. James, Mike, Steven, and a couple of FSU officials assembled for a few quiet words, mostly mollifying. FSU, it appeared, had never taken the controversy seriously. In this attitude, they took their cue from the Seminole Tribe. I was annoyed and agreed with Mike and the pan-Indian movement that it was time to require sports teams to take a good look at the derogatory attitudes at the basis of their Indian imagings. James was not moved by my commitment to what I saw as social justice. He was adamant. Finally, he got right up in my face and half shouted, "Hell, honey, THEY WIN! Now, when they start losing, I'll take the damn name back!" It was his own cultural brand of irrefutable logic, and I could only back down. It was the logic of a warrior mentality, and it appeared to be acceptable to most of the tribal citizens. They had even painted the gymnasium on the Hollywood Res in garnet and gold, FSU's colors. Their opinion was quite clearly expressed.

Mike Osceola continued his fight in other places. I continued to explain my opposition to the use of Indian mascots whenever James was willing to listen. At one point I recommended to James that he require FSU to prove their positive intentions to the tribe in the most tangible manner. If, I said, FSU really cared about the Seminoles, they could agree to give the tribe each year a mere 1 percent of their annual gross revenues from all of their "Seminole" branded products. Even at this time, that would have amounted to significant revenues. James was not interested in the idea.

Several years later I discussed the matter with the tribe's general counsel, Jim Shore. It was then that he told me that, in the not-too-distant past, he had discussed with white attorneys the tribe's legal standing for claiming proprietary right to the name "Seminole." He was advised at the time, he said, that the tribe had no legal standing to make or enforce such a claim. I argued that the response he had received was based on old, negative, social attitudes toward Indians and that, in the interim between his original question and now, social attitudes had changed. The tribe was much more likely to obtain a sympathetic hearing on this issue, at least. Certainly, history and documentation were on their side. Jim was uninterested. He was an extremely cautious man—one of the facts that would be at the heart of James's growing dissatisfaction with Jim over the coming years.

Neither, however, was James interested in taking on FSU over the use of the Seminoles' name. He certainly had not shied away from big fights with non-Indians before. Although he never specifically said so, I often wondered if his reticence might be in any way connected to the subject of the tribal-state agreement over tax-free tobacco sales. Perhaps at that time, while a sizeable but declining portion of the tribe's annual gross revenues (relative to rapidly increasing gaming revenues) still was coming from tobacco sales, he was reticent to initiate any fight that might provoke the state legislature to retaliate by reviewing and changing the tribe's lucrative tobacco sales agreement.

Later that same year I returned to Tallahassee with James, and with Peter Gallagher of the *Seminole Tribune,* to enjoy a private dinner with Wilma Mankiller (1945–2010), former principal chief of the Western Band of Cherokee Indians, who had come to Florida as an invited guest speaker at FSU. Again, neither Chief Mankiller nor FSU had consulted with the Florida Seminoles concerning the presence of another tribal representative. At a private dinner hosted by James, which was very cordial but politically formal, James announced that I would be remaining in Tallahassee to attend Chief Mankiller's presentation the next day. The point was not lost on the politically savvy chief. She understood that the Seminoles gave up none of their prerogatives to her or her tribe, and that the tribal chairman would be receiving a personal report on everything said by the "out of town" guest.

At her presentation the next day, to a packed-hall audience, Chief Mankiller responded to press questions regarding the FSU mascot issue with great diplomacy by saying that it was a local issue and the answer should be local as well. The press in Florida would have to look to the Florida Seminoles for responses. She was more interested, she said, in nationwide stereotypes. Indeed, the chief recently had signed a "Petition and Proclamation of the 1843–1993 International Indian Council," asking media mogul Ted Turner and his Atlanta Braves sports team to cease their use of the name and abandon their FSU-style tomahawk chop. Further, Chief Mankiller publicly disavowed non-Indian antagonisms to Indians' casino gaming as hypocritical; said that pseudo-Indian wannabes were damaging to Indians; and reminded listeners concerning sports mascots that "no other people would put up with such nonsense." Thus she made her point of view eminently clear and, at the same time, understood the political impropriety of restating it in the Florida case.

In 2001 the U.S. Commission on Human Rights issued a strong statement condemning the practice of using Indian images in sports, causing the National

Collegiate Athletic Association (NCAA) to revisit the controversy and distribute a "self-evaluation" in 2005, to help teams examine their use of potentially offensive imagery. When the NCAA also banned the participation of teams with Indian mascots in postseason games and issued a list of sports teams that it said used "hostile or abusive imagery" that included FSU, the university fought back and won an exemption. Then-FSU-president T. K. Wetherell had threatened to sue the NCAA, calling their characterization of FSU's relationship with the tribe "outrageous and insulting."[12] According to Bernard Franklin, senior vice president of NCAA, "The staff review committee noted the unique relationship between the university and the Seminole Tribe of Florida as a significant factor. The decision of a namesake sovereign tribe, regarding when and how its name and imagery can be used, must be respected even when others may not agree."[13]

James personally, and the tribe generally, became the target of a great deal of invective, in print and in person, both from other tribes and Indians and from non-Indian supporters of Indian causes. Even within the tribe itself, individual citizens expressed strong contradictory opinions, but the council would not revisit the issue. Today, the Hollywood gym still is painted garnet and gold. Many Seminole automobiles sport FSU bumper stickers. Anything that says "Seminole" has become a point of pride for tribal citizens, and if they have to enjoy a reflected pride from non-Indian football and basketball teams, then they are glad to have it.

In 2002 the FSU booster club moved forward with a plan to commission a larger-than-life-sized sculpture of their emblematic Seminole Indian, to be installed behind Doak Campbell Stadium football field on campus, and I was once again invited to consult regarding the accuracy of the image. The result was a bronze replica of the Seminole warrior and his spear and horse, with a specially rigged spear that could be set alight to herald the playing of each home game. The statue was dedicated, with fanfare and the participation of tribal representatives, on 10 October 2003. Once again I had reiterated the historical facts, and the boosters chose to remove the specific characterization of Osceola from the equation and make the image a more symbolic one, representing the honor, courage, and fighting spirit of the Seminole Indians generally. They would not, however, abandon the spear or the horse.

In 2005, FSU representatives met with the Tribal Council, asking the tribe to formally reconfirm its support for the university's use of Osceola and the "Seminole" mascot. By council resolution, the tribe agreed. FSU's President Wetherell flew down to meet with the council. At the council meeting on Friday, 17 June, the council passed a resolution in support of FSU's use of the name. "The Tribe's move comes as the NCAA completes a study on the issue of American Indians names by their member institutions."[14]

Hollywood council representative Max Osceola Jr., often the willing apologist for the tribe, told reporters that he considered it "an honor" to be associated with the university.[15] The Seminole Nation of Oklahoma's principal chief, Ken Chambers, publicly issued a statement of his tribe's support as well, thereby reversing earlier public statements from the SNO. In July 2005, the SNO Council voted overwhelmingly not to oppose the use of Indian names and mascots by college sports teams. SNO, frequently more amenable to blandishments than the Florida Seminoles, had been courted by FSU, through invitations to public events in Florida and scholarship offers to SNO students. In 2006, according to the organization American Indian Cultural Support, there remained at least 2,498 kindergarten, elementary, middle, and high schools still using Indian mascots nationwide, in addition to collegiate teams.

The Tribe's Own Museum

As a continuing commitment to the enlargement of his Big Cypress Res home, James, with the rubber stamp of the council, began work on two major undertakings early in the 1990s. One was the creation of a full-scale museum for the tribe, to be known as "Ah-Tah-Thi-Ki," a Miccosukee phrase meaning a place to learn: "If you don't know something, you go there to find out." The other was the creation of a canned hunting adventure that soon changed course and became an ecotour visitor attraction known as the Kissimmee Billie Swamp Safari. As with everything else that James and the tribe undertook, each was a unique and fascinating story in its own right.

The museum idea grew from a conception presented to James in 1989 by one of the many individuals, a young woman, whom he had hired to develop personal projects for him.[16] Such people came and went over the years—sometimes actually doing projects that were useful to the tribe and, at other times, simply siphoning off monies for themselves until James or one of the council reps, or the people themselves, balked and he let them slip away as quietly as he had permitted them to arrive. The pattern was so well established that the people had become very uneasy about anyone who appeared "out of nowhere," as it were, and worked directly for James.

If the person was a female, she was doubly suspicious because of the personal influence that she might wield (even though any such influence was always short-lived.) In some ways, my work could have fallen into this stereotype, and by the time I arrived in BC, only my determined scrupulousness kept me from being consigned to the same category. Sometimes local concerns were well founded and sometimes they were not, however. One BC resident, a man whom I had known for about a year at that point, asked me, out of a clear, blue sky one day, if I was having an affair with James. By this time, James's reputation with women had been long established. I responded, "What on earth would make you think that?" He said that both James and I wore black much of the time, and that was his only basis for wondering. I was reminded, yet again, what a fishbowl life in BC was.

By 1992 the idea for a museum of tribal history, to be open to the non-Indian public, had been permitted to reach the architectural planning stage. The council had, by resolution, created a museum board and had placed direction of the board in the hands of Billy L. Cypress. At the moment, Billy was one of two prominent men of the same name whose names confused outsiders (a third man of the same name having passed away only recently) and so, to distinguish them, they were referred to as "Museum Billy" and "Trail Billy," or "*nokósi(t)*" (Bear Clan) Billy" and "*tahkósaî(t)*" (Mole Clan) Billy." Tahkósaî(t) Billy was, and is, of course, the political leader of the Miccosukee Tribe.

Museum, or Bear Clan, Billy (1942–2004), was a Seminole who had earned a master of arts degree in education, had attained the rank of major in the U.S. Army Reserve, and had worked in Washington, DC, with the BIA for some years before returning to his tribe in Florida. He was an interesting individual who experienced flashes of brilliance interspersed with long periods of anxieties and misunderstandings. His wife, Carol Frank Cypress (Panther Clan, b. 1945), was a strong and intelligent woman who held Billy in her thrall, to his loving chagrin.

Billy was far more interested in publicity and public appearances and travel than in the day-to-day management of the museum, but he was determined to see the project to fruition, even though it was constantly over budget and behind schedule. The council was patient with his constant dithering and extremely lenient about cost overruns. In 1997 the council would finally abolish the museum authority and assert direct control, on the view that Billy had become entirely too independent in his outlook.[17] But he retained his nominal position as executive director, while a museum director and a staff managed the actual day-to-day operations of the museum in BC and the "museum" (preview center) on the Hollywood Res, now a part of the Hard Rock complex.

The original plan for the museum was to create a complex of ten buildings that was to take five years to construct and was to cost the tribe $10 million. When Billie took on the project, an architectural firm had already drawn plans and a site had been chosen. James decreed as the site for the multibuilding complex a sixty-acre cypress dome at the intersection of Snake Road (the main road through BC) and West Boundary Road, a site that had been his personal camp for many years. A very short distance behind this site James had built his personal residence. Actually, it was his second structure, the first having fallen down in midconstruction as a result of his having used no plans. James learned quickly, however, and the second held up. Here was the two-story house where Lesley went to work as nanny for James and Bobbie Lou. Here was the kitchen where James, barefooted, made morning coffee and we held our best conversations. Here was the yard where supplicants lined up each day to ask for loans. His ultimate plan was to use the house as a bed and breakfast for visitors and to build yet another residence behind the B&B for himself and his family. Other projects and considerations intervened constantly, however, and the B&B plan never came to fruition. Furthermore, the BC community was never happy with the idea of welcoming outsiders to the Res.

In no instance did there appear to be any differentiation between personal and tribal projects in terms of costs, but the tribe took this process in stride as the years went by and the projects became bigger, and council and board reps created their own personal/tribal projects. (More on this in chapters 9 and 10.) I was standing one bright day in BC near the landing strip with a Seminole friend, watching the tribal jet make its landing approach. "Does the cost of James's projects bother you?" I asked, referring to the constant intersection of tribal funds and personal rewards. She thought for a moment. "Oh, well," she said finally, "he does a lot for us, so I guess it's fair for him to do some things for himself." That was pretty much the standard—and traditional—view: reciprocity and equilibrium. That view could vary widely with the moment, however, as we shall see in the case of the Swamp Safari project and in the case of projects funded by James's successors for themselves.

The museum finally opened the doors of its first building in 1997, about five years later than planned, and severely over cost projections. Only one building was up—the public exhibition facility—and it had cost twice the original estimate, $2 million rather than $1 million. No artifact storage had been created and the entire interpretive emphasis was on only the last century and a half of Seminole history in Florida. But the exhibits were beautiful, and the opening ceremony was attended not only by Seminoles from all the reservations but also by representatives from Tallahassee to the Smithsonian Institution. Billy Cypress saw quite clearly that the museum existed with a dual mission: first and foremost was its commitment to encapsulate the history of the Seminole people for the Seminoles themselves and, secondarily, to make that history available to non-Indians.

He and the staff had obtained a number of the interpretive artifacts on loan from other institutions, but they also set about the process of obtaining their own artifacts for the exhibits, by buying them on the open art market. Unfortunately, this was and remains an extremely costly process. The irony of this process was not lost on Billy or the council, as they were forced to pay public art-market prices for clothing, beadwork pieces, and images of the Seminoles that had been obtained from them historically—some fairly, some not—in the first place. A unique feature of the interpretation was a diorama featuring life-sized mannequins wearing traditional clothing from the last century. The figures, ultimately forty-eight in all and made from life castings of living tribal citizens, present an immediacy unusual in any museum. A multiscreen introductory film, a $300,000 project in itself, touts the Seminole connection to gaming but also offers visitors an overview of modern Seminole life.

All legitimate museums depend partially on revenues from visitation to make up a portion of their annual budgets, but no museum, no matter how large or how high its visibility, can operate solely on such income. Other tribes, from the Tunica-Biloxi to the Eastern Cherokee to the Mashantucket Pequots have realized this, each asserting not only its pride in its own heritage but also its independence in the process. In the case of the Seminoles, James's philosophy was that the tribe should operate as autonomously as possible in every instance. He was fiercely independent in his outlook and saw the warrior spirit as the heart of Seminole survival. The tribe would support the museum, regardless of visitor income.

Down the road about four miles from the museum site was the 2,000 fenced acres of the Kissimmee Billie Swamp Safari, with its first buildings also in construction by 1992. Both of these enterprises were hampered by the same reality: BC was an isolated spot, seventy miles equidistant from either Florida coast, with no hotels or gas stations (except one small station with very irregular hours) and only a single restaurant, barely completed, at the safari. This detriment might also be turned into an advantage, however, given the number of visitors to South Florida annually, and the lure of Indians, nationally and internationally. As Billy Cypress said later, "People think we're in the middle of nowhere, but it all depends on how you look at it. We're in the middle of everything."[18]

At this writing, the museum has constructed four buildings and ribbons of walkways take visitors into the heart of a cypress dome where Seminole guides explain survival in the Everglades. School students from seven surrounding Florida counties go for field trips and eat their brown-bag lunches under chikî(t)s in the open-air world of the Seminoles. Visitors from all over Europe, especially Germans who are so attracted to American Indian history, find their way to this seemingly isolated spot. Above all, however, Seminole adults and children from the now-six reservations build greater pride in their heritage through museum programs created just for them.

A Controversial Visitor Attraction for BC

As the story—accepted as apocryphal even by the Seminoles—goes, during the United States' Wars of Removal in the first half of the nineteenth century, white soldiers were seeking a Seminole encampment when a young Seminole maiden sacrificed herself to protect her people. She ran out in front of the white men's horses and called out in her broken English, "Kiss I Me! Kiss I Me!" Her fate was sealed, but her people survived. We have documentary proof, of course, that the etymology of the word today used as the name of a central Florida town, "Kissimmee" (pronounced Kis SIM me), whose modern claim to fame is inextricably bound to a certain central Florida mouse, is actually a sixteenth-century Florida Indian word, its earliest meaning, however, unclear. A Spanish Roman Catholic missionary, a *doctrinero* (teacher of doctrine) at a mission in *Jizime,* was presumed killed in the revolt of the Mayaca-Jororo missions in 1697, near the location of the modern town.[19]

History notwithstanding, the story of the Seminole maiden was one of the genre that has most attracted the emotions of outsiders over the century and a half since the events of the Wars of Removal. James, constantly on the lookout to raise the status of the isolated BC Res to that of the capital of his kingdom, there decreed the creation of an enterprise based upon the single largest resource of the area: animals and woods. The original idea was to create what is known as a "canned hunt." He had seen one in Texas and, a hunter himself, liked the idea immediately.

The nexus of the Texas hunt and the chairman of the Seminole Tribe was a former state Game and Fresh Water Fish Commission (now, Florida Fish and Wildlife Conservation Commission) wildlife botanist named Jimmy McDaniel. James and Jimmy had gotten to know each other during James's panther trials, introduced by one of James's most nefarious connections, Robb Tiller, of whom much more later. Jimmy, who considered himself to have Creek Indian heritage, had supported James with favorable testimony that appeared to incorporate both the credibility of a state professional and the draw of esoteric Indian lore. The two men, with birth dates ten days and ten years apart (Jimmy, the elder), connected quickly. When James encountered anyone with whom he experienced a strong connection, he generally found ways to draw them close to him and keep them available for consultations and projects. Any negative characteristics that the person incorporated were ignored as long as they had even a single characteristic that might be valuable in some particular—even if as yet unknown—circumstance.

In this case the concept of creating a hunting business on the remote BC Res seemed a good one to James, but as word leaked out, non-Indian public sentiment was against such an enterprise. The salient elements of a canned hunt are several: the area of the hunt is finite, that is, enclosed by fencing, in this instance a 2,000-acre parcel of BC woods. Then the animals are fed regularly and encouraged to lose much of their natural fear of human contact so that when the hunters are taken into the area and placed on specific stands and platforms, they

are assured of seeing and having easy opportunities to kill animals. In this instance James and Jimmy decided to incorporate exotic animals, rather than only
indigenous varieties, as an added attraction. Animal rights activists and groups
from Dade (Miami) and Broward (Fort Lauderdale) counties arose in public
indignation at the plan, and James was forced to reconsider.

Rather than abandon the hunt plan concept completely, however, James erected
a screen. He quietly proceeded with the creation of the hunting area, but in an
even more isolated portion of the Res. Meanwhile, and more publicly, he began
the creation of the Kissimmee Billie Swamp Safari, which would be publicized
as an eco-attraction and would image the tribe as animal friendly guardians of
the Everglades. Even this idea was not without its obstacles, however, and they
emanated mostly from inside the tribe and, specifically, from the BC Res community.

When I first went to work for the tribe, it was on the BC Res where James
had invited me to live and teach. My home was in the guest lodge, a two-story,
four-bedroom house with all the "mod cons" in the middle of the safari site
and alongside a gopher-tortoise relocation area that was a cooperative project
of the tribe and the state. When I arrived, in the fall of 1992, a restaurant—
the Swamp Water Café—had been substantially completed and a "gift shop"—
a visitor orientation chickee—was just in the discussion stages of construction. A professionally carved sign had been installed out on the roadway across
from the entrance, about five hundred yards from the lodge. Each night for the
first several months of my residence there, we awoke to find the wooden sign
destroyed—peppered by shotgun blasts from community residents who were
determined to stop the construction of any business that would bring non-
Indians onto their Res. Further, some BC residents resented the name of the
enterprise as appearing to be a personal one rather than totally "theirs" (that is,
a tribal enterprise). James bowed to popular sentiment and began to refer to the
attraction simply as the "Swamp Safari," omitting the name "Billie" that some
felt bound the business to James personally.

In addition to the conceptual arguments between James and the community, there were administrative obstacles to be overcome as well. In 1992 and
'93, Dave and Debbie Holloway were living in the lodge also, and Dave was in
charge of the safari project. Interestingly, James had hired a couple who did not
really like Indians and who made that plain in words and actions, but Dave was
a Texan and purported to know animals and the sources for purchase of the ex-
otics that, James believed, would most attract visitors. The pairing of the Indians and the Holloways was, to put it diplomatically, an infelicitous one.

David antagonized employees and community residents alike. The more antagonistic he became, the more retribution they exacted. Padlocks were regularly cut, gasoline tanks emptied into local trucks, and both David and Debbie

became more and more unwelcome in the community. Despite periodic trips to Texas, ostensibly to purchase more elands, ostriches, and exotic cattle and deer, few new animals appeared on the safari grounds, and of those that did, the majority were either allowed to escape the grounds because of gates "accidentally" left open or padlocks cut or, it was assumed, disappeared as a result of being eaten by Florida panthers or alligators.

Tourists did slowly begin to seek out the safari, lured by its location, but the visitor tour element was functioning only by a hit-and-miss process. Through contacts made available to James by Robb Tiller, cast-off Chinese army jeeps were purchased and used to transport visitors over a mile-long course through the saw palmetto heads and hardwood hammocks and across the canals and water-filled trails of the safari property (winter is dry in South Florida and summer is very wet). Unfortunately, the jeeps had so many mechanical problems that they rarely made complete trips without overheating or completely breaking down. I recall one such tour with international VIPs, where the radiator exploded and spewed boiling water, narrowly missing the guests, and David had to get out into the knee-high water on the trail and use one of his expensive new boots to refill the radiator and, finally, get us back to base. The jeeps quickly ceased to be used and became stationary parts of the scenery. James finally tired of the Holloways and the controversies they engendered and left them to defend themselves in the community. James's way was not to confront but, rather, to visibly withdraw his support and protection from individuals who had earned his anger or outlived their usefulness. Dave and Debbie soon found a reason to leave the Res and Florida. James replaced them with Roy Diamond, by this time ex-husband of his administrative assistant, Pat Diamond.

Roy managed the attraction in a much more businesslike manner, but he had problems as well—both administratively and personally. A significant administrative obstacle had been, and continued to be, securing reliable personnel; indeed, securing *any* personnel. A few BC citizens were willing to work at the safari, but they were not always interested in punctuality or reliability. Moreover, the traditional attitude that Indian property was held in common made it difficult to convince tribal employees that equipment and other resources were not available for personal use.

Families of Mexican migrant workers from Montura Estates, a small, lower-income, housing development about twenty-five miles west by northwest of BC, became an alternative source of employees. Unfortunately, however, the low pay, the cost of daily travel, and personal attitudes made employment at the safari a revolving door. Roy's personal life, also undergoing stressful changes at the moment, together with the problem of finding and keeping employees, kept the complex in a state of constant anxiety.

James moved Roy out and sent Jimmy McDaniel (who had been sleeping on James's sofa, cooking for him and, generally, getting underfoot) to take over operations. Jimmy's focus, other than cooking (at which he was quite good), was the Hunting Adventures, and a number of complaints began to be lodged with James that the two enterprises were being permitted to overlap in far too public a manner. When an overly enthusiastic novice hunter brought a loaded shotgun into the Swamp Water Café and sat down with it across his lap, carelessly pointed right at me, I got into the fray also. The upshot was that James bought a trailer and had it placed inside the hunting area and moved Jimmy there. Jimmy hired his own son, Jamie, whose abrasive manner made his tenure short, and the safari management passed into the hands of another of James's old acquaintances, Tom Taylor.

Jimmy would remain in tribal employ for several more years, finally returning to his home and wife outside of Tallahassee in 2001, when James was suspended from office. Jimmy had delighted in a relationship with James that he saw as closer than did James. As James's interest in the South American world of indigenous peoples grew over this period (he was sure that, somewhere, he would encounter people whose language he would be able to understand), Jimmy delighted in setting up hunting trips to exotic locations.

When James began to tire of this particular sport, he and Jimmy began a new enterprise, based on the Hunting Adventures. This was the production of meat products, made from those animals shot by the hunters or culled from tribal herds, especially an ultimately moderately successful product, Chief's Jerky, and the subsidizing of a more successful seasoning product called Everglades Seasoning, based on the formula created by a neighbor of the BC Res, Boe Davis, who also was hired to oversee mass production and marketing of the product. The meat plant required the construction of a slaughterhouse on the hunting property that, after a couple of failed attempts to obtain FDA approval, was finally opened in 1995. The processing plant lost money in its early years but finally found its niche in processing beef for foreign and domestic markets.[20] The tribe has had some success with the seasoning product and continues to sell the item from its Web site today. The council has never shied away from supporting any enterprise that shows promise.

Tom Taylor and his wife quickly became the next subject of controversy in BC and across the tribe. James had encountered Tom almost twenty years earlier, and the two had liked each other, even though the conditions of their meeting were strange, to say the least. It had taken place while James was running Okalee Village on the Hollywood Res in the earliest days of his administrative experiences with the tribe. The tribe staged a public event for which nontribal groups were invited to set up tables on the grounds of Okalee to sell products or distribute information about their organizations. An application form was required, and somehow James managed not to be put off by the fact that Tom wanted to set up a table representing a South Florida KKK group. (An even larger irony in this situation is the fact that many such groups, whose amalgamation is based on bigotry and hatred, specifically exclude American Indians from their anger. Indians represent to them a warrior spirit, a degree of male bravery, and a commitment to personal freedom from authority that have little to do with the larger realities of Indian life but much to do with the unrealities of the lives of bigots. After the Swamp Safari opened, BC became a mecca for many such thinkers, and I had the opportunity to view them, firsthand. Their worlds were among the most convoluted I have ever witnessed.)

Although James had managed to ignore Tom's past association, there were others in the tribe who had not forgotten, and they let James know that, once again, he had made an unacceptable choice. The dissatisfaction was not helped by the fact that Tom also had worked as a prison guard for some of the intervening years since meeting James, and although he was kind and seemed easy going to people whom he liked personally, he was far less easygoing with persons whom he did not like and, all too frequently, that included community residents. James asked me to interview Tom, very quietly, and visit him in his home near St. Augustine to discover whether his attitudes still were overtly supportive of bigoted causes. I was undecided, and James was persuaded by local sentiment. Yet another director of the safari project passed into history.

The next director was the charm. Ed Woods appeared on the BC Res as the (at that time) life partner of a tribal citizen with whom he had a tumultuous relationship. That aspect of his life aside, once again James encountered an individual with whom he had military experience in common, and they formed a working bond. Ed was a former member of the U.S. Marine Corps who had been a part of the force surrounding the palace of Panamanian president Manuel Noriega. Interestingly enough, Ed is also an avid collector of Florida Indian projectile points, most of which he collects from Florida river bottoms, and about which he is extremely knowledgeable, and he works very well with students and other groups of visitors.

Subsequent to his hiring as director, Ed worked in almost all aspects of the operation of the safari and learned the process of ecotourism from the ground up. His personal involvement with tribal citizens that permitted him to be accepted by the BC community, a degree of Indian heritage that he also appears to embody, a fair if strident personality, and his administrative abilities have created for him a degree of success in his work that his predecessors could not achieve. His ability to get along with James certainly was a central element. His management of the safari would also at times include control of the Hunting Adventures and a small RV and camping ground on the BC Res. A moment would arrive when Ed would be called upon by the council to perform a specific and unpleasant task that would assure his survival for some years after the fall of James and make him the only James-appointee who would be able to survive the "purge." We shall discuss this later, in its own time.

In 1996 the Swamp Safari also was a money-losing operation ($2.2 million, together with the Hunting Adventures) and tribal authorities decided to move its accounting procedures to zero-based budgeting, thereby permitting past losses to be ignored in favor of only annual accounting. Today the safari supports itself through a steady if moderate visitation.

More Monuments

James's desire to diversify the economic base of the tribe was determined if not always productive. He had good instincts, but his process, based as it was on personal initiative rather than professional qualifications, always made success uncertain. One positive idea that did not quite pan out was the Brighton Turtle Farm project. This idea was a successor to the Brighton Catfish Farm project that had been tried in the 1970s and failed for lack of solid management. The five-hundred-acre Turtle Farm failed, quietly, ostensibly for the same reason. The project lost $289,597 in 1996 and almost twice as much in 1997.[21] Brighton residents complained that the manager was not being held sufficiently accountable for tribal funds, but James would not force the issue.

Tribal citizen Virgil Benny Motlow (Panther Clan, b. 1959) obtained a loan from the council to open a rope manufactory on the Immokalee Res that began with assertions of meticulous care and high-quality materials, but the business lost more than $150,000 in the first half of the fiscal year 1996–97.

One of the tribe's success stories was their ownership of Sheraton Four Points Tampa East Hotel, assessed at $9.25 million, and located on the Tampa Res. This was a particularly lucrative venture for the tribe and overlooked the entrance to the Tampa casino until James's removal and the replacement of everything on the Tampa Res by the Hard Rock hotel/casino complex. A ninety-six-room Days Inn motel, restaurant, and marina on Bahia Beach, on eastern Tampa Bay, a far less successful venture, was acquired by the tribe in March of 1996, for $2.15 million, and the tribe had plans to spend another $4 million to renovate the property. Later information acquired from the tribe's controversial administrator, Tim Cox, asserts that the Bahia purchase was promulgated by Jim Shore and a contract counsel, Eric Dorsky, and that both the purchase price and the tribe's rehab investment were far higher than the public information indicated.[22]

Two agricultural enterprises fared better for the tribe, although neither project was without its rocky beginnings. Seminole Brand Farms on the BC Res produced peppers, cucumbers, and squash. The nearby citrus groves featured lemons and grapefruit. The citrus groves, run by a tribal citizen, were still losing significant amounts of money in fiscal year 1996–97, but the tribe never withdrew its support, and the citrus groves in Brighton and BC continued as an integral part of the tribe's economy.

In the case of the produce farm, poor management was the original problem. Roy Pippin, a white man hired by James, was paid a $1 million management fee, even though he had bankrupted his own farm only six years earlier. The tribe paid for a double-wide trailer with decking and landscaping for Pippin and his wife, but the couple had personal difficulties and Pippin had professional difficulties. "He didn't produce like he thought he was going to produce," James told reporters when Pippin's contract was terminated.[23] The farm was $3.9 million in the red, with production and harvesting expenses nearly six times higher than sales.[24] The farming project has survived, nonetheless, with a succession of managers. It has never become a significant source of revenue for the tribe, but given the success of gaming, its failure to contribute significantly to the Seminole economy is not critical.

One example of a business that did make money for the tribe was its agreements with GTE (General Telephone and Electronics) in Collier County and Bell South in Indian River County to lease sites for cellular telephone towers. Although this income was not huge either, it had required no investment from the tribe and was producing revenues, although Jim Shore declined to reveal the amount.[25]

The continuing saga of the Micco aircraft deal is worth mentioning because it also highlights the Seminole way of doing business. About late 1993, James became interested in a small aircraft fabrication business. The deal was presented to him by Milt Kimble and Daniel Hunsinger, partners in Meyers Aircraft, developers of an improved version of the prototype Meyers 145 aircraft, which had been first certified in 1948 and had set numerous speed records in the 1960s.

The pair was pursuing an FAA certificate to manufacture and sell. The tribe would be required to invest (at the initial estimate) $2 million in order to acquire the supplemental Type Certificate, a working Meyers 145, a Meyers airframe suitable for modification, necessary tooling, and engineering working capital. The investment was to result in an FAA Type Certificate 3A1 for sales.

James, an avid pilot, and once again backed by the council, eventually spent $3 million to purchase the business and take over the forty-thousand-square-foot hangar in Fort Pierce, where the company was beginning to fabricate a light two-seater fixed-wing aircraft, now designated as the Micco SP-20, a single-engine, two-seat, sport/training aircraft. James had rechristened the company Micco Aircraft, Micco being an English translation of *mikkó*, the Miccosukee title for a civic leader of a village. Micco also was the name that James and Lesley had given to their first child and first son.

Despite the amount of money that the tribe invested in the business, however, and the expectation of certification, little progress was made over the next few years. Max Osceola Jr., still a tribal councilman, was named president of the company and was paid $80,000 a year for his title. He was given an office in the Fort Pierce hangar that he apparently never occupied. A reporter for *Aviation International News,* however, cited the president of the company as F. DeWitt Beckett.[26] When reporters asked why Max was worth such a salary when he had had no experience with aircraft, James responded, "He doesn't know a damn thing about airplanes . . . but Max does know marketing, all those types of things."[27] This was only minimally accurate, but it was an obvious way to provide extra income for an ostensible supporter on the council.

The original partnership with Kimble and Hunsinger mutated rapidly. Hunsinger left the partnership even before the letter of intent with the tribe was signed, and Kimble, ostensibly the working partner, disappeared. In May of 1996 at the annual required shareholders' meeting and election of a board of directors, Kimble was cited for having neglected his responsibilities. He had neither participated in the company's management nor in the meetings with shareholders. The agreement with the tribe stipulated three directors, two from the tribe and one to be determined by Kimble. But Kimble could not even be located. His notices were returned to the tribe by the U.S. Postal Service and the council declared the tribe's agreement with him to be ineffective, "based on [Kimble's] fraudulent representations." James and Max Jr. were reelected board members for another year.

On 18 November 1996, the Federal Aviation Administration granted the plane an experimental airworthiness certificate, permitting the company to test-fly the aircraft. The project languished, however, for lack of professional personnel. At the shareholders' meeting in March of 1997, James and Max Jr. were reelected yet again for another year.

When James was removed by the Tribal Council (including Max Jr.) in 2001, Micco Aircraft Company still was not producing or selling planes. Tim Cox, who would take over the tribe's administration during the final years of James's leadership, says that James knew that the plane would never be the principal moneymaker for the company. He believes, rather, that the purchase of the company was to provide the tribe with a venue for obtaining defense contracts. "If you can build planes then you can make parts. As an Indian, you can go to Boeing or Martin-Marietta and offer to work with them."[28]

But the entire process was ended when James was suspended. The council announced its desire to sell the company, and did so, for a mere $800,000. James, however, still confident that the business could become lucrative, a couple of years later would arrange a personal minority business loan through the BIA Eastern Area office in Nashville and buy the business for himself. He relocated it to Oklahoma and a smaller hangar in the town of Bartlesville, where he estimated that he could have access to an Indian workforce, and hangar space would cost three times less ($1–2 per square foot compared to $5–6 per square foot) than in South Florida. He has a Web site, a new manager (another in an ever-changing line), ex-tribal-pilot Peter Vedel as his international sales representative, and continuing optimism.

The end of the twentieth century became a period of high risk, high yield, high visibility, and high negative imaging for the Seminole Tribe. In particular, the *St. Petersburg Times* newspaper and two reporters, Jeff Testerman and Brad Goldstein, took on the tribe almost as a personal vendetta. Their determination to muckrake paid no attention to Seminole cultural values, placing data only in non-Indian context, never quite sure whether to praise James or damn him, and using any method at their disposal to obtain inside information, even to offering Pat Diamond anonymity if she would make internal documents available.[29] James countered their efforts by offering a $5,000 reward for the names of any tribal citizens or employees who gave proprietary information to any newspaper.

In 1997, Testerman and Goldstein challenged James to meet with them for a personal interview. James, the warrior, wanted a confrontation, but he was wont to shoot from the hip in such adversarial settings, and his responses could easily be taken out of context. Nevertheless, the interview was arranged, set for an open "neutral" area on Gulfport Beach (St. Petersburg). James would have let them hold the interview on tribal lands, but their lawyers would not permit it. "What they don't understand is the reservation is my world," James said. "Everywhere else is their world. There is no neutral site."[30] James went to the interview accompanied by controller Ted Boyd, housing director Joel Frank, *Seminole Tribune* reporter Pete Gallagher, SPD chief Tom Hernan, and Aviation Department director Charles Kirkpatrick.

The interview lasted for two hours and the reporters brought up every ostensibly negative thing that they had uncovered. When they pushed him over claims that tribal citizens were paying less than they should have for subsidized HUD housing, James shot back angrily, "So get your head out of your ass and don't talk to me in that fashion. I came here to talk to you on my own free will. You're not even paying my expenses. Okay? I'm trying to help you out so you can look good."[31]

The tribe also had suffered embarrassment from allegations of misuse of federal funding for some of its internal programs. In 1995, the tribe had a fifty-acre plot near Fort Pierce taken into trust, amid fears that another casino would result. This was not the case. By this time, about sixty tribal citizens, all descendants of four Seminole sisters, lived there and the tribe wanted to be able to deliver services to them in a manner consistent with those available on other reservations. In 1996 the property was declared a Res. In 1998 the tribe's housing authority was literally disbanded and reorganized, under a cloud of allegations concerning its practices. In addition, charges of illegal gaming practices, needless to say, continued unabated.

Florida attorney general Butterworth, never a fan of Seminole gaming, opined publicly that he was sure that Seminole gaming management was dishonest, and that the tribe was undoubtedly losing revenues—as were casino patrons. He cited the Mashantucket Pequot Tribe in Connecticut and the Shakopee Tribe in Minnesota as examples of honest and more lucrative gaming practices. "If they [the Seminoles] had done it the way some other tribes are doing it now, I believe they could be making a lot of money honestly. The people going to the tables would know the games were honest. . . . I would have much more of a comfort level."[32] Needless to say, Butterworth's concerns were hardly the same as those of the tribe. At this same time, however, within the tribe itself, James had begun to initiate a process of change, on his own initiative and not as a response to outside pressure, that would not be good for himself or the tribe, especially for himself.

8   Money Matters (More and More)

This was the mid-1990s and a time when a philosophical transition was taking place among tribal politicians. Tribal revenues were growing by leaps and bounds since the casinos had begun high-stakes bingo during the most recent legal battle with the State of Florida. James's usual approach was, "Let's just do what we [the tribe] want, and see what they [the feds] do about it." Greed kept the federal government trying to control tribes, even as white men's guilt usually kept their more overt actions at bay.

The tribe's annual gross revenues were over $130 million by the end of the final decade of the century, more than 80 percent of it from gaming revenues. In addition, total federal program funding to the tribe was $39.2 million: $12 million in health grants; $809,000 for law enforcement; and "several million" for water management.[1] The chairman's office line item was slightly more than $4.3 million. Each of the three big Res representatives (BC, Brighton, and Hollywood) had allocations of $2.4 million each, although they rarely managed to function within those numbers and, indeed, in fiscal year 1999 asked for and received increases to $3.6 million each. In addition, a line item for "general" council spending totaled slightly over $3.6 million. The two smaller Res allocations (those for Tampa and Immokalee) were $600,000 and $900,000 respectively, although by the same resolution, Immokalee received an increase to $1.2 million. The other, smaller reservations were included in the appropriations for the "big 3." By 1997, tribal dividends to individual citizens stood at $1,500 per month.

Council appropriations to each Res council representative were enlarging apace, although oversight on spending was, to all intents and purposes, nonexistent. In the cases of David Cypress, Mitchell Cypress, Max Osceola Jr., and Manuel ("Mando," now "Mondo") Tiger (Wind Clan, b. 1959), among others, they left James alone to pursue his projects. The animosity between James and David was ongoing, but David was content to snipe at James privately and agree

Figure 6. James E. Billie, chairman of the Tribal
Council, in his office, 1997. (Photograph by
Victor C. Ramos, courtesy of James Billie.)

with him publicly, because James was making money for the tribe and, by extension, for David. David would voluntarily make this process of economic self-
aggrandizement eminently clear in his later testimony in federal court, to the
amazement of the federal prosecutors and even FBI investigators (see chapters
10 and 11).

Board representatives, who had had fewer and fewer enterprises to fund and
whose funding was allocated by the council annually, were less profligate at this
point. In fact, the board had so little in the way of enterprises to oversee relatively speaking that, just prior to the tribalwide annual shareholders' meeting
of 1996, there was discussion among a number of tribal citizens concerning
whether the board should simply be disbanded and all tribal business operated
directly by the council. At this point the board oversaw wholesale distribution
of tobacco products, and had since 1982, distributing products to Smoke Shops
for nine locations in Hollywood, BC, Brighton, and Immokalee. It also continued to operate a tribal portion of the cattle program, an enterprise that was near
and dear to Seminole hearts, but never lucrative in the twentieth century.

In addition to tobacco sales and cattle the board also controlled citrus groves
in BC and Brighton, producing oranges, lemons, and grapefruit as well as fuel
sales for the citrus grove machinery, which combined to create a steady enterprise still functioning today. Planned sugarcane growing, a tentative (and, ul-

timately, relatively small) project, was just begun by 1997, and a planned plant and tree nursery for common and exotic varieties on the Hollywood Res failed to materialize. A planning and development function of the board, funded and directed partially by the BIA Seminole Agency, had existed since the 1970s. Integral to the internal administration of the tribe was the board's credit and finance department, overseeing the tribe's short-term loan and revolving credit programs. We have reviewed the latter function earlier, in chapter 6, and will address the former separately below.

Obviously, this possibility of deleting any or all of the board functions ignored the question of the "other side" of sovereignty: the primary function of the board was to serve as an incorporated entity that could open the doors of sovereign immunity sufficiently wide as to permit nontribal businesses to enter into money-making projects with the tribe on a legally protected footing, while permitting the larger sovereign immunity of the tribe to remain inviolable. Nevertheless, by this time major tribal borrowing to support development programs promulgated by James were being dealt with directly by the council, and it was the council that ultimately had to agree to any breach of sovereign immunity anyway. This is also the point at which Mitchell Cypress succeeded to the presidency of the board. Mitchell, brother of David, was a cattleman himself and popular with other cattlemen, whose governing body and conduit to council support had long been the board. Mitchell's general popularity assuaged doubts regarding board value, and the board remained.

Those who knew Mitchell and David best knew their down sides too, of course. The styles of both men are alike in their commitments to maintaining personal power. David, a quick thinker, periodically passes through publicly self-destructive bouts of substance abuse. At one time, David had aspirations to the chairmanship but yielded to his brother's ambitions. Nowadays his focus is predominantly on the internal affairs of the tribe but even more on feathering his own nest through business dealings peripheral to tribal lands and taking care of those persons useful to him. BC is "his" Res, and he takes all events there personally. In this he is very like James, but his level of anger is much higher and more visible and frequently makes his thinking arbitrary. Both brothers are fluent in their language (Miccosukee), although David's lexicon is considered rather colloquial by elders. David more and more prefers to occult himself, letting his hair grow past his knees in his version of warrior tradition, but clinging to his characteristic dark sunglasses even indoors.

Mitchell, much smoother in person than David, is also much more obviously desirous of high visibility. Mitchell looks outward to the non-Indian world, even though at this point he still understood very little of it. Almost all visitors to Mitchell's office are treated to an interpretation of the personal story behind a featured painting by Florida artist Guy LaBree. It depicts a dream Mitchell had some years ago of his riding into the spiritual sky to be reunited with his long dead wife. Usually, Mitchell's longtime personal assistant, Sally Tommie (Bird Clan, b. 1963, and liaison with the Fort Pierce community), recounts the story as Mitchell looks on. The Cypress brothers are hard to find when you need them; they are not very quick to absorb details, relying rather on assistants to synthesize information for them, and very prickly to deal with. As one very close associate says: "They both lose their tempers pretty fast. But, at least, if David gets mad at you, you know it's for something you've done, and he really lets you know it. But if Mitchell gets angry, he just goes off at everybody, he's like a shotgun: if you're in his way, you're likely to get hit!"[2]

Mitchell's sphere of interest was tribalwide politics. He counted on his Otter Clan for support, but slowly and conscientiously built rapport with the somewhat disaffected Creeks at Brighton. Obviously, even at this time, Mitchell's sights were set on the only position in the tribe higher than that of board president: council chairman. But Mitchell was patient. David quickly became content to exercise greater and greater control over BC, based principally on his constant support of elders on the Res, and to increase his opposition to James even as his (David's) increasing council representative's discretionary funding increased. Eventually, the Cypress brothers would become willing accomplices in a council coup, with the help of Max Jr. and Jim Shore, and aided by outside lawyers and investors, and precipitate a very public airing of the tribe's dirty laundry.

Power, the James Billie Way

For only slightly less than a quarter of a century James Billie walked a tightrope, both political and personal, for there is no differentiation in the Seminole world. He brought his people increasing economic returns and more visibility than they ever realized across Indian Country and non-Indian country. For himself, he gained increasing power and visibility also, more than he ever realized, and to a far greater extent than interested the other members of the council. He became a consummate manipulator, up to the very day when his entire system collapsed.

James found that the way to get things past the council was to think through the issues and decide what he considered to be "the most logical progression of thought and conclusion, and then flip it over completely—180°—and whatever is the complete opposite of the logical process/conclusion is what they will think and do."[3] He felt that if he ever was faced with a political opponent who thought logically, that person would be able to defeat him because he would know, instinctively, what James was up to. James never once considered that such insight might come from outside of the tribe, but that day was not far off.

He used a very effective trick at reelection times. For the first four months or so of the seven months leading up to an election he would make himself available to all comers and would hand out money, as tribal "loans," right and left. Then, about three months prior to the election he would simply—disappear! Never easy to find at the best of times, now finding him would become impossible. You could position yourself in a rocking chair on the porch of the Swamp Water Café and wait for hours. You could sit under the chikî(t) in his front yard. You could leave messages at the airport, and Ahfachkee School, and the SPD office.

He would be sighted in his plain black pickup, bumping along the dirt road to the far side of his cattle pasture. But he would have mysteriously gone by the time his location could be reported and word had spread—even though word could spread *very* quickly across BC. He would have "just" been seen taking off on his airboat, with a fishing pole stowed in the bow. Or, the helicopter would be missing from the airport. He could be in Tampa by the time that word got out, or he could be holed up anywhere between BC and the Okeefenokee Swamp, with a group of fellow musicians, recording a new album.

Wherever he disappeared to, he would reappear, just as mysteriously, about two weeks before the election. Supporters would organize barbecue dinner rallies for him on each Res during the months of his vanishment, and he would make brilliant entrances—and just as sudden exits—leaving just as people began to queue up to ask for money or favors or both. The system was simple. It was an adaptation of the drug pusher's game of giving and withdrawing drugs in order to "hook" users. James himself would disdain drug use and angrily decry alcohol abusers, but he appreciated the political value of the process. He never used drugs and was virtually abstemious with alcohol as well, taking only a glass or two of red wine on social occasions (muscadine is his favorite grape).

By his election-time disappearing ploy, James gave certain voters an analogous object lesson about the value of keeping their source in office. There were, of course, a significant number of voters who did not fall for the ploy, but even they afforded James status for the revenues he brought in to the tribe and the visibility that he was gaining for the tribe across Indian Country and nationally. James is a natural performer and showman with the heart of a warrior. The Maskókî people have always placed great value on these attributes.

As an illustration of this process in a broader application, I will recount a particularly revealing item. One morning, about 8:30 a.m., when his front yard was dappled with early sunlight falling through the thick oak branches and the birds were noisily seeking breakfast in the canal, he and I were drinking coffee in his kitchen. He was in cutoff jeans and T-shirt, and was barefooted, and we were in the middle of another great conversation when we began to hear voices out in the yard. This always annoyed him. He liked to begin his day peacefully, but it was only much later that he had a locking gate installed across his driveway, well back from the yard. He motioned me to follow him and we went out onto the porch.

At least seven men were already lined up outside the porch door, and he knew what they were there for. The first stepped up to him and launched in to an elliptical monologue about a business idea he had, and how much money he would need to pursue it. Neither he nor any of the men there had any real idea of the value of white men's money (recall that some Indians in the Northwest call white men's dollars "Frog Skins"); $15,000 had no more validity than $15 to some, but James knew that and that was not what interested him; he always applauded personal initiative, and as his own projects rarely required detailed planning, neither did he require it of others.

This morning, however, instead of speaking to the man, James turned to me, as if in surprise, and commented: "Look at that! Now, this guy voted against me in the last election and, now, look at him, standing here with his hand out and expecting me to give him a loan!" I surreptitiously looked around for a hole I might crawl into; I was very embarrassed for the man and, frankly, for myself. Apparently, however, that was exactly what James had in mind: requiring a Seminole man to beg, in front of a non-Indian woman. Each petitioner was forced to go through the same demeaning process before James agreed to give loans to all of them, but not without his imparting a stern gospel to each and all: When the next election comes around, remember who gave you this money!

James used his own determination to embarrass and, even more powerful, to shock, both for the psychological advantage they gave him in political settings and for the sheer emotional value that either or both provided in mixed company, especially in the company of women. In the moment when James gained the edge, he also gained the ascendancy. Once, a few years before I was invited to work for the tribe, James and I were sitting together at an archaeological conference in the Keys where I was a presenter. James was surrounded by academics, and it made him slightly uncomfortable. He murmured to me, "You know, I think I'm going to go back to college and get myself one of those degrees." "No you're not," I retorted too quickly. He glared at me, waiting for me to explain. "You couldn't afford to have a college degree because, then, you'd lose your edge! You like being the outspoken, uneducated little Indian too much. It puts people off their guard and gives you the advantage." I smiled as I said it, but the conversation ended there.

Even beyond the power to shock or merely embarrass, James was literally addicted to the use of sexual and scatological remarks in almost all settings. In his masterful second volume of his biography of Lyndon B. Johnson, Robert Caro describes the explicit nature of LBJ's sexuality and the power it gave him, and the description is such an apt one for James that it is impossible not to compare the two. Caro speaks of LBJ's roughness with his office staff. "And there was in all his abuse and inspections and orders an element of crudity—of that 'barnyard' talk that made men 'a bit embarrassed when it poured out in front of female members of the staff.' . . . His office conversation was permeated by sexual imagery. 'Take that tie off,' he would tell one of his male staffers. 'That knot looks like a limp prick.'"[4]

This is language that James understands, and not just with his small office staff but more particularly in public settings where he can singularize himself and gain the ascendancy in any discussion. He told a reporter some years later, recalling his "grandfathers" (anyone in his mother's clan and her mother's generation would have been his social "grandfather") that "their pivoting point on most subjects was always sex. . . . I remember listening to them as a small boy. They'd be talking seriously about something and then one would say, 'Heck, that's like having sex.' Little did I know that I'd pick it up. Now my son [Micco] is doing the same, and I've got to be very careful around him. Pretty soon he's copying me and laughing."[5]

It is important to realize that Indians in general and the Seminoles specifically are not prurient or repressed in their sexuality. These are non-Indian traits. Neither are the Seminoles licentious (with individual exceptions). They simply view human sexuality as an integral part of their humanity. They have social norms concerning sexual expression, most of which enjoin dignity and reservedness in public settings. But James was aware of white men's inhibitions and was interested in power.

I recall an insight that James provided into the workings of the Seminole mind (I was to realize quickly that it was the workings of his mind in particular). Shortly after I had begun my "history talks" at the field office in BC, James said: "You know, you have a Medicine man in your class." I responded, "Well, I thought that perhaps that might be so. He pays particularly close attention to everything I say. What does he want from me?" "He don't want *nothing* from you," James practically shouted. "What do you want from an alligator if you see him in your path? You don't *want* nothing. You just poke him a little to see which way he's gonna go!" In other cultures, this would be called "bear baiting." In the Everglades, it's "'gator baiting," and one of James's favorite sports. Either way, exercise caution.

Ironically, David Cypress's willingness to use sexual references, both in white man's and in Indian terms, was at least as obvious as that of James, and the rising economic base of the tribe only exacerbated their mutual distrust and disregard. Theirs was an unhappy relationship that could not help but bring back memories of the unhappy relationship of Jack Kennedy and Lyndon Johnson. Each needed the other for political reasons but reviled each other personally.

Vivian Crooks (non-Indian), who worked for the adult education program in BC for many years and together with her husband, Mike, owned a ranch not far west of the BC Res, recounted to me a moment when James's disdain of David was made especially clear to many in the tribe. The occasion was a tribal budget meeting held at an expensive hotel on Marco Island, over on Florida's west coast. When I began my relationship with the tribe in 1992 it was still James's practice to treat employees to three days of luxury at some beachfront hotel on the west coast or in Key West, ostensibly while the annual budget was being reviewed and finalized, but in actuality, they were just a few days of rewarding R&R. The whole trip was posh and at tribal expense. It was a given that employees would take families along although only close (nuclear) families were permitted, otherwise the entire tribe would have turned out. As with any tribal event, good food—and lots of it—was the core element of the trip.

By the later part of the 1990s, these events were discontinued, however, not for economic reasons so much as because the subject of the budget had begun to interest outsiders, especially reporters, and the council would no longer allow even line items, much less total budgetary figures, to become common knowledge. James even issued a tribalwide memorandum warning employees not to divulge any information from the budget, on pain of dismissal. To codify the proprietary nature of the information, the council also passed a resolution requiring that tribal financial statements not be made available to either non-Indians or the U.S. government.[6] Where he formerly had made complete copies of the finalized annual budget available to department heads, henceforth each department head was provided only with his or her own figures.

Anyway, at the event recalled by Vivian, a lovely dinner was over and people were seated on a restaurant's outside deck with cool drinks and David, drunk, walked over to the edge of the deck and took out his penis and relieved himself over the sands. James was appalled and angry and told David exactly what he thought of such rude behavior.[7] David knew full well that his actions would aggravate James, and James knew full well that David had done it for that very reason. James saw his own words and actions as always having a political value and David's as just profoundly crude. It was simply one more of the instances that alienated the two.

Dividends, Loans, and Deductions

Not all FR tribes give dividends to their citizens. Not all tribes have sufficient income to divide among their citizens, whether they might wish to or not. A number of tribes choose not to hand out monies on the premise that free money creates addiction and dissention. As late as the year 2005, only about 25 percent of all FR tribes distributed dividends based on gaming revenues.[8] The first

Seminole tribal dividends, or per capita payments to citizens from tribal profits, began as early as 1968, before the tribe had gaming. Tribal Council Resolution No. C-67-69 explained that the tribe had been the beneficiary of the proceeds from the sale of twenty acres of Hendry County land, amounting to $15,000, that had been willed to the tribe from the estate of a German businessman, Theodore Von Elmpt, who had passed away in 1965.[9]

In addition, the tribe's revenues from oil and gas rights leases from state Res lands, amounting to about $13,000 by 1968, were being held by Florida's Trustees of the Internal Improvement Fund and were scheduled to be released to the tribe by the end of the year. The total of the two amounts would be sufficient to permit a one-time $30 dividend. Each enrolled citizen, as well as those whose applications for enrollment were already in the tribal offices, would be eligible to receive the payout. Dividends for children under sixteen years would be paid to parents or guardians.

The fiscal year 1974 budget for the Seminole Tribe included an appropriation of $120,000 as a one-time dividend of $100 each to the 1,200 citizens.[10] Midway through Howard Tommie's chairmanship, however, tribal revenues dipped precipitously due to cancellation of three Hollywood leases, and the council suspended annual dividends. Howard suggested that, until matters improved, he could take his salary from various human resources (U.S. government) programs. The council not only found this acceptable but also in a pliant manner directed him to use these funds to raise his salary to $20,000. By 1978, conditions had eased sufficiently that the council could give $150, again as a one-time payment, to tribal citizens. However, any families with monies owing to the tribe would have $50 deducted from the dividend of the head of household (an obviously non-Indian term). The dividend was scheduled to be paid out just before the Christmas holiday.[11] (Many Indians were not interested in celebrating the Christian holiday, but all were interested in days off from white men's offices.)

After James took the reins and bingo monies began to trickle in, in the 1980s, a small dividend was reinstituted, and each citizen received, first, $150 a year and, then, in fiscal year 1982, $100 per quarter for three quarters and a fourth-quarter payment of $150.[12] In this latter instance the council specified those programs to which a Seminole might owe money and the priority order in which repayment deductions should be made. Unfortunately, the Social Security Administration and some other federal programs saw tribal distributions to citizens, albeit very small, as reasons to deny benefits to individual Indians. Over fifty tribal citizens lost precious income before the tribe passed Ordinance C-88-84, on 9 March 1984, to codify its per capita payment system (its dividends), in accordance with Public Law 98-64.[13] The council declared that it had sufficient expertise to administer and distribute per capita payments from funds that the federal government held for it annually, representing rents or other income from various leases of tribal lands. The council agreed that their distributions would not exceed the amount of the funds held by the government and that, conversely, any amounts over and above the amount taken in by the federal government would be deposited in the tribe's general account for the tribe's annual budget. This satisfied the requirements of the federal programs that had sought to deny benefits to tribal citizens. It did not, however, at the moment, have any impact upon gaming revenues and their application to dividends.

By 1985 the appropriation in the tribe's annual budget for dividends consumed $1,800,000 for total quarterly dividends of $300 per person, but a tight budget in the following year reduced the payout to $150 per quarter, and dividends fluctuated in this same range for the rest of the decade, as the tribe's economy fluctuated.[14] In fiscal year 1991 (beginning 1 July), dividends were budgeted at $760,000, with three payouts for a total of $400, for a total population of 1,900, which was approximately accurate.[15] For fiscal year 1992, dividends rose to a total of $1,200 per year, in three payouts, costing the tribe approximately $2,340,000.[16]

In fiscal year 1993, however, dividends were appropriated in two separate resolutions, but the official documents do not reflect totals consistent with past demographics; they reflect something oddly different. The first council resolution enabling a dividend payment for fiscal year 1993 indicates an appropriation of $3,150,000 for a one-time payout of $500.[17] For a population approaching 2,000, this should have required only $1 million at the most. A second council resolution during the same fiscal year and indicating a further appropriation for the same fiscal year totals $2,700,000 for another one-time payout, for a total of $1,000 in dividends in fiscal year 1993.[18] For the same population, this should have required only another $1 million. Consequently, an over appropriation of $3,850,000 for the fiscal year is indicated.

In 1992 the BIA issued to tribes with gaming income its "Guidelines to Govern the Review and Approval of Per Capita Distribution Plans" that capped the portion of gaming revenues that could be distributed to citizens and required the tribes to submit annual plans indicating the appropriations of gaming revenues. This was yet another determined attempt by the U.S. government to control the internal affairs of the FR tribes. As BIA eastern area supervisor Franklin Keel commented in a recent interview: "This has bothered me for a long time . . . because the U.S. government doesn't tell Donald Trump how to spend his money."[19] Nevertheless, the tribe submitted a plan for fiscal year 1995 that appropriated $25.2 million for per capita payments (dividends) to citizens and constituted slightly more than 30 percent of its estimated gaming revenues of $73,057,340 for that year.

This was a watershed era, financially, for the tribe as gaming revenues began to rise rapidly in the wake of James's decision to install slot machines, with or without government approval or a state compact. Nevertheless, the tribe had just entered a costly suit against the state over Class III gaming. The Pennsylvania Crime Commission issued its report targeting the Seminoles' Hollywood gaming managers. Costs were rising constantly for the hotel/restaurant project on the Tampa Res, and the tribe also was locked in negotiations with the BIA over trust land requests there. The National Indian Gaming Commission (NIGC) was not satisfied with Pan Am's management agreement for gaming at the Tampa Res either. The council was expending extraordinary funds for the purchase of stock for an offshore gaming venture in St. Maarten. At the same time, the council was locked in a contentious project with O. B. Osceola (Panther Clan, b. 1934) and his company, Coryi, Inc., over a new gaming venture on the Immokalee Res. In BC the bingo hall management was changing hands— again. All in all, the tribe was expending monies at a precipitous rate of speed. At the same time, however, gaming revenues were still seasonal; the largest revenues depended on the winter visitors—the snowbirds, who only began to come in following Labor Day, and revenues slowed down to a dribble after Easter, when the snowbirds returned to their northern homes. Although the tribal budget ordinance called for an annual reserve of 5–10 percent, this amount fluctuated each year with project requirements. It is certainly possible that the council was beginning to use the "per capita" line items as silent reserves for silent projects.

By 1997 tribal dividends had reached the astounding sum of $1,000 *per person per month*. Gaming revenues had topped $130 million per year, and Seminoles were beginning to accept higher and higher dividends as being their right as tribal citizens. I had had an exchange a couple of years earlier that brought their mindset home to me all too clearly. A Seminole friend in BC and I were talking one day, and I complimented him on his shiny new truck. This was a person who neither worked outside of the tribe nor for the tribe, at least not on any regular basis, so I knew that he had no regular income other than his dividends.

He responded, "I don't like it. I'm gonna get me a new one." I was surprised. I said, "But, ———, how are you going to do that—you haven't paid for this one yet?"

He answered, sullenly, "I don't care. I'll get the money from James."

"You mean, another loan?"

"Yeah."

"But, didn't you just get a loan to buy a new boat?"

"Yeah, so what?"

"Well, you must owe the tribe a lot of money already. How much do you owe?"

"$80,000."

"Good grief! You'll never be able to pay that back."

"I don't care. It's my money anyway!"

The Seminole tradition is community ownership. I couldn't argue. The line between traditional Seminole life and the requirements of the outside world were and are mutable. This was an instance, one of so many over hundreds of years, where cultural survival functioned on the premise of selective internalization of nontraditional elements. It may have been a process contrary to the processes of non-Indian society and values, but if it worked for the Seminoles, that was their business. There was, nonetheless, a limit to the council's acceptance of the growing problem of loans, a process that dovetailed into the subject of dividends. Both subjects, taken together, were parts of a growing awareness among tribal citizens that the former trickle of free money was rapidly becoming a torrent, and one that was not altogether a positive thing for the Seminoles. Two instances provide clear examples of the internal situation. I witnessed both.

The beautiful, new council chamber was crowded with Seminoles. Because of the distances between the outlying reservations and Hollywood, they didn't always turn out in numbers for council meetings anymore. Sometimes the council sent buses to pick them up. Only after James was deposed would the remaining council make such meetings moveable feasts and take them from Res to Res so that elders, especially, wouldn't have to travel in order to attend, and even the merest pretense of catering to the elders could have positive returns. But in this instance, there was an emotional issue on the agenda.

Now, James had two separate ways of dealing with agenda items when he knew they would be controversial. One was to have a pre-meeting meeting with a couple of the council reps, especially Max Jr. and Jack Smith Jr., from whom he knew he could get support. Then he would begin the meeting late so that people would be listless and filled up already on the cold drinks and bagels provided for them in the breezeway outside of the chamber. Next he would change the order of the agenda items without notice and handle only the small, cut-and-dried decisions before and during the normal lunch hour, thereby requiring the audience to sit through the normal lunch hour, very unhappily. (Seminoles do not adhere to fixed schedules, but they do not like missing meals.) Then he would announce a lunch break, usually from 1:00 p.m. until 2:30 p.m. Everyone would disperse. Then, he and the council would return early, purposely, and before the audience could reassemble (Seminoles are not interested in "punctuality") he would reconvene the council meeting and call a vote on the emotional issue and dispense with it in accordance with the prearranged vote, so the audience would return only to find that the subject already had been decided, whether to their liking or not.

But on the day that I am describing, he used a simpler and more direct method. The subject was dividends and their impact on education. Many Seminole elders still were not convinced that white man's education was necessary for Seminole children, despite council attempts over the years to support white man's education publicly, and in these families attendance at any school for white man's education was lackadaisical at best. As a counter to this disinterest, the parent-teacher support group from Ahfachkee School in BC had prepared a resolution to present to the council. The resolution called upon the council to support education through tighter control of dividends. Children who maintained a *C* average in school would continue to receive their dividends as usual. Students who did not meet this threshold would have their dividends withheld by the tribe and kept in a personal account that would once again become available when their grades rose. This put pressure on both the student and the parent or parents who would not have access to the money.

The resolution was presented by Melissa "Missy" Sanders (Panther Clan, b. 1971), a young and passionate educational supporter who also worked as an education counselor at Ahfachkee. She was nervous to begin with and was trying very hard to respect council protocol and procedures. James and the council simply ignored her. They carried on a conversation among themselves on the rostrum even as she spoke and would not even deign to respond to her questions or requests for attention. The poor young woman collapsed in tears. The audience supported her and became increasingly agitated, but to no avail. All the thought and good work of the BC group had been for naught. Certainly, tradition was against her; tribal leaders did not like to directly require anything of tribal citizens. Nevertheless, this was a situation and an era when such nontraditional considerations were appearing more and more often in tribal life. And the requirement for tribal leaders, in any era, to respect the rights of citizens to express themselves with dignity certainly had not ended. The supporters of white man's education retired the field, defeated.

The second controversial instance regarding dividends took place at another council meeting about a year later, in mid-1997. Hollywood voters had just re-elected Max Jr. a few weeks earlier to another two-year term, but by a very slim margin. One continuing dissatisfaction with Max Jr. was the fact that he did not (and does not) speak a tribal language. This, despite the fact that his mother, Laura Mae, was a political activist and was fluent in both tribal languages. Max was looking for some way to consolidate his voter base and raise his percentage of voter support. The most direct way, in his view, was to propose raising dividends. James certainly had used this same ploy himself, but at this moment he was dead set against such a move and told Max so. But this was a moment when the council reps also were really beginning to see the political potential in the distribution of their discretionary allowances (each rep had his own within the annual budget, to serve the Res he served). Within the coming years this line item would become a central element of contention between James and the council representatives. In the meantime, dividend monies came out of the gaming revenues and not out of any single rep's discretionary fund. Dividends were "free" money.

Max proposed that the individual dividend should be doubled, from $1,000 per person per month to $2,000. Ted Boyd, the tribal controller, was clearly very agitated at the prospect. "How much would it cost to raise the dividend?" Max asked. Ted had known well beforehand that Max was agitating for this raise, and he responded immediately, with total directness: "It would cost the tribe $30 million more a year. Right now, that would be an invitation to financial catastrophe." Amazingly, Max persisted. It had long been viewed within the tribe that most or all of the financial acumen in Max's family came from his wife of many years, Marge.

Once again, Max said, "But, we can afford that, can't we? How bad would it be?" Ted tried to compose himself and looked straight at Max and said, "It would be like a freight train coming down the track, and another train headed right for it. It would be a disaster." James stood against the raise, but the council outvoted him and agreed to the raise anyway. It was an extremely surprising defeat for James—the moment when the power of money outstripped James's personal power. Before the end of the calendar year, however, the council partially reversed itself and ordered the dividend lowered to $1,500 rather than $2,000, to begin in January 1998. Within a week of that fateful council meeting, however, Ted Boyd experienced a mild heart attack. He survived, but his days with the tribe were numbered.

The process of doling out monies in dividends as a standard element of the political process has only continued unabated since that time. James hired an outside accounting firm, on at least two occasions, to conduct classes on the Hollywood Res in money and money management, in the hope that the Seminoles would avail themselves of the opportunity to begin to understand the value and uses of white man's money, but the attempts were weak ones with only very limited success. The classes drew a small, self-selecting audience of people already predisposed to view money as a tool, and the classes quietly ended. In 2009, as this is being written, the monthly dividend has risen to $10,000 per tribal citizen per month. This is breathtaking, from a social and economic point of view, but also doable given the quantum leap in income that has been provided by the tribe's recent purchase of the entire Hard Rock company and its (once again controversial) gaming compact with Florida governor Charlie Crist (more on this later).

The other side of the coin, of which dividends are only one side, is the subject of tribal loans to individual citizens. This may seem difficult to rationalize in the minds of non-Indians, given the current amount of individual dividends.

In the case of both subjects, however, the tribal government is only functioning as a virtual recycling agent, within a tradition (discussed earlier) that views tribal income as a collectively held resource. When we add this reality to the fact that money in any significant amount has only been available to the Seminoles for about two short generations, it becomes simpler to realize how much the Seminoles still have to learn about white man's money. And, in all fairness, we should remember that there are many non-Indians who still have lessons to learn about handling money in a capitalist economy also. First, we must discuss the loan process, and then both the positive and the negative impacts that these monies have on Indians who are also very passionately committed to remaining Indians—whatever that may mean today.

～

Council Resolution No. C-67-69 (1969) had also directed that it would be the province of the board to decide how to handle the problem of individuals who owed monies to the board for "various accounts and loans." This passing mention is the entrée to a problem that had been growing for at least a decade before James Billie took office and already had become the source of much discontent.

James was constantly importuned for loans, and he gave them and used them to his political advantage, as we have witnessed, so loans were hardly the unilateral province of the board. (The subject of administrative "lines of authority" was one of total irrelevance to James or the council reps.) A Brighton loan program, however, was well established by 1985 and was run from the Res field office by a non-Indian woman who had been hired as the Community Action Program (CAP) officer, Ellen Click. Fred Smith worked closely with Ellen, especially after he became president of the board, in 1987, and he and Ellen soon married (his second marriage).

In 1984 the council acted on complaints from Brighton residents and ordered an audit of the Brighton "Sewing and Loan" programs on the premise that the programs had been administering an unauthorized loan program "for some time now."[20] Items such as patchwork jackets and other items of clothing were made by tribal citizens. When the items were sold, the makers received the price they asked and any profits were deposited in the sewing fund. Over time, the sewing fund became a resource for check cashing and short-term loans. A number of Brighton residents complained that Ellen Click, who was administering the program, was charging exorbitant interest rates. The council wanted to curtail the program. However, the complainants were eventually outnumbered and outvoiced. Ninety-nine Brighton residents signed a petition to keep the loan program, and the council relented. At the regular council meeting of 12 July 1985, the council approved the continuation of the "Brighton Payroll Account" and community loan program, run through the Community Action Program where Ellen Click worked. The loan program made cash available for short-term needs, and the Brighton residents saw it as too convenient to lose.[21] A dozen years later, James told reporters about the decision to keep the program. "The reason it's still there is because it's highly political in [Brighton]. Fred Smith was a very powerful political person and their family kind of run the Tribe over there and it just so happens that Ellen Click happens to be the wife of that very powerful political person. So nobody ever touched it."[22]

James had neither begun a tribal loan program nor did he alone run it. But the practice of giving out loans quickly took on a life of its own. James rationalized it as a way of teaching people to handle money: "All these people . . . the majority of the people did not have what you call borrowing capability. So we were trying to establish something. Let them learn how to pay on it."[23] In some instances, Seminoles asked for one-time loans large enough to underwrite business ventures: $30,000 perhaps for startup of a rope manufactory in Immokalee, or for construction of orange-picking machines for groves near Okeechobee. Many loans, however, were just to support small domestic issues that recurred, especially in the lives of elders who hardly spoke English much less understood the recurring nature of electric bills or telephone bills.

Telephone bills, especially, presented cultural problems for elders because of the tradition that kept a person from denying any request from a clan member who visited their homes. Younger relatives would visit their elders and would ask to use the telephone, and the elder would comply, only to learn when the bills came due that that person had extravagantly run up hundreds of dollars of charges for frivolous calls. The chairman would be asked for help, and he could hardly refuse. Many of the elders sacrificed their own comfort and security by having their telephones removed rather than having to refuse their relatives the use of them. People wanted car and boat loans. They borrowed to purchase everything from jewelry to exotic hunting dogs. They borrowed for bail bonds. The demand for cars, especially, and the need for cars to support program areas, became so great that, over the 1990s, the tribe began to take over as purchasing agent, partly because of its greater purchasing power and partly to preclude unscrupulous dealing by white auto dealers who unabashedly sought more than their fair share of tribal monies.

"There's a couple of older men on our reservation [BC] that I've known all my life," James told one reporter. "One of them belongs to the Wind clan, another one belongs to the Panther clan. And we know he wasn't gonna pay that loan off, but we gave it to him. We don't give a damn if he pays it back. So he's driving a very decent 19, maybe a '96 or '95, some sort of pickup truck. He says he doesn't have any money this month. Can you give me $500? We'll give him $500. And if somebody wants to politically challenge me on that, that was my decision."[24]

Very little was ever said about money provided to elders in the early days of the loan programs, but as dividends rose across the last decade of the century and loans rose precipitously as well, Ted Boyd advised James that the loan program needed to be regularized. In other words, tribal loans needed to be based on regulations, and they needed to be administered by a department rather than being handed out on the basis of political patronage from the chairman's office discretionary budget. Sometimes James complied with this. Sometimes he ignored it. Sometimes, if he became tired of being haunted by loan-seekers, he would have Pat Diamond hang a sign on the door of the chairman's outer office, announcing NO MORE LOANS UNTIL FURTHER NOTICE.

The result was negligible, however, because everyone knew that sooner or later when his dark mood passed, James would be available for renewed importuning. And this was a major problem when any program area or segment of tribal administration attempted to set limits or protocols. Tribal citizens knew that, just as with the mother who shouts threats at her child in the grocery store but never follows through, they couldn't really mean whatever they said because the most powerful person in the tribe would ignore the rules himself whenever it suited his political purpose. All a person had to do was go to the department and announce, "James says it's OK," in order to get what they wanted.

In the case of Ellen Click Smith and the Brighton loan program, the subject came to a head in 1996, after Fred's death, over a separate but intersecting problem. By that year tribal loans had reached $9.5 million and repayments were erratic, at best. The tribe charged 8.5 percent interest annually and the council passed a resolution permitting the accounting department to reserve one-half of an individual's monthly dividend payment to satisfy loan repayments. This was, of course, a contentious subject among many Seminoles. At Brighton, however, some community residents complained to the council that Ellen's loan practices for her personal program constituted "loan-sharking."[25] Jim Talik, the tribe's business manager, looked into the program and reported that interest rates, quoted to loan recipients at 10 percent, were actually annualized at 32 percent. Recipients would almost never get out from under such rates on their own.

James had tried to end the Brighton loan program, as mentioned earlier, but he said, "You gotta remember now, I'm voted in by some of the people that's on that reservation, so boy that group growled and protected [the program]. So we just left it alone."[26] But, when Fred passed away, his widow attempted to exercise her non-Indian right to be sole heir to his estate, especially his home in

Hollywood, on the Res. In this attempt, Fred's adult children challenged her. They complained to the council that Ellen was a non-Indian, that Fred had died without a will, and they vociferously wanted Ellen off the Res completely. Moreover, Ellen had tried to take the case into a state court, and the children were especially upset by this action. Ellen appeared at a council meeting in Hollywood and made her personal position, her position in control of a loan program, and her determination very clear. The Brighton loan program, left uncontrolled for too long, had finally come to a head in a very unpleasant way for the council.

The immediate problem of inheritance centered on the fact that neither opponent—Ellen nor Fred's children—had right completely on their side. Ellen, as a non-Indian, had no rights according to tribal tradition, even though tribal counsel Jim Shore took her side—against his own traditions. Nevertheless, the council, with community approbation, had made accommodations before in somewhat analogous cases, and they did not want the fight to go any further. The most positive case had involved Howard Tiger's widow, Winifred, who was a Cherokee rather than a Seminole. Nevertheless, she was highly respected and had worked hard for the tribe over the years in its education program, and her children and the Tiger family generally occupied a very positive place in the Seminole world. Consequently, she was quietly permitted to live on in her house on the Hollywood Res for all of her years after Howard's death. When she passed away in 2006, she was afforded burial on the Res, albeit in the Baptist church cemetery rather than the tribal cemetery, but she was staunchly Christian and wanted that.

In another very messy case that was unfolding at the same time as the Fred Smith case, the powerful Medicine man Pete Osceola, who lived down the Trail, was battling his own children over their mother's property inheritance, specifically a successful tourist shop down the Trail. The crux of the problem in the Fred Smith case was that tradition afforded no right of the children to inherit from the father. But neither did a husband have the right of inheritance from his wife, as in Pete Osceola's case. Father and mother traditionally came from separate clans. Children could inherit from their mothers, of whose clan they were members for life. In the old days, however, a father would have had few possessions other than his personal items to leave. Pete also took his case outside of the tribe, to white men's court. The Seminoles were not very supportive of his claims or his actions, which they felt were being encouraged by Pete's new wife, a tall blond Nordic non-Indian who appeared to care little about the tribe and its traditions, and whose very existence seemed to aggravate the situation. Beyond even all of this, not only was Pete a strong Medicine man, he also was a bundle carrier for one of the Green Corn ceremonial grounds. The Seminoles were ashamed that he would act in what seemed to them to be such an overtly greedy (read: non-Indian) manner. Pete did not take his situation to the council, although he did discuss it with James from time to time.

After much deliberation, the council finally found an acceptable method of settling the controversy between Ellen Click Smith and Fred Smith's children. The council agreed to buy Fred's Hollywood home, valued at approximately $75,000 by the tribe's real estate department, from Ellen and then sell it to the children for $1. In addition, the council voted to write off about $43,000 in an unpaid loan balance for President Smith.[27] This was a typical move in the case of deceased tribal citizens. Therefore, the council absorbed the brunt of the antagonistic impact of the Fred Smith inheritance situation and settled its own problems in house. As for the loans, the council also agreed to become the collection agent for Ellen's outstanding loans, agreeing to include nominal payments in the tribe's dividend deduction process on her behalf, further agreeing to take her cut off the top, even before collecting the tribe's repayment percentage.

According to the tribe's operations officer from 1998 to 2001, Tim Cox, the Brighton loan program run by Ellen Click Smith has continued. In 2003, after the chairman was out of the picture, the council voted to buy it out but the deal was never fully consummated. The price was set at $1 million, payable in ten installments of $100,000 each for ten months. Only the first payment was made, however, and a portion of the interest profits for the loans was assigned to Mitchell and David. Further, even before that moment, Jack Smith, as Brighton rep, had become a part of the process, taking a cut to cash dividend checks in Hollywood for loan recipients in Brighton. No one in the tribe questions these activities. Seminoles from BC and Brighton who continue to want money from the Brighton loan program do not balk at the process despite the fact that it clearly is a predatory one.[28]

Not only on Brighton Res did loan programs continue to function, and this was one of the holes through which the tribe was "hemorrhaging money" when Tim Cox took over operations. By April 2001, on the eve of Tim's departure, the total amount of loans out to tribal citizens from the tribe was $49,729,698: over $679,000 to a single individual and almost that much to James as the purchase price of the Weston home occupied by Lesley. The list of loan recipients totaled 114, the majority varying from $35,000 to $330,000. Loan monies were continuing to be disbursed by the tribe at the rate of almost $1 million per month. Our imaging of this process as positive or negative depends, nevertheless, on whether we view it as an element of a white man's capitalist system or as an element of a traditional system of sharing resources within an Indian society. Or, we might take the view that this is but another process of adapting

Old Ways to new opportunities and requirements. This judgment will have to be made over time.

~

Up to and beyond the end of the twentieth century, increasingly, the council reps were creating their own little fiefdoms on each Res, and even outside of the Res, using the rep's discretionary funds for each Res to bind supporters. "A majority on the Tribal Council, which controls the tribe's money, has maintained power in part by handing out cash and granting financial requests from tribal citizens. Since 2000, council members have spent more than $280 million as they chose from funds they control. The spending included luxury vehicles, televisions and stereo systems, and [they] paid for cosmetic surgery for tribal members."[29] Max Jr. told reporters, nevertheless, that there was "no favoritism" in council members' spending, despite clear evidence and sworn testimony to the contrary.

Beginning in the late 1990s, David Cypress, still council member for BC Res, together with a non-Indian confederate, Krishna Lawrence of Clewiston (an ex-employee of the tribe), had bought a boxing gym for themselves in Hollywood, using tribal monies. David and his brother, Mitchell, constructed luxury homes and compounds for themselves and their extended families in BC using tribal funds. Friends of David outside the tribe benefited also, most of all the confederate Lawrence, a Clewiston landscaper, purporting to have landscaped BC homes to the tune of $1 million during one year—on a Res where $1 million could have nearly rebuilt the entire community.[30]

I had only a single personal experience of David's avarice, but it was so obvious as to be unmistakable and so easily interjected as to be obviously practiced. I had made it a policy not to permit myself to be importuned by anyone outside of the tribe for access to tribal officials or other citizens. Nevertheless, everyone from individuals with "great money-making ideas" to insurance salesmen, companies touting investment schemes, and mobile phone salesmen attempted to use me as a conduit to Seminole money, and I was certainly one of the least importuned. James had a well-known policy of rewarding tribal citizens, and employees as well, if they brought successful moneymaking ventures to the tribe. I could have made money, but I could have lost a great deal of respect as well, and above all my position with the Seminoles was one of personal trust and discretion. They had already had far too many years of seeing evidence of non-Indians as greedy and desirous of personal gain.

So, I steadfastly resisted . . . until the son of a longtime personal friend asked me to speak to a friend of his and provide him with the opportunity to present a very small but lucrative business proposition to the tribe. The businessman, among other things a dealer in fireworks, wanted to lease a central, high-traffic, location on the Hollywood Res for seasonal fireworks sales, at a guaranteed profit to the tribe. The tribe had long ago created its own fireworks ordinance, but in a time when the emphasis of fireworks control was on sparklers and their potential as hazards.[31] Since that time the council regularly had permitted sales of fireworks by various citizens and subleasing by citizens of their business leases to outside companies for seasonal sales. In this instance, however, the dealer was determined that his offer should benefit the tribe as a whole rather than any single individual.

David Cypress agreed to meet with the man and hear his proposal, but David required me to be at the meeting. I was very uncomfortable but felt that I had no choice. We met in a Hollywood tribal office conference room, and David brought with him several members of his current entourage. The businessman and his wife/partner, Mr. and Mrs. Mark Rorabeck of Arizona, made their proposal. They were interested in using a piece of property that was not controlled by David. Nevertheless, without missing a beat, David asked: "Well, so what's in it for me? What's my share?" Mark was so taken aback that he hesitated, and David looked from one to the other of us, as if we were naive for not having anticipated this question. Mark answered that he was proposing this deal to the tribe rather than to any individual Seminole, but after a few more minutes of discussion David made it clear that a deal that did not include any personal profit for himself was not worth taking to the council, and the meeting ended.

To what extent was James the model for this system of self-aggrandizement among the tribe's politicians—the system of greed that ultimately led to his own downfall? He had said for years that he had built himself and only he could bring himself down. Certainly there was no single element or act that provided the cause and effect of his removal. By the late 1990s, the tribe's annual gross revenues were huge, and even while many tribal citizens were becoming addicted to white man's money, James was becoming jaded, and tired, and ready to make changes using a good deal less caution than he might even have exercised in years past.

Close to the end of his fifth term (1995–99), we sat late one weekday afternoon in his sumptuous Hollywood office: the carpet was thick and rich, the walls and occasional tables and the desk were covered with gifts that he had received from visitors and leaders from all over the world. The chairman's office was cantilevered out from the apex of the V-shaped building. One entire wall was of shaded glass and looked out over the front of this new and beautiful office building that the Seminoles had finally built after years of sharing shabby, tobacco-smoke-clogged office space with the BIA's Seminole Agency. Even the stillness of the air exemplified the powerful economic position that his tribe had come to occupy in recent years, after centuries of living and dying in this land that no white man had wanted. A lozenge-shaped reflecting pool separated the principal driveways, and the entire landscaping comprised plants that had cultural value to South Florida and, particularly, to the Seminoles. But James was moody and unsatisfied.

"I've just about had it," he said—obviously wanting me to disagree with him and possibly convince him otherwise. "I think I just won't run again. I'll just go ride my horses." (He especially loved Appaloosas and had sent out one Christmas card bearing a photo of himself, white Stetson hat clamped on his head and cigar clenched in his teeth, surveying his scrub pasture in BC.) I obliged, thinking it had just been a bad day. "Oh, come on, James. You're too far along in this process to quit now, and you love it. And you love the people. And they love you. You've accomplished too many valuable things to stop now." "No, I don't," he responded sullenly. "Too many complaints all the time. I've had enough of it all." "Well," I countered thoughtfully, obviously not realizing how close to the edge I was skating, "Maybe it's time for you to make a serious change in course, rather than quit." He looked up at me sharply, from under furrowed brows, waiting for the rest of my thought. "Perhaps it's time for you to stop being a politician and become a statesman," I said gently. It was too much. He had no intention of changing any of his habits. His eyes only grew smaller and brighter and his image turned into a glare. I quickly shifted the subject to one of less weight.

∽

Over the second half of James's administration, an increasingly limited number of themes was given centrality in the administration and growth of the tribe. One was the creation of an environmental program that centered on water management and water quality as an outgrowth of the East Big Cypress Case (EBCC) and its resolution in the water compact of 1987. Henceforth, contracts would proliferate each year for quality controls, enhanced water and sewer systems, lift stations, EPA surveys, and wetlands mitigation—all of which, of course, as a concomitant of population growth. These items were outlined for each fiscal year in annual work plans shared with the South Florida Water Management District (SFWMD).

Another concomitant of population growth was, naturally, the need for increased housing. This was a less difficult process on the BC, Brighton, and, even, Immokalee reservations where undeveloped or underdeveloped lands were available, even if they had to be purchased (as in Immokalee) or reclaimed environmentally or economically from lessees (as in BC and Brighton). In the pressured urban areas of Hollywood and Tampa, however, lands had first to be purchased in fee simple or leases repurchased, and the lands taken into trust before a combination of U.S./HUD or Native American Housing Assistance and Self-Determination Act (NAHASDA) and tribal funds could be used for housing construction.[32] The process of having lands taken into federal trust was a great deal less complex if the land in question was contiguous to an existing reservation. The late twentieth century was a moment when the U.S. secretary of the interior and the BIA were reacting negatively to a national unease at the creation of entirely new reservations, which might mean the creation of new gaming facilities.

From a population of just under 1,000 when the political Tribe was created in 1957, the Seminole tribal population had literally doubled in thirty-five years, but the rate of population growth had increased significantly especially since the mid-1970s. By 1999, the population had reached almost 2,400, but by 2009 it had almost reached 4,000 (see figure 5). Unfortunately, as mentioned earlier, this demographic bloom was an artificial one in that it was created by a radically increased number of outmarriages, with the result that a significant number of tribal citizens were poised on the threshold of tribal Q, and this, in turn, means that the generations being born even as this is being written may or may not be eligible for tribal enrollment. From time to time there have been some rumblings among tribal citizens about dropping the minimum Q requirement for enrollment to less than one-quarter. This certainly would be a "quick fix," but it would undoubtedly create serious difficulties in the long run, as generations with significantly diluted Seminole blood heritage might or might not have sufficient social heritage to carry on as a discrete culture group. In other words, in cultural terms the indiscriminate willingness to procreate and the lack of council guidance could rapidly dilute Seminole blood out of existence. Over the next decade of the twenty-first century—that is, in the very short term—it will be critical whether, and how, the current councils turn their attention to the very real crisis. The Seminoles, who are so adamantly determined to maintain their cultural boundaries—ergo, their cultural existence—are standing by inactively as their cultural boundaries erode beneath their very feet.

Another but relatively minor theme would require regular attention as tribal citizens tried their own hands at entrepreneurship on a small scale. Council meetings were replete in this period with requests for land leases for businesses to be run directly by citizens or to be subleased by citizens to non-Indians for the income. In most instances, the council agreed to the requests, as long as the tribe's land use committee had reviewed it and agreed, and as long as the amount to be paid to or by the lessee to the tribe was fixed at acceptable rates. These were reasonable amounts and the majority of the leases were to be renewed each year or two years. The process of leasing tribal lands to nontribal business interests for long terms (twenty-five years or longer), as earlier administrations had done on the premise of securing income, was on its way out. This next generation of long-term business dealings would take on the form of management contracts for tribal businesses, almost always for gaming facilities, or for gaming and ancillary hotel/restaurant and concession management. Gaming, in particular, was now providing such a spate of income that James's agenda could also include other long-term directions.

This was one of the recurring themes that, in this period, became a fugue. The population was growing. Although the U.S. government still provided support to the tribe in the form of grants to educational and social welfare programs, road construction, and housing subsidies, among other things, the constantly increasing requirements of the U.S. government pressed the tribe increasingly to acquire additional revenues. Further, the determination of James and the council to provide for the future of the tribe (not to mention themselves) weighed upon them all. James's answer to those needs encompassed a combination of approaches.

The most direct and least complex, relatively, was to acquire more land. (Recall his passionate comment that day on the BC airstrip, that he did not intend to fight the white men for power, he would "just buy the damn state back!") The problem, of course, was to approach land purchases quietly so the prospect of tribal money did not send prices skyrocketing, and the potential for tribal gaming did not prejudice prospective neighbors, fairly or unfairly. Two avenues were available to this end. The first was to incorporate wholly owned tribal entities that could function quietly in the marketplace. One such was McInturf Enterprises, Inc., with president Nancy McInturf as agent. McInturf was actually the married name (a marriage of short duration) of Nancy Motlow, an Immokalee resident and council liaison for the Immokalee community from time to time.

Late in 1991, McIE, Inc., began to buy acreage, along the Indian River, in St. Lucie County, on Florida's east coast, and on the southwest coast, in Collier County. The total of about two hundred acres cost the tribe $1.1 million. Part of the property would enlarge the tiny Immokalee Res. Part, two years later, would be taken into federal trust and declared the new Ft. Pierce Res. In another year, McIE, Inc., would acquire land at Yeehaw Junction, south of Orlando that would become a new site for the Green Corn Ceremony for Brighton residents. At $1,250 an acre for 2,500 acres, the site would cost the tribe slightly over $3.1 million. It was culturally important, however, for tradition dictated that a ceremonial ground should be closed and its location moved, in prescribed patterns over time.

Even as McIE, Inc., would continue to purchase lands with tribal funds in Tampa and greater Hillsborough County and St. Lucie County, the council was developing other entities to acquire or manage properties as well. Seminole Economic Development, Inc., Seminole Community Development Corporation, Seminole Properties I and II, and the Tampa Property Administrative Fund all sheltered the proprietary business of the tribe from public scrutiny. They required greater and greater tribal investments. They vested power in very few hands although, ostensibly, with council oversight and control. Directorships of the tribe's development entities were always in the hands of James, the tribal secretary/treasurer Priscilla Sayen, and/or tribal counsel Jim Shore and his administrative assistant Agnes Billie Motlow, and/or council vice chairman (and board president) Mitchell Cypress. This tiny power coterie was, of course, directed personally by James with the advice of two non-Indian employees who gained tremendous personal power with him in the late 1990s, Tim Cox and Dan Wisher. We will examine their roles more closely, beginning in chapter 10.

One prospective land deal was based upon direct purchase and involved another of James's grandiose plans. The land was in Osceola County and was offered by the Partin family, a family of successful businesspeople whose roots went deep into the twentieth century in Florida. A member of the family, an ex–Roman Catholic priest, brought the offer to the tribe. The location of the property, in central Florida not far from Orange County and Orlando, gave James the idea of a major tourist attraction, à la Disney World and Universal Studios, that he tentatively dubbed Indigenous World or, sometimes, Native America.

In early September 1998, the council approved the concept of the purchase. The parcel totaled slightly more than 3,000 acres and James was empowered to evaluate the property further, to negotiate a deal, and to expend the necessary funds relative to the due diligence, the closing costs, and any other reasonable requirements.[33] Six months later, preliminary land and environmental surveys had been completed and the acquisition still looked good to James, although his new tribal administrator, Tim Cox, did not favor the deal at all. The boundary survey had indicated a total of 3,544.98 acres. Groundwater and soil tests were still pending, but the council, by a unanimous vote of five/nil, still empowered the chairman to close the deal. S.T.O.F. Holdings, Ltd., would be the buyer, and the Partin Family Land Trust, the seller.[34] Although "Father" Robert was an enthusiastic broker, many Partin family members did not want to abandon lands that the family had accumulated so assiduously over so long a time.

All was not as well as it seemed with the deal, however. Father Robert, the Partin family's agent, visited James regularly and touted the history of the land, which might include a Seminole Wars battlefield, but the deal did not firm up. James was still excited about the purchase, however. He told Tim that it might be time for the tribe to create a Res there, move some tribal citizens up there from BC and Brighton and, perhaps, even relocate the tribe's headquarters there as well. It could be a major leap in the Seminoles' process of their own *reconquista*—their retaking of their Florida heartlands. It would have raised them to an entirely new level of statewide visibility and power.

James spoke to various Seminoles who excitedly pushed him for the possibility of individual ten-acre plots, which he had no intention of providing. In fact, within his envisioned scenario they might not get one-acre plots. Nor could the Seminoles understand that the land purchase would be in fee simple, at least until such time as it might be taken into federal trust as a Res. But until that time they would be individual landowners and would be required to pay taxes on the land. Rancor developed over these topics, along with so many others.[35]

The council was aware of James's tremendously costly plans for the site, and there was anxiety over taking the tribe so much deeper into debt. This was a moment when the tribe was once again becoming financially overextended. There was anger added to anxiety over the way James seemed more and more to be cutting the council out of the decision-making process. Ironically, the council members did not seem to feel any culpability for this, despite the fact that they had acquiesced regularly to the chairman's decisions, for two decades thus far, without any serious cavils. In fairness, the traditional way for Indians generally, including the Seminoles, to indicate disagreement or displeasure was through silence. But these were new times and the politicians were operating under a nontraditional set of rules.

A few months later the parcel had diminished slightly to 3,541.01 acres, and the selling price was $75 million, of which the seller was willing to finance most. But by September the larger deal "could not be consummated" and the family offered an alternative of 1,184 acres for $31.9 million. The council accepted this and closed the deal.[36] A second installment of land subsequently was negotiated and closed on, but the purchase was short-lived. As soon as James was suspended from office, the council repudiated this, among other of the chairman's dealings, and permitted all the property to revert to the Partin family, at an unnecessary loss to the tribe. Osceola County is one of the fastest-growing areas in the nation, and land is at a premium there. Over the final decade of the twentieth century, nevertheless, James and the council acquired properties in Tallahassee (Leon County), St. Augustine (St. Johns County), Melbourne (Brevard County), and Marion, Hillsborough, and Collier counties.

The other more complex and ultimately even more costly method of land acquisition for the tribe was to accept the blandishments of nontribal venture capitalists who more and more often approached James with offers of everything from airplanes to Miss Universe judgeships to land and development deals, in exchange for the opportunities to enter into management agreements at tribal gaming facilities, existing or yet to be constructed. These were multi-million-dollar deals that sometimes required substantial direct investments from the tribe, but could potentially return many millions more. There were just a few obvious obstacles in this approach.

The most basic was the fact that the number of established lending institutions ready to underwrite Indian business ventures was, as mentioned earlier, limited, and even those which would underwrite were hesitant. James expressed his anger more than once during this period at the tribe's experience with Barnett Banks, a Florida corporation. In early 1998 the tribe shifted some of its business to First National Bank, and James commented, "Back when we needed a little help, they were asking us for co-signers."[37] In James's mind this situation provided a rationale for entertaining offers from individual venture capitalists or consortia of such individuals, who reached out to him through various contacts already established or through "friends of friends."

The critical "downsides" of this process were several. First, James's business acumen and experiential base were not such as to provide him with completely sound judgment. Second, the personal advisors whom he chose were not at all culturally sensitive. In fact, they seemed to follow—inappropriately—the dictum of the warrior, U.S. Navy Admiral David Farragut: "Damn the torpedoes; full speed ahead." Then, the constantly rising tribal income buffered James and the tribe from complete failure, because the caliber of potential business investors varied widely. Sometimes, the outside people who approached him had direct access to big money, or indirect access to sources of big money. Sometimes they only had big ideas. The next downside was that these people, whether their financing was sound or not, were required, since 1988 and the passage of the National Indian Gaming Act, to be vetted by the U.S. government—including background checks by the FBI—on the premise of keeping organized crime with its admitted access to large sums of money out of Indian gaming.

In the 1990s, this put FR tribes interested in getting into or expanding gaming between the proverbial rock and a hard place. On the one side, getting "clean" money was difficult; on the other, taking available but "dirty" money was becoming less and less possible. James's response to this situation was to investigate such offers very gingerly, and only at second, third, or even fourth hand. The council entertained binding and nonbinding letters of agreement from consortia organized as corporations, limited liability partnerships (LLPs), and other funding aggregates. Despite large concepts that included everything from casinos and hotels and restaurants to golf courses and timeshares, most of these plans came to naught and often cost the tribe significant investments that it could not or did not choose to recoup.

It is important to keep in mind, nevertheless, that even as the number of deals presented to the tribe grew, and even as the BIA and the NIGC questioned the deals more and more closely, the members of the Tribal Council publicly supported all of James's moves. They gave the chairman, by official resolutions, the authority to negotiate deals, to expend funds, and to sign the letters of agreement. And the council resolutions always included the pro forma disclaimer, "Whereas, the Tribal Council . . . has reviewed said MOU [or MOA or LA], and it is otherwise fully advised." Almost invariably, the votes on such issues were unanimous: 5 for and 0 against, with no abstentions. Until almost the very moment when they turned against him, the council would abet the process. By the turn of the century, the council members would become so angry at the process of rapidly expanding business and change that James was attempting to drive through that they would suspend (in 2001) and, ultimately (in 2003), impeach their chairman in a process for which there was only a limited constitutional basis and no precedent. In the meantime, however, for an entire generation, over almost six terms of office, they either blindly trusted him or complicity agreed with him. The weight of evidence seems to support the latter.

9   The Beginning of the End

When I went out to BC to live, in late 1992, and literally on the morning after Hurricane Andrew passed over South Florida, the shock of the new began to overwhelm me. The Big Cypress, today the northern frontier of what remains of the Everglades, was dramatic in ways more personally impressive than I could have believed possible for a person who had lived less than 100 miles away from it for the last decade and whose historical Florida heritage had encompassed many of its wildernesses before.

Above all else was the vastness that contrasted so starkly with the "cheek-by-jowl" intensity of South Florida development. I came to call that east–west segment of I-75 known as Alligator Alley my personal time tunnel. White man's developments crept ever farther out of the urban environment into the dwindling Glades. Seminoles called the white people "ants" because of their seemingly unstoppable development, despite setback laws. But, as the residences gave way to water and sawgrass, broad vistas opened up and the pressures of the urban setting wafted away to be gradually replaced by recollections of centuries past and the Seminoles' stories, from their grandmothers' grandmothers, of surviving in this stark setting. There are few places left in Florida today where one can be so impressed by natural, undeveloped, and immense views such as this.

This was especially impressive at night on the BC Res, where there were no ambient city lights to gauze the stars. They literally seemed touchable. The voices of tiny screech owls were far larger than the birds themselves. I had heard that the cry of the Florida panther sounded eerily like that of a woman screaming, but I couldn't credit it until the first one I heard sent shivers up my spine. One of the most breathtaking of sights was the nighttime display put on by hundreds and hundreds of tiny fireflies—their wings shuddering in electrical brilliance—hovering over blossoming saw palmetto heads, some older heads thirty or forty feet in diameter. It was one show that Disney would never be able to fake.

The summer days pelted you with hurricane-season tropical rains and filled the mangrove sloughs with precious water that showed hardwood hammocks off in high relief for the life-saving places that they had been for the Seminoles and their ancestors for so many thousands of years. The dry winter cold, settling into the dense undergrowth of a land otherwise so wet, seeped into the bones no matter how many layers of clothing one wore. Mercifully short, South Florida winters in the Big Cypress and the Florida Everglades are nonetheless memorable. Alligators, snakes, mosquitoes, rain, heat, and the Seminole Indians—they all have formed a symbiotic relationship that most non-Indians would find utterly intolerable.

But the relationship with the land is so close for the Seminoles that each time I've asked them to identify what I view as photographs of *people* standing in woods, they've instinctively identified the trees first. "Now, see that big tree" they begin. "That's where the water tower is now." Then, and only then, once they've identified themselves with the landscape and nature, do they turn their attention to the people in the photograph. It's just like their view of what English speakers call *swamp*. To us, swamp is land with water over it. To the Seminoles, it's water, with land under it. To understand a language is to understand a people.

The BC Res was just on the cusp of losing some of its isolation when I arrived, as ecotourists and Indian lovers began to seek out a vestige of Indianness that was rare in the East or the southeastern United States. Moreover, events were moving with increasing rapidity in BC and across the tribe and inexorably overtaking the glorious isolation of life in the Big Cypress. Seminoles on the urban reservations had told me that the people in BC were "strange." They were, I realized, but not in the way they were imaged by the others. They were the people who were most at peace with the isolation of their setting and most determined to resist the onslaught of non-Indian life in as many ways as possible. They were the stalwarts who clung most determinedly to the Old Ways. Ironically, despite his own love of the Old Ways, it was James who was most determined to create development in BC, to make it the capital of his kingdom. The land and the people defeated him, however, at least for the moment.

∾

Late in 1992 the Kissimmee Billie Swamp Safari was still under construction. I awoke one morning to the screams of a young Mexican woman who had arrived at the Swamp Water Café to open up, only to find a twelve-foot alligator stretched out across the porch and in front of the door. He had climbed out of the adjacent canal and broken the fence to reach the porch, for reasons that we could not figure out. It took three men several hours to coax him back into the water. In those days, it was not unusual to find red Russian pigs, Watusi cattle, elands, or most any other creatures ambling across the front yard in the morning, as if to remind us humans that they had prior rights.

No construction had yet begun on the museum, but plans were under way. "James's crew," composed of Indian and Mexican workers, was busy fencing the Hunting Adventures property, and heavy equipment mishaps were frequent occurrences: one front-end loader would have to be sent into a bog to retrieve another. Community residents would go missing only to turn up in the custody of the Hendry County sheriff's office, calling James for bail money. He could be counted on to provide it regularly. Two years later, James directed the establishment of a tribal Wildlife and Parks Department and put Jimmy McDaniel formally in charge of the projects he had already headed since their inception a few years earlier. Now the Hunting Adventures would have its own line item in the annual budget, and it was envisioned that processing of the kills would turn into saleable meat products for the tribe and be, James hoped, another revenue-generating program area.

At that moment, James and Howard Tommie were not on good terms. This may have come about because Howard's lease payments for some of his Hollywood business sites were beginning to fall into arrears. Since he still received a percentage of the Hollywood bingo contract, however, money would not seem to have been the issue. The council would finally be forced to cancel some of his leases in a few years. There was also a rumor going around that Howard was planning to challenge James in the '95 election, to recover the chairman's seat as, indeed, he did—with an obvious lack of success. Robb Tiller had had baseball-style caps printed as campaign advertising for James to give out, and James gave me one—but, surreptitiously—and he warned me not to wear it on the Res. Tribal opinion was running strongly against Robb, and James did not want the caps—which everyone knew came from Robb—to remind them of the association. Ironically, he maintained the association. The tribe returned James to office for his fifth term, although his margin of victory had fallen.

David Cypress had been sent back to the council in 1991 and 1993, and would hold on to his seat in the 1995 elections, despite his personal battles and challenges from three BC candidates.

Mitchell Cypress ran against Fred Smith for board president in the same election, and won, partly on the basis of Fred's poor physical condition. His ability as a warrior was almost at an end. Mitchell freely underwrote birthday parties and personal gifts to useful individuals. Stanlo Johns and Willie Johns of Brighton actively worked for him.

Also by this time the process of handing out loans had once again gotten out of hand. The tribe had its own loan department now, with its own regulations, but James—ever the politician—continued to entertain requests for monies that he doled out from the chairman's discretionary fund. Pat Diamond was often annoyed with James for flouting all attempts at regularizing the loan system (among others) and agreeing to loans that might or might not ever be repaid. Because of her position as James's administrative assistant, she had been placed in the position of arranging for the loans that the chairman's office agreed to. In order to maintain some semblance of control, she consulted with Ted Boyd and Sal Giannettino, head of Information Systems (IS) for the tribe, to create the first integrated tribal member database. This was the accounting database that James would soon, with Dan Wisher's help, turn into the Big Red Button, as soon as he caught on to its informational value. For the first time it linked health, housing, and loan records for each individual so that their loan and re-payment histories could be reviewed before new loans were granted. Tribal citizens were constantly disgruntled that James's agreement to loan them monies might ultimately be denied because his decision was in conflict with the regulations. It was but one more grudge they stored up.

In Tampa, at the time, the Res had a new prevention officer, paid for through a federal Office of Substance Abuse grant. Pat Diamond and I sat through a community meeting at which the prevention officer touted the utility of her program, but though she shared her own personal history with substance abuse and recovery, it was already clear that her program would fail because she obviously failed to realize that she was working across cultural boundaries, and the success of the program depended more on the participants and their cultural expectations than on what she viewed as the beauty of her own culture-based program. If I could realize that after only my short time with the tribe, then I knew that the Seminoles certainly had realized it more rapidly than I. They did. They ignored her. She moved on.

In all fairness, the line between cultural understanding and cultural ignorance runs through a minefield. The new principal at Ahfachkee School, Marty Coyle, asked me to collaborate with the school's culture teacher, a tribal citizen, to create a Christmas program. I suggested that the students stage a play depicting the traditional Seminole creation story. Even though the occasion was a non-Indian holiday, the children could use the moment to reconfirm their own traditions. The teacher became furious with me because, she told others, I was trying to supplant Christianity. The people whom she told, however, were not all supporters of Christianity or the teacher, and they laughed heartily as they repeated her story to me.

Robb Tiller had brought James a potential investor, Dave Vopnford, who owned a chain of campgrounds. The idea was for Vopnford to take over the large, tin-roofed building that was the intermittently defunct BC bingo hall and the BC campground as well. The hall currently was being filled with U.S.

government surplus desks and other furniture and the Chinese army jeeps that Tiller had influenced James to acquire for potentially lucrative reasons. Vopnford proposed turning the bingo hall into an indoor campground, with amusements and activities inside and out, and incorporating the little campground across the road in the development. He wanted James to cut Tiller out of the deal, however, and they (James and Vopnford) finally cut a deal that failed, once again, to provide BC with the centrality that James had hoped for. More important, the deal deprived the tribe of promised income as it finally fell apart, with or without Tiller in the bargain.

The small campground on the edge of the BC airstrip across from the bingo hall, which the tribe had constructed first with HUD funding in 1988, was struggling along. Its location, in the Big Cypress, made it a draw for environmentalists and ecotourists and for some visitors just trying to get away from it all. But its development always had been minimal and its amenities almost nonexistent, and James never could seem to find the right combination of management skills and the right marketing niche. Prefab cabins occupied a small, flat piece of land exposed to the withering attacks of the South Florida sun. The Swamp Water Café at the Billie Swamp Safari was just basically completed so campers either had to accept the limited menu available or bring in their own supplies, or drive the forty-two miles to Clewiston to get them, since it was impossible to find variety in, or even depend on, the gas stations/convenience stores that opened and closed with irregularity on the Res.

Shortly after it opened James gave the management of the campground to one of his daughters, Bobbie Jamie Billie, who moved there enthusiastically but gradually lost interest. Almost two years later, the council assigned its management to an independent group, Campsite Management, Inc., that quickly realized the difficulty and lack of potential in the business. Otherwise, management of the struggling business intermittently was relegated to the current safari manager.[1]

In 1993, Robb Tiller brought Vopnford to BC to meet with James and present his grand vision for both the campground and the large bingo hall. In an unusual move for a businessman, Vopnford brought his mother and her sister along with him to the meeting, along with an unexplained young blond male, Larry. Vopnford, his gray-haired mother and aunt, James, Tiller, Larry, and I sat under the chickee in James's front yard for one long gentle evening and talked history. Various Seminoles stopped by. James roasted meat over the cook fire and ate one of the pieces first, in the Seminole tradition of illustrating to the guest that the food was worth eating and worthy of the host himself. It was obvious that the entire evening had been gently choreographed by both visitor and host, and that James was impressed with the guest and the proposal, and vice versa (it seemed).

On 4 August 1993, the council ratified an arrangement for management and marketing between the tribe and Thousand Adventures of Florida, Inc., David T. Vopnford, president, by which Thousand Adventures assumed the previous agreement for marketing and management assigned to Campsite Management, Inc., and added its own attractive plan.[2] The ultimate deal was a small one, relative to other business ventures the council obligingly entered into over the rest of James's leadership, but its short life, its termination, and the reasons for its termination all illustrate a process that was repeated too many times in the course of the tribe's business evolution and the leadership of James, backed by Mitchell, David Cypress, Max Osceola Jr., and Jack Smith.

The deal lasted only until the council terminated the agreement with Thousand Adventures of Florida, Inc., at their first meeting of the calendar year 1995.[3] They recited the failures of the contractor to perform according to the contract. Vopnford, a basic part of whose plan had been to create marketing materials and sell 1,000 memberships, had failed to provide the council with any membership materials and documents or the proposed rules and regulations for the enterprise. He had failed to provide accounting of any and all membership monies received, which were supposed to have been deposited in a special trust account from which tribal and business revenues were to have been derived. Vopnford had provided no reports of the trust fund status or even the basic inventory of assets that was a required part of the contract. Either Vopnford had sold memberships that were unrecorded and unaccounted for, or he had lost interest in the project early on and simply faded away. The tribal administrator, Larry Frank, sent official letters to Vopnford several times requesting the required documentation and accounting, but to no avail. Like a number of other projects entered into so easily by James and the council, and with such a lack of what businesspersons know as due diligence, the BC campground story was just one more.

More often than not the campground would straggle on, its management attached to that of the safari and, intermittently, to that of the Hunting Adventure. The safari finally began to show a profit, but only after the tribe's change to zero-based budgeting in fiscal year 2000 that no longer required the project to be dragged down by the significant amounts that the tribe had invested in its development, which would have taken many more years to amortize. By then the Hunting Adventures project had already shifted its revenue reliance to meat processing and the sale of cut-outs from tribal herds, the production and sale of the niche product Chief Jerky, and the sale of the acquired product Everglades Seasonings.

∾

The story of Robb Tiller, who brought the Vopnford deal to James and the tribe, is certainly one of the strangest in the history of James's association with strange characters. They had met years earlier, even before James's panther trials. In fact, it was Robb who had brought Jimmy McDaniel to James, although I had never asked how Robb and Jimmy had met. Robb had a facility for encountering people in high—and low—places and brokering relationships. James realized that some of his own tactics were abrasively direct, and he was impressed by the charm that Robb could use when he chose. Unerringly, Robb had gravitated toward James. The sine qua non of these brokered relationships was, it appeared, that they should offer some economic reward to the broker. James, nevertheless, realized that Robb harmed himself by not being content with bringing people together with James. He was, rather, determined to stay in the deal and command it.

James saw Robb as nonetheless valuable for his ability to find people and make them available to James. Robb's one positive attribute was that he was just intelligent enough not to attempt to meddle with the internal politics of the tribe. James remained his single conduit to tribal money and preferment, although at one point Robb did become engaged to a tribal citizen, Jo-Lin Osceola (Clan X, b. 1970, daughter of Joe Dan Osceola). The two, however, had mutually exclusive ambitions and the relationship ended.

Robb's ambition was to broker James to the outside world and ensconce himself in the lucrative position of power broker. Interestingly enough (to the rest of us who watched), James did not discourage this process. James sometimes told the story of a diving trip to the Bahamas, arranged by Robb early in their (his and James's) relationship. During a trip into deep waters to snorkel, James went into the water, and while he was there, Robb turned the boat back to the marina, leaving James distant and alone. James was quite sure that there had been no mistake—Robb had known that James was not on board. Fortuitously, James was picked up (after several anxiety-making hours in the water), but not by Robb. To my knowledge, Robb never apologized, and no one ever got a satisfactory answer from James about why he would continue an association with a person who would act in such a manner. My personal view is that Robb may have been providing James with an object lesson about the importance of treating Robb with proper deference. And, obviously, James got the message and was getting something out of the relationship, which continued on throughout James's chairmanship.

Under the heading of what I have called James's "'gator baiting," he once enjoyed an opportunity to annoy Robb tremendously, and he laughed about it for years. More important to the larger story of the tribe, the story highlights larger issues. It occurred during one of the annual hunting trips. James, the organizer, assigned trip participants to their sleeping tents, two to a tent. On this particular trip, James assigned Robb and Chris O'Donnell to the same tent.

Chris had worked for the tribe since late 1983, beginning as staff of the "Reservation Program" (such ambiguous designations usually being euphemisms for whatever-James-wanted programs) and moving upward to administrative assistant in the tribal administrator's office. She was absolutely devoted to James, enjoying a convenient sexual relationship with him, but only intermittently and never exclusively—Chris's own lack of exclusivity being only slightly less than that of James, and equally as well known. This reality will have a critical importance as the events of James's removal from power are played out.

According to James and others, it was not unusual for males and females to be assigned to share tents, and apparently it had not been an issue—until now. Chris was not bothered by the arrangement, but Robb was. First, he spent a day or so baiting Chris about her past relationship with James, calling her an "old girlfriend." This upset Chris, and she told Robb in no uncertain terms that she cared very much about James but would not resume a relationship with him, "even on Lesley's life!" James watched the uncomfortable scenario play itself out. He reported to me that Robb "got all fussy and fidgety" about sleeping in the same tent with Chris. When the hunters returned to BC, Robb took revenge on Chris by untruthfully telling Lesley that Chris wanted to resume her relationship with James, which upset Lesley very much and cost James a great deal of effort to calm her anger. Chris and Robb became permanently estranged over the events, but we shall watch as Chris continued to play a role in the events surrounding James's downfall.

So I said to James at one point, "If you know the weaknesses these people (such as Robb) have, and the problems of keeping them around, why do you do it?" (Pat Diamond used to refer to James as the puppet master—finding useful attributes in otherwise useless people and hanging them in his psychological closet until he needed them.) And he responded, "Because they do things for me. They get me into places I couldn't get into by myself." He was, in too many ways, still the half-blood Indian boy who never realized that there were other, and more legitimate, ways of getting into those places, such as by virtue of his own intelligence and position alone.

The complex relationship between James and Robb was fascinating. It carried a degree of emotionalism that seemed unusual in a purely political attachment, but there is always a degree of passion that transcends the purely utilitarian in power relationships. Each wanted to be near the other. Each needed the other as a potential source of self-aggrandizement and economic return. Each mistrusted the other and watched warily, askance. Each tried, constantly, to show the other up and embarrass the other. But each kept being drawn back to the other.

The association between James and Robb would continue almost into the period of estrangement between James and the council reps that would come to a head in the first year of the new, twenty-first, century. In the end, after Robb had been depositioned by federal authorities in their attempts to find charges against James (specifically, not the tribe), James told reporters: "Robb Tiller is a gentleman that—I'm not quite sure how to describe him, but if you believe in him . . . you . . . better go get a psychiatrist." Robb was constantly bringing potential deals to James, and "You'll get irritated at that. And you got Robb Tiller as a friend standing there, who's tryin' to act like your friend, but at the same time is using you as bait and you really don't know that he's using you as bait because he says he's your friend, but at the same time he's selling you by the ounce out there and you don't know it."[4]

One fascinating example of their eccentric relationship involved Federal Excess and Surplus Personal Property, a bingo hall full of worn-out government furniture, an expensive naval crane, and a tribal embarrassment that was really only tangential to a national scandal but had the potential to land James in federal prison. The nexus was Russell Hawkins, former chairman of the FR Sisseton-Wahpeton Sioux Tribe. James had come to know Hawkins in Indian Country leadership circles and through his annual hunting trips, some to Sioux territory.

In 1990, after recent amendments to the Indian Self-Determination Act, the BIA had notified the FR tribes that they were eligible to inspect and acquire government surplus property and use it for the benefit of the tribes. Each tribal governing body had to certify a screener who would view and choose the property. The property ranged from tired old file cabinets to high-value earthmoving and construction equipment that, after 1991, was coming back from duty in the Persian Gulf war. Hawkins's involvement appears to have been limited to permitting an arrangement that was beneficial to his tribe but quite illegal according to later decisions by federal authorities.

The arrangement involved allowing several non-Indians and one tribal citizen to form a company that would acquire pieces for the tribe and, subsequently, obtain the surplus pieces from the tribe for far-below-market-value prices. Ultimately they would resell them for tremendous profits, of which, according to court documents, the Sisseton-Wahpeton Tribe received only 10 percent, the screeners received 13 percent, and the outside company received the rest.[5] The *New York Times* reported, "Records show the lion's share of proceeds went to [the non-Indian] business associates. The tribe never saw millions of dollars' worth of gear ordered in its name. And it sold other equipment worth millions for a small fraction of its worth."[6] Some pieces of purchased property never even made it to the S-W Tribe; they went directly to the outside company and were sold without any profits going to the tribe.

One of the partners in the outside company, Dakota Machinery Exchange, and a screener for the S-W Tribe was an individual named Roger J. Raether. Raether was one of several who met with federal officials in an attempt to obtain a ruling on whether their purchase and resale process was legal. They decided to believe that it was, despite the fact that the manager of the Personal Property Services of the U.S. General Services Administration (GSA) issued a memorandum on 22 January 1992, halting all such transfers of excess property pending further investigation of the issue. A month later, the process was determined not to be in compliance with the GSA's interpretation of the law. Subsequently, it was determined that surplus property could be obtained by tribes only if it was intended for use in connection with a tribe's 638 (self-determination) contract with the BIA.

Meanwhile, in Florida, at the regular council meeting held on 13 March 1992, James proposed Robb Tiller as the screener for the Seminole Tribe, and the council confirmed him.[7] Tiller began to accumulate numerous versions of government cast-off furniture that, in turn, began to fill the old BC bingo hall. Pat Diamond at first signed all the purchase orders but, beginning to be wary of the growing number of purchases, passed the paperwork over to Chris O'Donnell in the tribal administrator's office. Unbeknownst to the tribe, however, several federal investigations of the purchases and sales were already in progress. In March of 1993, James kicked the process up a notch by dropping Robb as screener and asking the council to accept Roger Raether instead, as having a better track record at acquiring and selling.[8]

Within a short few months, the federal investigators tracked Raether to the Seminoles, but not before he had obtained for the tribe a 300-ton crane from a San Diego naval yard. Signing on behalf of the Seminoles, Raether sold the crane forward to his company. The sale price was documented at $34,000, and immediately another member of the company began trying to sell the same crane for $450,000. The federal authorities visited Hollywood and held conferences with Chris O'Donnell.

The GSA, the U.S. government's property management agency, stepped in and charged Raether, Hawkins, and another member of the company with conspiracy and lying to the agency about their purchases, including the crane the GSA had recovered before it could leave California. Raether and Hawkins went to trial and were convicted, but in 1996 the U.S. Court of Appeals for the Eighth Circuit reversed part of the Raether decision on a technicality, but confirmed the guilty verdict, and ordered a retrial. The case against Hawkins was not pressed, however. A year later, the Eighth Circuit once again heard the Raether case and affirmed his conviction.[9] James, although closely questioned by federal investigators, was not charged. Not until 1996, almost two years after

Raether had been convicted, did the council get around to reissuing the Seminole Tribe's screener's card, this time to James himself, but by then, the personal cost had become too high and it appears that he did not use it again.

Over the years, Robb Tiller left behind a trail of failed businesses of his own, including a yacht brokerage, an auto-leasing firm, and a diamond exchange. His business venture in 1998 required marriage to a Cuban woman. In March of that year, President Bill Clinton had lifted a two-year-old ban on travel restrictions to Cuba, permitting direct transport of food, medical supplies, and humanitarian aid to the country. Tiller was one of many who sought to take advantage of this thaw in relations. He obtained the use of a transport plane from a private investor, hangared it in Immokalee, and set up a Web site offering flight services to Havana and touting his ability to procure comely and subservient Cuban brides for interested men. By July of that year, however, his hangar rent was in arrears, his telephone services had been shut off, and Mr. and Mrs. Tiller had disappeared.[10] The FBI would, of course, locate him for questioning after 2001 when the council suspended James, prior to his impeachment, but Robb gave them nothing useful. He maintained at least a critical bit of loyalty to James (and, of course, to himself).

~

This last decade of the twentieth century was also the moment when Mitchell Cypress's star began to rise within the tribe. His personal story was one of overcoming adversities that his brother, David, had never been able to surmount permanently. James had told me that Mitchell Cypress and Jacob Osceola were two other individuals who had gone through Medicine training with Sonny Billie, at least through the initial four-day fast. There is, ostensibly, a bond among those who have gone through the training. James and Jacob have always appeared to support each other or, at the very least, not to publicly work against each other over the years. Not so with Mitchell.

James felt that Mitchell was a "flip-flop." He was always anxious lest he be viewed in any negative light by voters. He would go whichever way the political wind blew. He had a good head, James believed, but he deferred too much to James. James wanted Mitchell to stand on his own two feet. He finally would, to James's chagrin. In fact, many Seminoles said that Sonny Billie was doing bad Medicine on behalf of Mitchell and David, against James, and that is what killed Sonny. (Earlier, they also had said that Sonny was doing good Medicine, in support of James.) This may be, but if so, James did not see it and Sonny always maintained strong public support for James.

I also found Mitchell to be overly concerned about his public image, but not half as weak as James thought. "Why do you always have to do everything the tough way?" I asked Mitchell. "Why not help people?" Without need to consider, he replied "No, no, no. Make 'em tough. It's good. You'll find out who they

Figure 7. A trimmed cypress log awaits preparation beside the Wind Clan camp chikî(t), BC Res, 1997. (Photograph by P. R. Wickman.)

Figure 8. Henry John Billie (L) and Sonny Billie discuss the cypress log that will become a new dugout canoe, BC Res, 1997. (Photograph by P. R. Wickman.)

are." Why give them a compliment when you can give them a kick, he seemed to be saying. "Because the kick will make them get up and work. Leave them alone. Let them fight a little bit!" It is a warrior's philosophy, a survivor's philosophy.

Mitchell's wife had died several years earlier. He had been an inactive alcoholic for some years. The Discover Native America–event weekend in Jacksonville (see below) was his fourth anniversary, he told me, and I told him how proud I was of him. Mitchell told me about ceremonies and traditions for a man who had lost his wife. He took Medicine and was to refrain from sex for four months. In the old days, it had been four years, and there were some women in the tribe who still subscribed to the four-year requirement. Also, the widower was required to ask his mother-in-law what he should do for her and her clan and how he should best mourn for her daughter.

Mitchell's mother-in-law told him to take the Medicine and go through the ceremony at the next Green Corn and then come to her again. There was some payment involved for the Medicine man also (cow, horse, sheep, one to four bolts of cloth, or such). His Medicine was not totally complete until the next Green Corn, where an old man (another widower) was assigned to fetch him and lead him out to the central fire and walk him around the perimeter, four times, counterclockwise. After this, four men got up from a bench and greeted him as a brother. And these four men were men who had also lost wives, and they informed him that henceforward he would be a member of their ranks and if any other person should lose a mate, he would have the right and responsibility to go to that person and help them through their grief. As a result of this, he began to get better. He called on his mother-in-law again. She said he had been a good son to her and his wife's clan, but he should go back to his father's clan, although he could always come back to her clan again—an honor.

Mitchell was one of nine children, and taller than his siblings. He grew up with anger at his parents because there was some talk in the family that his mother may have had Mitchell by someone other than Jimmy Cypress. Frequently, he was sent to his maternal grandmother, and he felt that he was singled out, possibly because of the rumor that Jimmy Cypress was not his father. But Jimmy Cypress was not a person of good reputation within the tribe, and his negative history provided a constant impetus for Mitchell to keep his own reputation (relatively) untarnished.

Most of the negative side of Mitchell's reputation had to do with sexual exploits, and these were never viewed as very serious transgressions by the Seminoles, just as James's were not either. Again, as with so many other parts of Seminole life, sexuality—even in its twentieth-century version—was accepted, if it was not flaunted. This is why the whole subject of James's relationship with

Christine O'Donnell, which was touted to the non-Indian world as a reprehensible flaw, was such a transparent ploy to those who know the tribe and its proclivities. James's long-standing relationship with Chris simply provided Jim Shore and the council with an excellent target of opportunity. We will examine this situation in chapters 10 to 13.

Mitchell drank for about fifteen years. One dark night he and a friend were in his Beretta, drunk, about a mile beyond the BC community, on Snake Road, and he rolled the car. He and the friend wound up, unharmed, on the roof. Mitchell saw the beer can nearby and picked it up and flung it away and said, "That's it. That's enough." And he quit drinking. He attended AA meetings, but he knew that he could not, as they admonished, stay away from bars and other drinkers. In his case, the other drinkers were his people. He said: "You either want it [the alcohol] or you don't want it, and where you are doesn't matter." And I've seen Mitchell in bars, peacefully, with cups of coffee in front of him, when those around him were really drunk. "A man has to have two heads," Mitchell says frequently, and he is referring to a variety of circumstances.

Mitchell thought about running against James in this period, but thought better of it. Fred Smith told him to just stay on the board, and when he (Fred) retired, which might be soon Fred said, he would name his own successor, ostensibly Mitchell. In addition to his own natural ambitions, this is another reason why Mitchell ran for board president when Fred passed away unexpectedly in 1996. In the process, Mitchell seemed to gain a new degree of his own confidence in the process.

~

James's commitment to the Old Ways, his love of music and public performing, and his decision to boost the tribe's public visibility coincided with radically increasing gaming revenues in the mid-1990s, but not without tribal and nontribal contention fostered, as usual, by his unilateral decision making. One particular internal tribal story at the conjunction of these realities began with James Jumper (Panther Clan, 1940–1994), brother of James's partner Lesley Garcia's mother, Dolores Jumper (Panther Clan, b. 1947). Late in 1990, at James's instigation, the council appointed James Jumper as director of an American Indian Culture Project (AICP) for the tribe.[11]

James Jumper shortly requested and obtained monies from the council to stage a public event, in 1992, that was a pan-Indian tribal fair. The tribe had held public fairs before, but this one broadened the scope of the event. The problem stemmed from the fact that the event later was reported to the council as having lost, rather then made, money, and the council wanted the return of funds for which, in addition, no clear accounting could be made.

The unique feature of this situation was that James (Billie) was not among those who spoke out in favor of the accounting, and tribal citizens noticed this. In fact, James Jumper's position was that the monies had been a personal loan to him, and James Billie's silence concerning the matter, and the money, was permanent. No complete accounting was ever made. In July of 1992, James Jumper was summarily removed from his position as director of the AICP. Eight months later, when he applied to the council for permission to permit an advertising company to place a billboard on the home site that he leased from the tribe, the council saw an opportunity to recoup some of its funds and, undoubtedly, to slap at both Jameses. James Jumper could have his billboard contract, with an annual income of $11,500, but he would keep none of it. Half would go to the tribe for its agreement to the sublease; the other half would also go to the tribe, "pending settlement of other financial matters between James A. Jumper and the Seminole Tribe of Florida."[12] James Jumper died of what may have been a stroke, alone, in a motel room, a scant year and a half later.

The following year James authorized Jim McNeeley, an acquaintance of Pete Gallagher, to stage a much larger event, dubbed Discover Native America (DNA), in Orlando, again using tribal funds. The DNA was fairly well attended, despite poor weather, and McNeeley subsequently was hired again, twice more, to stage DNA events, in Jacksonville, Florida, and Nashville, Tennessee. In 1994 and '95, however, the Tribal Council voted against continuing an expenditure of funds for yet another off-Res activity for non-Indians, and the DNA events were cancelled.

DNA became yet another of James's "monuments" to enthusiasm and poor business. There was a great deal of expressed dissatisfaction within the tribe at James over this. In addition, Pete Gallagher, as a non-Indian, bore a great deal of responsibility in the eyes of citizens, too. Pete had come to James's attention some years before while he was working as a *St. Petersburg Times* reporter during James's panther trial. A year afterward, James had invited Pete to work for him, and Pete was an ardent defender of James—both inside and outside of the tribe—and of all of his policies and actions.

By mid-decade the James Jumper and the DNA affairs, together with other minor disaffections, had incited tribal citizens against James. The original canned safari hunting project had exposed the tribe to public ridicule. The safari had begun operations in BC, against the will of many in the local community, and its first director had excited much internal ill will also. Then, the tribe's time- and money-intensive suit against the State of Florida over gaming was decided—against the tribe—and the National Indian Gaming Commission (NIGC) was attempting to pressure the tribe to shut down the slot machines and poker tables that it had only so recently opened on the strength of possible success in the lawsuit. To further exacerbate a tense moment in the evolution of the tribe's political life, the tabloid *XS* published its Seminole gaming exposé highlighting alleged ties between the tribe and organized crime, proffering charges that James never denied.[13]

Further, these events were occurring over the same general period as the GSA's investigation of James, Russell Hawkins, Robb Tiller, and Roger Raether for their handling of government surplus purchases. This is also, of course, the same general period when James was charged with illegal hunting, and his annual hunting trips out West were permanently ended. James, the warrior, was in his element: there was fighting on multiple fronts. Even if some of his schemes failed, others paid off, and tribal income was steadily rising. The fact that the schemes might be overextending the tribe financially was a small concern. As James had said before, "The Seminoles have never been poor. We've always had housing; we could build a chickee. We've always had food; we could hunt and fish. So, if we lose all our money, no big deal."

∼

One bright spot in the Seminole (that is, James's) world, nevertheless, was a fairly well developed aviation department, even if it was not without its element of controversy. Travel, even without the hunting trips, was an integral and growing part of James's life. (It would only be a little nearer to the end of James's chairmanship when tribal citizens would begin to assert their interest in traveling on tribal planes and also would intensify the aviation department's schedule.)

The first aircraft had come into tribal ownership in the 1980s, through contraband forfeiture, during the tribe's earliest attempts to control the dissemination of drugs through and on the reservations. In 1991, with gaming revenues creating a working cushion for tribal enterprises, the council agreed to its first outright purchase of a TBM Model 700 aircraft, for $1.3 million.[14] In the same fiscal year, the private-use BC airstrip became a public-use facility. In the succeeding fiscal year, it was incorporated into the BIA Roads Program, and the airstrip was lengthened to accommodate jet aircraft. It was rapidly becoming a critical bit of infrastructure for James's development plan for BC.

The first tribal jet, an eight-passenger Hawker-Sidley, as well as a small fixed-wing craft and helicopters for tribal and forestry use were all part of the tribe's burgeoning aviation department. By the end of the 1990s the department had sold the Hawker, for a profit, and had acquired two sleek Turbo Commander aircraft, one under dubious circumstances.

Gary Fears was a Robb Tiller legacy, another of the individuals whom Robb introduced to James. Fears was interested in managing the Coconut Creek property that the tribe was negotiating to turn into a gaming casino. Local opposition was high, however, and the council was involved in litigation over their plans. James's recollection is that he wasn't sure that Fears could be taken seriously in his bid, so James told him to bring the tribe a Turbo Commander aircraft as a token of good faith, and he did. Fears told James that the aircraft was his to keep and urged James to enjoy it, and James did. James expressed the possibility that such a gift might be "jailbait," but he told the press that the gift had not influenced the tribe's decision regarding management of Coconut Creek, and he kept the plane. "I do not have any standards in my Tribe that says I can take donations or not take donations."[15]

In its earliest days, the tribe's aviation department was the sole province of James and, on occasion, of the other council members. Soon, tribal citizens began to complain that they were being denied access to this luxury, and James began to expand the department in order to meet their requirements.

Consequently, by 1999, the department had grown to a fleet consisting of a Gulfstream III (soon to be traded for a G IV), the two Turbo Commanders, a JetRanger II, and three helicopters: an AStar, a Hughes 500C, and a Bell 47G. The departmental staff comprised two qualified fixed-wing pilots and two rotor-wing pilots as well as an aviation mechanic, a line chief (a tribal citizen), a full-time flight attendant (also a tribal citizen), and a departmental secretary. The copilot and, by 1999, pilot, Peter Vedel was a tall, blond Dane who had been a pilot in his national Air Force. Peter was a serious and professional pilot who would not only survive James's ouster but would wind up, in 2009, as the international sales representative for Micco Aircraft, the evolution of the Meyers Aircraft Company, another of James's deals that quickly became contentious to the council, despite the fact that, in the short term, it became lucrative to Max Jr.[16]

The first tribal pilot was Charles Kirkpatrick, who, with his wife Havelina ("Harvey"), had moved from Texas to BC on James's promise to let him build and run a complete aviation department for the tribe. Charles's story is another one of those strange and complex ones that became all too typical in the tribe's modern history, especially in this period. Charles impressed James with his assertion that he had worked formerly for "the Company" (the CIA). He sometimes carried a handgun and was paranoid that everyone else in the aviation department was trying to undercut him with James.

Harvey, who was commuting back to Texas to complete a college degree, stayed away a bit too long, and Charles entered into a relationship with Tammy Diamond González, daughter of Pat and Roy Diamond and secretary for the aviation department. The relationship culminated in their divorces and remarriages, to each other. Sadly, their relationship and Charles's paranoia resulted in a serious and prolonged estrangement between mother and daughter—partly because of the pain caused to Tammy's husband and two small sons, and partly due to the fact that Charles, as so many others before him, sought to supplant Pat and position himself as a power broker to James. James's failure to quash such ambitions (especially those regarding Pat Diamond, who was well liked within the tribe) would only add Charles to the list of dissatisfactions with James that was growing within the tribe and, especially, within the council, even though James ridded himself of Charles at this point, as Charles's constant machinations became too much of a distraction.

This business of positioning one's self as a power broker is hardly one that is unique to Indians, generally, or to the Seminoles, specifically. It is, however, one that James failed to understand sufficiently, and one that would constitute a significant element of the tribalwide dissatisfaction that would lead David and Mitchell and Jim Shore to believe themselves justified in removing James, by whatever means. And all of the incidents and situations outlined here became separate skirmishes in the war that was about to erupt, roiling the waters of the seemingly placid lake and spilling over upon the all-too-public shores.

Gaming

The Next Chapter

The scope of Seminole business enterprises took a quantum leap in the 1990s, as radically expanded gaming income opened new vistas of investment possibilities to James and the tribe—and outside investors. One old obstacle remained, however, and a nationally watched renewed dispute ensued before gaming could be expanded as far as James envisioned. In 1986, former Broward County sheriff Bob Butterworth had been elected attorney general of the State of Florida. A popular servant of the people, he would be reelected to this position for a total of four terms, serving from 1986 through 2002, including his service as state chairman of Vice President Al Gore's unsuccessful campaign for the U.S. presidency in 2000, opposite Governor George Bush's state campaign chairman, Florida secretary of state Katherine Harris. Butterworth left office in 2002 to run an unsuccessful campaign for the state senate, losing to his opponent in a burst of growing statewide Republicanism, but not before he and the governor could once again attempt to balk the Seminoles over the issue of Indian gaming in Florida.

Butterworth had long held the view that Seminole gaming was mob controlled. He later told the *St. Petersburg Times,* "We always knew the mob was there. We just couldn't prove it."[1] Unfortunately, this view made him oppose Indian gaming completely. Butterworth served the administrations of three Florida governors—two Republicans and one Democrat. It was with the Democratic governor, Lawton Chiles—who had been a dependable supporter of the tribe on other Indian issues—that James and the council began to expand their visibility in Tallahassee and to expand their active lobbying for statewide Indian issues through the work of the Governor's Council on Indian Affairs.

The Governor's Council on Indian Affairs (GCIA), a frequently underfunded or nonfunded agency, was established by Executive Order 74-23 and was signed in 1974 by Governor Reubin Askew.[2] One responsibility of the GCIA is to advise the governor on matters affecting the rights and interests of the Indian people of the state. The other of GCIA's responsibilities is to provide educational, economic, social, and cultural advancement for Indian people in Florida. This latter it accomplishes through multiple federal grants that are the lifeblood of the agency.

Unfortunately, the wording of the original executive order is sufficiently ambiguous that the GCIA is required to provide its technical support to all individuals who proclaim themselves to be Indians, whether they are enrolled citizens of FR tribes or not. That is to say that part of the GCIA's hard-won grant funding supports wannabes. This fact has not been a paramount consideration in the life of the agency, however. One of its most successful and ongoing programs is its summer Florida Indian Youth Program and Leadership Academy, which provides hands-on experiences in upper-level education and political administration for about fifty young participants each year.

The executive order that established the GCIA requires that the chairmen of the two FR tribes headquartered in Florida (the Seminoles and Miccosukees) shall be the co-chairmen of the GCIA, and the rest of the board comprises five gubernatorial appointees, whose appointments are made with the advice of the co-chairmen. The majority of these five are always citizens of the two FR tribes. Despite this degree of control, however, the state has shown very limited interest in or support for the GCIA. The state budget for the fiscal years 1995–96 in fact contained no appropriation for the agency, and funding for that year came almost entirely from U.S. Department of Labor, Title IV funding.

It was in his capacity as the earliest director of the GCIA that James once again came to work with Osley Saunooke, an enrolled citizen and former chairman of the Eastern Band of Cherokee Indians of North Carolina. Saunooke also had been the first president of the United South and Eastern Tribes, or USET, at one time headquartered at Sarasota, Florida. Through Saunooke, James became acquainted with Robert Osley Saunooke, his son, an attorney. As James became increasingly disenchanted with Jim Shore, who became increasingly vocal in his bitterness at anything that James was doing at any given moment, James would take Robert Saunooke on his chairman's payroll as his personal counsel in a direct determination to circumvent what he saw as laborious and cumbersome attempts to obtain the legal support of the tribe's chief legal counsel, Jim Shore.[3]

Early on in its life the directorship of the GCIA passed to Joe Quetone, a Chickasaw Indian who has shepherded the agency ably ever since, despite the chronic funding problems. James and (Miccosukee chairman) Billy Cypress, the co-chairmen of GCIA, wearied of its limited power and efficacy over the years and in return gave it only their limited attention. In 1996, they pushed through a change in the bylaws that created the position of vice chairperson, the holder to be appointed on a rotational basis from the two FR tribes. Steven

Bowers became the principal tribal liaison with the GCIA and for the next few years remained active in promoting better relations among the tribe, the GCIA, and the political agencies of Broward County.

A major objective of this broadening of the tribe's image was a gaming compact with the state, as required by the Indian Gaming Regulatory Act of 1988. James wanted Class III gaming, which had been inelegantly defined by the U.S. Congress as "all forms of gaming that are not Class I gaming or Class II gaming." The council, following the requirements of the Indian Gaming Regulatory Act, passed Resolution C-106-91 on 29 January 1991, at a special meeting, with four votes for and none against (Vice Chairman Fred Smith being absent for health reasons, as he so often was this year). The tribe, wishing to "promote economic development, self-sufficiency, and a strong Tribal government," authorized the chairman to enter negotiations with the State of Florida. The NIGC permitted any tribe to enter into a compact with any state when that state already "permits such gaming for any purpose, by any person, organization, or entity," and this, the tribe asserted, the State of Florida already did.

James, therefore, quietly approached the governor, "Walkin' Lawton" Chiles, to offer the state a cut of the potential proceeds for its agreement. Chiles was particularly aware of the fact that three times over the preceding twenty years Florida voters had rejected referenda that would have legalized gambling across the state.[4] Pari-mutuel wagering at horse tracks and jai alai frontons already existed, paying the state nearly $100 million a year in state taxes, under heavy regulation, and he vociferously opposed statewide gambling or expanded gambling on the Indian reservations. Floridians generally also balked at broad-scale gambling. Chiles, a man of religiosity, among whose biggest backers were a vocal Baptist contingent in north and central Florida, opposed the Seminoles' plans for expanded gaming, as did the state's attorney general, Butterworth, despite the fact that each time James met with the governor, the percentage of his offering of a share for the state went up. Chiles, Butterworth and other prominent Florida politicians held out against expanded gaming, "believing it would further tarnish [*sic*] the state's reputation as a crime haven and erode the growth of productive enterprise."[5] Ultimately, the tribe's right to enhanced gaming would pit one sovereign against another in a landmark decision from the U.S. Supreme Court.

Even as James tried to forge a compact with the state, he determinedly proceeded with his own plans. He explored, among other avenues, the possibility that the tribe might take over closed U.S. military bases in Jacksonville, Orlando, Pensacola, or Homestead on which he would have opened casinos, but the deal was not looked upon favorably by the federal Base Realignment and Closure (BRAC) authorities.[6] In the meantime, I recall asking him in 1992 if he intended to wait for state agreement to expand the tribe's current gaming activities. He said, "I already have the [slot] machines. I have the room set up. All I have to do is unlock the door and flip on the light switch. I'm just gonna do it and see what they [the state and federal authorities] do."

In December of 1993 he did just that, adding 200 electronic video games to the Hollywood casino, and gaming revenues shot up exponentially. In March of 1994 the tribe opened another addition in Hollywood, for poker, but large enough physically to be ready for blackjack tables, dice games, and roulette wheels (even though James would no longer be in power when these finally arrived). In 1994, when a federal court ruled that the video games were just an electronic version of illegal slot machines, gaming provided approximately $45 million per year, or slightly over 60 percent of the tribe's annual gross revenues.[7] Weak attempts by federal authorities over the rest of the decade to shut down the machines did not deter the tribe.

The end was in sight for management of the Hollywood casino by Seminole Management Associates (SMA), however. Early in 1996 the NIGC rejected the renewal of their contract because some of the partners did not pass background checks, and the council turned the management over to JPW Consultants, which was just the SMA partners by another name. Consequently, the NIGC issued a notice of violation to the tribe on 30 May 1997, requiring that JPW should cease all management of the "Seminole Indian Bingo & Poker Casino" of Hollywood, and the tribe complied as of the same date, assuming direct control of the Hollywood gaming facility and agreeing to appoint an interim tribal manager until a full-time appointee could be decided upon. By the same notice, of course, the NIGC also had required that the tribe cease all of its Class III gaming, but just as the tribe saw the NIGC's interpretation of its machines as Class III as ambiguous, so also did it view the requirement to cease as nebulous. In November of 1999, the council unanimously voted to amend the tribe's gaming ordinance, enacted originally in 1993, to include pull tab games in addition to "games of bingo, . . . lotto, punch boards, tip jars, instant bingo, and other games similar to bingo."[8]

From 1990 through 1993, one of the three original members of the NIGC board was Joel Frank (Panther Clan, b. 1950), a Florida Seminole citizen and James's boyhood friend. A few years after his leaving the NIGC, their representatives would tell reporters that they had declined to respond to calls for an investigation of Seminole gaming partly because they were reluctant to embarrass Joel Frank. Joel responded that he had never heard such an allegation.[9] Joel is very sharp intellectually, hardly an unaware person. He was and remains very close to James, despite the fact that he has weathered James' removal and remains within tribal administration. Joel plays his cards very close to the vest, as the saying goes. When he returned to Hollywood, he took over the tribe's housing authority. When federal authorities cited the tribe over housing ac-

counting discrepancies early in 1998, the tribe finally abolished the old authority, laid off half the staff, and established a new authority to administer federal
grants. Joel has remained in control of the tribe's housing authority through
James's ouster and since.[10]

The NIGC's response to early criticisms of its actions and inactions was that
it viewed its role as one of assisting the Seminoles, as well as other tribes, in
their attempts to forge compacts with their states. The NIGC, never a strong
government agency, had a thirty-five-member staff to monitor gaming operations among 184 FR tribes in twenty-eight states. In relation to non-Indian
gaming, the State of Nevada alone, at the same time, had more than ten times
that number of staff to oversee only about half again as many gaming operations.

The Mashantucket Pequots' Foxwoods Resort Casino (Mashantucket [for-
merly Ledyard], Connecticut), for another example, reportedly took in more
than the slots at Donald Trump's Taj Mahal, the largest casino in Atlantic City.
"In a single 24-hour period last Nov. [1993], Foxwoods' 3,100 slot machines
brought in more than $2 million."[11] In 1993, approximately two hundred tribes
operated 180 bingo halls and fifty casinos across Indian Country. But although
Indian gaming produced an estimated gross of more than $6 billion per year,
all of it still equaled only 3 percent of the national gaming industry.

> In 1993, gross revenues nationwide from legal gambling surpassed $31.1
> billion a year, which is more than Americans spent on movie admissions,
> cable television and video rentals combined. In Florida, moral objections
> to casino gambling . . . waned considerably among voters [after] 1986, the
> last time the issue was considered. [After that time], thanks largely to the
> launch of its huge lottery in 1987, Florida far exceed[ed] the national av-
> erage in gambling per capita—even without casino gambling. In 1992,
> total legal wagering in Florida, including dog and horse racing, bingo,
> church-sponsored charitable games and the lottery, came to $4.1 billion,
> or $309 per Floridian, compared to a per capita figure of just $129 for the
> nation as a whole.[12]

Further, Florida was one of the top three "feeder states," with Floridians making more than one million visits to out-of-state casinos. Among the forty-one
national metropolitan areas that generated more than 500,000 visits to U.S. casinos, three were in Florida: Tampa Bay, Miami, and Fort Lauderdale, even
though the nearest full casinos at that time were thirteen to eighteen hours
away by auto.[13]

By 1994, even without a state compact, gaming revenues together with other
tribal enterprises, were generating $45 million per year for the Seminoles. By

1998 the tribe's percentage of gaming revenues topped $145 million, and the total gaming figure across Indian Country would equal 10 percent of all national gaming revenues, but still only 10 percent. Ultimately, the Seminole Tribe was unsuccessful in its pursuit of a tribal-state compact during James's tenure, but not before James and the council had taken their case all the way to the U.S. Supreme Court.

In 1991 James and the council had quit talking and brought their initial suit against the State of Florida in an effort to force a gaming compact. In its evolution through the court system, however, the crux of the suit was no longer gaming per se but, rather, the failure of the state to negotiate in good faith and, finally, the groundbreaking question of whether a state could even be required by the federal government—the U.S. Congress or the U.S. Supreme Court—to do so.

The Indian Gaming Regulatory Act (IGRA) stated, quite clearly, the responsibility of the state to negotiate with the tribe "in good faith."[14] Failure to do so, according to the law, could trigger mediation and, if such remained unfruitful, an appeal to the secretary of the interior. In September, however, the tribe chose to lodge its complaint in District Court, against the state and Governor Chiles, alleging that the respondents had "refused to enter into any negotiation for inclusion of [certain gaming activities] in a tribal-state compact, thereby violating the requirement of good faith negotiation."[15]

The District Court decision held that the tribe could sue the state. The Court of Appeals for the Eleventh Circuit (Atlanta, Georgia), however, when pressed by the state, parsed the decision, deciding with the District Court that Congress had, indeed, intended to abrogate the sovereign immunity of states, and had passed the IGRA under the Indian Commerce Clause of the U.S. Constitution. Nevertheless, the Eleventh Circuit also held, the Indian Commerce Clause had not given Congress the right to abrogate a state's Eleventh Amendment immunity from suit and, moreover, the District Court had erred in hearing the case, because it, therefore, had no subject matter jurisdiction over a tribal suit against a state.[16]

In reaching this decision, the Eleventh District consolidated the tribe's appeal with that of the Poarch Band of Creek Indians of Alabama brought under the IGRA also. The District Court had ruled against the Poarch Band and the later Supreme Court ruling considered the legal issues presented by the two appeals to be identical.[17]

James took counsel with the lawyer Bruce Rogow, a law professor from Nova Southeastern University School of Law, situated very close to the tribal headquarters in Hollywood. Rogow had guided the tribe successfully through its earlier gaming cases and appeals. Interestingly, Rogow was also the legal representative of Seminole Management Associates (SMA) and had come to James's acquaintance through his work on behalf of SMA partners. Subsequently, he had represented the tribe in, among other cases, its legal battles regarding shipboard casino gaming. The Court of Appeals decision had effectively closed off to the tribe any avenues for its legal right of redress, a basic element of the U.S. legal system, the tribe averred. Therefore, the only way to go was up—to the ultimate U.S. legal authority, the Supreme Court.

In 1995 the U.S. Supreme Court granted certiorari to hear the case.[18] On 27 March 1996, Chief Justice W. Rehnquist issued the majority opinion, with associate justices Stevens and Souter dissenting (Souter writing for the dissent). The core of the principal finding was: "We hold that, notwithstanding Congress' clear intent to abrogate the States' sovereign immunity, the Indian Commerce Clause does not grant Congress that power, and therefore § 2710 (d)(7) cannot grant jurisdiction over a State that does not consent to be sued."[19]

This was a startling slap to the U.S. legislative branch and opened the door to a spate of subsequent decisions from the Supreme Court further upholding states' rights against federal power. Decisions regarding ageism, sexism, wrongful dismissal, and related topics would follow, protecting states from litigants and thereby narrowing the rights of U.S. citizens to protect themselves by litigation from the unilateral actions of states. One lawyer commented that this decision would surely be viewed as one of the most important in twentieth-century history.[20]

My observation is that a most fascinating national irony ensues from this Supreme Court attitude. By tradition and law, the tribes deal directly with their only political equal, the U.S. federal government—not state governments. Tribes know this and consistently seek to maintain their government-to-government relationships with the U.S. government, above their relationships with their states. By its decision in the *Seminole Tribe of Florida v. Florida*, however, the Supreme Court opened the door for enhanced states' rights, at the expense of both the status of tribes and the status of the U.S. government, thereby echoing the beginnings of the national crisis of a century and a quarter earlier. The irony in this ideological turn by the Supreme Court is that it may be Indians who, by their continuing fight to preserve their sovereign legal status, which is to say, to preserve their government-to-government relationship with the federal government rather than with the states, may save the United States from fragmenting into its constituent parts once again.

The legal examples of the Seminoles were not lost on the Miccosukees (and James and Billy Cypress met to compare notes, quietly, about once a week or so, driving their inconspicuous vehicles deep into the Everglades for privacy). Nor was Billy one to back away from a fight with the United States or any other non-Indian officials. As the Seminoles presented their ultimately unsuccessful case to the Supreme Court, the Miccosukees were pursuing multiple suits;

against the secretary of the interior for failure to protect Indian rights; against the National Park Service for permitting flooding on the Miccosukees' trust lands; and against the U.S. Army Corps of Engineers, the South Florida Water Management District, and the state Environmental Protection Agency for weakening safe water standards in South Florida. Parts of these cases dovetailed into the Seminoles' fight over water management, although the Miccosukees were determined to force the state to accept the higher federal water standards for sheet water flowage across Miccosukee lands. Their cases, funded by gaming revenues, would struggle on.

It was in the year following the Supreme Court decision, 1997, when the NIGC finally rejected the tribe's contract with SMA to continue to run the Hollywood casino, saying that some of the company's shareholders did not pass background checks, as outlined above.[21] SMA had been associated with the tribe, in various deals, for seventeen years, surviving repeated allegations of corruption and mob management. In Hollywood, however, James had already ostensibly attempted to change management companies at the casino, giving power to "JPW Consultants," which was, however, just the old team of James P. "Skip" Weisman and Eugene P. "Butch" Moriarty (of SMA) under another name.

Under fire from the NIGC, the tribe finally bought out the SMA contract for approximately $60 million and finally took over the management of the Hollywood and Tampa operations for itself. Larry Frank (Otter Clan, b. 1953) was sent in to manage the Hollywood casino. Larry had no experience at such a task and was anything but a forceful administrator, but he was a tribal citizen and would report directly to James. Further, Ted Boyd, an Indian but not a Seminole, and the tribe's financial controller, was also appointed to oversee the finances of the casino, drawing a double salary for doing both jobs. This, again, was James's decision, with the acquiescence of the council, to send an individual to arrange the accounts for the casino and review those same accounts on behalf of the tribe. Bonnie Garris, Ted's quiet assistant who also reported directly, and personally, to James, assisted Ted and drew two salaries as well.

Shortly, Hollywood citizens objected, the NIGC objected, and Ted and Bonnie were relieved of their second jobs. At the end of 1995, the council finally had established a tribal gaming commission and established the position of gaming monitor, but the monitor's position remained unfilled until the beginning of 1997, when Roy Diamond was returned to the tribe's gaming operations as monitor. His principal responsibility was to oversee background checks on prospective employees in all of the tribe's casinos, in line with the requirements of the NIGC.

~

In addition to its more visible and more lucrative gaming operations in Hollywood and Tampa, the tiny casino on Brighton Res was contributing a steady, albeit small, stream of income to the tribe at this time. In business since the mid-1980s, by fiscal year 1999 the operation netted just over $110,000 annually, the least of any of the tribe's gaming operations. Brighton, approximately twenty miles southwest of the town of Okeechobee, has a potential for west and east coast draws but functioned at an isolated size and site despite expansion plans curtailed by environmental issues in 1999. A Brighton community resident, Marty Johns, ran the operation privately under a management contract, and almost in anonymity, until the NIGC served the tribe with a notice of violation for its failure to provide an annual audit for the casino covering fiscal year 1997 and ultimately levied a fine of $5,000. The tribe complied by hiring an auditing firm to provide the required annual audit and adopting policies and procedures acceptable to the NIGC.[22]

In order to bring the management of the Brighton casino into line with the others, the council also responded to NIGC contentions that no Brighton management contract had been submitted to it for review. The tribe asserted that no request for review of the Brighton contract had ever been received. The NIGC also asserted that Martin R. ("Marty") Johns managed the Brighton casino "independent of direct oversight or management control by the Tribe." The NIGC recommended that rather than a management contract the tribe could take direct control of the casino and hire Marty Johns as their manager. To this recommendation the tribe acceded in September of 2000.

~

The tribe's only completely unsuccessful gaming operation took place, ironically, in the one place James wanted success most—his own backyard, so to speak, on the BC Res. In 1986 the tribe had executed a contract for Big Cypress Million Dollar Jackpot, Inc. (BCMDJ, Inc.) to "finance, construct, improve, develop, manage, operate, and maintain" a gaming facility on the BC Res. Principals in BCMDJ, Inc., were Richard Knowlton, president, and William ("Billy") Van Horn, secretary/treasurer. The location on the Res was a central one, but the resulting facility was a giant tin-roofed building that would never manage to realize its potential.

The original agreement called for the corporation to create the facility and stage at least two or three large events per year. The cost of full-time operation would have been prohibitive. A year into this plan a supplemental agreement added a number of additional activities that the managers might offer at the facility—from auctions to sporting events to religious gatherings.[23] After yet another year of ostensibly high start-up costs and poor business, BCMDJ, Inc., submitted an operating budget to the tribe that asked for reimbursements in the amount of a little under $3.1 million and quickly assigned its functional interest in the operation to a consortium of investors calling themselves Cypress Associates, Ltd., of which Knowlton and Van Horn remained principals.

Thirty-two investors in New Jersey and Florida infused $3.2 million into the operation,with BCMDJ, Inc., retaining its interest as general partner, but even this was not enough.[24] Twice, accountants were hired by the council to review the books, and they concluded that Cypress Associates, Ltd., had $284,000 in unpaid liabilities together with other failures. The council demanded a $500,000 surety bond for their continued operation.

In fact, the tribe took Cypress Associates to court and the corporation wound up once again assigning its responsibilities to yet another entity, Investment Resources, Inc., on the condition, agreed to by both parties, that the new assignee would rectify the faults created by the earlier parties. This was not the case. The tribe's attorney informed management representatives that "the track record of both Jackpot and IRI to date had been substantially less than expected. Indeed, after more than three years of operation, the [BC] Bingo Hall has failed to produce any profit for either the Tribe or the managing group and indeed, has failed to break even,"[25] In November of 1990, the council terminated its agreements with BCMDJ, Inc., and Investment Resources, Inc.

James would not give up his dream. Even as the tribe terminated the previous contracts, it accepted an offer from a Georgia corporation, High Stakes Management, Inc., configured to do business as Grand Cypress Bingo, for management of the facility.[26] This permit lasted only for a few months and was revoked when High Stakes failed to pay its $20,000 per month commitment for two succeeding months or to establish an escrow fund to pay operating expenses and game prizes, as promised.[27]

The building languished, gathering dust, Everglades insects, and U.S. government surplus furniture and equipment. But the prospect of Indian gaming profits was still a lure, and the next entrepreneur was Joseph R. Ferrero, of Hyannis, Massachusetts, who called his consortium of investors Native Management Group. Early in 1996, it offered the tribe an exciting-sounding deal, for a total of $7,100,000, including refurbishing the tired old building, furnishing $2 million in operating capital, a $500,000 reserve, and a water treatment plant to serve the operation—an important piece of infrastructure in the Big Cypress. In April Global Equity Capital, LC, of Myrtle Beach, South Carolina, Thomas J. Butler, president, notified Ferrero that three entities had furnished firm commitments for financing. The three were First Fidelity, Ltd., of Gibraltar; Aces Gaming Group of Fort Lauderdale, Florida; and M.G.N.A. Consulting of Rensselaer, New York. They awaited contact and were ready to commit. A letter of intent was signed by Ferrero and the tribe—and was extended for six months, and extended for another six months, and amended, and amended. The agreement promised a 60:40 percent split in the tribe's favor, but the fiscal year 1998 budget still contained no projected disbursement for BC bingo.

The final chapters of the BC gaming story were just as unproductive as all the earlier ones had been. In mid-2000, with tribal gaming plans progressing well at Coconut Creek and continuing at all the other sites, James proposed to the council that rather than try to refurbish the old bingo hall building in BC, it would be simpler to add gaming to the Billie Swamp Safari. Again, the council obliged with its approval, but nothing ever came of the plan. In fact, the council was not against the concept of BC gaming, but by this time it had turned firmly against James and almost all of his projects. In March of 2001, James was suspended from office, and the council approved retaining a forensic auditor to review all of the tribe's finances. We shall revisit these events in the next chapter.

As for BC and James's grandiose visions for it, in April following his suspension and, consequently, without his presence at the meeting, the council agreed to a concept presented by a group calling itself Native Management Group, Ltd., that incorporated not only a gaming facility for BC as Phase I but, in a second phase, a theme park, hotel, golf course, and other commercial facets. The council required that there should be studies and reports on the plans before making any further moves, and nothing ever came of this deal either. David and Mitchell had already begun to construct luxury compounds for themselves and their families in BC, with tribal underwriting, but their dream of a tribal capital in the Big Cypress was not quite the same as that of James, and for the moment, at least, BC would remain the isolated community that it was.

～

Even as gaming management and management practices seemed to be evolving on the Florida mainland, James and the council were reaching out to a business venue offshore that might add a new and greater dimension to tribal gaming. From documents and newspaper reports, it appears that the tribe invested a relatively small amount, almost $800,000 over three years, in the Lightning Casino in St. Maarten, a Caribbean island administered by the Netherlands and identified by the U.S. State Department as a transshipment point for cocaine and heroin as well as a haven for money launderers.[28]

By two separate actions, in 1992 and one year later, the tribe had agreed to purchase a total of 138,600 shares of preferred capital stock in Offshore Enterprises, Ltd., a Turks and Caicos Islands corporation. The tribe's investment represented 19.8 percent of the total capital required by the offering corporation, for which it (the tribe) was to receive 3.34 percent interest in the company. According to the initial resolution, the chairman and the comptroller both recommended approval of the project, and the tribal counsel also had reviewed the offer for "legal sufficiency."[29]

Weisman and Moriarty, recently relieved of casino management in Hollywood, also were investors in the Caribbean venture, which, three years later, was just beginning to show a small profit. More important, however, was the allegation that a Hollywood employee had seen Weisman packing a box with money and sending it off to St. Maarten via UPS, with the implication that the casino there was a money laundering operation for the Hollywood casino. Further, it was alleged, such activities could not have occurred without the knowledge, explicit or implicit, of James. This information surfaced during the investigation of a case of wrongful dismissal brought by a former Hollywood casino guard, but Weisman and Moriarty, as SMA, offered to settle and the case was resolved out of court. Jim Shore told reporters, however, that the tribe was also negotiating with Weisman and Moriarty to set up an Internet gambling site on another Caribbean island, St. Kitts. That plan never came to fruition. The St. Maarten deal fell apart in the glare of public scrutiny, and the tribe's investment was not recovered. The idea of offshore gaming, however, would persist into a new game plan shortly.

⁓

Another aspect of the tribe's gaming empire had begun as early as 1982 when it acquired a 4.8-acre parcel in Coconut Creek, an incorporated municipality in northern Broward County, in exchange for Res land needed by the state to extend the Florida Turnpike.[30] A development proposal submitted to the tribe in 1985 awakened the council to the possibilities for use of the site. Nothing further was done for several years, however, until the tribe began to negotiate with the municipality of Coconut Creek for a utilities easement for the construction of retail shops on the property.[31]

Meanwhile, as the tribe expanded gaming on the Hollywood Res in Broward County, the council quietly began to buy up pieces of land surrounding the Coconut Creek parcel—not asking to have the extra lands taken into trust as Res lands but simply acquiring them in fee simple. In a parallel move, looking to the future, Gary Fears also began to acquire parcels surrounding the tribe's core property. Separately, they slowly and quietly acquired a total of 45 acres surrounding the original parcel. Toward the end of the decade the tribe announced plans to build a casino on the tiny central parcel, and after much local opposition based principally on the old arguments about organized crime and negative impact upon (non-Indian) gamblers, the tribe finally entered into a lucrative arrangement with the municipal government of Coconut Creek that has added upwards of $4 million per year to city coffers to provide utilities and other services to the casino—not to mention the rise in local payrolls and buying power. Due to NIGC resistance, Gary Fears never was able to become the active partner in the Coconut Creek operation that he and James had envisioned. Fears quietly shifted his interest in the project to Alan Ginsburg and a group of investors who would be more acceptable to federal regulators. He remained a quiet partner for some time, nevertheless, on his determination to recoup several millions of dollars that he had previously invested in the project.

The Seminoles, despite all fearful prognostications to the contrary, became good neighbors in Coconut Creek and would remain so until they announced that they had asked the U.S. secretary of the interior to take all of the remaining property into federal trust. This would enable them to increase their enterprise with the addition of a 1,500-room hotel, spa, parking garage, and 150,000 square feet of retail space, all of which would also add 5,000 jobs to the area. This move occurred in 2008, only after the council had ousted James, renegotiated his deal with developer David Cordish and with the Hard Rock owners, and had built one $400 million Hard Rock complex on the Hollywood Res and another on the completely rebuilt Tampa Res. At the time of this writing, the outcome of the Coconut Creek project awaits the decision of the new secretary of the interior, appointed by incoming President Barack Obama, on whether the tribe's nontrust acreage will be taken into trust for tribal use.

~

Meanwhile, the success of the tribe's gaming on Florida's west coast had opened the possibility of another venue, on the tiny Res of Immokalee. Its location was thirty miles inland, and about 150 miles southeast of Tampa and, therefore, an easy drive from the Gulf and an obvious draw for the entire lower southwest coastal area of the state. In 1988, council officials broached the idea and four months later a tribal citizen made the first viable offer for construction and management of the operation.[32] O. B. Osceola, doing business as Coryi Management, Inc., placed an offer before the council.[33] "OB" would obtain his own line of credit for a maximum project cost of $1.3 million and would otherwise spearhead the construction, furnishing, and hiring for the project. What he proposed was to be a one-stop-shop for the project, which was envisioned by James and the council as a relatively small but, nevertheless, potentially lucrative operation.

OB began making expensive changes to the plans almost immediately, but construction did not begin. The council agreed to an amended contract.[34] By the spring of 1992, Coryi had yet to fulfill its obligations, and the council agreed to another extension but obviously realized that the outlook for completion of the project at OB's direction was poor.[35] A year later, the council finally rescinded OB's contract for failure to perform.[36] The tribe contended that, among other failures, Coryi and OB had entered into "secret" construction agreements with the builder that increased the size and cost of the project. The project was completed amid much acrimony on both sides. The council ended its agreement with Coryi and reassigned the management contract to Charles W. Helseth, an old associate of James's, doing business as First American Gaming Corporation of Fort Lauderdale. The NIGC would not approve First American, so the tribe took over direct control.[37] James ultimately turned to his old supporters at Pan Am in Tampa, and in early 1998 the tribe and Pan Am entered into a consulting agreement for the Immokalee project, as a part of which Pan Am guaranteed the project loan in return for the management of the casino.[38]

Although OB had long been a friend of Jimmy Cypress, Mitchell and David's father, these decisions sparked a legal battle between OB and his family and the tribe that created permanent hard feelings with James, for whom friendship with Jimmy Cypress was no distinction. OB took the tribe into white man's arbitration. The council barred the family from even entering the Hollywood Res to pick up dividend checks. The council was especially incensed that tribal citizens would go into a white man's legal system and publicly fight their tribe. An arbitrator and a federal judge sided with OB and awarded the family almost $2.4 million of the $5 million they had sought. The tribe decided first to appeal, but finally in March of 1998 decided to forego the cost of further legalities and ratify the court judgment.[39] The tribe settled with Coryi for slightly less than the original award in an entry of judgment and agreement to forbear execution by and between Coryi, Inc., and the Seminole Tribe of Florida.

The management agreement between the tribe and Pan Am was not to be of long duration either, however. The agreement, submitted to the NIGC for approval by it and the BIA, was challenged by the NIGC on the grounds that the tribe had never submitted a management agreement to the commission. It held out to the tribe the prospect of a closure order for the Immokalee casino and a fine against the tribe. As a result the tribe and Pan Am agreed mutually to terminate their consulting agreement, and the tribe was able to negotiate a reduced penalty with the NIGC and the BIA.[40]

During the creation of the Immokalee bingo hall, Pan Am's Jim Clare also recommended to James that the tribe should further expand its gaming enterprises by purchasing ships that would be operated by commercial cruise lines and function as floating gambling operations—a premise that had debuted nationally only in 1991—running between Florida and Mexico. The tribe and Pan Am, under the business title of Coastal Gaming Group, Ltd., No. 1, with an interest in SeaCo, Ltd., would invest in both facets of the operation, and the council put more than $6 million into the first craft, a former French ferry christened *Imperial Princess* and rechristened the *Seminole Express*. Unfortunately, the ship was only the first of three that the tribe tried to buy, only to learn that they were unseaworthy and would require massive infusions of capital to bring the project to fruition. The project slowly sank into a legal quagmire over the gaming aspects and never got out of port.

Jim Talik, the business manager of some years for the board, was fired over the project (after James's ouster he would be rehired), when he tried to review it too closely and "feared exposure of a major cover up that the tribe had been swindled out of over $6 million."[41] It was one more of James's abortive projects that "littered the Seminole landscape like monuments," as Pat Diamond frequently described them (as was discussed in chapter 7). Nevertheless, the tide of monies running in to the tribe was far greater than the tide of monies running out—and the longer they could stay ahead of the flow, as it were, with growing revenues, the longer it would be before they would be inundated by it. The council representatives were becoming very disaffected by the weight of the loans piling up on the tribe, but, at least for the moment, the tribe still was ahead.

Pan Am & Associates continued its symbiotic relationship with the tribe in Tampa, however, at least for another few years. The Seminoles—individually and collectively—always prefer to do business with people they know and with whom they have come to have a level of comfort, regardless of whether that relationship benefits the non-Indians, as long as the tribe is included in the benefits with a sufficient degree of reciprocity. In this case, the reciprocal element of the relationship with Pan Am & Associates involved loans to James for business purchases (obviously, loans of monies made as profits from Seminole enterprises, to the Seminole chairman) and legal assistance in connection with Micco Enterprises, a personal business of James's that this time involved his Smoke Shop on the Miccosukee Res. Pan Am counsel Buddy Levy told reporters that he provided "a lot of pro bono work" for the tribe—a seemingly benign phrase that covered a multitude of dealings.[42]

As a result of their ongoing level of comfort with Pan Am management, the Tampa casino weathered several potential scandals. In 1990 it had survived a report from the U.S. inspector general's office concluding that the casino was "susceptible to fraud due to lack of any system of checks and balances between the management firms and the tribe."[43] A year later, eight people, including three casino employees, were fined or were sentenced to prison terms for conspiring to fix high-stakes bingo games and split casino profits. A bingo patron later filed suit against the casino management, alleging fraud and charging that Jim Clare knew about the scheme. Clare "vehemently denied knowing anything about the bingo fixing and a judge dismissed the lawsuit."[44]

By the end of the century the original Pan Am management contract for the Tampa casino was under fire from the NIGC and the BIA. The first contract, signed in 1980, provided for a twelve-year term with an automatic eight-year renewal. In the following year, the tribe had obtained a bank loan for $405,000 to add a tribal Smoke Shop, "museum" (to preserve the human remains discovered by the City of Tampa), and a Native Village for tourists on the Tampa Res, adjacent to the casino. In 1986, two years earlier than required by the original contract, the tribe exercised its option to extend the contract for another eight years, for which privilege Pan Am agreed to reduce its management fees from 47 to 40 percent and use its own funds to underwrite improvement of the facility for "large scale" bingo.

In 1988, following the passage of the National Indian Gaming Act, the National Indian Gaming Commission had required its chairman to notify all tribes operating casinos on management contracts created prior to 17 October of that year to submit the contracts for review by the NIGC. According to the Seminole Tribal Council, the commission chairman never requested a copy of the Pan Am contract for review. Regardless of that fact, the council approved a new contract, dated 9 June 1988, that was intended to continue the old contract and approve continued Pan Am management in two terms, from 1980 to 1992, and in a second term running from 1992 to 27 May 2000. The BIA eastern area supervisor, Bill Ott, signed off on this new contract on 14 June 1988. At the end of this new contract's second term, on 27 May 2000, the council passed a final resolution terminating their twenty-year association with Pan Am at the Tampa casino. By this action the tribe took over direct control of the Tampa casino, with manager John Fontana (husband of Jean Fontana, who worked for board chairman Mitchell Cypress) reporting directly to James and (ostensibly) to the council. By this time, however, the Hard Rock deal was clearly on the horizon, and the tribe was about to reach an entirely new plateau in tribal business and revenues.

∾

Buddy Levy, general counsel for Pan American, told reporters in 1997, "One of the reasons that we feel like we have such good relations with the tribe is we never get involved in any matters outside of the four corners of this building." While that obviously was not strictly accurate, it highlighted a certain degree of understanding of the nature of tribal politics that many other outsiders did not have. The subtle balance of power implicit in this understanding would soon come back to haunt James. As with any organization or entity generating large sums of money, a growing number of remora, lured by the smell of money, had drifted in and out of the lives of the Seminoles over the years. If James had been enticed by some of their blandishments and had permitted them to feed off of the tribe for a while, they had ultimately drifted away—either too small thinkers for James's visions, or too greedy too fast, or personally unacceptable to the council or tribal citizens.

This process began to take on entirely new and greater aspects in the later 1990s, however, as tribal revenues reached new heights and brought James and the tribe into even greater national and international visibility. In his life, several personal and professional lines were coalescing, and he was experiencing the more and less subtle rumblings of dissatisfaction. In 1994, for example, he had been through two operations to ameliorate his lifelong problem of pain from a bow-legged condition. He was told, expressly, by his doctors that he had to refrain from exerting undue pressure on his legs as they healed. But he had reached his fiftieth birthday that year, and although birthdays were only beginning to be of interest to Seminoles at the time, his own image as a leader with undiminished prowess was very much of interest to him. And so, at a tribalwide birthday celebration in the rodeo arena at BC, James decided to participate in a bull-riding competition. Everyone knew it was a mistake, but he was determined. It *was* a mistake. His image was damaged, but not irreparably (not as much as the damage to his legs), when the bull flipped him off, literally, in two seconds. Publicly, he had no choice but to take it well. Personally, he was much chagrined.

At this point James began to tire of the old ways of doing business (*his* old ways), and he began to seek methods of instituting change that satisfied his desire for rapidity and breadth of action. It was not too long after this moment when he expressed to me a desire to quit tribal leadership, and I mistakenly attempted to offer him the idea of lifting his field of vision from politics to statesmanship. He had told me often before that he liked my "take on things" because I "[came] at things from a completely different point of view" than did he. In this view, however, we were entirely too far apart.

In 1996, James's interest in wheeling and dealing took a decided upturn when no less a figure than Donald Trump made overtures to the tribe. This was, of course, the same Donald Trump who gloated at the U.S. Supreme Court decision against the Seminoles in their attempts to get the State of Florida to negotiate a gaming compact with the tribe. Referring to himself as "the biggest enemy of Indian gaming," Trump suddenly became one of several who wanted to take on the management of tribal gaming if Florida state law changed.[45]

Despite the fact that Trump had been a very vocal opponent of Indian gaming just a short time before, he saw the chance for enhanced profits now and began to court James. Trump sent representatives to the BC Res. He asked James "about the gaming atmosphere in Florida," to which James reportedly "offered an analogy which combined a whore, a finger, and the virtue of patience."[46] To further entice the tribe, nevertheless, Trump invited tribal leaders to visit him at his Taj Mahal casino in Atlantic City, New Jersey, for a Rod Stewart concert. He invited James—always involved in his own music—to open for the Beach Boys at a concert at Trump's (formerly Marjorie Merriweather Post's) estate in Palm Beach. James took along an alligator to impress the guests. Trump invited James to be a judge for the 1997 Miss Universe pageant in Miami.

Above all, Trump and James quietly joined forces to continue to lobby Tallahassee for a compact that would permit Class III gaming on the reservations. Together, Trump and the tribe contributed to hiring Mallory Horne, formerly a

powerful Florida legislator and close friend of Governor Chiles, to lobby on behalf of a compact. Trump was ready to contribute almost $1 million to the proj-
ect. Horne, a former speaker of the Florida House of Representatives as well
as president of the Florida Senate, had been, for many years, one of the most
powerful politicians in the state. He continued James's trend of offering larger
and larger cuts of gaming revenues to the state—finally reaching an offer of 45
percent—but even he could not convince Chiles. James's ardor cooled temporarily and Trump saw no possibility of rewards in the near future.

Another, and hilariously unlikely, gambit for gaming management came
around this same time from a small consortium of businessmen in Miami, including Jay Kislak, who owned one of the largest privately held mortgage ser-
vicing firms in the nation. Kislak was a Wharton graduate, a former U.S. Navy
pilot, and friend of and contributor to the Bush (42nd) campaign. He was, in addition, a former employer of mine. Jim Chapman, whose brick-making-machine
project James was currently supporting (more on this, below), and the group
that included Jay were among the many who wanted a gaming management
contract with the tribe. They had hoped to tempt the tribe by offering to buy a
resort at Hawks Cay, in the Florida Keys, and give it to the tribe as a gesture of
good will.

There was a planned Holocaust Memorial dinner in Miami, and Chapman
wanted James to attend. The objective was to introduce James to the group so
that they might ingratiate themselves. Ostensibly to this end, one of the group's
staff contacted Pat Diamond to see if they could get a Seminole patchwork
jacket to present to James at the dinner! Pat Diamond, knowing of my former
association with Jay, called me to see if the gambit could be for real. It was
surely the strangest bit of illogic that either Pat or I had encountered in some
time, and when she told James, he was, needless to say, no longer interested
in even hearing the group's proposal. He was willing to be courted by non-
Indians, but he was never willing to be insulted.

It was at this moment—when tribal revenues were enticing the likes of Steve
Wynn, chief executive of the Mirage in Las Vegas; Bill Bennett, former head of
Circus Circus; and Gary Fears, of an Illinois family that made millions in Illinois riverboat gambling—that James's dreams of his own power and of a quantum leap in business for the tribe began functionally to outstrip the ability or
interest of tribal citizens to accept change. And the line between the two—
James's vision and tribal interests—was formed by the council reps who had begun their own kingdom building, and they had the power, as James began to
push for change, to push back.

∽

A friend used to quote a cogent history professor whose mantra was that
"centuries have a bad habit of never beginning or ending on time." And so it

was with the twentieth century and its events, being brought to their dreadful conclusion inside the Seminole Tribe. It would take three years into the chronological twenty-first century for the old century to end. These years, moreover, would be ones of bitterness and warring, in ways far more public than the inner workings of the tribe had ever been before. These short three years would see the end of James Billie's twenty-four-year reign (in many ways, a term much more apt than mere tenure). Much of the internal upheaval would be played out on the pages of newspapers across the nation and would frighten much of Indian Country. The heretofore-placid lake waters would roil.

A number of other instances had already occurred across Indian Country in which tribal leaders had been brought down by internal factionalizations. Each was seen as a great sorrow by traditionalists among the Indians. Even more saddening, however, were the instances when one tribal faction or another had chosen to reach outside of the tribe for power and certification by seeking to involve the BIA or the FBI. In effect, it was a breaching of walls from the inside, thereby opening the internal workings of the tribe to outside scrutiny and, most sadly, the power of the U.S. government—the last power predisposed to support Indians in their fights to settle tribal disputes.

The next stage in the end of this generation of leadership would actually be a constellation of events, all of which seem to have been predicated on a shift in James's perception of his leadership role and the future direction of the tribe as he saw it. James was at the zenith of all he had accomplished for the tribe. "Yet," as a historian wrote of another high-visibility leader, "precisely at this point, he embarked on a course of new departures, introduced in politically maladroit ways, that threatened everything he had created."[47] This had a perfect application to James as well. He had said before that he had "made" himself and only he could bring himself down. Despite this, the fact is that he failed to recognize the downward slide when it began. Moreover, the larger reality is that it might not have been possible to stop the slide even if he had taken notice. A number of circumstances coalesced in the last few years of the century, more or less at the same time, to make the end almost inevitable.

Tribal dissatisfaction with James was growing, but if it had been solely a matter of dissatisfaction with James, he might have been able to weather the storm and continue in his leadership position. He certainly had been challenged before. But there were two other large elements to be considered. One was the internal havoc created by a small group of non-Indians whom James had hired to effect the changes he had in mind for the tribe. The other element was the looming and potentially brilliantly lucrative Hard Rock project, which, in its earliest concept, included only the construction of two casino/hotel complexes with commercial arcades, one in Hollywood and the other in Tampa. In its original form, no one (at least no one inside the tribe or on the council) saw the vast potential of this project, not even the tribal administrator who had brokered the deal.

It is difficult to explain how gradually anger at James grew over the last half of the last decade of the twentieth century. At the same time as his business deals were increasing radically in number, the tribe's dissatisfaction was increasing apace.

In 1994 and '95, as the State of Florida and the U.S. Supreme Court turned their decisions against the tribe (or, at the very least, that was the result), James appeared to be pushing the tribe into overdrive—seeking venture capitalists, business propositions, and investments, regardless of their degree of risk or how ill considered they might be. A certain type of entrepreneur was too frequently attracted to the high risk of investing in business with an FR Indian tribe almost as much as they were attracted to the potential for high yield. At the same time, James Billie's ego, his jaded view of his role as tribal leader, fueled by sniping from uninformed tribal citizens ("Indian fiddler crabs," he called them, from the old joke about a bucket of the tiny fiddler crabs where, when one tried to climb out, the others inevitably would grab him by the leg and pull him back in), the unctuous ministrations of the outsiders seeking access to tribal profits, and the constant and rising pressures from the U.S. government creating an ever-increasing need for increased revenues were pushing him to more and more daring actions.

The U.S. government, through the rules and regulations of its myriad agencies, seemed determined to hamstring the Indians. Consequently, James, the warrior, felt justified in using any means he could see as being at his disposal to continue to be the great Cash Cow. The speed of his movement was too fast for others in the tribe; his determination to move rapidly in order to take advantage of offers of outside support (risk be damned) drove him to a degree of secrecy that was antithetical to the rules of transparency as they were established for the tribe by the U.S. government, or even as they were interpreted by the tribe itself. James just went too far too fast.

Of course, it is important to recall once again that for almost two decades council representatives had been supporting James in his ventures, and they had been learning from his methods. When he said that if anyone ever figured out what he was up to they would be able to defeat him, he obviously did not realize the extent to which David and Mitchell and Max and Jim Shore, at least, were paying attention. In all of the years of James's tenure, right up to the council meeting of 24 May 2001, when Council Resolution C-133-01 suspended him, the council votes on his programs were almost invariably five/nil. That is, all four voting members voted with James. Any dissentions were smoothed out in the backroom pre-meeting meetings or over lunch at the Swamp Water Café. If James padded his own economy with personal businesses, they did also. If James hired his relatives or friends (or, often, his enemies—to keep them close), they did as well. Those actions occurred right along the shorelines that separated the Indian from the non-Indian world. In the Seminole Indian world, one takes care of clan, one takes care of one's loyalists, and if one does these things consistently one is permitted to take care of one's self as well. Indeed, one is expected to do so. Perhaps James's one step too far is that he became so tired of the process when he saw it mirrored in the actions of the council reps that he tried to limit them severely, and they turned on him: they perceived him as trying to climb out of the bucket, and they reached up and grabbed him by the leg and pulled him back in.

~

By 1999, council meetings had ceased to be one-day, bimonthly affairs and had stretched into multiday regular meetings interspersed with multiday special meetings called to conclude or just to ratify actions taken in the interstices. The story of Jim Chapman illustrates the process. Chapman was one of those individuals who reached James through a friend-of-a-friend, and who had an idea that was ready made for James's brand of creativity and entrepreneurship. He had designed a brick-making machine. The concept was to make use of low quality, freely available materials (such as straw and mud, at least) to produce a viable building product. The objective was to create a system of housing construction that would be economically available to third world nations and to lowest-income enclaves anywhere. Jim's initial target audience was in Nicaragua, but his practice audience was the Seminoles.

James was almost immediately intrigued by the concept and used $178,000 in funds from his chairman's office appropriation to support Chapman's experiments. James and Chapman formed a blind trust to support Chapman's experiments with the machine on the Hollywood and BC reservations. First, James sent Chapman to use the machine to construct a slaughterhouse and meat-processing plant inside the Hunting Adventures on the BC Res that was managed by Jimmy McDaniel. Not unexpectedly, the building was so poorly constructed that daylight streamed through the walls and Chapman (obviously not conversant with professional construction techniques) laid no foundation for the one-and-one-half-foot-thick concrete floor, which immediately began to dry, settle, and crack. Covering the cracks with a resinous substance only made matters worse, and it was necessary to pay a contractor to come in and tear out the floor and rebuild the building. It was the beginning of James's disenchantment with Jim Chapman.

Another possible venue for the brick-making machine was family housing, which was constantly an issue for the Seminoles in the 1990s. Each council meeting dealt with significant numbers of housing site leases and, following 1996 passage of US/NAHASDA, funding for housing construction. With the passage of this federal law, US/NAHASDA, banks were permitted to issue mortgage loans to Indians secured by tribal resources. The possibility that the tribe might be able to produce a suitable construction material for its own housing use was fascinating, no matter how many people told James that Chapman's machine just wasn't up to the task and never would be. Several initial attempts produced products so dry they crumbled before use. More attempts produced outsized bricks that did not crumble of their own weight but could not sustain the static load of a wall and floors and a roof. After more than a year of experimentation, three houses were constructed on the Hollywood Res, each clearly unsatisfactory.

By the time these were constructed, however, Chapman, and of course James, had made the leap to Nicaragua in search of possible government backing for rural housing construction projects there. It was at this point, as James and several more recent associates—Dan Wisher and Calixto García Vélez—began to make the necessary contacts with the government of Nicaragua, that Chapman's project fell by the wayside, both in Florida and in Latin America. It appeared too small by comparison with other and greater possibilities.

Gaming wealth was like a mushroom cloud that spread wider and wider over the tribe. From it emanated a growing sense of individual entitlement. Even the elders began to feel it, as the comforts it brought—among them air conditioning, prepared foods, and home helpers—eased their declining years in ways that their mothers and grandmothers never could have envisioned. At the top of the political system (a fictitious vertical power system instigated by whites, but functional nonetheless), the range of potential rewards was far greater and grew even faster as these individuals interfaced with the outside world and saw, more and more, the breadth of rewards available.

Max Jr.'s interest in fast cars, as an example, quickly gave way to a love of motorcycles. James took over Max's lease of a classic little red Corvette and kept the car until just after the council (including Max) suspended him in 2001. Max began to organize bike rallies for other Seminoles with similar interests, soon including nontribal biker enthusiasts as well. His interest in golf also gradually evolved into a tribalwide golf tournament. And these were merely the smaller interests in Max's life. His larger—and personally lucrative—business dealings would come to light in the court cases with which the council and Jim Shore sought to surround James and his non-Seminole associates, and as the Internal Revenue Service began to investigate the council representatives and their personal access to tribal monies.

In the early 1990s, Halloween contests had introduced the practice of offering cash prizes, usually of $35 or $50. By the other end of the decade, with the advent of Class II gaming (with what the NIGC charged was just Class III machines by another name), Max's golf tournaments offered substantially higher prizes. Even weekly bowling leagues for the elders provided cash and prizes for winners. Rapidly, people who had been raised in the ferocious Florida Everglades, without so much as potable water or plumbing (never mind *indoor* plumbing), began to establish expectations.

This is not to say that they were wrong to have such expectations; what is the real value of money if it cannot create some baseline comforts for human beings? But money, obtained out of a social context, is corrosive. A major fissure in the generational transmission of cultural information had occurred earlier in the century when HUD housing fragmented clan camps, and clan elders no longer had daily contact with succeeding generations. The old clan camps were not destroyed, but their values and uses tended more to the ritual rather than the daily social. By the 1980s, tribal revenues began to underwrite the acquisition of a new range of nontraditional material items—from pickup trucks and boats to exotic hunting dogs. Another decade of rising tribal income and personal dividends broadened the range of acquired items again appreciably. They included everything from kitchen appliances and gadgetry and home landscaping to personal vanity items such as hairdressing, manicures, and pedicures, and expensive jewelry and breast implants.

At the top of the new political ladder, personal tastes were satisfied in individual ways. For two decades by this point, citizen entrepreneurs had tried their hands at almost every conceivable business, supported by tribal loans. Their business acumen bordered on nil, but James continually agreed to loans on the premise that his people would learn by doing, just as he did. Despite this emotional belief, he radically overestimated their true interest even as he failed to realize their lack of experience of the outside world. The council constantly was besieged by requests for leases and subleases of tribal lands for envisioned enterprises such as flower shops, plant nurseries, hot dog stands, car washes, ice cream stands, and other food-vendor kiosks, especially on the Hollywood Res where the models of non-Indian urbanization were the most numerous. From the simple to the complex, most of the projects never materialized or faded into existence after two or three lease implementation extensions, only to fade out again, quietly, as individual loan balances rose up and up.

David Cypress acquired a growing number of business interests, but they survived: a pawnshop and a boxing gym on State Road 7/Highway 441 were very profitable. A non-Indian associate in Clewiston also profited greatly from David's patronage and largesse, acquiring nearly $1 million in overpriced landscaping contracts, among other extremely lucrative deals. (More on this in the following chapters.) Later, in 2006, as testimony in the tribe's court cases against

James became public information, many in the tribe attempted to remove David, even collecting a petition to remove him. At a community meeting in BC, they presented their petition, in accordance with the requirements of the constitution, only to have David call in SPD officers and direct them to remove his opponents. They refused to leave and SPD declined to use force on tribal citizens.[48] At a subsequent council meeting, more citizens faced David over the problem of tribal politicians' profiting from tribal businesses, and he raised his hands as if in surrender, proclaiming, "I know. I know. You're talking about me. I'm sorry. I'm sorry." But his empty protestations were all the citizens got for their efforts.[49]

Jack Smith contented himself with the ever-increasing Res appropriations that he could dole out to clan members and political supporters on the Brighton Res. Howard Tommie, Dorothy Tommie, Jacob Osceola, and Joe Dan Osceola have been among the most assiduous entrepreneurs, leasing and subleasing sites in Hollywood and BC and, in Howard's case, operating businesses in Oklahoma. For several years, Howard subleased a portion of his leased land on the northwest corner of the heavily trafficked State Road 7/Highway 441 and Stirling Road intersection to a hot dog vendor, selling from a colorful cart. The attendant was a curvaceous young woman, each day working in the South Florida sun clad only in a string bikini. She was quite successful. There was a joke inside the tribe about the number of men who had developed a liking for hot dogs. But this was certainly the smallest of Howard's business interests; his gaming returns were the largest.

All in all a relatively small but industrious number of tribal citizens were taking to white men's business. The fact that amassing individual wealth was not necessarily in line with tribal traditions was not a critical issue. The fact that some of them were amassing individual wealth at the expense of their tribe as a whole obviously would have to await another battle or perhaps even another war.

II   The Fourth Seminole War

"'We're trying to expand outward into the world of business,' says the Chief [in 1999]. 'On some of the islands they need beef, so I'm trying to have my Indian people provide and sell beef now. Then I'm going to Nicaragua and Honduras to introduce adobe block-making machines. They have this nice clay there and all they need is this machine that you pour clay into and—boom—it makes a block immediately. We're also selling in the Caribbean—kind of going around the world. . . . We're just learning how to spend money. And the only way to learn is you've got to have it in the first place. Finally it hits you. You realize that you have to learn how to save some, too. So in the white man's sense of the word, I'm not a businessman. I just happened to be here at the right time and made good decisions in the past 20 years. It seems like it's benefiting people. But in the overall picture, you never know.'"[1]

The questions that still arise—looking back on those last few years from about 1998 through that fateful spring of 2001—are whether events could have worked out differently if James had realized what he had created and the circumstances that he, principally, had set in motion, and whether he could have effected any substantive change. The preponderance of evidence weighs heavily against any other outcome.

James was seeing the picture clearly, but it was only from a single viewpoint—his own. Never did he see the depth of feelings that were arrayed against him from inside the tribe—feelings that had taken years to accumulate. By the time of his sixth political election victory he had ceased to question the validity of his own worldview.

Neither did he sufficiently realize the multiple and competing views of the tribe from the outside world looking in, and never did he take into consideration the power of those outside viewers to have an impact on his world. The two views that would have the greatest impact on his own future and the tribe's were those of the U.S. Federal Bureau of Investigation and those of a nationally known Baltimore developer named David Cordish—not wholly because of Cordish's unique characteristics, but, rather, because he represented quintessentially the hubris of a non-Indian looking from across the cultural divide and into the lucrative Indian world.

Regardless of all of those considerations, however, the acute precipitating condition was bound up principally in the degree of dissatisfaction that James had come to harbor after twenty years in office, his anger at the constant sotto voce harping that he had had to endure from his own constituency, and his determination to give the Seminoles what they wanted—whether they realized what they wanted or not. "James always said he wanted to spoil the people, but his desire to do it and the ability of the Tribe to make it happen were never the same thing," recalled Tim Cox, who probably got to know James in their short time together as well as or better than anyone ever had.[2]

James's imaging of the "Indian crabs" was a valid one, and one that he kept as a constant point of reference. In his anger, however, he constantly blocked out any consideration of the extent to which he had precipitated this condition. His was the ultimate warrior mentality, and it would admit of no other than a politically absolutist (to all intents, a military) solution to his current situation. And, although he did not fully realize it, his was a two-front war: he was fighting both within and without the tribe.

There is a special character—an especially sad character—to watching a nation of only a few thousand people who are, after all, in the most literal sense of the word "family" turn into angry, factionalized infighters, led by elected leaders who are driven by greed and their own angers to stage, literally, a bloody coup d'état. Their ancestors had fought for almost half a century to stave off the specter of domination by the U.S. government, and now they were frightened and greedy and giving in to new U.S. government pressures. And, even so, this might have been but a small scene on the world's stage if the stakes hadn't been so phenomenally high and the story so publicly ugly—and also if the cast of characters and their stories hadn't incorporated and illustrated so many cultural issues in both Indian and U.S. life and history.

⁓

It would be easy to blame the war on Tim Cox or Dan Wisher, the major characters in the drama of those final years (besides James) or, for that matter, on the supporting cast: Calixto García-Vélez and Alan Skavronak. A minor tier of irritants comprised the "old guard," Pete Gallagher and Robb Tiller, and a few others who also became targets of opportunity for the outside forces arrayed against James—not against the tribe but clearly, obviously, against James. Inside the tribe was the traditional cast of actors, led by Jim Shore: Mitchell, David, Max Jr., and Jack Smith, who became pawns.

In order to watch it unfold in its own time and manner, we must go into those last four years (four is always the number of power for the Seminoles) and recount the events. Much of the personal discontent that plagued James personally we have already recounted. And Pete and Robb were old actors in the drama, and if they had been the only actors they might have been negotiable obstacles in the path to continued power for James.

Robb was visible to the Seminole people and sometimes costly but still peripheral as far as internal decision-making was concerned. Pete created ongoing problems for James and himself because his position was inside the tribe and his machinations were all too clearly James's machinations. Pete's platform inside the tribe was as a reporter for the *Seminole Tribune*. This had annoyed the *Tribune*'s tribal staff from the moment of his hiring, in October of 1986, because Pete clearly occupied a favored spot with James, traveling with him on political occasions, setting up musical performing events for him (they had met partly through their musical connections), and writing the stories that glorified him to the readers of the *Tribune* both inside and outside of the tribe.

As James approached the winters of his discontent in the last years of the century, he ceased any pretense of neutrality or objectivity in the function of the newspaper and began to use it specifically and obviously as his own personal weapon, too much in the manner of a dictator. The *Tribune*'s longtime editor, Betty Mae Jumper, was tired by this moment. She was battling a recurrence of cancer, and her son's political opposition to James during the 1995 election had diminished her favored status with James tremendously. James's way, as I have mentioned previously, was not to confront but, rather, to simply turn the light of his attention—and, therefore, his protection—away from a disfavored individual and let the obviousness of his or her defenseless position take its course. Betty Mae was a fighter and not ready to give up the visibility that her editorship on the *Tribune* afforded her, but she was being pushed each day by the adversarial presence of Pete and two other non-Indian colleagues, Charles Flowers and Dan McDonald. Pete had engineered the hiring of these additional reporters through James's approbation and, as a consequence, the reporters felt able to openly ignore Betty Mae.

Second in command, nominally, at the *Trib* was Virginia Mitchell, who had been on the newspaper's staff almost since its inception. Virginia (Panther Clan, b. 1955) was every bit as aggressive as Betty Mae had ever been in her prime, and she went directly to the council members, especially from 1999 onward, with her constant complaints about the focus of the reporting of Gallagher, Flowers, and McDonald; about their lack of reportorial objectivity; and about their expense accounts, which, she contended, lined their pockets at the expense of the tribe.

She specifically complained that Pete lived in St. Petersburg, flew to Hollywood, stayed in a hotel, rented a car, and collected per diem "all at the Tribe's expense."[3] James sought to mollify this latter objection by assuming part of Pete's salary, paying it out of the chairman's office fund rather than out of the *Trib*'s budget. The ploy was transparent. In addition, Pete several times acted as the impresario for musical events underwritten by tribal funds—again with James's approbation.

At the time, however, any overspending coming out of the relatively small *Trib* budget was so flagrantly overwhelmed by overspending charges against the council as to almost completely eclipse Virginia's concerns. Shortly, Betty Mae would retire and James would remove Virginia from the editorship of the *Trib*. Pete, Charles, and Dan would have a short window of even greater latitude under the now de facto editorship of the chairman. Their window was shorter even than it might have been, however, because they ran head-on into the opposition of Tim and Dan. But these circumstances would only increase the volume of the anti-James Seminole chorus. The problems with the *Trib* were exacerbated by these actions and would become one of the more obvious problems the council would use against James in 2001 when, among other and far larger actions, "Jim Shore [would] help orchestrate the council's takeover of the *Tribune*."[4]

~

The story of Jim Chapman and the Terra Block machine was a minor one also, relatively speaking, until Chapman introduced the idea of taking the project to Nicaragua, and then the Nicaragua story took off in its own direction. His presence, however, illustrating yet another of James's ongoing deals at tribal expense, was another irritant to the council and the tribe. As it turns out, later news reporters made public yet another of James's complicated elements of the central plan.

Chapman, according to news reports, had been investigated by SPD in 1995 when he and James were part of a company called Sandy Beach Productions. "The background check showed Chapman had a lengthy arrest record involving auto theft, delivery of dangerous drugs, extortion, and fraud."[5] Indians are, generally speaking, not ones to take brushes with white men's law too seriously, on the premise that white men look for opportunities to find Indians in trespass of some law or another. Even so, they do have limits, and Chapman was a white man, and his background had been kept relatively quiet within the tribe.

Robert Saunooke, whom James hired in 2000 as his personal staff attorney (to cut Jim Shore out of the legal process), later told reporters that late in 1999 the Eastern Band of Cherokees had turned down a deal to open bingo on tribal land in North Carolina, put forward by "west Florida businessman Jim Chapman and Miami lawyer Martin Kalb." The NIGC, moreover, would not approve gaming without full tribal backing.

Although Chapman denied that the Seminoles were involved in the Cherokee deal, it certainly was reminiscent of the numerous attempts that James had made in the early and mid-1980s to ride the Seminoles' success in gaming to projects with other FR tribes. Saunooke said that James had thought about investing and had sent Tim Cox to North Carolina in the tribal jet to investigate. "Cherokee general counsel David Nash said tribal members ultimately turned their backs on Saunooke. 'He isn't in good standing here,' said Joe Martin, the Cherokee editor of *One Feather*, the tribal newspaper. After the bingo hall proposal, 'the tribe sort of shunned him.'"[6] Saunooke, who appears to have been taking this opportunity to denigrate Chapman even though he (Saunooke) also was an active part of the proposed deal, was quickly losing his credibility with the Seminole council as well, and he, too, would be fired in the coming purge.

As for Chapman, he and all of his ideas quickly fell by the wayside, but not before he, as too many others before, had been given access to the tribe and some of its monies, as James moved on to other and bigger projects.

The prospect of business in Nicaragua opened entirely new vistas to James. The easiest and most obvious transitional project was to purchase cattle land—an enterprise already close to the hearts of Seminoles, and one in which James had involved Jimmy McDaniel—in a country where cattle were already a major commercial element of the economy.

Shortly after Tim Cox, Dan Wisher, and Calixto García-Vélez became a part of the expansion plans, the council spent $2.4 million to buy 6,000 acres near Managua and another $1 million for 3,000 cattle. "If the tribe can't make money [on cattle] in Florida," a reporter naively asked later, "why invest more in Nicaragua?"[7] Tim responded that Nicaragua made sense because of cheap labor and land costs. This certainly made sense. If indeed the Seminoles' cattle business in Florida was not profitable—and it had not been thus far—then why should the tribe not look for some other place where it might have success?

The acreage that the tribe's money bought in Nicaragua included a ranch house that James enjoyed visiting. He loved horses, as had been mentioned earlier, and often chose to spend his time there even while David Cypress and other council reps and Tim, Dan, and Calixto preferred to seek out more salacious entertainment. Twice, at least, James took his new partner, María Santiago, to the ranch on the tribal jet, the Gulfstream (G) IV that he already would have arranged to trade up for a G V when the council removed him. The important point to realize here is that the council not only knew about the cattle ranch deal but also obviously was complicit and approving. In fact, following James's removal, the council would keep the ranch. We will go into the details of the projects in Nicaragua in chapter 12.

∾

At the same time, a story of even greater centrality and visibility for the tribe was rapidly growing out of the gaming issue—of course. Despite a lack of hard evidence in certain elements of the narrative, the many documented elements delineate an all-too-tired old story. For this and so many other reasons Jim Shore was becoming exponentially angry with James, his anger only fired by James's dissatisfactions with him. Jim is a member of the Bowers family, known for their deep, passionate, and unpredictable anger. He is also, however, a son of one of the most respected Medicine men of the twentieth century and, as such, as well as in respect to his blindness, accorded much deference among the Seminoles. He is a painstakingly slow decision maker, but also quite intelligent—in Pat Diamond's opinion the leading intellect of the tribe—and the two of them, Pat and Jim, were old friends who, especially in the period from 1999 through 2001, spoke almost daily by telephone. Their offices were only about twenty yards apart, on the fourth floor and no more distant than from mine there, but the more conditions deteriorated between James and Jim the more important it became for Pat Diamond and Jim to hide their friendship and information sharing.

At this point, Pat's long-simmering anger at James was heating up also. She was locked in a struggle with James, the council, and Tim over her determination to obtain a finder's fee for a cellular technology deal that had been brought to her attention by a business acquaintance outside of the tribe. She was asking for $1 million and James was offering $50,000, of which she asserted that he was also asking for a cut for his cooperation. Tim strenuously denies this, and the details (not to mention the precedents) make the possibility of any greed on James's part highly improbable. Tim was completely against paying any fee for actions that he viewed as having been completely within the scope of Pat's job. When James was suspended, Pat did not receive her fee, but she did manage to keep a job with the tribe, and her excellent salary, moving to Max's office. Her anger at James was, however, reaching a crescendo at the same moment as that of Jim.

Far less discreet about her relationship with Jim Shore was Chris O'Donnell, whose intermittent personal liaisons with him (and others) were all too well known, partly by her own very public admissions. Chris had had her own set of disappointments with James over the years, and most recently in particular. Moreover, negative events were swirling around Chris and James to degrees that could only reach a negative climax. For one thing, Chris had begun to become very disappointed with James as early as the moment when he had legally married Lesley. Chris never seemed to realize that James would never legally marry any non-Indian—herself or anyone else. This is further evidenced by the fact that he did not even divorce Lesley until several years after his impeachment, after he had begun living with María and after they (he and María) had had two children together.

As Chris later admitted, she was manipulated by Jim, Mitchell, and David into bringing sexual harassment charges against James at a politically useful moment, even though Tim asserts that Chris was already living with another Seminole citizen, Joe Don Billie (Panther Clan, b. 1950), at the time of the trip to New York when she later claimed that she became pregnant by James, and that she and Joe Don were sharing a room during that trip, which would have precluded her having the privacy of her room for a liaison with James.[8] Tim asserts that Chris and James had had sex a couple of days before the New York trip, however.

The story of Joe Don closely intersects that of both James and Chris, especially in this period. James had for some time been using Joe Don as a driver and general factotum, even though he was very aware of Joe Don's long-standing personal and political opposition, on the premise of the old axiom of keeping his enemies close. He had permitted Joe Don to learn to fly the helicopter, an enterprise to which Joe Don had taken quite successfully. Joe Don's lifestyle was consciously aggressive, and he had transmitted that consciousness to his son. James had taken Joe Don with him on several trips to Nicaragua, on one of which, as a show of power, James had taken away from him a prostitute with whom Joe Don was quite taken. Joe Don, badly hurt by James's insensitivity—clearly a display of power—soon afterward entered into a liaison with Chris, an action that he never would have taken before on the belief that it would have been inadmissible to trespass on James's "territory."

The few months following this New York excursion were a time of tremendous trauma for both Chris and Joe Don, as it turned out. Not too long afterward Joe Don's son was killed in a motorcycle accident. Joe Don was devastated. Within a short period Joe Don himself was permanently injured in a similar accident, becoming a quadriplegic. Chris and Joe Don remained close, she caring for him several days a week. Chris was clearly devastated by these events also, coming as they did during a time when she became pregnant, according to her assertions, although she was not sure whether the biological father was James or Joe Don.

These events all took place between September of 2000 and May of 2001. Chris informed James that she would not be returning to work. James arranged for her to be given what he thought of as a severance package that was later repudiated by the council, and Chris instituted her sexual harassment suit against James that would provide the council with its initial charge against the chairman and partly prompt his suspension. In fact, her harassment suit was formally entered on the same day that Tim left the tribe's employ. I am including some admittedly unsavory facts here, but only because they clearly give the lie to later actions and public statements of all the individuals concerned.

Enter the U.S. Federal Bureau of Investigation or, rather, reenter. According to tribal rumors it was in this same period that they began to pressure Mitchell and David in their homes. This was the moment, in mid-November of 2000, when David already had overspent his annual Res appropriation and wanted more. It was the moment when Tim informed him that he would not receive more. It was the eve of the council meeting of 18 November when David would nevertheless ask for another $1.5 million, and the council would approve it, regardless of Tim's disapproval, after several behind-the-scenes attempts to press Tim into supporting them against James.

The FBI had thus far obtained very little reward for all of its intense interest in James Billie over the years. It had maintained a growing dossier during the early years of the tribe's bingo establishment, documenting the involvement of various purportedly organized-crime-related individuals, although no successful prosecutions resulted. They had been bested, one might say, during their attempted prosecution of James's actions in the panther-killing affair some years earlier. The passage of the Indian Gaming Regulatory Act by the U.S. Congress in 1988 and the work of its NIG Commission only intensified the FBI's determination to find something actionable in the tribe's gaming, but, quite clearly, it was James the FBI wanted and not necessarily the tribe. Even the FBI's strange "Operation Cops and Indians," that came to a public head in 2001, hard on the heels of James's suspension, wound up as yet another embarrassment for the federal investigators, but their largest embarrassment—in the abortive federal lawsuit against Cox and Wisher—was yet to come.[9] Jim Shore, ostensibly a defender of his culture and his people, nevertheless would become the conduit to the FBI's much closer investigation of James and the council and their activities. He would, in real terms, open the back door into the fortress.

But before going any further into the investigation, we must review the status of the council's activities during this period, many of which were not at all irregular in the light of prevailing tribal requirements (and, especially, non-requirements) but were certainly irregular relative to the expectations of the non-Indian world. And, since so many of these activities were either introduced or furthered by two new actors on the Seminole tribal stage, Tim Cox and Dan Wisher, we must see how they came to their roles and how well they played them.

⌒

Dan Wisher was introduced to James by Charles Kirkpatrick, the tribe's first pilot. Dan and Charles were neighbors in River Bend Estates, a housing project of upper-end residential housing in the tiny town of La Belle, a principally agricultural town on Highway 80, about halfway between Clewiston and Fort Myers. Dan's field was computers; he had worked for some years for a manufacturing company as their information systems director in addition to having his own computer-consulting firm incorporated in Florida and a few other miscellaneous businesses. Dan's real love, however, was fishing, and that's why he was in La Belle.

James was having a small problem with the computer that had been installed in his home in BC. The reasons for his problem were several. First, there was a small electrical problem with the wiring. But James was not computer literate and not really interested in using computers. As I have mentioned before, James was always more interested in bottom lines than in details. He wanted to be given answers rather than to have to seek them out, but when he wanted information, he wanted it.

Another part of the computer problem, however, stemmed from larger tribal-wide problems with the current Information Systems (IS) Department still led, at that moment, by Sal Giannettino, who also had incurred the wrath of a number of Seminole employees across the five reservations who had to use his unwieldy and outmoded systems. Mary Jane Willie (Bird Clan, 1948–2003, a sister of Jim Shore), the tribal clerk, would not even permit Giannettino or any of his staff to enter her office because she was so dissatisfied with his systems and his lack of response to her office's needs. At the moment I also was a part of the chorus of dissatisfied customers asking for Sal's removal, and I was actively seeking outside computer support that would permit my department to circumvent the tribe's IS department altogether and become freestanding.

Charles took Dan to James's house in BC, and within a very short time Dan had the computer working properly again. He presented James with an invoice for $50 for his work. James was impressed; he was expecting to be presented with much larger charges. Dan was a big, bluff individual who was used to impressing listeners (and anyone around Dan was a listener, not a speaker) with his expansive knowledge of his subject, whatever that might be at the moment. Unfortunately, he also was used to an imperious style of management that was totally antithetical to the traditional Seminole style, and that would become obvious all too soon.

He and James quickly struck up a positive relationship. After a few conversations, James asked Dan to go into Hollywood and review the computer system that Sal previously had introduced to the tribe and to give him an appraisal of its utility and functionality. This process of simply dropping people into various situations, totally ignoring lines of authority and responsibility, was just one more of James's management characteristics. This was in the summer of 1998.[10] It didn't take Dan very long to find problems with the tribe's existing IS department, especially since Chris O'Donnell provided him entrée to the tribe's accounting records on instructions from James. Among other things it became obvious that Giannettino and one of his subordinates in the department had their own outside corporation, which was buying computer hardware and reselling it to the tribe at exorbitant prices. This was in addition to the fact that the equipment and the programs he introduced simply did not meet the tribe's needs.

Dan reported all of this to James and, subsequently, at the same council meeting where Sal Giannettino was terminated as head of the IS department, Dan Wisher was hired on an ostensible six-months contract, for $50,000, to run the IS department.[11] Dan entered the process of tribal administration at the nadir of Giannettino's popularity and at a moment when Pete Gallagher was agitating for two projects, which brought Dan and Pete into open conflict almost immediately in a process that set the unfortunate tone for Dan's interactions with other entrenched tribal employees. Pete was already in the process of setting up a tribal Web site, which he intended to manage. Dan saw the Web site as more properly being within the purview of the IS department, and the two quickly became bitter enemies. Further, Pete wanted to set up a live video feed from the Swamp Safari, and this was opposed, on economic grounds, not only by Dan but by Tim as well. Tensions rose quickly within the headquarters building.

In April of the following year Wisher got the "Solomon" system up and running and tracking of tribal expenditures, including that of the council reps, became a great deal easier. In July of 1999, James moved Dan out of the IS department, which, by this time, Dan had reorganized under competent supervision, and placed him within the chairman's office as a "technical advisor." Thus, the original six months, as it turned out, did not end until almost three years later, when James's leadership also was terminated and until Dan and Tim both were terminated as well. By that time Dan had parlayed James's approval into yet another round of the game of power brokerage that James had permitted around himself for so many years. Dan quickly had tired of the power struggles within the headquarters building in Hollywood. These included not only Pete and his *Trib* cohort but also Chris, George Johnson of real estate services, and the heads of purchasing and personnel. As the Nicaraguan deals began to take shape, Dan gladly departed the Hollywood offices for extended stays in Central America.

In the short run, however (and it was all really short run from this point), the presence of Dan Wisher and, shortly, Tim Cox, seemed to rejuvenate James. They had new ideas, and they brought new energy to James and the way he envisioned his leadership of the tribe proceeding at the very moment when that vision had been flagging. Advertently or inadvertently, they played directly into his belief in his own vision, which had already begun to separate itself from any belief, real or feigned, in a need for council support. In any meaningful manner, James had never had anyone to mentor him or set limits on his actions. So, in some ways, I suggested to Tim, he had been a surrogate parent to James. "Well, I think I was the voice of reason. I wouldn't tell him *not* to do anything;

I just told him what the consequences would be. [But] I really felt that, over the two years I was with the tribe, every single day was combat! And I had to outmaneuver, outthink, and outperform all the people that were standing around, wanting me to fail." It was a two-front war, I said. "No. A three-front war—the council."[12]

But the facade of council involvement and understanding was maintained, and this is an important point to keep in mind. At the least, the council maintained its tenuous hold on the chairman's various wheelings and dealings through its secretary/treasurer, Priscilla Sayen, who was officially charged, in almost every instance, with reviewing official documents—from larger and larger bank loans to land purchases to gaming management contracts to serving as an officer in the council's various business corporations and partnerships—and affixing her signature to them along with those of James and a very few others.

James often expressed his opinion that Pricilla was the most powerful official in the tribe: she signed checks, James did not. She had had experience working for the BIA and the IHS, but neither had given her the confidence that she needed to assert herself or to make decisions commensurate with her position. In reality, consequently, and in terms of actual power, Priscilla was a cipher. The council gave her responsibility to sign documents, but they gave her no authority to decide, and she took none. In her own view, she had been appointed by the council and could be removed by them just as easily, and this reality caused her no small amount of anxiety.

In a relatively few years Dan would be among those who would pay the price for arrogantly believing in their own vision for the tribe and their own belief in the permanence of power. By 2004, Dan would be gone; his computer staff would have almost completely turned over; and his vaunted accounting system would be replaced, yet again, by a council that expressed its own will, slowly but eventually. The more things change, the more they remain the same.

～

Timmy (not Timothy) Wayne Cox (non-Indian, b. 1969) actually came on the Seminole scene earlier than Dan Wisher, but in an altogether different context and not directly into the awareness of James. He was (and is) a cocky individual with a high intellect, an exceedingly rapid grasp of new subjects and details, an unsophisticated background, and a potent disregard for most authority. As Tim often says of himself, "I got BIG balls!"[13] He has an omnivorous mind, ironbound opinions, and not a few biases. As he often said, "Well, don't ask my opinion if you don't want to hear it!" Throw in his military experience and his determination to see the world as an ongoing war, and he and James Billie were made for each other.

Tim was a Georgia native who had met a Seminole woman, Amy Billie (Clan X, b. 1971), while they each were students at Georgia Southern College in Statesboro, Georgia, about sixty miles northwest of Savannah, and they married. Much later, Amy would bring Tim to Hollywood to attend a Tribal Fair and introduce him to her uncle, Hollywood council rep Max Osceola Jr. (Max's non-Indian wife and Amy's mother were sisters. Amy had been raised in Georgia rather than on the Res, but her love of her tribe was real.) At the fair, Tim met James also, but the two would have no time to connect.

Mr. and Mrs. Cox both finished their degrees, his in communications and hers in education. They moved to Americus, Georgia, where Tim joined the police force. According to his own description, he was "an overzealous officer," and his naturally combative nature led to disagreements that have since been parleyed by the press into serious problems under the heading of his having had "a checkered law enforcement past."[14] Tim sees the events alluded to as mountains that were really only molehills, but his aggressive nature makes it easy to see how disagreements could have occurred.

After several more moves, they both joined the U.S. Army Reserve in 1987, and Tim also began to pursue a master's degree in social administration. With no thought of moving to Florida, they bought land in North Georgia. Shortly, Amy was delivered of their second child, a son, who had some potentially serious health problems and needed access to state-of-the-art medical care that he did not appear to be receiving at the local facility. Amy spoke to Pat Diamond, and Pat acted with her usual alacrity to consult with James and have the infant moved to an Atlanta hospital where he recovered within a few days. Tim and Amy were exceedingly aware that it was through James's help their baby had been saved. In the spring of 1997 they moved to Florida.

Despite his gratitude toward James, and Amy's connection to the tribe, Tim was not willing to live on the Res. "I saw the Res as a slum."[15] Max Jr. offered to help the couple get a residence on the Res, but there was a waiting list and Tim and Amy did not want to cut ahead of the line. Moreover, Tim felt that as a non-Indian he would be at a disadvantage on the Res and "the Res was a high-crime area and I did not want to live with that."[16] Despite the validity of a part, at least, of this viewpoint, it was another evidence of Tim's belligerent outlook, and it would not win him any friends in his forthcoming work with the tribe.

"Amy and the children were getting $800 each from tribal dividends. But in 1997 the dividends were stopped for two months because the [state] court issued a closure order for the tribe's bingo; the tribe [was able to] stay it by court order, but it appeared [at that moment] that the tribe would lose the Class II pull tabs." James continued the gaming nonetheless. "In June and July the tribe didn't issue any dividend checks but in August the dividends rose to $1,000 and within a few months to $1,500." (The gaming closure order ceased when the state failed to file paperwork in a timely manner.)

Initially, Tim and Amy split a forty-hour workweek at one of Max's tobacco shops, until some weeks later, when Max directed Tim to the tribe's Gaming Monitor Department, where Roy Diamond was in charge of background checks for casino employees. During his tenure there Tim attended a tribal reception at Native Village, a small visitor attraction owned by James and his first wife, Bobbie Lou, on Highway 441/State Road 7 on the Hollywood Res. James was there, "and Amy was telling him about being here, and he looked at me and he said, 'Well, you ought to come over and work with the Tribe.' And I said, 'I already work with the Tribe,' and he responded, 'How come you didn't come to me?' and I said, 'I'm a grown man, I don't have to go to nobody.' So, he kinda laughed and he said, 'You gonna live on the Res?' and I said, 'Not if I can help it.' He laughed and said, 'That's a good idea.'"[17]

Three weeks later Tim received a call from the director of the tribe's Personnel Department, asking him to move over there and take over Indian Child Welfare Act (ICWA) investigations. The Indian Child Welfare Act was the federal law that brought Indian tribes into social welfare and legal processes involving Indian minors or minors who might be eligible for enrollment in FR Indian tribes.[18] It was enacted to provide the tribes with an opportunity to intercede for purposes of cultural preservation, "to establish standards for the placement of Indian children in foster or adoptive homes, [and] to prevent the breakup of Indian families." Agencies and courts from all over the United States are required to contact the appropriate FR tribe when there is any indication that a minor might be a citizen of, or eligible to be a citizen of, that tribe. It is a much overworked and underused law that is disregarded by numerous social systems and tribes themselves, to the detriment of future generations of American Indians.

But this was only the first of several program areas that Tim was going to be given to manage. In his relatively short time in personnel his intellect and rapid grasp of details stood out, and Tim also was given the management of the tribe's federally funded Drug-Free Workplace program, the tribe's own HMO, and its 401(k) program, the exempt status of which was in jeopardy at the time and took some months to straighten out. "I really didn't know how to do those things, but when I take over something new, I become a student of the subject. I read up on it and call people for help."[19]

This was classic. James's way was to throw a person into a situation and see how well he handled himself and how quickly he grasped the requirements of the job. Typically, James also watched to see how well an individual got along with tribal citizens. In this instance, however, James had another, and larger, agenda. He wanted to find someone who could grasp the essence of the changes that he was ready to implement and who had the intelligence and drive to see them through to fruition. At this moment and on this topic, tribal acceptance had become a secondary issue.

Tim was satisfied with the way he got along with others at the time, but he was aware nonetheless of his own contentious nature. "I know I'm a driven, goal-oriented personality. [But] most of the people I had to deal with . . . came to me with what I call bitches—a complaint with no alternative. You know, a complaint with no alternative leaves me with my original direction. And I give the example of, the easiest way to look like a bad guy is to be a good guy in a room full of bad guys. Because you're the one who stands out."[20]

In April of 1999, Chris O'Donnell called Tim and reported, "James just called and told me I need to get some help up here, someone educated who has some backbone." Chris wanted to take Tim upstairs, that is, to the fourth floor administrative suite, but at first James was concerned that Tim's marriage to a tribal citizen might incline him to partiality. That was a fair concern given the strength of clan relationships in every area of tribal life. It was the reason why there were so few Seminoles in SPD. It was one of the reasons why the council never had created a tribal court system. It was the way tribal politicians got themselves elected. It was a consideration that had an impact on everything from daily attendance at work to tribal hiring.

James met with Tim, and he "began by telling me he wasn't looking for friends, etc. So, I said, 'Wait a minute. If that's going to be an issue here, let's just forget it and I'll stay downstairs. Cause you're too old to be my friend.'"[21] Interestingly, this conversation seemed to set the tone for the entire relationship between James and Tim. They did become friends in the only way James knew how to form a friendship. Tim never held back, and James took it. It quite amazed those of us who had been in a position to watch James's previous relationships.

Problems with the lack of a full-time, officially appointed administrator reached a head a few months after the May 1999 elections and James's sixth re-election. The Phish concert was coming up on the BC Res (Pete Gallagher was spearheading this event, and it was shaping up to be the biggest thing the tribe had ever hosted). Coconut Creek casino was ready to go into construction. The new BC Field Office and Family Investment Center was in construction, just to name a few projects underway at the moment. James called a meeting of Ted Boyd, Bonnie Garris, Charles Helseth, Hugh Chang-Alloy, Tim, and a few others. Tim listened as each program head touted the need for more personnel and the enlargement of his or her program.

Finally, James said, "Tim, do you have anything to say?" and Tim, to whom discretion was rarely the better part of valor, responded, "In my opinion, you have nobody running this ship day to day. . . . You fly in, you're here for thirty minutes. Every tribal member within forty miles is piling in on top of you. You spend ten minutes with every department head, and you expect to know what's going on. If you'd hire somebody who can administrate, cut back on the size of these departments—otherwise, come in here and run the show yourself." James says, "Great. You're the guy." He instructed Tim to come up with a title for Chris, and Tim chose compliance officer, and to come up with a job description for Chris and himself. It was the whirlwind path to power, and it was the James Billie Way. The date was 17 September 1999.

James shortly presented Tim with a cell telephone, saying, "Here's your leash," and meaning it. James was prone to call those he trusted—or needed at whatever moment—at any hour of the day or night. But there came an instance, about a year and a half later, when Tim publicly barked at James for interrupting him with a call and put James on hold for almost five minutes, literally. James was still there when Tim switched back into the call.

At this initial moment, however, and despite the fact that he had been her choice, Tim and Chris did not get off to a good start. She had been performing most of the clerical responsibilities of the tribal administrator, and it was understood that she wanted to be appointed to the position officially. James had announced that he would serve, directly, as tribal administrator, but it obviously was not realistic for him to perform both the jobs of leader and administrator, and he was not, in fact, doing so. Chris told James that she had a number of loan requests on her desk, and he said to her, "Use some discretion." Tim, who was in the room at the time, recalled, "To me, that meant send the requests downstairs to the loan department and let them deal with them. [But, instead] Chris gave away $7 million in loans!" Of course, Tim filled out the check requisitions and gave them to Chris who, in turn, sent them over to Priscilla to be signed. But James was livid over such a giveaway, which included large loans to, among others, OB Osceola and his family, who certainly were not political supporters of James. Chris was so disheartened by James's anger that she stayed away from work for a large portion of the next ninety days.

Tim began his new assignment cautiously, but events rapidly began to overtake him. He first began to review accounts and accounting practices, to interview department heads, and to assess operations. He was stunned by much of what he found, especially as regarded the revenue-generating areas of the tribe's businesses—the largest of which, of course, were the casinos. Security ranged from lax to nonexistent. At Immokalee, there were no cameras in the money room, which is to say, no secure process of accountability. In Tampa, the money was counted and disbursed from the same room—a room with a drive-through window. Similar problems existed in each of the facilities and had to be addressed, frequently over the determined opposition of management.

Tim describes James as being "criminally biased." He says, "James seemed to think, 'Why would anybody steal from me when I would just give it to them?' He really did not want to accept the situation as I presented it. I called the first six months of showing James the realities of things 'the end of innocence.' Each time I showed him something, he was more amazed!"[22]

"I'd like to give myself credit [for the positive changes], but I can't. I'm smart, but not smart enough to have made that much difference," Tim says, regarding the significant jump in tribal profits that occurred after security and management practices were tightened up in the casinos.[23] In Immokalee alone, according to Tim, tribal profits rose 77 percent when better security measures were instituted. He is not asserting unscrupulousness specifically but, rather, lack of oversight and of best management practices. Another example that he cites is the number of pallets of bingo paper literally piling up in the supply area of the Tampa casino. The purchasing contract with the supply company simply called for deliveries of a set number of pallets on a set schedule, regardless of whether the supplies were needed. There was no oversight on the contract. The contract, as it turned out, belonged to David Cypress. And this reality led, in its turn, to the next phase of reorganization.

As soon as he felt that he had assessed the situation, Tim began to move, swiftly and confidently, to regularize the operations of the program areas, but at first, at least, he was swimming against a swiftly flowing tide. "The department heads, especially, had never been told 'no.' They had never been told, 'No, you can't take the entire department staff to that conference.' . . . I would tell them no, and they would show back up with a travel authorization signed by James! I went to see him and said, 'Take me out of this job. Put me back in personnel. If all you want is a secretary, you already have Chris O'Donnell. You tell me to do things but you won't support me. In six months or a year you're going to want to know why [the things you've told me to do] haven't been done, and you're going to blame me. And, if you blame me, the tribe will blame me. If the tribe blames me, my children will get grown and they will blame me. And that ain't goin' to happen!' So he said, 'What do you want?' and I said, 'Support me!' and he said, 'Alright, I'll give you enough rope.'"

The result was internal turmoil for almost a year. Tim sent out a shower of memoranda with new rules and regulations for everything, the objective being to reshape the tribe's infrastructure on a more businesslike model, and to contain spending. Change by fiat is never easy, however. The more he fulfilled James's expectations in the projects that James assigned to him, most of which were directly concerned with new, outside business interests and finances, the more responsibilities James piled on him. The more he realized of the tribe's potential for economic advancement, the more James's desire for action was only increased. The more he had to do, the less time he spent in the office and the more frustrated the directors became over the changing rules and over their inability to corner him to let him hear their concerns. Those who did manage to find him were furious. One department director literally attempted to slap him in the face. Some longtime staff quit, summarily. But Tim was a juggernaut; he plowed on.

Ted Boyd was one of the earliest casualties. Besides his confrontation with Max at the council meeting over the possibility of radically increased dividends, Ted was being heavily pressured by Tim over certain investments and high brokerage fees to which he was trying to commit the tribe. "Ted was good for the Tribe when the Tribe had only a little money—through the lean years—but as the tribe grew, he didn't know how to manage assets. Through the two years when I knew Ted, he was an absentee department head. Perhaps it was his heart condition, but he wasn't there."[24]

Ted's health gave way, and he shortly chose not to return to the tribe. Hugh Chang-Alloy was given control of accounting, but his tenure would not extend beyond that of James's. Bonnie Garris could not stay. She sent out a very large check that James told her not to send out, and he became very angry with her but would not have fired her. She chose to leave. The preschool program director would not introduce tribal languages into the curriculum. When the preschool students were brought into the council chamber for the 1999 inauguration ceremony and recited the U.S. Pledge of Allegiance but couldn't recite the Seminole Pledge, James was furious. Moreover, Max and the Hollywood community also were angry at this director because of her unwillingness to fire a subordinate who was known to be involved in an affair with the husband of one of Max's nieces. The community was determined to enforce its own norms, and its own traditions permitted it to do so. All of these events may or may not have been directly connected, but Tim Cox obviously was the nexus. In the eyes of tribal citizens he had brought turmoil to the tribe; the waters of the lake were roiling.

"In 1999, when I moved upstairs, I said [to myself] that I have two years to do this before they throw me out. By fiscal year 2000, the programs were pretty well on track. That was pretty easy. So it was time to go after the Tribal Council expenditures and allocations. That was the only other area to fix." The spending of the program areas had never been the biggest problem; it was principally a problem of regularizing their processes, of instituting sound business practices—and convincing them that there was a dependable process in place.

A very basic problem in this process was the fact that formerly the budgets had had little meaning, and everyone knew it. "Did James ever really worry about the budget?" I asked Tim. "No, James wasn't worried about that, because the budgets never really meant anything anyway. They were never real. They were numbers on a page that never tied into anything either. Not even the overall numbers meant anything either. I asked Ted before he left how he projected the income from year to year, and he said, 'Oh, I just add 2 percent to last year's.' But you can't do that with the tribe. Because, while I was there, there was a 72 percent increase in net! But Ted—and James—were content that, each year, the income had gone up."[25]

As the program areas were brought under control, however, the real problem became more and more visible. Trying to get discussions and decisions from the council reps was a serious and, ultimately, insurmountable problem. Even more important at this moment, however, was the fact that the council reps were becoming seriously addicted to the tribe's tremendous supply of money. They had become the biggest fish in the pond, and the most voracious. And the more Tim attempted to pin them down for answers, the more evasive they became.

"Trying to get answers from David Cypress, I've met with him in bars—the R&R [bar and pool hall] in Clewiston, in pool halls, the pool room in the back of the BC gym. He never wanted to meet for more than five minutes. I always had forty minutes of things to discuss. David would listen for five minutes and then tell me to give the paperwork to [his assistant]." (My own experience had been almost exactly the same: after hours of tracking David down to discuss issues with him, he would begin with, "Have you talked to James about this? Then, why are you coming to me?")

"I would lie in wait for Mitchell," Tim recalled, "but we got to a point where he would only want me to meet with [his assistants] Carolyn Billie and Sally Tommie. Max—I never could get an appointment with Max. I would see his truck at the [Hollywood] Smoke Shop early in the morning, or meet with him at his 'Harley House' (behind his home). [Even] James—I could get James's attention for about an hour but then his attention would wander and he would start rambling around the room looking for other things to amuse himself." Part of the problem was obviously a cultural one: the details of white man's business were myriad and tiresome. Part of the problem stemmed from Tim's own success: the council was pleased to have him conduct successful dealings that also buffered them from having to deal directly with the outside world. But another part of the problem was the council's own, and they were extremely unwilling to face it or accept change.

"And there was the council meeting where Max said to the council, 'Don't get mad at Tim for what's going on, be mad at us because we're directing him what to do.' You know, I would go to them and explain why we're getting screwed in whatever area, and I would say, 'Look, here's where you're getting screwed,' and they would say, 'Well, fix it.' And I would go to fix it, and I would find out that it was one of them doing the screwing!"

By the early fall of 2000, Tim, "Billie's hand-picked government operations manager, tried to enact a spending freeze. Cox's attempt to limit spending—

ignored by council members—set off a series of events that slowly disassembled Billie's administration."[26] Later that year, a *Miami Herald* reporter would break the story of the problems with the spending of the council reps. Tim, disgusted with the council's monumental overspending and individual greed, provided much information for the article. The *Herald*, at first concerned about the power of the tribe to retaliate, finally published the information nonetheless.

> Defining what benefits the tribe, as opposed to what benefits individual council members and their families, is an inexact science. . . . But documents obtained by *The Herald* show that some council members also catered to their own whims with the tribal allocations. Some leaders acquired luxury cars, rented limousines, drew thousands of dollars in cash and rang up thousands of dollars in charge-card bills. One spent money on a boxing gym. When several council members began to exceed their $5.1 million-a-year budgeted allocations late last year, the first hairline cracks in the tribe's long-stable political structure appeared. Within six months, those cracks had widened into divisions.
>
> Billie said the tribe's political troubles mounted when he warned his fellow councilmen to put the brakes on their spending. . . .
>
> "When tribes start earning large amounts of money from gaming, some [of them] struggle to handle the responsibility," said Doug Nash, an Idaho lawyer and member of the Nez Perce tribe who specializes in Indian gaming issues. For most it's a welcome dilemma, said Nash, who worked briefly for the Seminoles 20 years ago helping to write tribal ordinances. "Indian people have been, and for the most part still are, impoverished. Money is really a new twist," he said.[27]

Hugh Chang-Alloy, who had succeeded Ted Boyd, wrote a memo on 6 April warning the council that its spending might be breaking NIGC and IRS rules. A month later, Saunooke also wrote in a memo:

> "It has come to my attention that the Tribe, and its Tribal Council, are disbursing funds of the Tribe in such a matter [*sic; manner*] as to expose the Tribe, the Council Members and the individual Tribal members to tax and criminal liability." Billie said he believes his fellow council members were acting in the best interest of the tribe when they spent money from their allocations . . . [and] conceded he wasn't aware of how much money was being spent until his administrators pointed it out.
>
> Tim Cox, the operations officer who monitored almost every aspect of tribal government and business, said he was worried the tribe wouldn't be able to cover its expenses if spending was not curtailed. "It was appalling,"

Cox said. When council members exceeded their budgets, Cox sent them notices and showed them detailed accounting reports chronicling their top expenditures. Tribal Council members did not like being told how much money they could spend, Cox said. "They were absolutely livid."

Max said that the Tribe has its own way of sharing wealth. "You're not rich by how much you own but by how much you share. . . . To me it's a different philosophy. Instead of hunting [as traditionally], we're entrepreneurs."[28]

Of course, by 2001 the process of disassembly was no longer slow. This reality had become the principal internal cause of the war between James and the council. And the tribe's public visibility had made it the object of intense scrutiny. As Tim explains it, "The level of sophistication in their types of business dealings had skyrocketed, but the mindset just wasn't there yet. When you're making $20 to 30 million, you're of no interest to anybody. When you're making $300 to 500 million, you're a big fish now. You're a major employer. You have a major impact on the county, the state, and even the nation." The outside cause for the political disassembly came as a result of David Cordish and the Hard Rock deal, however, which was already far along in progress. A trumped-up sexual harassment suit, the FBI, and a hotel in Nicaragua were the opening salvos.

~

The story of the FBI and its ongoing interest in James and his affairs is a well-known one. As gaming revenues continued to spiral upward, internal elements of tribal life and tradition became the focus of outside observers. The newspaper reporters, in fact, went into a feeding frenzy—fueled by so many years of very restricted access to Seminole business and by the age-old lure of money. Three South Florida newspapers—the *Miami Herald,* the *Fort Lauderdale Sun-Sentinel,* and the *St. Petersburg Times*—bent their considerable resources to the acquisition of insider information. (Occasionally, the *Orlando Sentinel* or the *Jacksonville Times-Union* reprinted articles picked up by the wire services.) They slowly began to obtain tribal documents and surreptitiously interviewed any tribal citizens who were angry enough—and naive enough—to talk. Soon the story of the Seminoles and their international dealings would become international news.

The focus of the reporting was the wealth the tribe was amassing and the manner in which it was being spent. In particular, reporters reviewed council decisions that made significant amounts of monies available to tribal citizens. In all fairness, the commissioners of the NIGC treated the news reports temperately, making allowances for the fact that the Indian tribes were, indeed, using white men's money, but they were not products of the white man's world. In the case of the Seminoles, reporters were particularly incensed that council representatives were setting themselves up with lucrative personal deals funded by tribal monies.

Max Jr., the Hollywood rep, became the frequent public voice of the council and apologist for all of its actions. Nothing bothered Max. Many things profited him. He dealt easily with the non-Indian press, and he actually believed everything he said. He was the perfect choice. Mitchell only wanted to permit himself to be seen in a positive light. David angered too easily and gave away too much information. His confrontational, combative nature caused him to deny nothing and admit too much. The other two reps were too inexperienced in dealing with the outside world and their English often was insufficient. In the case of Jack Smith, whom Tim found to be quicker than the other council reps to grasp nuance, his health was quite poor. And the deals were labyrinthine. Those of David Cypress in particular, but even these were not yet as grand as the outside deals that James and Tim had set in motion, and in 1999 and in 2000 these took center stage as their details became known to reporters.

At a March 2001 council meeting, citizens asked James for explanations for the causes of their major complaints. One reporter who attended neatly summed up the various battles in the larger conflict. "In recent months tribal members have increasingly expressed their anger, suspicions and sense that the tribal government was keeping them in the dark. While some spoke up at meetings, others circulated typed pages of anonymous complaints. At the March meeting Billie addressed some of them. He talked about the FBI, saying the U.S. government will always investigate a successful tribe. He touched on the sexual harassment allegation, and said the tribe had bailed other top leaders out of similar problems."[29] Each of these items had its own trajectory, but the place where they intersected was right in the middle of the gigantic Hard Rock deal.

The story of the sexual harassment suit began in the summer of 2000; in many ways it was another outgrowth of the presence of Tim Cox, but it fit, quite conveniently, into the negotiations inside and outside of the tribe over the multi-million-dollar Hard Rock deal. Chris O'Donnell became a willing pawn. Chris, who had worked so hard for the tribe and specifically for James since 1982, also had enjoyed an intermittent sexual relationship of convenience (his and hers) with James almost since her hiring. James preferred to be on easy sexual terms with many of the women around him, and Chris knew this, the tribe knew this, and Chris enjoyed her job under these conditions. Nor were Chris's sexual expressions confined only to James, and this was well known both by her own open admissions and by tribal observation.

Although it had been Chris who had chosen Tim to be promoted to the administration office, she had hoped for him to become her subordinate rather than becoming his. Even though Chris was an excellent administrator when she was at her best, her first line of resort when frustrated was always substance abuse and a resultant loss of work time. Tim was far less inclined to tolerate this than James had been, and Chris's indignation only increased to new levels. Late in 2000, she finally quit her long-held position with the tribe. It stunned everyone. James approved and Tim arranged for her to be given a check for $125,000, ostensibly in payment for unused sick time. By April, however, in the midst of James's growing troubles, SPD was sent to serve her with papers banning her from entry into Res lands. Robert Saunooke, James's legal counsel, told reporters that she had been talking to tribal citizens and "creating a hostile atmosphere."[30] In fact, for the first time in all of their working years, she had been giving information to Lesley about James's sexual liaisons, and that was creating a very hostile atmosphere for him at home.

With assistance and direction from the tribe's outside counsels, Chris obtained the services of a Miami lawyer, Andrew Hall, who filed a lawsuit early in May 2001, charging sex discrimination, violation of the Pregnancy Discrimination Act, and inflicting emotional distress. Chris alleged that James had arranged $125,000 in "payoffs" after she became pregnant on a business trip with James, Lesley, and a daughter of James's to New York the previous July. Chris explained that she had been required to cease taking birth control pills because they interfered with a blood pressure medicine, and as a result of that situation she had become pregnant.

"Billie demanded she get an abortion or quit because 'the baby would look like him [and] dire consequences would follow,' if she stayed and had the baby, the suit said."[31] Following the abortion, her workplace became hostile. Chris O'Donnell was hired as an administrative assistant in the tribe's administrative office in 1982 and was propositioned by Billie in 1985, beginning a fifteen-year "'on demand'" sexual relationship. "'It was implied that these sexual relations were a condition of plaintiff O'Donnell's employment,' the suit said, claiming Billie regularly used his leadership position to coerce women employees into having sex with him."[32] The $125,000 severance pay was actually, the suit alleged, a combination of sick leave reimbursement, money to pay off her credit cards, and $5,000 for the abortion.

The assertion that "dire consequences" would follow the birth of a baby that might or might not look like James was a very weak argument, however. By long Seminole tradition, babies belong to their mothers, and this mother would not be able to give the baby a clan. She was not even a Seminole, although she was at least known to the tribe and liked by many. Even if James recognized the child and enrolled it, Seminoles have a positive attitude toward children, and this would be neither the first nor, undoubtedly, the last such instance in tribal history. Chris's story had much more value—specifically negative—outside of the tribe where different values prevailed and tribal values were not understood.

The lawsuit pressed by Chris O'Donnell was a transparent ploy on the part of Jim Shore and the council, but it served its purpose: it focused on James an even brighter spotlight outside of the tribe and put him in a most unflattering light, outside of the tribe anyway. James acted calmly in the face of reporters' questions, but his wrath showed through nonetheless. "'I'm not embarrassed by it, I'm just pissed off,' Billie said. But Billie, 57, said the Seminole culture sets them apart from white Americans as far as sexual behavior. 'Certain things you think are immoral, we kind of condone it,' Billie said. 'When they elected me, it wasn't because I was moral. . . . They think they're hurting me, but they're hurting themselves.'"[33]

James is both sincere and truthful here. For fifteen years the tribe had known of his intermittent sexual liaisons with Chris and with many others. None could fairly be called "relationships" as they had none of the characteristics of any personal, sustained affinity. He also told me that some years before the council had supported Mitchell when he had been named in a quiet paternity suit. As I have mentioned before, sexuality does not carry the social burden among the Seminoles that it does among some non-Indians. It was more strictly controlled historically than at this point, and it remains distasteful if it is public and embarrassing, but human sexuality is not inherently negative to the Seminoles.

Later, after James was removed from leadership and the Hard Rock deal had been completed, Chris would admit publicly that she had been put up to the charges and was pressured by Jim Shore and the council to make her charges against James public. (We will follow the case further in chapter 12.) Even with its limited degree of subtlety, moreover, the plan was obviously too complex to have been initiated inside the tribe. Its real value was as a critical element of the process of getting James out of the way of investor anxiety over the Hard Rock bond issue. All of this will become clearer as we follow the trajectory of Chris's case in the larger context of the tribe's gaming history and the next plateau in that story—the Hard Rock projects in Florida and the Nicaragua story.

The tribe had watched and heard, without much understanding, the intermittent but continuing battles that the council had been fighting with the U.S. government over gaming ever since James had come into power. In the 1980s, the council had signed the first management contract with Jim Clare and Pan Am for the Tampa bingo hall, eventually the Tampa casino. A number of problems became public over the years, despite which Clare and Pan Am and the tribe forged a close and profitable working relationship that continued up to 2000, when the tribe was finally pressured by the NIGC to buy out Clare's contract and take over management in Tampa directly. The increase in profit was enormous: the tribe's income jumped $424 million. By this time, however, the Hard Rock deal was firmly in the planning stage and David Cordish was the new Tampa partner. Even bigger profits were on the horizon.

The Immokalee casino had a long and troublesome history stemming from its first proposal by tribal citizen OB Osceola in 1988. When the agreement with OB failed to work out, OB took the tribe into litigation that finally ended in a costly settlement in 1998. In the short term, the tribe hired Seminole managers, but James quickly offered a management contract to an old supporter from the early GCIA and USET days, Charles Helseth, doing business as First American Gaming Corp., but the NIGC would not approve Helseth. Despite this fact, James kept Helseth close to his projects and in tribal employ for the remainder of James's tenure. Even when it became common knowledge that Helseth was making council information available to the FBI, shortly before federal investigators began to openly sit in on council meetings, he was not fired.[34] James still kept his friends close and his enemies closer, and above all, James maintained a calm reliance on his own innocence.

James subsequently invited Pan Am to take over in Immokalee in 1999. Pan Am's contract would end there within the year, however, a few months after the NIGC notified the tribe of its intention to challenge the tribe's agreement with Pan Am on the premise that the agreement was only a consulting contract, when, in fact, Pan Am had been managing the casino since its opening. The NIGC threatened substantial penalties and a possible closure order if the tribe continued its relationship with Pan Am without an acceptable management contract. The tribe relented and accepted a "mutual termination" with Pan Am and a "cessation of all payments" on 3 August 1999.[35] Once again the tribe took over direct management of the Immokalee operation.

The council gave Marty Johns the development and management contract for a gaming hall on the Brighton Res in the mid-1980s also. Brighton casino, the smallest and least lucrative of all the tribe's casinos, would nevertheless continue, quietly and profitably, even through the moment in September of 2000 when the NIGC fined the tribe for its failure to abide by federal regulations. The NIGC would require the tribe to take over direct management in Brighton, too; to which the council would agree, simply handing management back to Marty as an employee rather than a contractor. In other words, the NIGC was trying to force the tribe in the instance of each of its casinos to pay direct attention to the management and the revenues, rather than permitting the management contractors to function as quasi-autonomous agents without sufficient control over their profits.

The Coconut Creek property had come into tribal ownership in 1982, but plans for possible development dragged on until the mid- and late 1990s, when an acceptable finance and management group was found (acceptable to both the NIGC and the tribe) and a council agreement struck. The NIGC required revisions of the terms, however, until a third amended contract finally was accepted. In 1997 the tribe took back management of this operation also. Since at least 1998, the trust and nontrust lands at the Coconut Creek site were managed by a tribal corporation, Seminole Properties I, and its successor, Seminole Properties II, whose only director was Jim Shore. Finally, Phase I of the overall development project, the casino, opened to the public on 7 February 2000. The break-even point for Coconut Creek was $20 million, and it paid for itself in the first six months of operation.

The original concept for the Hard Rock complex on the Hollywood Res called for the closing and razing of the old Hollywood casino. But local sentiment was too much attached to it, and the final decision was to rename it the Hollywood Classic and keep it open. Guards there used to tell the stories, amusedly, of players who would line up at the doors after the hall closed for a single hour of cleaning to await the 6:00 a.m. reopening so that they could reclaim their "lucky" seats. Gamblers are a very superstitious lot.

Despite early attempts by James to remove the original interests from control, Moriarty and Weisman, doing business as Seminole Management Associates (SMA), remained in control in the Hollywood Classic. In 1992 and '93 the council agreed to try to push Seminole gaming beyond the Florida shores, putting money into the Offshore Enterprises in which SMA were partners, but the venture was short-lived and ended, with very little income for the tribe, amid charges of money laundering that were never proven. By 1996, when the U.S. Supreme Court issued its ruling in the tribe's case against the State of Florida, the tribe had created its own gaming commission and the position of gaming monitor (although the position would not be filled until the following year, by Roy Diamond, another "old retainer" of James's).

Under pressure once again from the NIGC, the council would approve a change of management at the Hollywood casino. The SMA contract was terminated, and a new management contract with JPW Associates was created. Once again, however, the NIGC balked; JPW and SMA were simply the same individuals, renamed. On 30 May 1997, the NIGC issued a notice of violation to the tribe, requiring that it cease its management contract with JPW. The tribe complied, but only after appealing the ruling. On 20 April 2001, only four days before the council suspended James from office, the Eleventh Circuit Court of Appeals issued its ruling, upholding the $3.4 million civil fine against JPW and upholding the NIGC ruling against JPW's management in Hollywood.[36]

Consequently, the tribe bought out the contract and took direct control of yet another of its gaming operations. The NIGC also required that the tribe shut down its pull tab machines, which the commission considered to be nothing more than thinly disguised Class III games. James had installed the machines during the process of the tribe's negotiations with, and suit against, the State of Florida, seeking a gaming compact that would include the state's agreement to Class III gaming on the reservations.

Two other ongoing Hollywood discussions concerned pieces of property in prime business locations. The old Hollywood casino, soon to be renamed Classic, fronted on State Road 7/Highway 441, the most heavily trafficked north–south axis through the Res. The most viable place for the tribe to create any other business development would be on the same road, but there were only two pieces of property with sufficient potential. Both of them quickly engendered hostility and controversy, one inside and the other outside of the tribe, and both became entangled ultimately in the Hard Rock story.

As early as 1996 I had begun lobbying James to use a site on the Hollywood Res for the construction of a tribal archives facility. My argument centered not only on the basic fact that the tribe had no such archives and already had lost far too much of its documentary history in its own failure and that of the BIA to preserve tribal documents, but also on the fact that what records the tribe currently was maintaining were being held in public storage facilities off the Res. Obviously this was insecure, as non-Res property provided none of the legal safeguards of Res land, and I was concerned that federal authorities could access tribal documents with impunity.

Once again, however, I was being naive for several reasons. For one thing, James was not concerned about the information contained in the publicly stored documents. For another, although I had no way of knowing it at the time, Jim Shore was about to make everything—tribal documents stored both off- and on-Res, including everything on the tribe's computer hard drives—available to federal investigators. And, of course, once that threshold had been crossed, the storage of records off-Res would no longer matter to the same extent as before. The only critical element was, and remained, the sovereign proprietary right of the tribe to protect its dealings. Nevertheless, and despite the fact that the tribe now has established its own document retention and imaging program within the accounting department, the tribe continues to dismissively store the documents of its program areas off-Res.[37]

Nevertheless, the site that I recommended was a lovely one, wooded and green and deep enough to set the building back from the road and protect it from direct visibility. It faced on Stirling Road, almost at its intersection with State Road 7/Highway 441, and had on it two small churches, one a Baptist church with a tribal membership, and the other a Hispanic church with no tribal membership. James, however, clearly wanted any archives to be located on the BC Res, his headquarters, but the potential logistical problems associated with such a location were too great, in my estimation.

James sent me to George Johnson, then the head of real estate services for the tribe, and we reviewed the history and current use of the Hollywood site that I preferred. In 1936, the State of Florida unilaterally had conveyed the property to the Florida Baptist Church, which later deeded it to the North American Mission Board. The tiny church had a staunch, albeit very small, membership of Seminoles who had converted to Christianity. The Mission Board later agreed to permit a Hispanic Iglesia Bautista to occupy a part of their site, for associations of religion rather than culture.

Johnson's finding, supported by James, was that the state had conveyed the property illegally. I had no idea at the time that the site was one that the council was quietly discussing for the location of another casino and hotel complex—not yet the Hard Rock deal, but a smaller deal based on offers from other outside entrepreneurs. But in late 1999, after Tim Cox was on board and the Hard Rock deal moved into negotiation for real, the council notified the Mission Board that it wanted the property. They offered to provide another site for the tribal church and even to construct a new building. It made the same offer to the Hispanic group. The Mission Board refused to discuss the offer, and tribal church members also were adamant that they would not be moved.

The tribe's lawyers interpreted the original state conveyance as having been a "constructive trust" in favor of the tribe, meaning that the tribe had the right to make its own decision about the property. The tribal Christians were incensed. Paul Buster, a former council member and Baptist preacher, was quoted as saying that "God's work comes first."[38] Another tribal preacher, from Brighton Res, Wonder Johns (Panther Clan, b. 1934), led the charge against the council, and the idea was quietly dropped.

This left James and the council with only one other viable choice. It was a larger piece of property, and it fronted right on State Road 7/Highway 441, but it was currently under lease and had been for some years. Tribal Lease No. 130 was between the tribe and R. Keith Christensen and Marian I. Christensen, and they operated a trailer park on the property that was used mostly by Canadian snowbirds. According to the articles of the original lease, executed on 19 July 1977, the tribe had the right to exercise the option to purchase the leasehold developments made on the property by the end of the contract period, on 19 July 1997, as long as the option was exercised by 19 July 1995. This option was, indeed, exercised by council resolution five days prior to the deadline.[39] All five council members voted in favor of the buyout. One day prior to the end of the buyout period, the council accepted a nonbinding letter of intent from a group calling itself Premier Entertainment Group of Florida, Inc., seeking a construction and management agreement for a gaming and hotel complex on the site and offering the tribe a contribution of $2 million toward the buyout of the lease.[40]

For many reasons, James and Christensen never had liked each other, and Christensen was not going to go quietly. This was July of 1997, almost two years before Tim Cox would be made tribal operations manager. Nevertheless, as a result of continuing legal battles, the Candlelight Mobile Home Park project became one of the first he was handed. Christensen had 66.85 acres occupied by about three hundred seasonal residents who owned or rented in the park, almost all Canadians, and he kept the park up well. He immediately began to appeal to the press and to castigate the tribe. In addition, "He said he was preparing a notice to the tribe demanding proper notice, as well as relocation costs, and had been authorized by his clients to seek an injunction if needed."[41] The tribe found, upon investigation, that Christensen was in breach of the lease by having permitted an entity unknown to the tribe to generate income and receive benefits from the park and contracting with a cable TV provider other than that with which the tribe had a contract. These actions were found to be in direct contravention of the lease requirements.

Despite much negative publicity, created to a great extent by Christensen's determination to paint the tribe as having performed an illegal taking, and subsequently not at all helped by Tim's abrasive and combative management style, the tribe moved forward with the buyout. In the process, the tribe received much adverse publicity that it accepted with equanimity. Barnett Bank agreed to a $6,720,000 loan (Christensen had asked for $10 million and finally settled for what the tribe considered to be a more equitable amount). The council agreed to yet another nonbinding letter of intent from yet another group, Reservation Resources Group, Ltd. (RRG, Ltd.), a Delaware corporation also seeking a construction and management agreement for the creation of a gaming, hotel, restaurant, and arcade complex. By two further resolutions, the council issued temporary occupancy permits to the park residents and appointed a firm to act as interim tribal managers and receivers to oversee the fair treatment of residents during their dispersal.

An extension of the letter of intent with RRG, Ltd., still was insufficient to solidify the deal, and by November of 1999, the council obviously had moved to a new and higher level of planning. Another council resolution indicated that the council had met with bankers, architects, general contractors, developers, and legal counsel, and "it is recommended that Project funding [for a much larger project] be obtained from the combination of a commercial bank loan and the issuance of revenue bonds."[42] This is the first mention of using a tribal bond issue as underwriting for such a project, and the bond issue will be the centerpiece of the soon-to-be solidified Cordish deal. It therefore authorized the chairman to execute suitable agreements with the necessary and appropriate companies in order to ensure that the planning and development activities would commence as soon as practicable.

On 7 June 2000, the council passed Resolution C-276-00, finally binding the tribe to an agreement—this one with Cordish Company for a hotel/casino operation on the Candlelight Park property. Max Jr. made the motion to accept and David Cypress seconded. Jack Smith was absent, but James and the other three constituted a quorum. On the 18th of the following month, the council broadened the scope of their agreement with Cordish, specifically naming his development company, Power Plant, and giving him the right to develop hotels and entertainment facilities on any tribal Res.

Among the fight with the tribe's Baptists, the public fighting over the re-taking of the Candlelight Park property, the rapidly increasing notoriety of the chairman over the potential sexual harassment suit, the poor publicity surrounding the cattle ranch in Nicaragua, and, soon, the growing questions about the Legends Hotel deal there that would ultimately involve Daniel Ortega and the eventual fall of the national president, only the potential profits of the Hard Rock project, both for the tribe and for the developer, could possibly assuage the fears of those involved and provide the impetus to keep the project going. In the meantime, the stories only became more complex and more public. The entry of developer David Cordish into the Seminole arena would radically change the nature and value of the entire fight.

〜

The year 1996 was the one in which Donald Trump had begun to pay court to James and the tribe in pursuit of a management contract that would give him the benefit of any gaming compact that the tribe might be able finally to arrange with the state. Trump's efforts would come to naught, but a "spin off" of his interest would have a tremendous impact upon the tribe and all of its future. Trump sent to Florida a representative, Richard Fields, who had reached Trump as a one-time manager for Trump's then wife, Marla Maples. Fields very quickly sized up the situation with the tribe, with James and his leadership, and with the potential for profit. When Trump relinquished his hopes of a Seminole partnership, Fields didn't. He left Trump's employ and subsequently went to work for David Cordish, a successful Baltimore developer.[43]

Not until three years after James's ouster did information concerning Fields's role in the tribal deal with Cordish and Power Plant, the Cordish corporation, become public, partly because Trump brought suit against Fields, claiming that Fields was the agent of his (Trump's) loss of the fabulously lucrative deal that one reporter described as "among the most envied and potentially profitable casinos in the Indian gambling industry . . . making the [Cordish] firm one of the highest-paid casino developers to ever strike a deal with an Indian tribe."[44] Revenue projections for the tribe's two Hard Rock casinos and complexes were for more than $4.7 billion net to the tribe over the first ten years, with over $1.3 billion in profit going to Cordish. From the experiences of two individuals directly involved on the Seminole side of the process, James and Tim, there appeared to have been more to the story, and other news stories—not to mention a federal court decision—bore them out.

When Tim Cox moved upstairs into administration, in April 1999, and into the tribal administrator's position on 17 September 1999, Trump's interest was over. Fields was living in Hollywood, Florida, not far from the tribal offices, and not far from Jim Shore's residence. The FBI was already listening in to council meetings, through the assistance of Charles Helseth, and federal investigators wanted much more direct access to tribal records. Jim Shore was the most obvious conduit, but he wasn't the only weak link in the chain. *Baltimore Sun* reporters Robert Little and Mike Adams did a masterful job of connecting almost all of the dots in the picture.

An examination of the Seminole Tribe's [Hard Rock] development deal, including a study of financial documents and court records, offers a revealing glimpse inside the boardrooms where the multibillion-dollar casino deal was crafted. Fields was the first of many enigmatic characters that Baltimore's celebrity development firm [Cordish Company and his subsidiary, Power Plant] embraced during its three-year plunge into tribal politics and gambling. It is, of course, the "plunge" into their politics that altered the future of the Tribe, apparently with Cordish's full understanding of what he was doing.

The Cordish Company eventually signed the deal with James E. Billie, the Seminole Tribe's alligator-wrestling chief, who was later ousted from office amid allegations of embezzlement, corruption and sexual harassment. Tribal official Timothy W. Cox—engaged as a Cordish Company business partner—was arrested by the FBI, accused of squandering Seminole riches through shadowy businesses in Nicaragua and Belize, and later cleared after an abortive federal trial. The Tribe's general counsel [Jim Shore], one of the Cordish Company's primary contacts, was shot three times as the deal neared completion.

The Cordish-led development team of respected bond lawyers, strategists, gambling experts and Wall Street financiers worked desperately to prevent events from sullying the project. They helped write and implement new tribal laws and issued lengthy legal opinions in hopes of pacifying nervous investors. And in the end, they pulled together the deal. Cordish calls it his proudest accomplishment.[45]

Obviously, this requires further explanation. One underlying story here concerns the ongoing determination of the FBI to gain access to tribal records and processes. Their interest was not secret, only their methods were. The stakes in the Hard Rock deal were higher than any had ever been for the tribe before. The fact that James Billie had brought them to this point was no longer a germane issue. In fact, the stakes for David Cordish were higher than his own ever had been before, and the tribe's current political infighting was a huge negative distraction in his eyes and, clearly, in the eyes of potential investors in the deal. Tribal infighting was becoming all too public. Even the Tribal Council members became very nervous and, obviously, willing to be guided by Cordish and his lawyers, since the man who had guided them for twenty years had now become their enemy.

Fields, however, was the obvious nexus among the Tribal Council (through Jim Shore), the FBI, and Cordish. His background was not in casino development, although he had worked with commercial casinos in Nevada in the 1980s when he led the national expansion of the Catch a Rising Star comedy club chain. In the summer of 1999, Fields also was making trips to visit the FR Seneca Nation in upstate New York, but tribal leaders banned him from the Res because of his association with Trump, who had publicly opposed Indian gaming in years past. Fields persisted, however, and overcame their objections.

David Cordish says he doesn't recall how or when he met Fields, and hardly acknowledges him except to praise his skills and integrity [which seems a profound accolade for someone who hardly knew him]. "He's hardly an employee of mine," Cordish said. "But I really think that whatever my arrangements might or might not be with him—I'm not even saying I have an arrangement with him—is a private matter."[46]

According to James and Tim, it was early 2000 when Fields introduced Cordish to the tribe. James, the council, and Tim met in the tribal offices in Hollywood with Cordish and Joseph S. Weinberg, a Cordish Company vice president. This initial meeting was not productive; Cordish proposed a hotel and casino with a Margaritaville theme. "Billie says he rejected the concept because he had once been snubbed at a political function by Jimmy Buffet, who had parlayed his popular song into a chain of theme restaurants."[47]

Cordish, a Baltimore native, fifty-nine years old at the outset of the Seminole project, had obtained a law degree and practiced for a short time with his father's firm, but developed other aspirations. From 1978 to 1981 he worked for the U.S. Department of Housing and Urban Development (HUD) as administrator of their Urban Development Action Grant program, giving out more than $1.5 billion in grants across the nation. He was introduced to business by an old friend who had hired him at HUD, and the thrill of the deal caught him, permanently. Through the company that he named Power Plant, Cordish became nationally known for development projects in Detroit, Charleston (Charleston Place), Houston (Bayou Place), and Niagara Falls, New York.

Baltimore Sun reporters Little and Adams quoted: "'OK, look, I could pontificate and say I'm doing this for social reasons, but that would not be fair for me to say,' said Cordish, whose company is the only five-time winner of the prestigious Urban Land Institute award of excellence. 'I'm thrilled to be doing this. I feel better about this project than any project we've ever done. But it's also a plain, ordinary business deal. . . . You know how when they have a diving meet, they grade the divers on the degree of difficulty?' he said. 'This has got five backflips in it.'"[48]

In another of several articles the *Sun* reported: "He has a private reputation as a shrewd negotiator with almost ruthless dedication to his convictions. . . . 'I love what I'm doing,' Cordish said. 'I love changing situations. I'm going to change the whole Seminole nation [*sic*], just like we changed parts of Baltimore and parts of Houston.'"[49] A very clear statement, indeed, although the hubris necessary to unilaterally choose to manipulate an entire people certainly was different from that necessary to change an inanimate landscape.

Following that first meeting in Hollywood, James sent Tim to Baltimore to learn more about Cordish and the company. Cordish later denigrated Tim to the reporters, suggesting that Tim was not a reliable source and claiming that he had spent no more than about ten seconds in Tim's company. Quite obviously, Cordish, having masterminded the separation of James and Tim from the tribe, also wanted to distance himself from them as well.

"The [*Baltimore*] *Sun* should be careful with Mr. Cox," Cordish said. "Cox, conversely, says that he spent about 20 hours in Cordish's company and offers a detailed and accurate description of the developer's Power Plant office, describing the layout, the furniture placement, artwork and distinctive architectural details. 'I made four trips to his office in Baltimore, including one with my wife, and I met with David Cordish every time,' Cox said. 'We had meals together, sat in on a conference call together, ate at the ESPN Zone downstairs. Ask him about that motorcycle video game. He likes that.'"[50] Cox was soon in frequent contact with the two men who would become the face of the Cordish Company in Florida—Joe Weinberg and Richard Fields.

In July of 2000, the council signed two deals with Cordish and Power Plant, one for two casinos—one on each of the Tampa and Hollywood reservations—and the other to arrange the financing. The financing would be arranged through a public bond issue that would quickly evolve into its own controversy, becoming the last straw that pushed Cordish to push the council to make its permanent break with its longtime leader.

On 8 January 2001, "Billie, Cox, Weinberg, Fields and assorted politicians and dignitaries gathered for a groundbreaking ceremony on the Hollywood reservation, crowded around a mound of sand sculpted into the shape of a guitar. The event had been delayed once before because the project's financing was shaky, but this time tribal officials and their development partners poked shovels in the dirt and triumphantly declared the complications resolved."[51] The allusion, of course, was to the sexual harassment suit against James, and the problems surrounding deals in Nicaragua involving not only the cattle ranch and the downtown Managua hotel deal, but also political misconduct charges that brought down the president of the country. We will examine these latter separately, in the next chapters.

The first meeting with Merrill Lynch and Co. and the bond attorneys who would figure out how to pay for the $455 million Hard Rock project was still three weeks away and the circumstances were already beginning to spook the wealthy investors that Cordish needed to make the deal work.

"People who buy tax-exempt bonds tend to be fairly conservative," said Perry E. Israel, an attorney who helped arrange the project's tax exempt bonds—the first time such financing has ever been used for an Indian gambling project. "As things got more and more—let's say things were unusual—then the investors got worried."

"I was being told repeatedly by the professionals trying to sell these bonds—J. P. Morgan, Merrill Lynch—that the leadership and the internal matters of the tribe were a big concern to the investment community—probably the biggest concern," said Ed Gray III, executive director of the Capital Trust Agency, a municipal agency that issued bonds for the casinos on the tribe's behalf. "For a while, the Cordish people were more into damage control than they were into development."

When rumors surfaced that former employee Christine O'Donnell was alleging that Billie had sexually harassed her, the tribe's leaders reportedly urged her to go public, despite the Seminoles' history of settling such claims. And here we reach the crux of the entire situation. "It was stated to me on various occasions that [tribal officials] could not do anything to James E. Billie concerning my termination until a lawsuit was filed concerning a sexual harassment charge against James E. Billie," O'Donnell said in a sworn affidavit filed two years later in a federal lawsuit Billie brought against the tribe.[52]

As we have already learned, Chris did indeed go public with her anger and allegations. In addition, the council's indignation over James's projects in Nicaragua as separate from, and in addition to, Tim's deals with Power Plant in that country and other parts of Latin America, together with Tim and Dan's business deals were obviously frightening to the council of the little tribe. Add to this the behind-the-scenes pressures of the FBI, and the situation rapidly became overwhelming. Only the machinations of an individual with the resources of a David Cordish, and an individual with so very much to lose in his own case, could find a way out of the public embarrassment, mollify the anxious investors, and close the fabulously lucrative deal.

On May 10, 2001, Cox resigned amid . . . federal and tribal investigations—the same day that O'Donnell filed her lawsuit in federal court. On May 24, 2001, citing the sexual harassment allegations against their longtime chairman and lingering questions about his handling of tribal finances, the other four members of the Seminole council unanimously voted to suspend Billie.

The ordinance [actually, a resolution] to suspend Billie was drafted by the tribe's legal counsel, Jim Shore, who testified later that he had help from Eric Dorsky, the tribe's outside counsel based in Davie, Fla. The day before the ordinance was approved, Dorsky spent the day in "multiple phone conferences with Joe Weinberg," according to the attorney's billing records.

There is no evidence that the Cordish Co. played any role in removing the tribe's chairman. But for more than a year, the Hard Rock development team was meeting and negotiating with the tribal attorneys and officials battling with Billie. Fields and Weinberg spoke with the tribe's lawyers and others involved in the deal nearly every day for long stretches, and sometimes several times a day. All shared a common interest—keeping Billie and his associates from causing more damage to their fragile project.

"I think it's very easy for him to point to this deal and say that this is what got him kicked out, but I don't believe it," Israel said. "If anything, maybe the questions we raised caused other members of the tribe to raise questions and that led to some of his problems. But I don't believe that either. I think even if this deal never took place he was going to face some problems. He did great things for the tribe. You can't deny that. But I think, maybe, in the end, he lost sight of the fact that his own interests and the interests of the tribe weren't always the same."[53]

In her later, sworn affidavit, signed 15 March 2003, Chris made it quite clear that Mitchell, David, and Jim Shore had repeatedly pushed her (her term) to the filing of the sexual harassment suit. Now, she swore that she had reviewed James's current complaint against the tribe, as well as Jim Shore's response, and she disagreed with Jim's position. Further, she confirmed that as regarded Jim Shore's real influence, "all matters of any significance were to be reviewed by Jim Shore and his office and that Jim Shore would advise the departments, Tribal Council, and Tribal members on how to proceed."[54] This latter statement specifically contradicted Shore's position that he was unaware of many of James's actions.

Nevertheless, James has no doubt in his mind whatsoever that Cordish was the mastermind behind his political removal from tribal leadership. He alleges that a few years following his removal, a Cordish representative contacted Chris O'Donnell and had her call James and offer to have him reinstated. James turned down the deal and, furthermore, told Chris that he no longer trusted her.[55]

La Ley del Deseo

The story of the tribe's movement into, and battles over, the Nicaraguan projects is a chapter in itself. It added a labyrinthine aspect to the entire political process that was only superficially grasped by reporters and outside viewers. To understand the Nicaraguan projects' place in the tribal story, we must reach back to see the evolution as an organic (not necessarily natural, but organic) outgrowth of James's desire for economic expansion.

"Controversy [growing inside the tribe in the summer of 2000] centers on the partially completed Legends Hotel in downtown Managua." Tim Cox and Dan Wisher borrowed "to complete the $7-million building," and Jim Shore told the *Seminole Tribune* that no tribal money was involved. This was obviously disingenuous. Cox and Wisher had set up Seminoles HR Americas; Tim reported that he only took the deal when the Tribal Council balked at it. Cox got some of the money from the Cordish Company and Saunooke advised that the pair, Cox and Wisher, give the tribe "a 10% stake in the deal." Jim Shore denied any knowledge of the Legends deal. "Wisher, 54, formerly the tribe's information systems consultant, has moved to Nicaragua and taken a position in the tribe's Foreign Affairs Department, Saunooke said."[1]

The original concept for tribal business in Nicaragua was one that evolved from several tangential projects. It was a rapid outgrowth of the earlier concept of Internet gaming and an extension of James's constant determination to diversify the tribe's economic base, lest economic conditions in Florida should diminish or halt gaming revenues. If land-based gaming should cease, at least the tribe would continue to have a revenue stream; if land-based gaming was able to continue, the tribe could double its revenues. By the opening years of the 1990s, gaming still provided only about 60 percent of the annual gross revenues of the tribe. As it worked out, even without the long-term rewards of offshore gaming, by the end of the century, it provided over 95 percent. The vast majority of tribal eggs were all in one basket. Unfortunately, James's ever-increasing drive for economic expansion, abetted by the council, also brought the tribe into a period of overextension—counterpoised against individual council reps' radically growing drives for personal profits—that only exacerbated matters.

The original idea for tribal entry into the business of offshore gaming was provided to James by Skip Weisman and his brother in 1996, just as they finally were being removed from management at the original Hollywood (later to be known as the Classic) casino. Tribal citizen Larry Frank was moved out of the tribal administrator's position and into direct tribal management of the casino as a result of NIGC pressures for the tribe to assume direct control of the operation. This is also the moment in which James decided to serve as his own tribal administrator, a short-lived and ineffective idea that would end with the appointment of Tim Cox to that position.

The council agreed to have Horkey and Associates, Accountants, which had worked as outside tribal auditors before, provide a feasibility study. Their study reported that, for an investment of $4.7 million the tribe would stand to gross as much as $720 million in three years of operation, split 50-50 with the outside management corporation. The findings were presented to the council in December of 1997, fourteen days after the feasibility study was presented and approved, and the project was approved by a vote of five/nil. Later, the council would aver that it had approved only the feasibility study.

In this same period, the tribe was operating its Tampa casino under a closure order from the state, and even though the state's case would eventually dissolve, moving gaming offshore seemed to be a rational new direction. Despite this fact, however, the tribe was involved in several large projects that had to be furthered first. A contract with Arthur Anderson and the RelTek companies to prepare the tribe's computer system for the potential Y2K problem was very costly and still only in the planning stages. The ongoing problem of Sal Giannettino and the IS department's poor functioning also inhibited computerization.

The first place chosen for the offshore gaming operations was the Central American nation of Belize. At a meeting with Tim—and with Jim Shore, Pete Gallagher (the upcoming Phish concert was another topic on the agenda), Mitchell, and a few others present—James announced that he was taking the tribe into offshore gaming operations. Jim Shore was cautious but James was determined, and Jim recommended that, at least, the tribe's name should not be used. "Well," he said, "I don't think you ought to do it but, if you're gonna do it, make sure you put it in another name, like we do the other corporations."[2] The resultant gaming site was called Casino Silk. Overtures to the governments of Guatemala, Costa Rica, and Belize indicated that Belize offered the most business-friendly atmosphere. Guatemala appeared to be angling to cut in and tax the games for themselves. Costa Rica was already saturated with gamers, and the national technological infrastructure was not capable of expanding at the moment. Belize seemed the obvious choice.

And it would have remained so if the weather had cooperated. For about a year and a half the tribe operated out of Belize. The set-up costs were less than expected, and, for $1.8 million, returns were also less than anticipated, but growing. A hurricane caused significant damage to the offices, however, and the operation was moved to Nicaragua where new telephone-line installations by U.S. companies offered a more dependable system. According to Tim Cox, council members never visited the Belize operation, but they did visit the setup in Nicaragua. And, by the time Casino Silk relocated to Nicaragua, the tribe already had established its other projects there.

Hurricane Mitch, which hit Nicaragua in 1998, had given James an idea to take his Terra Block machine there, but Dan was against the idea, thinking it was unworkable. In the meantime, Jimmy McDaniel had developed contacts in Central and South America through his hunting trips, on which he sometimes convinced James to join him, and he introduced James to Calixto García-Veléz, a grandson of the Cuban general of revolutionary fame. Calixto spent a short time working in the tribal offices in Hollywood and then moved full time to Managua to smooth the tribe's way in business with Nicaraguan authorities.

In addition to his famous name, the suave and urbane Calixto had excellent manners and a well-educated command of new-world Spanish, although his family had fallen into reduced circumstances since its immigration to Florida to flee Castro. Nevertheless, he impressed James and interested him in exporting tribal beef to Central America where, he said, cattle land could be had for $50 per acre, an idea also close to Jimmy's heart. James sent Calixto to Nicaragua to buy land for cattle and horses.

His first purchase was a 6,000-acre ranch with a rustic standing house, a lake, and its own defunct volcano, for which the tribe paid $2.6 million—a far cry from the $50 per acre originally touted by Calixto. Obviously, the tribe might have considered selling its beef in Florida rather than making such an expensive move out of the country. The most rational choice would seem to have been to sell to the Lykes Bros. operation, whose huge cattle lands abutted several of the reservations in South Florida. James, however, intensely disliked Lykes, whom he saw as having been a poor neighbor historically for environmental reasons. He told Tim, "I'd rather shut down than sell to those sons of bitches!"[3] So the tribe transferred some of its cattle operations, which had never been profitable in Florida, to a place where lower land, labor, and feed prices might increase the profitability.

James visited the ranch and found it rugged, rustic, and untamed, and immediately fell in love with it. Nicaragua's largest imports at the time were rice and beef, and the prospects for Seminole success looked good. The exception to successful prospects was the political condition of the country, but this was a constant in the lives of Nicaraguans. In fact, then-president Arnoldo Alemán, known to his people as "El Gordo," favored foreign investments in his country. Alemán had defeated former president José Daniel Ortega Saavedra (1985–1990) in the 1996 election by 48 percent to Ortega's 40 percent, but Ortega had refused to concede.

Alemán was under fire from Ortega's Sandinistas in long-running political and military battles for control of the country. Adding to the instability of the nation was the continuing imperialistic intervention of the U.S.-sponsored anti-Sandinista "Contras," begun during Ortega's first tenure and reaching the climax (but hardly the end) of their machinations in the international scandal of the Iran-Contra Affair. Alemán's administration constantly was under suspicion of embezzlement and bribery with, as it turned out, much reason. Partly as a result of great popular dissatisfaction Daniel Ortega's party would continue to maintain tremendous authority through the intervening years of his unsuccessful bids for the presidency, despite his defeats by U.S.-backed Violeta Chamorro (1990), Alemán (1996), and Enrique Bolaños (2001), until his eventual return to the presidency in 2006, in a politically instigated backroom deal known in Nicaragua as "el Pacto." The principal mechanism of his de facto if not de jure authority throughout the intervening years was the national judicial system in which the majority of the judges were known Sandinistas.

Both Ortega and Alemán—among the most visible power sources in Nicaragua—would become critical elements in the Seminoles' business outreach to that nation. Among other courtesies, James would provide rides for President Alemán on the tribal jet for trips to the Cayman Islands that would later be disclosed to be international money-laundering junkets. Tim and Dan would later become very public opponents of Alemán in publicity that would make the president their active enemy. Tim would meet several times personally with Daniel Ortega for cordial business and personal conversations that took on added importance when the tribe and the defendants—Dan, Tim, and Dan's son-in-law Mike Crumpton—attempted, eight times, to hobble one another with lawsuits in the country.

At its regular meeting of 10 September 1999, the Seminole Tribal Council had passed Resolution C-39-00 in support of economic development, giving James the authority to "pursue and obtain suitable business opportunities in Nicaragua" on the tribe's behalf. In addition, the resolution empowered the chairman to open a bank account with Banco Nicaragüense de Industria y Comercio, S.A. (BANIC), in the name of Seminole, S.A., the Tribe's Central American corporation, and gave him power of attorney. Nine days later, Tim received his promotion to tribal administrator and quickly applied for his first passport.

Calixto, at the same time, already had set up operational headquarters for himself and the tribe in Nicaragua. James gave him signature authority on a business account—James or Calixto could sign—to facilitate money transfers. Calixto rented a 3,500-square-foot house off the ranch, Las Colinas, for an amazing $3,000 per month. He set up tribal corporate offices in the BANIC building. The tribe sent down automobiles—a Ford Excursion and a Ford Expedition. For $330,000 James bought a lovely but also radically overpriced home across from the ranch and on a lake, from the Nicaraguan foreign minister. Repeated trips to visit their investment gave the council members, as well as Tim, Hugh, Dan (who soon was working out of Managua almost exclusively), and a few others the opportunity to enjoy the benefits of a money-hungry city. Nicaragua was the second poorest country in the Western Hemisphere; 45 percent of the country's citizens lived on less than $1 per day.[4] The city's downtown business section (among many other areas) had never been rebuilt after the devastating earthquake of December 1972. This was a country where American dollars could provide almost anything.

Tim recalls events of one trip to the tribe's ranch a few months later that highlights the council's complicity in the Nicaragua story and that, although it almost ended in disaster, in the process revealed much about the characters of the central people involved in this last chapter of the tribe's twentieth-century history. We might call it "The Story of James and the Volcano." Max Jr., Jack Smith, David, Mitchell, Calixto, James, Tim, and a few others were on a junket to visit the tribe's ranch in Nicaragua. During this trip the subject of the tribe's possible purchase of what would come to be called the Legends Hotel first came up. This is, of course, the hotel of which Jim Shore later would, on behalf of the tribe, disavow all knowledge.

There was an extinct volcano with a lake in its deep crater on the south end of the tribe's property. On this particular trip, James decided that he wanted to walk down to the lake's rim. Tim had sustained a small accident in BC shortly before the trip and had a gel cast on one foot. James never forced anyone to accompany him on any of his sometimes-dangerous whims, but he was acutely aware of the comments and characters of those who did or did not go with him. Jack Smith, Calixto, and the others wanted donkeys; there was a rough and very steep path down that had been hacked out of the grass and brush just for them. James, nevertheless, wanted to walk, and Tim declared he would go with him, cast and all. In the style of the Old Warriors, James frequently reconfirmed his right to leadership by virtue of his brash physical risk taking. The Seminoles always preferred strong leaders.

James thought that it might be possible to make some kind of recreational area around the lake—even though the angle of slope was very steep. James and Tim slid and almost tumbled down the slope, and James never even looked into the lake. He began to walk around the edge, in grass that was higher than his head, until he finally realized that he could no longer tell where he was. He had walked almost half a mile around. He and Tim had become separated, and Tim began to work his way back upward. By the time Tim regained the volcano's rim, James was still lost, although only he realized it. His only thought was to use his cell phone to contact the pilot, Peter Vedel, in the tribal helicopter to come to his rescue, although he really had no idea how.

Finally, unable to get a call through to the helicopter that he knew was circling somewhere near him, James called the tribal office in Florida—it took him over an hour to get a call through, but by moving up and up the slope he could finally get a signal—and spoke to Ida Díaz and had her call Peter in the helicopter and relay directions to him. "No, no—go right," James would call out, now watching the helicopter overhead. He still could not see the rest of his party. "No, no, tell him to come back the other way!" It was a long and arduous process. It had taken the party two and a half hours to trek down toward the crater lake and more than two and a half hours for Tim to get back out and much longer for James. He was half a mile from everyone else, and he could see the helicopter but no one else. And he drank about a gallon of water and was very near to heat stroke. It was just by luck that the helicopter, finally, spotted him.

His location, although he could not know it, was only a short distance from a clearing where the helicopter could put down and pick him up. So the helicopter dipped, and Ken Carlson, the copilot, decided to jump out to James to take him water and help him to the clearing. Unfortunately, Ken chose a spot to jump out where he thought he was only about ten feet off the grass—not realizing that the grass was almost ten feet tall itself—only to find out too late that he was really almost twenty feet off the ground; he promptly twisted his ankle. Moving slowly and painfully, it took another hour to direct the two of them to the clearing where they could be picked up.

David was amazed, and both he and Mitchell were clearly shaken up. They were not physical risk takers, and they were frightened by that kind of bravado, despite the image that they generally wished to project. They wanted to go home the next day. David said to Tim, in amazement and fright: "Why'd you do that?" And Tim, absorbed in the macho game, said, "Why wouldn't I? I did it because none of y'all thought I could. That's what real men do! Might not have been the smart thing, but real men don't always do the smart things to prove who they are." David said, "I don't ever want to go up against you in a fight!"[5]

Of course, David was referring to a physical fight, although the two of them had already come close to that point on previous occasions and for other reasons. But a legal fight was another matter, and in such an instance it was David and the council members who would clearly have the upper hand.

⁓

It was Calixto who first brought the possibility of the hotel investment to the attention of James and the others. As they were driving through downtown on their way back to Calixto's Las Colinas, he pointed out the building and its excellent location. The uncompleted 110-room hotel in downtown Managua was in default because the developer had overextended himself. James asked the others what they thought and the response was positive. The project balance was $3.5 million, and it would take at least another $3 million to finish it, with tax benefits for ten years as a result of a newly enacted tourism law. Once again, James's interest was piqued, David and Jack were supportive, and Priscilla Sayen, tribal secretary/treasurer, was advised.

Tim put together a briefing package for the council. George Johnson sent copies of the tribe's audited statements to the tribe's Nicaraguan law firm and the bankers, and, in May 2000, a meeting was set for the bankers and the tribe in Tegucigalpa, the capital city of Honduras. Tim was not excited about taking on a new and foreign project at this point. His recollection is that he was heavily invested in reorganizing the tribe's income operations at home, a project that he had barely had time to begin. Consequently, he put together what he considered to be an "outrageous" proposal: 10 percent down, the first two years interest free, and no collateral other then the building itself—which the bank already had.

After a couple of hours of hard negotiations the deal was fixed at a favorable 10 percent down, a ten-year repayment including two years interest free, and the rest financed at 6.25 percent above the international rate. James, who never wanted to sign any documents, designated Tim, Dan, and Calixto as signers representing the tribe. The group returned to Florida with yet another Nicaraguan enterprise.

Any excitement was short-lived. Within forty-eight hours James called Tim and informed him, "I don't think the tribe wants this [deal]." Tim was exasperated. If the tribe backed out of the deal, he told James, it would probably destroy its reputation in the country, and the Seminoles might lose their other project. This was a strange moment. The council members had been aware of the deal and had not disagreed. Why they changed their minds, literally over night, has never been disclosed. One possibility, certainly, is that James spoke with Mitchell and David, and they spoke with Jim Shore, all of whom (except James, of course) already felt an increasing determination to remove James from power and, consequently, did not want any more of "his" projects. Evidence of this attitude soon will be seen in the number of "James's" people and projects that were repudiated over the coming six months. Another possibility is that Jim Shore consulted with Cordish's attorneys, who, for the same reasons, advised against the tribe's extending itself further for the hotel purchase just when the Hard Rock bonds were in the offing.

Tim talked to Dan, who had construction experience, and convinced him that they (he and Dan) should take over the project. At first, James offered to participate, but he soon decided that such a personal involvement would be inappropriate and backed out of that, too. While the hotel project was moving forward in Nicaragua, the Hard Rock projects, with Cordish and Power Plant, were progressing in Florida. Tim recalls, "So, now I've got this hotel and a 5,000-square-foot restaurant on the fifth floor, and that's when I thought of making the Hard Rock Café in the hotel."[6]

~

Tim approached Cordish about participation in the financing, and the result was, first, the Tribal Council Resolution of 31 August 2000, giving Tim the tribe's approval to contract with Cordish and Power Plant in Central and South American Hard Rock development deals. And then, Tim arranged a personal deal with Cordish for $500,000, to be used to provide partial financing for the project. Illustrative of the relationship of Tim and Hard Rock is the fact that, at the time of his leaving the tribe, he had sold one Hard Rock in Costa Rica and had another in the works in Honduras.

The newspapers reported: "To help with [a] new effort—and, David Cordish says, to meet a demand of the Seminoles—Power Plant formed a partnership with Cox, enlisting him as a consultant and promising him 20 percent of any [Hard Rock] deal he could land [in Central America]. Cox had negotiated a deal to operate a Hard Rock Café at a hotel in Nicaragua, and Power Plant fronted him $500,000 for rent, according to a copy of Cox's contract with the developer."[7]

Council Resolution C-34-00 contravenes, quite clearly, the council's later public stance on this critical portion of this Hard Rock issue, as well as public statements made by David Cordish. In particular, Cordish's offhand remark that he contracted with Tim "to meet a demand of the Seminoles" is directly refuted by the language of the document. Because the situation and the details are laid out so clearly in the council resolution, here are the salient points, verbatim.

WHEREAS, The Seminole Tribe of Florida and Power Plant Entertainment, LLC entered into a development agreement on July 20, 2000 to develop Hotel/Casino and retail on the Hollywood and Tampa Reservations.

WHEREAS, Section 8.20 of the development agreement calls for Power Plant Entertainment LLC to disclose all business engagements with

Seminole Tribe of Florida members, employees and Officers and get written consent of the Tribal Council.

WHEREAS, Power Plant Entertainment LLC has gained preliminary approval from Hard Rock International to develop Hard Rock restaurants, Hotels and or casinos in Central and South America.

WHEREAS, Power Plant Entertainment LLC acknowledges that Tim W. Cox (Tribal Employee) was the originator of the Central and South American development idea and has been instrumental in developing the concept for the project and played a major role in the negotiations between Power Plant Entertainment LLC and Hard Rock International.

WHEREAS, Power Plant Entertainment LLC has expressed a desire to contract Tim Cox as a special consultant with this and other projects and intends to compensate him for this work with monetary payments and/or as a minority equity participant.

WHEREAS, The Tribal Council acknowledges that the Seminole Tribe of Florida will receive a portion of the profit from the Central and South American development and any other projects where Tim Cox is involved with Power Plant Entertainment LLC.

NOW THEREFORE BE IT RESOLVED: That the Seminole Tribe of Florida does hereby acknowledge and consent to the business agreement. . . .

BE IT FURTHER RESOLVED: That the Chairman . . . is hereby authorized to endorse the engagement.

The Resolution passed by a vote of 4/0 (Mitchell being absent), on a motion made by David R. Cypress and seconded by Max B. Osceola Jr.

Above all else, this official action by the council makes clear that the council knew and understood that Tim was to be paid by Power Plant. Consequently, when Jim Shore spoke to a reporter almost a year later, his comments were obviously inaccurate and calculated to cast Tim Cox as having performed an illegal action for which the tribe would go so far as to attempt to prosecute him. Jeff Testerman of the *St. Petersburg Times* wrote that Billie's "hand picked administrator helped negotiate the Hard Rock deal and pocketed $500,000 from the developers. He then cut a *secret* deal to open his own Hard Rock restaurant in Nicaragua. . . . 'It's a flat out conflict of interest, any way you slice it,' longtime tribal attorney Jim Shore told the *Seminole Tribune*" (emphasis added).[8] Further, the resolution makes it clear that the tribe expected to be cut in on any deal.

Construction of the hotel moved rapidly. By July work had begun, and it was arduous. Only the government owned any heavy construction equipment, and the work commenced, literally, by hand. By November the paperwork for the transfer of ownership was completed, and the rehabilitated hotel was dubbed the Legends Hotel. The name was a bit of a joke—it represented James. Tim and Dan told him he was a legend already.

Based on the council's action permitting Tim to act as an independent business agent in Central and South America, Cox and Wisher created an investment company, Inversiones Global, S.A. Tim later told reporters, and testified in federal court, that "essentially . . . the tribal company [Seminole S.A.] acted as a co-signer for Inversiones Global. Cox and Wisher had what he called a 'promise to sell,' an agreement that transferred the loan to them. Billie said . . . that he signed the document, as did other tribal council members."[9]

Cox also said that he and Wisher had written the tribe into the contract, permanently, for 10 percent of the deal. Jim Shore said that no loan papers for the two had been found, implying that the tribe had had no part in the deal. Tim's later actions indicate that he viewed the tribe as having not only a percentage of the profits but a percentage of the costs as well. James said that he wanted to stay out of the investment directly, because he wanted to keep the tribe distanced from the country's politics. These points of view are confusing but, nevertheless, distinctly different from the image that was promulgated to the press on the basis of official tribal comments.

In Central America and, especially, in Nicaragua in this time of the confused and still bloody animosities of Alemán's Liberal Alliance Party and Daniel Ortega's Sandinistas (an attempt on Alemán's life during the 1996 presidential campaign had resulted in the death of a bodyguard), there was no such thing as distancing the people or the tribe from the country's politics. Alemán had been elected on a strong anti-Sandinista platform, but Ortega and the party still counted many of the country's judges among their supporters.

Far from removing the tribe from national politics, Tim had quickly become an all-too-public opponent of the Alemán regime—with reason.

> We bought our rooms [that is, furniture for the hotel] from Steve Wynn in Las Vegas. He had refurbished The Desert Inn, . . . and we could buy complete rooms—everything from the beds and bedspreads to the lamps, except the TVs and telephones. We negotiated for days [with Wynn and, later, with the middleman] and got all the way down to $675 each for 110 rooms, that's about $74,000. . . . But it still would cost $233,000 to ship it! In the meantime, James decides that the tribe's going to pay for the furniture. . . . The tribe had kept 10 percent of the total deal but I wanted him to wait [until we knew the total cost]. James had come back to me while we were changing the ownership papers and said, "You know what? The country got to use the tribe's jet, and they used the tribe's name. You

should give the tribe 10 percent." . . . so James was determined to pay for the furniture, and I went down to pay for the shipping . . . and we ran into problems down there. Alemán wanted us to pay $50,000—for good will, apparently. He held up one of our shipping containers, of mattresses, on the premise that it's not furniture [even though] the container is marked "furniture." Dan and I actually went and met with Alemán and said, "We're bringing an international icon to Nicaragua, and you're nickel-and-dimeing us to death!" He spoke perfect English, and he had another three or four people with him who also spoke English. I'm not going to get arrested for bribing someone in Nicaragua, I told him. Have you ever heard of the words "Foreign Corruption Abroad Act?" BellSouth had just got hit with a Department of Justice citation for such practices—in Nicaragua! And sure enough, half an hour later, the container showed up. And later we had to give affidavits about this. We were actually the first ones to accuse Alemán of corruption, as early as July 2001. We were in the papers. We PAID to print it in the papers![10]

The year 2001 was, of course, a fateful one for the tribe and all concerned. By May when Tim resigned (and was fired) and James was suspended from office, the Legends Hotel and Hard Rock Café had been in operation for a year. Profits were skimpy, Tim contends, because they were being skimmed by hotel management in the absence of direct oversight. On 13 June 2001, barely three weeks after James, Tim, and Dan were no longer in tribal management, Tim was on his way back to Florida from Nicaragua when he received a telephone call from Dan saying, "We're being kicked out of the hotel." The tribe had instituted the first of what would eventually be eight lawsuits in Nicaragua, brought by both sides. Strangely, this one asserted that Tim and Dan were deceased and therefore that the tribe, as minority shareholder, intended to assume control of the hotel. This allegation would have been impossible, of course, had the tribe had no legal part in the deal.

But according to Nicaraguan documents obtained by the *St. Petersburg Times* and preliminary results of an investigation by Seminole General Counsel Jim Shore, millions of tribal dollars appear to have been routed to Nicaragua to buy, renovate and furnish the hotel. Then, records show, Cox and Wisher put together an option to buy the renovated hotel . . . which could be exercised at any time over the next seven years . . . [and] stipulated that Cox and Wisher could buy it for $3.5 million. That's the exact price paid to buy the hotel with what Shore believes was tribal money. . . . If it turns out the Seminoles own the hotel, it would make them partners with Cox. . . . The four-story Legends Hotel was only half complete when purchased. . . . It was finished with the assistance of Wisher's contractor son-in-law, Mike Crumpton, Shore said. Shore's best preliminary estimate of the tribe's investment? About $4 million. What part Billie played in the hotel deal is unclear. He is listed on Nicaraguan incorporation papers as the general manager and director of Seminole S.A., the name of the company that purchased the hotel in June 2000. The Seminole Tribal Council did not approve the hotel purchase, Shore said, though it did okay the cattle ranch purchase. While Cox and Wisher attempted to take over the hotel through their company Global Investors, Shore believes the paperwork was botched and the tribe still owns it. "It looks like the option is flawed," Shore said, because of an improperly executed power of attorney. "I think these two boys may have outsmarted themselves."[11]

At the same time, however, Jim Shore seems to be contradicting himself here. In his earlier statement, he believed that no documents indicated that the tribe had backed the purchase. Now, he seems to have found millions in tribal monies that have been used to buy, renovate, and furnish the hotel project. He makes no mention of the properly executed Council Resolution C-34-00 (mentioned above), giving the chairman the power to act on behalf of the council.

Tim stayed in Florida to gather documents. Dan and his son-in-law, Mike Crumpton, a contactor who was also a named defendant in this and later suits, flew to Costa Rica. On their return to Nicaragua a few weeks later, the two were jailed overnight but released on 4 July, and they returned to Costa Rica. A trial ensued, in which the defendants were charged with theft, fraud, and abuse of power. Ultimately, they fought the charges through Miami lawyers and through documents notarized by the Nicaraguan Consulate in Miami. The result, which came finally in October, was that the trio was found definitively not guilty.

This judgment was the fulcrum on which all the other legal battles in Nicaragua balanced, even though it was hardly the end of the legal battles with the tribe or the political battles with various Nicaraguan political factions. National elections in Nicaragua, held in November 2001, sent Enrique Bolaños, Alemán's former vice president and hand-picked successor, to the presidency with 56.3 percent of the 90 percent voter turnout, a margin of 14 percent over Daniel Ortega. International observers declared the elections fair and clean. Bolaños went into office on an anticorruption platform, immediately began to distance himself from Alemán, and denounced Ortega for having "destroyed" the country's economy during the 1980s. He criticized Ortega's close ties to Fidel Castro, Hugo Chávez, and Muammar al-Gaddafi, although there is every possibility that these charges were a part of the ongoing U.S. disinformation campaign.

Responding to public outcry, Bolaños finally stripped ex-president Alemán of his immunity, and by December of the following year, 2002, Alemán was indicted on charges of corruption. He was tried and convicted of money laundering, corruption, and embezzlement of $100 million and was adjudged guilty on 7 December 2003, for which Transparency International named him the ninth most corrupt leader in recent history.[12] Further, the United States moved to freeze accounts totaling $5 million that Alemán had hidden away in Florida banks. For reasons of poor health, however, he ultimately served the largest portion of his sentence under house arrest at his estate. The sentence would be overturned following Ortega's reelection in January 2009.

Among Bolaños's early actions as president was his decree lifting the immigration ban on Tim and Dan, who returned to the country in February 2002. This was in the midst of continuing legal turmoil over the hotel, and Tim was surprised to receive a message from Daniel Ortega indicating that he desired a meeting. Tim recalls:

> We had a female manager whose husband was an officer in the Sandinista party. She was aware of the turmoil, and she said, "Daniel Ortega wants to meet you." I didn't really know who Ortega was, but she said all the judges were Sandinistas too. I said, "Well, tell him to stop on by." And she said, No—you have to go to him. And I really didn't want to do it, but you don't say no to Daniel. [So] his people picked me up in a big SUV, patted me down, I was blindfolded, and taken to a compound in Managua. I had a translator but no one else from the tribe. Now, afterward, I went there with some other people. But at first, I didn't even know what he looked like, until he walked in and, then, I knew immediately who he was. He had the bearing and the presence, and I knew this was a leader. A very intelligent guy. Daniel could kill a lot of people, not because he had to but because he likes it. He said so. He said, "Twenty years ago I was impetuous, I was young, I didn't understand the impact of all my actions. I killed people during the war, not because I had to but because people around me were doing it and I liked to. If you're going to be a warrior, you have to be able to do that—not just kill, but kill because you like it! [Recall James's statement about being in the army and killing people.] Now, time has passed, I've changed. I'm a different man today. But I'll always live with that image. People are scared of me. . . . No one recognizes that the end does justify the means. I'll always be linked with Oliver North." Altogether, we met about five or six times, but most of the times were fairly short.[13]

They met again in June 2002, shortly before the FBI issued an arrest warrant for Tim, and he was required to return to Florida to be imprisoned.

This time I was there, Daniel Ortega sent a personal envoy to the hotel to set a meet. I said, "I don't know if that's wise—Daniel Ortega isn't well liked in the U.S. right now." They said, "Well. We'll send an SUV to pick you up and take you to the compound, and no one will ever know you were there." So I said, "Fine." I can't piss him off. So I went to the compound in Managua, and [he was there surrounded by his high-ranking officers] and several others you heard about during this time in the news. Daniel walks in. He's 6 feet tall. He's a fairly soft-spoken guy. He realizes that some of the decisions he made in the '80s were not clearly thought out. But he believes that Nicaragua is better off today than it was under [President Anastasio Somoza Debayle, who was overthrown in 1979]. So in his mind the end justifies the means. He says, "I didn't hold power that long, and I did hold an election. What people don't realize is that I'm the one who brought democracy back to Nicaragua. It wasn't the U.S. I didn't do what Somoza did. I got a bad rap. I only killed people who confronted me." So we had some very frank conversations. I said, "Well, I can't say that I agree with you completely, but I believe that you felt that you were doing the best things for the country." And of course, some of Ortega's successors—look at Violeta Chamorro, for example, is living now in Greece. She can't even go back to Nicaragua. Alemán is a thief. So ten years since I've been gone, and they've all been thieves. And [Ortega's] still living in a fortified compound: glass in the concrete, he still travels with an entourage [of bodyguards], you're still patted down before you get to the inner circle.[14]

From June 2001 through February 2002, Tim and the other defendants were not permitted to enter Nicaragua. Their management responsibilities were conducted by telephone and Internet. On 22 June 2002, Tim was arrested by the FBI, and he returned to Florida to imprisonment and the federal trial that finally ended with the judge's dismissal of the tribe's case. In January of 2003, his passport was returned, and in the next month Tim returned to Nicaragua for the last time. Altogether, during his trips, Tim and Daniel Ortega met for discussions several times and had dinner together several times. On a couple of those occasions they met at the hotel. "He had his fair share of corrupt people around him. Met with [one who asked me] 'What are you going to pay us to clean all this up?' That wasn't Ortega. . . . I don't think he knew that people around him were asking you for money. I told him that I was being asked for

$100,000 and told him who had asked me. And he would call them in and ask about it, and they would say, 'No, no, no, it was a misunderstanding.'"[15]

"So we went back in 2003, and I told him that he needed to get these Sandinistas under control because they're asking for money, and I don't have it, and they're not gonna get it. And he said, well, he couldn't control them. And I finally said to myself, well screw this. This is too dangerous. Anything we could pay, the tribe could pay more. . . . Then, all of a sudden, Alemán is in trouble. The judge is standing out in front of Alemán's house, on TV, with a gun in her hand, and pronouncing that Alemán would go to jail! So I told the tribe I would let them have the hotel for my investment in the construction and the land."[16]

I asked Tim if he felt that he still has a positive relationship with Daniel. Could he get back in to see him if he wanted? He responded quickly, "Absolutely." "Do you believe that he has exerted any political pressure on your behalf?" "Yes, on the criminal case. There were a lot of lies. I know he met with the judge. He said that the judge should not permit any monies received to influence the decision. And the judges were Sandinistas, so the judge listened. Daniel was testing me when he asked how much I was willing to pay to settle the case. I told him, 'None. I've spent all the money that I'm going to spend in Nicaragua on this issue.' And he said, 'That's a good place to be.' He asked me the same question several times, I think, figuring that he could come at the same question in different ways, and he might get a different answer. But he didn't."[17]

A couple of months later the tribe took physical possession of the hotel. Tim and Dan had obtained legal support for an "embargo" of the property, a version of receivership, but the tribe had obtained its own judicial order. Tim received a call in Florida from the hotel manager telling him that Nicaraguan officials had entered the hotel with guns and all representatives of Inversiones Global were required to quit the premises. In 2004, the tribe had given Calixto management of the hotel and had made a number of changes in the decor. The name was changed to Seminole Grand. The Hard Rock's signature guitar was torn off the building, and the interior had assumed a more local theme. Despite what may be viewed as the shortsightedness of these actions, the tribe's association with the Hard Rock company would not cease. By the end of the first decade of the twenty-first century, the Seminole Tribe of Florida would move to an entirely new and vastly larger plateau of business entrepreneurship, centering on the Hard Rock businesses worldwide.

13   A Change, of Course?

The end came swiftly, but its effects would drag on publicly and embarrassingly for years.

At the council meeting held on 24 May 2001, a continuation of the regular council meeting held on 10 March 2001, the council voted four/nil on a motion made by David Cypress and seconded by Jack Smith to suspend the tribal chairman, James Billie, from office after twenty-two years and almost six terms of leadership. As one might infer from the vote count, James was not present at the meeting. The official bases for the suspension were given as two and were laid out in four clear pages; a battery of lawyers had crafted them.

First was the fact that James had been named as defendant in "a case presently pending in the United States District Court for the Southern District of Florida captioned: *Christine O'Donnell v. James E. Billie,* Case No. 01-6797-CIV-Middlebrooks, which alleges serious misconduct against the Chairman both individually and during the performance of his duties as Chairman of the Tribal Council."

The other was that there were "newspaper reports [that] have alleged and purportedly documented the involvement of James E. Billie in matters which, if true, constitute gross neglect of duty and, in any event, charge misconduct which also clearly and adversely reflects upon the dignity and integrity of the Tribal Council as the constitutionally constituted governing body of the Seminole Tribe of Florida."[1]

The council decreed that James was not to serve in any capacity as a representative of the tribe, and his pay was suspended for the duration—the duration being whatever length of time it would take for the sexual harassment case to be resolved and for a forensic audit to be completed. Then, and only then, would the council decide on James's fate: reinstatement or removal. Since tribal politics provided no other recourse or avenue of redress, however, the action of the council in and of itself appeared to predict the outcome.

On 13 March 2001, the council had already passed Resolution C-91-01 to retain a forensic accountant to examine certain of the financial records of the tribe. The resolution explained, "Whereas Title 18, Section 1163 of the United States Code criminalizes embezzlement and theft from an Indian tribal organization . . . the Tribe's General Counsel will retain the forensic accountant . . . who will report its findings to the General Counsel, who will report to the Tribal Council and the Secretary/Treasurer of the Tribe."

The accountant was directed to concentrate his investigation on "the uses and misuses of Tribal moneys, funds, credits, goods, assets and other property . . . [and to] analyze, interpret, summarize and present the complex financial and business related issues confronted by the Tribal Council." Three items are made quite clear in this resolution. One is that the council members are admitting they actually had not understood all of the issues to which they had been signing their names over the years, regardless of the fact that in each instance the documents had stated quite clearly that they had been informed. Another is that the vote for the audit was passed by a vote of five/nil. That is, James was present at the meeting and approved the resolution—not the action one might presume of a guilty person. The third is that Jim Shore was being appointed the council's special prosecutor—its Kenneth Starr.

Reporters subsequently would make much of the unexpectedness of the council's suspension of its chairman, coming without warning as it appeared to do. This was inaccurate, however, as were so many of the details that outsiders were forced to seek out. As early as a few weeks following the Hollywood groundbreaking of the Hard Rock project, the council moved to negate the original financial contract with Cordish. The newspapers reported that the project was "stalled" because some council members objected to the financial structure James had advocated to complete the project.[2] This certainly was a clear sign to James that they were taking the reigns of control away from him, as if all of their earlier actions had not been clear signals. But in reality the Cordish agreement would be renegotiated—in Cordish's favor.

The first bond issue, for $315 million, [finally] closed in the summer of 2002, but only after a Cordish Co. subsidiary agreed to buy $40 million worth of the bonds and Hard Rock's parent, Rank Group PLC, bought $25 million. A ceremony was held on the Hollywood reservation beneath the Council Oak—a tree where Seminole leaders signed the tribe's modern constitution in 1957. A second bond issue, for $95 million, closed a year later.

As soon as the bonds were issued, the Cordish Co. was reimbursed for up to $20 million in expenses and also was to be paid $28.7 million in fees for developing and financing the project, according to its contracts.

But the true value of the Seminole Hard Rock deal for the company is in its projected long-term share of the casino's profits—more than $1.3 billion over a decade.[3]

By 10 May 2001, Tim had resigned, but the council, not willing to permit him to steal their thunder, had voted instead to fire him rather than accept his resignation. "[Then], at a May 11 council meeting, Billie sat on the council dais, waiting for the four council colleagues so the meeting could begin. None came. Finally Billie spoke into the microphone: 'Somebody call up Jim Shore and tell him to release the council members,' he said. The rest of the council, busy with its own secret agenda, never appeared and the meeting was postponed."[4] In reality, a regular meeting of the Tribal Council was held on 10 May, and James and all of the council reps were present. On the next day, the 11th, however, when the meeting was to have continued, James returned to find an audience but an empty dais. The council reps had indeed decided to continue the meeting—but without him. This certainly was another clear message. The meeting of the 10th would not be reconvened until 24 May—the day on which the council passed the resolution of suspension.

Finally, on the evening prior to the council's suspension resolution, Jim Shore once again contacted Pat Diamond—his private conduit into the chairman's office—and this time, according to Pat, asked her to perform a very unpleasant task on behalf of the council. She was saddened but had no choice. She was directed (she told me) to offer James a generous settlement if he would agree to resign outright the next day.[5]

There is yet another contradiction here. According to Tim Cox's recollection, it was Jim Shore himself and not Pat Diamond who contacted James on the evening before the council meeting. Further, Jim informed James that it was the council's intention to suspend him the next day, *with* pay. James countered with an offer to resign outright if the tribe would give him a settlement of $2 million and let him remove to Nicaragua and manage the tribe's cattle ranch there. Jim declined on behalf of the council. So James called Tim and reached him in Nicaragua at the Legends Hotel. Tim told him that if the council was determined to suspend him, James should write the resolution of suspension himself in order to maintain any degree of a favorable outcome. In fact, Tim reports that he wrote the resolution himself for James and faxed it to him where he was then living, in the guest lodge at the Swamp Safari in BC.

James called Tim again, the next day, and Tim asked, "What happened?" James reported of the meeting, "I didn't go." Tim was astounded. "Let 'em do what they're gonna do. Why should I care?" James said. "Because it's your livelihood, James," Tim retorted. James said that the council's decision had been to suspend him *without* pay. James had seen the growing animosity of the council reps, and had seen that many in the tribe were against him, but when the blow fell it still was quite a shock. The response of James the Warrior was classic. He was angry; he was determined; he would not capitulate.

The council had needed a mere fifteen minutes to take its official action. Shortly, Jim Shore would give a reporter another version of the reality behind the story: "Shore said that although the tribe is not currently negotiating with Billie, leaders would consider compensating him if he agreed to resign"[6]— obviously a restatement of the earlier, private offer that already had been declined, either in conversation with Jim Shore or with Pat Diamond. But the public moment, by then, was beyond negotiation, and the decision to suspend him without pay certainly may have been a power move by the council to force his hand on resignation.

Throughout the first quarter of 2001, the council had acted to make other changes in response to their previous dissatisfactions. It already had retained a forensic auditor and canceled the Gulfstream contract for the new G V for which James had contracted, even though it would cost the tribe $2 million for the cancellation. In late April, Jim Shore had arranged and the council had approved the reorganization of the *Seminole Tribune,* including the rehiring of Virginia Mitchell as editor. James was not present for the meeting.[7] Within two weeks (on 3 May), Pete Gallagher, Dan McDonald, and Charles Flowers were terminated. James was not present for this meeting either. Charles Flowers was.

"Flowers, who free-lanced for the paper for years and started working full-time in January, was covering the meeting at which he was fired. He said he watched in amazement as the four council members passed a resolution transferring authority over the paper from Billie to the entire council. At first, he was stunned. Then, he said, he felt betrayed. No one on the council had come to him with complaints about his stories, some of which Billie had reviewed before they went to press. 'In general, it was a very unfriendly, aggressive act that was wrongheaded and mean-spirited,' Flowers said."[8] This statement was disingenuous, at best, or oblivious, at worst. Flowers had been a central party in the ongoing feud between Pete and Betty Mae and Virginia, and he could not possibly have continued to believe that James could protect him when James's power was so publicly waning. Moreover, Tim Cox had been a vocal opponent of Flowers, Gallagher, and McDonald, and had made his sentiments known to Charles and to the council for some time.

At the same meeting at which the *Trib* reporters were terminated, Robert Saunooke's tenure was also ended. The resolution stated that the chairman's office had employed Saunooke in contravention of the tribal personnel policy, which is to say, circumventing the hiring procedure that required the approval of the council. Further, the resolution stated that Saunooke had "committed insubordination by and through recent comments published in the media," and that he would no longer be paid for any legal services, by which they signaled to James that he should not expect to use tribal funds to pay Saunooke to represent him (James) legally on a personal basis either.⁹ Saunooke would, however, continue to represent James for another year.

~

Almost four months after the council suspended James, he appealed to the eastern area supervisor of the BIA, Franklin Keel, headquartered in Nashville, to support his contention that the council had acted illegally when it suspended him.¹⁰ He had waited so long, he explained, because the Medicine man had told him to do so. The suspension amounted to a de facto removal, James asserted, and the tribal constitution and bylaws did not provide for such an action. He asked Keel to review the actions of the Tribal Council and advise him on four points. He asked whether the council had (1) acted within its authority, (2) afforded him due process, (3) granted him equal rights as a tribal "member," and (4) superseded the tribe's constitutional authority.

Supervisor Keel reviewed the matter and wrote a response to the council's action, asked his own in-house counsel to review it for appropriateness, and sent it along to the tribe. He supported James's contention that the council had acted outside of the authority of the constitution by a suspension that amounted to a removal when their allegations had not been proven and the constitution specified only the act of removal and not suspension. Further, the chairman had not been afforded the ten days' notice required nor had he been given the opportunity to appear before the council to reply to the charges.

As a consequence of the fact that the suspension amounted to a removal, Keel said, the constitution required that the council call an election, and if it did not, then the U.S. secretary of the interior was bound to do so. Finally, the appointment of another council member to replace the chairman indefinitely circumvented the scope of the bylaws' article permitting replacements for the chairman only on infrequent occasions, and not indefinitely. Consequently, Keel concluded, the effects of Resolution C-133-01 were "void and without effect."¹¹

Jim Shore was livid. He fired off a response that accused Keel of interfering in tribal affairs. He was "outraged," Keel's letter to James had been "fundamentally unfair," and his action "unthinkable." Most interestingly, Jim told Keel that "Mr. Billie has had the opportunity to avail himself of numerous internal Tribal remedies, which he has neglected and refused to do. Although Mr. Billie could have sought and requested reconsideration of the matter from the presently seated Tribal Council, he has chosen not to do so."¹² It is hard to imagine of what those numerous remedies might have consisted given the fact that the tribal body issuing the suspension, the council, was also the supreme appellate authority of the tribe. Jim even spoke to reporters about it. Jim "blasted Keel for adopting a 'one-sided version of the facts' that was 'not only precipitous but irresponsible.'"[13] "Of Frank Keel, Shore says: 'He's never returned my calls in four or five years.'"[14] It sounded far too much like a whine.

Regardless, very shortly Keel was instructed by his Washington, DC, superiors in the Department of the Interior/BIA that he would issue a letter of retraction. It appeared to the public that Keel himself had written the letter, but such was not actually the case. The letter said that Keel's earlier letter on behalf of James and on the issues on which he had "presumed" to give his opinion had been premature. "'The issues I commented on were first, and foremost, issues of tribal law that must be resolved through Tribal forums. . . .' Keel urged Billie and the tribal council to work toward a final resolution of the current disputes."[15]

According to Supervisor Keel, however, the retraction letter was not of his own composition. It was transmitted to him already written and lacking only his signature, which he was required to supply. He reasoned that the chain of actions led to only one conclusion. Jim Shore used his contacts in the office of then-Florida-governor Jeb Bush to pass along the council's wishes to Bush's brother in Washington, from whose office word was passed down to the Department of the Interior/BIA to issue a letter of retraction and cease any support for James Billie.[16]

In the same month, in a further move to attempt to clarify the problems with the council's actions, Keel wrote to the BIA's deputy commissioner of Indian affairs, Sharon Blackwell, in Washington, DC, in regard to eight separate 638 contract modifications currently awaiting review in his office. Mitchell had signed them in his capacity as acting council chairman. Keel said that the tribe's constitution (Article IV, Section 5) specifically prohibited appointment of the vice-chairman as acting chairman upon the removal of the chairman. The eight contracts totaled more than $1 million and therefore required a "properly authorized signature." In addition, Director Keel cited a similar situation involving the Seminole Nation of Oklahoma that had occurred in 2001 (and had resulted in an unsuccessful SNO lawsuit against the BIA) in which the BIA had "pointedly refused to acknowledge the actions of [what the BIA viewed as] an improperly constituted tribal council."[17] Therefore, would the BIA view the vice-chairman's signature as legal and sufficient? Despite repeated requests for clarification and advice, Keel never received any form of response to this request.[18]

Jim Shore subsequently told a reporter that the tribe's forensic audit was complete and had led to a current suit against James, Tim Cox, and Peter Ripich, but the sexual harassment suit was not over. As regards the audit, Shore subsequently would provide varying answers to this question and varying responses to those inside the tribe. The day following James's suspension, Jim Shore had told reporters that the audit was "ongoing and a tribal-wide thing not focusing on any one person."[19] As late as October of the following year, 2002, Jim Shore would tell a reporter that the audit was still "months away from completion," obviously using the matter of the audit as a means of delaying any final action on James's return to office until the council was ready to act.[20] This moment would not come until almost seven months later, at the end of James's current term.

~

The two-year period between the May 2001 suspension of the chairman and the political end of his current term of office, in May 2003, would be a crowded one. The tribe scrambled to file lawsuit after lawsuit, for the most part ineffectually, in an obvious effort to engage James, Tim Cox, and Dan Wisher, principally, in a tangle of costly litigations that would ensure their permanent political separation from the tribe. In this process the FBI would continue to participate.

The story of Chris O'Donnell's sexual harassment lawsuit—the first of James's legal troubles to break the surface of the lake—dragged on for almost another year and a half after the suspension, but it was still the smallest—albeit the most obvious—of the ploys used to set the chairman up for his ultimate removal. Finally, in October of 2002, the newspapers reported: "Seminole tribe settles sexual harassment lawsuit."[21]

When the story broke, Chris's final suit had been dismissed on the previous Tuesday following a confidential settlement. In October, U.S. District Judge Donald M. Middlebrooks called the allegations "disturbing" but dismissed the charges on the grounds that Indian tribes are exempt from Civil Rights Act provisions. Chris's lawyer, now Michael L. Cotzen, appealed, but an appellate judge affirmed the lower court's ruling. The suit was then refiled in circuit court in Broward County, where several counts were dismissed until only the count of intentional infliction of emotional distress remained. Neither her attorney nor James would discuss the settlement. "Asked about a financial settlement, Billie replied, 'I have no idea. Nothing has come out of my pocket.' . . . In settling the sick pay suit, Billie agreed to repay the tribe the $169,000 he directed Cox to pay O'Donnell in severance."[22]

~

At the end of May, following his suspension and with reporters following him, James had reverted to the one thing that always gave him joy, music. The Florida Folk Festival took place, as it had each year for over half a century, at the Stephen Foster Memorial grounds in White Springs, Florida (about ten miles north of Lake City, just north of I-10), on the Suwannee River. James often had been invited to perform on main stage, as had I. In fact, this is where he

Figure 9. Patricia Wickman, James, son Micco, and Lesley Garcia Billie enjoy a pleasant moment at the 1994 Florida Folk Festival, Stephen Foster Memorial, White Springs, Florida. (Photograph by P. R. Wickman.)

and I had met, many years earlier. He told the press that he wasn't angry about the recent actions of the council. "'I'm always in some kind of controversy,' [he said]. . . . He joked about his employment status, saying he would be joining his friends selling watermelons out of the beds of their pickup trucks. But, instead of watermelons, he joked, he would stand on Stirling Road near the tribal headquarters in Hollywood with a sign that read 'Ex-chairman will work for food.' 'Or sex for food,' he added."[23]

Privately, he had a tremendous anger, much of it focused on Jim Shore. In this period he began to refer to Jim Shore as "blind," not confining his blindness to his lack of physical sight, but referring to his intellectual shortsightedness. More and more he used this term to me and to others, especially inside the tribe. Tribal citizens were strongly factionalized at this point, and tempers were volatile on both sides of the issues.

It was at this moment that the FBI weighed in again, publicly, adding to the pressure by announcing that it was investigating gifts James had given to his current personal partner, María Santiago. María was one of a number of Hispanic employees who had worked at the Billie Swamp Safari, and they had met there. James and Lesley had pretty well gone their own ways personally, although Lesley was not one to take her diminished position calmly. María appeared to have come into James's life at a propitious moment. Perhaps it was just a matter of his finally being ready to settle down, or of needing emotional support through intense times, but it seemed that he had really found someone he could care about sincerely, at least for the moment. But he was far too much of a public figure for even this part of his life, for a short time at least, not to be dragged out into public view and examined.

The FBI questioned Ms. Santiago, who told them that James had paid for one month of her rent ($1,100), bought her a Rolex watch, jewelry, a truck, and a car. Much of this only came to light after an incident that took place late in the previous October, before James was suspended, when Lesley was arrested for accosting María in public, off the Res, robbing her of a diamond necklace that was another gift from James, and threatening to "slice her open and pull her guts out."[24] Lesley is a passionate young woman. As a result of her actions, Lesley faced felony charges of strong-armed robbery.

This confrontation with Lesley was actually María's second, the earlier one having taken place on the Broward Community College campus in Davie (greater Fort Lauderdale). After Lesley assaulted her there, María obtained a temporary restraining order. Lesley violated that order on this occasion, which was part of the basis of her arrest.

Lesley posted bond using a home in Weston as collateral. Weston is an upscale housing development on the far west side of Broward County, on the eastern edge of the sawgrass prairie that stretches away over about fifty miles to BC. The house reportedly cost $379,000, for which reporters found no recorded mortgage. This is because the tribe had fronted $360,000 for the purchase, as a loan to "Mr. and Mrs. Billie," on 31 August 2000, which James and Lesley agreed to repay with interest.[25] James was present at the council meeting and voted in favor of his own loan. There were no votes against the loan, although Mitchell was absent from the meeting.

In August of 2001, María obtained another temporary restraining order, with Lesley and her family sitting in the courtroom. Lesley did not testify because her felony charge was due to be heard later in the month. James's only comment on the restraining order (he did not attend the hearing) was, "They don't condone my love life. . . . But they do appreciate me being a good hunter and bringing in the meat."[26]

It was never his intention to live in the Weston house, however, nor did James continue to live in his old home in BC. He gave that up to Lesley, and in fact Lesley obtained a restraining order again James, which added the process of his disassociation from tribal politics. The political value of this move was to place in evidence James's lack of residence on the BC Res. In fact, he was living, at least part time, in a trailer on the BC Res belonging to one of his daughters; but this fact was officially ignored. The objective of the order was to make it appear that James no longer had any official residence on the Res, which would remove him from qualification to run for the chairmanship again because the tribe's constitution required that any candidate for an at-large office—and only the chairmanship and the board presidency were at-large offices—in order to be eligible to run must have had residence on the reservations for a minimum of ten months during the preceding four years.

By the time of the fracas between Lesley and María, James had relocated part time to the guest lodge at the Billie Swamp Safari in BC and most of the time to Moorehaven, on a small "ranch" that he bought for María. Lesley's principal residence was the house in Weston, but she traveled a good deal. Micco was in a private school in Orlando, and she spent much of her time there with him.

Interestingly, while these events had been playing out, both women had been pregnant. As James later reported, "My wife gave birth to my son [Red Heart] on June 6 [2001] and my girlfriend [María] gave birth on October 19 [2001]." Despite this seeming swirl of events, James and Lesley attempted a rapprochement. In July–August of 2001 they took the children on an 8,000-mile driving trip in an RV across the United States. A few weeks after their return, James told me nostalgically how beautiful it had been to watch the mother of his child nursing their infant. He recalled laughingly, "My other boys wanted to know why they couldn't do that too!"[27] Nevertheless, the trip was not a success, and his nostalgia was principally wishful thinking.

Privately, James always worried about his paternity (that is to say, about the fidelity of the mothers, upon whom he sometimes rightly projected his own infidelities) and sought to confirm it with DNA testing at each event. His children with Lesley and his children with María have been enrolled in the tribe, Red Heart by his mother and María's children by James. The children of James and Lesley are one-half Q (that is, half blood), and the children with María are one-fourth Q (one-quarter blood, the minimum threshold for citizenship in the Seminole Tribe). Despite her difficulties with Lesley, "Santiago says she has no intention of breaking up with Billie. 'We never make promises to each other,' she said. 'I'm not looking for marriage.'"[28] As has been mentioned previously, this is a conventional and self-serving facade.

A number of people, including myself, counseled with James then and since to take up some permanent residence on a Res if he did want to run again. The council required him to leave the Swamp Safari, however, once again failing to confront the issue openly but, rather, requiring a subordinate to take their message to James. At one point, a couple of years later, he did put a small trailer on a lot on the Brighton Res, but even this became a point of controversy. Most of his time was spent in Moorehaven with María and their growing family, and in reestablishing his chickee construction business.

His Smoke Shop business, on Miccosukee land "down the Trail," had been quickly lost, ultimately curtailing an important source of income. In early August 2003, James took $80,000 out of the shop to pay for Tim Cox's lawyer for the trial, a very generous act. That, together with his almost constant unrealistic calls upon the shop's income, meant that there were insufficient funds to pay for stock, and the store's inventory dwindled. The story of this business, on Miccosukee land, is actually very complicated. It involved a bank that was intimidated by FBI questioning and James's own profound lack of understanding of business and accounting at the practical level. Billy Cypress, then Miccosukee chairman, finally terminated James's lease and bought out the shop's remaining stock at a tremendously reduced price. In response to my questions to James about this matter, he simplified the story to his own benefit by asserting the failure of the Miccosukees to renew the lease in proper order and sufficient time, resulting in his loss of the shop and the income.[29] Details concerning these events came from Tim, who temporarily assisted James in reviewing the accounting and trying to hold on to the business.

With the change of James's official address in the tribal secretary's office to an address off-Res, his ability to run for the chairmanship again in the next election, coming up in 2007, was invalidated. He was well aware, however, that other candidates previously had run for office even though they were out of compliance with the residency requirement, and no one had challenged their ability to do so. Much of this reality stemmed from the fact that tribal housing on-Res was rapidly filling, but it seems that what he really wanted was for the people to rise up and support him. He wanted to return to office on a wave of popular support, although despite much vocal support and a couple of petition attempts this moment never came. His support never reached critical mass. He never spoke directly of this ultimate indignity, yet his pain was obvious to anyone who knew him. One event, coming in the opening days of the new year, would serve as the climax, we may see now, of all his aspirations: the attempted assassination of Jim Shore.

～

The remainder of the year following James's suspension was spent in maneuvering to regain his seat in various unsuccessful attempts. Some supporters circulated a petition for his reinstatement that was transmitted to the BIA in Washington but was disregarded by the council on the premise that its submission had exceeded the period allowed. James and Saunooke began a legal suit to have Jim Shore disbarred, but it was abortive. His current term still had two years to run and James tried to make the most of them. The off-term elections in May changed nothing for him. Other than the fact that John Wayne Huff unseated the incumbent, Jack Smith, for the Brighton representative's seat, the council remained the same. On the board, Paul Bowers, a more independent thinker, became the BC rep, replacing Mondo Tiger, who earlier had been supported by James, and David DeHass Jr. won the Hollywood seat. DeHass was less experienced while Paul Bowers was an old hand, at both cattle and politics.

At the inauguration ceremony on 4 June 2001, James attended and was treated most civilly by all. Big Shot (Moses Jumper Jr.), who was, as usual, the emcee for the event, introduced James and invited him to speak. James politely declined. At the end of the ceremony, I watched as the attendees formed a line for the traditional congratulatory shaking of hands with the newly elected officials. James joined the line and was courteously received by each of them.

Before the end of the calendar year, however, the council had acted to remove remnants of James's former administration. Personnel manager Diana Sgroi and IS manager Alan Skavronak were removed. Hugh Chang-Alloy lost his position as comptroller, allegedly because of his trips to Nicaragua with Tim. Jim Shore told reporters, "I think in the minds of the council members, these people were too closely associated with (former operations manager) Tim Cox. I think the council just felt safer taking them out."[30] Alan would retort by providing the technical expertise for Tim and James to create a short-lived Web site called Seminoletruth.com that blamed Jim Shore, especially, for the political upheaval in the tribe. Ultimately, the Web site would produce no results other than to further inflame both partisans and opponents within the tribe.

Shortly, SPD chief Thomas R. Hernan would be gone also. "In recent months Shore has been seeking a replacement for Tom Hernan, whom James picked. Billie had fired Hernan's predecessor and a handful of officers after they began investigating Billie's business partners and allegations of game fixing at tribal casinos. . . . '(Hernan) went overboard when the council wanted more security and he assigned a man to guard Billie,' Shore said with a laugh."[31] Tom Hernan was another of James's "old retainers." He had been hired as an SPD officer in 1986 and had risen through the ranks. He had had a close relationship with Chris O'Donnell through their work and was known by the tribe as one of "James's men." But he also had supported James and stood beside him in the Florida woods time and again to stop Seminoles who saw the traditional Green Corn Ceremony as an occasion for four days of drinking; James had been determined to clean up this central element of Seminole culture. In the turbulent atmosphere surrounding the turn of the twenty-first century, Tom had to make a choice about whom he would support, and he loyally bet on James.

The firing of Tom Hernan would come amid an intense escalation of emotions within the tribe that would climax with a rare—and almost fatal—event in the modern history of the tribe. James finally decided, after much hesitation, to bring suit against the council for what he strongly believed to have been their illegal actions. This critical point is ambiguous in the tribal constitution. It does not provide for a suspension of an official, although it does make provision for removal of an official for what might loosely be termed *moral turpitude*. Several years later the council would act to tighten up this provision. Even this section was ambiguous at the time, however.

This is the legal point that BIA supervisor Frank Keel had been making in his original letter in support of James. By suspending him without pay with what appeared to be no clear authority from the tribal constitution, the council was, to all intents and purposes, firing him without due process. Jim Shore, challenged by reporters, would only go so far as to say that the council's decision "draws on" the constitution.[32] In his deposition relative to the federal lawsuit that would begin late in the following year, however, Jim would respond much more clearly. When James's attorney, Robert Saunooke, asked, "For an elected official, not for an employee, is there a written policy in place to suspend an elected official?" Jim answered simply, "No."[33]

James had wavered in his decision to file the suit, and in fact he voluntarily dropped it after only a few weeks. Publicly, he preferred that the tribal citizens should rise up in his defense and force his reinstatement.[34] They did not. Privately, he was counseled by attorney Bruce Rogow that the tribe would certainly win. The failure of the tribal citizens to mount a successful petition should not be construed as a lack of support for him, however. It is important to remember that the traditional way for Seminoles (and many other American Indians) to display anger and disapprobation is through silence. Their personal, individual feelings do not necessarily rise to the level of public revolt on issues inside the tribe, although some would eventually be pushed to this point before too long.

Later, James explained, "'The tribe has a system called the four moons.'... 'If something happens, we give it four moons to see if we can iron things out. So I'm giving it four calendar months. Then I'll allow myself to go back to the people. I'm elected by the people, not by these two, three guys.'... I've always respected those guys whether I liked them or not, because they were elected by the people,' Billie said. 'So now I'm going back to the people.'"[35] At the same moment when James was making his public statements, however, the council was announcing to the Seminoles its pledge to raise dividends to $3,000 per month by the end of the year. Bread and circuses.

Three months after their suspension of James, the council finally agreed to a new and more favorable (to Cordish) contract with Power Plant, for $450 million. Negotiation on this revised contract had delayed the project for almost half a year, specifically the period when the council was maneuvering the removal of their chairman, but events began to move rapidly now.

In the same moment the council let lapse a $6.4 million deal to acquire a bank in South Florida. This had been a part of a larger and important project for the tribe: acquiring their own banking system that would, ostensibly, permit them to finance their own projects at much more favorable financial rates than those being charged by outside commercial institutions. Earlier decisions to join with other FR tribes that were creating a "Native American National Bank" banking network had failed when the project had fallen through, and a significant tribal investment had been lost. Now the council quietly repudiated another of their former chairman's ventures that had, in this case, already reached state levels in the negotiations. In addition, the council gave up a project to obtain FCC approval for an FM radio station that was to be centered in BC; this was another part of James's plan to centralize his government operations there. Mitchell wrote to the FCC and withdrew the tribe's application.

In September the council moved to initiate the first of its lawsuits. The suit was an outgrowth of the audit. Any legal points aside, however, the council was instituting what would soon clearly become a pattern of legal harassments against the trio—Tim, Dan Wisher, and Wisher's contractor son-in-law, Michael Crumpton—with only relatively limited return on the process. The first suit, an outgrowth of the forensic audit, was filed on Wednesday, 5 September, in federal court in Miami. The defendants were Tim and Peter T. Ripich, a former army buddy of Tim and a broker with Raymond James Securities in St. Petersburg; and the Raymond James company. Ripich left Raymond James in early 2001 and went to work for Prudential in their Coral Gables (Miami) office. The tribe also later named Prudential in another suit.

The charges were embezzlement, federal mail fraud, and violations of federal securities laws; they stemmed from actions in 1999 when James allegedly acted without council approval to authorize Tim to transfer the tribe's $30 million portfolio of blue-chip stocks to Ripich's control. At one point it appears that the investments rose as high as $60 million in value but plummeted to $10 million as a result of Ripich's "day trading in risky tech stocks, . . . constant churning of the . . . portfolio and [losses incurred when] Cox and Billie diverted millions to [what the suit alleged to be a sham] an Internet gambling company in Belize," and buying on margins.[36] The alleged unauthorized trading garnered Ripich $1.6 million in commissions and interest on the margin loans.[37] The tribe's suit sought $20 million in damages plus interest, costs, attorneys' fees, and unspecified punitive damages. Jim Shore finally told the press that the audit was complete.[38]

In mid-2002 a judge dismissed the original suit on jurisdictional grounds and referred the parties to arbitration. This arbitration issue would drag on through 2004, although charges against James and Tim were dropped in the process. The tribe filed another civil suit to recover the severance pay provided by James and Tim to Chris O'Donnell. James and Tim countersued and all parties finally dropped their suits. A separate suit brought against Prudential to regain the money transferred from the Raymond James account also was bounced from state to federal court. Prudential publicly called the suit "ludicrous" but, ultimately, lost.

The tribe refiled an additional civil suit against Dan Wisher, his son-in-law Michael Crumpton, and Michael Scott, a Wisher employee, on charges related to the Internet gaming site, the Virtual Data company; unauthorized use of tribal funds; and funding for the Legends Hotel and Hard Rock Café project in Managua. The suit even charged Tim with expending tribal funds to buy jewelry for a "girlfriend," a thing that he says he is entirely "too cheap to do. The jewelry was gifts for my wife, Amy, for our 10th anniversary."[39] The tribe shortly dropped these charges, perhaps as soon as it realized that Tim intended to fight back. He began by calling for depositions from tribal officials, almost none of whom responded. Tim also countered to this suit by calling for the tribe to repay him for $16,000 worth of expenses, which were quietly repaid to him by the tribe's lawyer, Don Orlovsky. This suit occurred and was being negotiated even as the federal suit was working its way through the legal system. It was finally dropped three weeks after the end of the central, federal, case described below.

Despite its lack of legal success, the tribe refiled its suit against James and Tim in January of 2003, a case that also lingered on into 2004. By this time Tim and his U.S. Army Reserve unit were being deployed to duty in the Iraq war, and he would obtain a continuance until he could return and respond to these charges. Robert Saunooke would be present to represent James, however. Again, much of the length of the case hinged on the difficulty of obtaining depositions from the tribe. Priscilla Sayen cooperated, and there was a single deposition from Jim Shore, which the judge compelled only after Jim had given his court testimony in the federal case. Council members openly ignored requests to depose them. Obviously, tribal officials were dragging their feet in every way possible.

In Miami, a federal grand jury had indicted Tim, Dan Wisher, and Dan's son-in-law on criminal charges of conspiracy to embezzle $2.7 million for investments in their own businesses. This trial was scheduled to begin early in December 2002. In legal terms it quickly became the centerpiece of all the council's legal duels with James—whether James was a named defendant or not.

As far as the tribe was concerned, however, it had only a single positive outcome: it kept the former chairman heavily and publicly engaged while the Hard Rock bond issue was being closed. It assuaged the anxieties of potential investors to see the tribe doing what appeared to be calling its erstwhile wayward leader to account. At the same time the case had at least two negative outcomes for the tribe. One concerned its inability, ultimately, to prove any of the charges made against the chairman. The other concerned the revelations of the financial dealings of the council members themselves, which were, by their own testimony, shown to be every bit as irregular as those of which they accused the chairman, albeit not (quite) as large.

The role of the FBI in the trial was intense and heavy handed. Tim recalls their actions in his regard as, without a doubt, the worst moment of his life. He was in Managua, Nicaragua, on the afternoon of 21 June 2002, in a meeting regarding the Legends Hotel and Hard Rock Café project when he received a telephone call from his wife, Amy, at home in Florida. It was the beginning of what he still calls the Seminole Civil War. It was, he recalls, "A tale which contains elements of sex, attempted murder, federal investigations, perjury, civil suits, foreign corruptions, foreign trials, federal trials, and acquittals. [It showed] that the basis of the Civil War, like many civil wars, was flawed and opposite the truth. [It showed] that the people who were pushing the hardest for the war had the most to gain and the most to hide by starting such a war."[40]

Amy informed Tim that FBI agents were in their home, and he asked to speak to one of them. Special Agent Tom Meyers informed him that they were there to arrest him and that he should come home as rapidly as possible. They haggled over how rapidly he could get there. He was terrified but tried to reassure his wife that all would be well. Amy, not a woman who intimidates easily, was terrified too. The agents had attempted to pressure her and the children by asking if she thought that her husband would cooperate in making a case against James or if he would prefer to go to jail and miss watching his children grow up. Intermittently, they also attempted to appear sympathetic to Amy and what she was going through. The effect was chilling.

Tim called his mother to let her know what was happening as well, so she wouldn't have to hear it on the television news. Next he called the airlines to arrange transportation home and then called the Miami attorney, David Mandell, who had represented him thus far. Mandell declined to represent him further, however, on the premise that Tim had not yet paid him all that he owed, and Tim was out of money. He did, however, call local federal prosecutor Edward Stamm and determine that bail would probably be set at $150,000, an amount clearly out of Tim's reach at that moment.

When he arrived in Miami the following afternoon, Tim was met by two U.S. Customs agents, two Miami-Dade police officers, and the two FBI agents, Meyers and Teamer. Tim, who had spoken to Meyers a number of times previously while the FBI agent had been sitting in on Tribal Council meetings, had boldly told Meyers that the least he could do if he were going to take Tim into custody immediately was to bring along food. Interestingly, Meyers soon gave Tim a super-sized Wendy's hamburger, fries, and a Dr. Pepper. It would be a few hours before he would be able to eat them, although even cold, he said, they provided some small comfort.

Meyers quickly told Tim directly, "You know what we want. If you give us

James most of your problems will go away." Teamer added, "You know, information is a commodity, and like all commodities the longer you wait to give it up the less valuable it will become." This would, of course, become the theme of their interrogation and several days of intense fears for Tim as he sat in a federal detention center in Miami before he was finally able to make bail. In the initial interrogation session, Meyers, who knew how much Tim loved his family, leaned across the table and in conversational tones, said, "Do you want your children to grow up without a daddy, because if you do not cooperate you are going to go to jail for at least ten years, and that means that you may get back in time to see [your daughter] graduate high school."

The agents' technique was to interrogate, intimidate, and then leave Tim alone to contemplate for a short while before resuming. After some hours of this gut-wrenching process, Tim finally said, "Enough is enough. You have my indictment and we are going to trial. It is obvious I am not going to confess because I do not know anything. I have told you all that I know. I had approvals for everything I did, and I have books at home that I will bring to trial to prove it." The agents called him a liar and accused him of being obstructive; they finally asked if he would be willing to sign a statement if they had one typed up. He agreed. When they returned, he found that they had prepared a statement that did not accurately reflect when he had been telling them, and he modified it before signing. This was the beginning of several days of incarceration designed to intimidate the defendant, and the process certainly worked. It did not, however, change his testimony or induce him to produce information incriminating James.

Tim later told the press that the FBI agents had started questioning people at the end of 2000. He was only one of a number from whom they tried to elicit information. "'They started actively knocking on doors,' Cox says of the agents. 'I believe they threatened the councilmen,' he asserts, 'particularly David Cypress and Mitchell Cypress.'"[41] If this is accurate, it worked, especially on Jim Shore, who was already predisposed to oppose James. In the process of preparing for the largest trial, which began in December of 2002, Jim literally gave the FBI investigators the tribe's entire computer hard drive. Every bit (and byte) of the tribe's proprietary information was made available to the U.S. government.[42] It was an appalling breach to those of us who were of the view that the records of a sovereign nation were absolutely proprietary, and that there existed a resulting need to maintain discretion regarding the release of tribal information. Later, Coconut Grove lawyer Marc Sarnoff, who had pressed several civil lawsuits against the tribe and put together theories of tribal corruption and money laundering, said that "'the FBI came to me over a year ago [in 2001] and said can we trust Jim Shore,' Sarnoff recalled. 'I said he was really the only guy there you could trust.'"[43] And, from the point of view of nontribal authorities, this was accurate. "The FBI contends [nevertheless] that their agents represented themselves in a professional manner and did not pressure anyone," reporters were told.[44]

Tim was not angry with the tribe, however. "He reserves his animosity for the FBI and the prosecutors. 'I spent $1.3 billion for the tribe. And they're questioning me about a $2.7 million transaction. That's like me giving you $100 and coming back later and asking you how you spent the money, [after I came] up with $99.80, and you say to me, "You fucking thief." That's the equivalent.' Because he was a demanding manager, Cox had an antagonistic relationship with employees from the moment he began. 'James called me "the hatchet man,"' Cox recollects. 'I was the one who was going to get everybody mad by changing the organization.'"[45] Cox has a cartoon taped on his wall from the *Seminole Tribune* (March 2001) in which he is speaking to the council and advising a spending freeze, a handful of arrows stuck in his butt. "I should have probably left then, but I'm tougher than I am smart."[46]

The trial began on 2 December 2002. Attorney for the defense for Tim, Ken Lipman, told the press, "The tribe's internal squabbles stem from jealousy and a fight over what to do with its fortune. 'The Seminoles' problems are in trying to find ways to spend money faster than they can make it,' Lipman said. 'They do a nice job.'"[47]

"Attorney Ken Lipman, . . . told jurors that Billie approved every penny the men spent and gave them the cash to set up an Internet gaming operation in the Caribbean. . . . 'We are sitting here because the government wished to indict Mr. Billie, wished to use these men to do it, and they would not cooperate,' Lipman said. 'These men did nothing different than what has been done at this tribe for many years.'"

Despite the significant charges and the immense effort that had gone into its preparation, the prosecution's case quickly began to unravel on the basis of testimony from former assistant comptroller Bonnie Garris and from Jim Shore himself. Bonnie testified that the council had routinely approved shaky business practices such as those currently on trial. Bonnie reported that as much as $850,000 had been transferred to her personal account in 1996 to pay for tribal festivities in Atlanta during the Summer Olympics. No one contended that Garris did anything wrong.

Shore told the court that "Billie saw the Internet as a potential source of at least $700 million over three years and a way to cement his position as the undisputed savior of the 2,500-member nation. But Shore said that he and other tribal elders worried that the gaming was illegal and could jeopardize existing casino operations spread throughout the state. . . . Lawyers for the men concede they created fake invoices to fend off the tribe's auditors. But they insist Billie approved everything. Much of Tuesday's testimony focused on the tribe's business practices and undercut several of the prosecution's prime arguments."[48] FBI agents testified also and admitted that gaming plans in the Caribbean and Central America did, indeed, appear to have been known to the council and to Jim Shore, and gaming companies alleged by the tribe to be shams were actually real, if short-lived.[49]

Finally, the case completely fell apart after James took the stand on the ninth day of the trial, for five hours of questioning. He testified without any immunity. He told the court that he was always looking for alternative sources of revenue for the tribe in case state and federal regulators ever succeeded in taking away the tribe's casinos. "Throughout the trial, the defendants called the case a domestic squabble among Indians, not something for the U.S. government to worry about. Billie supported that theory."[50] "Billie was never charged in the grand jury probe. Instead, he emerged Monday as the government's nemesis, testifying that he legally authorized every act prosecutors claim are crimes. . . . James called Jim Shore 'Too slow, too conservative.'"[51]

Without a doubt, a highlight of the testimony came when council rep David Cypress took the stand. His open and utterly ingenuous responses to the defense's questioning left no doubt as to the council's totally unrestricted view of its corporate spending. "'I have no problem with spending money; that's what I'm telling you,' Cypress testified Wednesday. . . . 'I bought Lexuses for anyone who asked for one. Give me a [sad] Hank Williams song, and I'll give you one, too.'"[52]

David's artless and unrepentant reporting of his flagrant spending of tribal funds shocked the court and reporters and even tribal citizens who had been unaware of the extent and amount of his enormous largesse. Among other very significant amounts, he gave $5.8 million (more than his annual appropriation) to Nationwide Landscaping, owned by David's friend and business partner Krishna Lawrence, a non-Indian.[53] He also approved disbursal of $1.2 million on sod from another company and gave Lawrence yet another $1.2 million directly. He and Lawrence also were partners in the Hollywood Warrior Boxing Gym that David had acquired with tribal funds. They were revealed to be associates in land sales deals that permitted Lawrence to turn over tribal land purchases for significant personal profits. His dealings with Lawrence were hardly the only ways in which David blithely distributed tribal funds. Nor was he the only council rep who made unilateral and unrestricted distributions of tribal monies. His distributions were, however, by far the largest and most widespread. He gave out monies to tribal citizens for everything from travel to autos and boats to jewelry and breast implants. He gave jobs to tribal citizens whom he favored, but especially to family members. His testimony was blatant, unregenerate, and fascinating to all who heard or read it.

A number of news articles would report these financial dealings, then and later, none of which would have been acceptable in the non-Indian world but few of which were really too upsetting to the Seminoles.[54] Spending tribal income on the desires of tribal citizens was acceptable. It echoed the multicentury tradition of the micco, a civic official, part of whose responsibilities it was to distribute goods, food, and other forms of wealth. Spending it on non-Indians was less acceptable. Spending it on one's self to the exclusion of the tribe was not acceptable at all. The tradition was that tribal leaders must take care of the tribe first—before themselves and before anyone outside the tribe. And it is for this reason that the same kind of voluptuous overspending by the same tribal officials continues today and will continue as long as tribal income can support it. This is what makes the council member's attempts to take their Indian leader into a white man's court and prosecute him for actions that they could not prove about him and were, at the same time, taking themselves, so ludicrous and so transparently self-serving.

The outcome of the brilliantly public courtroom drama came in mid-December when U.S. District Court Judge William Dimitrouleas pronounced the entire case unproven and dismissed the charges from the bench. He "issued his unusual ruling after two weeks of testimony in which nearly every government allegation was proven false—often by evidence prosecutors had gathered, but not shown to the jury. Most of the evidence came out during cross-examination by defense lawyers. . . . He told jurors he had rarely taken this step while sitting on the bench, but that the evidence forced a dismissal." Attorney Saunooke commented that any further suits could only be "malicious prosecution." Per defense attorney Alvin Entin: "Everything the government did was to try and slip around their own documents and their own witnesses. . . . The agents put together a disingenuous case and the prosecutors got stuck with it."[55]

Tim says that he spent $265,000 in defending himself, but "'I walked into the courtroom innocent, I walked out of the courtroom innocent.' Federal officials didn't have an estimate on the cost of the five-year investigation and prosecution of the case. However, at least three FBI, IRS, and Bureau of Indian Affairs investigators were devoted to it, and a financial analyst for the FBI testified that she spent two years on the case. Agents also made several trips to Nicaragua and Belize. Billie has been a target of a federal investigation since 1997."[56] One could just as well say, however, since 1979.

Despite their revelations concerning their own spending habits, no council reps would suffer the indignity of any criminal prosecutions. They would, however, become the subjects of Internal Revenue Service investigations relative to any U.S. tax obligations that they might have incurred in the process of distributing the tribe's wealth to individuals.[57] The individual citizens of FR tribes are legally bound by the United States to pay taxes, although the tribes, as an element of their sovereignty, are not.

Max Jr., in particular, has several times been audited and fined for nonpayment of back taxes. By 2007 he was earning $300,000 per year as a council rep plus $120,000 in dividends. He owed the tribe about $227,000 for tobacco purchases for his Smoke Shops from 1990. He told reporters that he was making payments. He owned Hollywood Choppers, a shop in the Hard Rock arcade that sells motorcycle-style apparel, as well as having a partnership in a company that sold furniture to the tribe. The IRS filed nine tax liens against him for irregularities from as far back as 1983. He paid off the first four but still owed $958,308 for the years 1993–2004. As a tribal citizen living on a Res, he owned no real estate, but he had four vehicles: a BMW, a Mercedes, and two motorcycles, a Harley and a Triumph. Max quoted Billy Cypress: "You know taxes, it's kind of like the federal government stole our land, and now they want you to pay for it."[58] In late 2007, Max would finally settle with the IRS for $270,000, ending other tax liens. Neither the IRS nor Max would comment on the settlement, but reporters quoted Max as having said earlier, "I didn't think Native Americans even had the word tax in their vocabulary."[59]

In the summer of 2007, the council approved a car wash business in the Hollywood Hard Rock parking garage for Max III, Max's son. Max told reporters clearly, "'I'm not going to hold it against my son that he is my son,' Osceola said. 'If there's a service or something that a Seminole-owned company can provide, we want to go there so they can prosper along with the tribal government. . . . I guess we have our own affirmative action program.'"[60]

David has been able repeatedly to arrange advantageous deals with the tribe. Among others, in 2007 the council acquired his Warrior Boxing Gym in Hollywood, in return for which the tribe deeded to him 534 acres of land near BC and an undisclosed amount of cash, although the gym was assessed at only $900,420 according to the Broward County property appraiser. Within a few days, David sold the entire land parcel for $4.5 million.[61] David declined to be interviewed by reporters about the tribal portion of the deal; Max, once again, spoke for him and for the council. One of David's daughters has an arrangement with the council for her services as a boxing promoter. Another has valet parking concessions for the Hard Rocks in Hollywood and Tampa.[62] In all fairness, it must be recalled that the Seminoles do not see this as any form of nepotism. Their tradition is to take care of the tribe first.

Here again we also must recall that the Seminoles are too small a tribe to be able to avoid business with clan or blood relatives. At the time of this writing, they still number only about four thousand. The problems with their system stem not so much from nepotism per se but rather from favoritism—that is, from the selective hiring of clan and nuclear family to the exclusion of less-favored or unfavored persons. Problems also stem from the lack of transparency that results in an unhealthy system of rumors and resulting antagonisms to the exclusion of a more healthy traditional political system of discussion and consensus. Of course, consensus decision-making is the very element that both James and the new generation of politicians have purposely shunted out of the traditional process.

~

Even as events in the criminal trial had been unfolding, events within the tribe had been moving on their own trajectory, and a rare one it was. On the evening of 9 January 2002, the turmoil building inside the tribe reached its zenith. Jim Shore finished his dinner in his private residence near the Hollywood Res. Chris O'Donnell, his longtime close associate, had been having dinner at a nearby steak house and had called to see whether he might want her to bring him something. He asked for a New York strip steak, baked potato, and corn on the cob. Jim lived alone and rarely cooked for himself. She left him between 7:30 and 8:30 p.m., after taking him the food and visiting for a short time. About 9:00 p.m., she called to see if he was still all right.[63]

Jim stretched out on the living room sofa across the room from sliding glass doors that gave onto a pool, patio, and surrounding hedge. He was listening to an audio book when he experienced a feeling that, amazingly, he did not immediately recognize as gunshots. He was able to call 911 and tell the operator, "I'm blind, and I don't know what happened. . . . I don't know if I've been shot at or [it's] an electrical thing. But my arm hurts—I feel some bleeding here."[64] Police and ambulance responded immediately, and Jim was not only still conscious but also was able to meet them calmly and open the door.

At nearby Memorial Regional Hospital, doctors readily identified three separate bullet wounds, one in the shoulder, another in the upper arm, and a third in the torso very near the heart. By the next day, however, Jim was able to answer questions from Hollywood police and federal agents, although he remained for a short time in critical condition. The attacker had used a rifle and fired from the far side of the pool, across the patio, and through the sliding glass doors. One news report said that there were only two bullet holes in the glass doors. It was a very strange attack, and although the police never said it, it seemed to many inside the tribe that any shooter who could group three shots so close together from such a distance and through plate glass certainly could have killed their target if that really had been their intention. The whole thing seemed to be more of a horrible warning than a real attempt at assassination.

The council immediately went on alert. The tribe went into shock. Jim's most ardent supporters, and even his most ardent critics, could not believe that anyone would go to such lengths. Even close friends expressed their disbelief. "'I was afraid for him, and I tried to discuss with him that he needed to be fearful,' said a close friend who requested anonymity for fear of retribution. 'He kind of blew it off. I don't think he ever thought [his enemies] were as nuts as

I did. I think he thought this was something that they could resolve like civilized gentlemen.' . . . 'I think it's too premature to say that this was some kind of professional hit, but I think it's safe to say that this was not a random act of violence,' Hollywood police Lt. Tony Rode said. 'It appears that Mr. Shore was targeted.'"[65] One of the tribe's outside attorneys saw it as a clear attempt to destabilize the government.[66] It didn't work.

SPD officers were posted at the entrance to the tribal headquarters in Hollywood and at Jim's residence. Rumors began to fly concerning the shooter, or who might have put "him" up to it. Pat Diamond's quiet belief was that it could have been a Nicaraguan citizen who got off the plane in Miami and was given a rifle and was put back on the plane the same day. Tim and James adamantly deny knowledge of, or responsibility for, any such actions. A reporter, obviously not realizing that such an inaccuracy was another element of the hostility plaguing the tribe at the time, commented that Jim Shore was the person "who effectively runs the tribe day to day."[67] Jim's ex-wife, Sue Baldwin, provided a cogent element of the story when she commented, "That's basically what he's been living for, trying to do the right thing for his people, or what he perceived to be the right thing."[68] It certainly was his *perception* of "the right thing," which was a greater catalyst in the events taking place inside the tribe than were any administrative powers he might have had.

Naturally, suspicion centered on James, but no evidence ever connected him directly to the shooting. The tribe officially offered a $50,000 reward, but no one ever collected. Given the influence that James had within the tribe and the amount of animosity that everyone knew he felt toward Jim, it certainly is possible that some supporter with too much emotion and too little sense performed the act thinking that he was doing James a favor.

Tribal concerns soon began to focus on a former employee, Sandy Arrendondo, of Afro-Hispanic heritage. Sandy was born in Clewiston, Florida, and had worked in the tribe's recreation department and in various other positions for some years.[69] Late in 2002, the council circulated flyers over all the reservations with a photo and the header "ALERT," announcing that "Sandy Arrendondo, date of birth 5-18-1963, has been trespassed from all reservations. If you see Sandy Arrendondo on any property owned by the Seminole Tribe of Florida please contact your local Seminole Police Department."[70]

Still, no shooter was ever found. No suspect was ever arrested. Local Hollywood police staged a reenactment of the crime a year and a half later, but it was to no avail.[71] The SPD sentry hut at the entrance to the tribal headquarters parking lot became a permanent part of life on the Res in Hollywood. Jim recovered and returned to work. He declined to live his life in hiding, he said, but he continued to travel in a chauffeured black sedan. He and the council continued to remove previous James Billie influences from tribal administration.

To replace Tim Cox, the council hired Ken Fields. Fields left his job as Hollywood's assistant city manager at the end of January 2002 to start work as the tribe's administrative officer, after seven years with the city of Hollywood. Fields had reached Florida from Carnegie Mellon University in Pittsburgh, and he had directed business operations at a software engineering company.[72] His tenure was not destined to be a long one, however. Unfortunately, Fields was one of many who came to tribal politics with two terminal flaws.

First, he believed the council members when they stated a desire to continue the administrative reforms that Tim Cox had begun. They did not state them, of course, as having anything to do with the Billie/Cox regime, but their premise was an ostensible desire to place the tribe on a sound business footing relative to the business practices of the non-Indian business world. Fields had no way of knowing, at the time, that they were perfectly willing to have the program areas continue to be controlled, but as individual politicians, they were absolutely unwilling to give up their own former practices. Most particularly, they were unwilling to give up their unrestricted access to tribal funds.

Second, Fields was sure that he brought to the tribe knowledge and experience that his employers did not have, and that they needed. Despite the fact that both of these premises were certainly accurate, he permitted this attitude to become all too apparent for tribal tastes. Individual citizens quickly began to complain that their access was being restricted and their desires were being thwarted or ignored. Even as the old tribal politicians began to move into a new generation of leadership, they knew the value of preserving certain of the old requirements of leadership, central among which was the requirement of personal access to power. Regardless of whether their requests were granted, Seminoles were determined to be permitted to have their say.

By the end of 2003, Fields stumbled into the same inherent problem as Tim had. He sent out a memorandum to the council reps notifying them that they were to be held to their monthly spending limits relative to their annual Res allocations. At only a quarter of the way into fiscal year 2004, David already had gone through 46 percent of his annual allocation. If they exceeded their monthly limits, Fields advised, no invoices or check requests from them would be honored.

By this time, the position of secretary/treasurer had been split and Priscilla had been relieved of her more contentious financial responsibilities. Mike Tiger had returned from his years of work with the Indian Health Service, most recently in Nashville, and the council welcomed him back as an educated individual who had disagreed politically with James for many years. They gave him the position of tribal treasurer, which relieved Priscilla tremendously, both of workload and of political involvement. Council invoices and check requests no longer had to be countersigned by Priscilla; now they went to Mike and then to the accounting department. Fields also did not realize the extent to which Mike Tiger and the council would accommodate each other.

At this same time Max Jr. sent out a $98,000 check as half payment for four Rolex watches that he gave as graduation presents to four tribal college graduates. Max obtained the watches through David Guderian of Tampa and his company, Kenco. Max and Guderian had formerly tried to obtain the Hard Rock contract for furnishings, but Cordish had hewed to the bid process and they were unable to qualify. At one point Mike Tiger mentioned to me that he was also thinking of going into the furniture business with Max.

And so it was that as late as 2007 the council reps were continuing in their by-now well-established patterns. Since 2000, the council reps had spent more than $280 million. Since 1999, David alone spent over $160 million—more than the others combined. In one eight-month period, more than $1 million in checks were to David and his children. Phil Hogan (Oglala Sioux), chairman of the NIGC, told reporters this "cries out for some inquiry, and they will receive that."[73] Priscilla said publicly that at one point while she was still treasurer, David was sending check requisitions directly to Sarah McDonald in accounting, and when she learned of it Priscilla told him she would suspend his account if he didn't send the requisitions to her to be signed first, as he should. "Asked what happened, she replied, 'He overrode me, you know.'"[74]

Ken Fields lasted in his position until 18 October 2006. The first reason handed out for his dismissal was that he was hiring cronies and not adhering to tribal personnel policy. This was a transparently convenient story, of course, that had proven its convenience in the past. Tribal citizens disliked him intensely and had all along. More likely is the fact that since 2003 the council had placed tribal citizen Amy Johns in his office as his assistant, and she was learning the business. Amy, a member of the Johns family of Brighton, already had a master's degree in public administration from Arizona State University. After about a year with Fields, she transferred to Mike Tiger's office for a year before returning to take over the tribal administrator's position when Fields was dismissed. She continues in that position to the date of this writing.

This was a standard policy in tribal governance, however, one that James had mentioned many times and had endeavored to utilize. The main difference between James's policies and those of the council after James left was that James had placed little or no reliance on academic background or training, choosing to place his reliance rather on untrained intelligence and ingenuity. The post-James council did seem to be choosing individuals with more specific training or experience. Nevertheless, in all fairness we must realize that as regarded training and experience, the tribe had now reached an era when there were more tribal citizens with training and experience from whom to choose than there had been formerly.[75]

The final year of James's last chairmanship was still filled with deep emotions among the Seminoles, but good things were happening for the tribe. They had not been materially harmed by the loss of James's leadership—and this fact acted to assuage the fears of some. Mitchell and David were no more liked by James's supporters than they had ever been. David continued to be the more abrasive of the two, but Mitchell's ability to maintain the continuity of tribal business during tumultuous times gave the Seminoles confidence. Tim Cox maintains that Mitchell was more politically savvy than he was generally given credit for being, and he was content to stand back as David, who had sublimated his own political aspirations to his brother's proven successes, continued to be the more confrontational and assertive.

Tribal revenues had climbed steadily during 1999 and 2000, but Cox asserts that was only due partially to his management. He believes that previous business practices had been so poor that the tribe was literally hemorrhaging its profits. Tim recalls, "Net revenue when I began work as the tribal administrator was $182 million, and gross was $580 million. When I left [in 2001] it was $650 million gross, with a net of $312 million."[76] Inordinate amounts of unaccounted-for monies were leaving the casinos in ways the tribe could not prove, as mentioned previously.

And, at that point, the Hard Rock deal had not even been consummated and thus had not begun to bring in revenues. Neither the Tampa nor the Hollywood Hard Rocks would open for business until 2004. The sexual harassment lawsuit was settled. Nevertheless, the tribe continued to keep Tim and Dan hamstrung in legal proceedings. In its initial suit, James was a named defendant. He was quietly dropped from subsequent proceedings, however.

This moment, moreover, was quite clearly the beginning of yet another generation of leadership, and despite the fact that it had taken a revolution to transition to it, the revolution had succeeded and the council was moving forward rapidly with changes in both style and content. There seemed no doubt that the end of James's official term, in 2003, would be his last. The council was acting independently of his leadership, and not in any tentative ways. No one inside the tribe believed, for a moment, that the settlement of any of the charges against James, Tim, or Dan would bring about the return of James to power.

Yet another ongoing lawsuit, this one against the managers whom James had brought to the tribe for the Coconut Creek casino, was moving through the courts. Gary Fears, originator of the Coconut Creek management agreement with the tribe, had been yet another legacy of Robb Tiller, who introduced him to James. Fears, whose management was disallowed by the NIGC, brought the more-reputable developer Alan Ginsburg into the deal and eased himself to a lucrative position at the far edge.

Out of tremendous profits, the tribe was obliged by its agreement to pay Alan H. Ginsburg and his management company 35 percent of net revenues after the original construction and start-up expenses were paid out. These payments averaged about $1.79 million per month, but after six months of payments the council and tribal attorneys ceased payments, questioning the validity of the original agreement. Ginsburg countersued, claiming that the tribe had inflated operating costs in order to diminish the amount of money due to the management. Jim Shore told reporters that his legal department had not been involved in the negotiations for the original deal, and this certainly may have been true, but Jim was using semantics here to avoid the fact that the council had acted on a resolution from his office to authorize the deal, albeit during James's administration.

According to Tim, Max had negotiated the Coconut Creek construction and management contract. Tim concluded, "Max gave away too much in the deal. He gave up 35 percent when other tribes were giving 20 percent. This was also too much because the prevailing philosophy when the tribe agreed to that contract was that since the Hollywood casino was doing $100,000 net at this time, you had tapped out the market. So no one ever thought that with all the competition [across the state]—the cruises to nowhere, the jai alai, the dog tracks, the horses, Miccosukees' casino, and the Seminoles' Hollywood casino, even Walt Disney World was only about two and a half hours away—there's no way you're going to get $100,000 out of this market!" But the doors opened and the place paid for itself in 120 days.

The tribe's lawsuit was finally settled, privately, in 2004, for an undisclosed amount somewhere between $150,000 and $200,000, and the tribe took over direct control of the last of its casinos. Despite predictions concerning a saturated market, the national demand for gaming does not seem to have been sated, and tribal profits continue unabated.

14   Coda

The end of James's current term was approaching. Another election would be held in May 2003, and James experienced a moment of desperation. Rather than wait on the tenuous success of a petition, James the Warrior would force the situation by simply marching in to headquarters and retaking his office, physically. Early in January 2003, he tried. First, he sent a letter to Priscilla on chairman's office letterhead informing her that "effective immediately I am resuming my position as the Tribal Chairman."[1] He went on to refer to the forensic audit that was used by the council as an element of his suspension. He reminded Pricilla (and, through her office, the council) that he had voted in favor of the audit and that the original intent was to audit "all the Councilmen and not just the Chairman's Office"—a critical point but an empty shot nonetheless.[2]

On Tuesday, 7 January, word spread through the building like wildfire that James had returned. Someone from Mitchell's office on the third floor called SPD. In the meantime, James found that all of the outer doors to the chairman's fourth-floor suite had been locked. SPD officers arrived quickly and tried to persuade him to leave, but he refused. More officers came. The possibility of a physical confrontation seemed imminent when the SPD chief arrived, and he and James were able to speak calmly. He convinced James to leave the building.

When James made it known publicly that he was planning to confront the council at its regularly scheduled meeting on Thursday, 9 January, the meeting was canceled. Despite the fact that its original premises for the suspension of the chairman had been removed, Brighton council rep John Wayne Huff told reporters he thought James should "stay away" from the office until the tribe was finished with its investigations. Hours after the confrontation at the tribal office, the council issued a public statement asserting that relative to the chairman's suspension they had acted in accordance with the tribal constitution and bylaws, and stood firm in their decision.[3]

The end, when it came, was practically anticlimactic. On Thursday, 27 February 2003, James Billie's political career effectively ended with the unanimous council's "Approval of Notification to James E. Billie Relative to Charges Which Warrant His Removal as Chairman of the Tribal Council of the Seminole Tribe of Florida," with an attached statement of charges containing nine counts.[4] He was charged with setting up business deals and spending tribal monies without council approval, among other charges. Once again it was Max Jr. who was willing to state the obvious. "In fact, councilor Max Osceola acknowledged that many of Billie's troubles stemmed from the way he operated rather than any specific wrongdoing."[5]

In order to comply with the ten-day notification period required by the constitution, a meeting was set by the council for Thursday, 13 March 2003 "to hear and consider his answer to the charges." The charges had been laid out in Resolution C-76-03 and accepted by the council on 27 February 2003: James had lied to the people and the council. He had treated tribal monies as his own. He had put allegiance to his non-Indian "friends" Tim Cox and Dan Wisher above his loyalty to the tribe. He had given monies to Tim and Dan to fight the tribe. He had conspired with them to "steal" the Legends Hotel from the tribe (the same hotel of which Jim Shore had, at an earlier point, disavowed all knowledge). James had, further, "defied the mandate of the Tribal Council" by requesting the assistance of the BIA. "Mr. Billie's actions, at the very least, are disruptive of the government of the Seminole Tribe of Florida, and, in the worse [sic] light, would be tantamount to treason."[6]

The resolution was accompanied by another statement of charges, including lies, deceit, and misrepresentation of crucial information. It expanded upon the original complaint to include the charge that James had "defied the mandate" of the Tribal Council by contacting Supervisor Keel of the BIA. Despite their very real political impact, these were clearly personal animosities and personal charges. At the very basis of any and every euphemism that the council could put forth as an ostensible legal charge, the reality was completely contained in the charge of "treason." James had spent too much time looking out for non-Indians and had slighted the tribe (at least in the eyes of the council).

The hearing that had begun on 13 March was adjourned for the council to consider the charges and responses, and it was reconvened on 18 March, when the council rendered a unanimous vote of impeachment. There was no further appeal or recourse. The same governing body that had brought the charges and decided on the suspension was also the court of last resort for their erstwhile leader. On 21 March 2003, Priscilla, in her capacity as tribal secretary, issued a memorandum to all departments with the subject, "Removal of James E. Billie as chairman," notifying the departments to "Please amend your stationary [sic] and letterhead to reflect this change."[7]

The council's action, coming as it did just prior to the at-large election, held on 12 May 2003, successfully supplanted James, thereby barring him from any immediate attempt to regain his chairman's seat by election for another four years. Mitchell handily beat out five competitors, with 55 percent of the 1,080 votes cast, to officially replace James as the tribe's new chairman. David was once again reelected to represent BC, and in Brighton, Roger Smith beat out the incumbent, John Wayne Huff, by a mere seven votes and seven other candidates by greater margins. In Hollywood, Max was reelected on a respectable margin of fifty-five votes.

For the board, Moses B. ("Moke") Osceola took the seat previously held by Mitchell, with a clear lead in a field of eight competitors. Among the challengers was Joel Frank, James's longtime friend, who was soundly defeated. Voters easily sent Paul Bowers back to the board from BC, a position he had held before. Johnny Jones took the Brighton seat formerly held by Alex Johns, who had not run, and David DeHass returned to the Hollywood seat for his second term.

The election proceeded without difficulty but not without challenge. James, through his attorney Robert Saunooke, complained to BIA officials that the council had lied about his residency just to keep him off the ballot. The complaint did no good. "'We have some new officials,' said master of ceremonies Moses Jumper Jr. 'We are going into a new era.'"[8]

Events proceeded swiftly from this point. In June the first phase of the Tampa Hard Rock project opened. Smaller than the Hollywood complex, and subject to the same local fears that have plagued Indian gaming everywhere, it nevertheless comprised 250 hotel rooms, had 1,800 video gaming machines, and was expected to add 2,000 new jobs to the area with a payroll of $20–25 million. The grand opening occurred in March 2004. During construction the council had broken up and relocated Res residents to new homes in the larger non-Indian community, with limited assistance. As dividends rose rapidly, individuals became financially secure.

At the end of the year the tribe first invited tribal citizens to take a hard-hat tour of the project in progress and next invited about six hundred nontribal guests to a preview showing of the Hollywood Hard Rock. Max proclaimed, "We are raising the level of sophistication for the tribe in the business world."[9] The anticipated visitation at the magnificent facility, when fully operational, was 20,000 persons per day. And already the hotel had received 60,000 reservations for what would soon be its five hundred rooms, 130,000 square feet of casino, 6,000-seat arena, four acres of pools with water slides and rock mountains, and a ninety-foot wall of water that doubles as a movie screen. CEO of gaming, Jim Allen (non-Indian), told the press, "We don't look at this as a casino . . . we look at this as a true entertainment destination."[10] The operation opened fully over 10–11 May 2004. Broward County officials were very positive about the operation. They were sure that the facility would raise the county's profile as a tourism destination. "'The Seminoles are one of the landmark tribes,' said David Palermo, director of media and public relations for the National Indian Gaming Association. 'They do with Class II gaming what many tribes can't do with full casino gaming.'"[11]

If tribal officials were cautious about giving James credit for these successes, the reporters were less so. "Today, the Seminoles' rise to wealth through gambling is owed largely to the brash, nose-thumbing style of the man who served as the tribe's chairman for two decades. . . . But whatever Billie, 59, might have lost in reputation over the years, he more than regained with a chest-beating manner that pushed the boundaries of Indian sovereignty and fueled the expansion of tribal gambling nationwide. [He was] . . . one of the most celebrated personalities in Indian country [*sic*]. . . . Today, the $15 billion that Indian tribes earn annually from gambling is more than the casino take in Atlantic City, N.J., and all of Nevada."[12]

At the same time that the new Hard Rock complexes were opening, Florida was mounting a public initiative to cut a slice of the gaming pie for itself. Floridians, for whom the subject of legalized gaming was becoming more and more of a hot-button issue, took the tribe to task for its proactive stance. Seminoles spent $5.6 million to run ads against the forthcoming vote on "Amendment 4, the initiative to bring taxed and regulated slot machines to seven South Florida venues."[13] A reporter saw this as hypocritical and called Max, who said he hadn't seen the commercials. "Osceola went on to say the council had decided it would be in the tribe's best interests to 'protect our assets.'"[14] Ultimately, the amendment was successful, but as it permitted only a limited application it did not have a significant impact on the tribe's gaming activities.

～

Inside the tribe the speed of change was increasing apace with its public image, and the changes were especially occurring in infrastructure. The accounting software the tribe had paid for on the advice of James's friend, Dan Wisher, had never been completely suitable. It was finally replaced by new software from Deloitte and Touche USA, L.L.P. The board approved the purchase of Lakeport Lodge, a small twenty-four-unit motel on the southeastern side of Brighton Res. This was the traditional annual lodging for the "boat people," as the Seminoles called the white people who came each year to fish in Lake Okeechobee. Miss Seminole, Cherelee Kristen J. Hall, represented the Florida Seminoles in the Miss Indian World pageant. Her talent was demonstrating the making of turtle-shell dance shakers. Joel Frank, now the tribe's director of grants and government relations, also had been the vice-chairman of Amerind Risk Management Corporation for three years. Amerind is an intertribal consortium created in the 1980s to challenge skyrocketing insurance costs and, with assistance from HUD, is a successful risk pool corporation.

The tribe's real estate services sold off another of James's legacies, five parcels of land in Chokoloskee, a tiny community down the southwest coast of the peninsula next to Everglades City, where James had given money each year for a festival in commemoration of the Smallwood family's early twentieth-century Indian trading post. Tribal citizens were offered first choice of the lots.

In addition, the council finally turned its attention to the long-standing problem of "Snake Road," the twenty-mile stretch connecting Alligator Alley with the BC Res. The road curved dangerously, was only two lanes, was unlighted and flanked by canals, and had been a death trap for too many years. Nine deaths had occurred there on its lonely stretches just since 1997. It was the bane of drunk drivers, of whom there still were too many. Snake Road also posed a hazard to all drivers because of cattle that would break the fence at night and stand—oblivious—on the road, and alligators that would sun themselves during the day, and buzzards that would be too full of roadkill to fly up in time to avoid crashing through the windshields of oncoming cars whose drivers were taking the curves too fast. Tourists, awed by the richness of the wildlife along the road, created their own hazards by stopping—completely—in their lane of traffic with less awareness of other drivers than the alligators and cows. Creating shoulders for the road was part of a larger process of tribal takeover of its own road maintenance. This project was part of taking back control of its own activities from the BIA. Miccosukee chairman Billy Cypress recalled that the curves had been built in to Snake Road because of Lady Bird Johnson, wife of then-president Lyndon B. Johnson. She had decreed its style as a part of her national road beautification projects.[15]

By the beginning of 2005, another tribal election was approaching, this one an off-year election in which only the council and board reps would stand. Among the candidates, David Cypress would sustain yet another round of tribal displeasure. Early in the year, I was contacted by tribal citizens who wanted to know what process was offered by the constitution for the removal of a tribal official. The constitution does offer a process for obtaining signatures on a petition of a requisite number of eligible voters for a recall. Tribal members petitioned to remove David on charges that included misuse and abuse of tribal funds and favoritism in his spending.

On 25 January 2005, Priscilla certified the signatures on the petition against David and sent him a letter listing nine charges. When the council met in the BC gym, tempers were running very high. Toi Andrews (Panther Clan, b. 1979, daughter of Maryjene Cypress Koenes) presented the petition. David angrily called SPD officers into the meeting and wanted SPD to remove her, physically if necessary. It was a tense moment. Men rose to her defense and surrounded her, and the SPD officers declined to become involved. Then the elder women, traditional voices of respect, surrounded her and made the council let her speak. The council then recessed for a mere ten minutes and came back and simply voted not to accept the petition. Max said he voted based on his "knowledge." In the tribe's political process, there was no recourse. It was a degree of arrogance that was new, even for David. It was also a clear signal of the degree to which the council had learned the power of standing together, even against the people themselves.

Two months later, however, Cypress won reelection by what the tribe's newspaper described as a landslide, with more votes than his four opponents combined.[16] David's base, which had always been among the elders to whom he catered liberally, amazingly returned him to office once again. Andrew Bowers, a lawyer with residences in Okeechobee (off-Res) and a permanent address on-Res, in Brighton, beat out Roger Smith for a two-year term on the council by only five votes, while Max held onto his council seat by only three votes. Gloria Wilson took the seat formerly held by David DeHass on the board, but otherwise the two bodies remained the same.

The following month, Florida governor Jeb Bush visited South Florida and took a short tour of the Hard Rock complex, telling reporters that he believed the moment might have come for the state to enter into a gaming compact with the Seminoles. Too late, said one reporter: "The tribe, after all, got snubbed in 1998 and still came out with a royal flush."[17] The reporter's overriding agenda, however, was not that the state should enter into a compact with the tribe per se, but rather that the state should see to it that non-Indians should gain a piece of the profits. This was not a unique point of view, nor was it even the most virulent. Opinions of Floridians who had watched for a decade as the tribe had attempted to move the state to a compact that would permit Class III gaming were deeply divided.

The regulations of the NIGC, instituted as a result of the Seminole lawsuit against the State of Florida for its failure to enter into negotiation with the tribe in good faith, permitted the tribe to apply to the U.S. secretary of the interior for permission to institute Class III gaming if the state would not negotiate. As Jeb Bush left office after his two terms, the tribe resumed its negotiations with the new governor, another Republican, Charlie Crist. The fact that the tribe could bypass the state and apply directly to the secretary of the interior was not lost on the governor or the legislature, although a final tug-of-war would have to play itself out before the tribe would finally get its compact. (We will visit their ultimate success in the epilogue.)

Newspapers around the state debated the issue of Indian gaming, and although supporters were many, opponents were vocal to extraordinary degrees. An article posted by the Fort Myers *News-Press* drew online comments from frighteningly uninformed readers. One reader commented, "I'm tired of the Seminoles thinking they are above the law."[18] Another, deeply biased, posted the opinion that "we should just go in and seize the casinos. Then round them all up and make them walk to Arkansas."[19]

The Seminoles realize that this was a continuation of the wars they had been fighting for survival for hundreds of years. No matter how much the social climate of the larger nation has changed today, bigotry and bias survive, and the issue of Indian gaming is certainly a "hot-button" issue for frightened individuals. Despite academic questions of whether they will continue as a people, holding their culture intact to any degree, and regardless of any unenlightened public sentiment, the Seminoles will use every method at their disposal, political and economic, to fight for their continuance. And the Florida Seminole people are fighters. Make no mistake.

~

A settlement, of sorts, between the tribe and their former chairman finally was reached in the following year, 2006. Five years after his suspension and public humiliation and three years after his impeachment, the council offered James a quid pro quo: he would issue a formal apology to his tribe—not for what he did but for the way he did it in such a heavy-handed and arrogant style. In return, the tribe would give him $600,000 in back pay and retirement benefits. A reporter who had been watching tribal politics for some years explained cogently: "Billie's ouster began an awkward public period for the normally secretive tribe. The dispute over finances and the political scandal not only lifted the veil from the Seminoles' inner workings, but also exposed the tribe's growing pains as it morphed into a major gambling enterprise."[20]

~

Two further episodes will finish the James Billie story, or at least it seems so at the moment. First is the coincidence of the tribe's settlement with their former leader with another opportunity for James to return to one of his foremost loves, aviation. As he told me the story, when the council ousted him, they closed the Micco Aircraft plant, despite the fact that an FAA certificate had been received, which was a milestone on the road to successful production and sales. Then the council sold the business for a fraction of its value to an individual who sold it again. Early in 2006, the current owner contacted James and offered to make him an officer of the company. The owner said James needed to help raise $1.5 million to get the company into production.

So James went to people he knew at Indian Town Bank in Martin County to seek support. They set certain conditions that included his providing a 20 percent equity. He had no idea at the time about how he would raise that amount of capital. But that was just before the tribe settled with him and the needed capital became available.

James forwarded the loan papers to BIA eastern area supervisor Frank Keel and asked him to review them. Supervisor Keel also helped him with a U.S. government "set aside" loan for Indian businesses. Subsequently, James has relocated the company to hangar space for production in Bartlesville, Oklahoma, where basic costs are about one-third of what they are in South Florida and a larger Indian work force is available.[21]

The Micco Aircraft project was never meant to be a full-time occupation for James. Nor was his chickee-building business, although he considered them to be enjoyable and entertaining. His music continues to occupy him as well, and Pete Gallagher continues to arrange performance venues for him from time to time. These are major elements of his life. His deep and abiding love, however, continues to be politics: he is a natural leader, whether his instincts are fully realized yet, even after all these years, or not.

The second episode took place in 2007, yet another election year for the tribe and one in which the at-large posts of chairman and president were once again available. James had been reminded, repeatedly, of the tribe's residency rule, by me and many others. His only concession to the requirement had been to place a trailer on a lot on Brighton Res and spend very little time there. He had not, therefore, applied to Priscilla's office to have his official residential address changed. Nevertheless, James the Warrior once again chose to believe that he would be afforded another opportunity.

The election was scheduled for 14 May. In March, James told the press that he was ready to run again. In April, he left for a short vacation in Puerto Rico, visiting with María's family. Supporters called him constantly, assuring him that they would be able to secure his freedom to run again. Brighton council rep Andy Bowers, in particular, spoke out about the inequity of barring any candidate based on enforcement of a residency requirement.

A special meeting of the tribe's council and its election board was hurriedly called in late April. The election board comprised nine members—three council-appointed representatives from each of the three "big reservations": BC, Brighton, and Hollywood. James believed that at least three of those election board members were predisposed to speak out and vote for him and that they could convince others. In a telephone call from Puerto Rico he expressed calm confidence to me that he would prevail. His confidence was, once again, misplaced. Andy Bowers was the only one to speak out in his favor.

"'The whole process was unfair,' said Andrew Bowers. . . . Asked why it was done, Bowers replied: 'The initials J.E.B.—that's the only reason.' . . . According to Carl Baxley, who attended the meeting, it 'was unusual, out of the norm of things, and it was a pretty clear indication of what the intent was: to make sure that James Billie was disqualified from the election.' . . . [Priscilla] Sayen was asked in an interview last week whether Billie could be disqualified if he did not live on one of the five Seminole reservations. She said although tribal rules specify that candidates must live on a reservation, the rules have not been enforced for years because of an acute reservation housing shortage. She also confirmed that no candidate otherwise qualified had ever been barred from the ballot because of residency.... According to Andrew Bowers, 'If you have been doing these things [waiving the residency rule] for years, then apply it to everybody. My argument is fairness.'"[22]

The argument was ineffective; the fairness doctrine did not apply. Ultimately, James was not the only dissatisfied politician. Priscilla's office had certified 1,640 tribal voters, of whom 1,100 ultimately cast ballots for the chairman's seat, which was handily retained by Mitchell. His only opponent was Moke Osceola, who chose to run for chairman rather than try to retain his board presidency. The only council upset was for Andy Bowers's seat. Roger Smith defeated him by a single vote in the traditional round-robin Brighton election in which former council rep John Wayne Huff also was defeated. David and Max were returned to their old positions for another term. For the board presidency, Richard Bowers beat out a field of five candidates that included tribal administrator Amy Johns. Otherwise, the board remained the same.

Three candidates challenged the results: Moke charged "procedural flaws and also some election flaws." The margin of error that he asserted turned out to be the number of off-Res voters who were only permitted to vote for the two at-large positions. A challenge from Tony Sanchez, who lost the board presidency to Richard Bowers, was denied, and in a recount of the Brighton votes Andy Bowers's loss to Roger Smith was confirmed.[23]

Once again, James accepted disappointment; this time, at least, with less anger. The press still remembered him as an exciting story nonetheless. "This is the chief whose audacious 1979 experiment with high-stakes bingo opened the way for the $25-billion-a-year Indian gaming industry; the tribal leader who defied the state and federal governments and fought off powerful corporate gambling interests and did more to bring wealth and influence to Native Americans than all the soul-stealing programs ever invented by the Bureau of Indian Affairs."[24] A fitting memorial for any politician, but especially for an Indian for whom warfare was not only a legacy but also a way of life.

Epilogue

It's another brilliantly sunny day in South Florida. You can see the heat shimmering off the roadway and feel the ocean breezes at the same time. You can drive east on the Stirling Road overpass over the Florida Turnpike and see all three sites. There's the old tribal office building site, a little back from the intersection of Stirling Road and Highway 441; it's a lovely parking lot now—if parking lots can be said to be lovely in any way. This one is asphalted and landscaped and palm treed into enticing perfection, even though it's larger than many Disney parking lots. From the overpass, you're only fifty yards away from the new tribal headquarters building on the south side, a four-story white monument to the determination of the Seminoles to orchestrate their lives without U.S. government intervention. This is a James Billie monument, possibly his best and most enduring.

Then, at the same time, you can turn your eyes northward and be hit by more blazing white. The covey of domed towers gathered in the sun is the Hard Rock casino complex about half a mile away. It's a Taj Mahal in its own right. Together, if you know the story, the three sites—the old tribal headquarters site (now a parking lot), the new tribal offices, and the Hard Rock—mark three critical points on the evolutionary trajectory of the Seminole people across the twentieth century. The symbolism is hard to miss. That now-gone low, dingy building was their childhood as wards of the white man's power, the new headquarters building marks their passage into political and financial adulthood, while the huge white towers with the giant guitar on the west shout, "This is who we are! We fought for it, and we won it. We're still the warriors we have been for thousands of years!"

The end of James Billie's reign was the beginning of a fourth generation in Seminole leadership. The Seminole people seem to have accepted Mitchell and David Cypress and their style of leadership, much of which they learned from

James Billie and the rest of which appears to center far more on money than on cultural preservation. This attitude may or may not support a future for the Seminole Indians as a distinct group. But history is not concerned with the art of the hypothetical. It looks only to the past, no matter how recent, and to the conditions the past creates today and for the future, if we allow it.

As I write the final pages of this book, in 2009, much has changed inside the Seminole Tribe of Florida. If the first rule of bureaucracy is to perpetuate itself, then it has. Despite some of the trappings of the old Indian consensus style of governance, there are more non-Indians employed by the tribe than ever before. More white lawyers are paid by the tribe than ever before. The contract that the tribe renegotiated with David Cordish as soon as James was ousted has now been abrogated by the same Tribal Council and litigated on the legal basis of ostensible unfairness to poor Indians.[1] In May of 2006, the tribe filed a lawsuit, this time against Cordish, to break what it characterized as an "illegal and unconscionable contract."[2] The final contract with Cordish and Power Plant, renegotiated at the end of James's tenure, required the tribe to pay Cordish 30 percent of the net gaming profits for ten years and 30 percent of hotel profits over fifteen years. Each of the partners certainly had profited handsomely.

The tribe needed all of the working capital it could retain, however. In 2006 the council entered into negotiations with Hard Rock International, headquartered in Orlando, to purchase the entire Hard Rock operation for $965 million. Negotiations had proceeded for a year previously. Hard Rock International's parent company, Rank Group, PLC, of England, was pleased with the deal, which was announced publicly in December 2006. A tribal delegation traveled to New York for the signing and partied atop the neon sign on the Manhattan Hard Rock. Jon Stewart of *The Daily Show* was completely at a loss for words as he ran the tape of Max—yet again speaking for the council—telling the crowd gathered below that the Indians had sold Manhattan for some wampum beads, but the Seminoles were now going to buy it back, "one hamburger at a time!"[3] In 2005, Rank Group had posted gross earnings of $690 million.

The purchase price was financed by the tribe and with debt. The tribe had "some sophisticated financial help from Merrill Lynch. . . . Industry journal *Casino City* estimates that Florida's Indian gaming revenue grew by 36.5 percent to $1.3 billion last year—almost all of that from the Seminoles' Hard Rocks."[4] In addition to the cafés and attendant businesses, one historical irony was realized by a single reporter with regard to the almost priceless collection of rock music memorabilia owned and exhibited by the Hard Rock chain. "In an ironic turnabout, the Seminoles now own artifacts revered in the white man's culture, and those relics are worth millions."[5] The deeper irony lies in the fact that the reporter did not realize that for many centuries white men have taken and bought and sold American Indian artifacts, a heritage many tribes are only now beginning to be able to regain by buying back the artifacts for themselves, frequently using the proceeds from gaming. Irony indeed.

In January of 2007, the Internal Revenue Service issued to the Seminoles two Technical Advice Memoranda (TAM) indicating that, in its opinion, the tribe had "improperly used tax-exempt bond proceeds to finance the original Hard Rock deal. The Tribe sold $345 million Series 2002 revenue bonds, with the help of Merrill Lynch and JP Morgan. The TAM concludes that such bond issues can be used by Tribes only when they finance an activity that qualifies as an essential government function. The TAM is almost identical to one issued recently to the Cabazon Band of Mission Indians in CA."[6] The IRS's "advice" appears to have done no damage to the tribe's operations, and in terms of "essential government functions" for an Indian tribe in Florida, it's hard to see how gaming could be anything else. By 2006, 228 FR tribes were using gaming to fund their governments, and 34 percent of gaming tribes gave dividends to their citizens.

If the objective of removing James Billie was to set the administration of the tribe on a more legal path of transparency and accountability, however, whether in Indian or white man's terms, then it hasn't. James is still building chickees and playing his guitar. The Tribal Council's members are more deeply than ever involved personally in lucrative tribal businesses. It's very much business as usual for the council reps, but the scale of events is growing ever larger. In a parallel manner, tribal dividends are keeping pace. Monthly payments to enrolled citizens stand currently at $10,000 each, still regardless of age.

Mitchell Cypress has been elected to a third term. Many of the tribal citizens complain about him, and he himself spread rumors that he would not run again after his first full elected term. He is a recovering alcoholic, dry for many years, and he has diabetes, or "sugar" as the Seminoles call it, that has gotten progressively worse due to hypertension and the stress of his position. His brother, David, continues in power also, despite the attempt of tribal citizens to oust him. Over the years he has permanently adopted the habit of wearing dark glasses indoors and out. He insists on wearing the thigh-length hair of an old warrior, but his crudely combative attitude is not in accord with the traditions he pretends to espouse. As the elders try to instill in the younger generations, "A good warrior never lets his enemy see his anger."

Monday, 20 August 2007: the fiftieth anniversary of the formation of the Seminole Tribe of Florida was celebrated in fine fashion. Politicians spoke, newspersons interviewed, everybody ate, and a spectacular two-hour fireworks display ended the evening. Mitchell Cypress told local newscasters, "We're going to the next level. We don't even know what that means yet, but we're ready to go on." Part of his vision of "the next level" obviously meant full Class III gaming, because the Seminoles were, once again, in serious discussions with the Florida governor. James Billie had tried to get Governor Lawton Chiles to enter into a gaming compact so the tribe could have Class III—full-blown blackjack and other games in which players play against the house rather than just against themselves. James offered "Walkin' Lawton" Chiles as much as 45 percent of the gross revenues, which could have meant more than $1.5 million (it was estimated at the time) for the state each year, but Chiles, true to his religious support base, turned James down.

Governor Charlie Crist was at least talking about percentages, but he also wants the state to have regulatory authority over the tribe in this regard. This, of course, would violate the tenets of the first victory James won, in 1981, when the U.S. Supreme Court confirmed the fact that the state had no authority to regulate an FR tribe, that is, a sovereign nation. Further, as a result of the Seminoles' willingness to take their fight all the way to the U.S. Supreme Court, the Department of the Interior issued a ruling permitting the secretary of the interior to permit Class III gaming in the absence of a compact with a state. This also seems strange in light of the clear historical government-to-government relationship that the federal—rather than state—government has had with FR tribes, but ultimately it was the leverage that the Seminoles needed to get their gaming compact with the governor.

In mid-2007, Secretary of the Interior Dick Kempthorne issued a letter to Florida governor Crist, giving him sixty days to conclude a compact with the Seminoles. The secretary declared that the tribe was entitled to Class III gaming. In response, the governor quickly found a philosophical rationale for acceptance. "'The risk is that we wouldn't get any money for the people,' said [Crist's chief of staff George] LeMieux, who said the state must negotiate 'in order to protect the taxpayer. So we will.'"[7]

Over the next year the governor and the tribe negotiated. The sticking points concerned the percentage of profits the tribe would give to the state and the degree of regulatory control that the tribe would permit the state. In the process the tribe once again resorted to the white man's legal system to force a compromise by asking a federal judge to force the Interior Department to act without state participation. In the meantime, in November, the suit was mooted when Crist signed a deal with the tribe.[8] The twenty-five-year deal called for an up-front payment from the tribe of $50 million, $125 million in the second year, and payments on a sliding scale from certain high-stakes games over the remainder of the term.

At the same time, the compact offered some protection to the Seminole Tribe against the indiscriminate proliferation of gaming competition statewide. The governor said that the deal limited gaming in Florida because Seminoles would be allowed to stop paying if the state allowed similar types of gaming elsewhere (excepting slot machines at horse and dog tracks and jai alai frontons, or gaming on Miccosukee lands if the state got a compact with them). The agreement also made an exception of Miami-Dade and Broward counties because voters statewide had already amended the constitution to permit slots there, to the ostensible benefit of education.

Per Joe Weinert, gambling industry analyst, "They're going to be able to attract a new class of gambler that in the past would have looked to Las Vegas.... People who want to open a $250,000 credit line to play baccarat now have the option of going to South Florida, which already has a base attraction of great weather and all of the lifestyle choices it has to offer."[9]

Despite the size of the figures and the potential for a revenue increase for Florida government, the deal was not a large one relative to other compacts nationally. "Industry analysts and public records show that Florida's compact with the Seminoles is dwarfed by others around the nation. [Also] it has less oversight and no permanent regulatory presence inside the casinos.... In comparison, Connecticut got $430 million last year from Mohegan Sun and Foxwoods [casinos]. California will get $400 million next year.... Broward County, Florida's slots pay 50 percent to Florida. In New York and Connecticut, State officials have permanent offices in the casinos. Seminoles will not. But Midwestern and Southwestern tribes are moving to lower percentages they pay to States."[10]

Almost a footnote to the historic agreement was the fact that "State Legislative leaders have already said they would challenge Crist's right to sign without Legislative approval."[11] Certainly this was not unrelated to the fact that almost on the same day economists announced that falling tax collections would leave the state with a $1 billion shortfall. State supreme courts in five states—New Mexico, Kansas, Rhode Island, New York, and Wisconsin—had ruled that their governors needed legislative approval for gaming compacts with tribes. Only in Mississippi had a federal court upheld the power of a governor to bind a state to a compact.[12]

The NIGC continued to monitor Seminole gaming and spending, but tribal implementation of the state compact moved swiftly. State legislators sought to stay tribal implementation, but the secretary of the interior approved the compact, the BIA did not intervene, and the Florida Supreme Court was not scheduled to hear the legislature's case until the end of January 2008, even though the compact would take effect on 29 December 2007.[13] Ultimately, a Tallahassee federal judge ruled that he would not stop Class III gaming while the governor and the legislature were arguing, because as had been so clearly adjudicated many years earlier, the state did not govern tribal lands.[14]

Varying court decisions at the state level failed to end the executive-legislative squabble. The state senate was inclined to support the governor and the tribe.

The house announced the formation of a committee to review the compact and promised a report by 3 March 2008, when the new session was scheduled to begin. The wrangling continued on into 2009, however, with the tribe already operating and advertising according to the compact. Finally, in mid-2009, after years of waiting for the state's Republican governor and Republican-dominated legislature to end their internal squabbling, and consequent years of loss of what could have been significant revenues to the state in a moment of profound national economic downturn, a legislative compromise was reached that permitted the legislature to feel included in the Seminole gaming compact. The bill gave the governor until 31 August 2009 to renegotiate with the tribe. The new legislative deal would significantly increase the state's share, and ostensibly funnel much-needed monies to statewide education.

~

"Cloying" is a highly underrated word in South Florida. During the first few months I lived in the Big Cypress, I actually didn't realize why so many Seminoles traveled around with towels draped around their necks. But I certainly felt the impressive weight of the heat, and I finally put the two together.

Mitchell and David, who had been born into the Everglades heat and grown up with it wrapped around them, finally began to construct their own oases—their tribally financed refuges from the heat. Of course, in BC, you can't stop the electricity from going out with annoying frequency or the water from coming out of the spigot or the showerhead a rusty, tannic-acid brown—no matter how much money you have or where you get your financing. But, all things considered, Mitchell and David have won. And Max. And Jim Shore. At least for the moment.

Business is booming at both Seminole Hard Rocks—and it's important to remember that the customer base—the people planted firmly in front of the slot machines and hugging the baccarat tables—are *not* Indians. They are the same people who live side by side with the people who have voted firmly against gaming in Florida, three times. And yet, jai alai frontons and dog tracks are multi-billion-dollar enterprises in the state. And, if you can convince voters that the money will profit education rather than just line the pockets of backers, you can slowly spread gaming into heretofore-unwelcoming quarters.

For twenty-two years, James was a bigger thinker than anyone else in the tribe. Now, his erstwhile protégés have gone him one better: instead of just buying the game or the name, they've bought the whole company. They've hired more "suits" than James ever thought of hiring, but they finally have the state compact, and the state finally has the obscenely large cut of the gaming profits that it so long scorned.

This fact, unfortunately, does not necessarily secure the future for the Florida Seminoles. On the contrary, it raises the risk level significantly. The more successful the Seminoles are, the more inured Floridians will become to gaming as an acceptable enterprise. The more acceptable it becomes, the sooner will arrive the moment when another statewide referendum will finally pass, and the Seminoles will lose their monopoly and their edge.

James knew this well, and he sought frequently to diversify the tribe's economic base, even if he didn't always make very good choices in the process. This next generation of warrior leaders has raised the stakes to an entirely new level. In each generation the question has loomed, will success destroy the Seminoles? The Seminoles have endured for thousands of years despite all the most direct and powerful efforts by Europeans and Euro-Americans to destroy them. Even Rome, however, finally crumbled under its own internal weight. When James said that he would be the one to destroy himself, he obviously didn't realize that the same admonition might apply to his people as well.

I said to Tim Cox in one of our numerous conversations, "Despite the historian's desire to avoid hypotheticals, we still often ask whether the times make the man or the man makes the times. The answer is, of course, it's a combination— sometimes a collision—of the two. What if his mother had lived? What if he had had a happy youth? What if James had grown up as a man who respected women and himself?" Tim, who was certainly in an excellent position to examine these questions, responded quickly:

> If all that had been different, then the tribe would be nowhere today. If James Billie didn't relish people thinking that he's a bad guy, if he didn't relish people thinking that he was crooked, then he never would have taken the actions that he took. Jim Clare, just before he died, and just after everything blew up, told me, "You know, I've offered James money over the years. I'd give James millions right now." He said, "You know how much James Billie has made me? In just the last five years, I have almost 200 million dollars! But he won't take any money." He said, "James did tell me, when it's all over, I may come back and want some hamburgers from you." But, if James didn't like that persona of being the bad guy, he never would have taken the risks. He never would have let people think that he was in bed with the bad guys. Of course, he wasn't. He was in bed with someone who was distantly associated with the bad guys. I've told James, "It's my role to let people know who the real James is; that you're not the bad guy you allowed people to paint you as."[15]

In the short run, at least, the last word may go to Jim Shore: As he told reporters when James was first suspended: "It's business as usual. Nothing is slowing down and the tribe is as strong as ever. If the turmoil is going to affect anyone it's not the tribe. The tribe is here forever. Some of us will come and go but the tribe will be here."[16]

In the long run, if Jim's optimism is well founded, the Seminoles will, once again, exercise control over their own fate. Despite the determination of the U.S. government to legislate the Indians out of existence, the Seminoles continue to image themselves as warriors. They will decide for themselves the degree to which they acquiesce and the number of years they, as a people, will survive.

Notes

Acknowledgments

1. *Indian Country* is a legal term defined in 18 USC § 1151, and includes reservations, allotments, and dependent Indian communities. For further discussion, consult Stephen L. Pevar, *The Rights of Indians and Tribes: The Basic ACLU Guide to Indian and Tribal Rights* (Carbondale: Southern Illinois University Press, periodically revised and reprinted).

Chapter 1

1. For enlarged discussions of these topics, I refer readers to one of my earlier works, *The Tree That Bends: Discourse, Power, and the Survival of the Maskókî People* (Tuscaloosa: The University of Alabama Press, 1999). For an analysis of warfare and its high social value among the southeastern tribes, see David H. Dye, "The Transformation of Mississippian Warfare: Four Case Studies from the Mid-South," in *The Archaeology of Warfare: Prehistories of Raiding and Conquest,* ed. Elizabeth N. Arkush and Mark W. Allen (Gainesville: University Press of Florida, 2006), 101–47.

2. Dye, "Transformation of Mississippian Warfare," 103.

3. James Billie, personal communication, 1994.

4. For a fuller discussion of the term "Seminole" and its origins, see Wickman, *The Tree That Bends,* 95–102, and passim.

5. Franklin Keel, eastern area supervisor for the Bureau of Indian Affairs, U.S. Department of the Interior, personal communication, 26 May 2006. Among traditional government tribes are, for example, the Onondaga and Cayuga.

6. Sonny Billie, as told to Dale Grasshopper, personal communication, 1993.

7. The clearest and most straightforward explanation of tribal sovereignty and the facets of its exercise today, couched within the parameters of federal laws that have circumscribed their exercise historically, is presented in Pevar, *The Rights of Indians and Tribes: The Basic ACLU Guide to Indian and Tribal Rights.*

8. Franklin Keel, eastern area supervisor, Bureau of Indians Affairs, Nashville, Tennessee, personal communication, 1998 et seq.

9. Kent Carter, director, Southwestern Regional Archives, National Archives and Records Administration (NARA), Fort Worth, Texas, personal communication, 1999.

10. Peter Skafte, "Conflict and Tacit Agreement: A Study of Seminole Social Interaction" (master's thesis, University of Florida, 1969), 41–42.

11. Harry A. Kersey Jr., *An Assumption of Sovereignty: Social and Political Transformation among the Florida Seminoles, 1953–1979* (Lincoln: University of Nebraska Press, 1996), 106.

12. BIA community services officer, Memorandum, 1968, 6, cited in Skafte, "Conflict and Tacit Agreement," 43.

13. For a larger account of the disaffection of the Indians toward the Spaniards, see John H. Hann, *Apalachee: The Land between the Rivers* (Gainesville: University Presses of Florida, 1988), 234–36.

14. *The Oxford Study Bible: Revised English Bible with Apocrypha,* Matthew 6:24 (New York: Oxford University Press, 1992), 1274.

15. Kersey, *Assumption of Sovereignty,* 82.

16. President Lyndon B. Johnson's Special Message to Congress, 6 Mar. 1978, and the Civil Rights Act of 11 Apr. 1978.

17. In addition to Kersey, *Assumption of Sovereignty,* see also Kersey's other two books of his Seminole trilogy, *Pelts, Plumes, and Hides: White Traders among the Seminole Indians, 1870–1930* (Gainesville: University Presses of Florida, 1975), and *The Florida Seminoles and the New Deal, 1933–1942* (Boca Raton: Florida Atlantic University Press, 1989).

18. For an excellent overview of this era and its impact upon the Removed Tribes in the West, see Angie Debo, *The Road to Disappearance* (Norman: University of Oklahoma, 1941). Obviously, despite earlier expectations, the Seminoles and their southeastern Maskókî kin have not disappeared.

19. See "An Act making Appropriations for the current and contingent Expenses of the Indian Department," 3 Mar. 1871, *U.S. Statutes at Large* 16:566. By an obscure rider attached to this otherwise innocuous piece of legislation, treaty making was ended, the sovereignty of the tribes was denigrated, and the power of the U.S. executive was diminished.

20. Mitchell Cypress, personal communication, 1995.

21. Kersey, *Assumption of Sovereignty,* and Kersey, *Pelts, Plumes, and Hides.*

22. On this subject, see, among others, John K. Mahon, *History of the Second Seminole War, 1835–1842* (1967; Gainesville: University Presses of Florida, 2006); Debo, *Road to Disappearance;* and Grant Foreman, *The Five Civilized Tribes: Cherokee, Chickasaw, Choctaw, Creek, Seminole,* 5th ed. (Norman: University of Oklahoma Press, 1974).

23. Two authors of American Indian women's history use this same point—that is, the dichotomy between Indian and white kinship systems, based on matriliny and patriliny respectively. See, for example, the conclusions of Carolyn Ross Johnston in her *Cherokee Women in Crisis: Trail of Tears, Civil War, and Allotment, 1838–1907* (Tuscaloosa: The University of Alabama Press, 2003), 146, and the comments of another Cherokee author, Rayna Green, in her *Women in American Indian Society* (New York: Chelsea House, 1992), discussed in Johnston, *Cherokee Women,* 145–46.

24. In *The Tree That Bends,* see especially 55, 61–66, and 89–95 for further discussions of the clan system.

25. Skafte, "Conflict and Tacit Agreement," 40.

26. The application of the term *city* to any southeastern Indian grouping is one that divides anthropological researchers. Many eschew the word, for their own reasons, while others have no difficulty with the term and the degree of social complexity that it implies. See, for example, the recent University of Florida publication, by Mallory McCane O'Connor, titled *Lost Cities of the Ancient Southeast* (Gainesville: University Press of Florida, 2009).

27. For further discussion of these clan systems, see Wickman, *The Tree That Bends*, 61–66.

28. For an excellent and colorful first-person account of the Green Corn Dance in the nineteenth century, see John Howard Payne, Autograph MS, in the Collections of Jay Kislak, Miami, Florida, and published posthumously in the *Continental Monthly* (Boston), I (1862): 17–29, and also in the *Chronicles of Oklahoma* 10 (1932): 170–95. In the twentieth century, Louis Capron has written first-person accounts of the Green Corn ceremonies for *National Geographic* magazine. His earlier account, "The Medicine Bundles of the Florida Seminole and the Green Corn Dance," was published in *Smithsonian Institution, Bureau of American Ethnology Bulletin 151, Anthropological Papers, No. 35,* 1953, 155–221.

29. This "old word" is still in use today. I have this information from two Brighton Creeks, each the daughter of a respected Medicine man.

30. *Miami Herald,* 13 May 1975, quoted in Kersey, *Assumption of Sovereignty,* 113.

31. Chairman Billy Cypress angrily rejects the assertion that *osani(t)* (Otter Clan) are the uncles of *tahkósai(t)*. He boasts that it is the reverse that is the case, although this is not at all consistent with information from the other clans. Rather, it is more consistent with the Seminoles' memories of why Mole Clan was nearly destroyed to begin with. Billy Cypress, personal communication, 1999.

Chapter 2

1. John H. Hann, ed. and trans., *Missions to the Calusa* (Gainesville: University of Florida Press, Florida Museum of Natural History, 1991), 220–25.

2. "Annual Report of the Seminole Agency to the Muscogee Area Office, Bureau of Indian Affairs, for the Fiscal Year Ending 30 June 1954," 3.

3. "Seminole Tribe of Florida: 20th Anniversary of Tribal Organization, 1957–1977," typescript program, Saturday, 20 Aug. 1977.

4. Francis Paul Prucha, *The Great Father: The United States Government and the American Indians,* 2 vols. in 1, unabridged (1984; Lincoln: University of Nebraska Press, 1995), xviii.

5. The tribe's own Reconstructed 1914 Roll (R1914) includes 187 individuals whose birth dates have been set prior to 1880 but who have not been identified on the R1880. Author's personal research.

6. There is no consistent and definitive source for infant or any other mortality figures for the Seminoles before the 1980s. There are only partial figures for various years.

7. *Florida Statistical Abstract* (Gainesville: University Presses of Florida, 1998).

8. See State of Florida Legislative Council and Legislative Reference Bureau, *Migrant Farm Labor in Florida: A Summary of Recent Studies* (Feb. 1961); and American Civil Liberties Union, "The Hands That Feed Us," *National Immigration and Alien Rights Project Report* No. 2 (Washington, DC: ACLU, Apr. 1986). In 1954, the number of migrant workers

in Florida was reported as 60,000 by the 1970 report of the Florida State Board of Health. These workers represented Puerto Rico, the Bahamas, the British West Indies, U.S. blacks, and U.S. whites. By 1986, U.S. blacks still comprised 40 percent of all citrus workers, but estimates of the total number of Florida migrant workers varied widely, from 100,000 to 150,000. Of all of these, approximately 75 percent were migratory inside the United States. In 2001, 80 percent of all farmworkers were men, and five out of six were Spanish speakers. See http://www.farmworkers.cornell.edu/pdf/facts_on_farmworkers.pdf. See also Southern Poverty Law Center, *Close to Slavery: Guestworker Programs in the United States* (Montgomery, AL: SPLC, 2007).

9. Clay MacCauley, "Seminole Indians of Florida," in *Bureau of American Ethnology Fifth Annual Report, 1883, 1884* (Washington, DC: Smithsonian Institution, 1887). On the subject of Florida "Seminole" Indian censuses, see the following articles: Harry A. Kersey Jr., "Florida Seminoles and the Census of 1900," *Florida Historical Quarterly* 60, no. 2 (1981): 145–60; and James W. Covington, "Some Observations concerning the July 1913 Census Taken by Agent Lucien Spencer," *Florida Anthropologist* 39, no. 3 (1986): 221–23.

10. Personal conversations with Betty Mae Jumper and several others who have requested anonymity; Amendment 3 to Tribal Council Ordinance C-3-59/Enrollment.

11. Kersey, *Assumption of Sovereignty,* 90.

12. *U.S. Statutes at Large* 60 (1946): 1049–56.

13. See Kersey, *Assumption of Sovereignty,* 135–52.

14. The Seminole Land Claim Case grew out of the U.S. Congress's passage of the Indian Land Claims Act, *U.S. Statutes at Large* 60 (1946): 1049–56.

15. The *Cobell v. Salazar* case, a.k.a. Individual Indian Monies Case (IIM) or the (Elouise) Cobell Case, was brought in 1996 as a class action suit against the BIA on behalf of 150,000 to 500,000 Oklahoma Indians (totals are controversial) whose land and mineral lease funds appear to have been lost or misused by the BIA since the late nineteenth century. According to some sources, it is the largest class action suit brought in U.S. history. The case was based upon treaties and agreements made by the U.S. government and the Indian Territory (Oklahoma) tribes, and, therefore, none of the Florida Indians were parties to the suit. The suit was brought to an unsatisfactory $3.4 billion settlement in 2009.

16. Betty Mae Tiger Jumper, personal communication, 1993; Rev. Lucius and Mrs. Carolyn Crenshaw, personal communication, 1994. See also William C. Sturtevant, "The Mikasuki Seminole: Medical Beliefs and Practices" (PhD diss., Yale University, 1955), 317. Sturtevant relates that twins of the opposite sex are accepted, but among same-sex twins the younger is believed to have been "caused by thunder," and its existence will strengthen one of the parents and cause the other to weaken and die. Therefore, it must be "let go," the Seminoles' euphemism for killed, usually by putting mud in its mouth and leaving it on a riverbank. I have heard two interpretations. Some people say that the differentiation is between fraternal and identical twins, regardless of their sex, the identical twins being the unacceptable pairing. One Seminole woman also recounted her memory of her mother's having seen a small bird that came immediately after the birth and sat at the *chiki(t)* and sang, and her mother interpreted the bird's presence as the spirit of one of her newborn twins, singing to the mother to take away her strength. The result was that the younger of the twins had to be let go. Then, the bird went away. (Name withheld by request.)

17. Andrew P. Canova, *Life and Adventures in South Florida* (Palatka, FL: n.p., 1885).

Canova's commander in the company of Florida Volunteers was Capt. Robert Mickler, my great-great-grandfather.

18. In the post–James Billie era, i.e., since 2003, Tribal Council meetings have been made "moveable feasts," being held on each of the reservations in turn and, thus, serving dual purposes: diminishing travel requirements for tribal citizens and catering to the old tradition of taking government to the people.

19. U.S. Department of Commerce, *Federal and State Reservations and Indian Trust Areas* (Washington, DC: U.S. Government Printing Office, 1974).

20. See Tribal Council Resolution C-04-81, 11 July 1980, by which the tribe accepts the human remains and C-110-84 by which the Tampa land is taken into federal trust.

21. See note 9, above.

22. Skafte, "Conflict and Tacit Agreement," 54.

23. Tribal Secretary Priscilla Sayen, personal conversation with the author, ca. 1998.

24. Prucha, *Great Father*, 1208.

25. Kersey, *Florida Seminoles and the New Deal*, 27–29.

26. NAHASDA, *U.S. Statutes at Large* 110: 4016, et seq.

27. The most comprehensive treatment of the U.S. government's 1950s and precursor attempts to cease its responsibilities (and in particular its economic responsibilities) to the FR tribes is to be found in Prucha, *Great Father*, 605–6 and 1017–70. For a discussion of the impact of the termination attempts on the Seminoles, see Kersey, *Assumption of Sovereignty*, chapter 2, 23–50.

28. *Public Papers of the Presidents of the United States: Lyndon B. Johnson, 1968–69* (Washington, DC: Government Printing Office, 1970), 335–44; and Executive Order 11399, "Establishing the National Council on Indian Opportunity," 6 Mar. 1968, 33 *Federal Register* 4245 (7 Mar. 1967), cited in Prucha, *Great Father*, 1099 and 1099n28.

29. Memorandum on legislative activity and problems, Robert L. Bennett to the Undersecretary of the Interior, 25 Apr. 1969, in Desk Files of Robert L. Bennett, 70A-2935, Legislation, box 150, cited in Prucha, *Great Father*, 1099 and 1099n29.

30. U.S. Congress, 83rd Cong., 2nd sess., "Termination of Federal Supervision over Certain Tribes of Indians, Joint Hearings before the Subcommittees of the Committee of Interior and Insular Affairs, on S. Doc. 2747 and H.R. 7321," Part 8, Seminole Indians, Florida, 1–2 Mar. 1954, 1122.

31. *U.S. Statutes at Large* 48: 984–88. The IRA was among the last elements of the reforms of the 1920s led by John Collier. See also Prucha, *Great Father*, 940–58, and Kenneth R. Philip, *John Collier's Crusade for Indian Reform, 1920–1954* (Tucson: University of Arizona Press, 1977), 160–244, passim.

32. For a discussion of this point, see Robert Thomas King, "The Florida Seminole Polity, 1858–1978" (Unpublished diss., University of Florida, 1978), 175.

33. See 25 USC 83, Sect's 1–11, also in Federal Register 43: 39362–64 (5 Sept. 1978).

34. Howard Tommie, oral history interview, 8–9, cited in Kersey, *Assumption of Sovereignty*, 127.

35. "Seminole Tribe of Florida: 20th Anniversary of Tribal Organization, 1957–1977," photoduplicated booklet.

36. Howard Tommie, interview with Harry Kersey, in Kersey, *Assumption of Sovereignty*, 117–18.

37. Rex Quinn, speech transcript (place and group not noted), 8 June 1981, 2, in the collections of the author.

38. See Tribal Council Resolution C-34-84, 7 Oct. 1983.

39. James Billie, speaking at the funeral of Rev. Bill Osceola, 1995.

40. U.S. Congress, 83rd Cong., 1st sess., 67 Stat. 586, 15 Aug. 1953. The tribe removed some requirements for state and federal compliance, and substituted its own authority. Its own liquor law had been codified in Ordinance C-2-65, 11 Sept. 1964.

41. Seminole Tribe of Florida, Inc., Board Resolution No. BD-34-78, and Seminole Tribe of Florida Council Resolution No. C-28-78. The board had already approved the land lease for the liquor shop when the council took up the issue. It approved a three-acre lease of land, for a period of fifty-five years, at a price of $6,000 per year or 10 percent of the net profits, whichever was greater. In regard to the tribal referendum, see Council Resolutions C-29-83, C-67-83, and C-129-85.

42. Allison Finn, "Amid Tears, Tribe Changes Leaders," *Miami Herald,* Tues., 5 June 1979, 1, 3BR.

43. Ibid.

44. Ibid.

Chapter 3

1. See Tribal Council Resolution C-31-86, 17 Oct. 1985, by which the Cessna was sold to James for $3,000 as being too costly for the tribe to repair; and C-117-87, 13 Mar. 1987, in regard to the Beechcraft.

2. William C. Sturtevant, "The Mikasuki Seminole: Medical Beliefs and Practices" (Unpublished diss., Yale University, 1955), 317.

3. Name of informants withheld by request. Jimmy Billie was a brother of Frank Billie and also was the father of the infamous agitator Bobby C. Billie.

4. Betty Mae Tiger Jumper, personal communication, 1993.

5. Name withheld for reasons of privacy.

6. Patsy West, *The Enduring Seminoles: From Alligator Wrestling to Ecotourism* (Gainesville: University Press of Florida, 1998), passim.

7. West, in her survey of the 1920s and '30s tourist attractions, *Enduring Seminoles,* assigns to them a positive value in the lives of the Seminoles. The Seminoles themselves do not remember their experiences as particularly positive. Above all, they did not appreciate being treated as zoo exhibits but felt pressured to obtain white man's money to survive. My negative opinion is obtained from personal interviews with, among others, Pete Osceola, William McKinley ("Wild Bill") Osceola, Annie Jimmie, and others.

8. William Sturtevant, "A Seminole Medicine Maker," in *In the Company of Man: Twenty Portraits by Anthropologists,* ed. Joseph B. Casagrande (New York: Harper and Brothers, 1960), 505–32. Josie did not report to Sturtevant that he (Josie) had killed the woman because she refused to have sex with him; he reported only that they had had an argument. Tribal citizens told me that the subject of the argument was sex.

9. Sonny Billie, personal conversations with the author, 1995–2001.

10. Mrs. Ann MacMillan, oral history interview with the author, 19 Sept. 2002. Ann's

husband, Hugh, was the brother of Neil MacMillan, and remembers many visits to the Cabbage Palm Ranch.

11. Oral history interview with Mrs. Nina Turner, 25 July 1995.

12. This moment occurred in January 1996.

13. Barbara Oeffner, *Chief: Champion of the Everglades, a Biography of Seminole Chief James Billie* (Palm Beach, FL: Cape Cod Writers, 1995), 39.

14. Joe Moosha, "Seminole Chief Retains a Sense of History," Hollywood (FL) *Sun-Tattler,* Thurs., 5 July 1979, 1A, 2A.

15. Ibid.

16. Ibid.

17. Ibid.

Chapter 4

1. John DeGroot, "James Billie: Born as Outcast, Leader Still Very Much a Man Alone," *Baltimore Sun,* from the *South Florida Sun-Sentinel, Sunshine Magazine,* 16 Feb. 1986.

2. Ibid.

3. Ibid.

4. *U.S. Statutes at Large* 62: 683, 757.

5. *U.S. Statutes at Large* 60: 1049–56, Sect. 2.

6. For a review of this period in greater national perspective, see Prucha, *Great Father,* esp. 1041–59.

7. Annual Report of the Secretary of the Interior for 1954, 242–43.

8. For a detailed review of this case, see Kersey, *Assumption of Sovereignty,* 135–53. See also Jim Shore and Jerry C. Straus, "The Seminole Water Rights Compact and the Seminole Indian Land Claims Settlement Act of 1987," *Journal of Land Use and Environmental Law* 6, no. 1 (1990): 1–24.

9. The original petition by the Seminole Indians of Florida (in 1957, the Seminole Tribe of Florida) was assigned Docket No. 73, except for the cause concerning the taking of lands for Everglades National Park that was severed and assigned Docket No. 73-A. The Seminole Nation of Oklahoma petition was assigned Docket No. 151. An attempt in Aug. 1951 by the group calling itself the Creek Nation East of the Mississippi, C. W. McGhee et al., representatives, also attempted to intervene in the Seminoles' petition and was assigned Docket No. 280. Finally, on 13 Sept. 1974, the ILCC severed Docket No. 280 and dismissed it. See NARA, RG 279, Docket No. 151, Box 1405, Folder 2.

10. "Florida Seminoles Favor 16 Million," *Alligator Times* 2, no. 1 (1976): 1; and Robert Liss, "U.S. Offers Seminoles $16 Million for Land; 25-Year Wrangle Ends," *Miami Herald* 22 Jan. 1976. For varying Florida Seminole sentiments, refer to Tribal Council Resolutions C-194-78, C-43-82, and C-98-87.

11. The Seminoles were not the only tribe in Indian Territory upon which the United States forced a clearly punitive treaty at this moment, abrogating all previous treaties. All of the so-called Five Civilized Tribes were each addressed: Choctaw, Chickasaw, Creek, Cherokee, and Seminole. In Article 2, each of the Five Tribes' treaties forced citizenship of slave descendants and freedmen upon the Indians. This is a very complex subject and largely

outside of the purview of the present work. For an in-depth review of this era and this subject, see, among other works, Angie Debo, *And Still the Waters Run: The Betrayal of the Five Civilized Tribes* (Norman: University of Oklahoma Press, 1989), ix–x; David E. Wilkins, *American Indian Sovereignty and the U.S. Supreme Court, The Masking of Justice* (Austin: University of Texas Press, 1997), 67; Wilma Mankiller and Michael Wallis, *Mankiller: A Chief and Her People, An Autobiography by the Principal Chief of the Cherokee Nation* (New York: St. Martin's Press, 1993), 128–29; Vine Deloria Jr. and Clifford M. Lytle, *The Nations Within: The Past and Future of American Indian Sovereignty* (Austin: University of Texas Press, 1984), 23–24; Vine Deloria Jr. and David E. Wilkins, *Tribes, Treaties, and Constitutional Tribulations* (Austin: University of Texas Press, 1999), 73, and *U.S. Statutes at Large* 60: 1049.

12. Richmond Tiger, former principal chief of the Seminole Nation of Oklahoma, personal communication to the author, 1996; and Chitto Hajo, a.k.a. Tom Palmer, former principal chief of the Seminole Nation of Oklahoma, personal communications to the author, 1996–2002.

13. See note 9, above.

14. Final award date, 27 Apr. 1976. Another $50,000 would be added in 1977 to compensate for the land taken by the U.S. government for Everglades National Park.

15. R. B. Plunkett Jr., Paul Moran, and Bob Schwartzman, "Seminoles' Shops Linked to Organized Crime Figures," *Fort Lauderdale News and Sun-Sentinel,* 22 July 1979, 1A, 16A.

16. James Billie, personal conversation with the author, 12 Aug. 1995.

17. See Council Resolutions C-9-78 (8 July 1977; 3 for and 1 against) and C-17-79 (11 July 1978; 3 for, 0 against, 2 abstentions).

18. Council Resolution C-82-79, 3 Jan. 1979.

19. See, e.g., Plunkett, Moran, and Schwartzman, "Seminoles' Shops Linked to Organized Crime Figures," 1A, 16A.

20. See *Vending Unlimited vs. State of Florida,* 364 So. 2d 5480 (1978), first brought in Broward County court, then transferred to Tallahassee by Broward County Judge Otis Farrington. The final decision on appeal, in favor of the Seminole Tribe, relied on the precedent of *Confederated Tribes of Colville vs. State of Washington,* 446 F. supp. 1339 (1978) for its favorable ruling. See *Washington v. Confederated Tribes,* 447 U.S. 134 (1980). See also, Mary Siegfried, "Seminole Tax Heads for Court," *Hollywood* (FL) *Sun-Tattler,* 6 Aug. 1977, 5A.

21. Siegfried, "Seminole Tax Heads For Court," 5A.

22. FL § (1985) sect. 210.05 (permanent tobacco agreement).

23. Plunkett, Moran, and Schwartzman, "Seminoles' Shops Linked to Organized Crime Figures," 1A, 16A; David Nickell, "Cashing In on Bingo: Are the Seminoles Married to the Mob?" *XS* magazine, 16 Feb. 1994.

24. Plunkett, Moran, and Schwartzman, "Seminoles' Shops Linked to Organized Crime Figures," 1A, 16A.

25. See, e.g., Les Kjos, "Seminoles in Time of Turmoil," UPI News, 10 June 2001. Michael Mayo, "Will the Anti-Gambling Seminoles Shut Their Casinos?" *South Florida Sun-Sentinel,* 7 Nov. 2004. At sunsentinel.com.

26. Patricia Diamond, personal communication, Oct. 1995.

27. *Seminole Tribe of Florida vs. State of Florida et al.,* Case No. 78-6116-Civ-NCR, U.S.

District Court for the Southern District of Florida, 17 Mar. 1978, also cited in Kersey, *Assumption of Sovereignty*, 162–74, 241n23. This was merely the beginning of numerous complaints and cross-complaints.

28. *Winters v. United States*, 207 U.S. 564 (1908); Shore and Straus, "The Seminole Water Rights Compact," 1.

29. Shore and Straus, "The Seminole Water Rights Compact," 1n1; Felix S. Cohen, *Handbook of Federal Indian Law* (1940; n.p: Bobbs-Merrill, 1982), 578–79.

30. The Florida Water Resources Act of 1972, Ch. 72-299, in Florida Statutes Ch. 373 (1989).

31. Florida Statute 285.06 (1989) (amended).

32. Kersey, *Assumption of Sovereignty*, 144–45.

33. Tribal Council Resolution C-43-82.

34. U.S. Congress, 101st Cong., 1st sess., "Statement of Mr. James Billie, Chairman, Tribal Council of the Seminole Tribe of Florida before the House Committee on Interior and Insular Affairs on H.R. 2838 and H.R. 2650," 14 Sept. 1989, 2.

35. Ibid., 3, 4, 7, 9, 11.

36. Tribal Council Resolution C-111-88.

37. *State of Florida v. Billie*, 497 So. 2d 889 (Fla. 2d DCA 1986); and *United States v. Billie*, 667 F. Supp. 1485 (S.D. Fla. 1987).

38. In the same year, the decision in *New Mexico v. Mescalero Apache Tribe*, 462 U.S. 324, 330 (1983) noted that the state conceded the tribe's exclusive jurisdiction over Indian hunting and fishing. See also Shore and Straus, "The Seminole Water Rights Compact," 6.

39. "Indian Leader Faces Trial in Panther Slaying," *New York Times*, 12 Feb. 1984.

40. Barbara Doctor, *Seminole Tribune*, 1, no. 6, 28 Dec. 1983, 1.

41. Author's oral history interview with Carlos Sloan, former Hendry County sheriff's deputy, 23 Jan. 2007. Mr. Sloan has a page for "H.C.S.O. Family" on MyFamily.com, on which he posts an undated [1978] newspaper article reporting the arrest, along with a mug shot of Jimmy Cypress taken at the time of his arrest.

42. Name withheld by request. Oral history interview with the author, 10 Jan. 2007.

43. James Billie, personal conversation with the author, 4 Jan. 2007.

44. *State v. Billie*, 497 So. 2d 889 (Fla. 2d DCA 1986).

45. *Department of Game v. Puyallup Tribe*, 414 U.S. 44, 49 (1973).

46. Robert Laurence, "The Bald Eagle, the Florida Panther, and the Nation's Word: An Essay on the 'Quiet' Abrogation of Indian Treaties and the Proper Reading of *United States v. Dion*," *Journal of Land Use and Environmental Law* 4, no. 1 (1988): 16.

47. Florida Statute § 380.055(8).

48. "Seminole Chief Denies Guilt in Panther Case," *New York Times*, 24 Apr. 1987.

49. Shore and Straus, "The Seminole Water Rights Compact," 6n34. See also Laurence, "The Bald Eagle, the Florida Panther, and the Nation's Word," 15–29.

50. *United States v. Dion*, 476 U.S. 734 (1986). Dwight Dion Sr. was an enrolled citizen of the FR Yankton Sioux Tribe of South Dakota who had been convicted of shooting four bald eagles on the tribe's reservation, in violation of the Endangered Species Act, and selling their carcasses in violation of the Eagle Protection Act and the Migratory Bird Treaty Act.

51. "Indian Leader Faces Trial in Panther Slaying," *New York Times*, 12 Feb. 1984.

52. Ibid. See also Philip Shabecoff, "Killing of a Panther: Indian Treaty Rights vs. Law on Wildlife," *New York Times,* 15 Apr. 1987.

53. Jon Nordheimer, "Jury Is Tied in Killing of Panther," *New York Times,* 27 Aug. 1987, and "Mistrial Declared in Panther Killing," *New York Times,* 28 Aug. 1987.

54. "Panther-Killing Case Dropped," *New York Times,* 10 Oct. 1987, and "Case Ended in the Death of a Panther," *New York Times,* 11 Oct. 1987.

55. In Brad Goldstein and Jeff Testerman, "Seminole Gambling: A Trail of Millions," *St. Petersburg Times,* 21 Dec. 1997, 6A.

56. Shore and Straus, "The Seminole Water Rights Compact," 7.

57. Kersey, *Assumption of Sovereignty,* 164 and 241n26; Stay Order, case no. 78-6116-Civ-NCR, SDF, 30 May 1984. See also USCoE Dredge and Fill Permit Application No. 85-IPD-20126, Dept. of the Army, 24 Sept. 1985.

58. *Oneida Indian Nation of New York v. State of New York,* 69 F. 2d 1070 (2d Cir. 1982), known as Oneida I.

59. The Trade and Intercourse Act, 22 July 1790, *U.S. Statutes at Large* 1: 137–38. The laws stated herein, originally designed to enforce Indian treaties and protect tribes against the nefarious dealings of whites, soon were seen to embody the basic features of federal Indian policy, including federal (rather then state) supremacy in relations with tribes and the requirement that even states could not obtain Indian lands, even by sale, unless by a treaty duly executed under the authority of the U.S. federal government. See Francis Paul Prucha, ed., *Documents of United States Indian Policy,* 3rd ed. (Lincoln: University of Nebraska Press, 2000), 14–15. See also Kersey, *Assumption of Sovereignty,* 164–65.

60. See, e.g., the American Indian Religious Freedom Act, *U.S. Statutes at Large* 92: 469ff., 11 Aug. 1978; Indian Child Welfare Act, *U.S. Statutes at Large* 92: 3069ff., 8 Nov. 1978; the Native American Graves Protection and Repatriation Act, *U.S. Statutes at Large* 104: 3048ff.; Archaeological Resources Protection Act, *U.S. Statutes at Large* 93: 721ff., 31 Oct. 1979; and Memorandum of President William J. Clinton of Government-to-Government Relations with Native American Tribal Governments, promulgated 29 Apr. 1994, in the *Federal Register,* 59: 22951–52, 4 May 1994.

61. Shore and Straus, "The Seminole Water Rights Compact," 7. The new negotiator, Timer Powers, seemed to have a genuine concern for settlement rather than standoff.

62. See Tribal Council Resolutions C-47-87 and C-01-88.

63. "Seminole Indian Land Claims Settlement Act of 1987," Public Law 100-228, 31 Dec. 1987. Despite its title, this is the settlement of the EBCC. Two further legal instruments would end the fight. First was the "Order Approving Settlement Agreement and Instructing Parties to Complete Performance of Settlement Agreement and Dismissing Case with Prejudice," issued by Judge Norman C. Roettger Jr., in the U.S. District Court for the Southern District of Florida, Case No. 78-6116-Civ, 29 Oct. 1987. Second was the Settlement Agreement itself, ibid.

64. See Tribal Council Resolution C-02-88.

65. Shore and Straus, "The Seminole Water Rights Compact," 24.

66. Ibid. The authors' use of the term *semi-autonomous* is, in itself, yet another bone of contention between Indians and whites. Its use is particularly hard in an article the first author of which is an Indian and chief legal counsel for his own tribe. The concept of "semi"

autonomy of a nation at the same time "sovereign" stems from the United States' acceptance of tribal sovereignty as clearly articulated in the U.S. Constitution, and the later declaration in a pair U.S. Supreme Court decisions, authored by Chief Justice John Marshall, that tribes were "domestic dependent nations." For more on this exceedingly complex subject, consult Prucha, *Great Father,* passim, and Pevar, *The Rights of Indians and Tribes: The Basic ACLU Guide to Indian and Tribal Rights,* to cite only two among many.

Chapter 5

1. U.S. Congress, 83rd Cong., 1st sess., Stat. 586, Public Law 277, 15 Aug. 1953.

2. Seminole Council Ordinance C-02-65, passed 11 Sept. 1964. Promulgated by Secretary of the Interior Stewart L. Udall, 3 Nov. 1964.

3. Tribal Council Resolution C-28-78, 12 Aug. 1977. The vote was 4 for, 0 against, with 1 abstention (Howard's).

4. Meeting 6 June 1978 of council and board, Resolutions C-142-78 and Bd-117-78.

5. Tribal Council Resolutions C-18-81, 11 July 1980, and C-19-81, of the same date. The former was the venture project agreement and the latter was the management agreement. Both were subject to BIA approval.

6. Tribal Council Resolution C-66-81, 14 Nov. 1980.

7. See Nickell, "Cashing In on Bingo: Are the Seminoles Married to the Mob?"; see also Pennsylvania Crime Commission, *Racketeering and Organized Crime in the Bingo Industry,* Apr. 1992; Kersey, *Assumption of Sovereignty,* 125.

8. Council Resolution C-79-79, 3 Jan. 1979.

9. See Nickell, "Cashing In on Bingo: Are the Seminoles Married to the Mob?"

10. Pennsylvania Crime Commission, *Racketeering and Organized Crime in the Bingo Industry.*

11. See Nickell, "Cashing In on Bingo: Are the Seminoles Married to the Mob?" 17.

12. Cited in ibid., 15.

13. See "Seminoles' Bingo Pays Off," *Palm Beach Post,* 1 Mar. 1982, 1–2; and Council Resolution C-21-80, 24 Aug. 1979.

14. Timmy Wayne Cox, interview with the author, 21 Jan. 2004, and per Seminole tribal chairman James Billie, personal communication, 1994.

15. U.S. Congress, 83rd Congress, 1st sess., 15 Aug. 1953, *U.S. Statutes at Large* 67: 588–90.

16. *Seminole Tribe of Florida vs. Robert Butterworth,* U.S. District Court, Southern Dist. of Florida, Fort Lauderdale Division, 491 F. Supp. 1015 (1980), holding entered 6 May 1980, enjoined Sheriff Butterworth from enforcing the state bingo statute on Indian land, on the basis that the state's regulation of bingo was only civil regulatory and could not be enforced on Indian lands. Judgment on appeal was rendered for the tribe on the same basis, in *Seminole Tribe of Florida vs. Robert Butterworth,* U.S. Court of Appeals, Fifth Circuit, Unit B, 5 Oct. 1981.

17. U.S. District Court for the Southern District of Florida, 491 D. Supp. 1015.

18. *Seminole Tribe of Florida v. Butterworth,* U.S. District Court, Southern District of Florida, No. 79-6680-Civ-NCR.

19. *United States v. Marcyes*, 557 F. 2d, U.S. Circuit Court of Appeals for the Ninth Circuit. The court held that a fireworks statute of the State of Washington was prohibitory rather than regulatory and concerned a dangerous item—fireworks—that could be bought on Res but carried off, to the detriment of the non-Indian population, whereas, in the case of the Seminoles, gaming was strictly an on-Res activity.

20. "Sheriff's Appeal against Seminole Bingo Heard in Atlanta," *Alligator Times*, 2 (1981), 1.

21. 5 Oct. 1981, *Seminole Tribe of Florida vs. Butterworth*, U.S. Court of Appeals, Fifth Circuit, No. 80-5496-658 F. 2d 310 (1981).

22. Cited in Nickell, "Cashing In on Bingo: Are the Seminoles Married to the Mob?" 14.

23. See Tribal Council Resolution C-04-81.

24. Jeff Testerman and Brad Goldstein, "Loyalty Pays Off for Tampa Partner," *St. Petersburg* [FL] *Times*, Dec. 1997.

25. Dana Treen, "Seminoles Find Card to Success," *Florida Times-Union*, 18 July 1993, C1, C4.

26. Former U.S. senator and close LBJ associate, George A. Smathers, personal communication to the author, 9 Nov. 1997.

27. Tribal Council Resolutions C-137-85, 13 July 1984, and C-55-85, 14 Dec. 1984, and C-14-84.

28. Tribal Council Resolution C-57-85, 14 Dec. 1984.

29. Tribal Council Resolution C-34-91, 27 Sept. 1990.

30. Tribal Council Resolution C-106-91, 29 Jan. 1991.

31. Quoted in Oeffner, *Chief: Champion of the Everglades*, 104–5.

32. Geneva Shore, an older sister of Jim, personal conversation with the author, 2002.

33. I heard this quotation from several individuals but especially from Pat Diamond, James's administrative assistant and close friend to Jim Shore, who was locked in her own love/hate relationship with James.

34. Seminole Tribe *News Brief*, 1, no. 2, 12 May 1983, single sheet.

35. Refer respectively to Tribal Council Resolutions C-12-84; C-43-84; C-44-84; C-45-84; C-46-84, C-39-85, C-47-85, C-49-85, and C-14-87; C-40-85, C-121-85, C-154-86, and C-05-87; C-60-85; C-48-86, C-49-86, C-87-86, and C-10-87; and C-68-84.

36. Dana Treen, "Miccosukees Look Ahead, Hold to Past," *Florida Times-Union*, 18 July 1993, C1, C5.

37. Nickell, "Cashing In on Bingo: Are the Seminoles Married to the Mob?" 16.

38. Ibid.

39. Ibid., 68.

40. *U.S. Statutes at Large* 102: 2467–76.

41. See 25 USC 2701(5) (1994), although the decision in *Three Affiliated Tribes of the Fort Berthold Reservation v. Wold Engineering, P.C.*, 467 U.S. 138 (1984), had held that state court jurisdiction would not interfere with the Indians' right to self-government. See Wayne L. Baker, "Seminole Speaks to Sovereign Immunity and Ex Parte Young," *St. John's Law Review* (Fall 1997): 11.

42. *California v. Cabazon Band of Mission Indians*, 480 U.S. Reports, 207–22, 25 Feb. 1987.

43. *U.S. Statutes at Large* 23: 385. See Prucha, *Documents of United States Indian Policy*, 166.

44. *U.S. Statutes at Large* 90: 585–86, 29 May 1976.

45. *U.S. Statutes at Large* 67: 588–90.

46. *U.S. Statutes at Large* 82 : 77, 11 Apr. 1968. See also Prucha, *Great Father*, 1044–45.

47. The subject of the intrusion of white men's law into Indian Country is so complex and frustrating to Indians as to make any attempt at simplifying the issues here run frighteningly close to the simplistic. For further explanations see any edition of *The Rights of Indians and Tribes: The Basic ACLU Guide to Indian and Tribal Rights*, ed. Pevar. For the broader non-Indian social matrix, see Prucha, *Great Father*, 1044–45.

The three basic canons require that the preponderance of decision-making weight should be accorded an Indian tribe and that, in any instance, the tribe's interpretation of treaties should be accepted. Taken together with the U.S. government's fiduciary responsibility to protect the tribes, and the newly espoused U.S. executive's "self-determination" policy for tribes, the tribes' separate attitudes toward state law enforcement on the reservations came to be of greater weight at this moment in U.S. social history than ever before. Over the years since, however, U.S., state, and local governments have sought to chip away at these rights.

48. Cynthia Parks, "What State's Doing about Swamp Ghetto," *Florida Times-Union and Jacksonville Journal*, Sunday, 7 June 1970, H1.

49. *U.S. Statutes at Large* 82: 77–81, 11 Apr. 1968.

50. Florida Statutes Annotated (1991), Sect. 285.18.

51. Pete Baker, interview with the author, 24 June 1997.

52. See Tribal Council Resolution C-109-74. The line item for Law and Order was $43,516.00.

53. See Tribal Council Resolution C-98-81, 16 Jan. 1981.

54. See http://www.floridastatefop.org/heroes_complete.asp. See also "Ex-Lawman Guilty of Drug Trafficking," *Dallas Morning News*, Jan. 1993, and Tex O'Neill, "Ex-Sheriff Pleads Guilty to Four Cocaine Charges," *Charlotte Observer*, 13 Feb. 1993, 3A.

55. Author's interview with Carlos Sloan, former Hendry County sheriff's deputy, 23 Jan. 2007.

56. See Ord. C-134-80 and Resolution C-77-82. For examples of forfeited aircraft, including one bought from the tribe by James personally, see Resolutions C-31-86, 17 Oct. 1985; C-50-86, 13 Sept. 1985; and C-117-87, 13 Mar. 1987.

57. See Tribal Council Resolution C-98-81. Seeley began work with the tribe on 16 Jan. 1981. Chief Chester Kowalski served until January 1984 (see Tribal Council Resolution C-80-84, 13 Jan. 1984); Richard McMonagle became the new chief per Tribal Council Resolution C-160-85, 31 May 1985; Thomas R. Hernan joined SPD as an officer on 2 Jan. 1986, per Tribal Council Resolution C-119-86, eventually rising to chief.

58. DeGroot, "James Billie: Born as Outcast."

59. See Tribal Council Resolution C-101-89, 6 Feb. 1989.

Chapter 6

1. Tribal Council Resolution C-21-94, passed 4 Aug. 1993.

2. Tribal Council Resolution C-94-91 thanks Joel for his service as he departs for Washington, DC.

3. The first proposal for this tribal service was submitted as early as 8 July 1979, but only began to take shape over the coming decade, as funds permitted.

4. By Tribal Council Resolution C-92-86, 6 Dec. 1985, the tribe requested additional funding from the Florida Higher Education Scholarship Program.

5. See, e.g., Tribal Council Resolutions C-01-59, 22 Aug. 1958; and C-66–75, 14 Mar. 1975.

6. Tribal Council Resolutions C-30-89, 20 Sept. 1988; and C-181-90 of 11 May 1990. Tribal Council Resolution C-156-91 of 21 May 1991 has attached a report outlining those factors, with the exception of the HTLV II factors (note 12, below).

7. Tribal Council Resolution C-89-91, passed 11 Jan. 1991.

8. "Seminole Tribe of Florida: 1959–1987," commemorative booklet produced by the Seminole Tribe of Florida, 1987, 4.

9. See http://www.redearth.org.

10. Indian Self-Determination and Education Assistance Act, Public Law 93-638, 4 Jan. 1975: "An Act to provide maximum Indian participation in the Government and education of Indian people; to provide for full participation of Indian tribes in the programs and services conducted by the Federal Government for Indians and to encourage the development of human resources of the Indian people; to establish a program of assistance to upgrade Indian education to support the right of Indian citizens to control their own educational activities; and for other purposes." The Tribal Council approved the negotiation of a 638 contract for its health program by Tribal Council Resolution C-57-76, 23 Jan. 1976.

11. Betty Mae Jumper, personal communications, 1997.

12. George W. Lowis, William A. Sheramata, Symalina Dube, Dipak Dube, Patricia R. Wickman, and Bernard J. Poiesz, "HTLV-II Risk Factors in Native Americans in Florida," *Neuroepidemiology* 18 (1999): 37–47; and Kirsi Huoponen, Antonio Torroni, Patricia R. Wickman, Daniele Sellitto, Daniel S. Gurley, Rosaria Scozzari, and Douglas C. Wallace, "Mitochondrial DNA and Y Chromosome-Specific Polymorphisms in the Seminole Tribe of Florida," *European Journal of Human Genetics* 5 (1997): 25–34.

13. Tribal Council Resolutions C-72-90 of 1 Dec. 1989; C-156-91 of 21 May 1991. By proposed amendment XXI to the Tribal Constitution, the Immokalee representative would have obtained a vote on the Tribal Council. See Tribal Council Resolution C-33-91, 28 Aug. 1990.

14. National Cattlemen's Beef Association statistics, 1997.

15. Susan Salisbury, "Tribe's Traceable Cattle Prime for BSE-Wary Japan," *Palm Beach Post*, 2004.

16. The basis for this revolving credit program was one of the reforms of the John Collier administration, in the 1930s. It was the Wheeler-Howard Act, *U.S. Statutes at Large* 48 Stat. 986, enacted 18 June 1934. Part of the purpose was to "promote economic development" among FR tribes and, to this end, the sum of $10 million was to be appropriated annually. In the Indian Financing Act, *U.S. Statutes at Large* 88: 77–83, enacted 12 Apr. 1974, Congress continued the successor acts of 26 June 1936, *U.S. Statutes at Large* 49 Stat. 1968; and 19 Apr. 1950, 64 Stat. 44. The 1974 act originally capped loans to tribes or individual Indians at $50,000 and created within the Department of the Interior the Indian Business Development Program.

17. Kersey, *Assumption of Sovereignty*, 94–95.

Chapter 7

1. Tribal Council Ordinance C-01-78, 12 Aug. 1977.

2. See Tribal Council Ordinances C-116-81 and C-117-81, enacted on 13 Mar. 1981.

3. See Tribal Council Ordinances C-05-82 and C-06-82, 14 July 1981; and Ordinances C-87-82 and C-88-82, of 8 Jan. 1982.

4. *Squire v. Capoeman,* 351 U.S. 1 (1956). See also Pevar, *The Rights of Indians and Tribes: The Basic ACLU Guide to Indian and Tribal Rights,* 2nd ed., 170–73. For specific aspects of individual Indian taxation conditions, cf. *Jourdain v. Commissioner,* 617 F. 2d 507 (8th Cir. 1980); *Hoptowit v. Commissioner,* 709 F. 2d 564 (9th Cir. 1983); *Anderson v. U.S.* 845 F. 2d 206 (9th Cir.), *cert. denied,* 488 U.S. 966 (1988); and *Choteau v. Burnet,* 283 U.S. 691 (1931).

5. For Priscilla's permanent appointment, see Tribal Council Resolution C-04-83 (Personnel Actions), passed Jan. 1983.

6. See New Jersey State Bar Foundation, at http://www.njsbf.org/njsbf/student/respect//winter03-1.cfm; Native American Mascots: Racial Slur or Cherished Tradition?

7. See Yahoo! Groups, http://groups.yahoo.com/group/NatNews/message/39441.

8. Jim Shore, personal communication to the author, 1998.

9. See, e.g., Jim's remarks in his op-ed piece, "Play with Our Name," in the *New York Times,* 27 Aug. 2005.

10. See http://www.collegefootballhistory.com/florida_state/history.htm.

11. Given our national experiences with Republican campaigners during the 2008 presidential election, we have been able to witness firsthand the negative effects of permitting pejorative statements and demeaning stereotyping to be repeated unchecked.

12. "NCAA Allowing Florida State to Use Its Mascot," *USA Today.* See http://www.usatoday.com/sports/college/2005-08-23-fsu-mascot-approved_x.htm.

13. Ibid.

14. Jeff Price, AP, "Tribe Supports FSU Nickname," *Miami Herald,* 18 June 2005.

15. "Oklahoma Seminoles OK Name," *USA Today.* See http://www.usatoday.com/sports/college/2005-08-11-fsu-mascot-support_x.htm.

16. By Tribal Council Resolution C-96-89 of 3 Feb. 1989, the tribe incorporated the museum as a not-for-profit entity.

17. Tribal Council Resolution C-151-98, passed 9 Jan. 1998.

18. "Grand Opening of the Ah-Tha [*sic*]-Thi-Ki Museum," commemorative issue, *Seminole Tribune,* 1997, 11.

19. John H. Hann, "The Florida Governor's Report on the Revolt of the Mayaca-Jororo Missions, February 1697," in Hann, *Missions to the Calusa,* 147. Hann opined that the word *Jizime* was probably a variant of *Atisime* and realizes that the word is the origin of the modern Kissimmee.

20. Jeff Testerman and Brad Goldstein, "Branching Out with Little Success," *St. Petersburg Times,* [21] Dec. 1997, 12A.

21. Ibid.

22. Tim Cox, interview with the author, 19 Mar. 2004. Tim cites the purchase price as having been $10 million plus another $15 million in rehab for a "resort" with only a marina as its salient feature and less than 10 percent occupancy.

23. Testerman and Goldstein, "Branching Out with Little Success."

24. Ibid.

25. Ibid.

26. Kirby J. Harrison, "Flying for the Tribe," *Aviation International News,* Apr. 1999, 55–56.

27. Testerman and Goldstein, "Branching Out with Little Success."

28. Timmy Wayne Cox, interview with the author, 23 Jan. 2004.

29. Pat Diamond, personal conversation with the author, 2003.

30. "*St. Petersburg Times* Interview with Chief Billie, Full Transcription," Nov. 1997. Posted on the Web site of the *Seminole Tribune,* at http://100.6.4.21/tribune/transcription .shtml.

31. Ibid.

32. Testerman and Goldstein, "Branching Out with Little Success."

Chapter 8

1. See http://www.fedspending.org.

2. Anonymous, at the request of the individual.

3. Personal conversation with the author, 12 Aug. 1995.

4. Robert A. Caro, *The Years of Lyndon Johnson: Master of the Senate* (New York: Alfred A. Knopf, 2002), 146–47.

5. Ethel Yari, "James Billie, Seminole Chief Leads His Tribe into the 21st Century," *Florida Living Magazine,* July 1999, 46.

6. Tribal Council Resolution C-222-94, 19 May 1994. The act referred to and relied upon a federal exemption for tribal proprietary records to be found in 5 USC 552 (b)(4).

7. Vivian Crooks, personal communication to the author, 25 Nov. 2003.

8. C. L. Henson, "Indian Gambling on Reservations—Seventeen Years Later," *American Studies Today Online,* 6 Nov. 2007. At http://www.americansc.org.uk/online/Gaming .htm. See also Henson's earlier article, posted at the same site on 21 Nov. 2005.

9. There is little information to be found concerning Herr Theodore Von Elmpt. There is no indication that he ever lived on his Hendry County property. His wife, Frau Theodore Von Elmpt, was living at Kaiserstrasse 34, Fürsorgeverein, Westfalen, Deutschland, in 1920. See *Gesamtverzeichnis der Teilnehmer an den Fernsprechnetzen in den Ober-Postdirektionsbezirkin Aachen, Cöln, Dortmund, Düsseldorf, Minden, und Münster in Westfalen* (Düsseldorf: A. Bagel, 1920), 1087.

On 31 May 1932, Herr Von Elmpt patented his design for a wooden chair with the U.S. Patent Office (Patent No. 1861331), on behalf of Munn and Company. The latter were not listed as his attorneys, although there was a firm of patent lawyers by that name in Washington, DC, at the time. The firm went out of business in 1960. There also was an H. L. Munn Lumber Company in Edinburgh, Scotland, that manufactured household furnishings and had been in business since 1891, as well as Munn and Company solicitors, doing business in Edinburgh as well. There also were other Von Elmpt families living in Northern Westphalia in the period of the 1880s through the 1930s, and several Von Elmpt males who were entering and leaving the United States, Mexico, and South America, most probably on business, so the family may have been a large and successful one. We have no exact idea of the reason for Herr Von Elmpt's interest in the Seminoles, but we do know that many Germans became intensely interested in American Indians in this period through the writings of the immensely popular author of young people's adventure stories, many set in the American West, Karl May (1842–1912). May's series is still in publication today and the Germans remain enamored of the romance of Indian life.

10. See Tribal Council Resolution C-21-74, 13 Aug. 1973.

11. See Tribal Council Resolution C-77-79, 11 Nov. 1978.

12. See Tribal Council Resolutions C-160-81 and C-34-82, 1 Sept. 1981.

13. Public Law 98-64, 97 Stat. 365, 25 USCS 117 (a), et seq., 2 Aug. 1983.

14. See Tribal Council Resolutions C-03-83 and C-31-84.

15. Tribal Council Resolution C-28-91, 31 July 1990.

16. Tribal Council Resolution C-168-91, 26 June 1991.

17. Tribal Council Resolution C-42-93, 13 Nov. 1992.

18. Tribal Council Resolution C-121-93, 12 Mar. 1993.

19. Franklin Keel, BIA eastern area supervisor, personal interview with the author, 14 Sept. 2006.

20. See Tribal Council Resolution C-164-85, 11 Jan. 1985.

21. See Tribal Council Resolution C-07-86, 12 July 1985.

22. "*St. Petersburg Times* Interview with Chief Billie, Full Transcription," Nov. 1997. Posted on the Web site of the *Seminole Tribune,* at http://100.6.4.21/tribune/transcription .shtml.

23. Ibid.

24. Goldstein and Testerman, "Seminole Gambling: A Trail of Millions," 7A.

25. Ibid.

26. Ibid.

27. Peter B. Gallagher, "New Year, New Budget for Tribal Council," *Seminole Tribune,* 20, no. 19, 23 Jan. 1998.

28. Tim Cox, interview with the author, 26 Jan. 2004.

29. Sally Kestin, Peter Franceschina, and John Maines, "Seminole Jackpot, Heady Days: The Tribe Has Access to Newfound Money," *Fort Lauderdale Sun-Sentinel,* Sun., 25 Nov. 2007, 1A, 24–28A. First of six parts.

30. Sally Kestin, Peter Franceschina, and John Maines, "Houses of Contrast, Cypress Brothers: The Tribal Leaders Enjoy Opulence; Most Seminoles Live Modestly," *Fort Lauderdale Sun-Sentinel,* Tues., 27 Nov. 2007, 1A, 10–11A. Third of six parts.

31. Tribal Council Ordinance C-03a-90, Fireworks Ordinance.

32. NAHASDA, *U.S. Statutes at Large* 110, passed 26 Oct. 1996.

33. Tribal Council Resolution C-43-99, 8 Sept. 1998.

34. Tribal Council Resolution C-205-99, 13 Mar. 1999.

35. Tim Cox, interviews with the author, 12, 14 Apr. 2004.

36. Tribal Council Resolution C-46-00, 9 Oct. 1999.

37. Gallagher, "New Year, New Budget for Tribal Council."

Chapter 9

1. See Tribal Council Resolution C-78-88, 8 Jan. 1988. The tribe pledged half of the proposed cost of $500,000 and obtained the other half from HUD.

2. Tribal Council Resolution C-32-94, 4 Aug. 1993.

3. Tribal Council Resolution C-103-95, 12 Jan. 1995.

4. "*St. Petersburg Times* Interview with Chief Billie, Full Transcription," Nov. 1997. Posted on the Web site of the *Seminole Tribune,* at http://100.6.4.21/tribune/transcription .shtml.

5. *USA v. F. Butch Oseby,* U.S. 8th Circuit Court of Appeals, No. 97-3207, Submitted 10 Mar. 1998. Filed 8 July 1998.

6. *New York Times,* "4 Are Indicted in Scheme Using Tribe to Obtain U.S. Equipment," 9 Oct. 1994.

7. Tribal Council Resolution C-205-92, 13 Mar. 1992.

8. By Tribal Council Resolution C-136-93, 12 Mar. 1993, Robb Tiller's screener card authority was terminated and, in the same meeting, by Tribal Council Resolution C-137-93, Raether was appointed.

9. For the original case against Raether and Hawkins, see 18 USC § 371 (1994). The reversal is U.S. Court of Appeals for the Eighth Circuit, 82 F. 3d 192, No. 95-3222SD, decided 22 Apr. 1996. The reconfirmation of the conviction is ibid. No. 97-1476SD, decided 30 Oct. 1997.

10. Clay W. Cone, "Immokalee-Based Air Service to Cuba Appears to Be Grounded," *Immokalee Independent,* 10 July 1998, 1A, 2A. Local Immokalee resident, Pam Brown, watched as Robb first parked a camper in a local church parking lot and kept me apprised of developments.

11. Tribal Council Resolution C-81-91, 9 Nov. 1990, retroactive to his hiring on 18 Oct. 1990.

12. See Seminole Council Resolutions C-38-93, 28 July 1992, for his termination as director; and C-99-93, of 12 Mar. 1993 for the assignment of income.

13. See Nickell, "Cashing In on Bingo: Are the Seminoles Married to the Mob?"

14. Tribal Council Resolution C-139-92, 20 Dec. 1991.

15. "*St. Petersburg Times* Interview with Chief Billie, Full Transcription."

16. See http://www.miccoaircraft.com.

Chapter 10

1. Brad Goldstein and Jeff Testerman, "Regulators Have Ties to Seminoles," *St. Petersburg Times,* 20 Dec. 1997, 1A.

2. Executive Order 74-23, signed on 10 Apr. 1974, by Governor Reuben O'Donovan Askew.

3. Tribal Council Resolution C-87-01, on 8 Mar. 2001, gave permanent status to Robert Osley Saunooke, who had been hired by the chairman's office since 20 Nov. 2000, at a salary of $150,000 per year.

4. The first and second referenda were held in 1978 and 1986. The most recent at this time was the referendum of 1994, in which two-thirds of those Floridians who cast ballots once again rejected full-scale gambling in Florida. See Phillip Longman, "Crapshoot: Casino Promoters Promise Floridians a Chance to Win Big (Part 1)," *Florida Trend,* May 1994, 30–36.

5. Ibid., 32.

6. Tribal Council Resolution C-96-95, of 12 Jan. 1995, authorizes the tribe to seek funding from the BIA for a feasibility study concerning the four bases.

7. Nickell, "Cashing In on Bingo: Are the Seminoles Married to the Mob?" 12.

8. See Tribal Ordinance C-02-94, enacted 30 Sept. 1993. See also Tribal Council Resolution C-113-00, passed 12 Nov. 1999, amending Sections 2-1, 4-1, 6-3, and 24-1 of the ordinance.

9. Goldstein and Testerman, "Regulators Have Ties to Seminoles."

10. Tribal Council Resolution C-176A-98, passed 13 Mar. 1998.

11. Nickell, "Cashing In on Bingo: Are the Seminoles Married to the Mob?" 13.

12. Longman, "Crapshoot: Casino Promoters Promise Floridians a Chance to Win Big (Part 1)," 30.

13. Ibid., 35.

14. The IGRA, 102 Stat., 2475, 25 USC § 2710 (d)(1)(C), requires a tribal-state compact under the Indian Commerce Clause of the U.S. Constitution, Art. 1, § 10, c1.3. The "good faith" requirement is in the IGCA, § 2710 (d)(3)(A).

15. *Seminole Tribe of Florida v. Florida,* U.S. Circuit Court of Appeals for the Eleventh Circuit, Atlanta, Georgia, 11 F. 3d 1016, 18 Jan. 1994.

16. Ibid.

17. *Poarch Band of Creek Indians v. Alabama,* 776 F. Supp. 550 (SD Ala. 1991), and 784 F. Supp. 1549 (SD Ala. 1992).

18. 513 U.S. (1995) and 517 U.S. 44 (116 S. Ct. 1114, 135 L. Ed. 2d 252 [1996]).

19. U.S. Supreme Court, 517 U.S. 44, *Seminole Tribe of Florida v. Florida,* No. 94-12, argued 11 Oct. 1995, and decided 27 Mar. 1996. Despite this decision, legalists cite three instances in which Eleventh Amendment exceptions exist. See Baker, "Seminole Speaks to Sovereign Immunity and Ex Parte Young," 11n19.

20. H. Lehman Franklin, JD, Statesboro, Georgia, personal conversation with the author, June 1997.

21. The tribe and the NIGC had entered into a memorandum of understanding concerning privacy safeguards for obtaining FBI background checks for casinos' "key employees and primary management officials." This did not begin the process of background checks but it codified procedures. See Tribal Council Resolution C-26-94, 4 Aug. 1993.

22. Tribal Council Resolutions C-25-99, 14 July 1998; and C-208-99, 23 Mar. 1999.

23. Tribal Council Resolution C-102-87, 2 Feb. 1987.

24. Tribal Council Resolutions C-59-88 and C-60-88, both 1 Aug. 1988.

25. Allen M. Lerner, of Lerner, Pearce, P.A., Fort Lauderdale, Florida, to Stan Taube, president, Investment Resources, Inc., of Minneapolis, Minnesota, and Alan Werkman, Esq., Deerfield Beach, Florida, 15 Aug. 1990.

26. Tribal Council Resolutions C-145-88, 24 June 1988; C-57-91, 9 Nov. 1990; C-58-91, 9 Nov. 1990; and C-97-91, 1 Nov. 1991.

27. Tribal Council Resolution C-97-91, 11 Jan. 1991.

28. Brad Goldstein, David Adams, and Jeff Testerman, "Seminoles Gain Entry in Caribbean Casino," *St. Petersburg Times,* 20 Dec. 1997, 13A.

29. See Tribal Council Resolutions C-36-93, 19 Aug. 1992, and C-07-94, 4 Aug. 1993.

30. Tribal Council Resolution C-107-86, 6 Dec. 1985, specifies the tract of land and authorizes the chairman to follow through on the development proposal submitted by a business developer. The proposal did not come to fruition. See also Jeff Testerman and Brad Goldstein, "Banking on Full-Scale Casinos," *St. Petersburg Times,* Dec. 1997.

31. Tribal Council Resolutions C-112a-88 and C-112b-88, 18 Mar. 1988.

32. Tribal Council Resolution C-33-89, 20 Sept. 1988.

33. Tribal Council Resolution C-103-90, 19 Jan. 1990.

34. Tribal Council Resolutions C-168-90, 11 May 1990; C-107-91, 21 Jan. 1991; and C-164-91, 26 June 1991.

35. Tribal Council Resolution C-225-92, 13 Mar. 1992.

36. Tribal Council Resolution C-72-94, 22 Nov. 1993.

37. Tribal Council Resolutions C-90-93, 12 Mar. 1993; and C-71-94, 22 Nov. 1993.

38. Tribal Council Resolutions C-144-94, 14 Jan. 1994; C-145-94, 28 Feb. 1994; and C-248-94, 20 May 1994. Also C-125-98 of 9 Jan. 1998.

39. See Jeff Testerman and Brad Goldstein, "King Bull," *St. Petersburg Times,* 21 Dec. 1997, 1A.

40. Tribal Council Resolution C-38-00, 3 Aug. 1999.

41. Jeff Testerman and Brad Goldstein, "Loyalty Pays Off for Tampa Partner," *St. Petersburg Times,* 20 Dec. 1997, 12A.

42. Ibid.

43. Ibid.

44. Ibid.

45. Jason Vest, "Trump's Gamble for Indian Wampun," *The Village Voice,* 1–7 July 1998.

46. Ibid., quoted from *The Seminole Tribune.*

47. This sentiment, so apropos for this moment in the modern life of the Seminoles, actually is taken from R. Laurence Moore's *Religious Outsiders and the Making of Americans,* cited in Jon Krakauer, *Under the Banner of Heaven: A Story of Violent Faith* (New York: Doubleday, 2003), 123, and is describing the actions of Joseph Smith soon after he and his Latter Day Saints followers entered Nauvoo, Illinois.

48. Maryjene Cypress Koenes, personal conversations with the author, 2003.

49. LaVonne Kippenberger, personal conversations with the author, 2006.

Chapter 11

1. Ethel Yari, "James Billie: Seminole Chief Leads His Tribe into the 21st Century," *Florida Living* (July 1999): 46–52.

2. All quotations from Tim Cox in this chapter, unless otherwise noted, are excerpted from interviews with the author conducted during January through April of 2004. The author extends sincere gratitude to Tim Cox for his willingness to share his invaluable information.

3. Jeff Testerman, "Chief's Hold on Seminoles Is Slipping," *St. Petersburg Times,* 29 Apr. 2001. At sptimes.com.

4. Ibid.

5. Jeff Testerman, "Chief's Ex-Pilot Set to Testify in Inquiry," *St. Petersburg Times,* 5 May 2001. At sptimes.com.

6. Ibid.

7. Testerman, "Chief's Hold on Seminoles Is Slipping."

8. Tim Cox, interview with the author, 11 Feb. 2004.

9. Jeff Testerman, "Seminole Backer's Role a Surprise," *St. Petersburg Times,* 1 July 2001. At sptimes.com.

10. On 14 June 1998.

11. Tribal Council Resolutions C-04-99 (Giannettino's termination) and C-07-99 (Wisher's employment), 7 July 1998.

12. Tim Cox, interview with the author, 21 Jan. 2004.

13. Tim Cox, interview with the author, 5 Apr. 2004.

14. Jeff Testerman, "Tribe's Operations Manager Earns Praise—and Criticism," *St. Petersburg Times,* 29 Apr. 2001. At ssptimes.com.

15. Tim Cox, interview with the author, 12 Jan. 2004.

16. Ibid. The quotes in the following paragraph are from this same interview.

17. Ibid.

18. Indian Child Welfare Act, *U.S. Statutes at Large* 92: 3069–76, 8 Nov. 1978.

19. Tim Cox, interview with the author, 12 Jan. 2004.

20. Ibid.

21. Ibid.

22. Tim Cox, interview with the author, 2 Feb. 2004.

23. Ibid.

24. Tim Cox, interview with the author, 16 Jan. 2004.

25. Tim Cox, interview with the author, 21 Jan. 2004.

26. Jeff Testerman, "Tribal Council Ousts Chief," *St. Petersburg Times,* 25 May 2001. At sptimes.com.

27. Erika Bolstad, "Seminole Leaders' Spending May Buy Trouble," *Miami Herald,* 5 Aug. 2001.

28. Ibid.

29. Tanya Weinberg, "After 22 Years, Seminole Leader's World Is Crumbling," *Fort Lauderdale Sun-Sentinel,* 10 June 2001. At sunsentinel.com.

30. Testerman, "Chief's Hold on Seminoles Is Slipping."

31. AP wire story, "Fired Worker Charges Seminole Chief Forced Her to Get Abortion," *Florida Times-Union,* Jacksonville, 10 May 2001.

32. Ibid.; and Jeff Testerman, "Woman Sues Tribal Chief over Sex Acts," *St. Petersburg Times,* 11 May 2001; Madeline Baró Díaz and Tanya Weinberg, "Ex-Worker Sues Chief for Sexual Bias, Firing," *South Florida Sun-Sentinel,* 11 May 2001, 1B, 2B; and Erika Bolstad, "Billie Faces Sexual Harassment Suit," *Miami Herald/Broward,* 11 May 2001, 2B.

33. Dara Kam, AP, "Removed Tribal Leader Says He Wasn't Elected for His Morals," *Naples Daily News,* 30 May 2001. At naplesnews.com.

34. This information concerning Helseth's cooperation was common knowledge in the tribal office building in early 2000. My information came directly from Mary Ella Gerchak, a tribal citizen who worked for Helseth. Helseth was frightened by the involvement of the

FBI and by knowledge that Jim Shore was cooperating with them. Helseth was not a strong individual, in any way.

35. Tribal Council Resolution C-38-00, 3 Aug. 1999.

36. Patrick Danner, "Lawsuit Gives Peek into Casino's Profit," *Miami Herald,* 24 Oct. 2002, Business Final, 1C.

37. Seminole Tribe of Florida, *Celebrating 50 Years of the Singing of Our Constitution and Corporate Charter* (Hollywood, FL: Seminole Communications, 2007), 105.

38. Jeff Testerman, "Seminoles Battle Baptists for Property," *St. Petersburg Times,* 13 July 2000. At sptimes.com.

39. Tribal Council Resolution C-04-96, 14 July 1995.

40. Tribal Council Resolution C-06-98, 18 July 1997.

41. Testerman, "Seminoles Battle Baptists for Property."

42. Tribal Council Resolution C-63-00, 12 Nov. 1999.

43. Robert Little and Mike Adams, "Enigmatic Partners Pursue a Rich Deal," *Baltimore Sun,* 15 Mar. 2004. At baltimoresun.com.

44. Roberto Santiago, "Trump: Partner Cheated Me Out of Deal," *Miami Herald,* 13 Apr. 2005, 1A.

45. Robert Little and Mike Adams, "A Developer Bets on Florida Fortune," *Baltimore Sun,* 14 Mar. 2004. At baltimoresun.com.

46. Ibid.

47. Robert Little and Mike Adams, "Enigmatic Partners Pursue a Rich Deal," *Baltimore Sun,* 15 Mar. 2004. At baltimoresun.com.

48. Robert Little and Mike Adams, "A Developer Bets on Florida Fortune," *Baltimore Sun,* 14 Mar. 2004. At baltimoresun.com.

49. Robert Little and Mike Adams, "'Great Things' Wherever He Goes," *Baltimore Sun,* 14 Mar. 2004. At baltimoresun.com.

50. Ibid.

51. Ibid.

52. Ibid.

53. Ibid

54. Christine O'Donnell, "Declaration of Christine O'Donnell under Penalties of Perjury," signed and notarized 15 Mar. 2003.

55. James Billie, telephone conversation with the author, 2 Jan. 2007.

Chapter 12

1. Jeff Testerman, "Tribe's Operations Manager Earns Praise—and Criticism," *St. Petersburg Times,* 29 Apr. 2001. At sptimes.com.

2. Tim Cox, interview with the author, 5 Apr. 2004.

3. Ibid.

4. For an excellent and succinct treatment of the nation's conditions and political problems, see, e.g., Joe DeRaymond, "Nicaragua Redux: The Strange Return of Daniel Ortega," *Counterpunch* e-zine, 22 Nov. 2006.

5. Tim Cox, interview with the author, 21 Jan. 2004.

6. Tim Cox, interview with the author, 5 Apr. 2004.

7. Jeff Testerman, "Chief's Hold on Seminoles Is Slipping," *St. Petersburg Times,* 29 Apr. 2001. At sptimes.com.

8. Ibid.; and Testerman, "Tribe's Operations Manager Earns Praise—and Criticism."

9. Erika Bolstad, "Managua Hotel at Center of Tribal Turmoil," *Miami Herald*, Broward, 24 June 2001, 1BR, 7BR.

10. Tim Cox, interview with the author, 5 Apr. 2004.

11. Jeff Testerman, "Tribe's Foreign Deals Get Scrutiny," *St. Petersburg Times,* 18 June 2001. At sptimes.com.

12. See, among many articles, "World Briefing/Americas: Nicaragua: Ex-President Ousted," *New York Times,* 20 Sept. 2002; David Gonzalez, "Nicaragua President Demands Corruption Trial for Predecessor," *New York Times,* 8 Aug. 2002; Eric Lichtblau, "U.S. Wants Foreign Leaders' Laundered Assets," *New York Times,* 23 Aug. 2003; "World Briefing/Americas: Nicaragua: 20-Year Sentence for Ex-President," *New York Times,* 9 Dec. 2003.

13. Tim Cox, interview with the author, 12 Apr. 2004.

14. Ibid.

15. Tim Cox, interview with the author, 5 Apr. 2004.

16. Tim Cox, interview with the author, 7 Apr. 2004.

17. Tim Cox, interview with the author, 5 Apr. 2004.

Chapter 13

1. Council Resolution C-133-01, 24 May 2001.

2. Baró Díaz and Weinberg, "Ex-Worker Sues Chief for Sexual Bias, Firing."

3. Little and Adams, "Enigmatic Partners Pursue a Rich Deal."

4. Jeff Testerman, "Tribe's Attorney Has No Room for Hate," *St. Petersburg Times,* 25 Apr. 2002. At sptimes.com.

5. Pat Diamond, personal conversation with the author, 15 June 2001.

6. Kam, "Removed Tribal Leader Says He Wasn't Elected for His Morals."

7. Tribal Council Resolution C-117-01, 25, Apr. 2001.

8. Erika Bolstad, "Seminole Board Takes Over Newspaper," [Miami] *Herald/Broward*, 7 May 2001, 1B, 2B.

9. Tribal Council Resolution C-120-01, 3 May 2001.

10. James E. Billie, chairman, to Franklin Keel, eastern area office superintendent [*sic*], BIA, 30 Aug. 2001.

11. Franklin Keel, director, BIA Eastern Regional Office, to James E. Billie, chairman, Seminole Tribe of Florida, 6 Sept. 2001.

12. Jim Shore, general counsel, Seminole Tribe of Florida, to Franklin Keel, director, BIA/Eastern Area Office, 7 Sept. 2001.

13. Jeff Testerman, "Letter Claims Seminole Leader Target of Probe," *St. Petersburg Times,* 17 Sept. 2001. At sptimes.com.

14. Tanya Weinberg, "Seminole Leader's Suspension Criticized," *Fort Lauderdale Sun-Sentinel,* 11 Sept. 2001, 5B.

15. Franklin Keel, director, BIA Eastern Regional Office, to James E. Billie, chairman, Seminole Tribe of Florida, 12 Sept. 2001; and Tanya Weinberg, "Indian Affairs Official

Backs Off Support for Ousted Chief Billie," *Fort Lauderdale Sun-Sentinel,* 14 Sept. 2001. At sunsentinel.com.

16. Franklin Keel, eastern area supervisor of the Bureau of Indian Affairs, personal conversations with the author, 14 Sept. 2006 and 1 June 2009.

17. Franklin Keel, director, BIA Eastern Regional Office, to Deputy Commissioner of Indian Affairs/Tribal Government Services, Washington, DC, 19 Sept. 2001.

18. Franklin Keel, personal communications with the author, 16 May 2006 and June 2009.

19. Erika Bolstad, "Seminole Leader Suspended Amid Finance Probe," *Miami Herald,* 25 May 2001, 1A, 2A.

20. Jeff Testerman, "Seminole Tribe Settles Sexual Harassment Lawsuit," *St. Petersburg Times,* 12 Oct. 2002. At http://www.pqasb.pqarchiver.com/sptimes.

21. Ibid.

22. Ibid.

23. Erika Bolstad, "Suspended Seminole Leader Takes New Troubles in Stride," *Miami Herald,* 27 May 2001.

24. Jeff Testerman, "FBI Looks into Gifts Billie Gave to Woman," *St. Petersburg Times,* 31 May 2001. At sptimes.com.

25. Tribal Council Resolution C-337-00, 31 Aug. 2000.

26. Erika Bolstad, "James Billie's Girlfriend Wins Legal Tiff with Wife," *Miami Herald,* 10 Aug. 2001.

27. James Billie, telephone conversation with the author, 20 Aug. 2001.

28. Bolstad, "James Billie's Girlfriend Wins Legal Tiff with Wife."

29. Pat Diamond, telephone conversation with the author, 7 Aug. 2003; and James Billie, telephone conversation with the author, 14 Aug. 2003.

30. AP. "Allies of Ousted Chief Are Fired," *Fort Lauderdale Sun-Sentinel,* 5 June 2001, at sunsentinel.com; and Jeff Testerman, "Tribal Council Fires Three," *St. Petersburg Times,* 5 June 2001. At sptimes.com.

31. Tribal Council Resolution, Personnel Actions, C-119-86, 1 Apr. 1986.

32. Tanya Weinberg, "Billie Sues Seminoles to Get His Job Back," *Fort Lauderdale Sun-Sentinel,* 7 June 2001. At sunsentinel.com.

33. Jim Shore, deposition, 6 Dec. 2002.

34. Erika Bolstad, "Ousted Leader Billie Sues Seminole Tribe," *Miami Herald,* 6 June 2001; Jeff Testerman, "Seminole Chief Files Lawsuit to Regain Tribal Council Post," *St. Petersburg Times,* 7 June 2001, at sptimes.com; Weinberg, "Billie Sues Seminoles to Get His Job Back"; and Jeff Testerman, "Suspended Seminole Leader Seeks a Rehearing," *St. Petersburg Times,* 20 June 2001, at sptimes.com.

35. Charles Flowers and Dan Ruck, "Seminole Chairman Works on Comeback," *South Florida Business Journal,* 31 Aug. 2001

36. Jeff Testerman, "Seminoles Sue Chief, Aide over Stocks," *St. Petersburg Times,* 6 Sept. 2001. At sptimes.com.

37. Jeff Testerman, "Seminoles May Have Lost Millions," *St. Petersburg Times,* 12 June 2001, at sptimes.com; and Testerman, "Seminoles Sue Chief, Aide over Stocks."

38. Weinberg, "Indian Affairs Official Backs Off Support for Ousted Chief Billie."

39. Tim Cox, interview with the author, 10 Mar. 2004.

40. Tim W. Cox, notes on his incarceration.

41. Wyatt Olson, "Gamblin' Men," *New Times,* 30 Jan.–5 Feb. 2003, 17–22.

42. This information was provided to the author on the day on which it occurred by an individual whose position it was to make the technological transfer, on condition of anonymity.

43. Jeff Testerman and Kathryn Wexler, "Seminole Tribe Attorney Shot at Home," *St. Petersburg Times,* 11 Jan. 2002.

44. Olson, "Gamblin' Men."

45. Ibid.

46. Ibid.

47. John Holland, "Trial Starts for 3 Men Accused of Stealing $2.7 million from Seminoles," *Fort Lauderdale Sun-Sentinel,* 3 Dec. 2002. At sunsentinel.com.

48. John Holland, "Testimony Weakens Seminole Fraud Case," *Fort Lauderdale Sun-Sentinel,* 4 Dec. 2002. At sunsentinel.com.

49. John Holland, "U.S. Agent Contradicts Gaming-Case Prosecutor," *Fort Lauderdale Sun-Sentinel,* 11 Dec. 2002, at sunsentinel.com; and John Holland, "FBI Analyst Testifies about Tribe Wire Transfers," *Fort Lauderdale Sun-Sentinel,* 13 Dec. 2002. At sunsentinel.com.

50. John Holland, "Former Seminole Leader Says He OK'd Millions for Internet Casino," *Fort Lauderdale Sun-Sentinel,* 17 Dec. 2002. At sunsentinel.com.

51. Jeff Testerman, "Billie Says He Okayed Gambling Project," *St. Petersburg Times,* 17 Dec. 2002. At sptimes.com.

52. John Holland, "Seminole Officials Went on Multimillion-Dollar Spending Spree with Gambling Profits," *Fort Lauderdale Sun-Sentinel,* 5 Dec. 2002. At sunsentinel.com.

53. For an excellent review of the relationship between David Cypress and Lawrence, see Sally Kestin, Peter Franceschina, and John Maines, "A Fast-Track Friendship," *South Florida Sun-Sentinel,* 28 Nov. 2007, 19A.

54. See, for example, the following articles, which include financial details and maps. Holland, "Seminole Officials Went on Multimillion-Dollar Spending Spree with Gambling Profits"; Sally Kestin, Peter Franceschina, and John Maines, "Seminole Jackpot," part 1 of 6, *South Florida Sun-Sentinel,* 25 Nov. 2007, 1A, 24A–28A; Kestin, Franceschina, and Maines, "Seminole Jackpot," part 2 of 6, *South Florida Sun-Sentinel,* 26 Nov. 2007, 1A, 22A–23A; Kestin, Franceschina, and Maines, "Houses of Contrast," part 3 of 6, *South Florida Sun-Sentinel,* 27 Nov. 2007, 1A, 10A; Kestin, Franceschina, and Maines, "Mountain of Debt," *South Florida Sun-Sentinel,* 27 Nov. 2007, 11A; Kestin, Franceschina, and Maines, "A Family Affair," part 4 of 6, *South Florida Sun-Sentinel,* 28 Nov. 2007, 1A, 18A; Kestin, Franceschina, and Maines, "A Fast-Track Friendship," *South Florida Sun-Sentinel,* 28 Nov. 2007, 19A; Kestin, Franceschina, and Maines, "Taxpayer Subsidies; Government Grants: The Tribe Continues to Get Lots of Federal Help," part 5 of 6. *South Florida Sun-Sentinel,* 29 Nov. 2007, 1A, 13A; and Kestin, Franceschina, and Maines, "NO CONSEQUENCES Council Spending: Federal Agencies Slow to Act on Violations," part 6 of 6, *South Florida Sun-Sentinel,* 30 Nov. 2007, 1A, 24A.

55. John Holland, "Trio Cleared as Judge Tosses Seminole Fraud Case," *Fort Lauderdale Sun-Sentinel,* 17 Dec. 2002, at sunsentinel.com; and John Holland, "Three Acquitted of Swindling Seminoles out of $2.7 Million," *Fort Lauderdale Sun-Sentinel,* 18 Dec. 2002, at sunsentinel.com.

56. Erika Bolstad, "Judge Throws Out Embezzlement Case against 3 Ex-Seminole Employees," *Miami Herald,* 18 Dec. 2002, 5B.

57. John Holland, "Feds Probe Tribe's Casino Profit," *South Florida Sun-Sentinel,* 21 Sept. 2003. As reprinted in the *Orlando Sentinel.*

58. Kestin, Franceschina, and Maines, "Mountain of Debt."

59. Sally Kestin and Peter Franceschina, "Seminole Official Is Freed of 3 Liens," *Fort Lauderdale Sun-Sentinel,* 4 Jan 2008, 1B, 7B.

60. Kestin, Franceschina, and Maines, "A Family Affair." For far greater details on this issue, see also the other segments of this six-part series, which ran on successive days.

61. Sally Kestin, "Seminole Land Deals Net Millions," *South Florida Sun-Sentinel,* 8 June 2008, 1A, 5A.

62. Kestin, Franceschina, and Maines, "A Family Affair."

63. This piece of information is not included in public news reports, but it was given to me by two tribal citizens who confided it at the time, on the basis of anonymity.

64. Vicky Agnew, Tanya Weinberg, and Jeff Shields, "Shooting of Seminole Tribal Counsel Was Planned Attack," *Fort Lauderdale Sun-Sentinel,* 11 Jan. 2002. At sunsentinel.com.

65. Daniel De Vise, Sara Olkon, and Elena Cabral, "Seminoles' Attorney Is Shot in Possible Murder Attempt," *Miami Herald,* 11 Jan. 2002.

66. Jeff Testerman and Kathryn Wexler, "Seminole Tribe Attorney Shot at Home," *St. Petersburg Times,* 11 Jan. 2002.

67. De Vise, Olkon, and Cabral, "Seminoles' Attorney Is Shot in Possible Murder Attempt."

68. Ibid.

69. Wanda Demarzo, "Focus Centers on Handyman in Shooting of Tribe Lawyer," *Miami Herald,* 21 Aug. 2003.

70. Flyer copy in the collections of the author.

71. Vicky Agnew, "Police Will Re-Stage Shooting of Seminole Lawyer in Hollywood," *Fort Lauderdale Sun-Sentinel,* 22 Nov. 2002. At sunsentinel.com.

72. Tanya Weinberg, "Seminoles Hire Hollywood Official for Administrator's Job," *Fort Lauderdale Sun-Sentinel,* 9 Jan. 2002. At sunsentinel.com.

73. Kestin, Franceschina, and Maines, "Seminole Jackpot."

74. Ibid.

75. For some statistics on Seminole education, see Elena Cabral, "Shifting Education's Focus—Seminoles Stress Survival of Culture," *Miami Herald,* 12 May 2003, final ed., 1A.

76. Tim Cox, interview with the author, 23 Jan. 2004.

Chapter 14

1. James E. Billie, chairman, to Priscilla Sayen, tribal secretary/treasurer, 3 Jan. 2003.

2. Ibid.

3. Elena Cabral, "Billie, Tribal Cops in Standoff," *Miami Herald,* 8 Jan. 2003.

4. Council Resolution C-76-03, 27 Feb. 2003.

5. John Holland, "Seminoles Plan Formal End of Chief Billie's Long Reign," *Fort Lauderdale Sun-Sentinel,* 28 Feb. 2003. At sunsentinel.com.

6. Council Resolution C-76-03, 27 Feb. 2003, "Statement of Charges," points 7, 8, 9.

7. Priscilla Sayen, tribal secretary, to all departments, 21 Mar. 2003, memorandum.

8. Jerry Berrios, "Seminoles Meet New Leaders," *Miami Herald,* 3 June 2003.

9. Jerry Berrios, "Small Tribe's Big Splash," *Miami Herald,* 5 Dec. 2003, 1A, 2A; and Michael Kelly, "Tribal Citizens Take Hard-Hat Tour of Seminole Hard Rock Hotel & Casino," *Seminole Tribune,* 19 Dec. 2003, 17.

10. Berrios, "Small Tribe's Big Splash."

11. Mimi Whitefield, Editor's Note: "Vegas-Style Glitz Arrives at Seminole Reservation," *Miami Herald,* Business Monday, 10 May 2004, 3; and Christina Hoag and Jerry Berrios, "Seminole Gaming Rocks & Rolls," *Miami Herald,* Business Monday, 10 May 2004, 22–26.

12. Robert Little and Mike Adams, "Chief Fought the Law, and Tribe Won," *Baltimore Sun,* 14 Mar. 2004. At baltimoresun.com.

13. Michael Mayo, "Will the Anti-Gambling Seminoles Shut Their Casinos?" *South Florida Sun-Sentinel,* 7 Nov. 2004. At sunsentinel.com.

14. Ibid.

15. *Seminole Tribune,* 19 Mar. 2004, 4; *Seminole Tribune,* 30 Apr. 2004, 6; *Seminole Tribune,* 21 May 2004, 7; and John Holland, "Perilous Everglades Route on a New Path," *South Florida Sun-Sentinel,* 29 Jan. 2005, 12B.

16. Official Tribal Election Returns.

17. Fred Grimm, "In My Opinion: Jeb Should've Told Seminoles to Deal Us In," *Miami Herald,* 21 June 2005.

18. See www.news-press.com, posting by "scubachick."

19. See www.news-press.com, posting by "38pitches."

20. Erika Bolstad, "Peace between a Tribe and Its Ex-Chief," *Miami Herald,* 23 Mar. 2006, 6B.

21. James Billie, telephone conversation with the author, 27 July 2006; see also Thom Smith, "Party People: Ex-Chief Billie Is Flying High," *Palm Beach Post,* 8 Oct. 2006, 4D.

22. Mike Clary, "Seminole Tribe Blocks Billie as Candidate for Chairman," *Fort Lauderdale Sun-Sentinel,* 25 Apr. 2007, 9B.

23. Jon Burstein, "Seminole Tribal Chairman Wins Re-Election; One Council Member Ousted," *Fort Lauderdale Sun-Sentinel,* 15 May 2007, at sunsentinel.com; Jon Burstein, "Seminole Chairman Wins 2nd Term," *Fort Lauderdale Sun-Sentinel,* 16 May 2007, at sunsentinel.com; and Roberto Santiago, "Tribal Election Upheld," *Miami Herald,* 25 May 2007, 2B.

24. Fred Grimm, "Chief Billie Shrugs Off His Fall from Power," *Miami Herald,* 17 May 2007, 3B.

Epilogue

1. John Holland, "Tribe Wants to End Deal with Casino Developers," *South Florida Sun-Sentinel,* 23 May 2006.

2. Jon Burstein, "Seminoles, Developer Reach Tentative $756 Million Deal," *Fort Lauderdale Sun-Sentinel,* 3 Mar. 2007.

3. Jon Stewart, *The Daily Show*, 11 Dec. 2006. See also Robert Barr, AP, "Seminoles Buy Parent Company of Hard Rock Casinos, Hotels, for $965 Million," *South Florida Sun-Sentinel*, 7 Dec. 2006.

4. Christina Hoag, "Rock 'N' Deal," *Miami Herald*, 8 Dec. 2006, 1A, 2A.

5. John Lantigua, "Gaming Lets Seminoles Turn Tables on Poverty," *Palm Beach Post*, 4 Feb. 2007, 1A, 6A.

6. Greg Smith, ed., *Native American Law Digest* 17, no. 1 (2007).

7. Dara Kam, "Interior Gives Florida Tribal Slots Deadline," *Palm Beach Post*, 28 June 2007, 4A.

8. Jon Burstein, "Governor, Seminoles Close to Slots Plan," *South Florida Sun-Sentinel*, 20 Aug. 2007, 8B. See also Dara Kam, "Crist OKs Gaming Deal with Seminoles," *Palm Beach Post, South County*, 15 Nov. 2007, 1A 7A.

9. Linda Kleindienst and John Holland, "Seminoles Hit Jackpot," *South Florida Sun-Sentinel*, 15 Nov. 2007, 1A.

10. John Holland, "Compact in 'Middle-Range,'" *South Florida Sun-Sentinel*, 15 Nov. 2007, 5B.

11. Kam, "Crist OKs Gaming Deal with Seminoles"; Kleindienst and Holland, "Seminoles Hit Jackpot."

12. Burstein, "Governor, Seminoles Close to Slots Plan."

13. See, among others, Linda Kleindienst and Ihosvani Rodriguez, "Official Seeks Delay of Tribal Gaming Compact," *South Florida Sun-Sentinel*, 21 Dec. 2007; AP, "Gambling Deal between Crist, Seminoles Receives Federal OK," *Palm Beach Post*, 3 Jan. 2008; Brendan Farrington, AP, "Seminole Gambling Compact with State Officially in Effect," *Fort Lauderdale Sun-Sentinel*, 8 Jan. 2008; and John Holland, "Is Compact Confusing? You Bet," *Fort Lauderdale Sun-Sentinel*, 24 Feb. 2008.

14. Randy Schultz, "Seminoles Up the Ante in Latest 'War,'" *Palm Beach Post*, 20 July 2008, 1E.

15. Tim Cox, interview with the author, 23 Jan. 2004.

16. Les Kjos, "Seminoles in Time of Turmoil," UPI News, 10 June 2001.

Bibliography

Newspapers

"4 Are Indicted in Scheme Using Tribe to Obtain U.S. Equipment." *New York Times.* 9 Oct. 1994.

Agnew, Vicky. "Police Will Re-Stage Shooting of Seminole Lawyer in Hollywood." *Fort Lauderdale Sun-Sentinel,* 22 Nov. 2002. At sunsentinel.com.

Agnew, Vicky, Tanya Weinberg, and Jeff Shields. "Shooting of Seminole Tribal Counsel Was Planned Attack." *Fort Lauderdale Sun-Sentinel,* 11 Jan. 2002. At sunsentinel.com.

"Around, Pilot: I Gave 'Cash Gift' to Ex-Seminole Chief." *Miami Herald,* 3 June 2002, 6B.

Associated Press. "Allies of Ousted Chief Are Fired." *Fort Lauderdale Sun-Sentinel,* 5 June 2001. At sunsentinel.com.

———. "Ex-Pilot Tells of Payments to Tribe Leader." *Fort Lauderdale Sun-Sentinel,* 3 June 2002. At sunsentinel.com.

———. "Fired Worker Charges Seminole Chief Forced Her to Get Abortion." *Florida Times-Union,* Jacksonville, FL, 10 May 2001.

———. "Gambling Deal between Crist, Seminoles Receives Federal OK." *Palm Beach Post,* 3 Jan. 2008.

———. "Indian Gambling Compact Goes into Effect, State Gets $50 Million." *Palm Beach Post,* 8 Jan. 2008.

———. "Shot Seminole Tribal Lawyer Now in Hiding." 4 Feb. 2002.

Athans, Marego, and Mike Adams. "Glamour, Glitz and the Wall." *Baltimore Sun,* 14 Mar. 2004. At baltimoresun.com.

Baró Díaz, Madeline, and Tanya Weinberg. "Ex-Worker Sues Chief for Sexual Bias, Firing." *South Florida Sun-Sentinel,* 11 May 2001, 1B, 2B.

Barr, Robert, AP. "Seminoles Buying Parent Company of Hard Rock Casinos, Hotels, for $965 Million." *South Florida Sun-Sentinel,* 7 Dec. 2006.

Bernard, Ricardo. "Use of Indian Names Debated." *Fort Lauderdale Sun-Sentinel,* 16 June 2000, 5B.

Berrios, Jerry. "Seminoles Meet New Leader." *Miami Herald,* 3 June 2003.

———. "Small Tribe's Big Splash." *Miami Herald,* 5 Dec. 2003, 1A, 2A.

Bolstad, Erika. "Billie Faces Sexual Harassment Suit." *Miami Herald/Broward*, 11 May 2001, 2B.

———. "Feds: Seminoles Wrong in Suspension." *Miami Herald*, 8 Sept. 2001.

———. "Hollywood Film Uses Slice of Seminole Reservation." *Miami Herald*, 1 July 2001.

———. "James Billie's Girlfriend Wins Legal Tiff with Wife." *Miami Herald*, 10 Aug. 2001.

———. "Judge Throws Out Embezzlement Case against 3 Ex-Seminole Employees." *Miami Herald*, 18 Dec. 2002, 5B.

———. "Managua Hotel at Center of Tribal Turmoil." *Miami Herald/Broward*, 24 June 2001, 1BR, 7BR.

———. "Meeting on Seminole Gambling Postponed by Interior Dept." *Miami Herald/Broward*, 16 May 2001.

———. "Ousted Leader Billie Sues Seminole Tribe." *Miami Herald*, 6 June 2001.

———. "Peace between a Tribe and Its Ex-Chief." *Miami Herald*, 23 Mar. 2006, 6B.

———. "Petition Drive Seeks Return of Seminole Leader." *Miami Herald*, 1 June 2001.

———. "Seminole Board Takes Over Newspaper." *Miami Herald/Broward*, 7 May 2001, 1B, 2B.

———. "Seminole Leader Suspended Amid Finance Probe." *Miami Herald*, 25 May 2001, 1A, 2A.

———. "Seminole Leaders' Spending May Buy Trouble." *Miami Herald*, 5 Aug. 2001.

———. "Seminole Portfolio at Center of Strife." *Miami Herald/Broward*, 17 Sept. 2001, 1B, 2B.

———. "Seminole Tribe: Ex-Chairman to Receive $600K [*sic*] for Apology." *Miami Herald*, 23 Mar. 2006, 1B, 2B.

———. "Seminoles Fire Manager Amid Rumors of U.S. Probe." *Miami Herald/Broward*, 11 May 2001, 1B, 2B.

———. "Seminoles' Pilot Flip-Flops on Tax Plea." *Miami Herald*, 26 Aug. 2001.

———. "Suspended Seminole Leader Takes New Troubles in Stride." *Miami Herald*, 27 May 2001.

———. "Tribe Rooted in Hardship Grows into Rich Enterprise." *Miami Herald*, 5 Aug. 2001.

Burstein, Jon. "Governor, Seminoles Close to Slots Plan." *South Florida Sun-Sentinel*, 20 Aug. 2007, 8B.

———. "Seminole Chairman Wins 2nd Term." *Fort Lauderdale Sun-Sentinel*, 16 May 2007. At sunsentinel.com.

———. "Seminole Tribal Chairman Wins Re-Election; One Council Member Ousted." *Fort Lauderdale Sun-Sentinel*, 15 May 2007. At sunsentinel.com.

———. "Seminoles, Developer Reach Tentative $756 Million Deal." *Fort Lauderdale Sun-Sentinel*, 3 Mar. 2007.

———. "Seminoles Submit Grand Casino Plan." *South Florida Sun-Sentinel*, 23 Jan 2007, 4B.

Cabral, Elena. "Billie, Tribal Cops in Standoff." *Miami Herald*, 8 Jan 2003.

———. "Former Manager of Tribe Indicted by Feds." *Miami Herald*, 25 June 2002, 1B, 2B.

———. "Road to Riches." *Miami Herald*, 11 May 2003. At nl.newsbank.com.

———. "Shifting Education's Focus—Seminoles Stress Survival of Culture." *Miami Herald*, 12 May 2003, final ed., 1A.

"Case Ended in the Death of a Panther." *New York Times*, 11 Oct. 1987.

Clary, Mike. "Culture Clash." *South Florida Sun-Sentinel,* 26 Nov. 2007, 22A–23A.

———. "Fast Fortune, Big Spending." *South Florida Sun-Sentinel,* 25 Nov. 2007, 1G–8G.

———. "Four Years after $60 Million Scandal, Ousted Leader of Seminoles Ready for Comeback." *Fort Lauderdale Sun-Sentinel,* 20 Apr. 2007, 1A, 2A.

———. "Seminole Tribe Blocks Billie as Candidate for Chairman." *Fort Lauderdale Sun-Sentinel,* 25 Apr. 2007, 9B.

Clary, Mike, and John Maines. "'Res Disease' Proving to Be a Real Killer." *Fort Lauderdale Sun-Sentinel,* 29 Sept. 2008, 1, 8.

Cone, Clay W. "Immokalee-Based Air Service to Cuba Appears to Be Grounded." *Immokalee Independent,* 10 July 1998, 1A, 2A.

Danner, Patrick. "Casino Company Fine Upheld." *Miami Herald,* 20 Apr. 2001.

———. "Lawsuit Gives Peek into Casino's Profit." *Miami Herald,* 24 Oct. 2002, Business final, 1C.

De Vise, Daniel, Sara Olkon, and Elena Cabral. "Seminoles' Attorney Is Shot in Possible Murder Attempt." *Miami Herald,* 11 Jan. 2002. At herald.com.

DeGroot, John. "James Billie: Born as an Outcast, Leader Still Very Much a Man Alone." *Baltimore Sun,* from the *South Florida Sun-Sentinel,* 16 Feb. 1986. At baltimoresun.com.

Demarzo, Wanda. "Focus Centers on Handyman in Shooting of Tribe Lawyer." *Miami Herald,* 21 Aug. 2003.

DeRaymond, Joe. "Nicaragua Redux: The Strange Return of Daniel Ortega." *Counterpunch* e-zine, 22 Nov. 2006.

DiPaola, Jim. "Seminole Warrior." *City Link,* 26 Dec.–1 Jan. 2002, 16–25.

Doctor, Barbara. *Seminole Tribune,* 1, no. 6 (28 Dec. 1983), 1.

Dorschner, John. "Bury My Heart on Custer Street." *Miami Herald Tropic,* 8 Apr. 1979.

———. "The Great Indian Bingo War." *Miami Herald Tropic,* 31 Oct. 1993, and *Seminole Tribune,* 20, no. 19 (23 Jan. 1998).

Driscoll, Amy. "The School That Slots Built." *Miami Herald,* 1 Nov. 2007, 1A, 2A.

"Ex-Lawman Guilty of Drug Trafficking." *Dallas Morning News,* Jan. 1993.

Fantz, Ashley. "Rare Portrait of Famed Chief Shown." *Miami Herald,* 18 Aug. 2006, 6B.

Farrington, Brendan, AP. "Seminole Gambling Compact with State Officially in Effect." *Fort Lauderdale Sun-Sentinel,* 8 Jan. 2008.

Finn, Allison. "Amid Tears, Tribe Changes Leaders." *Miami Herald,* Tues., 5 June 1979, 1, 3BR.

"Florida Seminoles Favor 16 Million." *Alligator Times* 2, no. 1 (Dec.–Jan. 1976), 1.

Florin, Hector. "Ruling on Seminole Leader's Suspension Is Called 'Premature' by Federal Official." *Miami Herald,* 15 Sept. 2001.

Flowers, Charles, and Dan Ruck. "Seminole Chairman Works on Comeback." *South Florida Business Journal,* 31 Aug. 2001. At southflorida.bcentral.com.

Franceschina, Peter. "Other Tribal Leaders Have Landed in Court over Use of Funds." *South Florida Sun-Sentinel,* 30 Nov. 2007, 25A.

Gallagher, Peter B. "New Year, New Budget for Tribal Council." *Seminole Tribune,* 20, no. 19 (23 Jan. 1998).

Goldstein, Brad, David Adams, and Jeff Testerman. "Seminoles Gain Entry in Caribbean Casino." *St. Petersburg Times,* 20 Dec. 1997, 13A.

Goldstein, Brad, and Jeff Testerman. "Regulators Have Ties to Seminoles." *St. Petersburg Times,* 20 Dec. 1997, 1A.

———. "Seminole Gambling: A Trail of Millions." *St. Petersburg Times,* 21 Dec. 1997, 6A.

González, David. "Nicaragua President Demands Corruption Trial for Predecessor." *New York Times,* 8 Aug. 2002

"Grand Opening of the Ah-Tha-Thi-Ki Museum." Commemorative issue, *Seminole Tribune* (1997).

Grimm, Fred. "Chief Billie Shrugs Off His Fall from Power." *Miami Herald,* 17 May 2007, 3B.

———. "In My Opinion: Jeb Should've Told Seminoles to Deal Us In." *Miami Herald,* 21 June 2005.

———. "No One Kept Tabs on Tribe's Expenses." *Miami Herald,* 5 Aug. 2001.

Guy, Kingsley. "Gambling: Debate Turning Nonsensical." *South Florida Sun-Sentinel,* 28 Nov. 2007, 31A.

Hafenbrack, Josh. "Casinos Face Two Futures in Two Bills." *Fort Lauderdale Sun-Sentinel,* 25 Mar. 2009, 6B.

———. "House Panel to Review Casino Deal with Seminoles." *Fort Lauderdale Sun-Sentinel,* 10 Dec. 2008.

———. "Seminole Gambling Compact in Trouble." *Fort Lauderdale Sun-Sentinel,* 5 Mar. 2009, 1, 12.

Harrison, Kirby J. "Flying for the Tribe." *Aviation International News* (Apr. 1999).

Hirth, Diane. "FSU Introduces Course on Seminole History." *Tallahassee Democrat,* 20 Sept. 2006. At tallahasseedemocrat.com.

Hitt, Jack. "The Newest Indians." *New York Times Magazine,* 21 Aug. 2005.

Hoag, Christina. "Rock 'N' Deal." *Miami Herald,* 8 Dec. 2006, 1A, 2A.

Hoag, Christina, and Jerry Berrios. "Seminole Gaming Rocks & Rolls." *Miami Herald/Business Monday,* 10 May 2004, 22–26.

Holland, John. "Billie Demands to Be Reinstated as Seminole Chairman." *Fort Lauderdale Sun-Sentinel,* 8 Jan. 2003. At sunsentinel.com.

———. "Case against Tribe Puts Park Residents in Limbo." *Fort Lauderdale Sun-Sentinel,* 15 Feb. 2008

———. "Compact in 'Middle-Range.'" *South Florida Sun-Sentinel,* 15 Nov. 2007, 5B.

———. "FBI Analyst Testifies about Tribe Wire Transfer." *Fort Lauderdale Sun-Sentinel,* 13 Dec. 2002. At sunsentinel.com.

———. "Feds Probe Tribe's Casino Profit." *South Florida Sun-Sentinel,* 21 Sept. 2003. As reprinted in the *Orlando Sentinel.*

———. "Former Seminole Leader Says He OK'd Millions for Internet Casino." *Fort Lauderdale Sun-Sentinel,* 17 Dec. 2002. At sunsentinel.com.

———. "Help Sought Halting Gaming." *Fort Lauderdale Sun-Sentinel,* 20 Sept. 2008.

———. "Interior Department: 'Good Riddance' to Gale Norton, but the Problems at Interior Remain." *Washington Spectator,* 32, no. 9 (1 May 2006), 1–2.

———. "Is Compact Confusing? You Bet." *Fort Lauderdale Sun-Sentinel,* 24 Feb. 2008.

———. "Perilous Everglades Route on a New Path." *South Florida Sun-Sentinel,* 29 Jan. 2005, 12B.

——. "Seminole Museum Opens in Broward." *South Florida Sun-Sentinel,* 18 May 2005.

——. "Seminole Officials Went on Multimillion-Dollar Spending Spree with Gambling Profits." *Fort Lauderdale Sun-Sentinel,* 5 Dec. 2002. At sunsentinel.com.

——. "Seminole Spending Draws IRS Attention." *Fort Lauderdale Sun-Sentinel,* 27 Dec. 2002, 1B, 2B.

——. "Seminole Tribe Elects New Leader, but Billie Challenges Result." *Fort Lauderdale Sun-Sentinel,* 14 May 2003. At sunsentinel.com.

——. "Seminole Tribe Hits Jackpot as Tracks Stumble." *Fort Lauderdale Sun-Sentinel,* [March?] 2008.

——. "Seminoles Plan Formal End of Chief Billie's Long Reign." *Fort Lauderdale Sun-Sentinel,* 28 Feb. 2003. At sunsentinel.com.

——. "Seminoles Seek to Expand Gambling." *Fort Lauderdale Sun-Sentinel,* 2 Feb. 2009.

——. "Seminoles Want Out of Casinos, Hotel Contract." *South Florida Sun-Sentinel,* 14 Oct. 2005.

——. "Testimony Weakens Seminole Fraud Case." *Fort Lauderdale Sun-Sentinel,* 4 Dec. 2002. At sunsentinel.com.

——. "Three Acquitted of Swindling Seminoles out of $2.7 Million." *Fort Lauderdale Sun-Sentinel,* 18 Dec. 2002. At sunsentinel.com.

——. "Trial Starts for 3 Men Accused of Stealing $2.7 Million from Seminoles." *Fort Lauderdale Sun-Sentinel,* 3 Dec. 2002. At sunsentinel.com.

——. "Tribal Leader's Allies Cleared." *Fort Lauderdale Sun-Sentinel,* 18 Dec. 2002. At sunsentinel.com.

——. "Tribe Wants to End Deal with Casino Developers." *South Florida Sun-Sentinel,* 23 May 2006. At sunsentinel.com.

——. "Trio Cleared as Judge Tosses Seminole Fraud Case." *Fort Lauderdale Sun-Sentinel,* 17 Dec. 2002. At sunsentinel.com.

——. "U.S. Agent Contradicts Gaming-Case Prosecutor." *Fort Lauderdale Sun-Sentinel,* 11 Dec. 2002. At sunsentinel.com.

——. "Yankees, Seminoles Strike Up Tasty Deal." *Fort Lauderdale Sun-Sentinel,* [March] 2008.

Hunt, April. "Frey Won't Wage County's Casino Fight." *Orlando Sentinel,* 4 Apr. 2001.

——. "Keller Plans Casino Fight." *Orlando Sentinel,* 1 June 2001.

——. "Keller Tries to Derail Casino." *Orlando Sentinel,* 29 June 2001. At orlandosentinel.com.

"In Best Interests of the Seminoles." Op-Ed. *St. Petersburg Times,* 15 June 2001. At sptimes.com.

"Indian Leader Faces Trial in Panther Slaying." *New York Times,* 12 Feb. 1984.

Jackson, Jerry W. "American Indians Discuss Opportunities: The Choctaws from Mississippi Shared How They've Diversified into Manufacturing." *Orlando Sentinel,* 23 Sept. 2003. At orlandosentinel.com.

Jalonick, Mary Clare. "Senate OKs Bill to Improve Health Care on Reservations." *Fort Lauderdale Sun-Sentinel,* 27 Feb. 2008.

Jordan, Don. "Seminole Charter School: Hope Alive for Dying Language." *Palm Beach Post,* 9 Dec. 2007, 1A, 8A.

Kam, Dara. "Court Declines to Hear Case over Gambling." *Palm Beach Post*, 12 Sept. 2008, 2A.

——. "Crist OKs Gaming Deal with Seminoles." *Palm Beach Post, South County*, 15 Nov. 2007, 1A 7A.

——. "Interior Gives Florida Tribal Slots Deadline." *Palm Beach Post*, 28 June 2007, 4A.

——. "New Panel Will Negotiate Gambling Deal with Tribe." *Palm Beach Post*, 10 Dec. 2008.

——. "Removed Tribal Leader Says He Wasn't Elected for His Morals." *Naples Daily News*, 30 May 2001. At naplesnews.com.

——. "Seminole Bed 'Taxes' Don't Go to State, Tribe Tells Lawmakers." *Palm Beach Post*, 12 Feb. 2009.

——. "Seminoles Would Hold Vegas Slots, Fold Card Games, under Proposal." *Palm Beach Post*, 10 Dec. 2008, 1A, 10A.

——. "Tourism Officials Deny Asking Seminoles to Charge Hotel Tax." *Palm Beach Post*, 13 Feb. 2009.

Karp, David. "Attorney: Seminole Casinos Didn't Launder Cash." *St. Petersburg Times*, 20 Apr. 2000. At sptimes.com.

——. "Tribe Inquiry Trapped Defendants, Lawyers Say." *St. Petersburg Times*, 21 Apr. 2000. At sptimes.com.

Kelly, Michael. "Tribal Citizens Take Hard-Hat Tour of Seminole Hard Rock Hotel & Casino." *Seminole Tribune*, 24, no. 17 (19 Dec. 2003), 17.

Kent, Cindy, comp. "People in the News." *Fort Lauderdale Sun-Sentinel*, 18 June 2001. At sunsentinel.com/business.

Kestin, Sally. "FEMA Paid Tribe's Hotel Tab." *South Florida Sun-Sentinel*, 29 Nov. 2007. At sunsentinel.com.

——. "Seminole Land Deals Net Millions." *South Florida Sun-Sentinel*, 8 June 2008, 1A, 5A.

Kestin, Sally, and Peter Franceschina. "Feds Look at Seminole Spending." *South Florida Sun-Sentinel*, 8 Dec. 2007, 1A, 10A.

——. "Seminole Official Is Freed of 3 Liens." *Fort Lauderdale Sun-Sentinel*, 4 Jan 2008, 1B, 7B.

Kestin, Sally, Peter Franceschina, and John Maines. "A Family Affair." Part 4 of 6. *South Florida Sun-Sentinel*, 28 Nov. 2007, 1A, 18A.

——. "A Fast-Track Friendship." *South Florida Sun-Sentinel*, 28 Nov. 2007, 19A.

——. "Grants Continued Despite Rule Violations, Records Show." *South Florida Sun-Sentinel*, 29 Nov. 2007, 13A.

——. "Houses of Contrast." Part 3 of 6. *South Florida Sun-Sentinel*, 27 Nov. 2007, 1A, 10A.

——. "Mountain of Debt." *South Florida Sun-Sentinel*, 27 Nov. 2007, 11A.

——. "NO CONSEQUENCES Council Spending: Federal Agencies Slow to Act on Violations." Part 6 of 6. *South Florida Sun-Sentinel*, 30 Nov. 2007, 1A, 24A.

——. "Seminole Jackpot." Part 1 of 6. *South Florida Sun-Sentinel*, 25 Nov. 2007, 1A, 24A–28A.

——. "Seminole Jackpot." Part 2 of 6. *South Florida Sun-Sentinel*, 26 Nov. 2007, 1A, 22A-23A.

———. "Taxpayer Subsidies: Government Grants: The Tribe Continues to Get Lots of Federal Help." Part 5 of 6. *South Florida Sun-Sentinel,* 29 Nov. 2007, 1A, 13A.

———. "Who Could Be Casino Winners?" *South Florida Sun-Sentinel,* 30 Dec. 2007, 1A, 6A.

King, Robert P. "Bush Wants U.S. out of Glades Cleanup." *Palm Beach Post,* 3 Feb. 2006, 1A, 6A.

Kjos, Les. "Seminoles in Time of Turmoil." UPI News, 10 June 2001.

Klas, Mary Ellen. "Senate to Offer 'Substantial' Compromise." *Miami Herald,* 5 May 2009.

Klas, Mary Ellen, and Gary Fineout. "Casino Developer a Big Donor to Ally of Crist." *Miami Herald,* 4 Aug. 2006.

Kleindienst, Linda, and John Holland. "Seminoles Hit Jackpot." *South Florida Sun-Sentinel,* 15 Nov. 2007, 1A.

Kleindienst, Linda, and Ihosvani Rodríguez. "Official Seeks Delay of Tribal Gaming Compact." *South Florida Sun-Sentinel,* 21 Dec. 2007.

La Corte, Rachel. "Seminoles to Elect New Chairman to Replace Ousted Leader Today." *Fort Lauderdale Sun-Sentinel,* 12 May 2003. At sunsentinel.com.

Lantigua, John. "Gaming Lets Seminoles Turn Tables on Poverty." *Palm Beach Post,* 4 Feb. 2007, 1A, 6A.

"Leading the Tribe, Issue: Seminoles' Council Makes Questionable Funding Decisions." Editorials. *South Florida Sun-Sentinel.* Jan. 2008, 26A.

Lichtblau, Eric. "U.S. Wants Foreign Leaders' Laundered Assets." *New York Times,* 23 Aug. 2003.

Liss, Robert. "U.S. Offers Seminoles $16 Million for Land; 25-Year Wrangle Ends." *Miami Herald,* 22 Jan. 1976.

Little, Robert, and Mike Adams. "Chief Fought the Law, and Tribe Won." *Baltimore Sun,* 14 Mar. 2004. At baltimoresun.com.

———. "A Developer Bets on Florida Fortune." *Baltimore Sun,* 14 Mar. 2004. At baltimoresun.com.

———. "Enigmatic Partners Pursue a Rich Deal." *Baltimore Sun,* 15 Mar. 2004. At baltimoresun.com.

———. "'Great Things' Wherever He Goes." *Baltimore Sun,* 14 Mar. 2004. At baltimoresun.com.

———. "Inquiries, Chief's Ouster Delayed Seminole Casinos." *Orlando Sentinel* (*Baltimore Sun*), 15 Mar. 2004. At baltimoresun.com.

Longman, Phillip. "Crapshoot: Casino Promoters Promise Floridians a Chance to Win Big (Part 1)." *Florida Trend,* May 1994, 30–36.

Lowry, Rich. "Sham Shamans: A Boom in Fake Indians." *New York Post,* 15 Mar. 2005, 35. (*National Review*).

Lucey, William. "James Billie at a Glance." *Fort Lauderdale Sun-Sentinel,* 20 Apr. 2007. At sunsentinel.com.

Mayo, Michael. "Will the Anti-Gambling Seminoles Shut Their Casinos?" *South Florida Sun-Sentinel,* 7 Nov. 2004. At sunsentinel.com.

Miller, Carol Marbin. "Court Rejects Tribe's Effort to Raise Boy." *Miami Herald,* 31 May 2007, 1A, 5A.

"Mistrial Declared in Panther Killing." *New York Times,* 28 Aug. 1987.

Moosha, Joe. "Seminole Chief Retains a Sense of History." *Hollywood Sun-Tattler,* Thurs., 5 July 1979, 1A, 2A.

"NCAA Allowing Florida State to Use Its Mascot." *USA Today.* At http://www.usatoday .com/sports/college/2005-08-23-fsu-mascot-approved_x.htm.

Nickell, David. "Cashing In on Bingo: Are the Seminoles Married to the Mob?" *XS* magazine, 16 Feb. 1994.

Nordheimer, Jon. "Jury Is Tied in Killing of Panther." *New York Times,* 27 Aug. 1987.

"Oklahoma Seminoles OK Name." *USA Today.* At http://.www.usatoday.com/sports/ college/2005-08-11-fsu-mascot-support_x.htm.

Olson, Wyatt. "Gamblin' Men." *New Times,* 30 Jan.–5 Feb. 2003, 17–22.

O'Neill, Tex. "Ex-Sheriff Pleads Guilty to Four Cocaine Charges." *Charlotte Observer,* 13 Feb. 1993, 3A.

"Panther-Killing Case Dropped." *New York Times,* 10 Oct. 1987.

Parks, Cynthia. "What State's Doing about Swamp Ghetto." *Florida Times-Union and Jacksonville Journal,* Sunday, 7 June 1970, H-1.

Piccoli, Sean. "Native Wisdom." *Fort Lauderdale Sun-Sentinel,* 25 June 2000, 1D, 10D.

Plunkett, R. B., Jr., Paul Moran, and Bob Schwartzman. "Seminoles' Shops Linked to Organized Crime Figures." *Fort Lauderdale News and Sun-Sentinel,* 22 July 1979, 1A, 16A.

Price, Jeff, AP. "Tribe Supports FSU nickname." *Miami Herald,* 18 June 2005.

Reid, Andy. "Seminole Tribute to Raise Presence of Art in Tampa." *Tampa Tribune,* 24 July 2003.

Rodríguez, Ihosvani. "Billie Convicted in Deaths of Sons." *South Florida Sun-Sentinel,* 3 Feb. 2005.

Sainz, Adrian, AP. "Indian Gaming Growth Slows, but Still up 11%." *Palm Beach Post,* [June] 2007.

Salisbury, Susan. "Source-Verified Beef Diminishes Worries." *Palm Beach Post,* 20 June 2005.

———. "Tribe's Traceable Cattle Prime for BSE-Wary Japan." [*Palm Beach Post,* n.d., 2004].

Santiago, Roberto. "The American Dream: Seminole Style." *Miami Herald,* 29 July 2007, 1A, 22A.

———. "Cities to Fight a Rule to Allow Casino Growth." *Palm Beach Post,* 27 Dec. 2007.

———. "Historic Find: A Letter to the Cowkeeper." *Miami Herald,* 5 June 2006, 1A, 2A.

———. "Native Pride." *Miami Herald,* 24 Nov. 2006, n.p.

———. "Ousted Leader Seeking Seat." *Miami Herald,* 30 Apr. 2007, 1B, 2B.

———. "Suing Seminoles over Injuries Hit-and-Miss Proposition." *Palm Beach Post,* 24 July 2005.

———. "Tribal Election Upheld." *Miami Herald,* 25 May 2007, 2B.

———. "Trump: Partner Cheated Me Out of Deal." *Miami Herald,* 13 Apr. 2005, 1A.

Satchell, Arlene. "From Pasture to Plate: Seminoles Add Beef Brand to Financial Empire." *Fort Lauderdale Sun-Sentinel,* 11 Mar. 2008, 1D, 2D.

Schultz, Randy. "Seminoles up the Ante in Latest 'War.'" *Palm Beach Post,* 20 July 2008, 1E.

Schwartz, Noaki. "Hollywood Residents Rally for More Security after Shooting of Seminole Lawyer." *Fort Lauderdale Sun-Sentinel,* 14 Jan. 2002. At sunsentinel.com.

"Seminole Chief Denies Guilt in Panther Case." *New York Times,* 24 Apr. 1987.

Seminole Tribal Council. "Stories Missed Tribe's Strong Local Impact." *Fort Lauderdale Sun-Sentinel,* 11 Dec. 2007.

"Seminole Tribe: Business Dispute Forces Out Manager." *Miami Herald,* [n.d. clipping].

Seminole Tribe News Brief, 1, no. 2, 12 May 1983, single sheet.

"Seminole Tribe Suspends Chief Jim Billie." Tampa bureau. *St. Petersburg Times,* 24 May 2001. At TampaBay.com.

Seminole Tribune. 24: 17, 19 Dec. 2003. [var.]

———. 25: 4, 19 Mar. 2004. [var.]

———. 25: 6, 30 Apr. 2004. [var.]

———. 25: 7, 21 May 2004. [var.]

"Seminoles' Bingo Pays Off." *The Palm Beach Post,* 1 Mar. 1982.

Shabecoff, Philip. "Killing of a Panther: Indian Treaty Rights vs. Law on Wildlife." *New York Times,* 15 Apr. 1987.

Shore, Jim. "Play with Our Name." *New York Times,* 27 Aug. 2005.

Siegfried, Mary. "Seminole Tax Heads for Court." *Hollywood Sun-Tattler,* 6 Aug. 1977, 5-A.

Smith, Greg, ed., *Native American Law Digest* 17, no. 1 (Jan. 2007).

Smith, Thom. "Party People: Ex-Chief Billie Is Flying High." *Palm Beach Post,* 8 Oct. 2006, 4D.

"*St. Petersburg Times* Interview with Chief Billie, Full Transcription." Nov. 1997. At http://100.6.4.21/tribune/transcription.shtml.

"Taste Is Issue on Downtown Hotel Plans." Op-Ed. *Tallahassee Democrat,* 7 June 2001. At tallahasseedemocrat.com.

Testerman, Jeff. "Billie Says He Okayed Gambling Project." *St. Petersburg Times,* 17 Dec. 2002. At sptimes.com.

———. "Chief's Ex-Pilot Set to Testify in Inquiry." *St. Petersburg Times,* 5 May 2001. At sptimes.com.

———. "Chief's Hold on Seminoles Is Slipping." *St. Petersburg Times,* 29 Apr. 2001. At sptimes.com.

———. "FBI Looks into Gifts Billie Gave to Woman." *St. Petersburg Times,* 31 May 2001. At sptimes.com.

———. "Gambling Activity by Seminoles Part of Federal Probe." *St. Petersburg Times,* 23 Jan. 1999.

———. "Letter Claims Seminole Leader Target of Probe." *St. Petersburg Times,* 17 Sept. 2001. At sptimes.com.

———. "Seminole Backer's Role a Surprise." *St. Petersburg Times,* 1 July 2001. At sptimes.com.

———. "Seminole Chief Files Lawsuit to Regain Tribal Council Post." *St. Petersburg Times,* 7 June 2001. At sptimes.com.

———. "Seminole Tribe Settles Sexual Harassment Lawsuit." *St. Petersburg Times,* 12 Oct. 2002.

———. "Seminole Tribe Sues Prudential over Funds." *St. Petersburg Times,* 13 Nov. 2002.

——. "Seminoles Battle Baptists for Property." *St. Petersburg Times,* 13 July 2000. At sptimes.com.

——. "Seminoles May Have Lost Millions." *St. Petersburg Times,* 2 June 2001, 1. At sptimes.com.

——. "Seminoles Sue Chief, Aide over Stocks." *St. Petersburg Times,* 6 Sept. 2001. At sptimes.com.

——. "Suspended Seminole Leader Seeks a Rehearing." *St. Petersburg Times,* 20 June 2001. At sptimes.com.

——. "Tribal Council Fires Three." *St. Petersburg Times,* 5 June 2001. At sptimes.com.

——. "Tribal Council Ousts Chief." *St. Petersburg Times,* 25 May 2001. At sptimes.com.

——. "Tribe Faulted for Not Warning Patrons about Sovereignty." *St. Petersburg Times,* 10 July 2005, 12B.

——. "Tribe's Attorney Has No Room for Hate." *St. Petersburg Times,* 25 Apr. 2002. At sptimes.com.

——. "Tribe's Foreign Deals Get Scrutiny." *St. Petersburg Times,* 18 June 2001. At sptimes.com.

——. "Tribe's Operations Manager Earns Praise—and Criticism." *St. Petersburg Times,* 29 Apr. 2001. At sptimes.com.

——. "Woman Sues Tribal Chief over Sex Acts." *St. Petersburg Times,* 11 May 2001. At sptimes.com.

Testerman, Jeff, and Brad Goldstein. "Banking on Full-Scale Casinos." *St. Petersburg Times.* Dec. 1997.

——. "Branching Out with Little Success." *St. Petersburg Times,* [21] Dec. 1997, 12A.

——. "King Bull." *St. Petersburg Times,* 21 Dec. 1997, 1A.

——. "Loyalty Pays Off for Tampa Partner." *St. Petersburg Times,* Dec. 1997.

Testerman, Jeff, and Kathryn Wexler. "Seminole Tribe Attorney Shot at Home." *St. Petersburg Times,* 11 Jan. 2002.

Tiger, Iretta. Letters to the Editor. "Billie, We Have Your Number." *City Link,* 9 Jan. 2002, 4.

"To the Point: First Step: Muzzle the Media." Op-Ed. *Miami Herald,* 8 May 2001, [I].

Treen, Dana. "Seminoles Find Card to Success." *Florida Times-Union,* 18 July 1993, C1, C4.

"Vegas Trip with Tribal Chief Was No Big Deal, King Says." *Miami Herald,* 5 Feb. 2004.

Vest, Jason. "Trump's Gamble for Indian Wampun." *Village Voice,* 1–7 July 1998.

Weeks, Judy. "A New Generation: Leaders for the Seminoles Tribe." *Florida Monthly,* Oct. 2007, 36.

Weinberg, Tanya. "After 22 Years, Seminole Leader's World Is Crumbling." *Fort Lauderdale Sun-Sentinel,* 10 June 2001. At sunsentinel.com.

——. "Billie Sues Seminoles to Get His Job Back." *Fort Lauderdale Sun-Sentinel,* 7 June 2001. At sunsentinel.com.

——. "Indian Affairs Official Backs Off Support for Ousted Chief Billie." *Fort Lauderdale Sun-Sentinel,* 14 Sept. 2001. At sunsentinel.com.

——. "Seminole Activists Push to Reform Tribal Politics, Government." *Fort Lauderdale Sun-Sentinel,* 10 Dec. 2001. At sunsentinel.com.

———. "Seminole Leader's Suspension Criticized." *Fort Lauderdale Sun-Sentinel,* 11 Sept. 2001, 5B.

———. "Seminoles Hire Hollywood Official for Administrator's Job." *Fort Lauderdale Sun-Sentinel,* 9 Jan. 2002. At sunsentinel.com.

———. "Seminoles Select New Member to Council." *Fort Lauderdale Sun-Sentinel,* 16 May 2001, 3B.

———. "Unanimous Tribal Council Vote Suspends Seminole Chairman." *Fort Lauderdale Sun-Sentinel,* 25 May 2001. At sunsentinel.com.

Wheelwright, Jeff. "Native America's Alleles." *Discover,* May 2005, 66–70.

Whitefield, Mimi. Editor's Note. "Vegas-Style Glitz Arrives at Seminole Reservation." *Miami Herald,* Business Monday, 10 May 2004, 3.

Wilson, Amy. "Expansion Planned for Hard Rock: Seminoles Aim to Add Units around Globe." *Palm Beach Post,* [June] 2007.

"Woman Accuses Tribal Leader of Harassment." N.p., n.d. (clipping).

"World Briefing/Americas: Nicaragua: 20-Year Sentence for Ex-President." *New York Times.* 9 Dec. 2003.

"World Briefing/Americas: Nicaragua: Ex-President Ousted." *New York Times.* 20 Sept. 2002.

Yari, Ethel. "James Billie: Seminole Chief Leads His Tribe into the 21st Century." *Florida Living,* July 1999, 46–52.

Manuscript Materials (including oral history interviews, lawsuit citations, U.S. congressional materials, and Internet URLs)

American Indian Religious Freedom Act (AIRFA). *U.S. Statutes at Large* 92: 469ff., 11 Aug. 1978.

"An Act Making Appropriations for the Current and Contingent Expenses of the Indian Department," 3 Mar. 1871. *U.S. Statutes at Large* 16: 566.

Anderson v. U.S. 845 F. 2d 206 (9th Cir.), *cert. denied,* 488 U.S. 966 (1988).

"Annual Report of the Seminole Agency to the Muscogee Area Office, Bureau of Indian Affairs, for the Fiscal Year Ending 30 June 1954."

Archaeological Resources Protection Act (ARPA). *U.S. Statutes at Large* 93: 721ff., 31 Oct. 1979.

Askew, Reuben O'D. Florida Governor, Executive Order 74-23, signed 10 Apr. 1974.

Baker, Pete. Interview with the author, 24 June 1997.

Billie, James E., Chairman, to Franklin Keel, Eastern Area Office Superintendent, BIA, 30 Aug. 2001.

———, to Priscilla Sayen, Tribal Secretary/Treasurer, 3 Jan. 2003.

Billie, Sonny, as told to Dale Grasshopper, 1993.

Buswell, James O., III. "Florida Seminole Religious Ritual: Resistance and Change." PhD diss., St. Louis University, 1972.

California v. Cabazon Band of Mission Indians, 480 U.S. Reports, 207–22, 25 Feb. 1987.

Capron, Louis. "The Medicine Bundles of the Florida Seminole and the Green Corn

Dance." Smithsonian Institution, Bureau of American Ethnology Bulletin 151, Anthropological Papers, No. 35, 1953, 155–221.

Carter, Kent, Director. Southwestern Regional Archives, National Archives and Records Administration, Fort Worth, TX, personal communication, 1999.

Choteau v. Burnet, 283 U.S. 691 (1931).

Clinton, William J. Memorandum of President William J. Clinton of Government-to-Government Relations with Native American Tribal Governments, Promulgated 29 Apr. 1994. *Federal Register* 59: 22951–52, 4 May 1994.

Cobell v. Salazar, a.k.a. Individual Indian Monies Case (IIM) or the (Elouise) Cobell Case was brought in 1996 as a class action suit against the BIA.

College Football History. At http://www.collegefootballhistory.com/florida_state/history.htm.

Confederated Tribes of Colville vs. State of Washington, 446 F. Supp. 1339 (1978).

Cornell Farmworker Program. At http://www.farmworkers.cornell.edu/pdf/facts_on_farmworkers.pdf.

Cox, Timmy Wayne. Interviews with the author, 2004 (Jan. 12, 16, 21, 23, 26; Feb. 2, 5, 6, 10, 11, 13; Mar. 10, 19, 24, 30, 31; Apr. 1, 2, 5, 7, 9, 12, 15).

———. Notes on his incarceration. Document in the collections of the author.

Crenshaw, Rev. Lucius, and Mrs. Carolyn. Interview with the author, 1994.

Crooks, Vivian. Interview with the author, 25 Nov. 2003.

Department of Game v. Puyallup Tribe, 414 U.S. 44, 49 (1973).

FedSpending.org. At http://www.fedspending.org.

Florida State Lodge. At http://www.floridastatefop.org/heroes_complete.asp.

Florida Statute § 380.055(8).

Florida Statutes Annotated (1991), Sect. 285.

Florida Water Resources Act of 1972, Ch. 72-299, in Florida Statutes Ch. 373 (1989).

Franklin, Lehman. Interview with the author, 7 June 1997.

Henson, C. L. "Indian Gambling on Reservations—Seventeen Years Later." *American Studies Today Online,* 6 Nov. 2007. At http://www.americansc.org.uk/online/Gaming.htm.

Indian Child Welfare Act. *U.S. Statutes at Large* 92: 3069ff., 8 Nov. 1978.

Indian Financing Act. *U.S. Statutes at Large* 88: 77–83, enacted 12 Apr. 1974.

Indian Gaming Regulatory Act (IGRA), 102 Stat., 2475, 25 U.S.C.

Indian Land Claims Act. *U.S. Statutes at Large* 60 (1946).

Indian Reorganization Act. *U.S. Statutes at Large* 48.

Indian Self-Determination and Education Assistance Act, PL 93-638, 4 Jan. 1975.

Johnson, Lyndon B., President. Special Message to Congress, 6 Mar. 1978, and the Civil Rights Act of 11 Apr. 1978.

Jourdain v. Commissioner, 617 F. 2d 507 (8th Cir. 1980).

Jumper, Betty Mae. Interviews with the author, 1993, 1997.

Keel, Franklin, Eastern Area Director for the Bureau of Indian Affairs, U.S. Department of the Interior. Interviews with the author, 26 May, 14 Sept. 2006; 2008; 1 Jun. 2009.

———. Director, BIA Eastern Regional Office to James E. Billie, Chairman, STOF, 6 Sept. 2001.

————. Director, BIA Eastern Regional Office to James E. Billie, Chairman, Seminole Tribe of Florida, 12 Sept. 2001.

————. Director, BIA Eastern Regional Office to Deputy Commissioner of Indian Affairs/ Tribal Government Services, Washington, DC, 19 Sept. 2001.

King, Robert Thomas. "The Florida Seminole Polity, 1858–1978." Diss., University of Florida, 1978.

Kippenberger, LaVonne. Interview with the author, 2006.

Koenes, Maryjene Cypress. Interview with the author, 2003.

Lerner, Allen M., of Lerner, Pearce, P.A., Fort Lauderdale, FL, to Stan Taube, president, Investment Resources, Inc., of Minneapolis, MN, and Alan Werkman, Esq., Deerfield Beach, FL, 15 Aug. 1990.

MacMillan, Ann, Mrs. Interview with the author, 19 Sept. 2002.

Micco Aircraft. At http://www.miccoaircraft.com.

Mitchell, Robert. Oral history interview, R. T. King, narrator, 7.15.1971, SEM 10AB, University of Florida, P. K. Yonge Library of Florida History, Doris Duke Indian Oral History Project.

National Archives and Records Administration, Record Group 279, Dockets 73, 73-A, 151 (Box 1405, folder 2).

Native American Graves Protection and Repatriation Act (NAGPRA). *U.S. Statutes at Large* 104.

Native American Housing Assistance and Self-Determination Act (NAHASDA). *U.S. Statutes at Large* 110.

New Jersey State Bar Foundation. Native American Mascots: Racial Slur or Cherished Tradition? At http://www.njsbf.org/njsbf/student/respect//winter03-1.cfm.

New Mexico v. Mescalero Apache Tribe, 462 U.S. 324, 330 (1983).

O'Donnell, Christine. "Declaration of Christine O'Donnell under Penalties of Perjury," signed and notarized 15 Mar. 2003.

Oneida Indian Nation of New York v. State of New York, 69 F. 2d 1070 (2d. Cir. 1982), known as Oneida I.

"Order Approving Settlement Agreement and Instructing Parties to Complete Performance of Settlement Agreement and Dismissing Case with Prejudice," issued by Judge Norman C. Roettger Jr., in the U.S. District Court for the Southern District of Florida, Case No. 78-6116-Civ, 29 Oct. 1987.

Palmer, Tom, a.k.a. Chitto Hajo. Interviews with the author, 1996–2002.

Payne, John Howard. Autograph MS, in the Collections of Jay Kislak, Miami, FL, and published posthumously in the *Continental Monthly* (Boston), I (1862), 17–29, and also in the *Chronicles of Oklahoma* 10 (1932), 170–95.

Pennsylvania Crime Commission. "Racketeering and Organized Crime in the Bingo Industry," Apr. 1992.

Poarch Band of Creek Indians v. Alabama, 776 F. Supp. 550 (SD Ala. 1991), and 784 F. Supp. 1549 (SD Ala. 1992).

Public Law 98-64, 97 Stat. 365, 25 USCS 117 (a), et seq., 2 Aug. 1983.

Quinn, Rex. Oral history interview, R. T. King, narrator, 12.13.1973, SEM 99AB, University of Florida, P. K. Yonge Library of Florida History, Doris Duke Indian Oral History Project.

———. Speech transcript (place and group not noted), 8 June 1981, in the collections of the author.

Red Earth. At http://www.redearth.org.

Sayen, Priscilla. Memorandum. To all departments, "Removal of James E. Billie as chairman," 21 Mar. 2003.

Schweitzer, Marianne Alagande. "Ethnography of the Modern Mikasuki Indians of Southern Florida." Master's thesis, Yale University, 1945.

"Seminole Indian Land Claims Settlement Act of 1987," Public Law 100-228, 31 Dec. 1987.

"Seminole Tribe of Florida 20th Anniversary of Tribal Organization, 1957–1977," typescript program, Saturday, Aug. 20, 1977.

Seminole Tribe of Florida v. Florida, U.S. Circuit Court of Appeals for the Eleventh Circuit, Atlanta, Georgia, 11 F. 3d 1016, 18 Jan. 1994.

Seminole Tribe of Florida v. Florida, U.S. Supreme Court, 517 U.S. 44, No. 94-12, argued 11 Oct. 1995, and decided 27 Mar. 1996.

Seminole Tribe of Florida vs. Robert Butterworth, U.S. Court of Appeals, Fifth Circuit, Unit B, 5 Oct. 1981.

———. U.S. District Court, Southern District of Florida, Fort Lauderdale Division, 491 F. Supp. 1015 (1980), holding entered 6 May 1980.

Seminole Tribe of Florida vs. State of Florida et al., Case No. 78-6116-Civ-NCR, U.S. District Court for the Southern District of Florida, 17 Mar. 1978.

"Sheriff's Appeal against Seminole Bingo Heard in Atlanta," *Alligator Times* 2 (1981): 1.

"Sheriff's Ties to Seminole Tribe under More Scrutiny." 13 May 2005. At indianz.com.

Shore, Jim. General Counsel, STOF, to Franklin Keel, Director, BIA/Eastern Area Office, 7 Sept. 2001.

Shore, Jim. Interview with the author, 7 Aug. 1998.

Skafte, Peter. "Conflict and Tacit Agreement: A Study of Seminole Social Interaction." Master's thesis, University of Florida, 1969.

Sloan, Carlos. Interview with the author, 23 Jan. 2007.

Smathers, George A., U.S. Senator. Interview with the author, 9 Nov. 1997.

Squire v. Capoeman, 351 U.S. 1 (1956).

State of Florida v. Billie, 497 So. 2d 889 (Fla. 2d DCA 1986).

Stewart, Jon. "The Daily Show." Comedy Central TV, 11 Dec. 2006.

Sturtevant, William C. "The Mikasuki Seminole: Medical Beliefs and Practices." Diss., Yale University, 1955.

Three Affiliated Tribes of the Fort Berthold Reservation v. Wold Engineering, P.C., 467 U.S. 138 (1984).

Tiger, Richmond. Interview with the author, 1996.

Trade and Intercourse Act, 22 July 1790. *U.S. Statutes at Large* 1: 137–38.

Turner, Nina, Mrs. Interview with the author, 25 July 1995.

United States v. Billie, 667 F. Supp. 1485 (S.D. Fla. 1987).

United States v. Dion, 476 U.S. 734 (1986).

United States v. Marcyes, 557 F. 2d, U.S. Circuit Court of Appeals for the Ninth Circuit.

U.S. Congress, 83rd Cong., 1st sess., 67 Stat. 586, 15 Aug. 1953.

U.S. Congress, 83rd Cong., 2nd sess. "Termination of Federal Supervision over Certain Tribes of Indians, Joint Hearings before the Subcommittees of the Committee of Interior and Insular Affairs, on S. Doc. 2747 and H.R. 7321," Part 8, Seminole Indians, Florida, Mar. 1–2, 1954, 1122.

U.S. Congress, 101st Cong., 1st sess. "Statement of Mr. James Billie, Chairman, Tribal Council of the Seminole Tribe of Florida before the House Committee on Interior and Insular Affairs on H.R. 2838 and H.R. 2650," 14 Sept. 1989.

U.S. Court of Appeals for the Eighth Circuit, 82 F. 3d 192, No. 95-3222SD, decided 22 Apr. 1996. (Raether)

U.S. Court of Appeals for the Eighth Circuit, 82 F. 3d 192, No. 97-1476SD. (Raether)

U.S. Presidential Executive Order 11399. "Establishing the National Council on Indian Opportunity," 6 Mar. 1968, 33 *Federal Register* 4245 (7 Mar. 1967).

U.S. Secretary of the Interior. *Annual Report,* 1954.

U.S. Statutes at Large 23.

U.S. Statutes at Large 49 Stat. 1968, 26 June 1936.

U.S. Statutes at Large 60.

U.S. Statutes at Large 62.

U.S. Statutes at Large 64 Stat. 44, 19 Apr. 1950.

U.S. Statutes at Large 67.

U.S. Statutes at Large 82.

U.S. Statutes at Large 90.

U.S. Statutes at Large 102.

USA Corps of Engineers Dredge and Fill Permit Application No. 85-IPD-20126, Dept. of the Army, 24 Sept. 1985.

USA v. F. Butch Oseby, U.S. Eighth Circuit Court of Appeals, No. 97-3207, submitted 10 Mar. 1998. Filed 8 July 1998.

Vending Unlimited vs. State of Florida, 364 So. 2d 5480 (1978).

Washington v. Confederated Tribes, 447 U.S. 134 (1980).

Wheeler-Howard Act, *U.S. Statutes at Large* 48 Stat. 986, enacted 18 June 1934.

Winters v. United States, 207 U.S. 564 (1908).

Yahoo! Groups. At http://groups.yahoo.com/group/NatNews/message/39441.

Published Materials

American Civil Liberties Union. "The Hands That Feed Us." National Immigration and Alien Rights Project Report No. 2. Washington, DC: ACLU, Apr. 1986.

Baker, Wayne L. "Seminole Speaks to Sovereign Immunity and Ex Parte Young." *St. John's Law Review* (Fall 1997).

BIA Community Services Officer. Memorandum, 1968, 6, cited in Skafte, "Conflict and Tacit Agreement," 43.

Canova, Andrew P. *Life and Adventures in South Florida.* Palatka, FL: n.p., 1885.

Caro, Robert A. *The Years of Lyndon Johnson: Master of the Senate.* New York: Alfred A. Knopf, 2002.

Cattelino, Jessica R. *High Stakes: Florida Seminole Gaming and Sovereignty.* Durham, NC: Duke University Press, 2008.

Cohen, Felix S. *Handbook of Federal Indian Law.* 1940. n.p: Bobbs-Merrill, 1982.

Covington, James W. "Apalachicola Seminole Leadership, 1820–1833." *Florida Anthropologist* 16, no. 2 (1963): 57–62.

———. "A Seminole Census, 1847." *Florida Anthropologist* 21, no. 4 (1968): 120–22.

———. "Some Observations concerning the Fort Caroline Slave Trade." *Florida Anthropologist,* 20, nos. 1–2 (1967): 10–18.

———. "Some Observations concerning the July 1913 Census Taken by Agent Lucien Spencer." *Florida Anthropologist* 39, no. 3 (1986): 221–23.

———. "Stuart's Town, the Yamassee Indians, and Spanish Florida." *Florida Anthropologist* 21, no. 1 (1968): 8–13.

———. "Trail Indians of Florida." *Florida Historical Quarterly* 58 (July 1979): 37–57.

Debo, Angie. *The Road to Disappearance.* Norman: University of Oklahoma Press, 1941.

———. *And Still the Waters Run: The Betrayal of the Five Civilized Tribes.* Norman: University of Oklahoma Press, 1989.

Deloria, Vine, Jr., and Clifford M. Lytle. *The Nations Within: The Past and Future of American Indian Sovereignty.* Austin: University of Texas Press, 1984.

Deloria, Vine, Jr., and David E. Wilkins. *Tribes, Treaties, and Constitutional Tribulations.* Austin: University of Texas Press, 1999.

Dye, David H. "The Transformation of Mississippian Warfare: Four Case Studies from the Mid-South." In *The Archaeology of Warfare: Prehistories of Raiding and Conquest,* edited by Elizabeth N. Arkush and Mark W. Allen. Gainesville: University Press of Florida, 2006, 101–47.

Florida Statistical Abstract. Gainesville: University Presses of Florida, 1998.

Foreman, Grant, *The Five Civilized Tribes: Cherokee, Chickasaw, Choctaw, Creek, Seminole,* 5th ed. Norman: University of Oklahoma Press, 1974.

Forum: The Magazine of the Florida Humanities Council, spring 2007.

Gallagher, Peter B. "The Rise and Fall of Chief Jim Billie: Flamboyant Chief Jim Billie Led the Seminoles out of Poverty When He Won the Battle to Build Gaming Casinos on Reservations." *Gulf Shore Life,* Oct. 2004. At http://www.gulfshorelife.com.

Gesamtverzeichnis der Teilnehmer an den Fernsprechnetzen in den Ober-Postdirektionsbezirkin Aachen, Cöln, Dortmund, Düsseldorf, Minden, und Münster in Westfalen. Düsseldorf: A. Bagel, 1920.

Hann, John H. *Apalachee: The Land between the Rivers.* Gainesville: University Presses of Florida, 1988.

———, ed. and trans. *Missions to the Calusa.* Gainesville: University of Florida Press, Florida Museum of Natural History, 1991.

Huoponen, Kirsi, Antonio Torroni, Patricia R. Wickman, Daniele Sellitto, Daniel S. Gurley, Rosaria Scozzari, and Douglas C. Wallace. "Mitochondrial DNA and Y Chromosome-Specific Polymorphisms in the Seminole Tribe of Florida." *European Journal of Human Genetics* 5 (1997): 25–34.

Johnson, Lyndon B. *Public Papers of the Presidents of the United States: Lyndon B. Johnson, 1968–69.* Washington, DC: Government Printing Office, 1970.

Kersey, Harry A., Jr. *Assumption of Sovereignty: Social and Political Transformation among the Florida Seminoles.* Lincoln: University of Nebraska Press, 1996.

———. "Economic Prospects of Florida's Seminole Indians." *Florida Planning and Development* 20 (December 1969).

———. "Florida Seminoles and the Census of 1900." *Florida Historical Quarterly* 60, no. 2 (October 1981): 145–60.

———. "The Florida Seminole Land Claim Case, 1950–1990." *Florida Historical Quarterly* 72, no. 2 (1993): 35–55.

———. *Pelts, Plumes, and Hides: White Traders among the Seminole Indians, 1870–1930.* Gainesville: University Presses of Florida, 1975.

———. "Private Societies and the Maintenance of Seminole Tribal Integrity, 1899–1957." *Florida Historical Quarterly* 56, no. 3 (1978): 297–316.

———. "Seminoles and Miccosukees: A Century in Retrospective." In *Indians of the Southeastern United States in the Late Twentieth Century,* edited by J. Anthony Paredes. Tuscaloosa: The University of Alabama Press, 1992.

———. *The Seminoles and the New Deal, 1933–1944.* Gainesville: University Presses of Florida, 1989.

King, R. T. "Clan Affiliation and Leadership among the Twentieth-Century Florida Indians." *Florida Historical Quarterly* 55, no. 2 (1976): 138–52.

Laurence, Robert. "The Bald Eagle, the Florida Panther, and the Nation's Word: An Essay on the 'Quiet' Abrogation of Indian Treaties and the Proper Reading of *United States v. Dion.*" *Journal of Land Use and Environmental Law* 4, no. 1 (1988).

Lowis, George W., William A. Sheramata, Symalina Dube, Dipak Dube, Patricia R. Wickman, and Bernard J. Poiesz. "HTLV-II Risk Factors in Native Americans in Florida." *Neuroepidemiology* 18 (1999): 37–47.

MacCauley, Clay. "Seminole Indians of Florida." Bureau of American Ethnology Fifth Annual Report, 1883, 1884. Washington, DC: Smithsonian Institution, 1887.

Mahon, John K. *History of the Second Seminole War.* 1967. Gainesville: University Presses of Florida, 2006.

Mankiller, Wilma, and Michael Wallis. *Mankiller: A Chief and Her People, An Autobiography by the Principal Chief of the Cherokee Nation.* New York: St. Martin's Press, 1993.

Moore, R. Laurence. *Religious Outsiders and the Making of Americans.* Cited in Jon Krakauer, *Under the Banner of Heaven: A Story of Violent Faith.* NY: Doubleday, 2003.

Oeffner, Barbara. *Chief: Champion of the Everglades, a Biography of Seminole Chief James Billie.* Palm Beach, FL: Cape Cod Writers, 1995.

Oxford Study Bible: Revised English Bible with Apocrypha, Matthew 6:24. New York: Oxford University Press, 1992.

Pevar, Stephen L. *The Rights of Indians and Tribes: The Basic ACLU Guide to Indian and Tribal Rights.* 2nd ed. Carbondale: Southern Illinois University Press, 1992.

Philip, Kenneth R. *John Collier's Crusade for Indian Reform, 1920–1954.* Tucson: University of Arizona Press, 1977.

Prucha, Francis Paul. *American Indian Policy: The Indian Trade and Intercourse Acts, 1790–1834.* Lincoln: University of Nebraska Press, 1962.

———. *Documents of United States Indian Policy.* 1975. 3rd ed. Lincoln: University of Nebraska Press, 2000.

———. *The Great Father: The United States Government and the American Indians.* 1984. Lincoln: University of Nebraska Press, 1995. Vols. 1 and 2, unabridged.

Seminole Tribe of Florida. *Celebrating 50 Years of the Signing of Our Constitution and Corporate Charter.* Hollywood, FL: Seminole Communications, 2007.

Shore, Jim, and Straus, Jerry C. "The Seminole Water Rights Compact and the Seminole Indian Land Claims Settlement Act of 1987." *Journal of Land Use and Environmental Law* 6, no. 1 (1990): 1–24.

Southern Poverty Law Center. *Close to Slavery: Guestworker Programs in the United States.* Montgomery, AL: SPLC, 2007.

Spoehr, Alexander. "Camp, Clan, and Kin among the Cow Creek Seminole of Florida." Anthropological Series Field Museum of Natural History 33 (1941): 1–27.

State of Florida Legislative Council and Legislative Reference Bureau. *Migrant Farm Labor in Florida: A Summary of Recent Studies.* Feb. 1961.

Sturtevant, William. "A Seminole Medicine Maker." In *In the Company of Man: Twenty Portraits by Anthropologists,* edited by Joseph B. Casagrande. New York: Harper and Brothers, 1960.

Tiger, Buffalo, and Harry A. Kersey Jr. *Buffalo Tiger: A Life in the Everglades.* Lincoln: University of Nebraska Press, 2002.

U.S. Dept. of Commerce. *Federal and State Reservations and Indian Trust Areas.* Washington, DC: U.S. Government Printing Office, 1974.

West, Patsy. *The Enduring Seminoles: From Alligator Wrestling to Ecotourism.* Gainesville: University Press of Florida, 1998.

Wickman, Patricia Riles. *The Tree That Bends: Discourse, Power, and the Survival of the Maskóki People.* Tuscaloosa: The University of Alabama Press, 1999.

Wilkins, David E. *American Indian Sovereignty and the U.S. Supreme Court: The Masking of Justice.* Austin: University of Texas Press, 1997.

Wilson, Edmund. *Apologies to the Iroquois: With a Study of the Mohawks in High Steel by Joseph Mitchell.* 1960. 1978. Syracuse, NY: Syracuse University Press, 1992.

Index

Page numbers in italics refer to illustrations.